GENERALS AND ADMIRALS OF THE THIRD REICH

GENERALS AND ADMIRALS OF THE THIRD REICH

For Country or Fuehrer

Volume 1: A–G

JAMES JACK WEBB

CASEMATE

Pennsylvania & Yorkshire

Published in the United States of America and Great Britain in 2024 by
CASEMATE PUBLISHERS
1950 Lawrence Road, Havertown, PA 19083, USA
and
47 Church Street, Barnsley, S70 2AS, UK

Hardback Edition: ISBN 978-1-95271-512-9
Digital Edition: ISBN 978-1-95271-513-6

A CIP record for this book is available from the British Library

Printed and bound in the United Kingdom by CPI Group (UK) Ltd, Croydon, CR0 4YY

Typeset in India by Lapiz Digital Services, Chennai.

For a complete list of Casemate titles, please contact:

CASEMATE PUBLISHERS (US)
Telephone (610) 853-9131
Fax (610) 853-9146
Email: casemate@casematepublishers.com
www.casematepublishers.com

CASEMATE PUBLISHERS (UK)
Telephone (0)1226 734350
Email: casemate@casemateuk.com
www.casemateuk.com

"A man who has seen three wars, never will wish another war. He must be a friend of peace. But I am not a pacifist. All my impressions of war are so bad, that I could be for it only under the sternest necessity—the necessity of fighting Bolshevism or of defending one's country."

Generalfeldmarschall and Reich President Paul von Hindenburg

Dedication

To My Close Friend and Fellow Researcher Michael Miller

Contents

Acknowledgements

I would like to thank my friend Michael Miller who helped guide me during the initial phases of this project. A noted author in his own right, he is also a great researcher. The other person who deserves major credit is my friend Fred Froberg, who, several years ago, took his own life on Christmas morning. Despite having grown children and a close family, the demons in his mind took what he and his family were not able to manage. Thus, making what is supposed to be a day of celebration into a day of eternal sorrow. Next, I would like to thank Theodor P. Savas of Savas Beatie Publishing. He took the time to look over my idea for this project and as a result, reached out to Ruth Sheppard, at Casemate Publishers, who in turn thought it was a project worth pursuing. I am grateful to them both for making a ten-year effort into reality. In addition, I want to thank Gordon Williamson, Marc Rikspoel, William Kramer, and the late Roger James Bender for their assistance with much-needed photos. I also want to thank Karlo Foder for providing essential information on the admirals of the Kriegsmarine.

Introduction

In these three volumes you will learn about the careers of over five thousand generals and admirals of the German Heer (Army), Luftwaffe (Air Force), Waffen-SS (Armed SS), and Kriegsmarine (Navy). These high-ranking officers lived during a unique time in which many experienced two world wars. World War I was a breeding ground for young officers and NCOs who would one day lead formations of their own into battle, but under a much different flag. For many of them, it would have been both an honor and an obligation to carry on the military bloodline they had inherited from their fathers and grandfathers. However, unlike the victorious celebrations that had followed the end of previous wars, this war ended in a stalemate of hopelessness and despair.

By the end of World War I, the Allies had not crossed into German territory and the Germans were also still very well armed and ready to carry on the war of attrition. Instead, the end of hostilities meant the end of Imperial Germany, the end of its army, and the abdication of its royal head, Kaiser Wilhelm II. By this time, it wasn't the Kaiser who was leading the German Army, but rather the future president, Generalfeldmarschall Paul von Hindenburg. Forced to follow the guidelines of the Treaty of Versailles, Germany had to disarm and destroy all its heavy weapons, aircraft, and armed naval vessels. Adding insult to injury, Germany also had to scale down its army to a 100,000-man peacetime formation. While the fortunate few continued their military careers, many thousands of veterans wandered the streets of Germany without work or any prospects for the future.

While hundreds of future generals and admirals were allowed to remain in the peacetime Reichswehr (Army) and Reichsmarine (Navy), there were just as many who were not. In the immediate post-war period, it was a free-for-all for any number of political formations to take control of the German government. Thousands of veterans took up arms to defend Germany against communist elements who had recently taken control of Russia. Even during the early days of post-war Germany, it was obvious that there were different ideologies between conservative Germans and the young Communist Party who posed a threat to Europe itself. This army of veterans who took on armed Communist formations acted in military-style formations called the "Freikorps" or "Free Corps." Once the Communists had been defeated, and the German Weimar Government formed, the Freikorps were dissolved, and these same veterans were left unemployed and with nothing to do.

Eventually, and with the improvement of the German economy, thousands of future senior officers were able to find employment with police formations throughout Germany, as well as in other fields of work. Joining the police force was an ideal job, as not only did it provide stability and regular pay, but many veterans found a sense of familiarity in the work as the police force was run like a military formation. Indeed, many were able to retain the officer or NCO rank they held in the Army, and allowed to wear the decorations which they had received for their service in World War I on their police uniform. One could say that these experiences helped mold the future generals and admirals of Germany, and to a certain extent, this is true.

Thousands of veterans joined the ranks, formations, and beliefs of the Nazi Party in its early years; but it wasn't until the Great Depression that their ranks really swelled with those who had served in the war. Most of those who joined were NCOs and enlisted ranks, with very few being officers. At that point, joining was more about supplying their basic needs than wearing a uniform and believing in Nazi ideology. Only when Hitler was appointed Chancellor by Reich President von Hindenburg on 30 January 1933, did these veterans and the peacetime German Reichswehr start to take the Nazis seriously. In Hindenburg's mind the Nazis were the lesser of two evils, being the only way to ensure that the German Communist Party did not take control of the Weimar Government and threaten the traditions and values of the German way of life. It was during these growing pains that the Reichswehr had to adapt to an ever-changing, volatile environment. There were still street fights between the Nazis and the Communists, the economy was still in shambles, and at any moment the Reichswehr could be called upon to restore order. The only bright light in an otherwise dismal situation was that—unknown to most Germans—Hitler was hell bent on disregarding the Treaty of Versailles, and would use all his energy and influence to not only rebuild the German economy, but to rebuild the German armed forces. This would prove a major hurdle for the Army, because even though Hindenburg had been a former Field Marshal and their Commander in Chief, he had abided by the policies of the Treaty and refused any expansion beyond the 100,000-man Army which it permitted. In other words, Hitler would also have to rebuild the Army from scratch.

With the death of President Paul von Hindenburg on 2 August 1934, the path was cleared for Hitler to combine the offices of President and Reich Chancellor, and clear out any members of government who stood in his way. There were two major components, or groups of people, that would assist Hitler in achieving his intended rebuilding of the economy and the Armed Forces: the industrial leaders and wealthy elite, and the Reichswehr generals and admirals.

Most industrial leaders and members of the elite held the belief "nothing ventured, nothing gained." They saw Hitler as a man filled with promise and modern vision, who would help rid them of the two biggest obstacles that were holding them back, the Treaty of Versailles, and the Great Depression. With the support of factory owners and the elite circles, Hitler was able to start adding modern weapons and armor to the depleted Reichsheer and Reichsmarine, put millions of people back to work to boost the economy, and gain the confidence and support of the German people. Major industrialists and other elite circles saw Hitler's vision as a way forward into a new, stronger Germany, the only way of bringing life back into factories that were lying idle. The production of arms and armor would put millions of people back to work, boost the economy, and rebuild the wealth lost after World War I and the early years of the Great Depression. The return of a strong Germany, and especially an army, would give elite circles and the aristocracy a sense of belonging, most of them having come from a military background.

In August 1934, General Werner von Blomberg, the newly appointed Minister of Defense, and his Chief of Staff, General Walther von Reichenau, an ardent Nazi and future General Field Marshal, took drastic measures to adapt the German Army into its new role as primary defender of the Third Reich. The first thing von Reichenau did (to the great satisfaction of Hitler), was to dishonorably discharge all German Jews from military service. Next, he ordered that the Nazi Party's national eagle and swastika be put on all military uniforms and headgear. The final and perhaps most significant change was the order that all members serving in the Armed Forces had to take an oath of loyalty to Hitler. As these drastic changes took place in the Army during 1934, Hitler moved to eliminate the leadership of his Brown Army, the Sturmabteilung (SA). The SA Chief of Staff, Ernst Roehm, a former officer at the head of almost 3,000,000 men, wanted the SA to replace the traditional Reichswehr and become the main army of the movement. Hitler knew that this would be disastrous; it would be impossible to achieve his goals of domination without the support of the German Army. Over three days (30 June–2 July 1934), and to the delight of the Army leadership, Roehm and most of the SA leadership were put up against the wall and executed by the S.S. There was now nothing standing in the way of Hitler, Blomberg, and next chapter of the German Army.

Thanks to the growth and revitalization of the German economy, the next four and a half years saw many milestones for the German Army. Having total disregard for the Treaty of Versailles and acting on his gut instinct that Great Britain and France would not enforce it, Hitler moved full speed ahead with his plans to rearm the military and expand its army to a size not seen since World War I. In March 1935, Hitler introduced conscription into the three major branches of the military, the Heer (Army), the Kriegsmarine (Navy) and the Luftwaffe (Air Force). In May of that same year, the Reichswehr was officially renamed as the Wehrmacht, a universal name for the entire Armed Forces. It was Hitler's desire to raise the Army itself to 36 divisions, which did not include specialty formations such as tank or panzer forces. For a country with a rich military history, and with Nazi Party formations organized along military guidelines, it came as no surprise that between 1935 and 1939, a total of 3.7 million men joined the Wehrmacht.

Now that millions of men were pouring into the Wehrmacht, it was time to provide them with weapons to operate with. The Treaty of Versailles had disarmed the German military, meaning that besides small arms for the Reichsheer (Army), and the most basic of surface vessels for the Reichsmarine (Navy), the new recruits had nothing to train with. But now the green light was given to the wealthy industrialists who had supported Hitler's rise to power. The steel and armament factories were able to operate at full production and provide the weapons that Hitler and the military so badly needed. The Heer was provided with higher-grade small arms, which included the latest automatic weapons. Several new types of artillery were also designed and produced; these would have devastating effects on enemy formations and cities. In addition, a new modern version of the tank, or panzer, was produced. This model would become the backbone of the Wehrmacht.

The Reichsmarine—or Kriegsmarine after the establishment of the Wehrmacht—was also given its fair share of modern industry. The days of the tiny vessels of the Weimar period were gone, and in their place, large surface ships such as battleships, destroyers, and auxiliary cruisers patrolled the shore of Nazi Germany. Not to be outdone by the panzers of the German Army, the Navy was also provided with its own modern version of the submarine, which would prove to be just as devastating and would send hundreds of ships to the bottom of the ocean.

While the Army and Navy had an established officer corps and organizational capacity to handle new recruits and equipment, the Air Force—Luftwaffe—had nothing. The Reichsheer and Reichsmarine had been allowed to have a small piecemeal force, but the German Air Service, part of both the Imperial Army and the Imperial Navy, had been forced to destroy all its aircraft. With no aircraft to operate, most of its pilots and personnel had been released from service. However, pilots were secretly trained in central Russia between 1924 and 1933, while inside Germany the Civil Air Service, Deutsche Lufthansa, was established in 1926, flying commercial passenger aircraft. Many pilots assumed the disguise of civil air pilots to get their initial training. There was also a para-military organization set up in 1933, the German Air Sports Association or DLV, which controlled all aircraft clubs in Germany. It was a front for past and future pilots of the Luftwaffe. During the same year, the Reich Air Ministry was established under Reich Minister Hermann Goering, to deal with the growth and administrative aspects of all air services in Germany. Both organizations became core elements for the future of the Luftwaffe. Once the Wehrmacht was created in 1935, the

Luftwaffe also benefited from the addition of fighter, dive bomber, bomber, and reconnaissance aircraft.

Now that Hitler's modern Army was becoming a reality, it was time to test the waters of both foreign diplomacy and his military. Starting off small, on 7 March 1936, Hitler sent 20,000 German troops to reoccupy the Rhineland. Despite this being a major violation of the Treaty of Versailles, Hitler's gamble that France and Great Britain would do nothing paid off. The next big test, and one that would again challenge Versailles, was giving military assistance to Nationalist Leader Francisco Franco during the Spanish Civil War from 1936 to 1939. While not wanting to use his entire military to help defeat the Republic and other foreign elements involved in the conflict, Hitler did send a sizable ground, air, and naval force to fight the campaign. By having a constant rotation of troops, pilots, naval officers, and personnel over a three-year period, vast numbers of the Wehrmacht gained much-needed experience on land, sea, and in the air during the campaign. After the conclusion of a successful military campaign, a victory parade was held in Germany and bemedaled men and officers beamed with confidence. In three years of war, only 300 men had been killed in action.

During the early rise of the Wehrmacht, and while troops were being led through the Rhineland and Spain, each branch of service had established its own high command of senior officers and operations staff that oversaw day-to-day functions as well as military operations. While Werner von Blomberg, now a Generalfeldmarschall, held the post of Minister of War in Hitler's Cabinet, the Army had Oberkommando des Heers (O.K.H.), which was formed in 1935. The O.K.H. was under the leadership of the Army Commander in Chief, Generaloberst Werner Freiherr von Fritsch, while his Chief of the General Staff was General der Artillerie Ludwig Beck. The Kriegsmarine or Navy had the Oberkommando der Marine (O.K.M.), which was formed in 1936. Its head was the Naval Commander in Chief, Grossadmiral Dr. Erich Raeder. Lastly, the Luftwaffe, or Air Force, had established the Oberkommando der Luftwaffe (O.K.L.), in 1935. Both the Reich Air Ministry and the O.K.L. were under the Luftwaffe Commander in Chief, Generaloberst, and later Generalfeldmarschall, Hermann Goering. Below him was his Inspector General of the Luftwaffe, General der Flieger, and later Generalfeldmarschall, Erhard Milch.

Although they had offered early support to Hitler, Defense Minister (now the Reich Minister of War), Generalfeldmarschall Werner von Blomberg, Werner Freiherr von Fritsch, and Ludwig Beck were beginning to develop mixed feelings about Hitler's intentions. With the last world war still fresh in their memories, none of the old school senior officers were in the mood for another full-blown conflict. Having sensed this and wanting to trade in these generals for more ardent supporters of Hitler, Generalfeldmarschall Goering and the Head of the SS, Heinrich Himmler, helped devise a plan which would force Blomberg and Fritsch to resign in January 1938.

As a result, the office of Reich Minister of War was dissolved, and Fritsch was replaced by the new Commander in Chief of the Army, Generaloberst Walther von Brauchitsch. In addition, the Oberkommando der Wehrmacht (O.K.W.), or German High Command, was set up as a mouthpiece for Hitler over all three branches of service. Its head was another ardent follower of Hitler, Generaloberst, and later Generalfeldmarschall, Wilhelm Keitel.

Hitler's next big gamble, and a much more personal one, concerned his birthplace, Austria. It was his deepest desire to unite the millions of Germans and Austrians under one flag. As early as the late 1920s, the Nazi Party had established roots in Austrian territory, and the more time that went by, the greater the call for unification, both in Austria and at home in Germany, became. However, behind closed doors, Hitler forced the Austrian Chancellor, Kurt Schuschnigg, to resign in March 1938, or else face the threat of a full-blown military invasion. As a result, and with pro-Nazi members of government in place, German forces marched peacefully into Austria, and Hitler was welcomed home by millions of fellow Austrians. It was another chapter in what was to be known as "The Flower War," in which the military was either allowed or forced their way into occupied or foreign territory without a single shot being fired. And again, the only thing the foreign powers could do was watch. It was this lack of response that allowed Hitler more time to build up his armed forces and once again challenge the foreign powers of Europe.

However, Hitler's next peacetime conquest was to be his last. Since the beginning of 1938, Hitler had desired to bring the predominant German population in the Czech Sudetenland into the greater German Reich. While Hitler was forcibly getting his way through foreign policy and putting pressure on the Czech President, Edvard Benes, the new Army Commander in Chief, Generaloberst Walther von Brauchitsch, drew up plans for the invasion of Czechoslovakia. In an attempt to maintain peace in Europe, the governments of France, Great Britain, and Italy gave in to Hitler's demands at the infamous Munich Agreement in September 1938. Rather than be protected as a sovereign state, Czechoslovakia became the victim of foreign policy. Adding insult to injury, President Benes was not even consulted over the immediate surrender of Czech territory. Surprisingly, openly opposing this act of aggression, as well as the invasion plans of von Brauchitsch, was the Army Chief of the General Staff, General Ludwig Beck, who feared this latest idea would lead to all-out war. When the occupation of the Sudetenland became a reality, Ludwig Beck resigned and was replaced by General Franz Halder. In March 1939 Hitler, in flagrant violation of the Munich Agreement, sent a large contingent of troops to occupy the remainder of Czechoslovakia. Once again, and despite promises to protect what was left of this state, France, Britain, and the rest of the world did nothing. This further invasion of Czechoslovakia not only embarrassed the French and British heads of state, but it also removed any remaining doubts as to Hitler's real intentions. The false sense of peace and security was finally at an end. The war that everyone had been trying to avoid was now to become a harsh reality. Hitler's generals and admirals were about to embark on a five-year conflict that would change the way war was to be fought. Not only was it to end the lives of millions of soldiers and civilians, but it was to be an ideological conflict that would challenge humanity itself.

***

The following biographies are arranged alphabetically, with each entry arranged as follows:

Last name, first name: highest rank (date of promotion), (branch of service); dates and places of birth and death. P for N.S.D.A.P. membership number (if applicable), SS for SS membership number. World War I service with highest rank and last unit or command. Year joined N.S.D.A.P., S.A., S.S. (if applicable). Promotion dates to general officer rank. Service 1933/4–1945 including postings and/or commands. Awards: senior political awards, Third Reich military awards, higher foreign military awards, other Third Reich political awards, Freikorps and Weimar awards, imperial German WWI awards and foreign WWI awards, etc. *(Dates are given as day.month.year)*

A

Abberger, Erich: Generalmajor (01.01.44), (Heer); born 06.04.09 in Koeln, died 03.05.88 in Wiesbaden. WWI: Oberleutnant in Pionier Bataillon 8. Attached to Kommandanteur Staff in Koenigsberg 10.1933–04.1935, Commander of Pionier Bataillon in Ulm (later Bataillon 5) 05.1935–03.1937, Commander of Instruction Courses for Officers at Pionierschule I in Berlin 04.1937–07.1939. WWII: Armee Pionier Officer for 5. Armee 08.1939–09.1939, Group Leader attached to General of Pioniers in O.K.H. 10.1939–09.1942, Pionier Leader of 11. Armee 09.1942–12.1942, Senior Pionier Officer 3, 05.1943–05.1945. Awards: 1939 Clasps to the 1914 Iron Cross 1st and 2nd Class, General Assault Badge, 1914 Iron Cross 1st and 2nd Class, 1914 Wound Badge in Black, Cross of Honor.

Abernetty, Otto: Generalmajor (01.07.40), (Luftwaffe); born 08.03.93 in Steinbach, died 02.07.40 from air accident over Chateaudun. WWI: in G.A.S. as Leutnant and Leader of Schlachtstaffel 13. Attached to Inspectorate for Luftwaffe Schulen in R.L.M. 10.1933–06.1934, Instruction Group Leader and later Commandant of Kampfflieger Schule at Prenzlau 09.1934–03.1936, Group Commander in K.G. 254, 03.1936–02.1937, Instruction Group Leader at Luftwaffe Kriegsschule Dresden 06.1937–02.1939. WWII: Chief of Department L (In 10) in R.L.M. 03.1939–08.1939, Ia to Luftwaffe Commander for Heeresgruppe Sud 08.1939–10.1939, Ia to Luftwaffe Commander for Heeresgruppe B 10.1939–11.1939, Commander of Luftwaffe in 18. Armee 11.1939–07.1940. Awards: 1939 Observer's Badge, 1939 Wound Badge in Gold, Pilot's Commemorative Badge, 1914 Iron Cross 1st and 2nd Class, 1914 Wound Badge in Black, 1914 Observer's Badge, Cross of Honor.

Abesser, Dr. Georg: General-Arzt (01.07.42), (Heer); born 07.08.89 in Schwammelwitz, died 03.08.77 in Itzehoe. Medical doctor by profession. WWI: Ober-Arzt (unit unknown). WWII: Commander of Sanitats Abteilung 30, 1938–01.1940, Korps Physician to XXXIX. Panzer Korps 02.1940–06.1943, Fuehrer Res. in O.K.H.

06.1943–09.1944, member of Standing Commission with X. Armee Korps 09.1944–04.1945. Awards: German Cross in Silver 07.09.43, 1939, Clasp to the 1914 Iron Cross 2nd Class, War Merit Cross 1st and 2nd Class with Swords, Eastern Front Medal, 1914 Iron Cross 2nd Class, Cross of Honor.

Abraham, Erich: General der Infanterie (16.03.45), (Heer); born 27.03.95 in Marienburg, died 07.03.71 in Wiesbaden. WWI: Leutnant der Res. in Infanterie Regiment 152. Promotions to Generalmajor 01.06.43, Generalleutnant 01.04.44. Kompanie Chef in Infanterie Regiment 18, 10.1935–10.1936, Kompanie Chef in Infanterie Regiment 105, 10.1936–02.1937. WWII: Commander of I. Bataillon, Infanterie Regiment 105, 02.1937–11.1939, Commander of II. Bataillon, Infanterie Regiment 266, 11.1939–04.1940, Commander of Infanterie Regiment 230, 04.1940–04.1942, Commander of 76. Infanterie Division 04.1942–10.1944, Commander of LXIII. Armee Korps 12.1944–05.1945. Awards: Oak Leaves 26.06.44 (516), Knight's Cross 13.11.42, German Cross in Gold 07.03.42, 1939 Clasps to the 1914 Iron Cross 1st and 2nd Class, Infantry Assault Badge in Bronze, West Wall Medal, 1914 Iron Cross 1st and 2nd Class, Cross of Honor.

General der Infanterie Erich Abraham. (Roger James Bender)

Abt, Alexander: Generalmajor (01.04.42); (Heer); born 14.03.92 in Danzig, died 01.03.70 in St. Wendel. WWI: Leutnant in Telegraph Bataillon 2. Commander of Nachrichten Abteilung at Muenster 10.1934–10.1935, Commander of Nachrichten Abteilung 16, 10.1935–10.1937. WWII: Commander of Signals Troops for Wehrkreis Kommando IX 10.1937–08.1939, Commander of Nachrichten Regiment 40, 08.1939–09.1939, Commander of Nachrichten Regiment 537, 09.1939–04.1940, Armee Nachrichtenfuehrer z.b.V. 555, 04.1940–08.1940, Signals Leader to Wehrmacht Befehlshaber of Belgium and Northern France 08.1940–11.1940, Fuehrer Res. in O.K.H. 11.1940–05.1941, Wehrmacht Signals Leader to Netherlands 05.1941–05.1942, Signals Leader West 05.1942–08.1944, Higher Signals Leader of Land Fortifications attached to O.B. West 08.1944–05.1945. Awards: 1939 Clasp to the 1914 Iron Cross 2nd Class, War Merit Cross 1st and 2nd Class with Swords, 1914 Iron Cross 1st and 2nd Class, Cross of Honor.

Adam, Kurt: Generalmajor (01.04.45), (Heer); born 08.07.97 in Stuttgart, died 24.01.73 in Munich. WWI: in G.A.S. Flieger Abteilung 226 and later Balloon Platoon 13. Advisor in Reich War Ministry 05.1933–06.1935, Batterie Chef in Artillerie Regiment 19, 10.1935–10.1936, Ia to 35. Division 10.1936–02.1939.

WWII: Ia to General Staff of Grenztruppen on Upper Rhein 03.1939–09.1939, Ia to XXV. Armee Korps 09.1939–09.1941, Chief of Staff to XXV. Armee Korps 10.1941–04.1943, Commander of Grenadier Regiment 07.1943–01.1944, Fuehrer Res. in Heeresgruppe Sud 01.1944–1945. Awards: German Cross in Gold 16.01.44, 1939 Clasps to the 1914 Iron Cross 1st and 2nd Class, Infantry Assault Badge in Silver, Eastern Front Medal, Pilot's Commemorative Badge, 1914 Iron Cross 1st and 2nd Class, 1914 Pilot's Badge, Cross of Honor.

Adam, Max: Konteradmiral (01.02.43), (Kriegsmarine); born 28.12.94 in Hamburg, died 22.10.78 in Hamburg. WWI: U-boat service as Marineingenieur-aspirant and Engineer on *U-92*. Attached to Marine Schule at Kiel 10.1934–09.1935, assignments unknown 09.1935–10.1938. WWII: Formation Engineer on Staff of Commander of Reconnaissance Forces 10.1938–05.1940, Engineer on Staff of Marine Gruppen Kommando West 05.1940–06.1942, Chief of Fuel Economy Department in O.K.M. 06.1942–09.1943, Chief of Supply Department of Quartermaster Office in O.K.M. 10.1943–05.1945. Awards: War Merit Cross 1st and 2nd Class with Swords, 1914 Iron Cross 2nd Class, 1914 Submarine Badge, Cross of Honor.

Adam, Wilhelm: General der Infanterie (01.04.35); born 15.09.77 in Ansbach, died 08.04.49 in Garmisch-Partenkirchen. WWI: Major and Commander of 17. Pionier Bataillon. Promotions to Generalmajor 01.02.30, Generalleutnant 01.12.31, allowed to wear uniform of honorary Generaloberst 01.01.39. Befehlshaber of Wehrkreis Kommando VII 10.1933–05.1935, Commander of VII. Armee Korps 05.1935–09.1935, Commander of Wehrmacht Academy 10.1935–02.1938, Oberbefehlshaber of Gruppen Kommando 2, 03.1938–11.1938. WWII: no further assignments, retired 05.1943. Awards: RK-Sachsen Albrecht Order 1st Class with Swords, 1914 Iron Cross 1st and 2nd Class, Bavarian Military Service Order 3rd Class with Swords, Cross of Honor.

Adam, Wilhelm: Generalleutnant z.V. (01.06.41), (Heer); born 27.10.77 in Tostedt, died 04.11.46 in Tblisi P.O.W. Camp. WWI: Major and Advisor in War Ministry. Promotion to Reichswehr Generalmajor 01.02.31. WWII: no assignments 03.1931–08.1939, Inspector of Transport Troops in O.K.H. 08.1939–05.1943, retired 08.1943. Awards: War Merit Cross 1st and 2nd Class with Sword, 1914 Iron Cross 1st and 2nd Class, Cross of Honor.

Adametz, Johann: Generalmajor (01.02.41), (Luftwaffe); born 10.04.79 in Vienna, died 05.06.63 in Vienna. WWI: Hauptmann and Staff Officer attached to Austrian 10. Armee. Transferred to German Wehrmacht 03.1938. WWII: attached to Luftflotte 4, 03.1938–08.1939, Chief of Department III (Radio Listening) attached to Luftflotte 4, 09.1939–03.1940, Commander of Signals Regiment 4 and Leader of Weather Office I in Luftflotte 4, 04.1940–01.1941, Signals Leader to Luftgau

Kommando XVII 01.1941–06.1941, retired 12.1941. Awards: War Merit Cross 1st and 2nd Class with Swords, Cross of Honor.

Adler, Hermann: Generalmajor (01.04.45), (Luftwaffe); born 20.11.90 in Berlin, died 26.01.67 in Junkersdorf. WWI: in G.A.S. as Leutnant der Res. (unit unknown). WWII: Advisor in R.L.M. 02.1936–01.1940, Advisor, Group Director and later Department Chief in O.K.W. 01.1940–09.1943, attached to Flieger Regiments 51 and later 22, 02.1944–06.1944, Commander of Flieger Regiment 93, 06.1944–09.1944, Commander of Fallschirm Regiment "Adler" 09.1944–05.1945. Awards: 1939 Clasps to the 1914 Iron Cross 1st and 2nd Class, Pilot's Commemorative Badge, 1914 Iron Cross 1st and 2nd Class, 1914 Pilot's Badge, Cross of Honor.

Adlhoch, Xaver: Generalmajor (01.11.42), (Heer); born 17.06.93 in Rottenburg, died 26.06.68 in Coburg. WWI: Oberleutnant and Kompanie Chef in Bavarian Res. Infanterie Regiment 7. Commander of I. Bataillon, Infanterie Regiment at Nuremberg 10.1934–10.1935. WWII: Commander of M.G. Bataillon 6, 10.1935–08.1939, Commander of Infanterie Regiment 236, 09.1939–10.1942, Standort Commandant of Wjasma 11.1942–10.1943, Commandant of Feldkommandantur 550, 10.1943–05.1944, retired 10.1944. Awards: 1939 Clasps to the 1914 Iron Cross 1st and 2nd Class, Infantry Assault Badge in Silver, 1914 Iron Cross 1st and 2nd Class, 1914 Wound Badge in Black, Cross of Honor.

Adolph, Ernst: Generalmajor z.V. (01.02.41), (Heer); born 08.04.73 in Heinde, died 02.06.55 in Goaslar. WWI: Major and Chief of Staff to XXXVIII. Reserve Korps. Recalled to military service without assignment 07.1935. WWII: Deputy Commander of Truppenubungsplatz at Bergen-Belsen 08.1939–06.1940, Commandant of Feldkommandantur 755, 06.1940–02.1942, Wehrmacht Commander of Dnjepropetrowsk 02.1942–05.1942, retired 05.1942. Awards: 1939 Clasp to the 1914 Iron Cross 2nd Class, War Merit Cross 1st and 2nd Class with Swords, RK-Hohenzollern, 1914 Iron Cross 1st and 2nd Class, 1914 Wound Badge in Black, Cross of Honor.

Adolph-Auffenberg, Gustav: Generalleutnant (01.09.43), (Heer); born 11.07.87 in Olmuetz, died 08.02.67 in Vienna. WWI: Hauptmann and Bataillon Commander in Infanterie Regiment 1. Promotion to Generalmajor 01.09.42. Staff Officer attached to Infanterie Regiment 3, 04.1937–03.1938, Commander of II. Bataillon, Infanterie Regiment 131, 06.1938–11.1938, attached to Staff of Infanterie Regiment 20, 11.1938–01.1939. WWII: Commander of III. Bataillon, Infanterie Regiment 85, 03.1939–10.1939, Commander of Infanterie Regiment 41, 10.1939–10.1940, Commander of Infanterie Regiment 453, 10.1940–09.1942, Commander of 285. Security Division 09.1942–09.1944, Commandant of Fortress Section Lower Danube 12.1944–05.1945. Awards: German Cross in Gold 20.03.42, 1939 Iron Cross 1st Class, 1939 Clasp to the 1914 Iron Cross 2nd Class, Infantry Assault

Badge in Silver, Eastern Front Medal, 1939 Wound Badge in Silver, 1914 Iron Cross 2nd Class, Cross of Honor.

Agricola, Kurt: Generalleutnant z.V. (01.08.43), (Heer); born 15.08.89 in Doebeln, died 27.12.55 in Bad Godesberg. WWI: Hauptmann on Staff of XIL. Armee Korps. Promotion to Generalmajor 01.01.38. Commander of Infanterie Regiment at Breslau 12.1934–10.1935, Commander of Infanterie Regiment 49, 10.1935–10.1937, Commander of Heer Processing Office 3, 10.1937–11.1938. WWII: without assignment 01.1939–08.1939, Wehrmacht Commandant of Oppeln 09.1939–12.1941, Commandant of Feldkommandantur 580, 12.1941–04.1945. Awards: German Cross in Gold 15.12.43, 1939 Clasps to the 1914 Iron Cross 1st and 2nd Class, 1914 Iron Cross 1st and 2nd Class, Cross of Honor.

Ahlfen, Hans von: Generalmajor (30.01.45), (Heer); born 20.02.97 in Berlin, died 11.09.66 in Oberdorf. WWI: Leutnant and Zugfuehrer in Baltic Sea Division. Company Chief in Pionier Bataillon at Hann-Muenden 10.1934–07.1935, Pionier Instructor at Kriegsschule 08.1935–08.1937. WWII: Group Director attached to Inspection of Pioniers in O.K.H. 10.1937–06.1940, Commander of Pionier Bataillon 40 (mot.) 07.1940–01.1941, Commander of Pionier Regiment Staff 617 (mot.), 01.1941–07.1942, attached to Staff of General of Pioniers to Heeresgruppe D 07.1942–07.1943, Pionier Leader to Heeresgruppe Norway 07.1943–10.1944, Pionier Leader to Armee Gruppe B 03.1945–05.1945. Awards: 1939 Clasps to the 1914 Iron Cross 1st and 2nd Class, General Assault Badge, 1914 Iron Cross 1st and 2nd Class, Cross of Honor.

Ahrens, Dr. Eberhard: Admiral-Arzt (01.09.41), (Kriegsmarine); born 13.01.92 in Wetter, died 29.06.45 in Malente. Medical doctor by profession. WWI: Naval Marinefeldhilfsarzt in Marine Corps Flanders. Attached to Kaiser-Wilhelm Medical Academy in Berlin after war, Ship Doctor for line ship *Hessen* 10.1933–10.1934, Ship Physician for battleship *Admiral Scheer* 11.1934–09.1935, attached to Medical Staff of Admiral of Eastern Sea 09.1935–10.1938. WWII: Chief Physician of Naval Hospital at Kiel-Hassee 09.1939–05.1940, Inspection Physician attached to Educational Inspectorate Staff 10.1938–09.1939, Chief Physician for Naval Hospital at Kiel-Hassee 09.1939–05.1940, Chief Physician to Marine Befehlshaber of France 05.1940–02.1941, Chief Physician of Naval Hospital at Kiel-Wik 02.1941–08.1942, Chief Physician on Staff of Marine Gruppen Kommando Sud 08.1942–09.1943, Chief Physician for Naval Hospital at Malente 11.1943–11.1944, retired 12.1944. Awards: War Merit Cross 1st and 2nd Class with Swords, 1914 Iron Cross 2nd Class, Cross of Honor.

Alberti, Konrad von: Generalmajor (01.04.43), (Heer); born 17.07.94 in Stuttgart, died 01.08.67 in Stuttgart. WWI: Oberleutnant and Adjutant to

Grenadier Regiment 119. Tactics Instructor at Kriegsschule Dresden 04.1934–10.1937. WWII: Commander of II. Bataillon, Infanterie Regiment 50, 10.1937–09.1939, Commander of Infanterie Regiment 284, 09.1939–11.1939, Commandant of Feldkommandantur 580, 11.1939–07.1941, Commandant of Feldkommandantur 240, 07.1941–05.1942, Commander of Infanterie Regiment 179, 06.1942–01.1943, Commander of Formation and Training Staff for XIII. Armee Korps 11.1943–10.1944, Commander of Battle Area XII South 11.1944–05.1945. Awards: Honor Roll Clasp 28.03.43, 1939 Clasps to the 1914 Iron Cross 1st and 2nd Class, Infantry Assault Badge in Silver, 1914 Iron Cross 1st and 2nd Class, 1914 Wound Badge in Black, Cross of Honor.

Albrecht, Conrad: Generaladmiral (01.04.39), (Kriegsmarine); born 07.10.80 in Bremen, died 18.08.69 in Hamburg. WWI: Korvettenkapitan and Chief of Zerstorer Flotille Flanders. Retained as part of Reichsmarine after war. Promotions to Reichsmarine Konteradmiral 01.04.30, Reichsmarine Vizeadmiral 01.10.32, Admiral 01.12.35. Chief of Marine Station for Eastern Sea 10.1932–07.1935, Commanding Admiral of Marine Station Eastern Sea 07.1935–10.1938. WWII: Marine Group Commander Eastern Sea 11.1938–10.1939, retired 12.1939. Awards: 1939 Clasps to the 1914 Iron Cross 1st and 2nd Class, Grand Cross of the Italian Order of the Crown, Grand Cross of the Hungarian Service Order, Commander's Cross of the Finnish Order of the White Rose 1st Class, German Olympic Games Decoration 1st Class, Red Eagle Order IV. Class with Swords, RK-Hohenzollern, 1914 Iron Cross 1st and 2nd Class, Oldenburg Friedrich-August Cross 1st and 2nd Class, Cross of Honor.

Generaladmiral Conrad Albrecht. (Bundesarchiv)

Albrecht, Prof. Dr. Othmar: General-Arzt z.V. (01.09.42), (Heer); born 29.10.71 in Graz, died 14.05.47 in Vienna. Medical doctor by profession. WWI: Austrian medical service as Oberstabs-Arzt (unit unknown). Transferred to German Wehrmacht 03.1938. WWII: Commander of Sanitats Abteilung of Wehrkreis Kommando XVII 08.1939–09.1943, no assignment 09.1943–02.1944, retired 02.1944. Awards: War Merit Cross 1st and 2nd Class with Swords, Cross of Honor.

Aldrian, Eduard: Generalleutnant (01.06.43), (Heer); born 26.04.88 in Pola, died 01.10.55 in Graz. WWI: Hauptmann and Battery Commander in Austrian Schwere Feld Artillerie Regiment 44. Promotion to Generalmajor 01.09.42. Transferred to German Wehrmacht 03.1938. WWII: Commander of Gebirgs Beobachter

Abteilung 38, 08.1938–10.1939, Commander of z.b.V. Artillerie Regiment Staff 619, 10.1939–11.1941, Commander of Artillerie 124, 11.1941–03.1943, Higher Commander of Artillerie 308, 03.1943–07.1943, Commander of 373. Croatian Division 08.1943–10.1944, Artillery Commander of 306. Infanterie Division 01.1945–05.1945. Awards: German Cross in Gold 14.03.43, 1939 Iron Cross 1st and 2nd Class, General Assault Badge, Eastern Front Medal, 1939 Wound Badge in Black, Croatian Order of the Crown of King Zvonimir 1st Class with Oak Leaves, Swords and Breast Star, Cross of Honor.

Allmendinger, Karl: General der Infanterie (01.04.43), (Heer); born 02.02.91 in Abstgmund, died 02.10.65 in Ellwangen. WWI: Oberleutnant and Adjutant in Fusilier Regiment 12. Promotions to Generalmajor 01.08.40, Generalleutnant 01.08.42. Attached to Staff of 1. Division 08.1934–10.1935, Ia to I. Armee Korps 10.1935–10.1937, Commander of Infanterie Regiment 35, 10.1937–11.1938. WWII: Chief of Abteilung 10 in Heeres General Staff 11.1938–10.1939, Chief of Staff to V. Armee Korps 10.1939–10.1940, Commander of 5. Infanterie Division 10.1940–01.1943, Commander of V. Armee Korps 07.1943–05.1944, temporary O.B. of 17. Armee 05.1944–07.1944, Fuehrer Res. in O.K.H. 07.1944–05.1945. Awards: Oak Leaves 13.12.42 (153), Knight's Cross 17.07.41, 1939 Clasps to the 1914 Iron Cross 1st and 2nd Class, Infantry Assault Badge in Silver, Eastern Front Medal, Finnish Freedom Cross 1st Class with Swords, 1914 Iron Cross 1st and 2nd Class, 1914 Wound Badge in Black, Cross of Honor.

Alt, Erich: Generalmajor (01.02.44), (Luftwaffe); born 26.06.87 in Nicolai, died 22.08.66 in Oberstedten. WWI: in G.A.S. as Hauptmann and Commander of Flieger Abteilung 37. Ib attached to Luftkreis Kommando IV in Muenster 03.1934–10.1937, Advisor in R.L.M. 11.1937–06.1938, Ib attached to Luftwaffe General Staff Kommando Austria 07.1938–01.1939. WWII: Chief of Operations to Luftflotte 4, 03.1939–07.1940, Quartermaster of Luftgau Kommando XVII 08.1940–01.1945. Awards: German Cross in Silver 1945, War Merit Cross 1st and 2nd Class with Swords, Pilot's Commemorative Badge, 1914 Iron Cross 1st and 2nd Class, 1914 Observer's Badge, Cross of Honor.

Alten, Georg von: Generalmajor z.V. (01.06.42), (Heer); born 30.11.75 in Altona, died 05.09.50 in Schelenberg. WWI: Major on Staff of Governor General for Warsaw. WWII: recalled to military service 08.1939, Commandant of P.O.W. Camp Stalag XI B 09.1939–05.1940, attached to Staff of Military Administration in occupied France 06.1940–09.1940, Commandant of Officer P.O.W. Camp IX D 09.1940–07.1941, Commandant of Stalag IX B 07.1941–1941, Commandant of Officer P.O.W. Camp IX A 1941–1942, Commandant of Stalag XVIII B 1942–07.1942, retired 07.1942. Awards: War Merit Cross 2nd Class with Swords, 1914 Iron Cross 1st and 2nd Class, 1914 Wound Badge in Black, Cross of Honor.

Alten, Hans-Henning von: Generalmajor (01.02.41), (Heer); born 09.08.90 Nisgawe, died 03.05.47 at Muenster P.O.W. Camp. WWI: Hauptmann on Staff of 232. Landwehr Division. Commander of II. Bataillon, Infanterie Regiment at Potsdam 10.1934–10.1935, attached to Staff of Gruppen Kommando 2, 10.1935–10.1936, Commander of Wachtruppe (later Wach-Regiment) Berlin 10.1936–05.1939. WWII: Wehrmacht Commander of Koblenz 06.1939–08.1940, Wehrmacht Commander of Muelhausen 01.1941–01.1942, Commandant of Feldkommandantur 607, 01.1941–11.1942, Fuehrer Res. in O.K.H. 11.1942–08.1943, Commandant of Feldkommandantur 1006, 08.1943–05.1945. Awards: 1939 Clasps to the 1914 Iron Cross 1st and 2nd Class, War Merit Cross 1st and 2nd Class with Swords, Commander's Cross of the Order of the Crown of Italy, RK-Sachsen-Albrecht Order 2nd Class with Swords, 1914 Iron Cross 1st and 2nd Class, Johann Ritter Order, Bavarian Military Service Order IV. Class with Swords, Cross of Honor.

Altrichter, Dr. Friedrich: Generalleutnant (01.04.43), (Heer); born 03.09.90 in Berlin, died 14.04.49 in Bediak P.O.W. Camp. WWI: Hauptmann and Staff Officer attached to 50. Reserve Division. Promotion to Generalmajor 01.04.41. Bataillon Commander in Infanterie Regiment at Potsdam 10.1934–10.1935, Bataillon Commander in Infanterie Regiment 9, 10.1935–10.1936, Leader of Lehrer Gruppe D at Kriegsschule Dresden 10.1936–05.1938, Commander of Infanterie Regiment 54, 05.1938–10.1938. WWII: Commander of Lehrer Gruppe A at Kriegsschule Dresden 11.1938–08.1939, Commander of Infanterie Regiment 188, 08.1939–01.1940, Infanterie Course Commander for 164. Infanterie Division 01.1940–08.1940, Commander of Infanterie Courses for 71. Infanterie Division 10.1940–03.1941, Commander of 1. Infanterie Division 07.1941–09.1941, Commander of 58. Infanterie Division 09.1941–04.1942, Commander of 154. Infanterie Division 06.1942–04.1945. Awards: German Cross in Gold 23.01.42, 1939 Clasps to the 1914 Iron Cross 1st and 2nd Class, Infantry Assault Badge in Silver, Eastern Front Medal, 1914 Iron Cross 1st and 2nd Class, Cross of Honor.

Altrock, Wilhelm von: Generalleutnant (01.04.43), (Heer); born 24.08.87 in Groeba, died 26.02.52 in Diedersen. WWI: Hauptmann and Commander of Sachsen Pionier Bataillon 4. Promotion to Generalmajor 01.04.40. Bataillon Commander in Infanterie Regiment at Dresden 10.1934–10.1935, Bataillon Commander in Infanterie Regiment 52, 10.1935–10.1936. WWII: Commander of Infanterie Regiment 83, 10.1936–03.1940, Commander of Truppenubungsplatz at Neuhammer 03.1940–05.1940, Commander of 379. Infanterie Division 05.1940–08.1940, Senior Commandant of Feldkommandantur 379, 08.1940–11.1943, Senior Commandant of Feldkommandantur 392, 11.1943–02.1944, Commandant of Feldkommandantur 559, 03.1944–08.1944, Fuehrer Res. in O.K.H. 08.1944–12.1944, P.O.W.

Commander for Wehrkreis Kommando XVIII 03.1945–05.1945. Awards: 1939 Clasps to the 1914 Iron Cross 1st and 2nd Class, 1914 Iron Cross 1st and 2nd Class, 1914 Wound Badge in Silver, Cross of Honor.

Alvensleben, Ludolf von: SS-Gruppenfuehrer und Generalleutnant der Waffen-SS und Polizei (09.11.43); born 17.03.01 in Halle, died 01.04.70 in Argentina. P-149345, SS-177002. Joined N.S.D.A.P. and S.A. in 1931, SA-Standartenfuehrer attached to Halle-Merseburg, joined S.S. in 1934. Promotion to SS-Brigadefuehrer 01.08.1940. Leader of SS-Fuss Standarte 46, 10.1934–07.1935, Leader of SS-Abschnitte X 12.1936–12.1937, attached to Staff of RFSS 12.1938. WWII: S.S.P.F. of Sinferopol 01.1942, S.S.P.F. of Crimea 05.1943, Leader and H.S.S.P.F. of SS-Oberabschnitte Elbe 01.1944–05.1945, member of Reichstag (WK 31 Wuerttemberg). Awards: Golden Party Badge (honorary), War Merit Cross 1st and 2nd Class with Swords, Crimea Shield, Gau Halle-Merseburg Commemorative Badge, Danzig Cross 1st Class, Reich Sports Badge in Silver, SA-Sports Badge in Bronze, German Horseman's Badge in Bronze, Degen, Ring.

Amann, Otto: Generalmajor (01.12.43), (Heer); born 11.01.92 in Osten, died 26.10.58 in Eichstadt. WWI: Oberleutnant in M.G. Kompanie of III. Bavarian Armee Korps. Training Commander in II. Bataillon, Infanterie Regiment at Regensburg 10.1934–10.1935, Commander of III. Bataillon, Infanterie Regiment 62, 10.1935–11.1938, Commander of III. Bataillon, Infanterie Regiment 85, 11.1938–03.1939. WWII: attached to Staff of Infanterie Regiment 85, 03.1939–08.1939, Commander of I. Bataillon, Infanterie Regiment 282, 08.1939–01.1940, Commander of Infanterie Replacement Regiment 10, 01.1940–07.1941, Commander of Infanterie Regiment 593, 07.1941–08.1942, Commander of Res. Grenadier Regiment 7, 05.1943–08.1943, Fuehrer Res. in O.K.H. 08.1943–05.1944, Wehrmacht Commander of Regensburg 05.1944–05.1945. Awards: 1939 Clasps to the 1914 Iron Cross 1st and 2nd Class, War Merit Cross 1st and 2nd Class with Swords, Infantry Assault Badge in Silver, 1914 Iron Cross 1st and 2nd Class, Bavarian Military Service Order IV. Class with Swords, Austro-Hungarian Military Service Cross 3rd Class with War Decoration, 1914 Wound Badge in Black, Cross of Honor.

Amann, Friedrich von: Generalleutnant z.V. (01.04.42), (Heer); born 08.03.70 in Berlin, died 29.03.53 in Halle-Saale. WWI: Major and Commander of Grenadier Regiment 7. Promotion to Generalmajor z.V. 01.12.40. WWII: recalled to military service 08.1939, Wehrmacht Commander of Breslau 08.1939–05.1942, Fuehrer Res. in O.K.H. 05.1942–05.1943, retired 05.1943. Awards: War Merit Cross 1st and 2nd Class with Swords, RK-Hohenzollern, 1914 Iron Cross 1st and 2nd Class, Cross of Honor.

Ammon, Carl von: Generalmajor (01.04.40), (Heer); born 27.07.78 in Berlin, died 23.09.46 in Wasserburg. WWI: Rittmeister and Advisor to Prussian War Ministry. WWII: Military Replacement Inspector of Stettin 06.1935–11.1944, retired 12.1944–05.1945. Awards: War Merit Cross 1st and 2nd Class with Swords, RK-Hohenzollern, 1914 Iron Cross 1st and 2nd Class, Austro-Hungarian Military Service Cross 3rd Class with War Decoration, Johann Ritter Order, Cross of Honor.

Ancker, Heinrich: Vizeadmiral (01.11.40), (Kriegsmarine); born 07.10.86 in Memel, died 15.05.60 in Hamburg. WWI: Kapitanleutnant and Adjutant to Staff of the II. Matrosen Division of Naval Station North Sea. Promotion to Konteradmiral 01.10.36. Naval Commandant of Wilhelmshaven 01.1933–09.1934, Commandant of line ship *Schlesien* 09.1934–09.1936, Commandant of Naval Arsenal at Kiel 09.1936–11.1937. WWII: Military Economics Inspector for Hamburg 11.1937–08.1942, Head of Reich Commission for Sea Office Hamburg 09.1942–02.1945. Awards: War Merit Cross 1st and 2nd Class with Swords, 1914 Iron Cross 1st and 2nd Class, 1914 Naval Wound Badge in Black, Cross of Honor.

Anders, Carl: Generalmajor (30.01.45), (Heer); born 31.08.93 in Guenz, died 28.01.72 in Prien. WWI: Oberleutnant and Adjutant to Infanterie Regiment 152. Kompanie Chef in Infanterie Regiment at Marienburg 10.1934–10.1935, Kompanie Chef in Infanterie Regiment 45, 10.1935–05.1937, Instructor for M.G. Zugfuehrer at Infanterie Schule in Doeberitz 05.1937–11.1938. WWII: Commander of II. Bataillon, Infanterie Regiment 45, 11.1938–02.1940, Commander of I. Bataillon, Infanterie Regiment 505, 02.1940–10.1940, Commander of I. Bataillon, Infanterie Regiment 581, 10.1940–11.1941, Commander of Grenadier Regiment 484, 11.1941–09.1944, Commander of 88. Infanterie Division 01.1945–05.1945. Awards: Knight's Cross 04.05.44, German Cross in Gold 14.02.42, 1939 Clasps to the 1914 Iron Cross 1st and 2nd Class, Infantry Assault Badge in Silver, Eastern Front Medal, 1914 Iron Cross 1st and 2nd Class, 1914 Wound Badge in Black, Cross of Honor.

Andersen, Kurt: Generalmajor (17.02.45), (Luftwaffe); born 02.10.98 in Hohenrade, died 09.01.03 in Bonn. WWI: NCO in Telegraph Bataillon I, Commander of II. Bataillon. Attached to R.L.M. 08.1935–03.1937, Batterie Chef in Flak Lehr Regiment 04.1937–06.1938. WWII: Flak Instruction Regiment 07.1938–06.1940, Commander of Flak Artillerie Schule II at Stolpmuende 06.1940–11.1942, Commander of Flak Regiment 153, 11.1942–06.1943, Commander of Luftwaffe Kriegsschule 6, 06.1943–03.1944, Flak Artillerie Inspector East 04.1944–01.1945, Commander of 23. Flak Division 02.1945–05.1945. Awards: Knight's Cross 21.12.42, 1939 Iron Cross 1st and 2nd Class, Flak War Badge, Ground Combat Badge, Baltic Cross 1st and 2nd Class, 1914 Wound Badge in Black, Cross of Honor.

Andrae, Alexander: General der Flieger (01.07.41), (Luftwaffe); born 27.04.88 in Koeslin, died 03.04.79 in Wiesbaden. WWI: Hauptmann on Staff of General Government of Antwerp. Promotions to Generalmajor 01.01.38, Generalleutnant 01.01.40. Transferred to Wehrmacht 07.1935, attached to Staff of Artillerie Regiment 12, 10.1935–07.1936. WWII: Commander of Luftwaffe Kriegsschule 11. 1936–08.1939, Inspector of Education and Training Affairs in R.L.M. 10.1939–03.1940, Commander of Air Region Staff 300 (Denmark) 03.1940–04.1941, Commander of Fortress Kreta 07.1941–08.1942, attached to R.L.M. 08.1942–05.1943, retired 05.1943, joined Heer as General der Artillerie in 04.1945. Awards: 1939 Clasps to the 1914 Iron Cross 1st and 2nd Class, 1939 Observer's Badge, 1914 Iron Cross 1st and 2nd Class, Cross of Honor.

Andre, Carl: Generalmajor (30.01.45), (Heer); born 24.05.94 in Freismissen, died 22.01.85 in Buckeburg. WWI: Leutnant and Adjutant to Infanterie Regiment 164. Kompanie Chef in Infanterie Regiment at Oldenburg 10.1934–10.1935. WWII: Commander of M.G. Bataillon 1, 10.1935–02.1940, Commander of Infanterie Regiment 521, 02.1940–04.1943, temporary Commander of 206. Infanterie Division 07.1943–10.1943, Fortress Commander of Bergen 12.1943–05.1945. Awards: German Cross in Gold 08.08.42, 1939 Clasps to the 1914 Iron Cross 1st and 2nd Class, Infantry Assault Badge in Silver, Eastern Front Medal, German West Wall Medal, RK-Hohenzollern, 1914 Iron Cross 1st and 2nd Class, 1914 Wound Badge in Black, Cross of Honor.

Andreas, Moritz: Generalleutnant (01.04.41), (Heer); born 16.04.84 in Ealing, died 13.16.64 in Hannover. WWI: Hauptmann and Commander of III. Bataillon, Infanterie Regiment 71. Promotion to Generalmajor 01.04.39. Commandant of Truppenubungsplatz at Koenigsbrueck 10.1934–04.1937, Landwehr Commander of Kuestin 04.1937–06.1938. WWII: Landwehr Commander of Luebben 06.1938–08.1939, Commander of 208. Infanterie Division 08.1939–12.1941, Senior Commandant of Feldkommandantur 242, 01.1942–09.1943, P.O.W. Commander for Heeresgruppe Sud 10.1943–02.1944, attached to Staff of Wehrkreis Kommando III 03.1944–09.1944, Defensive Replacement Inspector for Potsdam 10.1944–05.1945. Awards: 1939 Clasps to the 1914 Iron Cross 1st and 2nd Class, Infantry Assault Badge in Silver, Eastern Front Medal, RK-Hohenzollern, 1914 Iron Cross 1st and 2nd Class, 1914 Wound Badge in Black, Cross of Honor.

Angelis, Maximilian de: General der Artillerie (01.03.42), (Heer), born 02.10.89 in Budapest, died 06.12.74 in Graz. WWI: Hauptmann and Staff Officer in Austrian 2. Karstjaeger Brigade. Promotions to Generalmajor 15.03.38, Generalleutnant 01.08.40. Transferred to German Wehrmacht 03.1938, Inspector of Artillerie 08.1938–11.1938. WWII: Commander of Artillerie XV 11.1938–09.1939,

Commander of 76. Infanterie Division 09.1939–01.1942, Commander of XXXXIV. Armee Korps 03.1942–11.1943 and 12.1943–04.1944, O.B. of 2. Panzer Armee 09.1944–05.1945. Awards: Oak Leaves 12.11.43 (323), Knight's Cross 09.02.42, 1939 Iron Cross 1st and 2nd Class, Infantry Assault Badge in Silver, Eastern Front Medal, Cross of Honor.

Anger, Kurt: Generalmajor (01.10.39), (Heer); born 13.12.88 in Oliva, died 24.03.61 in Oberstaufen. WWI: Hauptmann on Staff of X. Armee Korps. Deputy Commander of Training in Halle/Saale 02.1934–06.1935, Commander of III. Abteilung, Artillerie Regiment at Naumburg 07.1935–09.1935, misc. assignments 09.1935–10.1936, Commander of I. Abteilung, Artillerie Regiment 31, 10.1936–10.1937. WWII: Commander of Artillerie Regiment 18, 10.1937–09.1939, Commander of Artillerie 110, 09.1939–04.1942, P.O.W. Commander for Wehrkreis Kommando XIII 08.1942–05.1945. Awards: 1939 Clasps to the 1914 Iron Cross 1st and 2nd Class, General Assault Badge, Eastern Front Medal, Crimea Shield, Commander's Cross of the Order of the Star of Romania with Swords and Breast Star, 1914 Iron Cross 1st and 2nd Class, Austro-Hungarian Military Service Order 3rd Class with War Decoration, 1914 Wound Badge in Black, Cross of Honor, Turkish Half-Moon Decoration.

Angermayer, Dr. Erwin: General-Arzt (01.06.42), (Heer); born 09.06.88 in Salzburg, died 20.03.63 in Salzburg. Medical doctor by profession. WWI: Ober-Arzt and Bataillon Medic to II. Bataillon, Austrian Infanterie Regiment 59. Transferred to German Wehrmacht 03.1938. WWII: Chief Physician to Wehrkreis XVII 04.1938–08.1939, Korps Physician to XVIII. Armee Korps 08.1939–10.1939, Division Physician to 59. Infanterie Division 10.1939–10.1940, Section Physician to Higher Kommando LX 10.1940–12.1941, Korps Physician to XXXVIII. Armee Korps 12.1941–05.1943, Fuehrer Res. in O.K.H. 05.1943–04.1945. Awards: 1939 Iron Cross 2nd Class, War Merit Cross 1st and 2nd Class with Swords, Eastern Front Medal, Cross of Honor.

Angern, Guenther: Generalleutnant (01.12.42), (Heer); born 05.03.93 in Kolberg, died 02.02.43 (suicide) in Stalingrad. WWI: Oberleutnant and Adjutant to Kavallerie Jaeger Regiment 6. Promotion to Generalmajor 01.09.41. Advisor on Inspection Staff of Kavallerie 10.1934–03.1935, Commander of Reiter Regiment at Fuerstenwalde 03.1935–10.1935, Commander of Reiter (later Kavallerie) Regiment 9, 10.1935–11.1938. WWII: Commander of 3. Schuetzen Brigade 11.1938–12.1939, Commander of 11. Schuetzen Brigade 12.1939–08.1941, Staff Officer and later Commander of 16. Panzer Division 09.1942–02.1943. Awards: Knight's Cross 05.08.40, German Cross in Gold 08.03.42, Honor Roll Clasp 22.07.41, 1939 Clasps to the 1914 Iron Cross 1st and 2nd Class, Tank Assault Badge in Silver, 1939

Wound Badge in Silver, German Horseman's Badge in Silver, 1914 Iron Cross 1st and 2nd Class, Cross of Honor.

Angerstein, Karl: Generalleutnant (01.04.43), (Luftwaffe); born 04.12.90 in Muehlhausen, died 20.09.85 in Feldkirchen. WWI: in G.A.S. as Oberleutnant and Leader of Bombenstaffel 18. Promotion to Generalmajor 01.04.41. Attached to Luftpolizei in Prussian Ministry of Interior 05.1933–10.1934, Leader attached to Luft Amt in Munich 10.1934–03.1937. WWII: Group Commander in K.G. 155 followed by K.G. 158, 07.1937–11.1939, Commander of II. Gruppe, K.G. 77, 11.1939–01.1940, Commander of K.G. 28, 01.1940–07.1940, Commander of K.G. 1 "Hindenburg" 07.1940–03.1942, Higher Commander of Kampfflieger und Stuka Schulen 07.1942–06.1943, temporary Commander of I. Flieger Korps 06.1943–11.1943, Special Duties Officer on Staff of General Unruh in O.K.W. 02.1944–09.1944, Officer Judge in Reichs War Court 01.1945–05.1945. Awards: Knight's Cross 02.11.40, German Cross in Gold 16.07.42, 1939 Clasps to the 1914 Iron Cross 1st and 2nd Class, Combined Pilot/Observer's Badge in Gold with Diamonds, Bomber Flight Clasp in Gold, Eastern Front Medal, Pilot's Commemorative Badge, RK-Hohenzollern, 1914 Iron Cross 1st and 2nd Class, 1914 Wound Badge in Silver, 1914 Pilot's Badge, Cross of Honor.

Ansat, John: Generalleutnant (01.08.42), (Heer); born 23.02.90 in Bersteningken, died 28.08.70 in Luebeck. WWI: Oberleutnant in Fusilier Regiment 1. Promotion to Generalmajor 01.08.40. Commander of Beobachter Abteilung 10.1935–10.1937. WWII: Commander of Artillerie Regiment 32, 10.1937–05.1940, Commander of Artillerie 134, 05.1940–12.1940, Commander of 102. Infanterie Division 12.1940–02.1942, Senior Commander of Artillerie 313, 06.1942–03.1945. Awards: German Cross in Gold 23.03.44, 1939 Clasps to the 1914 Iron Cross 1st and 2nd Class, Infantry Assault Badge in Silver, RK-Hohenzollern, 1914 Iron Cross 1st and 2nd Class, Cross of Honor.

Anton, Werner: Generalleutnant (01.07.44), (Luftwaffe); born 03.04.95 in Dresden, died 12.09.48 (from accident) at Wolfsburg P.O.W. Camp. WWI: in G.A.S. as Leutnant in Flieger Abteilung A 212. Promotion to Generalmajor 01.02.43. Transport Officer attached to Landes Polizei Inspectorate Staff in Sachsen-Thuringen 01.1934–07.1935, Transportation Officer attached to Staff of Luftkreis Kommando III 08.1935–04.1937, Batterie Chef in Flak Regiment 43, 10.1937–07.1938, Commander of Leicht Flak Abteilung 94, 08.1938–05.1939. WWII: Commander of I. Bataillon, Flak Regiment 7, 06.1939–10.1939, Commander of Flak Regiment 13, 10.1939–04.1941, Commander of Flak Brigade III and later Flak Brigade XV 12.1941–11.1942, Commander of 6. Flak Division 11.1942–05.1945. Awards: Knight's Cross 09.06.44, German Cross in Gold 29.04.43, 1939 Clasps to the

1914 Iron Cross 1st and 2nd Class, Flak War Badge, Kurland Cuff Band, Pilot's Commemorative Badge, RK-Military St. Heinrich's Order 20.11.16, 1914 Iron Cross 1st and 2nd Class, 1914 Observer's Badge, Cross of Honor.

Apell, Georg von: Generalleutnant (01.06.38), (Heer); born 21.10.84 in Wesel, died 30.03.45 in Lich. WWI: Hauptmann and Ia to 218. Infanterie Division. Promotion to Generalmajor 01.10.36. Commander of Infanterie Regiment 17, 11.1933–10.1936, Chief of Staff to XI. Armee Korps 10.1936–10.1937, Chief of Staff to Gruppen Kommando 2, 10.1937–11.1938. WWII: Commander of 9. Infanterie Division 12.1938–08.1940, attached to Wehrkreis IX 08.1940–5.1942, placed at disposal of O.K.H. 05.1942–06.1944, retired 06.1944. Awards: 1939 Clasps to the 1914 Iron Cross 1st and 2nd Class, Infantry Assault Badge in Silver, RK-Hohenzollern, 1914 Iron Cross 1st and 2nd Class, 1914 Wound Badge in Black, Cross of Honor.

Apell, Wilhelm von: Generalleutnant (01.04.43), (Heer); born 16.01.92 in Bueckeburg, died 07.03.69 in Baden-Baden. WWI: Oberleutnant and Kompanie Chef in VII. Res. Jaeger Bataillon. Promotion to Generalmajor 01.04.41. Commander of Halb Reiter Regiment at Erfurt 10.1934–02.1935, Commander of Kradschuetzen Bataillon 2, 02.1935–07.1938. WWII: Commander of Kavallerie Jaeger Regiment 11, 08.1938–02.1940, Commander of 9. Jaeger Brigade 02.1940–08.1941, Commander of 22. Panzer Division 09.1941–10.1942, attached to Wehrkreis Kommando XVII 10.1942–04.1943, Military Replacement Inspector for Vienna 04.1943–05.1945. Awards: Knight's Cross 14.05.41, 1939 Clasps to the 1914 Iron Cross 1st and 2nd Class, Tank Assault Badge in Bronze, Crimea Shield, 1914 Iron Cross 1st and 2nd Class, 1914 Wound Badge in Silver, Cross of Honor.

Generalleutnant Wilhelm von Apell. (Bundesarchiv)

Arenstorff, Hans-Adolf von: Generalmajor (01.10.43), (Heer); born 18.01.95 in Lohe, died 05.05.52 at Bryanke P.O.W. Camp. WWI: Leutnant and Ordnance Officer with 34. Infanterie Brigade. Attached to Staff of Reiter Regiment 13, 10.1935–10.1936. WWII: Commander of I. Abteilung, Kavallerie Regiment 13, 10.1936–09.1939, Commander of Aufklarungs Abteilung 152, 08.1939–12.1940, attached to Staff of 5. Schuetzen Brigade 12.1940–05.1941, Commander of 79. Jaeger Brigade 05.1941–01.1942, Commander of 16. Jaeger Brigade 01.1942–11.1942, Commander of 60. Infanterie Division (mot.) 11.1942–01.1943, captured at Stalingrad 01.1943. Awards: German Cross in Gold 14.01.42, 1939

Clasps to the 1914 Iron Cross 1st and 2nd Class, Infantry Assault Badge in Silver, Eastern Front Medal, 1914 Iron Cross 1st and 2nd Class, Cross of Honor, German Horseman's Badge in Silver.

Arnauld de la Periere, Friedrich von: Generalleutnant (01.01.41), (Luftwaffe); born 17.06.88 in Breslau, died 12.10.69 in Friedrichshafen. WWI: in Naval G.A.S. as Oberleutnant zur See in II. Marine Flieger Abteilung. Promotion to Generalmajor 01.02.39. Commander of Seeflieger Abteilung 03.1934–03.1935, Commander of Luftkreis Fliegerpark Brandis 04.1935–09.1936, several short term assignments 10.1936–11.1937, Department Chief in Supply Office of R.L.M. 11.1937–06.1939. WWII: Commander of Luftzeuggruppe 17, 07.1939–08.1943, Fuehrer Res. in O.K.L. 08.1943–08.1944, retired 08.1944. Awards: War Merit Cross 1st and 2nd Class with Swords, Naval Pilot's Commemorative Badge, 1914 Iron Cross 1st and 2nd Class, 1914 Naval Pilot's Badge, Cross of Honor.

Arnauld de la Periere, Lothar von: Vizeadmiral (01.02.41), (Kriegsmarine); born 18.03.86 in Posen, died 24.02.41 in air accident over Paris. WWI: U-boat service as Kapitanleutnant and Commandant of *U-139*. Promotion to Konteradmiral 01.06.40. Attached to Turkish Naval Academy 1932–1938. WWII: Naval Plenipotentiary for Danzig and Coastal Region 09.1939–03.1940, Naval Commander of Belgium and Netherlands 05.1940–06.1940, Naval Commander of Brittany 06.1940–12.1940, Naval Commander of Western France 12.1940–02.1941. Awards: 1939 Clasp to the 1914 Iron Cross 2nd Class, War Merit Cross 2nd Class with Swords, Pour le Mérite 11.10.16, RK-Hohenzollern, RK-Austro-Hungarian Leopold Order with War Decoration, 1914 Iron Cross 1st and 2nd Class, Prussian Crown Order IV. Class with Swords, Austro-Hungarian Military Service Cross 3rd Class with War Decoration, Turkish Silver Liakat Medal with Sabre, Turkish Half Moon, 1914 Submarine Badge, Cross of Honor.

Lothar von Arnauld de la Periere. (Bundesarchiv)

Arndt, Edgar: Generalmajor (01.07.43), (Heer); born 01.07.92 in Lissa, died 24.08.44 in action near Groghy. WWI: Oberleutnant and Adjutant to 5. Landwehr Infanterie Brigade. Bataillon Commander in Infanterie Regiment 25, 10.1934–09.1937. WWII: Military Training Director of Cottbus 10.1937–09.1939, Commander of Infanterie Regiment 337, 09.1939–03.1942, Commander of 708. Infanterie Division 07.1943–08.1944. Awards: 1939 Clasps to the 1914 Iron Cross 1st and 2nd Class, Infantry Assault Badge in Silver, Eastern Front Medal, 1939

Wound Badge in Gold, 1914 Iron Cross 1st and 2nd Class, 1914 Wound Badge in Silver, Cross of Honor.

Arndt, Karl: Generalleutnant (08.11.43), (Heer); born 10.03.92 in Gross-Kauer, died 30.12.81 in Balve-Langenholthausen. WWI: Hauptfeldwebel in Infanterie Regiment 46. Promotion to Generalmajor 10.03.43. Kompanie Chef in Infanterie Regiment at Frankfurt/Oder 10.1934–03.1935, Commander of I. Bataillon, Infanterie Regiment 68, 04.1935–01.1936, attached to Staff of Infanterie Regiment 68, 01.1936–07.1936, Commander of Ersatz Bataillon 67, 10.1936–11.1937, Staff Officer attached to 23. Division 11.1937–12.1938. WWII: Commander of II. Bataillon, Infanterie Regiment 68, 01.1939–02.1940, Commander of Infanterie Regiment 511, 02.1940–01.1943, Commander of 293. Infanterie Division 04.1943–11.1943, Commander of 359. Infanterie Division 11.1943–01.1945, Acting Commander of LIX. Armee Korps 01.1945–04.1945. Awards: Oak Leaves 01.02.45 (719), Knight's Cross 23.01.42, German Cross in Gold 02.07.44, 1939 Clasps to the 1914 Iron Cross 1st and 2nd Class, Infantry Assault Badge in Silver, Eastern Front Medal, 1914 Iron Cross 1st and 2nd Class, 1914 Wound Badge in Silver, Cross of Honor.

Arndt, Dr. Karl: General-Arzt (01.10.44), (Heer); born 01.04.89 in Fuerstenberg, died 23.01.43 (missing in action at Stalingrad and presumed dead). Medical doctor by profession. WWI: German medical service (rank and unit unknown). WWII: Division Physician to 62. Infanterie Division 08.1939–07.1942, Korps Physician to LI. Armee Korps 07.1942–01.1943. Awards: 1939 Clasp to the 1914 Iron Cross 2nd Class, War Merit Cross 1st and 2nd Class with Swords, Eastern Front Medal, 1914 Iron Cross 2nd Class, Cross of Honor.

Arnim, Friedemund von: Generalmajor (01.11.42), (Heer); born 06.01.94 in Kassel, died 03.06.75 in Wentorf. WWI: Oberleutnant on Staff of 2. Kavallerie Division. Adjutant to Kavallerie Kommando at Insterburg 12.1934–10.1935, Advisor on Staff of Inspection of Kavallerie 10.1935–10.1936, attached to Staff of Reiter Regiment 6, 10.1936–02.1938. WWII: Commander of Kavallerie Regiment 14, 02.1938–08.1939, Commander of Gebirgs Regiment 2, 10.1940–04.1941, Adjutant in O.K.H. 04.1941–11.1942, Commandant of Feldkommandantur 580, 12.1942–08.1943, Commandant of Feldkommandantur 602, 08.1943–09.1944, Fuehrer Res. in O.K.H. 09.1944–05.1945. Awards: War Merit Cross 1st and 2nd Class with Swords, General Assault Badge, 1914 Iron Cross 1st and 2nd Class, Bavarian Military Service Order IV. Class with Swords, Cross of Honor, German Horseman's Badge in Silver.

Arnim, Fritz von: Generalmajor (20.04.45), (Heer); born 24.08.92 in Gross-Fredenwalde, died 07.10.70 in Fredendorf. WWI: Leutnant der Res. in Military and Economic Staff in Romania. Attached to Military Replacement Inspection at

Koeln 04.1936–10.1936, attached to Artillerie Regiment 26, 11.1936–05.1938, attached to Staff of Commander of Artillerie 16, 06.1938–11.1938. WWII: attached to Staff of Commander of Artillerie 2, 11.1938–08.1939, Adjutant to 258. Infanterie Division 08.1939–06.1942, attached to Liaison Staff between Heeresgruppe Sud and Romanian VI. Armee Korps 06.1942–01.1943, Commander of Military District Kommando at Stargard 03.1943–05.1945. Awards: 1939 Iron Cross 1st Class, 1939 Clasp to the 1914 Iron Cross 2nd Class, Eastern Front Medal, 1914 Iron Cross 2nd Class, Austro-Hungarian Military Service Order 3rd Class with War Decoration, Cross of Honor.

Arnim, Hans-Jochen von: Generalmajor (02.11.42), (Luftwaffe); born 17.01.93 in Prenzlau, died 01.04.72 in Bad Toelz. WWI: in Naval G.A.S. as Leutnant zur See in II. Marine Flieger Abteilung. Advisor to Staff of Fliegerschule Warnemuende 01.1934–09.1935, Instructor at Seeflieger Schule 10.1935–02.1937, Seefliegerhorst Commandant of Hoernum 03.1937–03.1938. WWII: Seefliegerhorst Commandant of Puettnitz 04.1938–01.1941, Commander of Flieger Training Regiment 16, 01.1942–10.1942, Flughafenbereichs Commandant of 9-VII 01.1943–08.1943, Flughafenbereichs Commandant of 2-XII 09.1943–10.1944, retired 02.1945. Awards: War Merit Cross 1st and 2nd Class with Swords, Naval Pilot's Commemorative Badge, 1914 Naval Pilot's Badge, 1914 Iron Cross 2nd Class, Bavarian Military Service Order 4th Class with Swords, Cross of Honor.

Arnim, Hans-Juergen von: Generaloberst (03.12.42), (Heer); born 04.04.89 in Ernsdorf, died 01.09.62 in Bad Wildungen. WWI: Hauptmann and Bataillon Commander in Reserve Infanterie Regiment 93. Promotions to Generalmajor 01.01.38, Generalleutnant 01.12.39, General der Panzertruppe 17.12.41. Ia on Staff of Infanterie Fuehrer VI 03.1934–10.1935, Commander of Infanterie Regiment 68, 10.1935–02.1938, Commander of Heer Service Office 4 at Schweidnitz 02.1938–04.1939. WWII: attached to O.K.H. 05.1939–08.1939, Commander of 52. Infanterie Division 09.1939–10.1940, Commander of 17. Panzer Division 10.1940–11.1941, Commander of XXXIX. Panzer Korps 02.1942–12.1942, Oberbefehlshaber of 5. Panzer Armee 12.1942–03.1943, Oberbefehlshaber of Heeresgruppe "Afrika" 03.1943–05.1943, captured 05.1943. Awards: Knight's Cross 04.09.41, 1939 Clasps to the 1914 Iron Cross 1st and 2nd Class, Tank Assault Badge in Silver, Eastern Front Medal, RK-Hohenzollern, 1914 Iron Cross 1st and 2nd Class, 1914 Wound Badge in Silver, Cross of Honor.

Generaloberst Hans-Juergen von Arnim. (Bundesarchiv)

Arnim, Harry von: Generalmajor (01.10.41), (Heer); born 26.03.90 in Criewen, died 25.10.41 in action near Naroforminsk. WWI: Oberleutnant in Guards Infanterie Regiment. Department Commander in Reiter Regiment 13, 10.1935–09.1936, Department Commander at Kavallerie Schule at Hannover 10.1936–09.1938, attached to Staff of Senior Kavallerie Officers 4, 10.1938–03.1939. WWII: Commandant of Heeres Wehrkreis-Reit-und Fahrschule at Warendorf 04.1939–05.1940, Commander of Infanterie Regiment 479 5. 1940–10.1941. Awards: 1939 Clasps to the 1914 Iron Cross 1st and 2nd Class, Infantry Assault Badge in Silver, 1939 Wound Badge in Gold, 1914 Iron Cross 1st and 2nd Class, Cross of Honor, German Horseman's Badge in Silver.

Arning, Karl: Generalmajor (01.09.44), (Heer); born 10.02.92 in Berlin, died 17.11.64 in Hamburg. WWI: Oberleutnant and Ordnance Officer with 2. Guards Infanterie Brigade. Military District Officer in Osterode 05.1935–07.1936, Kompanie Chef in Infanterie Regiment 22, 10.1936–05.1939. WWII: Commander of II. Bataillon, Infanterie Regiment 3, 06.1939–05.1941, attached to Staff of Infanterie Regiment 3, 05.1941–10.1941, Commander of Infanterie Regiment 24, 10.1941–12.1943, attached to Heeresgruppe Nord Ukraine 04.1944–07.1944, Commander of 75. Infanterie Division 07.1944–04.1945. Awards: Knight's Cross 11.10.43, German Cross in Gold 30.04.43, 1939 Clasps to the 1914 Iron Cross 1st and 2nd Class, Infantry Assault Badge in Silver, Eastern Front Medal, 1939 Wound Badge in Silver, 1914 Iron Cross 1st and 2nd Class, 1914 Wound Badge in Black, Cross of Honor.

Arnold, Hugo: Generalmajor (01.12.43), (Luftwaffe); born 25.01.78 in Arnstadt, died 26.01.62 in Arnstadt. WWI: Feldwebel-Leutnant in Garde Feld Artillerie Regiment 6. Attached to Staff of Fahr Abteilung 6, 10.1933–09.1934, attached to Staff of Flak Regiment 7, 04.1935–09.1936. WWII: attached to Staff of Flak Regiment 4, 10.1936–08.1939, Commander of Flak Firing Grounds West Deep 08.1939–12.1943, retired 12.1943. Awards: 1939 Clasps to the 1914 Iron Cross 1st and 2nd Class, War Merit Cross 1st and 2nd Class with Swords, 1914 Iron Cross 2nd Class, Cross of Honor.

Arnold, Karl: Generalmajor (01.06.41), (Heer); born 08.03.90 in Anselmo, died 15.04.45 in action in Vienna. WWI: Hauptmann and Leader of 12. M.G. Sniper Bataillon. Attached to Staff of Infanterie Regiment 12, 10.1935–10.1936, Heeres Acceptance Inspector 2, 10.1936.10.1937, Attached to Ordnance Acceptance Office West in Hannover 10.1937–05.1938. WWII: Attached to Ordnance Acceptance Office of Vienna 06.1938–02.1941, Attached to Ordnance Acceptance Office of Brussels 02.1941–01.1944, Commandant of Feldkommandantur in the West (section unknown) 04.1944–11.1944. Awards: 1939 Clasp to the 1914 Iron Cross

2nd Class, War Merit Cross 1st and 2nd Class with Swords, 1914 Iron Cross 1st and 2nd Class, 1914 Wound Badge in Black, Cross of Honor.

Arnold, Wilhelm: Generalmajor (01.10.43), (Heer); born 20.09.94 in Eschwege, died 26.01.86 in Hannover. WWI: in G.A.S. as Oberleutnant in Flieger Kommando North. Commander of Nachrichten Abteilung at Stettin 10.1934–10.1935. WWII: Commander of Nachrichten Abteilung 42, 10.1935–08.1939, Commander of Nachrichten Regiment 632, 08.1939–10.1939, Commander of Nachrichten Regiment 521, 10.1939–12.1941, Signals Leader for 6. Armee 12.1941–01.1943, attached to Wehrkreis Kommando II 01.1943–08.1943, Signals Leader for Land Fortifications attached to Wehrmacht Befehlshaber of Norway 08.1943–04.1944, Office Group Chief for Signal Matters with Ersatz Armee 07.1944–04.1945. Awards: 1939 Clasps to the 1914 Iron Cross 1st and 2nd Class, General Assault Badge, Eastern Front Medal, 1939 Wound Badge in Gold, Pilot's Commemorative Badge, 1914 Iron Cross 1st and 2nd Class, 1914 Pilot's Badge, Cross of Honor.

Arnswaldt, Wolff-Ehrenreich von: Konteradmiral (01.01.45), (Kriegsmarine); born 23.03.98 in Radeluebbe, died 04.01.72 in Kassel. WWI: Leutnant zur See and Watch Officer with 17. Torpedobootsflotille. Instructor at Kuesten Artillerie Schule 09.1933–09.1935, 1. Artillery Officer on battleship *Deutschland* 09.1935–08.1937, attached to Naval Station Eastern Sea 09.1937–03.1938. WWII: 2. Admiral Staff Officer attached to Naval Station of Baltic Sea 03.1938–09.1939, 1. Admiral Staff Officer attached to Naval Station East 10.1939–07.1940, Commander of Sea Defenses at Flanders 07.1940–02.1941, Chief of Staff to Marine Befehlshaber of Black Sea 07.1941–06.1943, Chief of Staff to Inspection of Naval Artillerie 06.1943–07.1944, Commander of Sea Defenses at Kurland Bridgehead 07.1944–05.1945. Awards: 1939 Clasps to the 1914 Iron Cross 1st and 2nd Class, Kurland Cuff Band, Grand Officer's Cross of the Romanian Order of the Crown with Breast Star, 1914 Iron Cross 1st and 2nd Class, Cross of Honor.

Arps, Theodor: Vizeadmiral (01.04.42), (Kriegsmarine); born 02.02.84 in Neuenkirchen, died 28.04.47 in Garmisch-Partenkirchen. WWI: Kapitanleutnant on auxiliary cruiser *Kaiser Wilhelm der Grosse*, P.O.W. 10.1914–08.1919. Unknown status after end of war. Promotion to Konteradmiral 01.01.40. Group Leader in Naval Command 10.1933–09.1934. WWII: Department Chief for Naval Intelligence 10.1934–12.1939, Judge in Reichs War Court 01.1940–05.1945. Awards: War Merit Cross 1st and 2nd Class with Swords, 1914 Iron Cross 1st and 2nd Class, Cross of Honor.

Asal, Dr. Walther: General-Stabsarzt (09.11.44), (Heer); born 14.06.91 in Bruchsal, died 21.04.87 in Birkenfeld. Medical doctor by profession. WWI: Ober-Arzt and Medical

Adjutant to 52. Infanterie Division. Promotion to General-Arzt 01.09.41. Standort Arzt of Dresden 1936–1938. WWII: Division Physician to 4. Infanterie Division 1938–03.1940, Corps Physician to XI. Armee Korps 03.1940–08.1941, Group Physician to Panzer Gruppe "Afrika" 08.1941–09.1942, Inspector of Hospitals 09.1942–08.1944, Commander of Military Medical Academy 08.1944–03.1945. Awards: 1939 Clasps to the 1914 Iron Cross 1st and 2nd Class, War Merit Cross 1st and 2nd Class with Swords, Afrika Cuff Band, 1914 Iron Cross 1st and 2nd Class, Cross of Honor.

Ascheberg, Percy Freiherr von: Generalmajor (01.06.42), (Heer); born 11.06.80 in Gross-Buschhof, died 26.09.52 in Hamminkeln. WWI: in G.A.S. as Hauptmann and Leader of Flieger Abteilung 29. Attached to Heeres Service Office 4, 10.1935–09.1936. WWII: Military District Commander of Wesel 10.1936–07.1942, retired 07.1942. Awards: War Merit Cross 1st and 2nd Class with Swords, Pilot's Commemorative Badge, RK-Hohenzollern, 1914 Iron Cross 1st and 2nd Class, 1914 Pilot's Badge, Cross of Honor.

Aschenbrandt, Heinrich: Generalmajor (01.12.41), (Heer); born 30.06.84 in Wuerzburg, died 23.03.53 in Berlin. WWI: Hauptmann on General Staff of 19. Armee. Group Leader attached to Technische Amt of R.L.M. 10.1933–09.1935. WWII: Advisor in War Science Department of Reich War Ministry (later O.K.H.) 10.1935–07.1941, Commandant of Feldkommandantur 238, 07.1941–08.1944, Fuehrer Res. in O.K.H. 08.1944–12.1944, retired 12.1944. Awards: War Merit Cross 1st and 2nd Class with Swords, 1914 Iron Cross 1st and 2nd Class, 1914 Wound Badge in Black, Cross of Honor.

Aschenbrenner, Heinrich: Generalleutnant (01.08.44), (Luftwaffe); born 08.07.95 in Krankenhagen, died 11.12.60 in Bielefeld. WWI: in G.A.S. as Leutnant in Kampfgeschwader 2. Promotion to Generalmajor 01.08.42. Commander of Lehr Abteilung at Luftwaffe Nachrichtenschule Halle/Saale 10.1935–02.1937, Commander of Luftwaffe Nachrichten Ausbildungs Abteilung at Koehten 03.1937–03.1938. WWII: Commander of Luftwaffe Nachrichtenschule Regiment at Koethen 04.1938–08.1939, Luftwaffe Attaché to German Embassy in Moscow 10.1939–06.1941, Higher Signals Leader to Luftgau Kommando II 06.1941–09.1942, Senior Signals Leader to O.B of Luftwaffe 10.1942–04.1945. Awards: German Cross in Silver 01.09.42, 1939 Clasps to the 1914 Iron Cross 1st and 2nd Class, War Merit Cross 1st and 2nd Class with Swords, 1939 Observer's Badge, Pilot's Commemorative Badge, 1914 Iron Cross 1st and 2nd Class, 1914 Wound Badge in Black, 1914 Observer's Badge, Cross of Honor.

Assmann, Kurt: Vizeadmiral (01.01.41), (Kriegsmarine); born 13.07.84 in Nuremberg, died 26.07.62 in Bad-Homburg. WWI: Kapitanleutnant and Chief of Torpedobootsflotille Flanders. Promotion to Reichsmarine Konteradmiral 01.10.32. Leader of Marine Archives in O.K.M. 04.1933–01.1936. WWII: Chief of Kriegswissenschaftliche Abteilung in O.K.M. 01.1936–06.1943, retired 06.1943. Awards: War Merit Cross 1st and 2nd Class with Swords, Prussian Red Eagle Order IV. Class, RK-Hohenzollern, RK-Baden Order of the Zaehringer Lion 2nd Class with Swords, 1914 Iron Cross 1st and 2nd Class, Oldenburg Friedrich-August Cross 1st and 2nd Class, Cross of Honor.

Assmann, Max: Konteradmiral (Ing.) (01.02.43), (Kriegsmarine); born 28.12.94 in Hamburg, died 22.10.78 in Hamburg. WWI: Marineingenieuraspirant on *UC-92*. Lead Engineer for cruiser *Koenigsberg* 09.1932–09.1934, attached to Marineschule at Kiel 10.1934–09.1935, attached to Engineer Staff of Torpedo Boats 10.1935–10.1938. WWII: attached to Staff of Reconnaissance Surface Ships 10.1938–05.1940, Engineer Officer attached to Staff of Marine Gruppen Kommando West 05.1940–06.1942, Department Chief in O.K.M. 06.1942–09.1943, Chief of Nachschub Abteilung and later Nachschub Amtsgruppe of O.K.M. 10.1943–07.1945. Awards: War Merit Cross 1st and 2nd Class with Swords, 1914 Iron Cross 1st and 2nd Class, 1914 Submarine Badge, Cross of Honor.

Assmann, Dr. Walter: Generalleutnant (16.03.45), (Heer); born 22.07.96 in Muehlhausen, died 01.05.64 in Offenbach. WWI: Leutnant and Adjutant to 102. Res. Infanterie Brigade. Promotion to Generalmajor 01.09.44. Kompanie Chef in Infanterie Regiment at Heilbronn 10.1934–10.1935, Kompanie Chef in Infanterie Regiment 34, 10.1935–11.1938. WWII: Kompanie Chef in Grenz Infanterie Regiment 125, 11.1938–11.1939, Commandant of Staff Quarters for Wehrkreis XII 11.1939–04.1940, Commander of I. Bataillon, Infanterie Regiment 479, 06.1940, severely wounded and in hospital 06.1940–12.1940, Commander I. Bataillon, Infanterie Regiment 479, 12.1940–10.1941, temporary Commander of Infanterie Regiment 479, 10.1941–01.1942, Commander of Infanterie Regiment 478, 01.1942–11.1943, Fuehrer Res. in O.K.H. 11.1943–07.1944, Commander of 101. Jaeger Division 07.1944–05.1945. Awards: Knight's Cross 10.02.45, German Cross in Gold 25.04.42, 1939 Clasps to the 1914 Iron Cross 1st and 2nd Class, Infantry Assault Badge in Silver, Eastern Front Medal, 1939 Wound Badge in Black, 1914 Iron Cross 1st and 2nd Class, 1914 Wound Badge in Black, Cross of Honor.

Attig, Dr. Rudolf: General-Arzt (01.06.44), (Heer); born 14.04.93 in Giessen, died 27.01.81 in Bremen. Medical doctor by profession. WWI: German medical service (rank and unit unknown). WWII: Division Physician to 246. Infanterie Division 08.1939–04.1941, Division Physician to 17. Panzer Division 04.1941–06.1942, Corps Physician to XII. Armee Korps 06.1942–01.1943, Fuehrer Res. in O.K.H. 01.1943–12.1943, Army Physician to 10. Armee 12.1943–12.1944. Awards: 1939 Clasp to the 1914 Iron Cross 2nd Class, War Merit Cross 1st and 2nd Class with Swords, Eastern Front Medal, 1914 Iron Cross 2nd Class, Cross of Honor.

Audoersch, Oskar: Generalmajor (09.11.44), (Heer); born 27.02.98 in Colbiehnen, died 05.06.91 in Ulm. WWI: Leutnant and Adjutant to I. Bataillon, Infanterie Regiment 47. Kompanie Chef in Infanterie Regiment at Meiningen 10.1934–10.1935, Kompanie Chef in Schuetzen Regiment 2, 10.1935–04.1936. WWII: Advisor in Reich War Ministry (later O.K.H.) 04.1936–07.1940, Commander of Grenadier Regiment 394, 08.1940–01.1942, Department Chief in Office Group for Industrial Armaments in O.K.H. 01.1942–07.1944, Commander of 25. Panzer Division 08.1944–05.1945. Awards: German Cross in Gold 21.04.43, 1939 Clasps to the 1914 Iron Cross 1st and 2nd Class, War Merit Cross 1st and 2nd Class with Swords, Infantry Assault Badge in Silver, Eastern Front Medal, Silesian Eagle 1st and 2nd Class, 1914 Iron Cross 1st and 2nd Class, 1914 Wound Badge in Black, Cross of Honor.

Auer, Franz: Generalleutnant z.V. (01.01.43), (Heer); born 17.05.78 in Passau, died 15.08.67 in Staubing. WWI: Hauptmann and Ic on Staff of 6. Armee. Promotion to Generalmajor z.V. 01.11.38. WWII: employee in Heer Weapons Office in Suhl 04.1933–08.1939, recalled to military service 08.1939, Commissioner of Infanterie Weapons in Heer Waffen Abteilung of O.K.H. 08.1939–05.1941, Chief of Service Office in Paris for Heer Weapons Office 05.1941–12.1942, retired 04.1943. Awards: War Merit Cross 1st and 2nd Class with Swords, 1914 Iron Cross 1st and 2nd Class, 1914 Wound Badge in Black, Cross of Honor.

August, Kurt: General-Ingenieur (01.09.43), (Luftwaffe); born 14.06.94 in Hohenstein, died 05.12.81 in Munich. Engineer by profession. WWI: Leutnant der Res. in Feld Artillerie Regiment 21. WWII: attached to R.L.M. 06.1934–05.1945. Awards: War Merit Cross 1st and 2nd Class with Swords, 1914 Iron Cross 1st and 2nd Class, Cross of Honor.

Augsberger, Franz: SS-Brigadefuehrer und Generalmajor der Waffen-SS (21.06.44); born 10.10.05 in Vienna, died 19.03.45 in action in Neustadt. P-360700, SS-139528. Joined N.S.D.A.P. and S.S. in 1934. Attached to SS-Fuehrer Schule at Braunschweig 01.07.35–01.12.38. WWII: attached to SS-Gebirgs Division "Nord" 01.10.42, Commander of 20. Waffen Grenadier Division der SS (Estnische Nr. 1) 30.01.44–03.1945. Awards: Knight's Cross 08.03.45, German Cross in Gold 30.05.42, Honor Roll Clasp 1945, 1939 Iron Cross 1st and 2nd Class, Infantry Assault Badge in Bronze, 1939 Wound Badge in Gold, Reich Sports Badge in Bronze, SA-Sports Badge in Bronze, German Horseman's Badge in Silver, Degen, Ring.

Auleb, Helge: General der Infanterie (01.12.43), (Heer); born 24.03.87 in Gehren, died 14.04.64 in Duesseldorf. WWI: Hauptmann and Commander of I. Bataillon, Infanterie Regiment 117. Promotions to Generalmajor 01.02.39, Generalleutnant 01.12.40. Chief of Staff to Wehrkreis Kommando X 05.1935–10.1935, Chief of Staff to X. Armee Korps 10.1935–10.1936. WWII: Commander of Infanterie Regiment 77 followed by Infanterie Regiment 39, 10.1936–08.1939, Senior Quartermaster of 5. Armee 08.1939–10.1939, Senior Quartermaster of 2. Armee 10.1939–11.1939, Senior Quartermaster to Heeresgruppe A 11.1939–06.1940, Commander of 6. Infanterie Division 10.1940–01.1942, Fuehrer Res. in O.K.H. 01.1942–06.1942, Acting Commander of Crimea 04.1943–07.1943, Commander of Security Troops for Heeresgruppe A 09.1943–12.1943, German Troop Commander in Transnistria 12.1943–04.1944, German Troop Commander in North Romania 04.1944–06.1944, Commander of LXIX. Armee Korps 06.1944–05.1945. Awards: German Cross in Gold 26.12.41, 1939 Clasps to the 1914 Iron Cross 1st and 2nd Class, Infantry Assault Badge in Silver, Eastern Front Medal, 1914 Iron Cross 1st and 2nd Class, Cross of Honor.

Aulock, Hubertus von: Generalmajor der Res. (21.08.44), (Heer); born 02.10.91 in Kochelsdorf, died 18.01.79 in Norderstadt. WWI: Oberleutnant and Bataillon Adjutant in Infanterie Regiment 22. WWII: recalled to military service 08.1939, Headquarters Commandant for Korps Nachschub Fuehrer 403, 08.1939–05.1940, Headquarters Commandant for III. Armee Korps 04.1940–09.1940, attached to Staff of z.b.V. Regiment 800 "Brandenburg" 11.1940–04.1941, Chief of Commando Staff for Wehrmacht Befehlshaber of North-Western France 05.1941–08.1944, captured 09.1944. Awards: 1939 Clasps to the 1914 Iron Cross 1st and 2nd Class, 1914 Iron Cross 1st and 2nd Class, Cross of Honor.

Axthelm, Walther von: General der Flak Artillerie (01.04.44), (Luftwaffe); born 23.12.93 in Hersbrueck, died 06.01.72 in Traunstein. WWI: Oberleutnant in 8. Bavarian Feld Artillerie Regiment. Promotions to Generalmajor 19.09.40, Generalleutnant 01.10.42. Group Leader L3 attached to Reich War Ministry 04.1933–03.1935, Group Leader attached to Inspection of Flak Artillerie in R.L.M. 04.1935–08.1936. WWII: attached to Staff of Flak Regiment 103, 08.1936–05.1940, Commander of I. Flak Brigade 06.1940–03.1941, Commander of I. Flak Korps 03.1941–01.1942, Inspector of Flak Artillerie (L In 4) and General of Flak Weapons in R.L.M. 01.1942–03.1945. Awards: Knight's Cross 04.09.41, 1939 Clasps to the 1914 Iron Cross 1st and 2nd Class, Flak War Badge, 1914 Iron Cross 1st and 2nd Class, 1914 Wound Badge in Black, Cross of Honor.

General der Flak Artillerie Walther von Axthelm. (Bundesarchiv)

B

Baade, Ernst-Guenther: Generalleutnant (01.08.44), (Heer); born 20.08.97 in Gut Falkenhagen, died 08.05.45 of wounds at Bad Segeberg Military Hospital. WWI: Leutnant in Dragoon Regiment 9. Promotion to Generalmajor 20.03.44. Chief of 1. Schwadron, Reiter (later Kavallerie) Regiment 3, 10.1934–01.1939. WWII: Commander of Aufklarungs Abteilung 17, 08.1939–12.1939, Commander of I. Bataillon, Mounted Regiment 22, 12.1939–08.1941, Commander of Bicycle Bataillon 1, 10.1941–12.1941, Commander of Kradschuetz Bataillon 4, 12.1941–03.1942, Commander of Schuetzen Regiment 115, 04.1942–07.1942, Fuehrer Res. in O.K.H. 08.1942–04.1943, Commander of Wehrmacht Employment Staff for Italy 04.1943–10.1943, Commander of 90. Panzer Grenadier Division 12.1943–12.1944, attached to Wehrkreis Kommando III and later Wehrkreis Kommando XI 01.1945–03.1945, wounded by British fighter bombers 04.1945. Awards: Swords 16.11.44 (111), Oak Leaves 22.02.44 (402), Knight's Cross 27.06.42, German Cross in Gold 02.11.41, 1939 Clasps to the 1914 Iron Cross 1st and 2nd Class, 1 Tank Destruction Badge, Afrika Cuff Band, 1939 Wound Badge in Silver, 1914 Iron Cross 1st and 2nd Class, 1914 Wound Badge in Black, Cross of Honor.

Baader, Dr. Ernst: General-Arzt (01.12.44), (Heer); born 05.08.94 Waldshut, died 08.10.53 in Emmindingen. Medical doctor by profession. WWI: German medical service (rank and unit unknown). WWII: attached to Sanitats Abteilung 39, 11.1938–08.1939, Division Physician to 218. Infanterie Division 218, 08.1939–04.1940, Division Physician to 163. Infanterie Division 04.1940–10.1940, Chief Physician to Wehrmacht Plenipotentiary in Boehmen-Maehren 10.1940–05.1942, Corps Physician to LXXXVI. Armee Korps 11.1942–01.1944, Army Physician to 19. Armee 01.1944–05.1945. Awards: 1939 Clasp to the 1914 Iron Cross 2nd Class, War Merit Cross 1st and 2nd Class with Swords, 1914 Iron Cross 2nd Class, Cross of Honor.

Baarth, Juergen: Generalmajor (01.04.42), (Heer); born 06.04.90 in Stolp, died 09.05.61 in Nassau. WWI: Rittmeister and Squadron Chief in Hussar Regiment

5. Attached to Command Staff of Kraftfahr Abteilung at Magdeburg 01.1935–03.1935, Commander of Panzer Aufklarungs Abteilung 13, 01.1935–10.1935, Commander of Panzertruppen IX 10.1935–09.1937. WWII: Commander of Military District Remonteschule at Beeskow 10.1937–05.1942 and again 11.1943–08.1944, Commandant of Feldkommandantur 595, 06.1941–08.1943, Wehrmacht Commander of Koblenz 08.1944–11.1944. Awards: 1939 Clasps to the 1914 Iron Cross 1st and 2nd Class, 1914 Iron Cross 1st and 2nd Class, 1914 Wound Badge in Black, Cross of Honor, German Horseman's Badge in Silver.

Bach, Erich von dem: SS-Obergruppenfuehrer und General der Polizei (09.11.41); born 01.03.99 in Lauenburg, died 08.03.72 in a Munich prison. P-489101, SS-9831. WWI: Leutnant in Grenadier Regiment 10 "Koenig Friedrich-Wilhelm II." Served in Freikorps, joined N.S.D.A.P. and S.S. in 1931. Promotions to SS-Brigadefuehrer 15.12.33, SS-Gruppenfuehrer 11.07.34. Leader of SS-Oberabschnitte Nordost 01.10.34–01.07.035, Leader of SS-Oberabschnitte Sudost 01.12.36–01.12.38. WWII: H.S.S.P.F. of Russland-Mitte 30.01.42–15.05.43, Chief of Bandenkampfverbaende 30.01.44–09.11.44, Commander of Korps "von dem Bach" during Warsaw Uprising 1944, Commander of XIV. SS-Armee Korps, Member of Reichstag (WK 7 Breslau). Awards: Golden Party Badge (honorary), Knight's Cross 30.09.44, German Cross in Gold 23.02.43, 1939 Clasps to the 1914 Iron Cross 1st and 2nd Class, War Merit Cross 1st and 2nd Class with Swords, Anti-Partisan War Badge in Silver, Danzig Cross 1st Class, SA-Rally at Braunschweig Badge of Honor, Silesian Eagle 1st and 2nd Class, 1914 Iron Cross 1st and 2nd Class, 1914 Wound Badge in Black, Reich Sports Badge in Silver, SA-Sports Badge in Bronze, Degen, Ring.

SS-Obergruppenfuehrer Erich von dem Bach. (Bundesarchiv)

Bachelin, Helmuth: Generalmajor (01.10.44), (Heer); born 21.06.00 in Karlsruhe, died 21.08.75 in Hamburg. WWI: Leutnant in Feld Artillerie Regiment 14. Adjutant to Infanterie Regiment at Kolberg 10.1934–10.1935, Kompanie Chef in Infanterie Regiment 15, 10.1935–04.1937. WWII: Adjutant to 9. Infanterie Division 05.1937–06.1940, Group Director in Personnel Department of O.K.H. 10.1940–02.1942, Commander of Infanterie Regiment 36, 02.1942–09.1942, Director and later Commander of Courses for Hoehere Adjutanten in Personnel Department of O.K.H. 11.1942–02.1944, Chief of Zentral Abteilung in O.K.H. 04.1944–10.1944, Office Group Chief in Zentral Abteilung of O.K.H. 10.1944–05.1945. Awards: German Cross in Gold 05.04.43, 1939 Clasps to the 1914 Iron

Cross 1st and 2nd Class, Infantry Assault Badge in Silver, Eastern Front Medal, 1914 Iron Cross 1st and 2nd Class, 1914 Wound Badge in Black, Cross of Honor.

Bacher, Hermann: Generalmajor (01.12.42), (Heer); born 11.03.89 in Pola, died 06.10.64 in Salzburg. WWI: Hauptmann in Austrian Pionier Bataillon 2. Transferred to Wehrmacht 03.1938, attached to XVIII. Armee Korps 04.1938–11.1938, attached to Staff of Pionier Commander XVII 11.1938–05.1939. WWII: Pionier Leader to XI. Armee Korps 06.1939–06.1940, Pionier Leader to Panzer Gruppe 2, 06.1940–02.1941, Commander of Pionier Regiment 515, 02.1941–03.1942, Commander of Senior Construction Staff 23 in Caucasus 10.1942–02.1943, Higher Pionier Leader for crossing of Kerch Straight 02.1943–08.1943, Higher Pionier Leader of 23 for Kuban Bridgehead 08.1943–09.1943, Higher Pionier Leader 36, 10.1943–07.1944, Higher Pionier Leader to General Government (Poland) 09.1944–01.1945, Higher Pionier Leader 20, 01.1945–05.1945. Awards: German Cross in Gold 04.08.43, 1939 Iron Cross 1st and 2nd Class, General Assault Badge, Eastern Front Medal, Kuban Shield, Cross of Honor.

Bachmann, Johannes: Admiral (01.09.42), (Kriegsmarine); born 22.03.90 in Werdau, died 02.04.45 in action in Willebadessen. WWI: Oberleutnant zur See and Commandant of torpedo boat *G-8*. Promotions to Konteradmiral 01.04.39, Vizeadmiral 01.04.41. Leader attached to Kriegsmarine Service Office in Koenigsberg 09.1933–09.1935, Commandant of surface ship *Emden* 09.1935–08.1936. WWII: Chief of Staff to North Sea Naval Station 08.1936–08.1940, Coastal Commander of Eastern Frisia 08.1940–02.1941, Coastal Commander of German Bay 02.1941–06.1942, Naval Befehlshaber Western France 08.1942–01.1943, retired 05.1943. Awards: German Cross in Silver 05.03.43, 1939 Clasp to the 1914 Iron Cross 2nd Class, War Merit Cross 1st and 2nd Class with Swords, Coastal Artillery War Badge, RK-Sachsen Albrecht Order 2nd Class with Swords, 1914 Iron Cross 1st and 2nd Class, 1914 Naval Wound Badge in Black, Cross of Honor.

Back, Hans-Ulrich: Generalmajor (01.02.44), (Heer); born 26.08.96 in Saarbrucken, died 14.02.76 in Hagen. WWI: Leutnant in Infanterie Regiment 74. Kompanie Chef in Infanterie Regiment 60, 10.1935–03.1936, Leader of Transport Training in Infanterie Regiment 60, 04.1937–10.1937, Transport Officer on Staff of Schuetzen Regiment 4, 10.1937–01.1938. WWII: Commander of I. Bataillon, Schuetzen Regiment 2, 02.1938–11.1939, Commander of Schuetzen Regiment 2, 08.1939–08.1940, Commander of Grenadier Regiment 304, 08.1940–07.1942, Schnelltruppe Commander for Wehrkreis Kommando XVIII 11.1942–11.1943, Commander of 16. Panzer Division 11. 1943–08.1944, Commander of 178. Panzer Division 10. 1944–01.1945, Commander of Panzer Training Division "Tatra" 01.1945–02.1945, Commander of 232. Panzer Division 02.1945–03.1945. Awards: Knight's Cross

05.08.40, 1939 Clasps to the 1914 Iron Cross 1st and 2nd Class, Tank Assault Badge in Bronze, Eastern Front Medal, 1939 Wound Badge in Silver, 1914 Iron Cross 1st and 2nd Class, 1914 Wound Badge in Silver, Cross of Honor.

Admiral Otto Backenkoehler. (Williamson)

Backenkoehler, Otto: Admiral (01.04.43), (Kriegsmarine); born 01.02.92 in Goettingen, died 05.02.67 in Kiel. WWI: Oberleutnant zur See and Commandant of torpedo boat *V-5*. Promotions to Konteradmiral 01.10.40, Vizeadmiral 01.04.42. Commander of Torpedoschule 10.1933–09.1935, Commander of Marine Nachtrichtenschule 10.1933–09.1934, Commandant of surface ship *Koeln* 10.1935–10.1937, Chief of Staff to Flottenkommando 10.1937–10.1938. WWII: Chief of Staff to Baltic Sea Naval Station 10.1938–10.1939, Chief of Staff to Fleet Kommando 10.1939–07.1940, Chief of Torpedo Abteilung in O.K.M. 08.1940–03.1943, Chief of Marinewaffen Abteilung in O.K.M. 03.1943–04.1944, Chief of Kriegsmarine Armaments in O.K.M. 05.1944–05.1945. Awards: Knight's Cross of the War Merit Cross with Swords 03.01.45, German Cross in Silver 07.08.43, 1939 Clasps to the 1914 Iron Cross 1st and 2nd Class, High Seas Fleet War Badge, 1914 Iron Cross 1st and 2nd Class, Cross of Honor.

Backhaus, Paul: Generalmajor (01.04.44), (Luftwaffe); born 11.10.89 in Koeln, died 23.12.60 in Padersborn. WWI: in G.A.S. as Hauptmann and Commander of Flieger Abteilung A 259. Commander of Fliegergruppe Liegnitz 08.1934–09.1936. WWII: Commander of Fliegergruppe Paderborn 10.1936–09.1939, Fliegerhorst Commandant of Sagan-Kuepper 10.1939–05.1940, Fliegerhorst Commandant of Gossalier 05.1940–04.1941, Commander of Luftzueggruppe at Warsaw 04.1941–08.1942, Commander of Luftzeuggruppe Finland 08.1942–08.1944, attached to Luftgau Kommando VIII 09.1944–01.1945, retired 01.1945. Awards: 1939 Clasps to the 1914 Iron Cross 1st and 2nd Class, Pilot's Commemorative Badge, RK-Wuerttemberg Friedrich Order 1st Class with Swords, 1914 Iron Cross 1st and 2nd Class, Austro-Hungarian Military Service Order 3rd Class with War Decoration, 1914 Pilot's Badge, Cross of Honor.

Bade, Hans-Albert: Generalmajor (01.04.43), (Heer); born 01.01.79 in Beckendorf, died 06.04.59 in Potsdam. WWI: Hauptmann and Commander of III. Bataillon, Infanterie Regiment 31. WWII: attached to Kriegswissenschaftliche Abteilung of Heeres General Staff 08.1935–03.1942, Department Director (GR 7) East in Heeres General Staff of O.K.H. 03.1942–10.1942, Advisor with Inspector of Education and Training Affairs 10.1942–05.1943, retired 05.1943. Awards: War Merit Cross 1st and 2nd Class with Swords, RK-Hohenzollern, 1914 Iron Cross 1st and 2nd Class, 1914 Wound Badge in Black, Cross of Honor.

General der Artillerie Paul Bader. (Bundesarchiv)

Bader, Paul: General der Artillerie (01.07.41), (Heer); born 20.07.83 in Lahr, died 28.02.71 in Emmendingen. WWI: Hauptmann and Adjutant to Feld Artillerie Brigade 39. Promotions to Generalmajor 01.12.35, Generalleutnant 01.01.38. Commander of Artillerie Regiment at Ludwigsburg 10.1934–09.1935, Commander of Artillerie 2, 10.1935–03.1937. WWII: Commander of 2. Infanterie Division 04.1937–10.1940, Commander of 3. Infanterie Division (mot.) 10.1940–05.1941, Commander of LXV. Armee Korps 05.1941–04.1942, Wehrmacht Befehlshaber of Serbia 07.1941–08.1943, Commander of XXI. Gebirgs Korps 08.1943–10.1943, Fuehrer Res. in O.K.H. 10.1943–03.1944, retired 03.1944. Awards: German Cross in Gold 29.01.43, 1939 Clasps to the 1914 Iron Cross 1st and 2nd Class, Infantry Assault Badge in Bronze, 1914 Iron Cross 1st and 2nd Class, 1914 Wound Badge in Black, Cross of Honor.

Bader, Robert: Generalmajor (20.04.45), (Heer); born 14.03.99 in Landau, died 10.05.45 in action near Iglau. WWI: Leutnant in Bavarian Infanterie Regiment 2. Advisor in Reich War Ministry 05.1934–06.1935, Advisor in 2. Abteilung of Heeres General Staff 07.1935–10.1937, Kompanie Chef in Infanterie Regiment 19, 10.1937–06.1938, attached to General Staff of Heeres Gruppen Kommando 2, 06.1938–11.1938, Special Purpose Officer attached to O.B. des Heeres 11.1938–02.1939. WWII: Ia to 3. Gebirgs Division 03.1939–09.1940, Quartermaster of 15. Armee 01.1941–11.1941, Quartermaster of 12. Armee 11.1941–09.1942, Quartermaster of 6. Armee 09.1942–08.1943, Chief of General Staff to XXV. Armee Korps 08.1943–12.1944, Commander of 4. Gebirgs Division 02.1945–04.1945. Awards: German Cross in Silver 19.02.43, 1939 Iron Cross 1st Class, 1939 Clasp to the 1914 Iron Cross 2nd Class, War Merit Cross 1st and 2nd Class with Swords, Eastern Front Medal, 1914 Iron Cross 2nd Class, Cross of Honor.

Bader, Rudolf: Generalmajor (01.01.45), (Heer); born 03.05.98 in Konstanz, died 03.06.83 in Freiburg. WWI: Leutnant der Res. in Feld Artillerie Regiment 76. Batterie Chef in Artillerie Regiment at Ulm 01.1935–10.1935. WWII: Batterie Chef in Artillerie Regiment 5, 10.1935–08.1939, Commander of II. Abteilung,

Artillerie Regiment 125, 08.1939–04.1942, Commander of Artillerie Regiment 253, 05.1942–09.1944, Commander of 560. Volks Grenadier Division 11.1944–05.1945. Awards: German Cross in Gold 08.10.43, 1939 Clasps to the 1914 Iron Cross 1st and 2nd Class, General Assault Badge, Eastern Front Medal, Baltic Cross 1st and 2nd Class, 1914 Iron Cross 1st and 2nd Class, Cross of Honor.

Badinski, Kurt: Generalleutnant (01.01.43), (Heer); born 17.05.90 in Grebenstein, died 27.02.66 in Oldenburg. WWI: Oberleutnant and Adjutant of 22. Infanterie Brigade. Promotion to Generalmajor 01.02.42. Tactics Instructor at Infanterie Schule Dresden 01.1935–10.1936. WWII: Commander of I. Bataillon, Infanterie Regiment 16, 10.1936–08.1939, Commander of Infanterie Regiment 489, 08.1939–01.1942, Commander of 23. Infanterie Division 02.1942–07.1942, Fuehrer Res. in O.K.H. 07.1942–09.1942, Commander of 269. Infanterie Division 09.1942–11.1942, Wehrmacht Commander of Bergen 11.1942–11.1943, Commander of 276. Infanterie Division 11.1943–08.1844, captured 08.1944. Awards: Knight's Cross 11.10.41, 1939 Clasps to the 1914 Iron Cross 1st and 2nd Class, Infantry Assault Badge in Silver, Eastern Front Medal, RK-Hohenzollern, 1914 Iron Cross 1st and 2nd Class, 1914 Wound Badge in Black, Cross of Honor.

Baecher, Rudolf: Generalmajor z.V. (01.02.41), (Heer); born 23.06.80 in Bremen, died 03.12.47 in Luebeck. WWI: Hauptmann and Bataillon Commander in 36. Feld Artillerie Brigade. WWII: recalled to military service 08.1939, Commander of Artillerie Ersatz Regiment 22, 08.1939–03.1940, Commander of Artillerie Regiment 213, 1940–08.1941, Commander of Artillerie Ersatz Regiment 5, 08.1941–1943, retired 08.1943. Awards: 1939 Clasps to the 1914 Iron Cross 1st and 2nd Class, General Assault Badge, RK-Hohenzollern, 1914 Iron Cross 1st and 2nd Class, 1914 Wound Badge in Black, Cross of Honor.

Baeke, Dr. Franz: Generalmajor (01.04.45), (Heer); born 28.02.98 in Schwarzenfels, died 12.12.78 in Hagen. WWI: Vizefeldwebel in Fuss Artillerie Regiment 7. Attached to Aufklarungs Abteilung 6, 04.1937–07.1939. WWII: Zugfuehrer in Panzer Jaeger Abteilung 65, 08.1939–01.1940, Kompanie Chef in Panzer Jaeger Abteilung 65, 01.1940–05.1941, Panzer Squadron Leader in Panzer Regiment 11, 05.1941–11.1941, Ordnance Officer on Staff of Panzer Regiment 11, 11.1941–06.1942, Commander of II. Abteilung, Panzer Regiment 11, 06.1942–07.1943, Commander of Panzer Regiment 11, 07.1943–07.1944, Commander of 106. Panzer Brigade "Feldherrnhalle" 07.1944–01.1945, Commander of 13. Panzer Division 03.1945–05.1945. Awards: Swords 21.02.44 (49), Oak Leaves 01.08.43 (262), Knight's Cross 11.01.43, 1939 Iron Cross 1st Class, 1939 Clasp to the 1914 Iron Cross 2nd Class, Tank Assault Badge Grade V (100), 3 Tank Destruction Badges, Eastern Front Medal, 1939 Wound Badge in Gold, Reich Sports Badge in Gold, 1914 Iron Cross 2nd Class, Cross of Honor.

Baentsch, Alfred: Generalleutnant (01.01.43), (Heer); born 05.02.94 in Magdesprung, died 31.01.43 of wounds near Voronezh. WWI: Leutnant in Infanterie Regiment 158. Promotion to Generalmajor 01.06.42. Bataillon Commander in Infanterie Regiment at Braunschweig 10.1934–07.1935, Instructor at Kriegsschule 08.1935–07.1938, Advisor and Group Leader in Abteilung 7 of Heeres General Staff 08.1938–07.1939. WWII: Quartermaster to Heeresgruppe C 08.1939–11.1939, Quartermaster to 2. Armee 11.1939–03.1940, Chief of Heeres Affairs Department in O.K.H. 11.1940–06.1942, Commander of 82. Infanterie Division 07.1942–01.1943. Awards: 1939 Clasps to the 1914 Iron Cross 1st and 2nd Class, War Merit Cross 1st and 2nd Class with Swords, 1939 Wound Badge in Gold, 1914 Iron Cross 1st and 2nd Class, 1914 Wound Badge in Silver, Cross of Honor.

Baer, Karl: Generalmajor (01.01.44), (Heer); born 08.10.94 in Freckenfeld, died 13.01.44 in action in Loshkarevska. WWI: Leutnant with Bavarian Feld Artillerie Regiment 12. Chief of Nachrichten Zug in Artillerie Regiment 7, 10.1935–10.1936, Batterie Chef in Artillerie Regiment 33, 10.1936–11.1937. WWII: Commander of I. Abteilung, Artillerie Regiment 25, 12.1937–08.1939, Commander of Artillerie Ersatz Regiment 25, 08.1939–10.1939, Commander of Artillerie Regiment 238, 01.1940–10.1942, Commander of Artillerie Regiment 110, 10.1942–05.1943, Commander of Grenadier Regiment 681, 05.1943–01.1944. Awards: German Cross in Gold 27.11.41, Honor Roll Clasp 28.03.43, 1939 Clasps to the 1914 Iron Cross 1st and 2nd Class, General Assault Badge, Eastern Front Medal, 1939 Wound Badge in Gold, 1914 Iron Cross 1st and 2nd Class, Cross of Honor.

Baerenfanger, Erich: Generalmajor (20.04.45), (Heer); born 12.01.15 in Menden, died 01.05.45 (suicide) in Berlin. WWII: Grenadier Regiment 123 from Platoon Leader to Commander of III. Bataillon 11.1938–10.1943, attended Regimental Commander's Course 02.1944–06.1944, Inspector of Heeres Youth Leadership and Inspector of H.J. Military Training Camps 07.1944–04.1945. Awards: Swords 23.01.44 (45), Oak Leaves 17.05.43 (243), Knight's Cross 07.08.42, German Cross in Gold 26.12.41, Honor Roll 14.08.42, 1939 Iron Cross 1st and 2nd Class, Infantry Assault Badge in Silver, Eastern Front Medal, Crimea Shield, 1939 Wound Badge in Gold, Golden HJ Honor Badge.

Generalmajor Erich Baerenfanger. (Bundesarchiv)

Baerens, Friedrich: Generalmajor (01.12.43), (Luftwaffe); born 22.04.88 in Satow, died 02.01.67 in Gauting. WWI: in G.A.S. as Hauptmann in Feld

Flieger Abteilung 37. WWII: Advisor to Luftgau Kommando IV Dresden 10.1935–05.1940, Advisor to Feld Luftgau Kommando Belgium and Northern France 06.1940–03.1942, attached to Staff of Flughafenbereichs Commandant 3-VI 04.1942–07.1942, Flughafenbereichs Commandant of 7-IV 10.1942–01.1943, Flughafenbereichs Commandant of 4-VIII 02.1943–05.1944, Fuehrer Res. in O.K.L. 05.1944–12.1944, retired 12.1944. Awards: War Merit Cross 1st and 2nd Class with Swords, Pilot's Commemorative Badge, 1914 Iron Cross 1st and 2nd Class, 1914 Observer's Badge, Cross of Honor.

Baessler, Erich: Generalleutnant (01.01.44), (Heer); born 05.08.90 in Obreforsterei, died 11.05.57 in Bremen. WWI: Oberleutnant and Ordnance Officer on Staff of XXI. Res. Armee Korps. Promotion to Generalmajor 01.01.42. WWII: Commander of II. Bataillon, Infanterie Regiment 65, 10.1935–08.1939, Commander of Infanterie Ersatz Regiment 22, 08.1939–12.1939, Commander of Infanterie Regiment 399, 12.1939–11.1941, Fuehrer Res. in O.K.H. 11.1941–04.1942, Commander of 377. Infanterie Division 04.1942–12.1942, Fuehrer Res. in O.K.H. 12.1942–06.1943, temporary Commander of 12. Luftwaffe Feld Division 06.1943–10.1943, Commander of 19. Luftwaffe Feld Division 10.1943–07.1944, Fuehrer Res. in O.K.H. 07.1944–10.1944, Commander of 191. Res. Infanterie Division 12.1944–05.1945. Awards: German Cross in Gold 18.10.41, Honor Roll Clasp 29.09.41, 1939 Clasps to the 1914 Iron Cross 1st and 2nd Class, Infantry Assault Badge in Silver, RK-Hohenzollern, 1914 Iron Cross 1st and 2nd Class, Cross of Honor.

Baessler, Johannes: Generalleutnant (01.02.44), (Heer); born 03.05.92 in Grasegrund, died 09.11.44 of wounds in a Vienna military hospital. WWI: Oberleutnant and Adjutant to 82. Res. Infanterie Brigade. Promotion to Generalmajor 01.02.42. Ia to 3. Kavallerie Division 08.1934–10.1935, Ia to 1. Panzer Division 10.1935–09.1936, Ia on Staff of Panzertruppen Kommando 09.1936–03.1938, Ia to XVI. Armee Korps 04.1938–11.1938. WWII: Commander of Panzer Regiment 4, 11.1938–09.1939, Chief of Staff to XI. Armee Korps 09.1939–02.1942, Commander of 9. Panzer Division 04.1942–07.1942, Fuehrer Res. in O.K.H. 11.1942–04.1943, Commander of 242. Security Division 07.1943–08.1944, in hospital due to wounds 08.1944–11.1944. Awards: German Cross in Gold 08.01.43, 1939 Clasps to the 1914 Iron Cross 1st and 2nd Class, Tank Assault Badge in Bronze, Eastern Front Medal, 1939 Wound Badge in Gold, 1914 Iron Cross 1st and 2nd Class, Cross of Honor.

Baethke, Dr. Paul: General-Arzt (01.10.44), (Heer); born 27.01.95 in Elbholz, died 23.01.53 in Luechow. Medical doctor by profession. WWI: German medical service (rank and unit unknown). WWII: Division Physician to 215. Infanterie Division 08.1939–08.1940, Commander of 695. (mot.) Heeres Medical Bataillon

08.1940–06.1942, Corps Physician to XVII. Armee Korps 06.1942–06.1944, Army Physician to 18. Armee 06.1944–05.1945. Awards: 1939 Clasp to the 1914 Iron Cross 2nd Class, War Merit Cross 1st and 2nd Class with Swords, Eastern Front Medal, 1914 Iron Cross 2nd Class, Cross of Honor.

Baeumker, Adolf: Ministerialdirigent (01.01.38), (Luftwaffe); born 14.07.91 in Breslau, died 04.03.76 in Bad Godesberg. Civil Servant by profession. WWI: in G.A.S. as Oberleutnant (unit unknown). WWII: Department Chief (LC) in R.L.M. 05.1933–05.1944, Civil Servant in R.L.M. 05.1944–05.1945. Awards: War Merit Cross 1st and 2nd Class with Swords, Pilot's Commemorative Badge, RK-Hohenzollern, RK-Sachsen Albrecht Order 2nd Class with Swords, 1914 Iron Cross 1st and 2nd Class, 1914 Observer's Badge, Cross of Honor.

Bahlke, Rudolf: General-Intendant (01.01.41), (Heer); born 04.04.88 in Berlin, died 07.08.78 in Stettin. Administrative Officer by profession. WWI: Administrative Officer (rank and unit unknown). WWII: Chief Intendant to Wehrkreis Kommando V (dates unknown). Awards: War Merit Cross 1st and 2nd Class with Swords, Cross of Honor.

Bahn, Egmont: Generalmajor (01.08.43), (Heer); born 09.08.92 in Nieder-Hermsdorf, died 18.01.49 in Mengebostel. WWI: Oberleutnant in Hussar Regiment 16. Attached to Staff of Commander for Truppenubungsplatz at Bergen 07.1936–11.1938. WWII: Bataillon Commander in Infanterie Regiment 12, 11.1938–08.1939, Bataillon Commander in Infanterie Regiment 467, 08.1939–01.1940, Commander of Infanterie Regiment 320, 01.1940–02.1943, Commander of Heeres Weapons Schule in Norway 06.1943–12.1944, attached to Wehrmacht Befehlshaber of Italy 01.1945–05.1945. Awards: 1939 Clasps to the 1914 Iron Cross 1st and 2nd Class, Infantry Assault Badge in Silver, Eastern Front Medal, 1914 Iron Cross 1st and 2nd Class, Austro-Hungarian Military Service Cross 3rd Class with War Decoration, 1914 Wound Badge in Black, Cross of Honor.

Baier, Albrecht: Generalleutnant (01.01.43), (Heer); born 28.07.93 in Frankfurt am Main, died 17.01.53 in Weinheim. WWI: Oberleutnant and Batterie Fuehrer in Feld Artillerie Regiment 3. Promotion to Generalmajor 01.02.42. Ia to 2. Division 10.1934–09.1935, Ia to II. Armee Korps 09.1935–10.1937. WWII: Commander of Artillerie Regiment 73, 10.1937–09.1939, Chief of Staff to Wehrkreis XXI 10.1939–02.1940, Chief of Staff to XXXIX. Armee Korps 02.1940–09.1940, Chief of Staff to Wehrkreis XXI 09.1940–02.1942, Commander of 102. Infanterie Division 02.1942–05.1942, Commander of 342. Infanterie Division 08.1942–11.1943, Commander of 297. Infanterie Division 02.1944–05.1945. Awards: German Cross in Gold 31.08.43, 1939 Clasps to the 1914 Iron Cross

1st and 2nd Class, Eastern Front Medal, RK-Hohenzollern, 1914 Iron Cross 1st and 2nd Class, 1914 Wound Badge in Black, Cross of Honor.

Baier, Eberhard: Generalleutnant (01.03.45), (Luftwaffe); born 20.08.95 in Frankfurt, died 21.02.83 in Wiesbaden. WWI: in G.A.S. as Leutnant in Jasta 18. Promotion to Generalmajor 01.04.42. Special Duties Officer attached to R.L.M. 04.1933–03.1935, Gruppe Commander in S.G. 162, 04.1935–03.1936, Commander of S.G. 162, 04.1936–01.1937, Commander of S.G. 165, 04.1937–1938. WWII: Commander of L.G. 2, 11.1938–08.1939 and at same time Fliegerhorst Commandant of Juterbog-Waldlager 06.1939–08.1939, Commander of Stuka Geschwader 1, 09.1939–07.1940, Commander of Stuka Schule 1, 08.1940–07.1941, Director of III. Luftwaffe Control Commission in France 08.1941–06.1943, Advisor and later representative of Personnel Employment in R.L.M. 06.1943–03.1945. Awards: 1939 Clasps to the 1914 Iron Cross 1st and 2nd Class, 1939 Pilot's Badge, Pilot's Commemorative Badge, 1914 Iron Cross 1st and 2nd Class, 1914 Pilot's Badge, Cross of Honor.

Balck, Hermann: General der Panzertruppe (01.11.43), (Heer); born 07.12.93 in Danzig, died 29.11.82 in Erbenbach. WWI: Leutnant in 10. Jaeger Bataillon. Promotions to Generalmajor 01.08.42, Generalleutnant 01.01.43. Attached to Staff of Commander of Frankfurt/Oder 10.1934–10.1935, Commander of Radfahrer Bataillon 1, 10.1935–11.1938. WWII: Administrator attached to Staff of Inspector of Motorized Troops in O.K.H. 11.1938–10.1939, Commander of Grenadier Regiment 1, 10.1939–12.1940, Commander of Panzer Regiment 3, 12.1940–05.1941, Commander of 2. Panzer Brigade 05.1941–06.1941, placed in charge of settling Heeres motor vehicle situation within O.K.H. 07.1941–11.1941, General of Schnelltruppen attached to O.B. of Heeres 11.1941–05.1942, Commander of 11. Panzer Division 05.1942–03.1943, Fuehrer Res. in O.K.H. 03.1943–11.1943, Commander of XXXXVIII. Panzer Korps 11.1943–08.1944, Oberbefehlshaber of Heeresgruppe G 09.1944–12.1944, O.B. of 6. Armee 12.1944–05.1945. Awards: Diamonds 31.08.44 (19), Swords 04.03.43 (25), Oak Leaves 20.12.42 (155), Knight's Cross 03.06.40, 1939 Clasps to the 1914 Iron Cross 1st and 2nd Class, Tank Assault Badge in Silver, RK-Hohenzollern, 1914 Iron Cross 1st and 2nd Class, 1914 Wound Badge in Gold, Cross of Honor.

General der Panzertruppe Hermann Balck. (Bundesarchiv)

Balla, Erich: Generalmajor (01.08.43), (Heer); born 15.03.85 in Puetz, died 11.08.43 in action in Bialystock. WWI: Hauptmann and Bataillon Commander (unit unknown). WWII: Military Training Director at Tilsit 10.1934–09.1939, Commander of Infanterie Regiment 301, 09.1939–11.1942, Fuehrer Res. in O.K.H. 11.1942–05.1943, Commander of Ersatz Grenadier Regiment 11, 05.1943–08.1943. Awards: German Cross in Gold 11.12.41, 1939 Clasps to the 1914 Iron Cross 1st and 2nd Class, Infantry Assault Badge in Silver, Eastern Front Medal, 1939 Wound Badge in Gold, RK-Hohenzollern, 1914 Iron Cross 1st and 2nd Class, Cross of Honor.

Ballauff, Werner: SS-Brigadefuehrer und Generalmajor der Waffen-SS (01.05.43); born 21.09.90 in Duesseldorf, died 10.01.73 in Duesseldorf. P-585143, SS-66679. WWI: Oberleutnant on Staff of 7. Kavallerie Division, P.O.W. 12.1914–11.1919. Joined N.S.D.A.P. and S.A. in 1931, joined S.S. in 1933. Z.b.V. SS-Oberabschnitte Nord 01.10.34, attached to III. Sturmbann, SS-Standarte 2 "Germania" 01.07.35, Leader on Staff of SS-Standarte 1 "Deutschland" 01.12.36, Leader of III. Sturmbann, SS-Standarte 1 "Deutschland" 01.12.37, attached to SS-Standarte 3 "Der Fuehrer" 01.12.38. WWII: Deputy Commander of SS-Waffen Junkerschule at Braunschweig 30.01.42, Commander of SS-Waffen Junkerschule at Braunschweig 15.05.43–09.11.44. Awards: 1939 Iron Cross 1st Class, 1939 Clasp to the 1914 Iron Cross 2nd Class, War Merit Cross 1st and 2nd Class with Swords, 1914 Iron Cross 2nd Class, 1914 Wound Badge in Black, Cross of Honor, Reich Sports Badge in Silver, SA-Sports Badge in Gold, Degen, Ring.

Baltzer, Martin: Vizeadmiral (01.04.45), (Kriegsmarine); born 10.11.98 in Stettin, died 03.04.71 in Beckum. WWI: Leutnant zur See on liner *Prinz Regent Luitpold*. Promotion to Konteradmiral 01.01.43. Training Officer for surface ship *Karlsruhe* 09.1933–07.1934, attached to Inspectorate of Education for Kriegsmarine 08.1934–10.1936, Commandant of destroyer *Max Schultz* 04.1937–10.1938. WWII: First Adjutant on Staff of Baltic Sea Naval Station 10.1938–05.1942, Commandant of light cruiser *Koeln* 05.1942–12.1942, Chief of Naval Personnel Department in O.K.M. 01.1943–05.1945. Awards: 1939 Iron Cross 1st Class, 1939 Clasp to the 1914 Iron Cross 2nd Class, War Merit Cross 1st and 2nd Class with Swords, Auxiliary Cruiser War Badge, 1914 Iron Cross 2nd Class, Cross of Honor.

Baltzer, Martin: Generalmajor (01.04.41), (Heer); born 04.10.89 in Strehla, died 13.08.55 in Wiesbaden. WWI: Oberleutnant on Signals Staff of 208. Infanterie Division. Commander of Nachrichten Abteilung at Koenigsbrueck 10.1934–10.1935, Commander of Nachrichten Abteilung 14, 10.1935–03.1937, attached to Staff of Heeres Nachrichtenschule 04.1937–11.1938. WWII: Commander of Nachrichtentruppe XII 11.1938–08.1939, Signals Leader to 1. Armee 08.1939–09.1943, Signals Leader with Wehrmacht Befehlshber of Norway 09.1943–04.1944, Fuehrer Res. in

O.K.H. 04.1944–08.1944, attached to Special Staff I in O.K.H. 09.1944–01.1945, Commander of 172. Infanterie Division 01.1945–05.1945. Awards: 1939 Clasps to the 1914 Iron Cross 1st and 2nd Class, War Merit Cross 1st and 2nd Class with Swords, Eastern Front Medal, 1914 Iron Cross 1st and 2nd Class, Cross of Honor.

Baltzer, Richard: Generalleutnant (01.10.39), (Heer); born 01.06.86 in Danzig, died 10.05.45 in Prague. WWI: Hauptmann on Staff of Field Railway Affairs. Promotion to Generalmajor 16.03.36. Commander of Infanterie Regiment 25, 06.1936–02.1938. WWII: Landwehr Commander of Allenstein 03.1938–08.1939, Commander of 217. Infanterie Division 08.1939–04.1942, Fuehrer Res. in O.K.H. 04.1942–08.1942, Commander of 156. Infanterie Division 08.1942–12.1943, Commander of 182. Infanterie Division 03.1944–05.1945. Awards: German Cross in Gold 31.01.42, 1939 Clasps to the 1914 Iron Cross 1st and 2nd Class, Infantry Assault Badge in Silver, Eastern Front Medal, 1914 Iron Cross 1st and 2nd Class, Cross of Honor.

Baltzer, Robert: Generalleutnant (01.04.43), (Heer); born 03.07.92 in Danzig, died 08.03.43 in Kiev. WWI: Hauptmann on Staff of Telegraph Troops. Promotion to Generalmajor 01.04.41. Commander of Nachrichten Abteilung at Potsdam 10.1934–07.1935, Instructor at Heeres Nachrichtenschule 08.1935–03.1937. WWII: Lehrer Gruppe Commander at Heeres Nachrichtenschule 04.1937–08.1939, Commander of Heeres Nachrichtenschulen 09.1939–03.1940, Signals Leader for 2. Armee 03.1940–03.1943. Awards: German Cross in Silver 30.11.42, War Merit Cross 1st and 2nd Class with Swords, Eastern Front Medal, 1914 Iron Cross 1st and 2nd Class, Cross of Honor.

Bamberg, Dr. Georg: Generalmajor (01.02.41), (Heer); born 06.10.87 in Waldenburg, died 18.11.79 in Ottrau. WWI: Hauptmann and Commander of II. Bataillon, Res. Infanterie Regiment 106. Attached to Staff of Infanterie Regiment 62, 10.1935–11.1938. WWII: Wehrmacht Commander of Kaiserslautern 11.1938–10.1941, Wehrmacht Commander of Riga 10.1941–04.1944, Wehrmacht Commander of Braunschweig 04.1944–11.1944, Fuehrer Res. in O.K.H. 11.1944–05.1945. Awards: 1939 Clasp to the 1914 Iron Cross 2nd Class, War Merit Cross 1st and 2nd Class with Swords, RK-Sachsen Military St. Heinrich's Order 05.11.18, 1914 Iron Cross 1st and 2nd Class, 1914 Wound Badge in Black, Cross of Honor.

Bamler, Rudolf: Generalleutnant (01.04.43), (Heer); born 06.05.96 in Osterburg, died 13.03.72 in Gross-Glienicke. WWI: Oberleutnant and Adjutant to Feld Artillerie Regiment 59. Promotion to Generalmajor 01.04.42. Attached to Reich War Ministry 12.1934–05.1938, Chief of Abwehr Abteilung III in O.K.H. 05.1938–02.1939. WWII: Commander of Artillerie Regiment 74, 03.1939–08.1939, Chief of Staff to Wehrmacht Befehlshaber of Danzig-West Prussia 09.1939–10.1939,

Chief of Staff to Wehrkreis XX 10.1939–11.1940, Chief of Staff to XXXXVII. Armee Korps 11.1940–05.1942, Chief of General Staff to Wehrmacht Befehlshaber of Norway 05.1942–04.1944, Commander of 12. Infanterie Division 06.1944, captured 06.1944. Awards: German Cross in Gold 12.03.42, 1939 Clasps to the 1914 Iron Cross 1st and 2nd Class, Eastern Front Medal, 1914 Iron Cross 1st and 2nd Class, Cross of Honor.

Banse, Gustav: Generalmajor (01.04.42), (Luftwaffe); born 19.04.93 in Schwerin, died 01.08.65 in Luebeck. WWI: in G.A.S. as Leutnant der Res and Adjutant to Flieger Gruppenfuehrer 3. Schwadron Chef in Fahr Abteilung Luebeck 11.1934–09.1935, joined Luftwaffe in 10.1935, Commander of Fliegergruppe Goettingen 10.1935–10.1938, attached to Staff of K.G. 253 "Legion Condor" 11.1938–03.1939. WWII: Commandant of Luftzeuggruppe 8, 07.1939–10.1939, Commandant of Luftzeuggruppe 12, 10.1939–09.1940, Commandant of Luftzeuggruppe Western France 10.1940–07.1943, Quartermaster to Feld Luftgau Kommando XXV 07.1943–01.1944, Fuehrer Res. in O.K.L. 01.1944–09.1944, attached to Motor Transport Affairs in O.K.W. 01.1945–02.1945. Awards: War Merit Cross 1st and 2nd Class with Swords, Pilot's Commemorative Badge, 1914 Iron Cross 1st and 2nd Class, 1914 Observer's Badge, Cross of Honor.

Barckhausen, Franz: General der Artillerie (01.07.43), (Heer); born 21.12.82 in Rittergut, died 03.05.56 in Berlin. WWI: Hauptmann and Commander of II. Bataillon, Infanterie Regiment 102. Promotions to Generalmajor 01.04.36, Generalleutnant 01.03.38. Inspector of Feldzug Inspection 04.1934–03.1935, Heeres Feldzeugmeister 04.1935–10.1937, Commander of Artillerie 24, 10.1937–04.1938, Authorized Representative of O.K.W. for Skoda Works in Prague and Pilsen 09.1938–04.1939. WWII: Director of German military mission in Slovakia 05.1939–11.1939, Armaments Inspector Ober-Ost Krakau 11.1939–06.1940, Chief of Military Economic and Armaments Staff for France 07.1940–04.1943, retired 08.1943. Awards: German Cross in Silver 31.08.43, War Merit Cross 1st and 2nd Class with Swords, Silesian Eagle 1st and 2nd Class, RK-Hohenzollern, 1914 Iron Cross 1st and 2nd Class, Cross of Honor.

Barde, Konrad: Generalmajor (01.03.45), (Heer); born 13.11.97 in Alt-Rosenberg, died 04.05.45 (suicide) in Traunstein. WWI: Leutnant in Feld Artillerie Regiment 602. Batterie Chef in Artillerie Regiment 44, 10.1936–02.1938, Commander of I. Abteilung. WWII: Artillerie Regiment 44, 03.1938–11.1940, Commander of IV. Abteilung, Artillerie Regiment 104, 11.1940–03.1942, Commander of Artillerie Regiment 104, 03.1942–02.1944, Fuehrer Res. in O.K.H. 02.1944–06.1944, Commander of Artillerie 186, 07.1944–09.1944, Fuehrer Res. in O.K.H. 09.1944–12.1944, Commander of 198. Infanterie Division 01.1945–04.1945. Awards: Knight's Cross 05.01.43, German Cross in Gold 26.12.41, 1939 Clasps to the 1914 Iron Cross 1st and 2nd Class, General Assault Badge, Eastern Front Medal, 1914 Iron Cross 1st and 2nd Class, Cross of Honor.

Barelmann, Heinrich: Ministerialdirigent (01.07.42), (Luftwaffe); born 11.05.79 in Oldenburg, died 27.06.62 in Oldenburg. Civil Servant by profession. WWI: served (rank and unit unknown). WWII: Department Chief in R.L.M. 07.1935–08.1939, Department Chief (LD 7) in Office Gruppe Construction for Administration in R.L.M. 08.1939–05.1944, retired 05.1944. Awards: 1939 Clasp to the 1914 Iron Cross 2nd Class, War Merit Cross 1st and 2nd Class with Swords, 1914 Iron Cross 2nd Class, Austro-Hungarian Military Service Cross 3rd Class with War Decoration, Cross of Honor.

Barends, Erwin: Generalmajor (01.06.41), (Heer); born 03.06.80 in Hamburg, died 29.03.52 at Voikovo P.O.W. Camp. WWI: in G.A.S. as Hauptmann and Flieger Abteilung Commander (unit unknown). WWII: Commander of Military District Commando at Neu-Strelitz 10.1936–08.1939, Commander of Infanterie Regiment 632, 08.1939–08.1940, again Commander of Military District Commando at Neu-Strelitz 08.1940–11.1940, Commander of Infanterie Regiment 570, 11.1940–10.1942, retired 10.1942. Awards: 1939 Clasps to the 1914 Iron Cross 1st and 2nd Class, Infantry Assault Badge in Silver, Pilot's Commemorative Badge, RK-Hohenzollern, 1914 Iron Cross 1st and 2nd Class, 1914 Pilot's Badge, Cross of Honor.

Barenthin, Walter: Generalmajor (01.03.44), (Heer and Luftwaffe); born 13.01.88 in Berlin, died 28.02.59. WWI: Hauptmann in Pionier Regiment 25. Kompanie Chef in Pionier Bataillon 7, 06.1936–10.1937, Staff Officer attached to Lockdown Service Gruppe in Regensburg 11.1937–04.1938, Pionier Staff Officer attached to XVII. Armee Korps 05.1938–05.1939. WWII: Commander of Pionier Bataillon 216, 09.1939–03.1941, transferred to Luftwaffe 04.1941, attached to Pionier Leader of XI. Flieger Korps 04.1941–10.1942, Commander of Luftwaffe Jaeger Regiment 11.1942–03.1943, Supplemental and Schule Commander for XI. Flieger Korps 05.1943–09.1943, Commander of 3. Fallschirm Division 09.1943–02.1944, Commander of Training and Replacement Units of Fallschirm Armee 02.1944–12.1944, Commander of Fallschirmjaeger Training and Replacement Division 12.1944–03.1945. Awards: German Cross in Gold (date unknown), 1939 Clasps to the 1914 Iron Cross 1st and 2nd Class, Kreta Cuff Band, Afrika Cuff Band, 1939 Wound Badge in Silver, 1914 Iron Cross 1st and 2nd Class, 1914 Wound Badge in Black, Cross of Honor.

Barlen, Karl: General der Flieger (01.04.44), (Luftwaffe); born 17.07.90 in Traden-Trarbach, died 25.03.56 in Rod. WWI: in G.A.S. as Oberleutnant in Feld Flieger Abteilung 8. Promotions to Generalmajor 20.04.39, Generalleutnant

01.04.41. Advisor and Group Leader attached to Personnel Office of R.L.M. 11.1933–03.1936, Commander of Fernaufklarungs Gruppe 115 and Fliegerhorst Commandant of Goeppingen 03.1936–03.1937, Chief in Personnel Department of R.L.M. 04.1937–01.1939. WWII: Office Gruppe Chief of Personnel Department in R.L.M. 02.1939–03.1943, Commandant of Schutzzone Slovakia 04.1943–05.1945. Awards: German Cross in Gold (date unknown), 1939 Clasps to the 1914 Iron Cross 1st and 2nd Class, War Merit Cross 1st and 2nd Class with Swords, Spanish Cross in Bronze without Swords, Combined Pilot-Observer's Badge, Bulgarian Military Service Order 1st Class with War Decoration, Pilot's Commemorative Badge, 1914 Iron Cross 1st and 2nd Class, Oldenburg Friedrich August Cross 1st and 2nd Class, 1914 Pilot's Badge, 1914 Austro-Hungarian Pilot's Badge, Cross of Honor.

Barnewitz, Dr. Hans-Joachim: General-Arzt (01.03.45), (Heer); born 18.08.92 in Berlin, died 19.04.65 in Luebeck. Medical doctor by profession. WWI: German medical service (rank and unit unknown). WWII: Division Physician to 228. Infanterie Division 08.1939–02.1940, Division Physician to 6. Infanterie Division 02.1940–06.1941, Physician attached to German Liaison of Italian High Command in Africa 06.1941–10.1941, Corps Physician to German Afrika Korps 10.1941–09.1942, Fuehrer Res. in O.K.H. 09.1942–05.1943, Commander of Sanitats Abteilung "Thorn" 05.1943–11.1944, Corps Physician to Wehrkreis XII 01.1945–05.1945. Awards: German Cross in Silver 02.06.44, 1939 Clasp to the 1914 Iron Cross 2nd Class, War Merit Cross 1st and 2nd Class with Swords, Afrika Cuff Band, 1914 Iron Cross 2nd Class, Cross of Honor.

Barsewisch, Karl-Henning von: Generalmajor (01.05.44), (Luftwaffe); born 02.10.95 in Karlsruhe, died 19.11.81 in Wedel. WWI: Oberleutnant in Infanterie Regiment 167. Attached to Fernaufklarungs Gruppe 24, 08.1938–12.1938. WWII: attached to Luftwaffe Staff of Wehrmacht O.B. East 01.1939–05.1940, Chief of Operations to Luftwaffe Commander of 4. Armee 10.1940–07.1941, Luftwaffe Commander for Panzer Gruppe 2, 07.1941–06.1942, Chief of Operations and later Chief of Staff to General of Fernaufklarungs attached to O.K.H. 06.1942–11.1942, General of Reconnaissance Aircraft (L In 1) in R.L.M. 11.1942–05.1945. Awards: German Cross in Gold 10.01.44, 1939 Clasps to the 1914 Iron Cross 1st and 2nd Class, Eastern Front Medal, Reconnaissance Flight Clasp in Gold, 1939 Pilot's Badge, 1914 Iron Cross 1st and 2nd Class, Cross of Honor.

Bartcky, Viktor: Generalmajor (01.08.41), (Heer); born 13.09.91 in Dresden, died 23.08.41 in action near Kiev. WWI: Oberleutnant and Regimental Adjutant (unit unknown). Bataillon Commander in Infanterie Regiment 96, 10.1934–11.1938. WWII: Commander of Infanterie Regiment 52, 11.1938–02.1940, Commander of Infanterie Regiment 513, 02.1940–08.1941. Awards: 1939 Clasps to the

1914 Iron Cross 1st and 2nd Class, Infantry Assault Badge in Silver, 1939 Wound Badge in Gold, RK-Sachsen Military St. Heinrich's Order 24.07.17, 1914 Iron Cross 1st and 2nd Class, 1914 Wound Badge in Black, Cross of Honor.

Bartenwerffer, Gustav von: Generalmajor z.V. (01.02.42), (Heer); born 10.06.72 in Nancy, died 08.01.47 in Berlin. WWI: Oberstleutnant and Staff Officer (unit unknown). WWII: recalled to military service 08.1939, temporary Chief of Military Administration for District A in North-Western France 1940–07.1941, Commandant of Feldkommandantur 758, 07.1941–09.1942, retired 09.1942. Awards: War Merit Cross 1st and 2nd Class with Swords, RK-Hohenzollern, 1914 Iron Cross 1st and 2nd Class, 1914 Wound Badge in Black, Cross of Honor.

Barth, Otto: Generalmajor (09.11.44), (Heer); born 18.06.91 in Dresden, died 03.05.63 in Erlangen. WWI: Oberleutnant and Adjutant in 32. Infanterie Division. Batterie Chef in Artillerie Regiment 4, 09.1936–02.1938. WWII: Commander of I. Abteilung, Artillerie Regiment 17, 03.1938–12.1940, Commander of Artillerie Regiment 17, 12.1940–05.1943, Fuehrer Res. in O.K.H. 05.1943–09.1943, Course Director at Artillerie Schule 09.1943–07.1944, Commander of 30. Infanterie Division 08.1944–02.1945, Commander of 21. Luftwaffen Feld Division 02.1945–05.1945. Awards: Knight's Cross 08.05.43, German Cross in Gold 09.10.42, 1939 Clasps to the 1914 Iron Cross 1st and 2nd Class, German Army High Command Commendation Certificate 05.10.42, General Assault Badge, Eastern Front Medal, Kurland Cuff Band, RK-Sachsen Military St. Heinrich's Order 07.05.18, 1914 Iron Cross 1st and 2nd Class, 1914 Wound Badge in Black, Cross of Honor.

Barton, Gottfried: Generalmajor (01.02.41), (Heer); born 29.03.85 in Vienna, died 13.01.77 in Vienna. WWI: Rittmeister in Austrian 12. Gebirgs Jager Division. Transferred to German Wehrmacht 03.1938. WWII: Commander of Wehrkreis-Reit-und Fahrschule at Schlossdorf 08.1938–06.1941, Commander of Brigade 203, 06.1941–08.1942, Commander of 203. Security Division 08.1942–01.1943, Fuehrer Res. in O.K.H. 01.1943–06.1943, retired 06.1943. Awards: War Merit Cross 1st and 2nd Class with Swords, RK-Military Maria Theresia Order 1917, Cross of Honor.

Bartsch, Dr. Erich: General-Veterinar (01.10.41), (Heer); born: 04.01.90 Leipzig, died 09.10.41 in action in Russia. Medical veterinarian by professsion. WWI: German medical service as Ober-Veterinar (unit unknown). WWII: Division Veterinar to 14. Infanterie Division 1938–02.1940, Korps Veterinar to XXVII. Armee Korps 02.1940–10.1941. Awards: 1939 Clasp to the 1914 Iron Cross 2nd Class, War Merit Cross 1st and 2nd Class with Swords, 1939 Wound Badge in Gold, German West Wall Medal, 1914 Iron Cross 1st and 2nd Class, Cross of Honor.

Barwinski, Otto: General-Richter (01.06.42), (Heer); born 12.09.90 Gross-Purden, died 30.09.69 in Berlin. Jurist by profession. WWI: service unknown. WWII: attached to Heeres Legal Department of O.K.H. 06.1936–05.1940, Reich War Official with Reichs War Court 05.1940–05.1945. Awards: War Merit Cross 1st and 2nd Class without Swords, Cross of Honor.

Basler, Moritz: Generalmajor (01.01.38), (Heer); born 24.12.86 in Wartenberg, died 13.07.41 of natural causes in Salzburg. WWI: Hauptmann and Staff Officer to Austrian Insonzo Armee. Transferred to German Wehrmacht 03.1938, attached to Command Staff of Infanterie Regiment 26, 10.1938–01.1939. WWII: Fuehrer Res. in O.K.H. 02.1939–01.1940, attached to Staff of Field Equipment Commander for III. followed by Wehrkreis XII 02.1940–05.1940, Field Equipment Commander for Wehrkreis XIII 05.1940–10.1940, Field Equipment Commander for Wehrkreis XVIII 10.1940–07.1941. Awards: War Merit Cross 2nd Class with Swords, Cross of Honor.

Basse, Hans von: Generalleutnant (01.04.42), (Heer); born 23.04.87 Kamen, died 10.10.79 in Baden-Baden. WWI: Hauptmann on Staff of 183. Infanterie Division. Promotion to Generalmajor 01.04.40. Commander of Infanterie Regiment 60, 10.1935–04.1939. WWII: injured and recovering from automobile accident 04.1939–05.1940, Commander of Division 182, 05.1940–05.1941, Commander of 225. Infanterie Division 05.1941–09.1942, Fuehrer Res. in O.K.H. 09.1942–01.1943, retired and called back to service 01.1943–07.1943, General with Special Duties on Staff of 18. Armee 07.1943–08.1944, Senior Field Commandant of Section 397, 09.1944–10.1944, Fuehrer Res. in O.K.H. 10.1944–02.1945, retired 02.1945. Awards: 1939 Clasps to the 1914 Iron Cross 1st and 2nd Class, Infantry Assault Badge in Silver, Eastern Front Medal, 1914 Iron Cross 1st and 2nd Class, 1914 Wound Badge in Black, Cross of Honor.

Basse, Max von: Generalmajor (01.04.42), (Heer); born 30.03.83 in Kamen, died 13.02.47 in Wiesbaden. WWI: Hauptmann and Bataillon Commander in Res. Infanterie Regiment 13. Leader of Welfare and Supply Department at Hannover 10.1933–05.1938. WWII: Leader of Wehrkreis Kommando VIII Welfare and Supply Department of VIII. Armee Korps 06.1938–01.1942, Leader of Wehrkreis Kommando XII Welfare and Supply Department of XII. Armee Korps 01.1942–07.1942, retired 07.1942. Awards: War Merit Cross 1st and 2nd Class with Swords, RK-Hohenzollern, 1914 Iron Cross 1st and 2nd Class, 1914 Wound Badge in Silver, Cross of Honor.

Bassenge, Gerhard: Generalmajor (01.01.43), (Luftwaffe); born 18.11.97 Ettbingen, died 13.03.77 in Luebeck. WWI: in G.A.S. as Leutnant in Jasta 2. Group Leader and Advisor attached to R.L.M. 01.1934–02.1937, Commander of Fliegerschule and Fallschirm Schule I in Stendal 03.1937–05.1938, attached to General Staff of Luftwaffe 10.1938–05.1939. WWII: Chief of Staff to Luftgau Kommando XVII 06.1939–01.1940, Chief of General Staff to Luftflotte 2, 01.1940–07.1940, Chief of General Staff to Luftflotte 5, 08.1940–10.1940, Flughafenbereichs Commandant for Africa 06.1941–09.1942, Commander of 19. Luftwaffe Feld Division 10.1942–01.1943, captured 05.1943. Awards: German Cross in Gold 27.07.42, 1939 Clasps to the 1914 Iron Cross 1st and 2nd Class, Parachutist Badge, "Jagdstaffel Boelcke Nr 2, 1916/18" Commemorative Cuff Band, Pilot's Commemorative Badge, 1914 Iron Cross 1st and 2nd Class, 1914 Wound Badge in Black, 1914 Pilot's Badge, Cross of Honor.

Bassewitz-Behr, Georg Henning Graf: SS-Gruppenfuehrer und Generalleutnant der Waffen-SS und Polizei (20.04.43); born 21.03.00 in Luetzow, died 31.01.49 at Magadan P.O.W. Camp. P-458315, SS-35466. WWI: Fahnenjunker attached to 2. Kurassier Regiment "Koenig." Joined N.S.D.A.P. in 1930, joined N.S.K.K. and S.S. in 1931. Promotion to SS-Brigadefuehrer 01.01.42. Attached to Staff of SS-Oberabschnitte Nord 01.10.34–01.07.35, attached to Staff of SS-Hauptamt 01.12.36–01.12.38, Leader of Hauptabteilung I in SS-Hauptamt and later SS-Fuehrungshauptamt in regards to Inspection of SS Motorized Units. WWII: Leader of SS-Abteilung (mot.) in Kommandostab RFSS, S.S.P.F. of Dnjepropterowsk 30.01.42, S.S.P.F. of Mogilew, Leader of SS-Oberabschnitee Nordsee and H.S.S.P.F. 15.05.43–09.11.44. Awards: 1939 Iron Cross 1st and 2nd Class, War Merit Cross 1st and 2nd Class with Swords, Eastern Front Medal, German Social Welfare Decoration 3rd Class, Cross of Honor, Reich Sports Badge in Silver, SA-Sports Badge in Bronze, German Motor Sports Badge in Silver, Degen, Ring.

Bastian, Max: Admiral (01.04.38), (Kriegsmarine); born 28.08.83 in Berlin, died 11.03.58 in Wilhelmshaven. WWI: Kapitanleutnant and Second Admiral Staff Officer on Staff of Reconnaissance Force for Baltic Sea. Promotions to Reichsmarine Konteradmiral 01.09.33, Vizeadmiral 01.12.35. Commander of Line Ships 10.1932–09.1934, Second Admiral of Eastern Sea Station 10.1934–09.1935, Chief of General Marine Office in O.K.M. 09.1935–04.1938, attached to O.K.W. 04.1938–09.1938. WWII: President of Reich War Court 09.1939–10.1944, retired 11.1944. Awards: Knight's Cross of the War Merit Cross with Swords 12.10.44, War Merit Cross 1st and 2nd Class with Swords, Grand Officer Cross of the Spanish Imperial Order of Joch und den Pfeilen, Finnish Freedom Cross

Admiral Max Bastian. (Josef Charita)

2nd Class with Swords, RK-Hohenzollern, 1914 Iron Cross 1st and 2nd Class, Cross of Honor.

Bauer, Ernst von: Generalmajor (01.10.44), (Heer); born 20.06.96 in Elberfeld, died 25.09.45 in Kembs. WWI: Leutnant and Adjutant to I. Bataillon, Infanterie Regiment 68. Kompanie Chef in Infanterie Regiment at Muenster 10.1934–10.1935, Kompanie Chef in Infanterie Regiment 39, 10.1935–10.1936. WWII: Adjutant to 2. Infanterie Division 10.1936–03.1940, Adjutant to II. Armee Korps 07.1940–05.1943, Commander of NCO Panzertruppe Schule at Arnswalde 09.1943–03.1944, Battle Commandant of Montpellier 04.1944–09.1944, Commander of 189. Infanterie Division 10.1944–02.1945. Awards: 1939 Clasps to the 1914 Iron Cross 1st and 2nd Class, Eastern Front Medal, 1914 Iron Cross 1st and 2nd Class, 1914 Wound Badge in Black, Cross of Honor.

Bauer, Heinrich: General-Ingenieur (01.04.41), (Luftwaffe); born 15.04.76 in Memel, died 13.09.60 in Gauting. Engineer by profession. WWI: service unknown. Leader of Gruppe LC II 6 in R.L.M. 10.1933–06.1938. WWII: Department Chief (LC 3) in R.L.M. 07.1938–05.1945. Awards: War Merit Cross 1st and 2nd Class with Swords.

Bauer, Paul: Generalmajor z.V. (26.08.39), (Heer); born 18.06.80 in Steingaden, died 14.02.48 in Munich. WWI: Hauptmann on Staff of the 39. Bavarian Res. Division. Promotion to Reichswehr Generalmajor 01.12.32. WWII: recalled to military service 08.1939, Commander of 189. Infanterie Division 10.1939–04.1941, Fuehrer Res. in O.K.H. 04.1941–07.1941, Commandant of Feldkommandantur 247, 07.1941–12.1941, retired 12.1941. Awards: 1939 Clasp to the 1914 Iron Cross 2nd Class, 1914 Iron Cross 1st and 2nd Class, Bavarian Military Service Cross IV. Class with Swords, Cross of Honor.

Bauer, Dr. Otto: General-Veterinar (01.06.44), (Heer); born 31.08.74 Muehlhausen, died 11.10.46 in Braunschweig. Medical veterinarian by profession. WWI: Oberstabs-Arzt (unit unknown). WWII: Korps Veterinar to XI. Armee (later Ersatz) Korps 08.1939–05.1945. Awards: War Merit Cross 1st and 2nd Class with Swords, RK-Sachsen Albrecht Order 2nd Class with Swords, 1914 Iron Cross 1st and 2nd Class, Cross of Honor.

Baumeister, Dr. Wilhelm: General-Arzt (01.10.42), (Heer); born 07.12.87 in Disteln, died 19.01.63 in Muenster. Medical doctor by profession. WWI: Assistant Physician (unit unknown). WWII: Division Physician to 2. Light Division 1938–02.1941, Corps Physician to VIII. Armee Korps 02.1941–12.1942, Army Physician to 6. Armee 03.1943–05.1945. Awards: German Cross in Silver 03.12.43,

1939 Clasp to the 1914 Iron Cross 2nd Class, War Merit Cross 1st and 2nd Class with Swords, Eastern Front Medal, 1914 Iron Cross 2nd Class, Cross of Honor.

Baumgartner, Richard: Generalmajor (01.12.39), (Heer); born 21.02.86 in Hainburg, died 17.10.79 in Graz. WWI: Hauptmann in Austrian 28. Trench Bataillon. Transferred to German Wehrmacht 03.1938, Staff Officer attached to Higher Pionier Officer 507.1938–06.1939. WWII: attached to Pionier Staff of Heeres Gruppen Kommando 1, 06.1939–10.1939, Commander of Pionier Regiment 628, 10.1939–02.1940, Commander of High Construction Staff 14, 02.1940–11.1941, Higher Pionier Officer 4 Wiesbaden 11.1941–09.1944, Fuehrer Res. in O.K.H. 09.1944–0.1945. Awards: War Merit Cross 1st and 2nd Class with Swords, Cross of Honor.

Baur de Betaz, Wilhelm: Generalleutnant (01.08.43), (Luftwaffe); born 17.02.83 in Metz, died 26.05.64 in Lindenfels. WWI: in G.A.S. as Hauptmann and Commander of Flieger Abteilung A 275. Promotion to Generalmajor 01.07.41. Vice President of D.L.V. 03.1933–12.1934, Commander of Luftgau Reserve 13, 04.1935–04.1937. WWII: Group Director in Kriegswissenschaftliche Abteilung of R.L.M. 05.1937–09.1939, Chief of Staff to Hoehere Flieger Ausbildungs Commander 4, 09.1939–03.1940, Commander of z.b.V. Kampfgruppe Norway 03.1940–09.1940, Flughafenbereichs Commandant to Greifswald and later Doeberitz 09.1940–05.1942, attached to Special Staff in O.K.W. 05.1942–10.1942, Chief of Economic Staff in Norway 11.1942–09.1944, Fuehrer Res. in O.K.L. 09.1944–05.1945. Awards: German Cross in Gold (date unknown), 1939 Clasps to the 1914 Iron Cross 1st and 2nd Class, Pilot's Commemorative Badge, RK-Hohenzollern, 1914 Iron Cross 1st and 2nd Class, Wuerttemberg Friedrich Order 1st Class with Swords, Austro-Hungarian Military Service Cross 3rd Class with War Decoration, 1914 Pilot's Badge, Cross of Honor, Turkish Half Moon.

Baurmeister, Hans-Joachim: Generalmajor (09.11.44), (Heer); born 28.10.98 in Glogau, died 12.02.50 at Voikovo P.O.W. Camp. WWI: Feld Artillerie Regiment 282. Attached to Staff of Artillerie Abteilung at Ohrdruf 10.1934–10.1935, Batterie Chef in Artillerie Regiment 74, 10.1935–10.1936, Commander of II. Abteilung, Artillerie Regiment 73, 10.1936–11.1938. WWII: Tactics Instructor at Kriegsschule Potsdam 11.1938–10.1939, Commander of Artillerie Regiment 23, 03.1940–01.1942, Course Director at Artillerie Schule I 01.1942–04.1943, Commander of Artillerie 130, 04.1943–02.1944, Commander of 290. Infanterie Division 11.1944–04.1945. Awards: German Cross in Gold 21.10.43, 1939 Clasps to the 1914 Iron Cross 1st and 2nd Class, German Army High Command Commendation Certificate 28.11.41, War Merit Cross 1st and 2nd Class with Swords, 1914 Iron Cross 1st and 2nd Class, 1914 Wound Badge in Black, Cross of Honor.

Bayer, Dr. Alfred: General-Arzt (01.04.42), (Heer); born 24.09.88 in Ulm, died 07.02.52 in Ulm. Medical doctor by profession. WWI: German medical service (rank and unit unknown). WWII: Division Physician to 7. Infanterie Division 1938–04.1940, Corps Physician to XXVIII. Armee Korps 11.1940–09.1941, Army Physician to Panzer Armee "Afrika" 09.1941–01.1943, Army Physician to 1. Armee 07.1943–11.1944, Corps Physician to Replacement VII. Armee Korps 01.1945–05.1945. Awards: War Merit Cross 1st and 2nd Class with Swords, Afrika Cuff Band, 1914 Iron Cross 2nd Class, Cross of Honor.

Bayer, Friedrich: Generalleutnant (01.10.40), (Heer); born 01.11.87 in Krotoschin, died 05.08.53 at Voikovo P.O.W. Camp. WWI: Hauptmann and Commander of III. Bataillon, Infanterie Regiment 13. Promotion to Generalmajor 01.10.38. WWII: Commander of Infanterie Regiment 77, 10.1936–10.1939, Wehrmacht Commander of Strasbourg 07.1940–03.1941, Commander of 217. Infanterie Division 04.1942–09.1942, Commander of 347. Infanterie Division 09.1942–10.1943, Commander of Division 408, 11.1943–06.1944, captured 09.1944. Awards: 1939 Clasps to the 1914 Iron Cross 1st and 2nd Class, Infantry Assault Badge in Silver, 1914 Iron Cross 1st and 2nd Class, Cross of Honor.

Bayerlein, Fritz: Generalleutnant (01.05.44), (Heer); born 14.01.99 in Wurzburg, died 31.01.70 in Wurzburg. WWI: Unteroffizier in Bavarian Infanterie Regiment 9. Promotion to Generalmajor 01.03.43. Attached to Staff of 15. Division 10.1935–12.1936, Kompanie Chef in M.G. Bataillon 6, 10.1937–11.1938, Ib to XV. Armee Korps 11.1938–03.1939. WWII: Ia to 10. Panzer Division 04.1939–02.1940, Ia to XIX. Armee Korps 02.1940–06.1940, Ia to Panzer Gruppe Guderian 06.1940–11.1940, Ia to 2. Panzer Armee 11.1940–08.1941, Chief of General Staff of Afrika Korps and later Panzer Armee "Afrika" 10.1941–03.1943, Commander of 3. Panzer Division 10.1943–01.1944, Commander of Panzer Lehr Division 01.1944–01.1945. Awards: Swords 20.07.44 (81), Oak Leaves 06.07.43 (258), Knight's Cross 26.12.41, German Cross in Gold 23.10.43, Honor Roll Clasp 05.03.45, 1939 Iron Cross 1st Class, 1939 Clasp to the 1914 Iron Cross 2nd Class, Tank Assault Badge in Bronze, Afrika Cuff Band, 1939 Wound Badge in Silver, 1914 Iron Cross 2nd Class, 1914 Wound Badge in Black, Cross of Honor.

Bazing, Richard: Generalmajor (01.11.42), (Heer); born 19.12.94 in Diedenhofen, died 22.05.87 in Bonn. WWI: Oberleutnant and Ordnance Officer to Infanterie Regiment 243. Commander of Pionier Bataillon 33, 05.1936–11.1938. WWII: Commander of Pioniers in Wehrkreis VI 11.1938–08.1939, Pionier Leader to Wehrmacht Mission in Romania 10.1940–06.1942, Pionier Leader to 20. Gebirgs Armee 06.1942–09.1943, General of Pioniers to Heeresgruppe F 09.1943–11.1944, Fuehrer Res. in O.K.H. 11.1944–05.1945. Awards: 1939 Clasps to the 1914

Iron Cross 1st and 2nd Class, Commander's Cross of the Order of the Star of Romania with Swords, Commander's Cross of the Hungarian Service Order with Swords and War Decoration, Finnish Freedom Cross 1st Class with Swords, RK-Wuerttemberg Friedrich Order 2nd Class with Swords, RK-Wuerttemberg Military Service Order, 1914 Iron Cross 1st and 2nd Class, 1914 Wound Badge in Black, Cross of Honor.

Becher, Karl: Generalmajor (12.03.43), (Heer); born 29.01.85 in Theerbude, died 23.01.57 in Bielefeld. WWI: Senior NCO in Fuss Garde Regiment 4. Commander of III. Bataillon, Infanterie Regiment at Rastenburg 10.1934–10.1935, Commander of III. Bataillon. WWII: Infanterie Regiment 23, 10.1935–10.1939, Commander of Infanterie Regiment 250, 03.1940–09.1940, Commander of Infanterie Regiment 228, 09.1940–12.1941, Commander of Infanterie Regiment 547, 12.1941–11.1942, Fuehrer Res. in O.K.H. 11.1942–06.1943, Wehrmacht Commandant of Koenigsberg 06.1943–02.1945. Awards: 1939 Clasps to the 1914 Iron Cross 1st and 2nd Class, Infantry Assault Badge in Silver, Eastern Front Medal, 1914 Iron Cross 1st and 2nd Class, 1914 Wound Badge in Black, Cross of Honor.

Bechler, Helmut: Generalmajor (30.01.45), (Heer); born 02.06.98 in Gruen, died 09.01.71 in Kassel. WWI: Leutnant and Signals Officer to II. Bataillon, Infanterie Regiment 182. Attached to Infanterie Regiment at Koenigsbrueck 10.1934–03.1935, Kompanie Chef in Infanterie Regiment at Koenigsbrueck 04.1935–10.1935, Kompanie Chef in Infanterie Regiment 53, 10.1935–11.1937. WWII: attached to IV. Armee Korps 11.1937–08.1939, Commander of I. Bataillon, Infanterie Regiment 173, 08.1939–10.1941, Commander of Infanterie Regiment 173, 02.1942–03.1943, Fuehrer Res. in O.K.H. 03.1943–10.1943, Commander of Grenadier Regiment 504, 10.1943–08.1944, Commander of 85. Infanterie Division 11.1944–02.1945. Awards: Knight's Cross 26.03.44, German Cross in Gold 19.12.41, 1939 Clasps to the 1914 Iron Cross 1st and 2nd Class, Infantry Assault Badge in Silver, Eastern Front Medal, 1939 Wound Badge in Silver, Silesian Eagle 1st and 2nd Class, 1914 Iron Cross 1st and 2nd Class, 1914 Wound Badge in Black, Cross of Honor.

Becht, Ernst: Generalmajor (01.04.42), (Heer); born 24.05.95 in Dieuze, died 01.09.59 in Idar-Oberstein. WWI: Leutnant assigned to Field Railway Operations. Commander of Panzer Abwehr Abteilung 5, 10.1935–09.1936, Abteilung Chief in Reich War Ministry 10.1936–01.1938. WWII: Gruppe Chief in (WRo) of O.K.W. 02.1938–02.1943, Chief of Military Economic Staff Inland of O.K.W. 03.1943–07.1943, Fuehrer Res. in O.K.H. 08.1943–03.1944, attached to Delegation of 4-Year Plan 08.1944–04.1945. Awards: War Merit Cross 1st and 2nd Class with Swords, Finnish Freedom Cross 1st Class with Swords, 1914 Iron Cross 1st and 2nd Class, Cross of Honor.

Beck, Dr. Fritz: General-Intendant (01.06.40), (Luftwaffe); born 03.01.90 in Dresden, died 05.07.70 in Wiesbaden. Administrative Officer by profession. WWI: Leutnant in Feld Artillerie Regiment 192. Member of N.S.D.A.P. Intendant in Luftkreis Kommando I in Koenigsberg 02.1936–05.1937, Personal Advisor in R.L.M. 05.1937–01.1939. WWII: Department Chief in R.L.M. 02.1939–09.1939, Intendant to Luftgau Kommando II 09.1939–02.1941, Intendant to Luftgau Kommando XI 02.1941–05.1941, Intendant to Luftgau Kommandos XI and XII at same time 05.1941–09.1943, Intendant to Feld Luftgau Kommando Belgium and Northern France 09.1943–09.1944, Intendant to Luftgau Kommando XIV 09.1944–05.1945. Awards: War Merit Cross 1st and 2nd Class with Swords, 1914 Iron Cross 1st and 2nd Class, Cross of Honor.

Beck, Ludwig: General der Artillerie (01.10.35), (Heer); born 29.06.80 in Biebrich, died 20.07.44 (suicide) in Berlin for part in attempted assassination of Adolf Hitler. WWI: Major on Staff of Armee Gruppe "Deuschen Kronprinz." Promotions to Reichswehr Generalmajor 01.02.31, Reichswehr Generalleutnant 01.12.32, honorary uniform of Generaloberst z.V. 01.11.38. Chief of Troop Office in Reich War Ministry 10.1933–06.1935, Chief of Heeres General Staff 07.1935–08.1938, retired 10.1938. Awards: RK-Hohenzollern, 1914 Iron Cross 1st and 2nd Class, Cross of Honor.

Becke, Erwin: Generalmajor (01.12.42), (Heer); born 29.11.81 in Harburg, died 22.10.57 in Hannover. WWI: Hauptmann and Ia to 79. Infanterie Division. WWII: Director of Military Economics Office in Hannover 05.1935–11.1941, Armaments Inspector for Hannover 11.1941–01.1943, retired 01.1943. Awards: War Merit Cross 1st and 2nd Class with Swords, 1914 Iron Cross 1st and 2nd Class, Cross of Honor.

Becker, Dr. Bruno: General-Intendant (01.05.44), (Heer); born 08.05.94 in Dresden, died 24.05.72 in Munich. Administrative Officer by profession, WWI: service unknown. WWII: Armee Gruppe Intendant (dates and units unknown). Awards: War Merit Cross 1st and 2nd Class without Swords, Cross of Honor.

Becker, Carl: Generalleutnant (01.10.43), (Heer); born 16.01.95 in Varel, died 24.03.66 in Heidelberg. WWI: Leutnant in Infanterie Regiment 91. Promotion to Generalmajor 01.04.43. Attached to I. Bataillon, Infanterie Regiment at Osnabrueck 10.1934–10.1935, Kompanie Chef in Infanterie Regiment 37, 10.1935–01.1937, Commander of III. Bataillon. WWII: Infanterie Regiment 37, 02.1937–05.1940, Commander of Infanterie Regiment 18, 12.1940–01.1943, Commander of 253. Infanterie Division 01.1943–05.1945. Awards: Oak Leaves 14.04.45 (829), Knight's Cross 29.10.42, German Cross in Gold 18.10.41, Honor Roll Clasp 29.09.41, 1939 Clasps to the 1914 Iron Cross 1st and 2nd Class, German Army High Command Commendation Certificate 04.10.41, Infantry Assault Badge in Silver, Eastern Front

Medal, German West Wall Medal, RK-Hohenzollern, 1914 Iron Cross 1st and 2nd Class, 1914 Wound Badge in Gold, Cross of Honor.

Becker, Dr. Ernst: General-Arzt (01.10.38), (Heer); born 07.05.84 in Irxleben, died 14.01.62 in Haldensleben. Medical doctor by profession. WWI: Feld-Arzt (unit unknown). WWII: Oberstarzt attached to Reich Welfare and Utilities Court of Wehrmacht 02.1935–08.1939, Corps Physician to XXIII. Armee Korps 08.1939–11.1940, Corps Physician to Wehrkreis XI 11.1940–12.1944. Awards: War Merit Cross 1st and 2nd Class with Swords, 1914 Iron Cross 2nd Class, Cross of Honor.

Becker, Franz: Generalmajor (01.08.42), (Heer); born 28.04.93 in Altdamm, died 11.03.76 in Koeln. WWI: Oberleutnant and Adjutant to Infanterie Regiment 77. Instructor at Infanterie Schule (later Kriegsschule) at Dresden 04.1934–12.1936, Commander of II. Bataillon, Infanterie Regiment 3, 01.1937–05.1939. WWII: Commander of Truppenubungsplatz at Baumholder 06.1939–10.1940, Commander of Infanterie Regiment 3, 10.1940–01.1942, Commander of Truppenubungsplatz at Muenster 07.1942–06.1944, assigned to Special Duties for Oberbefehlshaber of Heeresgruppe Nord Ukraine 07.1944–01.1945. Awards: 1939 Clasps to the 1914 Iron Cross 1st and 2nd Class, Infantry Assault Badge in Silver, Eastern Front Medal, Cross of Honor.

Becker, Fritz: Generalleutnant (01.04.43), (Heer); born 07.03.92 in Heidberg, died 11.06.67 in Herzberg. WWI: Oberleutnant and Adjutant in 77. Res. Infanterie Brigade. Promotion to Generalmajor 01.04.42. Commander of I. Bataillon, Infanterie Regiment at Muenster 10.1934–10.1935. WWII: Commander of I. Bataillon, Infanterie Regiment 64, 10.1935–08.1939, Commander of Infanterie Regiment 60, 08.1939–05.1942, Commander of 370. Infanterie Division 09.1942–06.1944, Commander of 389. Infanterie Division 09.1944–03.1945. Awards: Knight's Cross 06.04.43, German Cross in Gold 22.11.41, 1939 Clasps to the 1914 Iron Cross 1st and 2nd Class, Infantry Assault Badge in Bronze, Eastern Front Medal, 1939 Wound Badge in Black, German West Wall Medal, 1914 Iron Cross 1st and 2nd Class, 1914 Wound Badge in Black, Cross of Honor.

Becker, Hellmuth: SS-Brigadefuehrer und Generalmajor der Waffen-SS (01.10.44), born 12.08.02 in Alt-Ruppin, died 28.02.53 at Stalingrad (executed as P.O.W.). P-1592593, SS-113174. Joined N.S.D.A.P. in 1933, joined S.A. in 1932, joined SS in 1933. Attached to I. Sturmbann, SS-Standarte 2 "Deutschland" 01.10.34–01.07.35, attached to I. SS-T.V. Sturmbann "Oberbayern" 01.12.36, Leader of I. Sturmbann, 1. SS-T.V. Standarte "Oberbayern" 01.12.37–01.12.38. WWII: Commander of I. Bataillon, SS-Totenkopf Infanterie Regiment 1, Commander of SS-Totenkopf Kampfgruppe "Becker," Commander of SS-Panzer Grenadier Regiment, "Totenkopf"

15.05.43, Commander of SS-Panzer Grenadier Regiment 36, attached to SS-Fuehrungshauptamt 30.01.44, Commander of 3. SS-Panzer Division "Totenkopf" 09.11.44. Awards: Oak Leaves 21.09.44 (595), Knight's Cross 07.09.43, German Cross in Gold 26.09.42, 1939 Iron Cross 1st and 2nd Class, Infantry Assault Badge in Bronze, Demjansk Shield, Eastern Front Medal, 1939 Wound Badge in Black, Reich Sports Badge in Silver, SA-Sports Badge, Degen, Ring.

SS-Brigadefuehrer Hellmuth Becker. (Marc Rikmenspoel)

Becker, Hermann: Generalleutnant (01.11.42), (Luftwaffe); born 09.08.93 in Niederglauchau, died 06.02.45 (executed by Wehrmacht) at Fort Zinna. WWI: in Naval G.A.S. as Leutnant zur See attached to Seefliegerstationen at Zeebruegge. Promotion to Generalmajor 01.11.40. Commander of Fliegergruppe Keil 11.1934–02.1936, Commander of Seeflieger Schule 03.1936–03.1938. WWII: Commander of Sea Air Service Units 04.1938–12.1939, Inspector of Air Service Units in R.L.M. 12.1939–09.1943, Fuehrer Res. in O.K.L. 10.1943–12.1944, brought up on charges and lost rank and all rights 12.1944. Awards: War Merit Cross 1st and 2nd Class with Swords, 1939 Wound Badge in Gold, Naval Pilot's Commemorative Badge, 1914 Iron Cross 2nd Class, 1914 Naval Pilot's Badge, Cross of Honor.

Becker, Prof. Dr. Karl: General der Artillerie (01.10.36), (Heer); born 14.12.79 in Speyer, died 08.04.40 (suicide) in Berlin. WWI: Hauptmann and Advisor with Artillery Test Commission. Promotions to Reichswehr Generalmajor 01.02.33, Reichswehr Generalleutnant 01.10.34. President of Reichs Research Council 03.1937–02.1938. WWII: Chief of Heer Weapons Office in O.K.H. 03.1938–04.1940. Awards: 1914 Iron Cross 1st and 2nd Class, Cross of Honor.

General der Artillerie Prof. Dr. Karl Becker. (Bundesarchiv)

Becker, Paul: Admiral-Richter (01.05.44), (Kriegsmarine); born 23.05.81 in Worms, died 11.09.63 in Kiel. Jurist by profession. WWI: Oberleutnant der Res. in Infanterie Regiment 118. WWII: Senior Judge for Baltic Sea Naval High Command 10.1936–05.1944, retired 08.1944. Awards: War Merit Cross 1st and 2nd Class with Swords, 1914 Iron Cross 1st and 2nd Class, Cross of Honor.

Becker, Wilhelm: Generalleutnant (01.07.43), (Luftwaffe); born 27.10.97 in Hanau, died 09.01.64 in Goettingen. WWI: in G.A.S. as Leutnant in Jasta 30. Promotion to Generalmajor 01.08.41. Advisor in R.L.M. 12.1933–03.1935, Fliegerhorst Commandant of Goeppingen 07.1935–1936, Group Leader in Technische Amt of R.L.M. 1936–02.1937, attached to Staff of Luftkreis Kommando V 03.1937–09.1937. WWII: Department Chief in Economic Staff of O.K.W. 10.1937–10.1942, Chief of Field Economic Office in O.K.W. 11.1942–09.1944, Fuehrer Res. in O.K.L. 09.1944–05.1945. Awards: War Merit Cross 1st and 2nd Class with Swords, Finnish Freedom Cross 1st Class with Swords, Pilot's Commemorative Badge, 1914 Iron Cross 2nd Class, 1914 Wound Badge in Black, 1914 Pilot's Badge, Cross of Honor.

Beckmann, Alfred: Generalmajor z.V. (01.02.41), (Heer); born 07.07.77 Herford, died 21.04.46 in Bad Honnef. WWI: Major and Ia to 11. Infanterie Division. Attached to Staff of Military Replacement Inspection at Giessen and later in Koblenz 11.1934–04.1936, attached to Staff of IX. Armee Korps 05.1936–07.1936. WWII: without assignment 07.1936–08.1939, Commander of Restraum Kommandantur I 08.1939–11.1939, attached to Staff of General Kommando Eifel 11.1939–08.1940, Commandant of Feldkommandantur 758 and later Feldkommandantur 199, 08.1940–08.1941, Fuehrer Res. in O.K.H. 08.1941–06.1943, retired 06.1943. Awards: War Merit Cross 1st and 2nd Class with Swords, 1914 Iron Cross 1st and 2nd Class, 1914 Wound Badge in Black, Cross of Honor.

Beelitz, Dietrich: Generalmajor (01.05.45), (Heer); born 14.03.06 in Diedenhofen, died 06.09.02. Adjutant to I. Bataillon, Infanterie Regiment at Stettin 10.1934–08.1935, attached to Staff of Kriegsschule and General Staff of Heeres 08.1935–07.1937, attached to Household Department of General Staff of Heeres 08.1937–03.1939. WWII: Group Director in Household Department of O.K.H. 04.1939–05.1940, Ia to 97. Infanterie Division 12.1940–04.1942, on Staff of Chief of Heeres Personnel Department in O.K.H. 11.1942–12.1943, Ia to Heeresgruppe C followed by 10. Armee 12.1943–05.1945. Awards: German Cross in Gold 05.05.42, 1939 Iron Cross 1st and 2nd Class, Eastern Front Medal.

Beeren, Karl von: Generalleutnant (01.05.43), (Heer); born 10.02.90 in Eissen, died 13.09.61 in Wiedenbrueck. WWI: Oberleutnant and M.G. Officer in Infanterie Regiment 15. Promotion to Generalmajor 01.02.42. Commander of Ausbildungs Bataillon of Infanterie Regiment at Paderborn 10.1934–10.1935, Commander of II. Bataillon, Infanterie Regiment 64, 10.1935–10.1937, attached to Staff of Infanterie Regiment 79, 10.1937–11.1938. WWII: Military Commander of Koeln 11.1938–08.1939, Commander of Infanterie Regiment 193, 08.1939–02.1942, Commander of 280. Infanterie Division 04.1942–11.1944, Commander of Division 526, 12.1944–01.1945, in hospital 01.1945–04.1945. Awards: 1939 Clasps to the 1914 Iron Cross 1st and 2nd Class, Infantry Assault Badge in Silver, Eastern Front

Medal, 1914 Iron Cross 1st and 2nd Class, 1914 Wound Badge in Black, Cross of Honor.

Behlendorf, Hans: General der Artillerie (01.10.41), (Heer); born 13.08.89 in Allenstein, died 16.03.61 in Baden-Baden. WWI: Hauptmann and Adjutant with z.b.V. General Kommando 51. Promotions to Generalmajor 01.03.38, Generalleutnant 01.02.40. Leader of Abteilung P4 in Reich War Ministry 11.1934–01.1938, Commander of Artillerie 31, 02.1938–07.1939. WWII: Commander of 34. Infanterie Division 07.1939–12.1941, Commander of LXXXIV. Armee Korps 05.1942–04.1943, Fuehrer Res. in O.K.H. 04.1943–12.1944, retired 12.1944. Awards: Knight's Cross 11.10.41, 1939 Clasps to the 1914 Iron Cross 1st and 2nd Class, Infantry Assault Badge in Silver, Eastern Front Medal, 1939 Wound Badge in Black, German Red Cross Decoration 1st Class, RK-Hohenzollern, 1914 Iron Cross 1st and 2nd Class, Cross of Honor.

Behr, Heinrich von: Generalleutnant (01.11.42), (Heer); born 08.09.87 in Koenigsberg, died 16.11.51 in Hardtwiesen. WWI: Hauptmann in Infanterie Regiment 95. Promotion to Generalmajor 01.11.40. Commander of I. Bataillon, Infanterie Regiment 12, 10.1935–05.1937. WWII: Commander of Infanterie Regiment 45, 06.1937–12.1940, Commander of 173. Res. Infanterie Division 12.1940–02.1944, Commander of Division Formation Staff "Grafenwohr" 07.1944–02.1945. Awards: 1939 Clasps to the 1914 Iron Cross 1st and 2nd Class, Infanterie Assault Badge in Silver, 1914 Iron Cross 1st and 2nd Class, Cross of Honor.

Behr, Heinrich Freiherr von: Generalmajor (01.04.45), (Heer); born 26.06.02 in Roennen, died 14.08.83 in Bonn. Adjutant to Senior Signals Officer attached to Inspector of Kavallerie 10.1934–10.1935, Kompanie Chef in Nachrichten Abteilung 39, 10.1935–03.1937. WWII: Course Director at Heeres Sportschule Wuensdorf 04.1937–09.1939, Commander of Nachrichten Abteilung 198, 09.1939–04.1940, Commander of Panzer Nachrichten Abteilung 39, 04.1940–09.1941, Commander of Nachrichten Abteilung in German Afrika Korps 01.1942–11.1942, Commander of Panzer Grenadier Regiment 200, 07.1943–12.1944, Commander of 90. Panzer Grenadier Division 12.1944–04.1945. Awards: Oak Leaves 09.01.45 (689), Knight's Cross 23.02.44, 1939 Iron Cross 1st and 2nd Class, Close Combat Clasp in Bronze, General Assault Badge, Afrika Cuff Band, Baltic Cross 1st and 2nd Class.

Behr, Max von: SS-Gruppenfuehrer und Generalleutnant der Waffen-SS (30.01.44); born 10.01.79 in Reddenau, died 27.12.51 in Lindau. P-5849115, SS-276063. WWI: Major i.G. attached to Romanian General Staff. Joined N.S.D.A.P. in 1937, joined S.A. in 1933, joined S.S. in 1936. Promotion to SS-Brigadefuehrer 30.01.38. Leader on Staff of SS-Hauptamt 01.12.36, Leader on Staff of RFSS 01.12.37–01.12.38. WWII: SS-Standort Commandant of Vienna 30.01.42, SS-Standort Commandant of Berlin 15.05.43–09.11.44, N.S.D.A.P.-Oberdienstleiter. Awards: War Merit Cross 1st and 2nd Class with Swords, Grand Officer's Cross of the Italian Order of the Crown, RK-Hohenzollern, RK-Sachsen Ernestine House Order 1st Class with Swords, RK-Wuerttemberg Friedrich Order 2nd Class with Swords, 1914 Iron Cross 1st and 2nd Class, Austro-Hungarian Military Service Cross 3rd Class with War Decoration, Turkish Half Moon, Cross of Honor, Degen, Ring.

Behrend, Hermann-Heinrich: Generalmajor (04.17.45), (Heer); born 25.08.98 in Perleberg, died 19.06.87 in Soltau. WWI: Leutnant in Infanterie Regiment 43. Kompanie Chef in Infanterie Regiment at Paderborn 10.1934–10.1935, Kompanie Chef in Infanterie Regiment 64, 10.1935–12.1936, Metals Defense Representative of General Kommando III at Rheinmetall Brosig AG and Werke Tegal/Berlin 03.1937–12.1938. WWII: Director of NCO courses for Infanterie Regiment 16, 02.1939–08.1939, Commander of I. Bataillon, Infanterie Regiment 489, 08.1939–09.1941, Commander of Patrol Group Service with O.B. Ukraine 12.1941–08.1942, Commander of Patrol Group Service for O.B. Norway 08.1942–12.1942, Commander of Patrol Group Service for Travel Transport Centre 12.1942–05.1943, Commander of Grenadier Regiment 154, 05.1943–10.1943 and 12.1943–06.1944, Commander of Grenadier Regiment 529, 07.1944–12.1944, Division Leader's Course 02.1945–03.1945, Commander of 490. Infanterie Division 04.1945–05.1945. Awards: Swords 26.04.45 (148), Oak Leaves 06.03.44 (421), Knight's Cross 15.07.41, 1939 Clasps to the 1914 Iron Cross 1st and 2nd Class, Infantry Assault Badge in Silver, 1939 Wound Badge in Gold, Eastern Front Medal, 1914 Iron Cross 1st and 2nd Class, 1914 Wound Badge in Black, Cross of Honor.

Behrens, Wilhelm: Generalleutnant (01.09.44), (Heer); born 23.08.88 in Berlin, died 15.08.68 in Lotte. WWI: Oberleutnant and M.G. Officer in Ulan Regiment 11. Promotion to Generalmajor 01.01.42. Attached to Staff of Reiter Regiment 38, 10.1934–04.1935, attached to Infanterie Regiment 10, 05.1935–09.1935, Commander of II. Bataillon, Infanterie Regiment 10, 10.1935–09.1938. WWII: Department Chief in Heeres Waffenmeisterschule in Berlin 10.1938–10.1939, Commander of Infanterie Regiment 106, 10.1939–12.1939, Commander of 328. Infanterie Division 12.1939–01.1942, in hospital 01.1942–04.1942, Commander of 193. Infanterie Division 06.1942–06.1944, retired 09.1944. Awards: Knight's Cross 27.03.42, German Cross in Gold 09.12.41, 1939 Clasps to the 1914 Iron Cross 1st and 2nd Class, Infantry Assault Badge in Silver, Eastern Front Medal, RK-Hohenzollern, 1914 Iron Cross 1st and 2nd Class, 1914 Wound Badge in Silver, Cross of Honor.

Behrendt, Hans: Generalleutnant (01.10.43), (Luftwaffe); born 28.07.92 in Breslau, died 24.07.59 in Schulenburg. WWI: in G.A.S. as Oberleutnant in

Flieger Abteilung 45. Promotion to Generalmajor 01.11.41. Advisor in Reich War Ministry 07.1933–09.1934, Advisor in R.L.M. 10.1934–05.1935, Instructor and later Lead Instructor for Fliegergruppe Tutow 06.1935–02.1937, Fliegerhorst Commandant of Giebelstadt 03.1937–01.1939. WWII: Commander of K.G. 27 "Boelcke" 02.1939–11.1940, Commander of Kampfflieger Schule II at Hoersching 11.1940–1942, Inspector of Personnel of Luftwaffe in R.L.M. 1942–04.1945. Awards: 1939 Clasps to the 1914 Iron Cross 1st and 2nd Class, 1939 Observer's Badge, Pilot's Commemorative Badge, 1914 Iron Cross 1st and 2nd Class, 1914 Observer's Badge, Cross of Honor.

Behschnitt, Walter: Generalleutnant (01.09.40), (Heer); born 13.08.85 in Reichenbach, died 20.10.70 in Frankfurt am Main. WWI: Hauptmann on Staff of Chief of Field Railway Affairs. Promotion to Generalmajor 01.10.37. Commander of Infanterie Regiment at Kassel 10.1934–10.1935, Commander of Infanterie Regiment 15, 10.1935–10.1937, Commander of Heeres Service Office 9, 10.1937–11.1938, Commandant of Fortifications for Aachen 11.1938–03.1939. WWII: Commander of 15. Infanterie Division 04.1939–10.1939, Commander of 166. Infanterie Division 11.1939–04.1940, Commander of 254. Infanterie Division 04.1940–03.1942, Military Replacement Inspector for Hannover 05.1942–04.1945. Awards: German Cross in Gold 06.09.42, 1939 Clasps to the 1914 Iron Cross 1st and 2nd Class, Eastern Front Medal, 1914 Iron Cross 1st and 2nd Class, 1914 Wound Badge in Black, Cross of Honor.

Beisswaenger, Hugo: Generalleutnant (01.08.44), (Heer); born 13.10.85 in Stuttgart, died 28.05.63 in Ulm. WWI: Oberleutnant and Chief of 2. Batterie, Feld Artillerie Regiment 29. Promotion to Generalmajor 01.06.43. Commander of V. Abteilung, Artillerie Regiment at Ulm 10.1934–10.1935, Commander of II. Abteilung, Artillerie Regiment 41, 10.1935–03.1936. WWII: Advisor, Chief of Staff and later Department Chief with Inspector of Artillerie (In 4) in O.K.H. 03.1936–11.1941, Commander of Panzer Artillerie Regiment 116, 11.1941–11.1942, General with Chief of Heeres Armaments in O.K.H. 04.1943–02.1945. Awards: 1939 Clasps to the 1914 Iron Cross 1st and 2nd Class, War Merit Cross 1st and 2nd Class with Swords, Eastern Front Medal, 1914 Iron Cross 1st and 2nd Class, 1914 Wound Badge in Black, Cross of Honor.

Beisswaenger, Walter: Generalmajor (01.04.43), (Heer); born 29.06.94 in Schloss Stolberg, died 25.12.84 in Munich. WWI: Oberleutnant and Adjutant to II. Abteilung, Feld Artillerie Regiment 49. Commander of IV. Abteilung, Artillerie Regiment at Ludwigsburg 10.1934–10.1935, Commander of I. Abteilung, Artillerie Regiment 51, 10.1935–10.1936, Commander of I. Abteilung, Artillerie Regiment 72, 10.1936–12.1938. WWII: Advisor in Weapons Office of O.K.H. 01.1939–09.1939, Commander of Artillerie Regiment 195,

09.1939–10.1940, Department Chief in Heeres Weapons Office of O.K.H. 10.1940–05.1943, Commander of Artillerie 101, 05.1943–11.1943, attached to Staff of Commander of Artillerie 120, 01.1944–04.1944, Commander of Artillerie 485, 08.1944–03.1945. Awards: 1939 Clasp to the 1914 Iron Cross 2nd Class, War Merit Cross 1st and 2nd Class with Swords, General Assault Badge, 1914 Iron Cross 2nd Class, Cross of Honor.

Below, Gerd-Paul von: Generalmajor der Res. (20.04.45), (Heer); born 30.11.92 in Strasburg, died 09.12.53 at Voikovo P.O.W. Camp. WWI: Oberleutnant in Ulan Regiment 9. WWII: recalled to military service and attached to Infanterie Regiment 4, 09.1935–08.1939, Commander of I. Bataillon, Infanterie Regiment 374, 08.1939–11.1941, Commander of Grenadier Regiment 374, 11.1941–01.1943, taken ill in military hospital then Fuehrer Res. in O.K.H. 01.1943–01.1945, Commander of z.b.V. Division Stab 615, 02.1945–05.1945. Awards: Knight's Cross 28.02.43, 1939 Clasps to the 1914 Iron Cross 1st and 2nd Class, Infantry Assault Badge in Silver, Eastern Front Medal, 1914 Iron Cross 1st and 2nd Class, Cross of Honor.

Beltinger, Dr. Arthur: General-Arzt z.V. (01.12.41), (Heer); born 27.05.81 in Ingolstadt, died 17.10.64 in Rosenheim. Medical doctor by profession. WWI: German medical service (rank and unit unknown). WWII: Chief Physician to Military Befehlshaber of Krakau 09.1939–10.1939, Korps Arzt to Wehrkreis Kommando XVIII 10.1939–05.1945. Awards: War Merit Cross 1st and 2nd Class with Swords, 1914 Iron Cross 2nd Class, Cross of Honor.

Benda, Hans: Admiral-Oberstabsintendant (01.05.44), (Kriegsmarine); born 19.08.77 in Metz, died 27.02.51 in Schleswig-Holstein. Administrative Officer by profession. WWI: Naval Official and Department Chief in Reichsmarineamt. Promotions to Admiral-Intendant (date unknown), Admiral-Stabsintendant (date unknown). WWII: Chief of Naval Administration Office in O.K.M. 11.1939–02.1945. Awards: German Cross in Silver 18.03.45, War Merit Cross 1st and 2nd Class with Swords, 1914 Iron Cross 1st and 2nd Class, Cross of Honor.

Bender, Waldemar: Konteradmiral z.V. (01.07.42), (Kriegsmarine); born 28.12.85 in Danzig, died 06.12.50 in Kiel. WWI: U-boat service as Kapitanleutnant and Staff Officer with III. Submarine Flotilla. Chief of Nautical Abteilung in Marineleitung 09.1932–09.1935. WWII: not in service 09.1935–09.1939, at disposal of Kriegsmarine 09.1939–05.1941, Chief of Staff to Naval Shipyard at Drontheim 05.1941–05.1942, Senior Shipyard Director at Horten Naval Shipyard 05.1942–03.1943, Commander of Sea Water Way "Kaiser Wilhelm" Channel 06.1943–01.1945. Awards: War Merit Cross 1st and 2nd Class with Swords, 1914 Iron Cross 1st and 2nd Class, 1914 Submarine Badge, Cross of Honor.

Beneckendorf und von Hindenburg, Oskar von: Generalleutnant z.V. (01.04.42); (Heer), born 31.01.81 in Koenigsberg, died 13.02.60 in Bad Harzburg. Son of Generalfeldmarschall and Reichspresident Paul von Hindenburg. WWI: Hauptmann and Ia to 20. Infanterie Division. Promotion to Generalmajor z.V. 01.09.40. WWII: Commander of 422. Infanterie Division 10.1939–03.1940, Commander of 401. Infanterie Division 03.1940–01.1941, P.O.W. Commander for Wehrkreis I 01.1941–12.1944. Awards: War Merit Cross 1st and 2nd Class with Swords, RK-Hohenzollern, 1914 Iron Cross 1st and 2nd Class, Cross of Honor.

Bengsch, Dr. Otto: General-Arzt (30.01.45), (Luftwaffe); born 28.07.79 in Guscht, died 15.07.54 in Bad Schwartau. Medical doctor by profession. WWI: Marine-Oberstabsarzt (unit unknown). WWII: Department Physician in Luftwaffe Hospital 4 in Wismar 11.1938–12.1940, Chief Physician of Luftwaffe Hospital 4 in Wismar 01.1941–1945. Awards: War Merit Cross 1st and 2nd Class with Swords, German Horseman's Badge in Silver, 1914 Iron Cross 1st and 2nd Class, Cross of Honor.

Benicke, Dr. Fritz: Generalleutnant (01.05.44), (Heer); born 11.08.94 in Charlottenburg, died 14.03.75 in Starnberg. WWI: Oberleutnant and Pionier Leader to 76. Res. Infanterie Division. Promotion to Generalmajor 01.07.43. WWII: Commander of 47. Pionier Bataillon 10.1935–03.1940, Pionier Leader to Panzer Gruppe 1 (later Panzer Armee 1) 12.1940–06.1943, Commander of 25. Panzer Grenadier Division 11.1943–04.1944, Higher Pionier Leader for Wehrkreis Kommando XI 08.1944–12.1944, Defensive Line Commander for Wehrkreis Kommando XXI 12.1944–05.1945. Awards: German Cross in Silver 26.01.43, War Merit Cross 1st and 2nd Class with Swords, 1914 Iron Cross 1st and 2nd Class, 1914 Wound Badge in Black, Cross of Honor.

Benkendorff, Dr. Rudolf: Ministerialdirigent (01.11.44), (Luftwaffe); born 05.08.90 in Hamburg, died 04.08.73 in Hamburg. Civil Servant and Meteorologist by profession. WWI: Leutnant der Res. in Res. Jaeger Bataillon 18. Leader of Air Weather Service in R.L.M. 04.1933–10.1934, Leader of Weather Service for Luftkreis Kommando VI 10.1934–06.1939. WWII: Chief Meteorologist to Luftflotte 2, 06.1939–06.1943, Chief of Weather Service of Luftwaffe in O.K.L. 06.1943–05.1945. Awards: 1939 Clasp to the 1914 Iron Cross 2nd Class, War Merit Cross 1st and 2nd Class with Swords, German West Wall Medal, 1914 Iron Cross 1st and 2nd Class, 1914 Wound Badge in Black, Cross of Honor.

Benthack, Georg: Generalmajor (01.12.44), (Heer); born 02.03.94 in Hamburg, died 17.08.73 in Hamburg. WWI: Leutnant der Res. with Fuss Artillerie Regiment 16. WWII: attached to Staff and later Batterie Chef to Beobachter Abteilung 20, 10.1936–10.1939, Commander of 20. Beobachter Bataillon 10.1939–11.1941, Course Instructor at Artillerie Schule II at Jueterbog 11.1941–03.1943, Commander of Artillerie Regiment 619, 08.1943–12.1943, Festung Artillerie and later Fortress Divisional Commander of Crete 12.1943–05.1945. Awards: Knight's Cross 21.05.45, 1939 Clasps to the 1914 Iron Cross 1st and 2nd Class, Heer Flak Badge, 1914 Iron Cross 1st and 2nd Class, Cross of Honor.

Bentivegni, Franz-Eccard von: Generalleutnant (30.01.45), (Heer); born 18.07.96 in Potsdam, died 04.04.58 in Wiesbaden. WWI: Leutnant in Garde Feld Artillerie Regiment 2. Promotion to Generalmajor 01.08.44. Batterie Chef in Artillerie Regiment 23, 10.1935–06.1936, attached to Staff of IX. Armee Korps 07.1936–03.1938, Ia to 26. Division 04.1938–02.1939. WWII: Department Chief in Abwehr III of O.K.W. 03.1939–09.1943, Department Chief of Amt Ausland, Abwehr III in O.K.W. 09.1943–03.1944, Commander of 170. Infanterie Division 05.1944–03.1945. Awards: German Cross in Silver (date unknown), 1939 Clasps to the 1914 Iron Cross 1st and 2nd Class, War Merit Cross 1st and 2nd Class with Swords, RK-Hohenzollern, 1914 Iron Cross 1st and 2nd Class, 1914 Wound Badge in Black, Cross of Honor.

Berchem, Otto Freiherr von: Generalmajor (01.04.44), (Luftwaffe); born 21.01.77 in Landshut, died 29.05.49 in Haggen. WWI: Major and Staff Officer in Austrian Feld Armee. Transferred to German Wehrmacht 03.1938, attached to Luftgau Kommando V in Munich 1938–01.1939. WWII: Intelligence Officer attached to General Staff of Luftflotte 3, 02.1939–04.1945. Awards: War Merit Cross 1st and 2nd Class with Swords, German Red Cross Decoration 1st Class, Red Eagle Order IV. Class, 1914 Iron Cross 1st and 2nd Class, Bavarian Military Service Order IV. Class with Swords, Cross of Honor.

Bercken, Werner von: Generalleutnant (01.08.44), (Heer); born 08.02.97 in Oppeln, died 29.02.76 in Roettgen. WWI: Leutnant and Adjutant to II. Bataillon, Grenadier Regiment 7. Promotion to Generalmajor 01.02.44. Kompanie Chef in Infanterie Regiment at Frankfurt/Oder 10.1934–10.1935, Kompanie Chef in Infanterie Regiment 68, 10.1935–09.1936. WWII: Commander of III. Bataillon, Infanterie Regiment 50, 10.1936–12.1939, Course Instructor at Infanterie Schule 12.1939–08.1940, Commander of Infanterie Regiment 509, 11.1940–12.1941, Commander of Infanterie Regiment 84, 12.1941–11.1943, Commander of 102. Infanterie Division 02.1944–04.1945. Awards: Knight's Cross 23.10.44, German Cross in Gold 01.06.44, 1939 Clasps to the 1914 Iron Cross 1st and 2nd Class, Infantry Assault Badge in Silver, Eastern Front Medal, 1914 Iron Cross 1st and 2nd Class, 1914 Wound Badge in Silver, Cross of Honor.

Berendes, Heinrich: Generalmajor z.V. (01.03.42), (Heer); born 30.07.81 in Thorn, died 17.03.61 in Dortmund. WWI: Hauptmann and Adjutant to 15. Res. Infanterie Division. Commander of Military District Commando II in Dortmund

10.1933–12.1937. WWII: no assignment 12.1937–05.1940, Commandant of Feldkommandantur 752, 06.1940–07.1941, Commandant of Feldkommandantur 246, 03.1942, Commandant of Feldkommandantur 755, 03.1942–02.1943, retired 08.1943. Awards: 1939 Clasps to the 1914 Iron Cross 1st and 2nd Class, 1914 Iron Cross 1st and 2nd Class, Cross of Honor.

Berendt, Waldemar: Konteradmiral (31.10.29), (Kriegsmarine); born 16.04.78 in Goerlitz, died 16.08.78 in Bayreuth. Psychologist by profession. WWI: Marine-Stabsingenieur on torpedo boat. Psychologist attached to Naval Station North Sea 05.1933–03.1939. Awards: 1914 Iron Cross 1st and 2nd Class, Cross of Honor.

Berg, Kurt von: Generalleutnant (01.11.40), (Heer); born 26.07.86 in Offenburg, died 15.03.52 in Freiburg. WWI: Hauptmann and Ia to 221. Infanterie Division. Promotion to Generalmajor 01.03.38. Commander of Artillerie Regiment at Fulda 10.1934–10.1935, Commander of Artillerie Regiment 45, 10.1935–10.1937, Commander of Artillerie 15, 10.1937–04.1939. WWII: Military Replacement Inspector for Koblenz 05.1939–02.1940, Commander of 556. Infanterie Division 02.1940–08.1940, Military Replacement Inspector for Koblenz 08.1940–12.1944, Commander of Division "von Berg" 01.1945–05.1945. Awards: 1939 Clasps to the 1914 Iron Cross 1st and 2nd Class, RK-Hohenzollern, 1914 Iron Cross 1st and 2nd Class, Cross of Honor.

Berg, Martin: Generalmajor (01.08.44), (Heer); born 04.04.05 Arensberg, died 02.04.69 in Bahrendorf. Kompanie Chef in Infanterie Regiment 67, 10.1935–10.1936. WWII: Kompanie Chef in Infanterie Regiment 82, 10.1936–05.1940, Commander of II. Bataillon, Infanterie Regiment 82, 05.1940–05.1942, Commander of Grenadier Regiment 166, 05.1942–03.1944, Commander of 1. Ski Infanterie Brigade (later Division) 05.1944–10.1944, in hospital due to illness 12.1944–05.1945. Awards: Knight's Cross 30.12.43, German Cross in Gold 21.02.42, 1939 Iron Cross 1st and 2nd Class, Close Combat Clasp in Bronze, Infantry Assault Badge in Silver, Eastern Front Medal, 1939 Wound Badge in Silver, Reich Sports Badge in Bronze.

Bergen, Hans: Generalleutnant (01.10.43), (Heer); born 05.03.90 in Munich, died 17.02.57 in Landshut. WWI: Hauptmann in Bavarian Infanterie Regiment 10. Promotion to Generalmajor 01.10.41. Commander of I. Bataillon, Infanterie Regiment 62, 10.1935–03.1936, major car accident and recovery 03.1936–10.1938. WWII: attached to Staff of Infanterie Regiment 62, 10.1938–08.1939, Commander of Infanterie Regiment 179, 08.1939–04.1940, Commander of Infanterie Regiment 187, 05.1941–11.1941, Commander of 323. and later Commander of 299. Infanterie Division 02.1942–05.1943, Commander of 390. Field Training Division

05.1943–11.1944, Commander of Division 526, 12.1944–3.1945. Awards: Knight's Cross 09.07.41, 1939 Clasps to the 1914 Iron Cross 1st and 2nd Class, German Army High Command Commendation Certificate 03.07.41, Infantry Assault Badge in Silver, Eastern Front Medal, 1939 Wound Badge in Silver, 1914 Iron Cross 1st and 2nd Class, 1914 Wound Badge in Black, Cross of Honor.

Berger, Adolf: Generalmajor (01.08.43), (Heer); born 30.07.96 in Wesel, died 05.08.43 in action near Shablikino. WWI: Leutnant in Dragoon Regiment 21. Attached to Heeres Gasschule 10.1935–05.1936, Advisor in WaPruf 9 of O.K.H. 10.1936–1939. WWII: Commander of Aufklarungs Abteilung 105, 1939–01.1941, Regiment Staff Commander of Werfertruppe 1, 01.1941–04.1942, Commander of Werfer Artillerie Regiment 304 5.1942–06.1942, Commander of Werfertruppe 4, 06.1942–08.1943. Awards: 1939 Clasps to the 1914 Iron Cross 1st and 2nd Class, Heer Flak Badge, 1939 Wound Badge in Gold, 1914 Iron Cross 1st and 2nd Class, Cross of Honor.

Berger, Gottlob: SS-Obergruppenfuehrer und General der Waffen-SS (21.06.43); born 16.07.96 in Gerstetten, died 05.01.75 in Stuttgart. P-426875, SS-275991. WWI: Leutnant der Res. and Adjutant to III. Bataillon, Infanterie Regiment 476. Joined N.S.D.A.P. in 1931, joined S.A. in 1930, SA-Oberfuehrer, joined S.S. in 1936. Promotions to SS-Brigadefuehrer 20.04.39, SS-Gruppenfuehrer 20.04.41. Attached to Staff of SS-Oberabschnitte Sudwest 01.12.1936, Leader on Staff of RFSS 01.12.1937, attached to Staff of SS-Hauptamt 01.12.1938. WWII: Chief of Amt VI and Amt X in SS-Hauptamt, Chief of SS-Hauptamt 30.01.42–05.1945, President of German-Croat Society, Inspector-General of P.O.W.s, N.S.D.A.P.-Hauptdienstleiter, Member of Reichstag (WK 22 Duesseldorf-Ost). Awards: Golden Party Badge (honorary), Golden HJ Honor Badge with Oak Leaves, Knight's Cross of the War Merit Cross with Swords 15.11.44, German Cross in Silver 01.09.44, 1939 Clasps to the 1914 Iron Cross 1st and 2nd Class, War Merit Cross 1st and 2nd Class with Swords, German Social Welfare Decoration 2nd Class, German Olympic Games Decoration 1st Class, Grand Cross of the Croatian Order of the Crown of King Zvonimir with Oak Leaves, Swords and Breast Star, Commander's Cross of the Order of the White Rose of Finland with Swords, RK-1914 Iron Cross 1st and 2nd Class, 1914 Wound Badge in Silver, Cross of Honor, SA-Sports Badge in Gold, Degen, Ring.

SS-Obergruppenfuehrer Gottlob Berger. (Josef Charita)

Berger, Hanns: Generalmajor (01.02.42), (Heer); born 18.12.93 in Glogau, died 09.02.42 of wounds at a military hospital in Riga. WWI: Oberleutnant in Fuss Artillerie Regiment 15. WWII: Commander of I. Abteilung, Artillerie Regiment 54, 10.1935–08.1939, Commander of Artillerie Regiment 18, 09.1939–02.1942. Awards: German Cross in Gold 26.12.41, 1939 Clasps to the 1914 Iron Cross 1st and 2nd Class, General Assault Badge, 1939 Wound Badge in Gold, Reich Sports Badge in Gold, 1914 Iron Cross 1st and 2nd Class, 1914 Wound Badge in Black, Cross of Honor.

Berger, Dr. Karl: General-Veterinar (01.12.42), (Heer); born 24.12.85 in Bromberg, died 12.01.52 in Ploen. Medical veterinarian by profession. WWI: Ober-Veterinar (unit unknown). Division Veterinar to 11. Division 1938–11.1938. WWII: Korps Veterinar to XXIV. Armee Korps 1939–12.1940, Korps Veterinar to L. Armee Korps 12.1940–02.1941, Korps Veterinar to LIII. Armee Korps 02.1941–12.1941, attached to Veterinar Ersatz Abteilung 3, 12.1941–12.1942, retired 08.1943. Awards: War Merit Cross 1st and 2nd Class with Swords, German West Wall Medal, 1914 Iron Cross 1st and 2nd Class, Cross of Honor.

Berger, Lothar: Generalmajor (20.04.45), (Heer); born 31.12.00 in Halberstadt, died 05.11.71 in Bad Schwartau. WWI: Fahnrich in Infanterie Regiment 16. Kompanie Chef in Infanterie Regiment at Halberstadt 10.1934–10.1035, Kompanie Chef in Infanterie Regiment 12, 10.1935–10.1936, Kompanie Chef in Infanterie Regiment 66, 10.1936–05.1939. WWII: Commander of III. Bataillon, Infanterie Regiment 84, 06.1939–10.1940, Commander of I. Instruction Bataillon at Infanterie Schule 10.1940–01.1943, Commander of Grenadier Regiment 336, 01.1943–09.1943, Commander of Jaeger Regiment 721, 10.1943–01.1945. Awards: Oak Leaves 28.03.45 (806), Knight's Cross 05.08.40, 1939 Clasps to the 1914 Iron Cross 1st and 2nd Class, Infantry Assault Badge in Silver, 1914 Iron Cross 1st and 2nd Class, 1914 Wound Badge in Black, Cross of Honor.

Bergmann, Friedrich: Generalleutnant (01.03.38), (Heer); born 10.05.83 in Ingolstadt, died 21.12.41 in action near Syavki. WWI: Hauptmann and 2. Staff Officer to 6. Bavarian Reserve Division. Promotion to Generalmajor 01.03.36. Commander of Artillerie 5, 10.1935–12.1936. WWII: Commander of 27. Infanterie Division 01.1937–10.1940, Commander of 137. Infanterie Division 10.1940–12.1941. Awards: German Cross in Gold 19.12.41, 1939 Clasps to the 1914 Iron Cross 1st and 2nd Class, Infantry Assault Badge in Silver, 1939 Wound Badge in Gold, RK-Hohenzollern, 1914 Iron Cross 1st and 2nd Class, Cross of Honor.

Berka, Waldemar: Generalmajor (01.03.41), (Heer); born 03.08.80 in Breslau, died 09.04.65 in Minden. WWI: Hauptmann and Commander of I. Bataillon, Res. Infanterie Regiment 37. Attached to Staff of Military Replacement Kommando

VIII 03.1935–09.1935, Leader of Zweigstelle Oppeln 10.1935–03.1937. WWII: Commander of Wehrbezirks Kommando in Neisse 04.1937–10.1942, retired 10.1942. Awards: War Merit Cross 1st and 2nd Class with Swords, Pour le Mérite 23.06.18, RK-Hohenzollern, 1914 Iron Cross 1st and 2nd Class, Cross of Honor.

Berlin, Wilhelm: General der Artillerie (01.10.44), (Heer); born 28.04.89 in Koeln, died 15.09.87 in Hamburg. WWI: Hauptmann and Chief of 1. Schwere Freiwilligen Batterie. Promotions to Generalmajor 01.03.40, Generalleutnant 01.03.42. Commander of II. Abteilung, Artillerie Regiment at Jueterbog 10.1934–04.1935, Commander of II. Abteilung, Artillerie Lehr Regiment 05.1935–04.1936, Artillery Commander attached to Staff of Panzertruppen Kommando 05.1935–10.1937. WWII: Commander of Artillerie Regiment 33, 10.1937–09.1939, Commander of Artillerie 101, 09.1939–10.1940, Commander of Artillerie Schule II at Jueterbog 10.1940–04.1943, Commander of 227. Infanterie Division 06.1943–02.1944, attached to Heeres General Staff 07.1944–02.1945. Awards: Knight's Cross 06.03.44, 1939 Clasps to the 1914 Iron Cross 1st and 2nd Class, War Merit Cross 1st and 2nd Class with Swords, Finnish Freedom Cross 1st Class with Swords, RK-Hohenzollern, 1914 Iron Cross 1st and 2nd Class, Cross of Honor.

Bernard, Curt: Generalleutnant (01.10.39), (Heer); born 09.12.86 in Berlin, died 02.12.54 in Goettingen. WWI: Rittmeister and Ia to 7. Landwehr Division. Promotion to Generalmajor 01.01.38. Chief of Staff to VIII. Armee Korps 03.1935–09.1935, Commander of 3. Schuetzen Brigade 10.1935–03.1937. WWII: Chief of General Staff to Heeres Gruppen Kommando 4, 04.1937–08.1939, Fuehrer Res. in O.K.H. due to stroke 08.1939–12.1940, Commander of 178 Division (mot.) 12.1940–05.1942, Fuehrer Res. again 05.1942–06.1943, retired 06.1943. Awards: 1939 Clasps to the 1914 Iron Cross 1st and 2nd Class, 1914 Iron Cross 1st and 2nd Class, Cross of Honor.

Berndt, Dr. Walter: General-Stabsintendant (01.10.42), (Luftwaffe); born 09.02.97 in Bochum, died 24.07.73 in Mainz. Administrative Officer by profession. WWI: service unknown. Promotion to General-Intendant 20.02.40. Intendant to Luftkreis (later Luftwaffen Kommando) VI in Keil 04.1934–05.1939. WWII: Intendant to Luftgau Kommando XI 06.1939–02.1941, Chief Intendant to Luftflotte 4, 09.1941–05.1945. Awards: War Merit Cross 1st and 2nd Class with Swords, Cross of Honor.

Berndt, Dr. Wilhelm: SS-Brigadefuehrer und Generalmajor der Waffen-SS (09.11.44); born 02.08.89 in Hamburg, died 16.05.45 in Berlin. P-4054776, SS-229196. Medical doctor by profession. WWI: Physician attached to Grenadier Regiment 89. Joined N.S.D.A.P. in 1933 and S.S. in 1934. Attached to SS-Sanitats Abteilung Nordwest 01.12.37, attached to Sanitats Abteilung SS-T.V.-K.L. 01.12.38,

Leader of SS-Sanitats Staffel for SS-Standarte "Germania." WWII: attached to SS-Sanitats Amt 30.01.42, attached to SS-Fuehrungshauptamt 15.05.43–30.01.44, Chief of Amt A II in SS-Hauptamt 09.11.44–05.1945. Awards: 1939 Clasps to the 1914 Iron Cross 1st and 2nd Class, War Merit Cross 2nd Class with Swords, 1939 Wound Badge in Black, 1914 Iron Cross 1st and 2nd Class, Cross of Honor, Reich Sports Badge in Gold, SA-Sports Badge in Bronze, Ring.

Bernecker, Erich: Generalleutnant (01.07.41), (Heer); born 11.05.85 in Lenkeningken, died 28.10.41 in action near Valki. WWI: Hauptmann and General Staff Officer. Promotion to Generalmajor 01.06.38. Attached to Staff of Commander of Artillerie I in Koenigsberg 10.1935–12.1937, Commander of Artillerie Regiment 30, 01.1938–03.1939. WWII: Commander of Artillerie 5, 04.1939–09.1939, Commander of Artillerie 31, 09.1939–07.1940, Commander of Artillerie 124, 07.1940–10.1941. Awards: 1939 Clasps to the 1914 Iron Cross 1st and 2nd Class, General Assault Badge, 1939 Wound Badge in Gold, 1914 Iron Cross 1st and 2nd Class, Cross of Honor.

Berner, Erhard-Heinrich: Generalmajor (20.04.45), (Heer); born 12.09.94 in Schellerhau, died 25.07.60 in Hannover. WWI: Oberleutnant der Res. and Adjutant to III. Bataillon, Res. Infanterie Regiment 106. WWII: Kompanie Chef in Infanterie Regiment 5, 10.1935–08.1939, Commander of Infanterie Ersatz Bataillon 322, 09.1939–02.1940, Commander of III. Bataillon and later Commander of II. Bataillon, Infanterie Regiment 508, 02.1940–05.1941, Fuehrer Res. in O.K.H. 05.1941–04.1942, Commander of Unteroffizier Schule at Jauer 04.1942–10.1942, Commander of Jaeger Regiment 28, 12.1942–02.1945, Commander of 76. Infanterie Division 02.1945–05.1945. Awards: Knight's Cross 18.01.45, German Cross in Gold 24.12.41, Honor Roll Clasp 17.06.44, 1939 Clasps to the 1914 Iron Cross 1st and 2nd Class, Infantry Assault Badge in Silver, Eastern Front Medal, 1914 Iron Cross 1st and 2nd Class, Cross of Honor.

Bernhard, Friedrich-Gustav: Generalleutnant (01.08.42), (Heer); born 05.10.88 in Gut Radau, died 30.12.45 (executed) at Bryansk. WWI: in G.A.S. as Hauptmann in Flieger Abteilung A-242. Promotion to Generalmajor 01.08.40. Commander of Nachrichten Abteilung at Stettin 10.1934–10.1935. WWII: Commander of Nachrichtentruppen II 10.1935–08.1939, Signals Leader to 7. Armee 08.1939–11.1939, Signals Leader to 18. Armee 11.1939–08.1940, Signals Leader to Heeresgruppe A 08.1940–10.1941, Commandant of Feldkommandantur 532, 04.1942–05.1945. Awards: German Cross in Gold 17.03.44, 1939 Clasps to the 1914 Iron Cross 1st and 2nd Class, Pilot's Commemorative Badge, 1914 Iron Cross 1st and 2nd Class, 1914 Wound Badge in Black, 1914 Pilot's Badge, Cross of Honor.

Bernuth, Julius von: Generalmajor (01.04.42), (Heer); born 12.08.97 in Metz, died 12.07.42 after air accident over Sokranja. WWI: Leutnant and Bataillon Adjutant in Infanterie Regiment 365. Kompanie Chef in Infanterie Regiment at Munich 10.1934–10.1935, Kompanie Chef in Gebirgs Jaeger Regiment 100, 10.1935–03.1936, Ia to 17. Division 03.1936–07.1937. WWII: Tactics Instructor at Kriegsschule 08.1937–09.1939, Chief of Staff to XXVI. Panzer Korps 10.1939–03.1940, Chief of Staff to XV. Panzer Korps 03.1940–10.1940, Chief of Training Department of Heeres General Staff in O.K.H. 10.1940–06.1941, Chief of General Staff to 4. Panzer Armee 01.1942–07.1942. Awards: Blood Order (Reichswehr), Knight's Cross 05.08.40, 1939 Clasps to the 1914 Iron Cross 1st and 2nd Class, 1939 Wound Badge in Gold, 1914 Iron Cross 1st and 2nd Class, 1914 Wound Badge in Black, Cross of Honor.

Berthold, Friedrich: Generalmajor (07.01.41), (Luftwaffe); born 26.01.89 in Ingolstadt, died 03.12.78 in Munich. WWI: in G.A.S. as Hauptmann and Commander of Flieger Abteilung 304b. Leader of Flughafens Munich 07.1934–11.1936, Leader of Air Office Nuremberg 12.1936–03.1937. WWII: Director of Air Office at Munich 04.1937–08.1939, Director of Gruppe V of Luftgau Kommando VII 09.1939–11.1939, Deputy Adjutant to Luftflotte 3, 12.1939–04.1940, Flughafenbereichs Commandant of Morlaix and Bretagne 08.1940–07.1941, Special Duties Officer with Feld Luftgau Western France 08.1941–05.1942, Flughafenbereichs Commandant of 2-III 05.1942–06.1943, Flughafenbereichs Commandant of 6-XII 07.1943–03.1945. Awards: War Merit Cross 1st and 2nd Class with Swords, Pilot's Commemorative Badge, RK-Hohenzollern, 1914 Iron Cross 1st and 2nd Class, 1914 Pilot's Badge, Turkish Half Moon, Cross of Honor.

Berthold, Gerhard: Generalleutnant (10.06.43), (Heer); born 12.03.91 in Schneeberg, died 14.04.42 in action at Korolevka. WWI: Oberleutnant and Adjutant in Infanterie Regiment 102. Promotion to Generalmajor 01.09.41. Attached to General Staff of Heeres 07.1935–09.1937, Ia to Staff of VIII. Armee Korps 10.1937–11.1938. WWII: attached to Staff of Infanterie Regiment 17, 11.1938–08.1939, Commander of Infanterie Regiment 82, 08.1939–11.1939, Commander of Infanterie Regiment 17, 12.1939–08.1941, Commander of 31. Infanterie Division 08.1941–04.1942. Awards: Knight's Cross 04.12.41, 1939 Clasps to the 1914 Iron Cross 1st and 2nd Class, Infantry Assault Badge in Silver, 1939 Wound Badge in Gold, 1914 Iron Cross 1st and 2nd Class, 1914 Wound Badge in Black, Cross of Honor.

Bertram, Georg: Generalleutnant (01.08.39), (Heer); born in 31.08.82 Danzig, died 27.10.53 in Bad Pyrmont. WWI: Rittmeister and Bataillon Commander in Infanterie Regiment 115. Promotion to Generalmajor 01.10.35. Commandant of

Stettin 10.1935–03.1937. WWII: General for Special Duties in Reich War Court 04.1937–10.1942, Senior Commandant of Feldkommandantur 589, 11.1942–07.1943, Senior Commandant of Feldkommandantur 670, 06.1943–01.1944, Commandant of Feldkommandantur 533, 01.1944–09.1944, Rear Area Commander for 1. Fallschirm Armee 10.1944–12.1944, Rear Area Commander for 15. Armee 12.1944–01.1945, Rear Area Commander for 25. Armee 01.1945–05.1945. Awards: German Cross in Silver 26.12.44, War Merit Cross 1st and 2nd Class with Swords, 1914 Iron Cross 1st and 2nd Class, 1914 Wound Badge in Black, Cross of Honor.

Bertram, Oskar: Generalleutnant (01.06.41), (Luftwaffe); born 04.11.90 in Gera, died 12.08.65 in Wiesbaden. WWI: Oberleutnant in Feld Artillerie Regiment 59. Promotion to Generalmajor 01.06.39. Commander of Fahr Abteilung 4, 10.1933–03.1935, Commander of I. Abteilung, Flak Regiment 10, 04.1935–09.1936, Commander of Flak Regiment 4, 10.1936–06.1939. WWII: Higher Commander of Festung Flak III 06.1939–04.1940, Commander of Air Defense Kommando 2, 04.1940–08.1941, Commander of 2. Flak Division 09.1941–01.1942, Officer Judge attached to Reichs War Court 01.1942–06.1943, Commander of all Luftwaffe Transport and Motor Units 1943–12.1944. Awards: War Merit Cross 1st and 2nd Class with Swords, 1914 Iron Cross 1st and 2nd Class, 1914 Wound Badge in Black, Turkish Half Moon, Cross of Honor.

Besch, Helmut: Generalmajor (01.11.42), (Heer); born 17.04.92 in Strasbourg, died 13.10.74 in Tuebingen. WWI: U-boat service as Oberleutnant zur See and Watch Officer on *U-141*. Commander of I. Bataillon, Infanterie Regiment 33, 10.1935–11.1935. WWII: Commander of Truppenubungsplatz at Heuberg 12.1935–06.1940, Commander of Truppenubungsplatz at Harskamp 06.1940–03.1942 and again 05.1944–04.1945, Commander of Truppenubungsplatz in Galicia then Zolkiev 03.1942–04.1944. Awards: 1939 Clasps to the 1914 Iron Cross 1st and 2nd Class, Baltic Cross 1st and 2nd Class, 1914 Iron Cross 1st and 2nd Class, 1914 Submarine Badge, Cross of Honor.

Bessel, Arnold von: Generalmajor (01.06.41), (Heer); born 24.05.82 Wiesbaden, died 19.07.45 of natural causes while in custody in a Paris hospital. WWI: Hauptmann and Bataillon Commander in Infanterie Regiment 57. Training Leader in Gumbinnen 03.1936–08.1937. WWII: Training Leader in Karlsruhe 09.1937–08.1939, Commander of Infanterie Regiment 326, 08.1939–05.1941, Commander of 709. Infanterie Division 05.1941–07.1942, P.O.W. Commandant in Wehrkreis Kommando XX 07.1942–11.1942, P.O.W. Commandant in Operations Area II 11.1942–10.1943, retired 01.1944. Awards: 1939 Clasps to the 1914 Iron Cross 1st and 2nd Class, Infantry Assault Badge in Silver, Eastern Front Medal, Commander's Cross of the Order of the Star of Romania with Swords, 1914 Iron Cross 1st and 2nd Class, Cross of Honor, German Horseman's Badge in Silver.

Bessell, Hans: Generalmajor (01.04.43), (Heer); born 24.02.93 in Magdeburg, died 11.02.79 in Koeln. WWI: Oberleutnant in Pionier Bataillon 11. Attached to Staff of Pionier Bataillon at Magdeburg 07.1935–10.1935, Commander of Pionier Bataillon 43, 10.1935–03.1936, Commander of Pionier Bataillon 26, 04.1936–11.1936, attached to Heer Nachrichtenschule at Halle/Saale 11.1936–03.1938, attached to Festung Pionier Stab 22, 04.1938–11.1938. WWII: Commander of Festung Pionier Stab 22, 11.1938–10.1939, Commander of Construction Truppe 5, 04.1940–01.1941, Commander of Special Duties Pionier Staff 673, 05.1941–06.1942, Higher Pionier Leader 2, 06.1942–03.1943, Commander of Front Line Construction Staff in Italy 03.1943–11.1943, Festung Pioneer Fuehrer XIII 07.1944–01.1945. Awards: German Cross in Silver 24.11.44, 1939 Clasp to the 1914 Iron Cross 2nd Class, War Merit Cross 1st and 2nd Class with Swords, Eastern Front Medal, 1914 Iron Cross 1st and 2nd Class, Austro-Hungarian Military Service Cross 3rd Class with War Decoration, 1914 Wound Badge in Black, Cross of Honor.

Betche, Wilhelm: Konteradmiral z.V. (01.02.41), (Kriegsmarine); born 24.10.79 in Rostock, died 12.12.41 in Rostock. WWI: Oberleutnant (Ing) at U-Boot Schule. WWII: not in service 09.1932–09.1939, attached to K.M. Service Office in Hamburg 09.1939–05.1941. Awards: War Merit Cross 2nd Class with Swords, 1914 Iron Cross 2nd Class, Cross of Honor.

Bethcke, Dr. Hans: General-Veterinar (01.01.44), (Heer); born 25.03.89 in Ulm, died 20.07.57 in Munich. Medical veterinarian by profession. WWI: Ober-Veterinar (unit unknown). WWII: Division Veterinar to 7. Division 1938–1939, Korps Veterinar to Hoehere Kommando z.b.V. XXXVII 1939–12.1940, Korps Veterinar to XVII., XXX. and XXXIII. Armee Korps (dates unknown), Armee Veterinar to 16. Armee (dates unknown). Awards: 1939 Clasp to the 1914 Iron Cross 2nd Class, War Merit Cross 1st and 2nd Class with Swords, Eastern Front Medal, Crimean Shield, Kurland Cuff Band, RK-Sachsen Order of the White Falcon 2nd Class with Swords, 1914 Iron Cross 1st and 2nd Class, Mecklenburg-Schwerin Military Service Cross 1st and 2nd Class, Turkish Half Moon, Cross of Honor.

Bettenhaeuser, Werner: Vizeadmiral (01.02.43), (Kriegsmarine); born 03.05.86 in Meine, died 11.09.59 in Halver. WWI: Marine-Oberingenieur for torpedo boats. Promotion to Konteradmiral 01.10.36. WWII: Commander of Marine Schule at Kiel 09.1931–11.1939, placed at disposal of Kriegsmarine 01.1940–07.1941, Director of Naval Equipment and Repair Service in Libau 07.1941–02.1943, Chief of Senior Shipyard Staff for Eastern Territories 02.1943–08.1943, retired 08.1943. Awards: War Merit Cross 1st and 2nd Class with Swords, 1914 Iron Cross 1st and 2nd Class, 1914 Naval Wound Badge in Black, Cross of Honor.

Betz, Paul: Generalmajor (01.05.44), (Heer); born 10.07.95 in Harburg, died 09.05.44 in action in Sevastopol. WWI: Leutnant in Pionier Bataillon 30. WWII: Instructor at Kriegsschule in Munich 10.1937–08.1939, Course Director at Pionier Schule II 10.1939–02.1940, Commander of 2. Pionier Lehr Bataillon 02.1940–05.1941, Commander of Pionier Bataillon 900 05.1941–11.1941, Commander of z.b.V. Pionier Regiment Staff 700, 07.1942–12.1943, Battle Group Commander and Fortress Commandant of Sevastopol 12.1943–05.1944. Awards: Knight's Cross 16.06.44 (posthumously), German Cross in Gold 10.02.44, Honor Roll Clasp 29.06.44, 1939 Clasps to the 1914 Iron Cross 1st and 2nd Class, General Assault Badge, Eastern Front Medal, 1939 Wound Badge in Gold, 1914 Iron Cross 1st and 2nd Class, 1914 Wound Badge in Black, Cross of Honor.

Betzel, Clemens: Generalleutnant (01.01.45), (Heer); born 09.06.95 in Ulm, died 27.03.45 in action in Danzig. WWI: Oberleutnant in Bavarian Fusilier Artillerie Regiment 1. Promotion to Generalmajor 01.07.44. WWII: Commander of II. Abteilung, Artillerie Regiment 93, 08.1939–01.1941, Commander of III. Abteilung, Artillerie Regiment 103 and later Regimental Commander 01.1941–03.1944, Commander of 4. Panzer Division 05.1944–09.1944, Commander of 529. Infanterie Division 09.1944–03.1945. Awards: Oak Leaves 11.03.45 (774), Knight's Cross 05.09.44, German Cross in Gold 11.03.43, 1939 Clasps to the 1914 Iron Cross 1st and 2nd Class, German Army High Command Commendation Certificate 19.09.43, General Assault Badge, Eastern Front Medal, 1939 Wound Badge in Gold, 1914 Iron Cross 1st and 2nd Class, Cross of Honor.

Betzler, Dr. Maximilian: General-Veterinar (01.08.42), (Heer); born 09.05.91 in Ulm, died 21.03.88 in Geislingen. Medical veterinarian by profession. WWI: Ober-Veterinar (unit unknown). WWII: Leader of Lehrgangs II at Heeres Veterinary Academy 1938–06.1941, Armee Veterinar to Panzer Gruppe 4 (later 4. Panzer Armee) 06.1941–1941, Commander of Lehrgruppe II at Heeres Veterinary Academy 1941–02.1942, Armee Veterinar to 2. Panzer Armee 02.1942–1945. Awards: 1939 Clasp to the 1914 Iron Cross 2nd Class, War Merit Cross 1st and 2nd Class with Swords, Croatian Order of the King of Zvonimir 1st Class with Breast Star and Swords, RK-Wuerttemberg Friedrich Order 2nd Class with Swords, 1914 Iron Cross 1st and 2nd Class, Cross of Honor.

Beukemann, Helmuth: Generalleutnant (01.05.43), (Heer); born 09.05.94 in Hamburg, died 13.07.81 in Hamburg. WWI: Oberleutnant and Adjutant to Infanterie Regiment 165. Promotion to Generalmajor 01.11.42. Tactics Instructor at Kreigsschule in Munich 10.1934–11.1938. WWII: Commander of I. Bataillon, Infanterie Regiment 89, 11.1938–01.1940, Commander of Infanterie Regiment 382, 01.1940–08.1942, Commander of 75. Infanterie Division 09.1942–07.1944, Commander of z.b.V. Division 539, 09.1944–05.1945. Awards: Knight's Cross

14.05.41, German Cross in Gold 20.01.44, 1939 Clasps to the 1914 Iron Cross 1st and 2nd Class, German Army High Command Commendation Certificate 01.05.41, Infantry Assault Badge in Silver, 1939 Wound Badge in Silver, RK-Hohenzollern, 1914 Iron Cross 1st and 2nd Class, 1914 Wound Badge in Black, Cross of Honor.

Beust, Henning Freiherr von: General-Richter (15.04.45), (Heer); born 17.05.92 in Jena, died 09.07.65 in Scharbeutz. Jurist by profession. WWI: Leutnant in Hussar Regiment 14. WWII: Court Judge for X. Armee Korps in Hamburg 11.1935–08.1939, judge at Reichs War Court 11.1939–12.1942, Heeresgruppe Judge to Heeresgruppe D 12.1942–1943, Legal Advisor to Oberbefehlshaber West 1943–05.1945. Awards: War Merit Cross 1st and 2nd Class with Swords, 1914 Iron Cross 1st and 2nd Class, 1914 Wound Badge in Silver, Cross of Honor.

Beutler, Otto: Generalmajor (01.10.43), (Heer); born 16.03.94 in Chemnitz, died 21.07.44 in action in Brody Pocket. WWI: Leutnant in Hussar Regiment 19. Advisor in Reich War Ministry 08.1934–10.1937, Ia to 14. Division 10.1937–04.1939. WWII: Ia to IV. Armee Korps 05.1939–10.1939, Chief of Staff to IV. Armee Korps 10.1939–06.1942, Chief of Staff to Economics Office in O.K.H. 08.1942–09.1943, Commander of 340. Infanterie Division 06.1944–07.1944. Awards: German Cross in Gold 03.03.42, 1939 Clasps to the 1914 Iron Cross 1st and 2nd Class, Eastern Front Medal, 1939 Wound Badge in Gold, RK-Sachsen Albrecht Order 2nd Class with Swords, 1914 Iron Cross 1st and 2nd Class, Cross of Honor.

Beuttel, Kurt: Generalleutnant (01.03.41), (Heer); born 06.03.86 in Waldshut, died 02.05.56 in Munich. WWI: Hauptmann and Bataillon Commander in Infanterie Regiment 76. Promotion to Generalmajor 01.03.38. Commander of Infanterie Regiment at Osnabrueck 10.1934–10.1935, Commander of Infanterie Regiment 37, 10.1935–01.1937, Fuehrer Res. in O.K.H. 02.1937–10.1937, Heeres Field Equipment Commander for Wehrkreis Kommando XIII 10.1937–07.1938. WWII: Heeres Field Equipment Commander for Wehrkreis Kommando XVII 08.1938–09.1941, Commandant of Feldkommandantur 365, 01.1942–08.1944, retired 12.1944. Awards: War Merit Cross 1st and 2nd Class with Swords, 1914 Iron Cross 1st and 2nd Class, Cross of Honor.

Bey, Erich: Konteradmiral (25.12.43), (Kriegsmarine); born 23.03.98 in Hamburg, died 26.12.43 in action on battleship *Scharnhorst* in North Sea. WWI: Leutnant zur See and Watch Officer in 5. Torpedobootsflotille. Referent attached to Training Abteilung of Marineleitung (later O.K.M.) 09.1934–03.1937, attached to 2. Zerstorer Division 04.1937–04.1938, Chief of 3. Zerstorer Division 05.1938–10.1938, Commandant of Zerstorer Division "Friedrich Ihn" 10.1938–04.1939. WWII: Chief 4. Zerstorer Flottille 04.1939–05.1940, Chief of Destroyers 05.1940–12.1943. Awards: Knight's Cross 09.05.40, 1939 Iron Cross 1st Class, 1939 Clasp to the 1914

Iron Cross 2nd Class, Narvik Shield, Destroyer's War Badge, 1939 Wound Badge in Gold, 1914 Iron Cross 2nd Class, Cross of Honor.

Beyer, Dr. Franz: General der Infanterie (01.07.44), (Heer); born 27.05.92 in Bautzen, died 15.10.68 in Bad Wiessee. WWI: Oberleutnant zur See and Adjutant on liner *Westfalen*. Promotions to Generalmajor 01.02.42, Generalleutnant 01.01.43. Attached to Staff of Infanterie Regiment 66, 10.1935–10.1936, Commander of III. Bataillon, Infanterie Regiment 66, 10.1936–03.1939. WWII: Commander of Infanterie Regiment 131, 04.1939–12.1941, Commander of Infanterie Regiment 331, 02.1942–02.1943, Commander of Infanterie Regiment 44, 03.1943–01.1944, Commander of LXXX. Armee Korps 08.1944–05.1945. Awards: Knight's Cross 12.09.41, 1939 Clasps to the 1914 Iron Cross 1st and 2nd Class, Infantry Assault Badge in Silver, 1914 Iron Cross 1st and 2nd Class, 1914 Wound Badge in Silver, Cross of Honor.

Beyer, Hans-Heinrich: Generalmajor (01.10.43), (Luftwaffe); born 19.09.81 in Berlin, died 05.03.64 in Goettingen. WWI: Hauptmann in Infanterie Regiment 50. WWII: Advisor in Wehrkreis-Fursorge-und Versorgungs Abteilung of Wehrkreis Kommando III 07.1936–11.1940, Commander of Luftwaffe Construction Regiment 2 in Luftgau Kommando VI 01.1941–10.1943, retired 10.1943. Awards: War Merit Cross 1st and 2nd Class with Swords, RK-Hohenzollern, 1914 Iron Cross 1st and 2nd Class, 1914 Wound Badge in Black, Cross of Honor.

Bickel, Karl: Generalmajor (01.10.43), (Heer); born 17.01.91 in Ingolstadt, died 11.12.69 in Leoggries. WWI: Oberleutnant in Bavarian Infanterie Regiment 8. Commander of III. Bataillon, Infanterie Regiment at Nuremberg 10.1934–10.1935, Commander of III. Bataillon, Infanterie Regiment 63, 10.1935–07.1938, Training Leader 2 at Aachen 08.1938–07.1939. WWII: Training Leader at Hirschberg 04.1939–08.1939, Commander of Infanterie Regiment 318, 08.1939–05.1940, Commandant of Feldkommandantur 815, 08.1940–02.1944, Commandant of Feldkommandantur 626, 05.1944–09.1944, State Minister and Military District Commander for Boehmen-Maehren 09.1944–05.1945. Awards: 1939 Clasp to the 1914 Iron Cross 2nd Class, War Merit Cross 1st and 2nd Class with Swords, Eastern Front Medal, German West Wall Medal, Eastern People's Decoration 2nd Class in Silver with Swords, RK-Baden Order of the Zaehringer Lion 2nd Class with Swords, 1914 Iron Cross 1st and 2nd Class, Bavarian Military Service Order 2nd Class with Swords, Cross of Honor.

Bieber, Martin: Generalmajor (01.01.45), (Heer); born 10.11.00 in Tabarz, died 19.10.74 in Duesseldorf. WWI: Leutnant with Fusilier Regiment 39. Kompanie Chef in Infanterie Regiment at Osnabrueck 06.1935–10.1935, Kompanie Chef in Infanterie Regiment 37, 10.1935–10.1936, Kompanie Chef in Infanterie

Regiment 39, 10.1936–11.1938. WWII: Ordnance Officer on Staff of Infanterie Regiment 26, 11.1938–08.1939, Ordnance Officer on Staff of 86. Infanterie Division 08.1939–12.1939, Commander of II. Bataillon, Infanterie Regiment 167, 01.1940–03.1942, Commander of Infanterie Regiment 184, 09.1942–07.1943, Commander of Division Gruppe 86, 11.1943–08.1944, Commander of 271. Volks Grenadier Division 09.1944–05.1945. Awards: Oak Leaves 02.09.44 (566), Knight's Cross 28.07.43, German Cross in Gold 02.01.42, 1939 Clasps to the 1914 Iron Cross 1st and 2nd Class, Infantry Assault Badge in Silver, Eastern Front Medal, West Wall Medal, 1939 Wound Badge in Silver, 1914 Iron Cross 1st and 2nd Class, 1914 Wound Badge in Black, Cross of Honor.

Biedermann, Wolf Freiherr von: Generalmajor (01.04.41), (Luftwaffe); born 11.07.90 in Herbesthal, died 14.05.64 in Wiesbaden. WWI: Oberleutnant and Kompanie Chef in Infanterie Regiment 178 followed by service in G.A.S. Advisor in R.L.M. 10.1934–09.1935, Fliegerhorst Commandant of Stade 10.1935–03.1939. WWII: Fliegerhorst Commandant of Salzwedel 04.1939–1940, Fliegerhorst Commandant of Halberstadt 1940–09.1942, Commander of 7. Luftwaffe Feld Division 09.1942–03.1943, Commander of Waffentechnischeschule 2 Merseburg 01.1944–01.1945, attached to III. Flieger Ersatz Bataillon 02.1945–05.1945. Awards: War Merit Cross 1st and 2nd Class, Pilot's Commemorative Badge, RK-Sachsen Albrecht Order 2nd Class with Swords, RK-Sachsen Military Service Order 2nd Class with Swords, 1914 Iron Cross 1st and 2nd Class, 1914 Pilot's Badge, Cross of Honor.

Biegeleben, Arnold Freiherr von: Generalleutnant (01.08.37), (Heer); born 16.04.83 in Darmstadt, died 11.10.40 of natural causes in Jullouville. WWI: Hauptmann and Commander of III. Abteilung, Feld Artillerie Regiment 25. Promotion to Generalmajor 01.05.35. Kavallerie Commander at Hannover 05.1935–02.1936, Higher Kavallerie Officer 2, 04.1936–10.1937, Higher Kavallerie Officer 4, 10.1937–02.1938. WWII: Commander of 6. Infanterie Division 03.1938–10.1940. Awards: Knight's Cross 05.08.40, 1939 Clasps to the 1914 Iron Cross 1st and 2nd Class, Infantry Assault Badge in Silver, German Westwall Medal, RK-Hohenzollern, 1914 Iron Cross 1st and 2nd Class, Cross of Honor.

Biehler, Ernst-Friedrich: Generalmajor (20.04.45), (Heer); born 07.06.03 in Ulm, died 26.05.97 in Karlsbad. Attached to Infanterie Regiment at Ludwigsburg 10.1934–08.1935, Company Leader in Infanterie Regiment 13, 10.1935–09.1937, attached to Staff of Infanterie Regiment 13, 10.1937–12.1938. WWII: Regimental Adjutant to Infanterie Regiment 13, 01.1939–08.1939, attached to Staff of XXV. Armee Korps 12.1939–04.1940, Ic on Staff of 26. Infanterie Division 06.1940–11.1940, Ic on Staff of 24. Infanterie Division 11.1940–01.1942, Ia to 24. Infanterie Division 01.1942–10.1943, Ia to 9. Luftwaffe Feld Division 11.1943–01.1944, Instructor at Kriegsschule at Hirschberg 01.1944–07.1944, Commander of Infanterie Regiment 358, 11.1944–01.1945, attached to Staff of Fortress Frankfurt-Oder 01.1945–05.1945. Awards: Knight's Cross 08.05.45, German Cross in Gold 10.07.43, 1939 Iron Cross 1st and 2nd Class, War Merit Cross 1st and 2nd Class with Swords, Eastern Front Medal, 1939 Wound Badge in Black.

Biehler, Franz: General-Intendant (07.11.41), (Heer); born 15.10.95 in Berlin, died 25.11.74 in Wolfenbuettel. Administrative Officer by profession. WWI: service unknown. WWII: Ministry Official in O.K.W. 05.1939–10.1942, General-Intendant in O.K.W. 10.1942–1944, Office Group Chief of Gruppe W.V. 1944–05.1945. Awards: War Merit Cross 1st and 2nd Class without Swords, Cross of Honor.

Biel, Werner von: Generalmajor z.V. (01.06.42), (Heer); born 14.09.74 in Wichmannsdorf, died 10.06.55 in Bad Harzburg. WWI: Major and Chairman of 1. Remote Commission. Advisor in Remonte Inspection of Reich War Ministry 04.1934–03.1938. WWII: Chairman of 1. Remonte Commission 08.1939–07.1942, retired 07.1942. Awards: War Merit Cross 1st and 2nd Class with Swords, 1914 Iron Cross 1st and 2nd Class, Cross of Honor.

Bieler, Bruno: General der Infanterie (01.10.41), (Heer); born 18.06.88 in Gumbinnen, died 22.03.66 in Dorfmark. WWI: Hauptmann and Staff Officer (unit unknown). Promotions to Generalmajor 01.03.38, Generalleutnant 01.03.40. Commander of Infanterie Regiment 55, 10.1935–10.1937. WWII: Chief of Staff to II. Armee Korps 10.1937–09.1939, Commander of 73. Infanterie Division 09.1939–10.1941, Commander of VI. Armee Korps 01.1942–11.1942, Commander of LXXXVI. Armee Korps 11.1942–05.1943, Commander of Wehrkreis Kommando XI 08.1943–12.1944. Awards: Knight's Cross 26.10.41, German Cross in Gold 20.11.42, 1939 Clasps to the 1914 Iron Cross 1st and 2nd Class, Infantry Assault Badge in Silver, Eastern Front Medal, Crimea Shield, Silesian Eagle 1st and 2nd Class, 1914 Iron Cross 1st and 2nd Class, Cross of Honor.

Bielfeld, Peter: Generalleutnant (01.02.42), (Heer); born 23.04.88 in Siegersdorf, died 09.03.63 in Glucksburg. WWI: Hauptmann on Staff of Marine Korps Flanders. Promotion to Generalmajor 01.02.40. Commander of I. Bataillon, Infanterie Regiment at Rastenburg 10.1934–09.1935, Commander of I. Bataillon, Infanterie Regiment 23, 10.1935–03.1936. WWII: Commander of Truppenubungsplatz at Altengrabow 04.1936–08.1939, Commander of Infanterie Regiment 194, 08.1939–12.1939, Wehrmacht Commander of Posen 01.1940–09.1943, Fuehrer Res. in O.K.H. 09.1943–03.1944, P.O.W. Commander for Wehrkreis

XXI 03.1944–03.1945. Awards: War Merit Cross 1st and 2nd Class with Swords, 1914 Iron Cross 1st and 2nd Class, Cross of Honor.

Bieneck, Hellmuth: General der Flieger (01.07.41), (Luftwaffe); born 07.11.87 in Krotoshin, died 08.03.72 in Koeln. WWI: in G.A.S. as Hauptmann and Staff Leader in K.G. 4 and later K.G. 7. Promotions to Generalmajor 01.01.38, Generalleutnant 01.01.40. Ausbildungsleiter attached to Inspection of Fliegerschulen 04.1934–03.1935, Chief of Staff to Kommando of Fliegerschulen 04.1935–09.1936, Hoehere Flieger Commander 5, 10.1936–06.1938, Commander of 4. Flieger Division 07.1938–01.1939. WWII: Commander of Z Higher Luftwaffe Schule at Gatow 02.1939–08.1939, Commander of Luftwaffe for Armee Gruppe C and later B 08.1939–12.1939, Commander of Higher Luftwaffe Schulen 01.1940–02.1941, Commander of Luftgau Kommando II 02.1941–01.1943, Commander of Luftgau Kommando I 08.1943–08.1944, Fuehrer Res. in O.K.L. 08.1944–12.1944. Awards: German Cross in Silver 21.04.43, 1939 Clasps to the 1914 Iron Cross 1st and 2nd Class, War Merit Cross 1st and 2nd Class with Swords, Combined Pilot-Observer's Badge, Pilot's Commemorative Badge, RK-Hohenzollern, 1914 Iron Cross 1st and 2nd Class, 1914 Pilot's Badge, Turkish Liakat Medal in Silver with Sabre, Turkish Half Moon, Cross of Honor.

Bieringer, Ludwig: Generalmajor (01.07.43), (Heer); born 12.08.92 in Metz, died 22.01.75 in Hannover. WWI: Oberleutnant in Fusilier Artillerie Regiment 137. Attached to Staff of Abteilung VI of Kavallerie Schule 05.1934–10.1935, Commander of Kraftfahr Abteilung 7, 10.1935–10.1937, Instruction Group Leader at Heeres Nachschub Schule in Hannover 10.1937–11.1938. WWII: Course Director at Kraftfahrtruppen Schule in Hannover 11.1938–08.1939, Heeres Supply Commander 541, 08.1939–08.1940, Heeres Supply Commander 561, 09.1940–06.1942, Supply Commander to Heeresgruppe A 09.1942–04.1943, Field Commandant of Besancon and later Field Commandant of Draguignan 11.1943–08.1944, captured 08.1944. Awards: 1939 Clasps to the 1914 Iron Cross 1st and 2nd Class, Eastern Front Medal, 1914 Iron Cross 1st and 2nd Class, Cross of Honor.

Biermann, Otto: Generalmajor (01.04.41), (Heer); born 27.07.73 in Gut Neumuehlen, died 01.05.45 in Berlin. WWI: Major on Staff of Army High Command. WWII: Advisor and Group Director with Inspection of Fortresses 10.1933–06.1940, attached to General of Pioniers and Fortresses in Metz 06.1940–12.1940, Department Chief in Fortress Branch of O.K.H. 12.1940–05.1943, Fuehrer Res. in O.K.H. 11.1943–07.1944, retired 07.1944. Awards: War Merit Cross 1st and 2nd Class with Swords, Prussian Red Eagle Order IV. Class with Swords, RK-Hohenzollern, 1914 Iron Cross 1st and 2nd Class, 1914 Wound Badge in Black, Cross of Honor.

Biess, Paul: Generalleutnant z.V. (01.04.42), (Heer); born 26.12.72 in Ossig, died 01.06.49 in Berlin. WWI: Major and Commander of Res. Infanterie Regiment 17. Promotion to Generalmajor z.V. 01.02.41. Recalled to military service 01.1939. WWII: attached to Staff of Wehrkreis VIII 01.1939–06.1940, P.O.W. Commander for Wehrkreis Kommando IX 10.1940–04.1942, retired 01.1943. Awards: War Merit Cross 1st and 2nd Class with Swords, 1914 Iron Cross 1st and 2nd Class, Cross of Honor.

Bilharz, Eugen: Generalmajor (01.02.41), (Heer); born 06.08.86 in Baden-Baden, died 08.12.63 in Baden-Baden. WWI: Hauptmann and Commander of II. Bataillon, Infanterie Regiment 32. Instructor at Heeres Gasschutz Schule in Berlin 02.1935–04.1936, Leader of Heeres Field Equipment for Wehrkreis Kommando VIII 07.1936–11.1938. WWII: Field Equipment Commander for Wehrkreis Kommando III 11.1938–12.1940 and 04.1941–09.1941, Commander of Feldzeuggruppe 2 Westen 09.1941–03.1944, Commander of Liaison Staff for Commandant of Feldkommandantur 996, 06.1944–09.1944, Fuehrer Res. in O.K.H. 09.1944–01.1945. Awards: War Merit Cross 1st and 2nd Class with Swords, RK-Sachsen Albrecht Order 1st Class with Swords, RK-Sachsen Military Service Order 2nd Class with Swords, 1914 Iron Cross 1st and 2nd Class with Swords, 1914 Iron Cross 1st and 2nd Class, Cross of Honor.

Bingler, Dr. Kurt: General-Stabsarzt (01.06.42), (Heer); born 12.10.88 Mudau, died 22.01.72 in Garmisch-Partenkirchen. Medical doctor by profession. WWI: German medical service (rank and unit unknown). Promotion to General-Arzt 01.06.40. WWII: Division Physician to 1. Gebirgs Division 1938–08.1939, Corps Physician to VII. Armee Korps 08.1939–02.1941, Chief Physician to Military Befehlshaber of France 02.1941–01.1942, Army Physician to 20. Gebirgs Armee 01.1942–09.1944, Corps Physician to Ersatz XVIII. Armee Korps 09.1944–05.1945. Awards: German Cross in Silver 27.09.44, War Merit Cross 1st and 2nd Class with Swords, Finnish Freedom Cross 1st Class with Swords, 1914 Iron Cross 1st and 2nd Class, 1914 Wound Badge in Black, Cross of Honor.

Biron, Walther: General-Stabsrichter (01.05.44), (Luftwaffe); born 16.09.90 in Graudenz, died 24.02.46 in Neu-Ulm. Jurist by profession. WWI: Leutnant der Res. in Feld Artillerie Regiment 209. Promotion to General-Richter (date unknown). Oberlandgerichtsrat for Marienwerder 01.1933–02.1936. WWII: Advisor to Reichs War Court 10.1936–09.1942, Senate President in Reich War Court 10.1942–05.1945. Awards: War Merit Cross 1st and 2nd Class with Swords, 1914 Iron Cross 1st and 2nd Class, Cross of Honor.

Bisle, Artur: Generalmajor (01.04.43), (Heer); born 14.10.88 in Weiden, died 06.12.58 in Munich. WWI: Oberleutnant in 1. Bavarian Jaeger Bataillon. Attached to Staff of Infanterie Regiment 19, 10.1935–12.1937, Training Leader at Sonthofen 01.1938–05.1938, Training Leader at Landeck/Tirol 07.1938–06.1939. WWII: Training Director at Landsberg, Lech 07.1939–10.1939, Commander of Infanterie Regiment 316, 10.1939–09.1942, Field Commandant at Blios, Tunis, Vienna, Reval and later at Liebau 12.1942–01.1945. Awards: 1939 Clasps to the 1914 Iron Cross 1st and 2nd Class, Infanterie Assault Badge in Silver, Eastern Front Medal, Bavarian Military Service Order IV. Class with Swords, 1914 Iron Cross 1st and 2nd Class, Austro-Hungarian Military Service Cross 3rd Class with War Decoration, 1914 Wound Badge in Black, Cross of Honor.

Bismarck, Georg von: Generalleutnant (01.08.42), (Heer); born 15.02.91 in Neumuehl, died 31.08.42 in action at El Alamein. WWI: Oberleutnant and Adjutant to 6. Res. Jaeger Bataillon. Promotion to Generalmajor 01.03.42. Commander of Kraftfahr Abteilung at Koenigsberg 10.1934–11.1938. WWII: Commander of Schuetzen Regiment 7, 11.1938–12.1940, Commander of 20. Schuetzen Brigade (later 20. Panzer Division) 12.1940–12.1941, Commander of 21. Panzer Division 02.1942–08.1942. Awards: Knight's Cross 29.09.40, 1939 Clasps to the 1914 Iron Cross 1st and 2nd Class, Tank Assault Badge in Silver, 1939 Wound Badge in Gold, RK-Hohenzollern, 1914 Iron Cross 1st and 2nd Class, Cross of Honor.

Generalleutnant Georg von Bismarck (right) with Generalfeldmarschall Erwin Rommel. (Bundesarchiv)

Bismarck, Kurd von: Generalmajor (01.04.41), (Heer); born 10.07.79 in Berlin, died 05.01.43 of natural causes in Potsdam. WWI: Major on Staff of III. Armee Korps. WWII: Commander of Military District Kommando at Potsdam 10.1933–07.1942, retired 07.1942. Awards: War Merit Cross 1st and 2nd Class with Swords, RK-Hohenzollern, 1914 Iron Cross 1st and 2nd Class, Cross of Honor.

Bittrich, Wilhelm: SS-Obergruppenfuehrer und General der Waffen-SS (01.08.44); born 26.02.94 in Wernigerode, died 19.04.79 in Wolfratshausen. P-829700, SS-39177. WWI: in G.A.S. as Leutnant der Res. attached to Jasta 4. Joined N.S.D.A.P., joined S.S. in 1932. Promotions to SS-Brigadefuehrer 19.10.41, SS-Gruppenfuehrer 01.05.43. Attached to SS-Fliegersturme, Leader of I. Sturmbann, SS-Fuss Standarte 2, 01.10.34, attached to I. Sturmbann, SS-Standarte 1 "Deutschland" 07.1935, Leader of II. Sturmbann, SS-Standarte 1

"Deutschland" 01.12.36–01.12.37, Leader of I. Sturmbann, SS-Standarte 3 "Der Fuehrer" 01.12.38. WWII: attached to SS-Fuehrungshauptamt 30.01.42, Commander of SS-Kavallerie Brigade, Commander of SS-Kavallerie Division "Florian Geyer," Commander of SS-Panzer Grenadier Division "Hohenstaufen" 15.05.43, Commander of 9. SS-Panzer Division "Hohenstaufen" 30.01.44, Commander of II. SS-Panzer Korps 09.11.44–05.1945. Awards: Swords 06.05.45 (153), Oak Leaves 28.08.44 (563), Knight's Cross 14.12.41, German Cross in Gold 06.03.43, 1939 Clasps to the 1914 Iron Cross 1st and 2nd Class, Pilot's Commemorative Badge, 1914 Iron Cross 1st and 2nd Class, 1914 Wound Badge in Black, 1914 Pilot's Badge, Cross of Honor, SA-Sports Badge in Bronze, Degen, Ring.

SS-Obergruppenfuehrer Wilhelm Bittrich. (Marc Rikmenspoel)

Biwer, Franz: Generalmajor (01.09.41), (Luftwaffe); born 29.06.91 in Euskirchen, died 02.01.62 in Euskirchen. WWI: in G.A.S. as Oberleutnant in Artillerie Flieger Abteilung 224. Instruction Leader for Kampfflieger Schule at Jueterbog 10.1934–09.1935, Commander of Fighter Flight Class at Oldenburg 1936–10.1938. WWII: Fliegerhorst Commandant of Neu-Kuhren 11.1938–1942, Hoehere Flieger Ausbildungs Commander in Luftgau Kommando XVII 1942–03.1943, Luftwaffe Inspector 17 in R.L.M. 05.1943–04.1944, retired 04.1944. Awards: War Merit Cross 1st and 2nd Class with Swords, 1939 Observer's Badge, Croatian Order of the Crown of King Zvonimir 1st Class with Swords and Breast Star, Pilot's Commemorative Badge, 1914 Iron Cross 1st and 2nd Class, 1914 Wound Badge in Silver, 1914 Observer's Badge, Cross of Honor.

Blanckensee, Siegfried von: Generalmajor (20.04.45), (Heer); born 11.09.92 in Zipkow, died 08.05.45 (suicide, location unknown). WWI: Leutnant in Grenadier Regiment 5. Chief of 1. Kompanie, Infanterie Regiment at Kolberg 10.1934–10.1935, Chief of 1. Kompanie, Infanterie Regiment 4, 10.1935–10.1936, Chief of 1. Kompanie, Infanterie Regiment 94, 10.1936–11.1938. WWII: Commander of I. Bataillon, Infanterie Regiment 96, 11.1938–08.1939, Commander of I. Bataillon, Infanterie Regiment 458, 08.1939–10.1940, Commander of Infanterie Regiment 458, 10.1940–02.1942, Commander of Acceptance Office for Officer Applicants in Wehrkreis Kommando VI 11.1942–09.1944, Commander of Security Regiment 113, 11.1944–05.1945. Awards: 1939 Clasps to the 1914 Iron Cross 1st and 2nd Class, Infantry Assault Badge in Silver, Eastern Front Medal, 1914 Iron Cross 1st and 2nd Class, Cross of Honor, Reich Sports Badge in Silver.

Blaschke, Prof. Dr. Hugo: SS-Brigadefuehrer und Generalmajor der Waffen-SS (01.10.44); born 14.11.81 in Neustadt, died 06.12.59 in Nuremberg. P-452082, SS-256882. Dentist by profession and personal dentist to Adolf Hitler and other leading members of Party and Government. Joined N.S.D.A.P. in 1931, joined S.S. in 1935. Attached to SS-Hauptamt 01.07.35, Leader on Staff of SS-Hauptamt 01.12.36–01.12.38. WWII: attached to SS-Sanitats Amt 30.01.42, attached to D. St. Reichsarzt-SS und Polizei 15.05.43, Oberster Zahn-Arzt (Senior Dentist) in D. St. Reichsarzt-SS und Polizei 30.01.44–05.1945. Awards: War Merit Cross 1st and 2nd Class with Swords, Degen, Ring.

Blaskowitz, Johannes: Generaloberst (01.10.39), (Heer); born 10.07.83 in Paterswalde, died 05.02.48 (suicide) at Nuremberg Prison. WWI: Hauptmann and Divisional Staff Officer. Promotions to Reichswehr Generalmajor 01.10.32, Reichswehr Generalleutnant 01.12.33, General der Infanterie 01.08.36. Inspector of Waffen Schulen in Reich War Ministry 02.1933–03.1935, Commander of II. Armee Korps and Befehlshaber of Wehrkreis II 06.1935–11.1938. WWII: O.B. of Heeres Gruppen Kommando 3, 11.1938–08.1939, O.B. of 8. Armee 08.1939–10.1939, O.B. Ost (Poland) 10.1939–05.1940, Oberbefehlshaber of 1. Armee 10.1940–05.1944, Oberbefehlshaber of Heeresgruppe G 05.1944–09.1944 and 12.1944–01.1945, Oberbefehlshaber of Netherlands 01.1945–05.1945. Awards: Swords 25.04.45 (146), Oak Leaves 29.10.44 (640), Knight's Cross 30.09.39, German Cross in Silver 30.10.43, 1939 Clasps to the 1914 Iron Cross 1st and 2nd Class, War Merit Cross 1st and 2nd Class with Swords, RK-Hohenzollern, 1914 Iron Cross 1st and 2nd Class, 1914 Wound Badge in Black, Cross of Honor.

Generaloberst Johannes Blaskowitz. (Bundesarchiv)

Blaul, Dr. Friedrich: General-Stabsarzt (01.08.41), (Luftwaffe); born 20.11.89 in Metz, died 03.10.47 in Linden. Medical doctor by profession. WWI: Ober-Arzt (unit unknown). Promotion to General-Arzt 01.08.39. Physician for Luftwaffe Gruppe 3, 04.1938–01.1939. WWII: Chief Physician to Luftflotte 3, 02.1939–07.1942, Fuehrer Res. in O.K.L. 09.1942–08.1943, Chief Luftwaffe Physician in Kurheimes-Bad Sachsen 04.1944–05.1945. Awards: War Merit Cross 1st and 2nd Class with Swords, 1914 Iron Cross 1st and 2nd Class, 1914 Wound Badge in Black, Cross of Honor.

Blaurock, Edmund: Generalleutnant (01.04.45), (Heer); born 12.10.99 in Nuremberg, died 25.01.66 in Nuremberg. WWI: Leutnant in Bavarian Feld Artillerie

Regiment 8. Promotion to Generalmajor 01.10.44. Attached to Training Abteilung in Reich War Ministry 05.1934–06.1935, attached to Abteilung 4 of Heeres General Staff 07.1935–10.1937, Batterie Chef in Artillerie Regiment 27, 10.1937–06.1938. WWII: Ia to 8. Infanterie Division 06.1938–02.1941, Ia to 9. Armee 03.1941–04.1942, Chief of Staff to XXXXIII. Armee Korps 04.1942–11.1943, Chief of Staff to XXVIII. Armee Korps 11.1943–02.1944, Commander of Grenadier Regiment 324, 02.1944–10.1944, Commander of 56. Infanterie Division 10.1944–03.1945. Awards: Oak Leaves 19.02.45 (746), Knight's Cross 27.07.44, German Cross in Gold 04.06.44, 1939 Iron Cross 1st Class, 1939 Clasp to the 1914 Iron Cross 2nd Class, Eastern Front Medal, 1914 Iron Cross 2nd Class, 1914 Wound Badge in Black, Cross of Honor.

Bleckwenn, Wilhelm: Generalmajor (30.01.45), (Heer and Kriegsmarine); born 21.10.06 in Berge, died 10.10.89 in Saarbruecken. Kompanie Officer attached to M.G. Bataillon 1, 10.1935–10.1937, Kompanie Chef in M.G. Bataillon 10, 10.1937–07.1938. WWII: Kompanie Chef in M.G. Bataillon 14, 11.1938–01.1940, Commander of I. Bataillon, Grenz Infanterie Regiment 127, 01.1940–11.1940, Commander of Infanterie Regiment 487, 01.1942–08.1944, Commander of 708. Volks Grenadier Division 11.1944–01.1945, transferred to Kriegsmarine as Konteradmiral 01.03.45, Commander of 1. Marine Infanterie Division 02.1945–05.1945. Awards: Oak Leaves 10.10.44 (621), Knight's Cross 06.04.44, German Cross in Gold 14.04.42, 1939 Iron Cross 1st and 2nd Class, Close Combat Clasp in Silver, Infantry Assault Badge in Silver, Eastern Front Medal, German West Wall Medal, 1939 Wound Badge in Silver, German Horseman's Badge in Gold.

Generalmajor Wilhelm Bleckwenn. (Bundesarchiv)

Bleyer, Eugen: Generalleutnant (01.06.44), (Heer); born 20.11.96 in Mainz, died 18.03.79 in Bad Toelz. WWI: Leutnant and Adjutant to III. Bataillon, Infanterie Regiment 186. Promotion to Generalmajor 01.12.43. Kompanie Chef in Infanterie Regiment at Koenigsberg 10.1934–10.1935, Schwadron Chef in Cycling Bataillon 1, 10.1935–10.1936, attached to Staff of 29. Division 10.1936–11.1938. WWII: Adjutant to Wehrmacht Commander of Erfurt 11.1938–08.1939, Commander of II. Bataillon, Infanterie Regiment 355, 08.1939–02.1940, Commander of I. Bataillon, Infanterie Regiment 36, 03.1940–03.1941, Commander of Infanterie Regiment 379, 03.1941–04.1943, Commander of 258. Infanterie Division 10.1943–09.1944,

Commander of 181. Infanterie Division 10.1944–05.1945. Awards: Knight's Cross 14.12.41, 1939 Clasps to the 1914 Iron Cross 1st and 2nd Class, Infantry Assault Badge in Silver, Eastern Front Medal, 1939 Wound Badge in Gold, West Wall Medal, 1914 Iron Cross 1st and 2nd Class, 1914 Wound Badge in Black, Cross of Honor.

Block, Dr. Adolf: General-Richter (1944), (Heer); born 17.10.93 in Buedingen, died 24.11.90 in Buedingen. Jurist by profession. WWI: service unknown. WWII: Auxiliary Judge of Reichs War Court and Administrator of Reichs War Bar 08.1939–01.1943, Senior Judge to 1. Panzer Armee 01.1943–05.1945. Awards: War Merit Cross 1st and 2nd Class with Swords, Cross of Honor.

Block, Johannes: General der Infanterie (01.07.44), (Heer); born 17.11.94 in Buschdorf, died 26.01.45 in action near Kielce. WWI: Leutnant in I. Bataillon, Infanterie Regiment 146. Promotions to Generalmajor 01.09.42, Generalleutnant 21.01.43. Kompanie Chef in Infanterie Regiment 4, 07.1934–12.1936, Commander of I. Bataillon. WWII: Infanterie Regiment 4, 02.1937–05.1940, Commander of Infanterie Regiment 202, 03.1940–05.1942, Commander of 294. Infanterie Division 09.1942–12.1943, Commander of LVI. Panzer Korps 06.1944–01.1945. Awards: Blood Order (Infanterie Schule), Oak Leaves 22.11.43 (331), Knight's Cross 22.12.41, 1939 Clasps to the 1914 Iron Cross 1st and 2nd Class, Infantry Assault Badge in Silver, Eastern Front Medal, 1939 Wound Badge in Gold, 1914 Iron Cross 1st and 2nd Class, Cross of Honor.

Block, Lothar von: Generalmajor (01.02.42), (Heer); born 21.05.89 in Luebben, died 03.03.67 in Bonn. WWI: Oberleutnant in Res. in Infanterie Regiment 261. Attached to Staff of Wehrkreis IV 10.1934–10.1935, Commander of II. Bataillon, Infanterie Regiment 9, 10.1935–03.1938, attached to Staff of Infanterie Regiment 9, 04.1938–11.1938. WWII: Commander of Grenz Infanterie Regiment 123, 11.1938–04.1940, Office Chief for Suitability Examinations and Acceptance in Wehrkreis Kommando XX and later Wehrkreis Kommando IV 06.1940–02.1943, P.O.W. Commander for Wehrkreis Kommando IV 02.1943–04.1945. Awards: War Merit Cross 1st and 2nd Class with Swords, 1914 Iron Cross 1st and 2nd Class, 1914 Wound Badge in Gold, Cross of Honor, Johann Ritter Order.

Block, Paul: Generalmajor (01.03.45), (Heer); born 10.10.95 in Koenigsberg, died 22.07.56 in Kehl. WWI: Leutnant der Res. in Pionier Bataillon 11. Kompanie Chef in Pionier Bataillon 11, 10.1935–11.1938. WWII: Commander of Pionier Bataillon 56, 11.1938–08.1939, Commander of I. Bataillon, Eisenbahn Pionier Regiment 2, 08.1939–11.1940, Commander of Eisenbahn Pionier Regiment 5, 11.1940–12.1941, Commander of Eisenbahn Pionier Regiment 4, 09.1942–10.1943, Commander of 3. Eisenbahn Pionier Brigade 10.1943–04.1945. Awards: German Cross in Silver 19.12.44, 1939 Clasps to the 1914 Iron Cross 1st and

2nd Class, War Merit Cross 1st and 2nd Class with Swords, Baltic Cross 1st and 2nd Class, 1914 Iron Cross 1st and 2nd Class, 1914 Wound Badge in Silver, Cross of Honor.

Blomberg, Werner von: Generalfeldmarschall (20.04.36), (Heer); born 02.09.78 in Stargard, died 14.03.46 in Nuremberg. P-3805226. WWI: Major and Ia to 7. Armee. Promotions to Reichswehr Generalmajor 01.04.28, Reichswehr Generalleutnant 01.10.29, Reichswehr General der Infanterie 30.01.33, Reichswehr Generaloberst 31.08.33. Reich Minister and Befehlshaber of German Army 05.1933–05.1935, Reich War Minister and Oberbefehlshaber of Wehrmacht 06.1935–01.1938, dismissed and forced to retire 02.1938. Awards: Golden Party Badge (honorary), Combined Pilot/Observer's Badge in Gold with Diamonds, Pour le Mérite 03.06.18, RK-Hohenzollern, 1914 Iron Cross 1st and 2nd Class, 1914 Wound Badge in Black, Cross of Honor.

Generalfeldmarschall Werner von Blomberg. (Bundesarchiv)

Blomeyer, Karl: Generalmajor (01.12.43), (Heer); born 22.01.84 in Koblenz, died 10.10.59 in Bad Oeynhausen. WWI: Hauptmann and Bataillon Commander in Feld Artillerie Regiment 100. Training Leader at Meseritz 10.1934–03.1935. WWII: attached to E-Officer Korps 03.1935–08.1939, Commander of Border Watch Section 23, 08.1939–12.1939, Commander of Infanterie Regiment 307, 12.1939–11.1940, Commander of Infanterie Regiment 341, 11.1940–12.1942, P.O.W. Camp Commander 05.1943–04.1944, retired 07.1944. Awards: 1939 Clasps to the 1914 Iron Cross 1st and 2nd Class, Infantry Assault Badge in Silver, 1914 Iron Cross 1st and 2nd Class, Cross of Honor.

Bluecher, Johann-Albrecht von: Generalmajor (01.08.42), (Heer); born 11.11.92 in Potsdam, died 14.05.72 in Bonn. WWI: Oberleutnant in Dragoon Regiment 17. Attached to Staff of Reiter Regiment at Schwedt 10.1934–04.1935, Instructor at Kriegsschule in Hannover 05.1935–10.1937, Instructor at Gasschutz Schule 10.1937–11.1938. WWII: Course Director at Heeres Gasschutz Schule 11.1938–10.1939, Commander of Rocket Troops 1, 02.1940–09.1940, Commander of Werfertruppen Schule 09.1940–10.1942, Commander of Werfertruppe 2, 02.1943–02.1944, Inspector of Smoke Troops and Gas Defense 08.1944–05.1945. Awards: 1939 Clasps to the 1914 Iron Cross 1st and 2nd Class, War Merit Cross 1st and 2nd Class with Swords, 1914 Iron Cross 1st and 2nd Class, Mecklenburg-Schwerin Military Service Cross 1st and 2nd Class, Cross of Honor.

Bluemke, Friedrich: Generalmajor (01.08.44), (Heer); born 18.02.98 in Rahnwerder, died 04.09.44 of wounds in Odessa P.O.W. Camp. WWI: Leutnant in Infanterie Regiment 42. Attached to Reich War Ministry 10.1933–10.1936, Kompanie Chef in Infanterie Regiment 27, 10.1936–10.1937. WWII: Ia to 23. Infanterie Division 10.1937–09.1940, Chief of Staff to XIV. Armee Korps followed by XXXXII. Armee Korps 06.1941–06.1942, Commander of Infanterie Regiment 347, 08.1942–01.1944, Commander of 257. Infanterie Division 07.1944–08.1944. Awards: Knight's Cross 06.11.43, Honor Roll Clasp 07.10.43, 1939 Clasps to the 1914 Iron Cross 1st and 2nd Class, Infantry Assault Badge in Silver, Eastern Front Medal, Crimea Shield, 1914 Iron Cross 1st and 2nd Class, 1914 Wound Badge in Black, Cross of Honor.

Bluemm, Oskar: Generalleutnant (01.04.40), (Heer); born 26.06.84 in Zwiesel, died 12.12.51 in Ursberg. WWI: Hauptmann and Adjutant to 22. Bavarian Infanterie Brigade. Promotion to Generalmajor 01.04.38. Commander of Infanterie Regiment at Bayreuth 10.1934–10.1935, Commander of Infanterie Regiment 42, 10.1935–11.1938. WWII: Infanterie Commander 7, 11.1938–08.1939, Commander of 57. Infanterie Division 08.1939–11.1942 and 04.1942–10.1942, Commander of 407. Infanterie Division 11.1942–05.1945. Awards: Knight's Cross 23.11.41, 1939 Clasps to the 1914 Iron Cross 1st and 2nd Class, German Army High Command Commendation Certificate 22.09.41, Infantry Assault Badge in Silver, Eastern Front Medal, 1914 Iron Cross 1st and 2nd Class, Cross of Honor.

Blum, Dr. August: General-Stabsarzt (01.08.42), (Heer); born 17.08.89 in Reichensachsen, died 25.05.52 in Reichensachsen. Medical doctor by profession. WWI: Assistenz-Arzt (unit unknown). Promotion to General-Arzt 01.08.40. WWII: Division Physician to 15. Division 1938–08.1939, Korps Arzt to IX. Armee Korps 10.1939–02.1941, Chief Medical Physician to Wehrmacht Befehlshaber of Belgium and Northern France 02.1941–04.1944, retired 07.1944. Awards: War Merit Cross 1st and 2nd Class with Swords, 1914 Iron Cross 1st and 2nd Class, Cross of Honor.

Blumenreuter, Dr. Carl: SS-Gruppenfuehrer und Generalleutnant der Waffen-SS (09.11.44); born 16.11.81 in Berlin, died 11.07.69 in Groemitz. P-5916337, SS-276523. Medical doctor by profession. WWI: Oberleutnant der Res. and Adjutant to Gas Dienst of A.O.K. 4. Joined N.S.D.A.P. in 1937, joined S.S. in 1936. Promotion to SS-Brigadefuehrer 09.11.42. Attached to Sanitats Abteilung SS-T.V. 01.12.36, attached to Sanitats Abt. SS-V.T. 01.12.37, attached to Sanitats Abt. SS-T.V.-K.L. 01.12.38. WWII: Hauptabteilungs Leader in Abteilung III, SS-Sanitats Amt, SS-Fuehrungshauptamt 30.01.42, attached to D. St. Reichsarzt-SS und Polizei 15.05.43, Sanitats Zeugmeister in D. St. Reichsarzt-SS und Polizei 30.01.44–05.1945. Awards: War Merit Cross 1st and 2nd Class without Swords,

Luftschutz Honor Badge 1st Class, 1914 Iron Cross 1st and 2nd Class, Cross of Honor, SA-Sports Badge in Bronze, Degen, Ring.

Blumentritt, Guenther: General der Infanterie (01.04.44), (Heer); born 10.02.92 in Munich, died 12.10.67 in Marburg. WWI: Oberleutnant and Adjutant to 20. Infanterie Brigade. Promotions to Generalmajor 01.11.41, Generalleutnant 01.12.42. Attached to Staff of Wehrkreis Kommando VII 07.1935–10.1935, Ia to VII. Armee Korps 10.1935–10.1937, Commander of I. Bataillon, Infanterie Regiment 19, 10.1937–10.1938. WWII: Chief of Abteilung 4 in Heeres General Staff 11.1938–08.1939, Ia in General Staff of Heeres Gruppe A 10.1939–10.1940, Chief of General Staff to 4. Armee 10.1940–01.1942, Deputy Chief of Staff to Heeres General Staff in O.K.H. 01.1942–09.1942, Chief of General Staff to Heeresgruppe D 09.1942–01.1943 and 06.1944–09.1944, Oberbefefehlshaber of 25. Armee 01.1945–03.1945. Awards: Oak Leaves 18.02.45 (741), Knight's Cross 13.09.44, German Cross in Gold 26.01.42, 1939 Clasps to the 1914 Iron Cross 1st and 2nd Class, Eastern Front Medal, RK-Hohenzollern, 1914 Iron Cross 1st and 2nd Class, 1914 Wound Badge in Black, Cross of Honor.

Bock, Fedor von: Generalfeldmarschall (19.07.40), (Heer); born 03.12.80 in Kuestrin, died 04.05.45 from British fighter aircraft strafing in Oldenburg. WWI: Major and Ia to Heeresgruppe "Deutscher Kronprinz." Promotions to Reichswehr Generalmajor 01.02.29, Reichswehr Generalleutnant 01.02.31, General der Infanterie 01.03.35, Generaloberst 15.03.38. O.B. of Armee Oberkommando 3, 10.1935–03.1938. WWII: O.B. of Armee Oberkommando 1, 11.1938–08.1939, O.B. of Heeresgruppe Nord 08.1939–10.1939, O.B. of Heeresgruppe B 10.1939–06.1941, O.B. of Heeresgruppe Mitte 06.1941–12.1941, O.B. of Heeresgruppe Sud 01.1942–06.1942, placed at disposal of the Fuehrer 07.1942–05.1945. Awards: Knight's Cross 30.09.39, 1939 Clasps to the 1914 Iron Cross 1st and 2nd Class, Silesian Eagle 1st and 2nd Class, Pour le Mérite 01.04.18, RK-Hohenzollern, 1914 Iron Cross 1st and 2nd Class, Cross of Honor.

Generalfeldmarschall Fedor von Bock. (Roger James Bender)

Bock, Max: General der Infanterie (01.12.40), (Heer); born 23.10.78 in Sackrau, died 12.11.45 in transit to Russian P.O.W. camp. WWI: Major on Staff of Chief of Field Railway Affairs. Promotions to Generalmajor 01.01.36, Generalleutnant 01.02.38. Recalled to military service as Oberst without assignment 01.1935,

Commander of Heeres Service Office 2, 01.1936–03.1937. WWII: Commander of 11. Infanterie Division 04.1937–10.1939, Commander of Wehrkreis Kommando XX 10.1939–02.1943, retired 04.1943. Awards: German Cross in Silver 30.04.43, 1939 Clasps to the 1914 Iron Cross 1st and 2nd Class, War Merit Cross 1st and 2nd Class with Swords, RK-Hohenzollern, 1914 Iron Cross 1st and 2nd Class, Cross of Honor.

Bock von Wuelfingen, Detlef: Generalmajor (01.12.43), (Heer); born 10.12.95 in Kassel, died 30.12.84 in Burgstemmen. WWI: Oberleutnant in Infanterie Regiment 188. WWII: Commander of Nachrichten Bataillon 28, 10.1935–03.1940, Commander of Signals Regiment 589, 03.1940–12.1940, Signals Leader to 15. Armee 04.1941–06.1942, Wehrmacht Signals Officer for Budapest 06.1942–01.1943, Commander of Signals Regiment 521, 02.1943–04.1943, Commander of Infanterie Regiment 311, 06.1943–08.1943, Signals Leader to Wehrmacht Mission in Romania 09.1943–03.1944, Fuehrer Res. in O.K.H. 04.1944–07.1944, Commandant of Feldkommandantur 681, 09.1944, captured 09.1944. Awards: 1939 Clasps to the 1914 Iron Cross 1st and 2nd Class, 1914 Iron Cross 1st and 2nd Class, Austro-Hungarian Military Service Cross 3rd Class with War Decoration, Cross of Honor.

Bock von Wuelfingen, Ferdinand: Generalleutnant (01.04.38), (Heer); born 10.06.83 in Neu-Vorweck, died 22.05.56 at Schloss Miltenberg. WWI: Hauptmann and Commander of II. Abteilung, Feld Artillerie Regiment 11. Promotion to Generalmajor 01.02.35. WWII: Military Replacement Inspector for Berlin 10.1934–06.1943, retired 06.1943. Awards: War Merit Cross 1st and 2nd Class with Swords, 1914 Iron Cross 1st and 2nd Class, Cross of Honor.

Bockelberg, Hans: General-Stabsrichter (01.03.45), (Heer); born 18.01.90 in Nienburg, died 29.11.55. Jurist by profession. WWI: service unknown. Promotion to General-Richter 01.05.43. WWII: Chief of Heeres Legal Office in O.K.H. 1939–1945. Awards: War Merit Cross 1st and 2nd Class with Swords.

Bodecker, Karl von: Konteradmiral z.V. (01.07.42), (Kriegsmarine); born 29.01.75 in Friedenthal, died 20.10.57 in Bueckeburg. WWI: Korvettenkapitan and Commander of gun boat *Jaguar*, P.O.W. 11.1914–01.1920. Service unknown 02.1920–08.1939. WWII: placed at disposal of Kriegsmarine 09.1939–07.1941, Shipyard Construction Director in Eastern Territories 07.1941–11.1941, Chief of Senior Shipyard Staff of Eastern Territories 12.1941–02.1943, retired 02.1943. Awards: War Merit Cross 1st and 2nd Class with Swords, RK-Hohenzollern, 1914 Iron Cross 1st and 2nd Class, Cross of Honor.

Bodecker, Karl-Adolf von: Generalmajor (01.04.45), (Heer); born 07.08.96 in Peine, died 28.09.83 in Bad Pyrmont. WWI: Leutnant in Dragoon Regiment 5.

Schwadron Chef in Reiter Regiment 12, 10.1934–09.1935, Kompanie Chef in Pionier Bataillon 14, 10.1935–09.1936, Adjutant to 28. Division 10.1936–11.1938. WWII: Commander of Pionier Bataillon 59 (mot.) 11.1938–03.1941, Chief Personnel Officer (IIa) to XXXXVII. Panzer Korps 03.1941–03.1942, Ia to General of Pioniers for Heeresgruppe Mitte 03.1942–03.1943, Pionier Leader to 7. Armee 03.1943–09.1944, Higher Pionier Leader to O.B. of Replacement Armee 09.1944–05.1945. Awards: 1939 Clasps to the 1914 Iron Cross 1st and 2nd Class, General Assault Badge, Eastern Front Medal, 1914 Iron Cross 1st and 2nd Class, Cross of Honor.

Bodenhausen, Erpo Freiherr von: Generalleutnant (01.11.43), (Heer); born 12.04.97 in Arnstein, died 09.05.45 (suicide) in Grobina. WWI: Leutnant in Dragoon Regiment 5. Promotion to Generalmajor 20.04.43. Chief of Ausbildungs Schwadron in Reiter Regiment at Hannover 10.1934–10.1935, Chief in 2. Schwadron, Reiter Regiment 13, 10.1935–05.1936, Adjutant on Staff of 12. Division 05.1936–10.1936, attached to Kavallerie Regiment 13, 10.1936–11.1938. WWII: Commander of II. Abteilung, Kavallerie Schuetzen Regiment 8, 11.1938–12.1940, Commander of Schuetzen Regiment 28, 12.1940–05.1942, Commander of 23. Schuetzen Brigade 05.1942–11.1942, Commander of 12. Panzer Division 05.1943–04.1945. Awards: Knight's Cross 17.12.43, German Cross in Gold 03.01.42, 1939 Clasps to the 1914 Iron Cross 1st and 2nd Class, Tank Assault Badge in Silver, Eastern Front Medal, Kurland Cuff Band, 1914 Iron Cross 1st and 2nd Class, 1194 Wound Badge in Black, Cross of Honor.

Bodenschatz, Karl: General der Flieger (01.07.41), (Luftwaffe); born 10.12.90 in Rehau, died 25.08.79 in Palma. P-7991185. WWI: in G.A.S. as Oberleutnant in J.G. 1 "Richthofen." Promotions to Generalmajor 01.02.38, Generalleutnant 01.01.40. First Adjutant to Goering as Reich Minister of R.L.M. 04.1933–03.1938. WWII: Chief of Minister Office in R.L.M. und Chief Luftwaffe Liaison at Fuehrer Headquarters 04.1938–05.1945. Awards: Golden Party Badge (honorary), German Cross in Silver 30.05.42, War Merit Cross 1st and 2nd Class with Swords, Combined Pilot/Observer's Badge in Gold with Diamonds, 20.07.44 Wound Badge in Gold, Finnish Freedom Cross 1st Class with Oak Leaves and Swords, Bulgarian Grand Officer's Cross of the Military Service Order, German Olympic Games Decoration 1st Class, Aeronautical Research Membership Badge, "J.G. Freiherr von Richthofen Nr. 1, 1917/18" Commemorative Cuff Band, Pilot's Commemorative Badge, 1914 Iron Cross 1st and 2nd Class, RK-Baden Order of the Zaehringer Lion 2nd Class with Swords, Bavarian Military Service Order IV. Class with Swords, 1914 Observer's Badge, 1914 Wound Badge in Silver, Turkish Half Moon, Cross of Honor.

Boeckh-Behrens, Hans: Generalleutnant (01.09.43), (Heer); born 27.11.98 in Wernigerode, died 13.02.55 at Voikovo P.O.W. Camp. WWI: Leutnant in

Fusilier Regiment 36. Promotion to Generalmajor 01.07.42. Kompanie Chef in Infanterie Regiment at Deutsch-Eylau 10.1934–10.1935, Kompanie Chef in Infanterie Regiment 3, 10.1935–07.1936, Tactics Instructor at Kriegsschule 08.1936–06.1939. WWII: Chief of General Staff to Korps Kommando z.b.V. 08.1939–09.1939, Ia to 16. Armee 10.1939–01.1942, Chief of General Staff to 16. Armee 01.1942–07.1943, Commander of 32. Infanterie Division 09.1943–05.1945. Awards: Knight's Cross 09.12.44, German Cross in Gold 30.01.43, 1939 Clasps to the 1914 Iron Cross 1st and 2nd Class, Infantry Assault Badge in Silver, Eastern Front Medal, Kurland Cuff Band, 1914 Iron Cross 1st and 2nd Class, 1914 Wound Badge in Black, Cross of Honor.

Boeckmann, Herbert von: General der Infanterie (01.04.42), (Heer); born 24.07.86 in Bremen, died 10.03.79 in Baden-Baden. WWI: Hauptmann on Staff of Political Department of Feld Armee. Promotions to Generalmajor 01.08.38, Generalleutnant 01.08.40. Chief of Ausbildungs Abteilung in Reich War Ministry 09.1934–10.1935, Commander of Infanterie Regiment 2, 10.1935–10.1938. WWII: Chief of Staff to I. Armee Korps 11.1938–08.1939, Chief of General Staff to 3. Armee 08.1939–10.1939, Commander of 11. Infanterie Division 10.1939–01.1942, Commander of L. Armee Korps 03.1942–07.1942, Fuehrer Res. in O.K.H. 07.1942–03.1943, forced to retire 03.1943. Awards: Knight's Cross 04.12.41, 1939 Clasps to the 1914 Iron Cross 1st and 2nd Class, Infantry Assault Badge, Eastern Front Medal, 1914 Iron Cross 1st and 2nd Class, Cross of Honor.

Boege, Ehrenfried-Oskar: General der Infanterie (01.06.44), (Heer); born 11.11.89 in Ostrowo, died 31.12.65 in Hildesheim. WWI: Oberleutnant and Adjutant in 38. Reserve Infanterie Brigade. Promotions to Generalmajor 01.04.42, Generalleutnant 01.01.43. Tactics Instructor at Kriegsschule in Dresden 01.1935–10.1936, Commander of III. Bataillon, Infanterie Regiment 84, 10.1936–11.1938. WWII: Commander of Course A at Kriegsschule in Potsdam 11.1938–08.1939, temporary Commander of Fuehrer Headquarters 08.1939–10.1939, Commander of Infanterie Regiment 161, 12.1939–07.1940, Commander of Infanterie Regiment 7, 07.1940–02.1942, Commander of 197. Infanterie Division 02.1942–11.1943, Commander of XXXXVIII. Armee Korps 06.1944–09.1944, O.B. of 18. Armee 09.1944–05.1945. Awards: Oak Leaves 21.09.44 (594), Knight's Cross 22.12.41, German Cross in Gold 13.01.43, 1939 Clasps to the 1914 Iron Cross 1st and 2nd Class, Infantry Assault Badge in Silver, Eastern Front Medal, Kurland Cuff Band, 1914 Iron Cross 1st and 2nd Class, Cross of Honor.

Boehaimb, Johannes: Generalmajor (20.04.45), (Heer); born 17.11.95 in Freising, died 02.09.72 in Weilheim. WWI: Leutnant and Bataillon Adjutant in Infanterie Regiment 124. Commander of II. Bataillon, Infanterie Regiment 103, 10.1935–09.1936. WWII: Commander of II. Bataillon, Infanterie Regiment 71 (mot.)

10.1936–08.1939, Commander of Infanterie Regiment 543, 08.1939–05.1940, Commander of Infanterie Ersatz Regiment 254, 05.1940–08.1940, Commander of Infanterie Regiment 278, 08.1940–03.1941, Commander of Infanterie Regiment 53 (mot.) 03.1941–11.1941, Director of Infanterie Training at German Mission in Romania 11.1941–12.1944. Awards: 1939 Clasps to the 1914 Iron Cross 1st and 2nd Class, Infantry Assault Badge in Silver, 1914 Iron Cross 1st and 2nd Class, Cross of Honor.

Boehlke, Hellmuth: Generalleutnant (01.08.44), (Heer); born 07.02.93 in Luban, died 08.04.56 in Bad Mergentheim. WWI: Leutnant der Res. and Kompanie Chef in 2. Jaeger Bataillon. Promotion to Generalmajor 01.01.44. Kompanie Chef in Infanterie Regiment 55, 10.1935–04.1937. WWII: Commander of II. Bataillon, Infanterie Regiment 21, 05.1937–02.1940, Commander of Infanterie Regiment 46, 02.1940–03.1941, Commander of Grenadier Regiment 430, 03.1941–10.1942, Commander of Infanterie Regiment 134, 02.1943–11.1943, Commander of 334. Infanterie Division 02.1944–04.1945. Awards: Oak Leaves 25.01.45 (716), Knight's Cross 24.09.42, German Cross in Gold 27.10.41, 1939 Clasps to the 1914 Iron Cross 1st and 2nd Class, Infantry Assault Badge in Silver, Eastern Front Medal, 1914 Iron Cross 1st and 2nd Class, 1914 Wound Badge in Black, Cross of Honor.

Boehm, Hermann: Generaladmiral (01.04.41), (Kriegsmarine); born 18.01.84 in Rybnik, died 11.04.72 in Kiel. WWI: Kapitanleutnant and Commandant of torpedo boat *V-128*. Promotions to Reichsmarine Konteradmiral 01.10.34, Vizeadmiral 01.04.37, Admiral 01.04.38. Chief of Staff to Flottenkommando 09.1932–10.1933, Commandant of line ship *Hessen* 10.1933–09.1934, Befehlshaber of Reconnaissance Surface Ships 09.1934–09.1937, Commanding Admiral of Marine Station North Sea 10.1937–10.1938. WWII: Flotten Chef 11.1938–10.1939, placed at disposal of O.B. of Kriegsmarine 10.1939–03.1940, Marine Befehlshaber of Norway 04.1940–01.1943, retired 05.1943. Awards: German Cross in Gold 20.11.41, 1939 Clasps to the 1914 Iron Cross 1st and 2nd Class, High Seas Fleet War Badge, Spanish Cross in Gold with Swords, Grand Cross of the Italian Order of the Crown, Grand Cross of the Hungarian Service Order, Grand Cross of the Spanish Service Order, Spanish War Cross (Spain), RK-Hohenzollern, 1914 Iron Cross 1st and 2nd Class, Oldenburg Friedrich-August Cross 1st and 2nd Class, Turkish Silver Liakat Medal with Sabre, 1914 Naval Wound Badge in Black, Cross of Honor.

Boehm-Bezing, Diether von: General der Kavallerie z.V. (01.02.43), (Heer); born 09.11.80 in Lueben, died 30.11.74 in Ebenhausen. WWI: Rittmeister and Commander of II. Bataillon, Res. Infanterie Regiment 7. Promotions to Reichswehr Generalmajor 01.10.33, Generalleutnant z.V. 01.02.41. Commander of Reiter Brigade at Stettin 10.1934–09.1935, Commander of 2. Kavallerie Division 10.1935–03.1936, Commandant of Breslau 10.1936–01.1937, Landwehr Commander of Breslau

02.1937–09.1937. WWII: left military service 09.1937–08.1939, recalled to military service 08.1939, Commander of 252. Infanterie Division 08.1939–03.1942, Commander of 153. Infanterie Division 06.1942–12.1942, retired 02.1943. Awards: German Cross in Gold 19.12.41, 1939 Clasps to the 1914 Iron Cross 1st and 2nd Class, Infantry Assault Badge in Silver, Eastern Front Medal, RK-Hohenzollern, 1914 Iron Cross 1st and 2nd Class, Cross of Honor.

Boehm-Tettelbach, Alfred: General der Infanterie z.V. (01.12.40), (Heer); born 28.03.78 in Erstein, died 12.07.62 in Berlin. WWI: Major on Staff of Chief of Field Railway Affairs. Promotions to Reichswehr Generalmajor 01.11.30, Reichswehr Generalleutnant 01.10.32. Instructor at Kriegsschule 06.1935–10.1938. WWII: Special Purpose Officer in Heeres 11.1938–09.1939, Commandant of Feldkommandantur 581, 09.1939–01.1940, Commander of Hoeheres Kommando z.b.V. XXXVII 03.1940–05.1942, Commander of LXXXII. Armee Korps 05.1942–11.1942, retired 02.1943. Awards: German Cross in Silver 15.01.43, War Merit Cross 1st and 2nd Class with Swords, RK-Hohenzollern, 1914 Iron Cross 1st and 2nd Class, Cross of Honor.

General der Infanterie Franz Boehme. (Bundesarchiv)

Boehme, Franz: General der Infanterie (01.08.40) later Gebirgstruppe (23.03.44), (Heer); born 15.04.85 in Zeltweg, died 29.05.47 (suicide) in Nuremberg Prison. WWI: Hauptmann on Staff of Austrian 1. Infanterie Division. Promotions to Generalmajor 01.04.38, Generalleutnant 01.06.39. Transferred to German Wehrmacht 03.1938, Infanterie Commander 23, 11.1938–06.1939. WWII: Commander of 32. Infanterie Division 07.1939–06.1940, Commander of XVIII. Armee Korps 10.1940–11.1943, Military Befehlshaber of Serbia 04.1943–08.1943, Deputy Commander of XVIII. Armee Korps and Befehlshaber of Wehrkreis Kommando XVIII 12.1943–06.1944, Fuehrer Res. in O.K.H. 07.1944–12.1944, Wehrmacht Befehlshaber of Norway and O.B. of 20. Armee 01.1945–05.1945. Awards: Knight's Cross 29.06.40, German Cross in Gold 10.02.44, 1939 Iron Cross 1st Class, 1939 Clasp to the 1914 Iron Cross 2nd Class, Infantry Assault Badge in Silver, Finnish Freedom Cross 1st Class with Oak Leaves and Swords, Heer Bergfuehrer Badge, 1914 Iron Cross 2nd Class, Numerous Austrian Awards, Cross of Honor.

Boehme, Hermann: Generalleutnant (01.04.44), (Heer); born 29.11.96 in Freiberg, died 29.10.68 in Munich. WWI: Leutnant and Adjutant to III. Bataillon, Infanterie Regiment 177. Promotion to Generalmajor 01.10.43. Kompanie Chef in Infanterie

Regiment 10, 10.1935–12.1935, Ia to 8. Division 01.1936–03.1938. WWII: Ia to II. Armee Korps 03.1938–11.1939, Group Director in Defense Operations Staff of O.K.W. 11.1939–06.1940, Chief of Staff to German Armistice Commission 06.1940–03.1943, Commander of 73. Infanterie Division 09.1943–05.1944, captured 05.1944. Awards: German Cross in Silver (date unknown), War Merit Cross 1st and 2nd Class with Swords, 1939 Clasps to the 1914 Iron Cross 1st Class, Infantry Assault Badge in Silver, RK-Sachsen Military St. Heinrich's Order 01.11.17, 1914 Iron Cross 1st and 2nd Class, 1914 Wound Badge in Silver, Cross of Honor.

Boehme, Dr. Robert: General-Intendant (01.05.44), (Heer); born 22.10.76 in Berlin, died 15.03.56 in Berlin. Administrative Officer by profession. WWI: service unknown. Attached to Abteilung attached to the O.K.H. (dates unknown). Awards: War Merit Cross 1st and 2nd Class with Swords, 1914 Iron Cross 2nd Class, Cross of Honor.

Boehmer, Hans: Generalmajor (30.01.45), (Luftwaffe); born 21.10.86 in Mainz, died 30.10.78 in Palma. WWI: in G.A.S. as Rittmeister and Commander of Flieger Abteilung 224. Leader of Flight Training Office at Paderborn 04.1935–10.1935, Commander of Luftgau Res. 10, 01.1936–09.1936, Commander of Luftgau Res. 11, 10.1936–04.1937, Quartermaster 2 on Staff of Luftwaffe Gruppen Kommando 2, 02.1938–02.1939. WWII: Quartermaster 1 to Luftflotte 2, 03.1939–10.1939, Ia to Air Region Staff 14, 10.1939–11.1940, Ia to Luftgau Staff 300 and later Luftgau Staff 2, 02.1941–03.1942, Flughafenbereichs Commandant of Fuerth 03.1942–07.1944, Flughafenbereichs Commandant of 5-IV 07.1944–01.1945. Awards: 1939 Clasps to the 1914 Iron Cross 1st and 2nd Class, Eastern Front Medal, German West Wall Medal, Pilot's Commemorative Badge, 1914 Iron Cross 1st and 2nd Class, 1914 Wound Badge in Black, 1914 Observer's Badge, Turkish Silver Liakat Medal with Sabre, Cross of Honor.

Boehmer, Kurt: Konteradmiral (01.02.43), (Kriegsmarine); born 31.12.92 in Magdeburg, died 01.10.44 in action near Gasseln. WWI: Leutnant zur See and Watch Officer on *U-17* and later *U-22*. Chief of 1. Raumbootsflottille 09.1933–09.1935, attached to Inspectorate of Torpedo Boats and Mine Ships 09.1935–09.1936, attached to Inspectorate of Surface Blocking Weapons 10.1936–07.1937. WWII: First Officer on *Admiral Scheer* 07.1937–01.1940, Commander of Special Formation of North Sea 01.1940–05.1940, Chief of Staff to Befehlshaber of Safety for North Sea 06.1940–10.1940, Commander of Minesweepers North 10.1940–03.1942, Commander of Minesweepers East 03.1942–06.1944, Commander of 9. Security Division 06.1944–10.1944. Awards: Knight's Cross 06.10.40, 1939 Iron Cross 1st Class, 1939 Clasp to the 1914 Iron Cross 2nd Class, Minesweepers-Sub Chasers-Escort Vessels War Badge, 1939 Wound Badge in Gold, Spanish Cross in

Silver without Swords, Finnish Freedom Cross 1st Class with Swords, 1914 Iron Cross 2nd Class, 1914 Submarine Badge, Cross of Honor.

Boehringer, Gustav: Generalleutnant (01.01.44), (Heer); born 07.07.92 in Strassburg, died 20.02.74 in Konstanz. WWI: Oberleutnant and Kompanie Chef in 21. Pionier Bataillon. Promotion to Generalmajor 01.02.42. Commander of Pionier Bataillon at Ulm 10.1934–10.1935, Commander of Pionier Bataillon 45, 10.1935–09.1936. WWII: Department Chief for Pioniers in Reich War Ministry (later O.K.H.) 10.1936–11.1940, Commander of z.b.V. Pionier Staff Regiment 700, 11.1940–07.1941, Pionier Leader to 11. Armee 07.1941–08.1942, General of Pioniers in Heeresgruppe A 08.1942–05.1943, General of Pioniers in Heeresgruppe Sud and later Nord Ukraine 05.1943–05.1945. Awards: Knight's Cross of the War Merit Cross with Swords 06.10.44, German Cross in Silver 30.09.42, 1939 Clasps to the 1914 Iron Cross 1st and 2nd Class, War Merit Cross 1st and 2nd Class with Swords, Eastern Front Medal, Crimea Shield, 1914 Iron Cross 1st and 2nd Class, 1914 Wound Badge in Black, Cross of Honor.

Boelsen, Dr. Hans: Generalleutnant (01.03.45), (Heer); born 06.03.94 in Emden, died 24.10.60 in Frankfurt am Main. WWI: Leutnant and Ordnance Officer on Staff of 242. Infanterie Division. Promotion to Generalmajor 01.06.44. Kompanie Chef in Infanterie Regiment at Giessen 10.1934–10.1935, Kompanie Chef in Infanterie Regiment 36, 10.1935–10.1936, Kompanie Chef in Infanterie Regiment 115, 10.1936–11.1937, Course Instructor for Staff Offices in 33. Division 11.1937–12.1937, assignments unknown 01.1938–10.1938. WWII: Tactics Instructor at Potsdam Kriegsschule 11.1938–10.1939, First Adjutant of Wehrkreis XXII 10.1939–03.1940, First Adjutant to Panzer Gruppe "von Kleist" 03.1940–07.1940, First Adjutant to Panzer Gruppe 1, 07.1940–05.1941, Commander of 160. Kradschuetzen Infanterie Bataillon 07.1941–12.1941, Commander of Instruction Staff III at Infanterie Schule Doeberitz 03.1942–01.1943, Commander of 111. Panzer Grenadier Division 05.1943–11.1943, Fuehrer Res. 05.1943–09.1944, Commander of 18. Panzer Grenadier Division 09.1944–02.1945. Awards: Knight's Cross 17.09.43, German Cross in Gold 17.11.41, Honor Roll Clasp 18.08.43, 1939 Clasps to the 1914 Iron Cross 1st and 2nd Class, Infantry Assault Badge in Bronze, 1939 Wound Badge in Silver, 1914 Iron Cross 1st and 2nd Class, 1914 Wound Badge in Black, Cross of Honor.

Boemers, Hans: Generalleutnant (01.07.44), (Heer); born 20.04.93 in Bueckeburg, died 15.01.64 in Braubach. WWI: Oberleutnant and Adjutant to Feld Artillerie Regiment 58. Promotion to Generalmajor 01.04.42. Attached to Heeresfeldzeugmeisterei 04.1935–12.1936, Commander of I. Abteilung, Artillerie Regiment 70, 12.1936–10.1937, Commander of Artillerie Regiment 34, 10.1937–11.1938.

WWII: Commander of Artillerie Regiment 70, 11.1938–11.1939, Commander of Artillerie 145, 01.1941–03.1942, Commander of 65. Infanterie Division 07.1942–01.1943, Commander of Heeres Feldzeuggruppe 3, 01.1943–02.1944, Field Equipment Inspector for Ersatz Armee 02.1944–05.1945. Awards: German Cross in Gold 19.12.41, 1939 Clasps to the 1914 Iron Cross 1st and 2nd Class, General Assault Badge, Eastern Front Medal, 1914 Iron Cross 1st and 2nd Class, Cross of Honor.

Boenicke, Walter: General der Flieger (01.03.35), (Luftwaffe); born 15.12.95 in Radisleben, died 21.04.47 (suicide) at Muenster P.O.W. Camp. WWI: in G.A.S. as Leutnant in Flieger Abteilung A 13. Promotions to Generalmajor 01.09.41, Generalleutnant 01.09.43. Advisor in Personalamt of R.L.M. 04.1934–03.1935, attached to Staff of Reich War Ministry 07.1935–03.1938, Fliegerhorst Commandant of Stargard 04.1938–01.1939. WWII: Department Chief in R.L.M. 02.1939–06.1940, Chief of Staff to I. Flieger Korps 06.1940–11.1941, Chief of Staff to Fortress Commander at Crete 11.1941–06.1942, Chief of General Staff to Luftwaffe Commander for Heeresgruppe Mitte 06.1942–10.1943, Commander of 3. Flieger Division 01.1944–04.1944, Fuehrer Res. in O.K.L. 05.1944–02.1945. Awards: Knight's Cross 14.05.44, German Cross in Gold 14.01.44, 1939 Clasps to the 1914 Iron Cross 1st and 2nd Class, Kreta Cuff Band, 1939 Wound Badge in Black, Combined Pilot-Observer's Badge, Pilot's Commemorative Badge, RK-Hohenzollern, 1914 Iron Cross 1st and 2nd Class, 1914 Observer's Badge, Cross of Honor.

Boenigk, Oskar Freiherr von: Generalmajor (01.02.41), (Luftwaffe); born 25.08.93 in Siegerdorf, died 30.01.46 in Kretschendorf P.O.W. Camp. WWI: in G.A.S. as Oberleutnant and Commander of J.G. 2. Staff Officer attached to Jagdflieger Schule Schleissheim 09.1934–10.1935. WWII: Fliegerhorst Commandant of Perleberg 03.1936–10.1939, Flughafenbereichs Commandant of 1-VIII Breslau 12.1939–11.1942, retired 05.1943. Awards: War Merit Cross 1st and 2nd Class with Swords, Pilot's Commemorative Badge, Silesian Eagle 1st and 2nd Class, Pour le Mérite 25.10.18, RK-Hohenzollern, RK-Sachsen Ernestine House Order 2nd Class with Swords, 1914 Iron Cross 1st and 2nd Class, 1914 Pilot's Badge, Cross of Honor.

Boening, August: Konteradmiral (01.01.45), (Kriegsmarine); born 15.08.91 in Duisburg, died 01.07.64 in Eckernforde. WWI: Marine Pay Master for Halb Flottille. Instructor at Marine Schule Muerwick 09.1933–04.1935, attached to Marine Nachrichtenschule 04.1935–09.1935, Administrative Officer for U-Flottille *Weddigen* 09.1935–05.1937, Administrative Staff Leader attached to Staff of U-Boats 05.1937–04.1939. WWII: Personnel Advisor on Staff of North Sea Naval Station 04.1939–01.1940, General Advisor in Naval Personnel Office of O.K.M. 01.1940–06.1943, Department Chief for Food Supply and Clothing for Marine

Gruppen Kommando Baltic Sea 06.1943–05.1945. Awards: War Merit Cross 1st and 2nd Class with Swords, 1914 Iron Cross 1st and 2nd Class, Turkish Silver Liakat Medal with Sabre, Turkish Half Moon, Cross of Honor.

de Boer, Johannes: Generalleutnant (01.04.44), (Heer); born 05.09.97 in Hamburg, died 14.03.86 in Hamburg. WWI: Leutnant der Res. in Feld Artillerie Regiment 223. Promotion to Generalmajor 01.10.43. Attached to Staff of II. Abteilung, Artillerie Regiment 56, 10.1935–10.1936, Batterie Chef in Artillerie Regiment 56, 10.1936–10.1937. WWII: Commander of I. Abteilung, Artillerie Regiment 58, 10.1937–09.1939, Commander of Artillerie Regiment 22, 10.1939–04.1943, attended course for divisional leaders 05.1943–07.1943, Commander of 26. Infanterie Division 08.1943–11.1944, Commander of 280. Infanterie Division 11.1944–05.1945. Awards: Knight's Cross 19.06.40, German Cross in Gold 22.01.42, 1939 Iron Cross 1st Class, 1939 Clasp to the 1914 Iron Cross 2nd Class, General Assault Badge, Eastern Front Medal, Crimea Shield, 1914 Iron Cross 2nd Class, Cross of Honor.

Boesler, Walter: General-Stabsintendant (01.09.44), (Heer); born 19.12.86 in Koenigsberg, died 15.02.57 in Reutlingen. Administrative Officer by profession. WWI: Feld-Intendant to 18. Landwehr Division. Promotion to General-Intendant 01.10.39. Advisor in Abteilung 3 of Reich War Ministry 06.1935–10.1937. WWII: Korps Intendant to X. Armee Korps 11.1937–06.1940, Chief Intendant to Wehrmacht Befehlshaber of Netherlands 06.1940–11.1942, Chief of Amtsgruppe V-III in O.K.H. 11.1942–05.1945. Awards: German Cross in Silver 31.01.45, War Merit Cross 1st and 2nd Class with Swords, 1914 Iron Cross 2nd Class, Cross of Honor.

Boesser, Karl: Generalmajor (01.04.42), (Heer); born 07.10.76 in Ploen, died 17.05.45 (presumed dead). WWI: Major and Bataillon Commander in Feld Artillerie Regiment 44. WWII: attached to Inspector of Transport Troops in O.K.H. 03.1938–04.1942, attached to Administration branch of O.K.H. 04.1942–04.1943, retired 08.1943. Awards: War Merit Cross 1st and 2nd Class with Swords, RH-Hohenzollern, 1914 Iron Cross 1st and 2nd Class, Cross of Honor.

Boettcher, Hermann: Generalleutnant (01.11.39), (Heer); born 10.05.84 in Hannover, died 20.07.69 in Stuttgart. WWI: Hauptmann and Commander of Motor Bataillon 15. Promotion to Generalmajor 01.08.37. Commander of Infanterie Regiment at Goerlitz 10.1934–10.1935, Commander of Infanterie Regiment 30, 10.1935–11.1938. WWII: Landwehr Commander of Hannover 11.1938–08.1939, Commander of 216. Infanterie Division 08.1939–09.1940, Commander of 148. Infanterie Division 11.1940–04.1943, Commandant of Feldkommandantur 590, 05.1943–09.1944, Wehrmacht Commander of Glatz 01.1945–05.1945. Awards: 1939 Clasps to the 1914 Iron Cross 1st and 2nd Class, Infantry Assault Badge in

Silver, 1914 Iron Cross 1st and 2nd Class, 1914 Wound Badge in Black, Cross of Honor.

Boettcher, Karl: Generalleutnant (01.03.42), (Heer); born 25.10.89 in Thorn, died 09.02.75 in Bad Wimpfen. WWI: Hauptmann and Commander of 149. Fuss Artillerie Bataillon. Promotion to Generalmajor 01.03.40. Commander of I. Abteilung, Artillerie Regiment 59, 10.1935–10.1936, Commander of Artillerie Regiment 1, 10.1936–03.1939. WWII: Commandant of Kattowitz 04.1939–08.1939, Commander of Artillerie 104, 09.1939–12.1941, Commander of 21. Panzer Division 12.1941–11.1942, Commander of 345. Infanterie Division 11.1942–03.1943, Commander of 347. Infanterie Division 10.1943–12.1943, Senior Commander of Artillerie 305, 03.1944–03.1945. Awards: Knight's Cross 13.12.41, 1939 Clasps to the 1914 Iron Cross 1st and 2nd Class, General Assault Badge, Afrika Cuff Band, 1914 Iron Cross 1st and 2nd Class, Cross of Honor.

Boettge, Kurt: Generalmajor (01.10.41), (Luftwaffe); born 13.12.92 in Arnsberg, died 19.09.46 in Shogborough Military Hospital. WWI: in G.A.S. as Oberleutnant in Flieger Abteilung 37. Kompanie Chef in Flieger Ersatz Regiment in Oschatz 06.1935–1937, Fliegerhorst Commandant of Handorf 1937–03.1939. WWII: Commander of Flieger Training Regiment 31, 04.1939–1941, Flughafenbereichs Commandant of 1-I 1941–02.1945. Awards: War Merit Cross 1st and 2nd Class with Swords, Combined Pilot-Observer's Badge, Golden HJ Honor Badge, Reich Sports Badge in Gold, Pilot's Commemorative Badge, 1914 Iron Cross 1st and 2nd Class, 1914 Observer's Badge, 1914 Austro-Hungarian Pilot's Badge, Cross of Honor.

Boettger, Dr. Hugo: General-Veterinar (01.08.42), (Heer); born 21.10.83 in Kastel, died 02.04.53 in Hamburg. Medical veterinarian by profession. WWI: Ober-Veterinar in Hussar Regiment 10. WWII: Deputy Korps Veterinar to X. Armee Korps 04.1936–08.1939, Korps Veterinar to Wehrkreis X 08.1939–01.1944, retired 05.1944. Awards: War Merit Cross 1st and 2nd Class with Swords, 1914 Iron Cross 2nd Class, Cross of Honor.

Boettger, Karl: Generalmajor (01.04.41), (Heer); born 15.11.91 in Bad Frankenhausen, died 11.07.65 in Bremen. WWI: Oberleutnant and 2. Adjutant to Commander of Kowno. Commander of III. Bataillon, Infanterie Regiment at Koenigsbrueck 10.1934–10.1935, Commander of III. Bataillon, Infanterie Regiment 53, 10.1935–09.1936. WWII: Chief of Clothing Department in Reich War Ministry (later O.K.H.) 10.1936–07.1943, attached to Chief of Heeres Armaments and O.B. of Ersatz Armee 11.1943–03.1944, Commandant of Feldkommandantur 674, 04.1944–04.1945. Awards: War Merit Cross 1st and 2nd Class with Swords, RK-Sachsen Albrecht Order 2nd Class with Swords, 1914 Iron Cross 1st and 2nd Class, 1914 Wound Badge in Black, Cross of Honor.

General der Artillerie Friedrich von Boetticher. (Josef Charita)

Boetticher, Friedrich von: General der Artillerie (01.09.40), (Heer); born 14.10.81 in Bethelsdorf, died 28.09.67 in Bielefeld. WWI: Major and Ia to 241. Infanterie Division. Promotions to Reichswehr Generalmajor 01.10.31, Reichswehr Generalleutnant 01.10.33. WWII: Military Attaché in Washington and later Mexico 04.1933–06.1942, attached to Senior Quartermaster IV in O.K.H. 06.1942–12.1942, attached to Wehrmacht Central Office in O.K.W. 12.1942–05.1945. Awards: Knight's Cross of the War Merit Cross with Swords 27.05.42, War Merit Cross 1st and 2nd Class with Swords, RK-Sachsen Military St. Heinrich's Order 09.11.18, RK-Hohenzollern, 1914 Iron Cross 1st and 2nd Class, Cross of Honor.

Boetticher, Dr. Hans: General-Richter (1944), (Heer); born 08.09.99 in Prinzenthal, died 23.09.88 in Munich. Jurist by profession. WWI: service unknown. WWII: Judge with Heeres Plenipotentiary in Boehmen-Maehren 08.1939–12.1940 and 10.1941–07.1942, Judge with O.K.H. 12.1940–10.1941, Chief Judge attached to Wehrmacht Befehlshaber of France 07.1942–09.1944, Chief Judge to Heeresgruppe G 09.1944–05.1945. Awards: War Merit Cross 1st and 2nd Class with Swords, Cross of Honor.

Bogatsch, Rudolf: General der Flieger (01.07.41), (Luftwaffe); born 14.09.91 in Breslau, died 05.06.70 in Beis. WWI: Oberleutnant on Staff of z.b.V. Command 54. Promotions to Generalmajor 01.10.38, Generalleutnant 01.01.40. Chief of Staff to Inspection of Flak Artillerie in R.W.M. 09.1933–09.1934, Commander of Flak Abteilung Lankwitz 10.1934–09.1935, High Commander of Flak Artillerie III in Dresden 10.1935–09.1937, Chief of Luftwaffe Administrative Office in R.L.M. 11.1937–11.1938. WWII: Commander of Army Flieger Units and Inspector of Reconnaissance Units in R.L.M. 02.1939–05.1942, Commander of Luftgau Kommando XVII 08.1942–09.1943, Fuehrer Res. in O.K.L. 09.1943–03.1944, attached to Luftflotte "Reich" 03.1944–09.1944, Commander of IV. Flak Korps 09.1944–05.1945. Awards: Knight's Cross 20.03.42, 1939 Clasps to the 1914 Iron Cross 1st and 2nd Class, Flak War Badge, 1939 Observer's Badge, 1914 Iron Cross 1st and 2nd Class, Cross of Honor.

Bogen, Erich von: Generalleutnant (01.07.44), (Heer); born 14.08.93 Bromberg, died 03.09.72 in Emden. WWI: in G.A.S. then transferred to Infanterie as Oberleutnant and Adjutant to Fuess Infanterie Regiment 34. Promotion to Generalmajor 01.02.43. Attached to Inspection 2 in Reichswehr Ministry 02.1933–03.1937,

Commander of I. Bataillon, Infanterie Regiment 27, 03.1937–10.1937. WWII: Commander of II. Bataillon, Infanterie Regiment 89, 10.1937–09.1939, Commander of Infanterie Regiment 202, 09.1939–05.1940, Commander of Infanterie Regiment 154, 05.1940–08.1941, attached to Panzertruppen Schule 09.1941–09.1942, General with Special Duties assigned to Heeresgruppe Mitte 03.1943–05.1944, captured 05.1944. Awards: Honor Roll Clasp 07.04.44, 1939 Clasps to the 1914 Iron Cross 1st and 2nd Class, Infantry Assault Badge in Silver, 1939 Wound Badge in Silver, Pilot's Commemorative Badge, 1914 Iron Cross 1st and 2nd Class, 1914 Wound Badge in Black, 1914 Observer's Badge, Cross of Honor.

Bogendoerfer, Friedrich Ritter von: Generalmajor z.V. (01.11.41), (Heer); born 05.05.69 in Buttelbronn, died 04.01.45 of natural causes in Nuremberg. WWI: Oberstleutnant and Commander of Bavarian Infanterie Regiment 26. WWII: recalled to military service 08.1939, Senior Commandant of Feldkommandantur 589, 03.1940–1942, retired 1943. Awards: War Merit Cross 1st and 2nd Class with Swords, Pour le Mérite 08.11.18, RK-Bavarian Military Max Joseph Order 08.11.18, RK-Hohenzollern, 1914 Iron Cross 1st and 2nd Class, Cross of Honor.

Bohlmann-Combrinck, Theodor: Generalmajor (01.12.43), (Heer); born 18.11.91 in Delmenhorst, died 18.11.56 in Bad Honnef. WWI: Leutnant in Infanterie Regiment 20. Kompanie Chef in Schuetzen Regiment 1, 10.1935–06.1937, attached to Staff of II. Bataillon, Schuetzen Regiment 1, 06.1937–11.1938. WWII: Commander of II. Bataillon, Schuetzen Regiment 1, 11.1938–12.1939, Commander of Schuetzen Regiment 111, 12.1939–05.1942, Schnelltruppen Commander for Wehrkreis Kommando IV 05.1942–11.1943, Panzertruppen Commander for Wehrkreis Kommando IV 02.1944–05.1945. Awards: Knight's Cross 08.08.41, 1939 Clasps to the 1914 Iron Cross 1st and 2nd Class, Tank Assault Badge in Bronze, Eastern Front Medal, 1939 Wound Badge in Silver, RK-Sachsen Order of the White Falcon 2nd Class with Swords, 1914 Iron Cross 1st and 2nd Class, Oldenburg Friedrich-August Cross 1st and 2nd Class, 1914 Wound Badge in Black, Cross of Honor.

Bohnstedt, Edgar: Generalrichter z.V. (25.07.44), (Heer); born 05.06.72 in Craemersdorf, died 13.03.46 in Traunstein. Jurist by profession. WWI: Hauptmann der Res. and War Judge for 12. Infanterie Division. Judge for Gruppe 2 at Koenigsberg 01.1934–09.1937, retired 09.1937. WWII: recalled to military service without assignment 07.1944. Awards: 1914 Iron Cross 1st and 2nd Class, Cross of Honor.

Bohnstedt, Wilhelm: Generalleutnant (01.04.42), (Heer); born 05.10.88 in Schmarsow, died 11.08.47 in Hameln. WWI: Hauptmann on Staff of Res. Infanterie Regiment 270. Promotion to Generalmajor 01.04.40. Commander of Infanterie Regiment at Glogau 10.1934–10.1935. WWII: Commander of Infanterie Regiment

51, 10.1935–06.1940, Commander of 32. Infanterie Division 10.1940–01.1942, Inspector of Infanterie in O.K.H. and Chief of Heeres Armaments Department in O.K.H. 05.1942–01.1945, Fuehrer Res. in O.K.H. 01.1945–05.1945. Awards: Knight's Cross 13.10.41, 1939 Clasps to the 1914 Iron Cross 1st and 2nd Class, Infantry Assault Badge in Silver, Eastern Front Medal, 1194 Iron Cross 1st and 2nd Class, 1914 Wound Badge in Black, Cross of Honor.

Boie, Claus: Generalmajor (01.12.42), (Heer); born 10.01.91 in Koenigsberg, died 28.08.83 in Lueneburg. WWI: Oberleutnant in Infanterie Regiment 165. Commander of II. Bataillon, Infanterie Regiment at Leipzig 10.1934–10.1935, Commander of II. Bataillon, Infanterie Regiment 11, 10.1935–11.1937, Staff Officer Instructor at Koenigsbrueck 11.1937–12.1937, assignments unknown 01.1938–10.1938. WWII: Commander of Infanterie Regiment 130, 11.1938–06.1940, Commander of Infanterie Regiment 44, 07.1940–09.1941, Commander of Infanterie Regiment 572, 09.1941–11.1942, Commandant of Feldkommandantur 541, 10.1942–04.1944, Commandant of Feldkommandantur 497, 04.1944–08.1944, captured 08.1944. Awards: 1939 Clasps to the 1914 Iron Cross 1st and 2nd Class, Infantry Assault Badge in Silver, Eastern Front Medal, RK-Hohenzollern, 1914 Iron Cross 1st and 2nd Class, Bavarian Military Service Order IV. Class with Swords, Cross of Honor.

Boineburg-Lengsfeld, Hans Reichsfreiherr von: Generalleutnant (01.12.42), (Heer); born 09.06.89 in Eisenach, died 20.11.80 in Felsberg. WWI: Oberleutnant on Staff of 8. Kavallerie Division. Promotion to Generalmajor 01.10.41. Adjutant to 4. Reiter Brigade 10.1934–01.1935, attached to Staff of Reiter Regiment at Gera 05.1935–10.1935, Commander of II. Bataillon, Schuetzen Regiment 1, 10.1935–11.1938. WWII: Commander of Schuetzen Regiment 1, 11.1938–10.1939, Commander of 4. Schuetzen Brigade 10.1939–10.1940, Commander of 7. Schuetzen Brigade 10.1940–09.1941, Commander of 23. Panzer Division 09.1941–12.1942, Fuehrer Res. in O.K.H. 12.1942–04.1943, Wehrmacht Commandant of Greater Paris 05.1943–08.1944, Fuehrer Res. in O.K.H. 09.1944–05.1945. Awards: Knight's Cross 19.07.40, 1939 Clasps to the 1914 Iron Cross 1st and 2nd Class, Tank Assault Badge in Silver, RK-Sachsen Albrecht Order 2nd Class with Swords, RK-Sachsen Order of the White Falcon 2nd Class with Swords, 1914 Iron Cross 1st and 2nd Class, Cross of Honor.

Bolbrinker, Ernst: Generalmajor (01.07.44), (Heer); born 23.10.98 in Graz, died 02.07.62 in Bielefeld. WWI: Leutnant in Infanterie Regiment 144. Attached to Staff of II. Abteilung, Panzer Regiment 1, 03.1937–10.1937, Kompanie Chef in Panzer Regiment 1, 10.1937–11.1937. WWII: Chief of 7. Kompanie, Panzer Regiment 1, 1938–10.1939, Headquarters Commandant for XVI. Armee Korps 11.1939–09.1940, Commander of I. Abteilung, Panzer Regiment 5,

09.1940–8.1941, Group Director in O.K.H. 06.1942–02.1943, attached to Staff of Inspector of Panzertruppen in O.K.H. 02.1943–05.1945. Awards: Knight's Cross 15.05.41, 1939 Clasps to the 1914 Iron Cross 1st and 2nd Class, Tank Assault Badge in Bronze, Afrika Cuff Band, 1939 Wound Badge in Black, 1914 Iron Cross 1st and 2nd Class, Cross of Honor.

Boltenstern, Walter von: Generalleutnant (01.08.42), (Heer); born 26.11.89 in Breslau, died 19.01.52 at Voikovo P.O.W. Camp. WWI: Hauptmann and Ordnance Officer on Staff of 79. Reserve Division. Promotion to Generalmajor 01.08.40. Adjutant to Wehrkreis Kommando III 10.1934–10.1935, Adjutant to Generalkommando of III. Armee Korps 10.1935–10.1937. WWII: Commander of Infanterie Regiment 71, 10.1937–05.1940, Commander of 29. Infanterie Division (mot.), 07.1940–12.1941, Commander of 179. Infanterie Division (mot.), 01.1942–02.1943, attached to Reichs War Court 02.1943–05.1944, retired 05.1944. Awards: Knight's Cross 13.08.41, 1939 Clasps to the 1914 Iron Cross 1st and 2nd Class, Infantry Assault Badge in Bronze, Silesian Eagle 1st and 2nd Class, 1914 Iron Cross 1st and 2nd Class, 1914 Wound Badge in Black, Cross of Honor.

Boltenstern, Werner von: Generalmajor (01.03.45), (Heer); born 04.06.97 in Leipzig, died 31.01.85 in Hannover. WWI: Leutnant and Bataillon Adjutant in Grenadier Regiment 9. Kompanie Chef in Infanterie Regiment at Kolberg 10.1934–10.1935, Kompanie Chef in Infanterie Regiment 4, 10.1935–12.1935, attached to Personnel Office of Reich War Ministry 12.1935–03.1936. WWII: Advisor in Heeres Personnel Office of Reich War Ministry (later O.K.H.) 04.1936–09.1940, Department Chief in Heeres Personnel Office of O.K.H. 10.1940–04.1942, Commander of Infanterie Regiment 4, 06.1942–05.1943, Fuehrer Res. in O.K.H. 05.1943–09.1943, Commander of Formation Staff for Division 402, 11.1943–12.1943, Fortress Commandant of Stavanger 01.1944–05.1945. Awards: 1939 Clasps to the 1914 Iron Cross 1st and 2nd Class, War Merit Cross 1st and 2nd Class with Swords, Infantry Assault Badge in Silver, 1914 Iron Cross 1st and 2nd Class, Cross of Honor.

Boltze, Arthur: Generalleutnant z.V. (01.02.41), (Heer); born 18.03.78 in Hohstedt, died 07.11.54 in Jugenheim. WWI: Major and Commander of II. Bataillon, Infanterie Regiment 179. Promotion to Reichswehr Generalmajor 01.02.33. WWII: recalled to military service 09.1939, Commander of 154. Infanterie Division 12.1939–08.1942, retired 08.1942. Awards: 1939 Clasps to the 1914 Iron Cross 1st and 2nd Class, Infantry Assault Badge in Silver, RK-Sachsen Military St. Heinrich's Order 30.11.14, RK-Hohenzollern, 1914 Iron Cross 1st and 2nd Class, Cross of Honor.

Bonatz, Ernst: Generalmajor (01.08.41); (Luftwaffe), born 15.03.91 in Stendal, died 14.05.58 in Bad Harzburg. WWI: in G.A.S. as Oberleutnant and Leader of Schlachtstaffel 18. Attached to Staff of Luftkreis Kommando II 04.1934–02.1936, Commander of Flieger Gruppe 212 in Cottbus 03.1936–02.1937, Group Leader in R.L.M. 03.1937–03.1938, Department Chief in Personnel Office of R.L.M. 04.1938–06.1939. WWII: Amtsgruppe Chief of Personnel in R.L.M. 07.1939–04.1942, Military Replacement Inspector for Weimar 11.1942–05.1945. Awards: War Merit Cross 1st and 2nd Class with Swords, Pilot's Commemorative Badge, 1914 Iron Cross 1st and 2nd Class, Bavarian Military Service Order IV. Class with Swords, 1914 Wound Badge in Black, Austro-Hungarian Military Service Cross 3rd Class with War Decoration, 1914 Pilot's Badge, Cross of Honor.

Boner, Alfred: Generalmajor (01.08.44), (Luftwaffe); born 02.01.02 in Berlin, died 05.03.88 in Rhauderfehn. Attached to Staff of Reich War Ministry 10.1933–09.1934, attached to R.L.M. 10.1934–06.1935, Advisor and later Group Leader attached to Staff of Signals Chief in R.L.M. 07.1935–05.1939. WWII: Department Chief and Chief of Operations in Communications Office Group of O.K.L. 01.1939–12.1939, Signals Leader to II. Flieger Korps 01.1940–07.1942, Signals Leader to XII. Flieger Korps 08.1942–09.1943, Senior Signals Leader of Luftflotte Reich 02.1944–05.1945. Awards: Knight's Cross of the War Merit Cross with Swords 20.04.45, 1939 Iron Cross 1st and 2nd Class, War Merit Cross 1st and 2nd Class with Swords.

Bonger, Dr. Karl: General-Veterinar (01.06.42), (Heer); born 13.04.87 in Beetzendorf, died 15.01.70 in Beetzendorf. Medical veterinarian by profession. WWI: Ober-Veterinar (unit unknown). WWII: Division Veterinar to 1. Division 1938–08.1939, Korps Veterinar to XXXXV. Hoehere Kommando and later to LXXXIII. Armee Korps 08.1939–07.1943, retired 07.1943. Awards: War Merit Cross 1st and 2nd Class with Swords, German West Wall Medal, 1914 Iron Cross 1st and 2nd Class, Cross of Honor.

Bonin, Reimar von: Konteradmiral (01.01.41), (Kriegsmarine); born 03.10.90 in Berlin, died 18.05.76 in Bad Liebenzall. WWI: Kapitanleutnant and Chief of 11. Halb Flotilla. Chief of Organizational Department in Marineleitung 10.1933–09.1934, Chief of Staff to Inspectorate for Education of Kriegsmarine 09.1934–06.1937. WWII: Naval Attaché to German Embassy in Helsinki 07.1937–09.1944, Commander in Naval District Eutin then Vienna 11.1944–04.1945. Awards: War Merit Cross 1st and 2nd Class with Swords, Finnish Freedom Cross 1st Class with Swords, 1914 Iron Cross 1st and 2nd Class, Cross of Honor.

Bonness, Otto: SS-Brigadefuehrer und Generalmajor der Waffen-SS (30.01.45); born 04.04.89 in Salzdahlem, died 02.10.54 in Hagen. P-671592, SS-21294. WWI: Unterzahlmeister for Infanterie Regiment 25. Joined N.S.D.A.P. and S.S. in

1931. Attached to SS-Hauptamt 01.07.35, attached to Fuehrung Stab of SS-V.T. 01.12.36, attached to Staff of R.u.S.H.A. 01.12.37–01.12.38. WWII: attached to W.V.H.A. 30.01.42, Leader on Staff of H.S.S.P.F. Serbia 15.05.43, Leader on Staff of H.S.S.P.F. Italy 30.01.44, Leader on Staff of H.S.S.P.F. Serbia 09.11.44. Awards: War Merit Cross 1st and 2nd Class with Swords, Social Welfare Decoration 3rd Class, 1914 Iron Cross 2nd Class, Cross of Honor, German Horseman's Badge in Silver, Degen, Ring.

Borchers, Friedrich: Generalmajor (01.12.42), (Heer); born 11.12.79 in Glogau, died 25.01.59 in Horinghausen. WWI: Hauptmann and Commander of Pionier Bataillon 2. Heer Service Office 9, 10.1935–09.1936. WWII: attached to Staff of IX. Armee Korps 10.1936–08.1939, Commander of Festung Pionier Stab 20, 09.1939–10.1939, Commander of Senior Construction Staff 40, 10.1939–10.1941, Commander of Senior Construction Staff 14, 10.1941–08.1942, retired 01.1943. Awards: War Merit Cross 1st and 2nd Class with Swords, RK-Hohenzollern, 1914 Iron Cross 1st and 2nd Class, Cross of Honor.

Bordihn, Adolf: Generalleutnant (01.11.42), (Heer); born 24.01.89 in Deutsch-Krone, died 20.01.58 in Braunschweig. WWI: Oberleutnant with Formation Staff of Turkish 14. Pionier Bataillon. Promotion to Generalmajor 01.11.40. Attached to Fortress Inspection III 10.1935–09.1936. WWII: Fortress Inspector IV 10.1936–08.1939, Commander of Senior Construction Staff 12, 08.1939–12.1939, Fortress Pionier Leader IV then XIII 12.1939–01.1941, Pionier Leader to 15. Armee 01.941–05.1943, Commandant of Fortifications for Upper Rhine 05.1943–10.1944, Higher Pionier Leader to Lower Silesia 10.1944–05.1945. Awards: German Cross in Silver 30.10.43, War Merit Cross 1st and 2nd Class with Swords, General Assault Badge, 1914 Iron Cross 1st and 2nd Class, Cross of Honor.

Bork, Max-Hermann: Generalleutnant (01.7.44), (Heer); born 01.01.89 in Forsthaus, died 04.07.73 in Twielenfleth. WWI: Leutnant in Infanterie Regiment 176. Promotion to Generalmajor 01.04.43. Attached to Staff of Wehrkreis Kommando VI 10.1934–10.1935, Kompanie Chef in Infanterie Regiment 23, 10.1935–07.1936, Ia to 9. Division 08.1936–03.1938, Ia to 45. Division 04.1938–11.1938. WWII: attached to Abteilung 5 of Heeres General Staff in O.K.H. 11.1938–08.1939, Department Chief in Field Transport Matters of Heeres General Staff 01.1940–01.1942, Chief of Staff to LIII. Armee Korps 01.1942–02.1943, Chief of General Staff to 6. Armee 03.1943–04.1944, Commander of 47. Volks Grenadier Division 09.1944–03.1945. Awards: Knight's Cross 09.05.45, German Cross in Gold 16.08.42, 1939 Clasps to the 1914 Iron Cross 1st and 2nd Class, Eastern Front Medal, 1914 Iron Cross 1st and 2nd Class, 1914 Wound Badge in Black, Cross of Honor.

Bormann, Dr. Ernst: Generalmajor (01.10.44), (Luftwaffe); born 05.11.97 in Kirchbrack, died 01.08.60 in Duesseldorf. WWI: in G.A.S. as Leutnant in Jasta "Boelcke." Advisor in R.L.M. 09.1934–03.1935, Staffelkapitan in K.G. "Boelcke" 04.1935–05.1938, Commander of III. Gruppe, J.G. "Richthofen" 06.1938–10.1938. WWII: Commander of Gruppe I., Kampf Lehr Geschwader at Greifswald 11.1938–07.1940, Commander of Pilot Fuehrer Schule at Geblingen 08.1940–02.1941, Commander of K.G. 76, 02.1941–01.1943, Flieger Fuehrer of Crimea 02.1943–06.1943, Flughafenbereichs Commandant of 5-VIII 10.1944–5.1945. Awards: Oak Leaves 03.09.42 (119), Knight's Cross 05.10.41, 1939 Clasps to the 1914 Iron Cross 1st and 2nd Class, Eastern Front Medal, Bomber's Flight Clasp in Gold, 1939 Pilot's Badge, "Jagdstaffel Boelcke Nr. 2, 1916/18" Commemorative Cuff Band, Pilot's Commemorative Badge, Silesian Eagle 1st and 2nd Class, 1914 Iron Cross 1st and 2nd Class, 1914 Pilot's Badge, Cross of Honor.

Bormann, Ulrich: Generalmajor (30.01.45), (Heer); born 20.06.85 in Glatz, died 14.01.72 in Geisenheim. WWI: Hauptmann on Staff of Stage Inspection 18. WWII: Military District Commander of Hirschberg 10.1936–08.1941, Commander of Infanterie Ersatz Regiment 128 (mot.) 09.1941–07.1942, Commandant of Feldkommandantur 198, 11.1942–08.1944, Commandant of Feldkommandantur 593, 09.1944–05.1945. Awards: 1939 Clasps to the 1914 Iron Cross 1st and 2nd Class, War Merit Cross 1st and 2nd Class with Swords, 1914 Iron Cross 1st and 2nd Class, Austro-Hungarian Military Service Cross 3rd Class with War Decoration, Cross of Honor.

Borne, Kurt von dem: Vizeadmiral (01.09.42), (Kriegsmarine); born 24.11.85 in Bromberg, died 31.01.46 in Russian captivity. WWI: Kapitanleutnant and Artillery Officer on small cruiser *Coeln*. Promotion to Konteradmiral 01.07.40. Economic Officer attached to Marineleitung 10.1933–01.1936. WWII: Chief of Economic Department in O.K.M. 06.1936–11.1939, Amtsgruppe Chief for Economics in O.K.M. 11.1939–10.1942, Chief of Naval Armaments and Economic Office in O.K.M. 11.1942–07.1944, retired 09.1944. Awards: German Cross in Silver 31.07.44, War Merit Cross 1st and 2nd Class with Swords, 1914 Iron Cross 1st and 2nd Class, Bavarian Military Service Order IV. Class with Swords, Johann Ritter Order, Cross of Honor.

Bornemann, Karl: Generalleutnant z.V. (01.06.41), (Heer); born 15.09.85 in Znain, died 20.02.79 in Vienna. WWI: Hauptmann and Ia to Austrian 10. Gebirgs Brigade. Promotion to Generalmajor z.V. 01.08.39. Transferred to German Wehrmacht 03.1938. WWII: Fuehrer Res. in O.K.H. 04.1938–08.1939, Commander of Division 148, 09.1939–01.1940, Commander of z.b.V. Division 442, 01.1940–01.1944, Wehrmacht Commander of Wuerzburg 04.1944–05.1945. Awards: German Cross in

Gold 23.02.43, 1939 Iron Cross 1st Class, 1939 Clasp to the 1914 Iron Cross 2nd Class, Infantry Assault Badge in Silver, 1914 Iron Cross 2nd Class, Cross of Honor.

Bornscheuer, Paul: Generalmajor (01.12.44), (Heer); born 20.08.92 in Theodorshalle, died 30.09.83 in Bruehl. WWI: Leutnant and Batterie Officer in Feld Artillerie Regiment 80. Attached to Staff of Artillerie Regiment 19, 04.1936–10.1936, Batterie Chef in Artillerie Regiment 9, 10.1936–08.1938. WWII: Commander of II. Abteilung, Artillerie Regiment 70, 11.1938–04.1940, Commander of Artillerie Regiment 311, 05.1940–10.1940, Commander of Artillerie Regiment 146, 10.1940–10.1942, Fuehrer Res. in O.K.H. 10.1942–09.1943, Commander of Artillerie 316, 03.1944–05.1945. Awards: German Cross in Gold 19.09.42, 1939 Clasps to the 1914 Iron Cross 1st and 2nd Class, German Army High Command Commendation Certificate 27.10.44, General Assault Badge, 1914 Iron Cross 1st and 2nd Class, Cross of Honor.

Borowietz, Willibald: Generalleutnant (01.05.43), (Heer); born 17.09.93 in Ratibor, died 01.07.45 from accident at Clinton, Mississippi P.O.W. Camp. WWI: Oberleutnant and Bataillon Adjutant in Infanterie Regiment 156. Promotion to Generalmajor 01.01.43. Attached to Staff of Kraftfahrtruppen Schule 10.1935–10.1937, attached to Staff of Panzertruppen Schule 10.1937–01.1939. WWII: attached to Kommando Stab of Chief of Schnellen Truppen in O.K.H. 02.1939–09.1939, Commander of Panzer Jaeger Bataillon 50, 09.1939–06.1941, Commander of Schuetzen Regiment 10 (later Brigade) 06.1941–11.1942, Commander of 15. Panzer Division 11.1942–05.1943, captured 05.1943. Awards: Oak Leaves 10.05.43 (235), Knight's Cross 24.07.41, German Cross in Gold 14.06.42, 1939 Clasps to the 1914 Iron Cross 1st and 2nd Class, German Army High Command Commendation Certificate 12.04.41, General Assault Badge, Eastern Front Medal, Silesian Eagle 1st and 2nd Class, 1914 Iron Cross 1st and 2nd Class, 1914 Wound Badge in Black, Cross of Honor.

Borowski, Heinrich: Generalmajor (01.04.41), (Heer); born 23.06.80 in Mewe, died 08.04.63 in Celle. WWI: Hauptmann and Commander of I. Abteilung, Feld Artillerie Regiment 403. Attached to Military Replacement Inspection Elbing 10.1935–03.1939. WWII: Artillery Instructor for Landwehr Commander of Elbing 04.1939–09.1939, Commander of Artillerie Regiment 228, 09.1939–12.1940, Commander of Artillerie Regiment 85, 12.1940–04.1941, Commander of 704. Infanterie Division 04.1941–09.1942, retired 11.1942. Awards: 1939 Clasps to the 1914 Iron Cross 1st and 2nd Class, General Assault Badge, 1914 Iron Cross 1st and 2nd Class, 1194 Wound Badge in Black, Cross of Honor.

Both, Friedrich von: Generalmajor z.V. (01.06.42), (Heer); born 22.02.71 in Marburg, died 31.10.45 from accident in Kassel. WWI: Major and Commander of Feld Artillerie Regiment 278. WWII: Wehrmacht Commander of Bordeaux and later Commander of Truppenubungsplatz at Wildflecken 07.1940–06.1942, retired 11.1942. Awards: War Merit Cross 1st and 2nd Class with Swords, RK-Hohenzollern, 1914 Iron Cross 1st and 2nd Class, 1914 Wound Badge in Black, Cross of Honor.

Both, Kuno-Hans von: General der Infanterie (01.06.40), (Heer); born 09.04.84 in Zabern, died 22.05.55 in Ehlen. WWI: Hauptmann and Commander of I. Bataillon, Res. Infanterie Regiment 90. Promotions to Generalmajor 01.01.37, Generalleutnant 01.10.38. Commander of Infanterie Regiment at Luebeck 10.1934–10.1935, Commander of Infanterie Regiment 6, 10.1935–10.1936, Commander of Kriegsschule at Hannover 10.1936–11.1938. WWII: Commander of 21. Infanterie Division 11.1938–10.1939, Commander of I. Armee Korps 10.1939–04.1943, Security Troop Commander for Heeresgruppe Nord 04.1943–04.1944, Rear Troop Commander for Heeresgruppe Sud 07.1944–05.1945. Awards: Knight's Cross 09.07.41, German Cross in Gold 09.09.42, 1939 Clasps to the 1914 Iron Cross 1st and 2nd Class, Infantry Assault Badge in Bronze, Eastern Front Medal, Pour le Mérite 10.04.18, RK-Hohenzollern, 1914 Iron Cross 1st and 2nd Class, 1914 Wound Badge in Black, Cross of Honor.

General der Infanterie Kuno-Hans von Both. (Bundesarchiv)

Bothmer, Richard von: Generalmajor (01.12.44), (Heer); born 27.05.90 in Dieuze, died 10.03.45 (suicide) in Jungsdorf. WWI: Oberleutnant in Infanterie Regiment 138. Commander of I. Bataillon, Infanterie Regiment at Kassel 10.1934–10.1935, Commander of I. Bataillon, Infanterie Regiment 87, 10.1935–10.1936, Commander of I. Bataillon, Infanterie Regiment 111, 10.1936–11.1938. WWII: Wehrmacht Commander of Salzburg 11.1938–08.1939, Commander of Infanterie Regiment 499, 08.1939–04.1941, German Locations Officer in Naples 04.1941–01.942, Commandant of Feldkommandantur 768, 01.1942–03.1943, Commandant of Feldkommandantur 1032, 09.1943–12.1944, Battle Commander for Bonn 12.1944–03.1945. Awards: 1939 Clasps to the 1914 Iron Cross 1st and 2nd Class, Infantry Assault Badge in Silver, RK-Hohenzollern, 1914 Iron Cross 1st and 2nd Class, 1914 Wound Badge in Black, Cross of Honor.

Botsch, Walter: Generalleutnant (01.09.44), (Heer); born 27.02.97 in Braunsbach am Kocher, died 07.01.69 in Schwabisch Gmund. WWI: Leutnant and Chief of 3. M.G. Kompanie, Infanterie Regiment 124. Promotion to Generalmajor 01.09.43. Attached to Staff of Wehrkreis Kommando V (later V. Armee Korps) 10.1934–09.1936, Kompanie Chef in Infanterie Regiment 35, 10.1936–09.1937. WWII: attached to Military Economic Staff in Wehrmacht Amt of Reich War Ministry (later O.K.W.) 09.1937–10.1939, Ia to XXX. Armee Korps 10.1939–10.1940, Chief of Staff to XXX. Armee Korps 10.1940–06.1943, Chief of General Staff to 19. Armee 08.1943–01.1945. Awards: Knight's Cross 08.05.45, German Cross in Gold 22.06.42, 1939 Clasps to the 1914 Iron Cross 1st and 2nd Class, Eastern Front Medal, Crimea Shield, 1914 Iron Cross 1st and 2nd Class, 1914 Wound Badge in Silver, Cross of Honor.

Botzheim, Erich Freiherr von: Generalleutnant z.V. (1940), (Heer); born 10.01.71 in Schloss Mattsies, died 28.03.58 in Munich. WWI: Oberstleutnant and Commander of Bavarian Artillerie Regiment 13. Promotion to Reichswehr Generalmajor 16.07.23. WWII: recalled to military service 08.1940, Commandant of P.O.W. Camp Oflag IV 08.1940–02.1941, P.O.W. Commander for Wehrkreis Kommando IV 02.1941–06.1942, retired 08.1942. Awards: War Merit Cross 1st and 2nd Class with Swords, Prussian Red Eagle Order IV. Class with Swords, RK-Hohenzollern, 1914 Iron Cross 1st and 2nd Class, Bavarian Military Service Order 3rd Class with Swords, Cross of Honor.

Bourquin, Alexander: Generalleutnant (01.08.44), (Heer); born 21.05.96 in Nazereth, died 05.12.66 in Braunschweig. WWI: Leutnant in Infanterie Regiment 103. Promotion to Generalmajor 01.01.44. Kompanie Chef in Infanterie Regiment at Plauen 10.1934–10.1935, Kompanie Chef in Infanterie Regiment 31, 10.1935–10.1936, Instructor at Kriegsschule in Munich 10.1936–04.1938. WWII: attached to Command Staff of Kriegsschule at Wiener-Neustadt 04.1938–08.1939, attached to Staff of Hoehere Kommando z.b.V. XXXVII 09.1939–11.1939, Commander of I. Bataillon, Infanterie Regiment 282, 01.1940–10.1940, Commander of Infanterie Regiment 446, 10.1940–09.1941, Offizier Schule Instructor followed by Wehrmacht Commander of Wiener-Neustadt 12.1941–01.1943, Deputy General of Ost Truppen (Foreign Volunteers from Eastern Europe) 01.1943–09.1943, Commander of 114. Jaeger Division 12.1943–09.1944, Inspector of Foreign Volunteer Units in O.K.H. 01.1945–05.1945. Awards: 1939 Clasps to the 1914 Iron Cross 1st and 2nd Class, Infantry Assault Badge in Silver, RK-Sachen Military St. Heinrich's Order 01.06.17, 1914 Iron Cross 1st and 2nd Class, Cross of Honor.

Boysen, Wolf: Generalleutnant (01.09.42), (Heer); born 26.04.85 in Bitsch, died 20.01.71 in Guetersloh. WWI: Hauptmann and Commander of I. Bataillon,

Infanterie Regiment 170. Promotion to Generalmajor 01.08.39. Commander of I. Bataillon, Infanterie Regiment 103, 10.1935–09.1936, attached to Staff of Infanterie Regiment 30, 10.1936–03.1937. WWII: Commander of Infanterie Regiment 7, 04.1937–10.1939, Military Replacement Commander for Weimar 12.1939–05.1942, Military Replacement Inspector for Kattowitz 05.1942–02.1945. Awards: 1939 Clasps to the 1914 Iron Cross 1st and 2nd Class, RK-Hohenzollern, 1914 Iron Cross 1st and 2nd Class, Cross of Honor.

Brabaender, Hans: Generalleutnant (01.01.43), (Heer); born 28.11.89 in Russow, died 26.10.82 in Hamburg. WWI: Oberleutnant in 2. Jaeger Bataillon. Promotion to Generalmajor 01.11.41. Commander of Ausbildungs Bataillon, Infanterie Regiment at Giessen 10.1934–10.1935, Commander of II. Bataillon, Infanterie Regiment 57, 10.1935–01.1938. WWII: Commander of Jaeger Regiment 68, 02.1938–09.1939, Commander of Jaeger Regiment 71, 10.1939–12.1939, Commander of Infanterie Regiment 267, 12.1939–12.1940, Commander of Infanterie Regiment 241, 12.1940–12.1941, Commander of 416. Infanterie Division 12.1941–06.1943, Commander of 270. Infanterie Division 08.1943–05.1945. Awards: 1939 Clasps to the 1914 Iron Cross 1st and 2nd Class, Infantry Assault Badge in Silver, 1914 Iron Cross 1st and 2nd Class, Cross of Honor.

Braemer, Walter: General der Kavallerie z.V. (01.09.42), (Heer); born 07.01.83 in Koenigsberg, died 13.06.55 in Hamburg. P-4012329, SS-223910. WWI: Rittmeister on Staff of XXVI. Reserve Korps. Promotions to Reichswehr Generalmajor 01.10.32, Generalleutnant z.V. 01.07.41. Joined N.S.D.A.P. and S.S., SS-Gruppenfuehrer 20.04.44. Recalled to military service 07.1938. WWII: Commandant of Feldkommandantur 580, 08.1939–05.1941, Wehrmacht Commander of Ostland (Eastern Territories) 06.1941–04.1944, Fuehrer Res. in O.K.H. 04.1944–01.1945. Awards: German Cross in Silver (date unknown), 1939 Clasps to the 1914 Iron Cross 1st and 2nd Class, War Merit Cross 1st and 2nd Class with Swords, RK-Hohenzollern, 1914 Iron Cross 1st and 2nd Class, Degen, Ring.

Braeuer, Bruno: General der Fallschirmtruppe (01.06.44), (Luftwaffe); born 04.02.93 in Willmansdorf, died 20.05.47 (executed) in Athens. WWI: Senior NCO in Infanterie Regiment 155. Promotions to Generalmajor 01.09.41, Generalleutnant 06.09.42. Commander of I. Bataillon, Luftwaffe Regiment "General Goering" 11.1935–08.1937, Commander of IV. (Fallschirm) Bataillon, Luftwaffe Regiment "General Goering" 09.1937–03.1938, Commander of I. Bataillon, Fallschirmjaeger Regiment 1, 04.1938–12.1938. WWII: Commander of Fallschirmjaeger Regiment 1, 01.1939–09.1942, Commander of Festung Kreta and of Luftgau Stab Kreta 02.1943–05.1944, Fuehrer Res. in O.K.L. 06.1944–03.1945. Awards: Knight's Cross 24.05.40, German Cross in Gold 31.03.42, 1939 Clasps to the 1914 Iron Cross 1st and 2nd Class, Ground Combat Badge, Parachute Badge, Kreta Cuff Band, Afrika Cuff Band, 1914 Iron Cross 1st and 2nd Class, Cross of Honor.

Braeuer, Walter: General-Stabsintendant der Marine (01.08.43), (Kriegsmarine); born 02.11.80 in Giesmannsdorf, died 06.01.55 in Bad Harzburg. Administrative officer by profession. WWI: Hauptmann der Res. on Staff of VI. Armee Korps. Promotion to General-Intendant der Marine 21.03.42. Service unknown 1919–01.1939. WWII: retired in 01.1939 but reactivated 03.1942, Chief Intendant to Wehrmacht in Romania 04.1942–06.1944, hospital stay at Potsdam 08.1944–02.1945. Awards: German Cross in Silver 12.10.44, War Merit Cross 1st and 2nd Class with Swords, 1914 Iron Cross 1st and 2nd Class, Cross of Honor.

Brahms, Dr. Wilhelm: Admiral-Arzt z.V. (01.02.41), (Kriegsmarine); born 14.08.80 in Sande, died 13.12.66 in Bremen. Medical doctor by profession. WWI: Marine-Oberstabsarzt and Ship Physician. WWII: recalled to military service 08.1939, Chief Physician of Naval Hospital at Bremen 09.1939–05.1941, Chief Physician of Naval Hospital at Bedburg-Hau 06.1941–01.1944, retired 01.1944. Awards: War Merit Cross 1st and 2nd Class with Swords, 1914 Iron Cross 1st and 2nd Class, Cross of Honor.

Brakert, Otto: Generalmajor (10.04.43), (Luftwaffe); born 20.12.94 in Grevesmuehlen, died 30.04.70 in Munich. WWI: Leutnant der Res. in Feld Artillerie Regiment 269. Batterie Chef in Flak Abteilung in Luebeck 04.1935–06.1936. WWII: Fliegerhorst Commandant of Koelleda 07.1936–07.1941, attached to Staff of Luftzeuggruppe at Rostov 11.1941–10.1942, Commander of Luftzeuggruppe for Athens 01.1943–06.1943, Truppe Commander of Luftgau Kommando XVII 03.1944–05.1945. Awards: 1939 Clasp to the 1914 Iron Cross 2nd Class, War Merit Cross 1st and 2nd Class with Swords, 1914 Iron Cross 2nd Class, Cross of Honor.

Brand, Albrecht: Generalleutnant (01.10.39), (Heer); born 14.01.88 in Neisse, died 31.12.69 in Ebernberg. WWI: Hauptmann attached to Armee General Staff. Promotion to Generalmajor 01.10.37. Commander of Artillerie Regiment at Naumburg 10.1934–10.1935, Commander of Artillerie Regiment 14, 10.1935–06.1936. WWII: Commandant of Fortifications at Koenigsberg 06.1936–08.1939, Commander of 311. Infanterie Division 08.1939–11.1939, Commandant of Fortifications at Koenigsberg 11.1939–12.1941, Commandant of Fortifications for East Prussia 12.1941–07.1943, Chief of Heeres Museum 10.1943–05.1945. Awards: 1939 Clasps to the 1914 Iron Cross 1st and 2nd Class, 1914 Iron Cross 1st and 2nd Class, 1914 Wound Badge in Silver, Cross of Honor.

Brand, Fritz: General der Artillerie (01.08.40), (Heer); born 22.04.89 in Berlin, died 26.11.67 in Weilheim. WWI: Hauptmann attached to Armee General Staff. Promotions to Generalmajor 01.08.37, Generalleutnant 01.08.39. Commander of

Artillerie Regiment at Schwerin 10.1934–10.1935, Commander of Artillerie Regiment 12, 10.1935–10.1937, Commander of Artillerie Regiment at Jueterbog 10.1937–02.1938. WWII: Inspector of Kriegsschulen 03.1938–08.1939, Commander of 78. Jaeger Division 09.1939–10.1939, General der Artillerie attached to O.B. of Heeres 10.1939–10.1943, Fuehrer Res. in O.K.H. 10.1943–03.1945. Awards: Knight's Cross of the War Merit Cross with Swords 24.12.44, German Cross in Silver 23.09.43, 1939 Clasps to the 1914 Iron Cross 1st and 2nd Class, 1914 Iron Cross 1st and 2nd Class, Cross of Honor.

General der Artillerie Fritz Brand. (Josef Charita)

Brandenberger, Erich: General der Panzertruppe (01.08.43), (Heer); born 18.07.92 in Augsburg, died 21.06.55 in Bonn. WWI: Oberleutnant and Batterie Chef in Bavarian Feld Artillerie Regiment 6. Promotions to Generalmajor 01.08.40, Generalleutnant 01.08.42. Group Leader in Ausbildungs Abteilung of Reichswehr Ministry (later Reich War Ministry) 09.1933–10.1935, attached to Abteilung 4 in General Staff of Heeres 10.1935–10.1936, Commander of Artillerie Regiment 74, 10.1936–01.1939. WWII: Chief of Staff to Grenztruppen Kommando Eifel 03.1939–09.1939, Chief of Staff to XXIII. Armee Korps 09.1939–02.1941, Commander of 8. Panzer Division 02.1941–01.1943, attached to LIX. Armee Korps 01.1943–03.1943, Commander of XVII. Armee Korps 08.1943–11.1943, Commander of XXIX. Armee Korps 11.1943–06.1944, Oberbefehlshaber of 7. Armee 08.1944–02.1945. Awards: Oak Leaves 12.11.43 (324), Knight's Cross 15.07.41, 1939 Clasps to the 1914 Iron Cross 1st and 2nd Class, Tank Assault Badge in Silver, Eastern Front Medal, West Wall Medal, 1914 Iron Cross 1st and 2nd Class, 1914 Wound Badge in Black, Cross of Honor.

General der Panzertruppe Erich Brandenberger, left. (Bundesarchiv)

Brandes, Ferdinand: Ministerialdirektor (04.05.42), (Kriegsmarine); born 30.04.79 in Bad Salzuflen, died 19.04.74 in Bad Salzuflen. WWI: Naval Construction Department of Reichsmarineamt (rank unknown). WWII: recalled to military service 08.1939, Amtsgruppe Chief for Ships-Machinery Construction (K II) in O.K.M. 10.1939–11.1944, retired 12.1944. Awards: German Cross in Silver 17.01.45, War Merit Cross 1st and 2nd Class with Swords.

Brandes, Friedrich: Naval Senior Construction Director (09.11.44), (Kriegsmarine); born 02.12.79 in Nordassel, died 11.11.50 in Nordassel. Scientist by profession. WWI: Scientific Assistant and Official in Torpedo Lab of Reichsmarine. Service unknown 1919–02.1934. WWII: Director then President of Naval Chemical Physical Test Institute 03.1934–05.1945. Awards: War Merit Cross 1st and 2nd Class with Swords.

Brandt, Arthur: Generalmajor (01.01.43), (Luftwaffe); born 12.12.87 in Stolbey, died 13.04.67 in Birkenwerder. WWI: in G.A.S. as Hauptmann der Res. (unit unknown). Commander of Fliegergruppe Jueterbog 05.1933–12.1935, Commander of Luftzeug Office at Schwerin-Gerries 01.1936–12.1937, attached to Legion Condor 01.1938–03.1938. WWII: Commandant of Luftzeuggruppe 7, 04.1938–1942, Flughafenbereichs Commandant of 8-XII 1942–08.1943, attached to Flieger Ersatz Bataillon in Luftgau Kommando XII 09.1943–05.1944, attached to Luftwaffe Kommando at Ploesti oil fields 06.1944–08.1944, captured 08.1944. Awards: War Merit Cross 1st and 2nd Class with Swords, Spanish Cross in Bronze with Swords, Pilot's Commemorative Badge, RK-Hohenzollern, 1914 Iron Cross 1st and 2nd Class, 1914 Pilot's Badge, Cross of Honor.

Brandt, Friedrich-Wilhelm: Generalleutnant (01.12.34), (Heer); born 17.08.79 in Naumburg, died 13.01.39 in Wuerzburg. WWI: Hauptmann and Artillery Staff Officer attached to XXV. Res. Korps. Promotion to Reichswehr Generalmajor 01.4.33. Commander of 15. Division 10.1935–03.1936, retired 03.1936. Awards: RK-Hohenzollern, 1914 Iron Cross 1st and 2nd Class, Cross of Honor.

Brandt, Georg: General der Kavallerie z.V. (01.12.40), (Heer); born 24.08.76 in Wolterdorf, died 21.04.45 (suicide) in Berlin. WWI: Major and Chief of Staff to z.b.V. Kommando 67. Promotions to Reichswehr Generalmajor 01.02.29, Reichswehr Generalleutnant 01.02.30. WWII: recalled to military service 08.1939, Commander of Hoehere Kommando XXXIII 08.1939–05.1942, retired 08.1942. Awards: 1939 Clasps to the 1914 Iron Cross 1st and 2nd Class, RK-Hohenzollern, 1914 Iron Cross 1st and 2nd Class, Cross of Honor.

Brandt, Heinz: Generalmajor (01.07.44), (Heer); born 11.03.07 in Berlin, died 21.07.44 of wounds from 20.07.44 attempt on Hitler's life in Rastenberg. Attached to Staff of Kriegsschule 10.1936–03.1938, attached to Staff of 25. Division 04.1938–03.1939. WWII: Chief Personnel Officer (IIa) of 25. Infanterie Division 04.1939–10.1939, Ia to 297. Infanterie Division 02.1940–11.1940, Ia in Operations Department of O.K.H. 11.1940–07.1944. Awards: 1939 Iron Cross 1st and 2nd Class, War Merit Cross 1st and 2nd Class with Swords, 20.07.44 Wound Badge in Gold (posthumously), German Olympic Games Decoration 2nd Class.

Brandt, Prof. Dr. Karl: SS-Gruppenfuehrer und Generalleutnant der Waffen-SS (20.04.44); born 08.01.04 in Muelhausen, died 02.06.48 (executed) at Landsberg Prison. P-1009617, SS-260353. Medical doctor by profession. Joined N.S.D.A.P. in 1932, joined S.S. in 1934. Promotion to SS-Brigadefuehrer 30.01.43. Attached to Staff of SS-Oberabschnitte Ost 01.10.34–01.07.35, Leader on Staff of SS-Hauptamt 01.12.36–12.1938. WWII: attached to "LSSAH" 01.10.42, attached to SS-Fuehrungshauptamt 15.05.43–05.1945 SS-DALs, Personal Escort Physician to Hitler, Generalkommissar of Fuehrer for Sanitation and Health 08.1944–05.1945, Heer General-Arzt der Res., performed medical experiments in concentration camps. Awards: Golden Party Badge (honorary), SA-Sports Badge in Bronze, Degen, Ring.

Brasack, Curt: SS-Brigadefuehrer und Generalmajor der Waffen-SS (30.01.45); born 06.04.92 in Schoenebeck, died 28.09.78 in Hamburg. P-276498, SS-8216. WWI: Leutnant der Res. attached to Feld Artillerie Regiment 27. Joined N.S.D.A.P. in 1930, joined S.S. in 1931. Leader of SS-Fuss Standarte 91, 01.10.34–01.12.36. WWII: Leader of SS-Abschnitte XXX 01.12.37–01.12.38–09.11.44, Commander of SS-Artillerie Regiment "Das Reich," Commander of SS-Artillerie Regiment 54 "Nederland," Artillery Commander of VII. SS-Gebirgs Korps, Artillery Commander of IV. SS-Panzer Korps. Awards: German Cross in Gold 19.10.44, 1939 Clasps to the 1914 Iron Cross 1st and 2nd Class, General Assault Badge, 1939 Wound Badge in Black, SA-Rally at Braunschweig Badge of Honor, 1914 Iron Cross 1st and 2nd Class, Cross of Honor, Reich Sports Badge in Gold, SA-Sports Badge in Bronze, Degen, Ring.

Brauchitsch, Walther von: Generalfeldmarschall (19.07.40), (Heer); born 04.10.81 in Berlin, died 18.10.48 in Hamburg. WWI: Major on Staff of Guards Res. Corps. Promotions to Reichswehr Generalmajor 01.10.31, Reichswehr Generalleutnant 01.10.33, General der Artillerie 20.04.36, Generaloberst 04.02.38. Befehlshaber of Wehrkreis Kommando I and Commander of I. Armee Korps 06.1935–03.1937, Befehlshaber of Gruppen Kommando 4, 04.1937–01.1938. WWII: Oberbefehlshaber of German Army 02.1938–12.1941, placed in reserve at disposal of the Fuehrer 12.1941–05.1945. Awards: Golden Party Badge (honorary), Knight's Cross 30.09.39, 1939 Clasps to the 1914 Iron Cross 1st and 2nd Class, Breast Star to the German Red Cross Decoration, Grand Cross of

Generalfeldmarschall Walther von Brauchitsch. (Michael Miller)

the Order of the White Rose of Finland with Breast Star and Swords, Grand Cross of the Finnish Cross of Freedom with Breast Star and Swords, RK-Hohenzollern, 1914 Iron Cross 1st and 2nd Class, Cross of Honor.

Brauer, August: Generalmajor z.V. (01.10.41), (Heer); born 11.11.80 in Lueneburg, died 22.03.53 in Verden. WWI: Oberleutnant on Staff of XV. Armee Korps. Commander of Military District Kommando at Bremen 04.1934–12.1937, retired 12.1937. WWII: recalled to military service 08.1939, Commander of Artillerie Regiment 269, 09.1939–02.1940, Commander of Artillerie Regiment 554, 02.1940–08.1940, Commander of Artillerie Regiment 187, 08.1940–11.1940, Commander of Artillerie Regiment 332, 11.1940–03.1943, retired 03.1943. Awards: 1939 Clasps to the 1914 Iron Cross 1st and 2nd Class, General Assault Badge, 1914 Iron Cross 1st and 2nd Class, Cross of Honor.

Brauer, Johannes-Oskar: Generalmajor (01.10.44), (Heer); born 11.03.95 in Stargard, died 15.11.80 in Bremen. WWI: Leutnant in Infanterie Regiment 147. E-Officer attached to Military Economic Inspection VI in Muenster 07.1936–01.1938. WWII: Kompanie Chef in Infanterie Regiment 96, 02.1938–08.1939, Commander of III. Bataillon, Infanterie Regiment 368, 08.1939–07.1942, Commander of Infanterie Regiment 397, 07.1942–07.1944, Commander of 562. Volks Grenadier Division 07.1944–01.1945. Awards: German Cross in Gold 03.08.42, 1939 Iron Cross 1st Class, 1939 Clasp to the 1914 Iron Cross 2nd Class, Infantry Assault Badge in Silver, Eastern Front Medal, Demjansk Shield, 1914 Iron Cross 2nd Class, 1914 Wound Badge in Black, Cross of Honor.

Braumueller, Erwin: Generalmajor (01.11.43), (Luftwaffe); born 03.10.81 in Berlin, died 13.02.55 in Travemuende. WWI: Hauptmann and Commander of 30. Fuss Artillerie Bataillon. Advisor attached to Technische Amt of R.L.M. 01.1935–12.1938. WWII: Chief of Military Economics Department (G L 2) in R.L.M. 12.1938–06.1940, Armaments Inspector A for North-West France 07.1940–04.1941, Chief of Military Economic Staff Southeast in Belgrade 04.1941–04.1945. Awards: War Merit Cross 1st and 2nd Class with Swords, 1914 Iron Cross 1st and 2nd Class, Austro-Hungarian Military Service Cross 3rd Class with War Decoration, Cross of Honor.

Braumueller, Hans: Generalmajor (01.06.41), (Heer); born 03.03.83 in Hannover, died 04.03.56 in Langelsheim. WWI: Hauptmann and Commander of II. Bataillon, Feld Artillerie Regiment 10. WWII: Director of Psychological Test Center for Wehrkreis IX 05.1933–03.1944, retired 03.1944. Awards: War Merit Cross 1st and 2nd Class with Swords, 1914 Iron Cross 1st and 2nd Class, 1914 Wound Badge in Black, Cross of Honor.

Braun, Georg: Generalleutnant (01.11.41), (Heer); born 27.10.87 in Oberrode, died 14.11.41 in action near Kharkov. WWI: Hauptmann and Bataillon Commander in Res. Infanterie Regiment 83. Promotion to Generalmajor 01.12.39. Commander of III. Bataillon, Infanterie Regiment 15, 12.1935–09.1936, Instructor at Kriegsschule Dresden 10.1936–07.1937, Commander of Infanterie Regiment 73, 08.1937–09.1938. WWII: Commander of Kreigsschule Hannover 10.1938–09.1939, Commander of 68. Infanterie Division 09.1939–11.1941. Awards: 1939 Clasps to the 1914 Iron Cross 1st and 2nd Class, Infantry Assault Badge in Silver, 1939 Wound Badge in Gold, RK-Hohenzollern, 1914 Iron Cross 1st and 2nd Class, Cross of Honor.

Braun, Julius: Generalleutnant (01.04.44), (Heer); born 15.03.95 in Erlangen, died 08.05.62 in Ellingholfen. WWI: Oberleutnant and Commander of Bayern Gebirgs Artillerie Batterie 10. Promotion to Generalmajor 01.04.43. Commander of I. Abteilung, Artillerie Regiment at Nuremberg 10.1934–10.1935, Commander of III. Abteilung, Artillerie Regiment 7, 10.1935–11.1938, Commander of II. Abteilung, Artillerie Regiment 7, 11.1938–07.1939. WWII: Commander of Artillerie Regiment 115, 08.1939–02.1941, Commander of Artillerie Regiment 114, 02.1941–09.1942, Commander of Artillerie 134, 09.1942–04.1943, Commander of 4. Infanterie Division 08.1943–05.1944, Senior Commander of Artillerie 318, 09.1944–05.1945. Awards: German Cross in Gold 26.12.41, 1939 Clasps to the 1914 Iron Cross 1st and 2nd Class, General Assault Badge, Crimea Shield, Commander's Cross of the Romanian Order with Crown and Swords, 1914 Iron Cross 1st and 2nd Class, Bavarian Military Service Order IV. Class with Swords, Cross of Honor.

Braune, Friedrich: Konteradmiral (01.01.41), (Kriegsmarine); born 06.10.89 in Fehrbellin, died 29.06.71 in Flensburg. WWI: Oberleutnant zur See and Watch Officer on torpedo boat *V-187*, P.O.W. 08.1914–11.1918. Chief of Ship Stamm Division of North Sea 10.1932–03.1935, Chief of Staff to Staff II of Admiral of North Sea 04.1935–09.1936, Commander of Schiff Stamm Regiment for Eastern Sea 10.1936–09.1937, Commander of 1. Schiff Stamm Regiment 10.1937–10.1938. WWII: Commander of Naval District Commando in Kolberg 11.1938–12.1939, Officer Judge of Reichs War Court 12.1939–03.1941, Senior Director of Naval Shipyard at Bergen 04.1941–05.1942, Judge for Jury Court in Berlin 09.1942–04.1945. Awards: War Merit Cross 1st and 2nd Class without Swords, 1914 Iron Cross 1st and 2nd Class, 1914 Naval Wound Badge in Black, Cross of Honor.

Brauner von Haydringen, Josef: Generalleutnant (01.03.41), (Heer); born 04.10.86 in Tulln, died 27.04.54 at Perov-Uralsk P.O.W. Camp. WWI: Hauptmann on Staff of Austrian 115. Infanterie Brigade. Promotion to Generalmajor 01.04.39. Transferred to German Wehrmacht 03.1938, attached to Infanterie Regiment 6, 07.1938.

WWII: Commander of Infanterie Regiment 132, 08.1938–11.1939, Chief of Staff to Grenz Abschnitte Sud 02.1940–05.1940, Chief of Staff to Military Commander in General Government 05.1940–05.1941, Commander of 101. Leichte Division 06.1941–04.1942, Commander of 187. Infanterie Division 08.1942–01.1944, Commandant of Feldkommandantur 531, 05.1944–05.1945. Awards: German Cross in Gold 23.01.42, 1939 Iron Cross 1st Class, 1939 Clasp to the 1914 Iron Cross 2nd Class, Infanterie Assault Badge in Silver, Eastern Front Medal, 1914 Iron Cross 2nd Class, Cross of Honor.

Brause, Adolf-Hans: Generalmajor (01.08.42), (Heer); born 09.10.77 in Farnrode, died 19.11.59 in Berlin. WWI: Hauptmann on Staff of Chief of Field Railway Affairs. WWII: Advisor in Heeres Armaments Office of O.K.H. 02.1938–08.1939, attached to Staff of Chief for Heeres Armaments and O.B. of Ersatz Army 09.1939–09.1942, retired 09.1942. Awards: War Merit Cross 1st and 2nd Class with Swords, 1939 Wound Badge in Black, 1914 Iron Cross 1st and 2nd Class, Cross of Honor.

Brause, Franz-Hermann: Generalmajor (28.02.43), (Heer); born 02.01.82 in Chemnitz, died 02.08.69 in Gifhorn. WWI: Hauptmann and Bataillon Commander in Res. Feld Artillerie Regiment 24. Recalled to military service 07.1938. WWII: without assignment 07.1938–08.1939, Advisor in General Heeres Office of O.K.H. 09.1939–01.1943, retired 02.1943. Awards: War Merit Cross 1st and 2nd Class with Swords, 1914 Iron Cross 1st and 2nd Class, Cross of Honor.

Brednow, Fritz: General-Intendant (01.01.37), (Heer); born 20.01.87 in Neu-Stettin, died 23.08.64 in Goslar. Administrative Officer by profession. WWI: service unknown. WWII: Intendant to Wehrkreis VIII 01.1937–04.1943, retired 05.1943. Awards: War Merit Cross 1st and 2nd Class with Swords, 1914 Iron Cross 2nd Class, Cross of Honor.

Bredow, Hasso von: Konteradmiral (01.01.41), (Kriegsmarine); born 31.03.83 in Neuruppin, died 16.10.66 in Koeln. WWI: Kapitanleutnant and First Artillery Officer on liner *Koenig Albert*. WWII: Leader of Psychological Naval Office in Kiel 10.1933–09.1939, Commander for Office of Qualification Tests at Kiel 10.1939–06.1940, Naval Commander for Pomeranian Coast 06.1940–03.1943, retired 05.1943. Awards: 1939 Clasps to the 1914 Iron Cross 2nd Class, Red Eagle Order IV. Class, RK-Sachsen Albrecht Order 1st Class with Swords, 1914 Iron Cross 1st and 2nd Class, Johann Ritter Order, Cross of Honor.

Bredow, Hermann von: Konteradmiral (01.11.42), (Kriegsmarine); born 04.11.93 in Wilhelmshaven, died 10.03.54 in Westerland. WWI: Leutnant zur See and Outpost Commander. Attached to Weapons Department in Marineleitung/O.K.M.

10.1933–11.1935, Commandant of Marine Artillerie Schiff Schule *Brummer* 02.1936–08.1937. WWII: Commander of 5. Schiff Stamm Abteilung 01.1938–04.1939, Naval Fortress Commander of Memel 04.1939–07.1940, Commander of Sea Fortifications at Kristiansand 09.1940–01.1945, Gas and Air Protection Inspector of Kriegsmarine in O.K.M. 02.1945–05.1945. Awards: 1939 Clasps to the 1914 Iron Cross 1st and 2nd Class, 1914 Iron Cross 1st and 2nd Class, Cross of Honor.

Brehmer, Walter: Generalmajor (01.03.43), (Heer); born 28.06.94 in Nordhausen, died 19.09.67 in Hamburg. WWI: Oberleutnant Pionier Bataillon, 7. Kavallerie Division. Commander of I. Abteilung, Schuetzen Regiment 1, 10.1935–07.1938. WWII: Commander of Kavallerie Schuetzen Regiment 10, 08.1938–09.1941, Commander of 9. Schuetzen Brigade 09.1941–05.1942, Wehrmacht Commander of Erfurt 06.1942–08.1943, Commander of 325. Security Division 08.1943–07.1944, Fuehrer Res. in O.K.H. 07.1944–12.1944, attached to Heeresgruppe F 12.1944–04.1945. Awards: Blood Order (Infanterie Schule), 1939 Clasps to the 1914 Iron Cross 1st and 2nd Class, General Assault Badge, Eastern Front Medal, 1939 Wound Badge in Black, 1914 Iron Cross 1st and 2nd Class, Cross of Honor.

Breitenstein, Charles: Ministerialdirigent (30.01.45), (Kriegsmarine); born 15.07.98 in Berlin, died 31.08.63 in Immenstadt. Civil Servant by profession. WWI: service unknown. Service unknown 1919–09.1939. WWII: Chief of Department for Electro-Technology (K II L) in Head Office Warship Construction of O.K.M. 10.1939–11.1944. Awards: War Merit Cross 1st and 2nd Class with Swords, 1914 Iron Cross 2nd Class, Cross of Honor.

Breith, Friedrich: Generalleutnant (01.04.43), (Heer); born 25.05.92 in Kirchheimbolanden, died 09.07.82 in Munich. WWI: Oberleutnant and 1. Ordnance Officer on Staff of 3. Bavarian Infanterie Division. Promotion to Generalmajor 01.04.42. Commander of III. Abteilung, Artillerie Regiment at Nuremberg 10.1934–10.1935, Commander of III. Abteilung, Artillerie Regiment 17, 10.1935–10.1937. WWII: Commander of Artillerie Regiment 35, 10.1937–04.1940, Commander of Artillerie 127, 04.1940–12.1941, Commander of Artillerie Schule I and later II 01.1942–05.1944, Commander of 4. Gebirgs Division 07.1944–05.1945. Awards: German Cross in Silver 22.07.44, War Merit Cross 1st and 2nd Class with Swords, Eastern Front Medal, German West Wall Medal, 1914 Iron Cross 1st and 2nd Class, Bavarian Military Service Order IV. Class with Swords, 1914 Wound Badge in Black, Cross of Honor.

Breith, Hermann: General der Panzertruppe (01.03.43), (Heer); born 07.05.92 in Primasens, died 03.09.64 in Wachtberg. WWI: Oberleutnant and Adjutant to 241. Infanterie Brigade. Promotions to Generalmajor 01.08.41, Generalleutnant 01.11.42. Attached to Kraftfahr Ausbildungs Kommando at Zossen 08.1934–10.1935,

Commander of II. Abteilung, Panzer Regiment 5, 10.1935–11.1938. WWII: Commander of Panzer Regiment 36, 11.1938–02.1940, Commander of 5. Panzer Brigade 02.1940–11.1940, Commander of 3. Panzer Division 10.1941–10.1942, Commander of III. Panzer Korps 01.1943–05.1945. Awards: Swords 21.02.44 (48), Oak Leaves 31.01.42 (69), Knight's Cross 03.06.40, 1939 Clasps to the 1914 Iron Cross 1st and 2nd Class, Tank Assault Badge in Silver, Eastern Front Medal, 1939 Wound Badge in Gold, RK-Hohenzollern, 1914 Iron Cross 1st and 2nd Class, Cross of Honor.

Breithaupt, Franz: SS-Obergruppenfuehrer und General der Waffen-SS (20.04.44); born 08.12.80 in Berlin. died 29.04.45 (shot by own aide) in Prien. P-602663, SS-39719. WWI: Hauptmann attached to 9. Kavallerie Division. Joined N.S.D.A.P. in 1931, joined S.S. in 1932. Promotions to SS-Brigadefuehrer 09.11.38, SS-Gruppenfuehrer 15.08.42, z.b.V. RFSS 01.10.34. Attached to SS-Hauptamt 01.07.35, attached to Staff of SS-Hauptamt 01.12.36–01.12.38. WWII: Leader on Staff of RFSS 30.01.42, Chief of Hauptamt SS-Gericht 15.05.43–1945, Polizei President. Awards: War Merit Cross 1st and 2nd Class with Swords, German Red Cross Decoration 1st Class, German Social Welfare Decoration 2nd Class, German Olympic Games Decoration 1st Class, RK-Hohenzollern, 1914 Iron Cross 1st and 2nd Class, 1914 Wound Badge in Silver, Cross of Honor, Degen, Ring.

Breithaupt, Joachim: Generalmajor (01.12.42), (Luftwaffe); born 28.01.83 in Wandlitz, died 18.07.60 in Brake-Lemgo. WWI: Naval Airship Service Kapitanleutnant and Airship Commander. Advisor for Air Ships in R.L.M. 04.1933–01.1939. WWII: Flughafenbereichs Commandant of Neu-Brandenburg 01.1939–06.1940, Flughafenbereichs Commandant of Laon 06.1940–12.1942, retired 05.1943. Awards: War Merit Cross 1st and 2nd Class with Swords, 1920 Airship Commemorative Badge, Badge, RK-Hohenzollern, 1914 Iron Cross 1st and 2nd Class, Cross of Honor.

Brekle, Dr. Richard: General-Arzt z.V. (01.05.41), (Heer); born 30.03.79 in Stuttgart, died 12.09.41 of natural causes in Stuttgart. Medical doctor by profession. WWI: Assistenz-Arzt (unit unknown). WWII: recalled to military service 08.1939, Corps Physician to Wehrkreis V 08.1939–09.1941. Awards: German Red Cross Decoration 1st Class, 1914 Iron Cross 1st and 2nd Class, Cross of Honor.

Bremer, Friedrich: Generalleutnant (01.10.38), (Heer); born 19.06.86 in Goettingen, died 22.03.45 in Goettingen. WWI: in G.A.S. as Observer in Brieftauben Abteilung 10 (rank unknown). Promotion to Generalmajor 01.01.37. Commander of Artillerie Regiment 3, 10.1933–02.1936, Commander of Artillerie 3, 03.1936–02.1938, Commander of 34. Infanterie Division 03.1938–03.1939. WWII: Special Purpose Officer attached to O.B. des Heeres 04.1939–02.1942, retired 02.1942. Awards:

Pilot's Commemorative Badge, 1914 Iron Cross 1st and 2nd Class, 1914 Observer's Badge, Cross of Honor.

Brenken, Walter: Generalmajor (01.06.42), (Heer); born 26.02.83 in Muenster, died 02.01.52 in Bad Ems. WWI: Rittmeister and Ia to 6. Reserve Division. WWII: Military District Commander for Koblenz 10.1935–07.1942, retired 07.1942. Awards: War Merit Cross 1st and 2nd Class with Swords, 1914 Iron Cross 1st and 2nd Class, Cross of Honor.

Brennecke, Kurt: General der Infanterie (01.02.42), (Heer); born 16.12.91 in Ringelheim, died 30.12.82 in Bonn. WWI: Hauptmann and Adjutant to 26. Infanterie Brigade. Promotions to Generalmajor 01.08.38, Generalleutnant 01.08.40. Commander of Kraftfahr Abteilung at Stettin 10.1934–05.1935, Chief of Staff to Wehrkreis Kommando VII and VII. Armee Korps 06.1935–11.1938. WWII: Chief of General Staff to Heeres Gruppen Kommando 6, 11.1938–08.1939, Chief of General Staff to 4. Armee 08.1939–10.1940, Chief of General Staff to Heeresgruppe C 10.1940–06.1941, Chief of General Staff to Heeresgruppe Nord 06.1941–01.1942, Commander of XXXXIII. Armee Korps 02.1942–01.1943, Commander of Courses for Divisional Commanders 06.1943–05.1945. Awards: Knight's Cross 12.07.42, German Cross in Gold 13.10.41, 1939 Clasps to the 1914 Iron Cross 1st and 2nd Class, Infantry Assault Badge in Silver, Eastern Front Medal, 1914 Iron Cross 1st and 2nd Class, 1914 Wound Badge in Black, Cross of Honor.

Brenner, Karl: SS-Gruppenfuehrer und Generalleutnant der Polizei (15.03.44); born 19.05.95 in Mannheim, died 14.02.54 in Karlsruhe. P-3460685, SS-307786. WWI: Leutnant in Feld Artillerie Regiment (unit unknown). Joined H.J. in 1926, HJ-Bannfuehrer, joined N.S.D.A.P. in 1935, joined S.S. in 1938. Promotion to SS-Brigadefuehrer 30.01.42. Leader on Staff of SS-Hauptamt 01.12.38. WWII: Inspector of Ordnungspolizei for Salzburg 30.01.42, Befehlshaber of Ordnungspolizei in Salzburg 15.05.43, Commander of 6. SS-Gebirgs Division "Nord" 30.01.44–1945. Awards: Knight's Cross 27.12.44, German Cross in Gold 16.06.44, 1939 Clasps to the 1914 Iron Cross 1st and 2nd Class, War Merit Cross 1st and 2nd Class with Swords, Infantry Assault Badge in Silver, 1939 Wound Badge in Gold, Golden HJ Honor Badge, RK-Baden Order of the Zaehringer Lion 2nd Class with Swords, 1914 Iron Cross 1st and 2nd Class, 1914 Wound Badge in Silver, Cross of Honor, Reich Sports Badge in Gold, German Horseman's Badge in Silver, Degen, Ring.

Breuning, Eric Alfred: Konteradmiral (01.01.43), (Kriegsmarine); born 16.10.97 in Rottweil, died 28.11.78 in La Palmas. WWI: Fahnrich zur See on liner *Kaiserin*. Advisor for Sperrversuchkommando 04.1932–09.1934, 3. Admiral Staff Officer attached to Befehlshaber of Reconnaissance Surface Ships 09.1934–10.1936. WWII:

Advisor for Mine Affairs in Operations Department of O.K.M. 10.1936–09.1942, Commander of 3. Security Division 09.1942–05.1943, Commander of Security Forces West 06.1943–09.1944, Chief of Staff to North Sea Operational Staff in O.K.M. 10.1944–05.1945. Awards: German Cross in Gold 24.09.44, 1939 Iron Cross 1st Class, 1939 Clasp to the 1914 Iron Cross 2nd Class, Commander's Cross of the Romanian Order of the Star with Swords, Finnish Freedom Cross 2nd Class with Swords, 1914 Iron Cross 2nd Class, Cross of Honor.

Breusing, Hero: Generalmajor (01.05.44), (Heer); born 02.06.94 in Charlottenburg, died 07.02.73 in Koblenz. WWI: Leutnant in Feld Artillerie Regiment 213. Advisor in Heeres Waffen Amt of Reichswehr Ministry 06.1934–04.1935, Leader and later Department Chief in Wa B6 of Reich War Ministry 05.1935–10.1937. WWII: Commander of Panzer Aufklarungs Abteilung 41, 10.1937–02.1940, Commander of Panzer Regiment 2, 03.1940–05.1941, Commander of Panzer Regiment 203, 07.1941–03.1943, Commander of 122. Infanterie Division 05.1944–09.1944, Wehrmacht Commander of Litzmannstadt 09.1944–1945. Awards: 1939 Clasps to the 1914 Iron Cross 1st and 2nd Class, Tank Assault Badge in Silver, Eastern Front Medal, Finnish Freedom Cross 1st Class with Swords, 1914 Iron Cross 1st and 2nd Class, Cross of Honor.

Briesen, Arthur von: Generalmajor (01.10.42), (Heer); born 26.09.91 in Metz, died 15.05.81 in Koblenz. WWI: Oberleutnant on Staff of A.O.K. Infanterie Regiment 3 at Rostock 10.1934–03.1935, attached to Staff of III. Bataillon, Infanterie Regiment at Rostock 04.1935–10.1935, Commander of III. Bataillon, Infanterie Regiment 27, 10.1935–11.1938. WWII: attached to Staff of Infanterie Regiment 27, 11.1938–04.1939, Wehrmacht Commander of Prague 05.1939–02.1944, attached to Staff of Wehrmacht Commander for Boehmen-Maehren 07.1944–11.1944, Fuehrer Res. in O.K.H. 12.1944–05.1945. Awards: 1939 Clasps to the 1914 Iron Cross 1st and 2nd Class, War Merit Cross 1st and 2nd Class with Swords, RK-Hohenzollern, RK-Sachsen Albrecht Order 2nd Class with Swords, RK-Sachsen Service Order 2nd Class with Swords, 1914 Iron Cross 1st and 2nd Class, Johann Ritter Order, Cross of Honor.

Briesen, Kurt von: General der Infanterie (01.08.40), (Heer); born 03.05.86 in Anklam, died 20.11.41 in action near Andreyevka. WWI: Hauptmann and Ia to 239. Infanterie Division. Promotions to Generalmajor 01.08.37, Generalleutnant 01.08.39. Commandant of Neu-Stettin 04.1934–10.1935, Commander of Infanterie Regiment 69, 10.1935–01.1938. WWII: Commander of 30. Infanterie Division 02.1938–11.1940, Commander of LII. Armee Korps 11.1940–11.1941. Awards: Knight's Cross 27.10.39, 1939 Clasps to the 1914 Iron Cross 1st and 2nd Class, 1939 Wound Badge in Gold, RK-Hohenzollern, 1914 Iron Cross 1st and 2nd Class, 1914 Wound Badge in Black, Cross of Honor.

Vizeadmiral Helmuth Brinkmann. (Roger James Bender)

Brinkmann, Helmuth: Vizeadmiral (01.02.44), (Kriegsmarine); born 12.03.95 in Luebeck, died 26.09.83 in Drissen. WWI: Leutnant zur See and Watch Officer on torpedo boat *S-133*. Promotion to Konteradmiral 01.09.42. Advisor attached to Reich War Ministry 01.1933–03.1935, Commandant of aviso *Grille* 05.1935–05.1938, Advisor attached to Marinewehr Abteilung in O.K.M. 05.1938–10.1938. WWII: Chief of Naval Defense Department in O.K.M. 10.1938–07.1940, Commander of heavy cruiser *Prinz Eugen* 08.1940–08.1942, Chief of Staff to Marine Gruppen Kommando Sud 08.1942–11.1943, Marine Befehlshaber of Black Sea 11.1943–11.1944, Second Admiral of Baltic Sea 01.1945–05.1945. Awards: Knight's Cross 17.05.44, German Cross in Gold 25.03.42, 1939 Clasps to the 1914 Iron Cross 1st and 2nd Class, High Seas Fleet War Badge, Commander's Cross of the Italian Order of the Crown, Commander's Cross of the Hungarian Service Order with Breast Star and Swords, Grand Officer's Cross of the Bulgarian Military Service Order with War Decoration, Romanian Order of Michael the Brave 3rd Class, Grand Officer's Cross of the Romanian Order of the Crown with Swords, 1914 Iron Cross 1st and 2nd Class, Cross of Honor.

Britzelmayr, Karl: Generalmajor (01.12.44), (Heer); born 26.05.94 in Passau, died 09.03.68 in Landshut. WWI: Oberleutnant and Ordnance Officer to Prinz Oskar von Preussen. Kompanie Chef in Infanterie Regiment at Landshut 10.1934–10.1935, Kompanie Chef in Infanterie Regiment 62, 10.1935–11.1936, attached to Staff of Infanterie Regiment 62, 11.1936–05.1938, attached to Command Staff of Inspection for Western Fortifications 06.1938–11.1938. WWII: Leader of Exploratory Staff of Fortifications in Glogau 02.1939–08.1939, Commander of III. Bataillon, Infanterie Regiment 179, 08.1939–11.1940, Commander of Grenadier Regiment 217, 10.1941–08.1943, Commander of 347. Security Division 09.1944–11.1944, Commander of 19. Volks Grenadier Division 11.1944–04.1945. Awards: Knight's Cross 02.02.42, German Cross in Gold 09.06.43, 1939 Clasps to the 1914 Iron Cross 1st and 2nd Class, Infantry Assault Badge in Silver, Eastern Front Medal, West Wall Medal, 1914 Iron Cross 1st and 2nd Class, 1914 Wound Badge in Black, Cross of Honor.

Brockdorff-Ahlefeldt, Walter Graf von: General der Infanterie (01.08.40), (Heer); born 13.07.87 in Perleberg, died 09.05.43 of natural causes in Berlin. WWI: Hauptmann on Staff of IV. Armee Korps. Promotions to Generalmajor 01.04.37,

Generalleutnant 01.03.39. Commander of Infanterie Regiment 8, 03.1934–02.1938. WWII: Commander of 23. Infanterie Division 03.1938–06.1940, Commander of II. Armee Korps 06.1940–01.1943. Awards: Oak Leaves 27.06.42 (103), Knight's Cross 15.07.41, 1939 Clasps to the 1914 Iron Cross 1st and 2nd Class, Demjansk Shield, Eastern Front Medal, 1914 Iron Cross 1st and 2nd Class, 1914 Wound Badge in Black, Cross of Honor.

Brodowski, Fritz von: Generalleutnant (01.02.41), (Heer); born 26.11.86 in Kolberg, died 20.10.44 in action in Besancon. WWI: Rittmeister and Bataillon Commander in Guards Grenadier Regiment 3. Promotion to Generalmajor 01.01.37. Commander of Reichswehr Acceptance Office at Ulm/Donau 10.1934–04.1935, Military Replacement Inspector for Ulm 04.1935–05.1938. WWII: Military Replacement Inspector for Stuttgart 06.1938–08.1941, Commander of Feld Ersatz Division B 08.1941–09.1942, Commander of Special Purpose Division 404, 09.1942–03.1943, attached to Wehrmacht Commander of Belgium-Northern France 12.1943–04.1944, Commander of Kampfgruppe "von Brodowski" 09.1944–10.1944. Awards: 1939 Clasps to the 1914 Iron Cross 1st and 2nd Class, War Merit Cross 1st and 2nd Class with Swords, 1939 Wound Badge in Gold, RK-Hohenzollern, 1914 Iron Cross 1st and 2nd Class, 1914 Wound Badge in Black, Cross of Honor.

Broeking, Fritz: Ministerialdirektor (26.09.41), (Kriegsmarine); born 11.03.77 in Gevelsberg, died 29.12.61. Engineer by profession. WWI: Chief of Marine Construction Affairs for Torpedo and U-Boats (rank unknown). WWII: service unknown 1919–09.1939, Department Chief for Naval Construction and Electro Technology for U-Boats in O.K.M. 10.1939–12.1944, retired 12.1944. Awards: German Cross in Silver 12.01.44, War Merit Cross 1st and 2nd Class with Swords, 1914 Iron Cross 2nd Class, Cross of Honor.

Broich, Friedrich Freiherr von: Generalleutnant (05.01.43), (Heer); born 01.01.96 in Strasbourg, died 24.09.74 in Leoni. WWI: Oberleutnant in Ulan Regiment 9. Promotion to Generalmajor 01.01.43. Adjutant to 1. Kavallerie Division 12.1933–10.1935, attached to Inspectorate 3 of Reich War Ministry 10.1935–11.1938. WWII: Commander of II. Bataillon, Kavallerie Regiment 6, 11.1938–08.1939, Commander of Kavallerie Regiment 6, 09.1939–12.1939, Commander of Kavallerie Regiment 21, 12.1939–09.1940, Commander of Kavallerie Regiment 22, 09.1940–09.1941, Commander of 24. Schuetzen Brigade 12.1941–10.1942, Commander of 10. Panzer Division 02.1943–05.1943, captured 05.1943. Awards: Knight's Cross 29.08.42, German Cross in Gold 02.11.41, 1939 Clasps to the 1914 Iron Cross 1st and 2nd Class, Infantry Assault Badge in Silver, 1914 Iron Cross 1st and 2nd Class, 1914 Wound Badge in Black, Cross of Honor.

Bronsart von Schellendorf, Heinrich: Generalmajor (01.09.44), (Heer); born 21.09.06 in Neustrelitz, died 22.09.44 in action in Dieuze. Adjutant to Reiter Regiment 6, 10.1934–09.1937. WWII: Schwadron Chef in Reiter Regiment 6, 10.1937–08.1939, Schwadron Chef in Reiter Aufklarungs Abteilung 179, 09.1939–10.1939, Commander of Aufklarungs Abteilung 36 (mot.) 11.1939–12.1942, Commander of Panzer Grenadier Regiment 13, 02.1943–03.1944, Chief Personnel Officer for A.O.K. 8, 05.1944–09.1944, Commander of 111. Panzer Brigade 09.1944. Awards: Oak Leaves 12.02.44 (394), Knight's Cross 10.09.43, German Cross in Gold 24.05.42, 1939 Iron Cross 1st and 2nd Class, General Assault Badge, Eastern Front Medal, 1939 Wound Badge in Gold, German Horseman's Badge in Gold.

Bruch, Hermann: Generalleutnant (01.11.40), (Luftwaffe); born 28.05.93 in Heiligenmorschel, died 15.06.76 in Neustadt. WWI: in Naval G.A.S. as Oberleutnant zur See in II. Marine Flieger Abteilung. Promotion to Generalmajor 01.10.39. Commander of Naval Aircraft 04.1934–09.1935, Chief of Zentral Abteilung in R.L.M. 10.1935–09.1936, Chief of Staff to Luftwaffe Commando in Kiel 10.1936–03.1939. WWII: Commander of Naval Luftwaffe East 06.1939–04.1940, Commander of Sea Luftwaffe 04.1940–04.1941, Commander of Luftwaffe for Northern Norway 04.1941–07.1942, Military Administrative and Production Inspector in Economic Staff East 12.1942–10.1944, attached to Luftgau Kommando III 10.1944–01.1945. Awards: German Cross in Silver 1945, 1939 Clasp to the 1914 Iron Cross 2nd Class, War Merit Cross 1st and 2nd Class with Swords, Naval Pilot's Commemorative Badge, 1914 Iron Cross 1st and 2nd Class, Bavarian Military Service Order IV. Class with Swords, 1914 Naval Pilot's Badge, Cross of Honor.

Bruckmann, Hans: Generalmajor (01.04.44), (Heer); born 07.09.81 in Ulm, died 08.11.62 in Baden-Baden. WWI: Hauptmann and Ia to 19. Infanterie Division. Military Representative to Budapest 05.1937–08.1937. WWII: Representative and later Military Attaché to Sofia 09.1937–12.1942, Fuehrer Res. in O.K.H. 12.1942–02.1943, Wehrmacht Commander of Colmar 03.1943–02.1944, Fuehrer Res. in O.K.H. 03.1944–05.1944, retired 05.1944. Awards: War Merit Cross 1st and 2nd Class with Swords, RK-Hohenzollern, 1914 Iron Cross 1st and 2nd Class, Cross of Honor.

Bruder, Dr. Kuno: General-Veterinar (01.04.41), (Heer); born 20.09.86 in Rombach, died 23.10.64 in Tuebingen. Medical veterinarian by profession. WWI: Ober-Veterinar (unit unknown). WWII: Korps Veterinar to XI. Armee Korps 1935–08.1939, Armee Veterinar to 4. Armee 08.1939–11.1944, Heeres Veterinar to Heeresgruppe H 11.1944–05.1945. Awards: German Cross in Silver 13.12.44, 1939 Clasp to the 1914 Iron Cross 2nd Class, War Merit Cross 1st and 2nd Class with Swords, Eastern Front Medal, 1914 Iron Cross 1st and 2nd Class, Bavarian Military Service Order IV. Class with Swords, Cross of Honor, Reich Sports Badge in Gold.

Bruecker, Otto-Hermann: Generalleutnant (20.04.45), (Heer); born 17.10.99 in Berlin, died 12.12.64 in Weinheim. WWI: Gefreiter in 20. Pionier Bataillon. Promotion to Generalmajor 01.10.44. Attached to Staff of Infanterie Leader V 04.1935–10.1935, attached to Staff of 9. Division 10.1935–12.1936, attached to Staff of Landwehr Commander of Hanau 01.1937–01.1937, assignment unknown 02.1937–09.1937, Kompanie Chef in Infanterie Regiment 5, 10.1937–09.1938. WWII: Intelligence Officer to II. Armee Korps 09.1938–04.1940, Ia to XXIV. Armee Korps 04.1940–04.1942, Ia to 7. Armee 04.1942–12.1942, Commander of Grenadier Regiment 419, 01.1943–05.1944, Commander of 6. Grenadier (later Volks Grenadier) Division 07.1944–04.1945. Awards: Knight's Cross 14.04.45, 1939 Iron Cross 1st and 2nd Class, Eastern Front Medal, 1939 Wound Badge in Black, Cross of Honor.

Bruehl, Ferdinand: Generalmajor (09.11.44), (Heer); born 09.11.96 in Eltville, died 09.04.68 in Aschaffenburg. WWI: Leutnant and First Ordinance Officer in VIII. Armee Korps. Attached to Artillerie Regiment at Muenster 10.1934–10.1935, Batterie Chef in Artillerie Regiment 16, 10.1935–09.1936. WWII: Batterie Chef in Artillerie Regiment 26, 10.1936–08.1939, Commander of III. Abteilung, Artillerie Regiment 26, 08.1939–11.1940, Commander of III. Abteilung, Artillerie Regiment 107, 11.1940–06.1941, Commander of Artillerie Regiment 198, 06.1941–05.1944, Commander of 563. Volks Grenadier Division 08.1944–02.1945. Awards: German Cross in Gold 14.04.42, 1939 Clasps to the 1914 Iron Cross 1st and 2nd Class, German Army High Command Commendation Certificate 27.02.44, General Assault Badge, 1914 Iron Cross 1st and 2nd Class, Cross of Honor.

Bruendel, Carl: Generalmajor (01.09.44), (Heer); born 26.12.88 in Hamburg, died 12.09.57 in Ratzeburg. WWI: Leutnant in Infanterie Regiment 140. Attached to National Chinese Army 10.1935–11.1938. WWII: attached to Staff of Landwehr Commander for Luebben 03.1939–02.1941, Commander of Panzer Jaeger Bataillon 208, 02.1941–06.1942, Commander of Grenadier Regiment 510, 06.1942–03.1943, Grenadier Regimental Commander in Division E 08.1943–09.1944. Awards: German Cross in Gold 19.12.41, 1939 Clasps to the 1914 Iron Cross 1st and 2nd Class, German Army High Command Commendation Certificate 20.08.41, General Assault Badge, Eastern Front Medal, 1914 Iron Cross 1st and 2nd Class, 1914 Wound Badge in Black, Cross of Honor.

Bruening, Josef: Generalmajor (01.04.45), (Heer); born 18.10.93 in Wiedenbruck, died 03.02.69 in Wiedenbruck. WWI: Leutnant and Ordnance Officer to Infanterie

Regiment 458. Tactics Instructor at Kriegsschule Hannover 10.1935–10.1938. WWII: Commander of III. Bataillon, Infanterie Regiment 17, 11.1938–03.1940, Commander of Infanterie Regiment 431, 10.1940–05.1942, Commander of Schule VIII for Officer Aspirants of Infanterie 09.1942–06.1944, Commander of Truppenubungsplatz at Muenster 09.1944–05.1945. Awards: German Cross in Gold 29.01.42, 1939 Clasps to the 1914 Iron Cross 1st and 2nd Class, Infantry Assault Badge in Silver, Eastern Front Medal, RK-Hohenzollern, 1914 Iron Cross 1st and 2nd Class, 1914 Wound Badge in Silver, Cross of Honor.

Bruhn, Johannes: Generalmajor (01.11.44), (Heer); born 10.07.98 in Neumunster, died 20.11.54 in Luebeck. WWI: Leutnant der Res. in Feld Artillerie Regiment 505. Attached to I. Abteilung, Artillerie Regiment at Halberstadt 04.1935–10.1935, attached to Staff of II. Abteilung, Artillerie Regiment 59, 10.1935–02.1936, attached to Command Staff of Artillery Courses at Jueterbog 02.1936–08.1937. WWII: Commander of II. Abteilung, Artillerie Regiment 39, 09.1937–09.1939, Commander of Schwere Abteilung Abteilung 606, 08.1939–09.1940, Commander of Artillerie Regiment Staff 818, 07.1941–10.1942, Commander of Artillerie 149, 04.1943–08.1944, Commander of 553. Volks Grenadier Division 09.1944–11.1944. Awards: Knight's Cross 20.12.43, German Cross in Gold 17.11.41, 1939 Iron Cross 1st Class, 1939 Clasp to the 1914 Iron Cross 2nd Class, General Assault Badge, 1914 Iron Cross 2nd Class, Cross of Honor.

Brunner, Josef: Generalleutnant (01.10.43), (Luftwaffe); born 30.10.89 in Stadl-Paura, died 15.01.67 in Lambach. WWI: Oberleutnant and Leader of Austrian Flieger Kompanie 36. Promotion to Generalmajor 01.09.41. Transferred to German Wehrmacht 03.1938, attached to Staff of K.G. 157, 06.1938–11.1938, Fliegerhorst Commandant of Langenhagen 12.1938–06.1939. WWII: attached to Fernaufklarungs Gruppe 14, 07.1939–02.1941, Commander of Luftwaffe for Heeresgruppe Nord 02.1941–02.1942, Luftwaffe Commander attached to Oberbefehlshaber West 02.1942–1943, Commander of Air Base at Dresden 1943–06.1944, Higher Commander for Luftwaffe Kriegs und Offizier Schulen 06.1944–02.1945. Awards: 1939 Iron Cross 1st Class, 1939 Clasp to the 1914 Iron Cross 2nd Class, War Merit Cross 1st and 2nd Class with Swords, 1914, Pilot's Commemorative Badge, 1914 Iron Cross 2nd Class, 1914 Observer's Badge, Cross of Honor.

Bruns, Walter: Generalmajor (01.04.42), (Heer); born 11.12.89 in Hannover, died 20.02.67 in Neckargemund. WWI: Hauptmann with 904. Air Defense M.G. Bataillon. Commander of I. Bataillon, Infanterie Regiment at Flensburg 10.1934–07.1935, Commander of I. Bataillon, Infanterie Regiment 26, 10.1935–10.1937, Commander of II. Bataillon, Infanterie Regiment 46, 10.1937–06.1939. WWII:

Commander of Infanterie Regiment 21, 07.1939–09.1939, Military Attaché in Madrid and Lisbon 10.1939–10.1941, Senior Commandant of Feldkommandantur 570, 06.1942–09.1944, Commander of 89. Infanterie Division 09.1944–03.1945. Awards: 1939 Clasps to the 1914 Iron Cross 1st and 2nd Class, 1914 Iron Cross 1st and 2nd Class, Bavarian Military Service Order IV. Class with Swords, 1914 Wound Badge in Black, Cross of Honor.

Bruns, Walter: Generalmajor (01.06.42), (Heer); born 15.09.91 in Kirberg, died 15.04.57 in Goettingen. WWI: Hauptmann in 185. Pionier Bataillon. Attached to Heeres Feldzeugmeister 04.1935–10.1936, Mine Device Inspector 10.1936–03.1937. WWII: Heeres Device Inspector B 03.1937–08.1939, Commander of Construction Staff 47, 08.1939–04.1940, Commander of Rhine Crossings 04.1940–05.1941, Commander of Bridging Staff "Bruns" in Heeresgruppe Nord 05.1941–05.1942, Commander of Truppenubungsplatz at Harskamp 05.1942–01.1943, Commander of Heeres Waffenmeisterschule 01.1943–01.1945. Awards: 1939 Clasp to the 1914 Iron Cross 2nd Class, War Merit Cross 1st and 2nd Class with Swords, 1914 Iron Cross 1st and 2nd Class, Cross of Honor.

Buch, Fritz von: Generalmajor z.V. (01.03.43), (Heer and Luftwaffe); born 24.01.76 in Braunsberg, died 04.04.59 in Kassel. WWI: Major and Commander of Guards Feld Artillerie Regiment 7. Recalled to military service 07.1938, no assignment 07.1938–07.1939. WWII: Commander of Artillerie Regiment 9, 08.1939–10.1940, Commander of Artillerie Regiment 606 (mot.) Staff 10.1940–11.1941, Commander of Panzer Artillerie Regiment 128, 11.1941–12.1942, transferred to Luftwaffe in 06.1943, Senior Artillery Commander of Fallschirm Armee 03.1944–02.1945. Awards: German Cross in Gold 26.06.42, 1939 Clasps to the 1914 Iron Cross 1st and 2nd Class, General Assault Badge, Eastern Front Medal, RK-Hohenzollern, RK-Sachsen Albrecht Order 1st Class with Swords, 1914 Iron Cross 1st and 2nd Class, Austro-Hungarian Military Service Cross 3rd Class with War Decoration, Cross of Honor.

Bucher, Wolfgang: Generalmajor (01.02.44), (Heer); born 15.07.98 in Leipzig, died 19.02.44 in action near Cherkassy. WWI: Leutnant in Infanterie Regiment 107. Attached to Staff of Artillerie Commander V 10.1935–02.1936, attached to Staff of 25. Division 03.1936–09.1936, Kompanie Chef in Infanterie Regiment 119, 10.1936–03.1937. WWII: Ia to 11. Infanterie Division 04.1937–08.1939, Ia to I. Armee Korps 09.1939–09.1940, Senior Quartermaster of 18. Armee 09.1940–03.1942, Senior Quartermaster for Heeresgruppe Nord 03.1942–12.1943, Commander of Infanterie Regiment 417, 12.1943–02.1944. Awards: German Cross in Gold 23.02.44, German Cross in Silver 15.02.43, 1939 Clasps to the 1914 Iron Cross 1st and 2nd Class, War Merit Cross 1st and 2nd Class with Swords, Eastern Front Medal, 1939 Wound Badge in Gold, 1914 Iron Cross 1st and 2nd Class, Cross of Honor.

Buchholz, Ulrich: Generalleutnant (01.02.44), (Luftwaffe); born 22.12.93 in Landsberg, died 20.06.74 in Moelln. WWI: in G.A.S. Leutnant in Jasta 20. Promotion to Generalmajor 01.12.41. Commander of Fahr Abteilung 2, 03.1934–06.1935, Adjutant and IIa on Staff of Luftkreis Kommando IV in Muenster 07.1935–09.1937. WWII: Fliegerhorst Commandant of Neuruppin 10.1937–08.1939, Hoehere Flieger Ausbildungs Commander 6 in Prague 09.1939–03.1940, Commander of Transport Geschwader z.b.V. 3, 03.1940–01.1943, Transport Fliegerfuehrer 1, 05.1943–11.1944, temporary Commander of 2. Flieger Division 10.1944–02.1945. Awards: German Cross in Gold 12.07.43, 1939 Clasps to the 1914 Iron Cross 1st and 2nd Class, Transport Flying Clasp in Gold, 1939 Pilot's Badge, Commander's Cross of Romania with Breast Star and Swords, Pilot's Commemorative Badge, 1914 Iron Cross 1st and 2nd Class, 1914 Wound Badge in Silver, 1914 Pilot's Badge, Cross of Honor.

Bucholz, Wilhelm: Admiral-Richter (01.05.44), (Kriegsmarine); born 16.04.96 in Hannover, died 19.08.55 in Hamburg. Jurist by profession. WWI: service unknown. WWII: Judge attached to Baltic Sea Naval Station 1934–03.1941, Chief Judge and Chief of North Sea Naval Station Legal Department 03.1941–02.1945. Awards: War Merit Cross 1st and 2nd Class with Swords, Cross of Honor.

Buchterkirch, Ernst: Generalmajor (01.02.41), (Heer); born 10.06.88 in Stolp, died 22.07.41 of natural causes in Stettin. WWI: Hauptmann attached to Gun Test Commission. Commander of Truppenubungsplatz at Zossen 01.1932–11.1938, Commander of Truppenubungsplatz at Wildflecken 11.1938–04.1939. WWII: Wehrmacht Commander of Stettin 05.1939–07.1941. Awards: 1939 Clasps to the 1914 Iron Cross 1st and 2nd Class, 1914 Iron Cross 1st and 2nd Class, 1914 Wound Badge in Black, Cross of Honor.

Buck, Albert: Generalmajor (01.07.42), (Heer); born 23.01.95 in Stuttgart, died 06.09.42 in action near Novorossik. WWI: Leutnant in Res. Infanterie Regiment 246. WWII: Commander of III. Bataillon, Infanterie Regiment 56, 10.1935–10.1939, Commander of Infanterie Regiment 305, 11.1939–04.1942, Commander of 198. Infanterie Division 04.1942–09.1942. Awards: Knight's Cross 17.07.41, German Cross in Gold 13.09.42, 1939 Clasps to the 1914 Iron Cross 1st and 2nd Class, German Army High Command Commendation Certificate 01.07.41, Infantry Assault Badge in Silver, Eastern Front Medal, 1939 Wound Badge in Gold, 1914 Iron Cross 1st and 2nd Class, Cross of Honor.

Buddenbrock, Jobst Freiherr von: Generalmajor (01.12.44), (Heer); born 21.06.95 in Ohlau, died 30.08.57 in Guetersloh. WWI: Leutnant in Guards Feld Artillerie Regiment 3. Commander of II. Abteilung, Artillerie Regiment at Schweidnitz 10.1934–10.1935, Commander of II. Abteilung, Artillerie Regiment

28, 10.1935–04.1939. WWII: attached to Staff of Artillerie Regiment 28, 04.1939–08.1939, Commander of Artillerie Regiment 162, 08.1939–11.1940, Commander of Artillerie Regiment 188, 05.1941–03.1943, Commander of Artillerie 103, 10.1943–06.1944, Commander of Artillerie 120, 09.1944–04.1945. Awards: German Cross in Gold 24.03.43, 1939 Clasps to the 1914 Iron Cross 1st and 2nd Class, General Assault Badge, Eastern Front Medal, German Westwall Medal, 1914 Iron Cross 1st and 2nd Class, 1914 Wound Badge in Silver, Cross of Honor.

Budnowski, Dr. Otto: Generalstabs-Veterinar (01.04.32), (Heer); born 25.05.74 in Danzig, died 21.09.56 in Berlin. Medical veterinarian by profession. WWI: Oberstabs-Veterinar (unit unknown). WWII: recalled to military service 08.1939, Leitender Veterinar Officer to O.B. East (occupied Poland) 08.1939–05.1940, Leitender Veterinar assigned to Stettin 07.1941–1942, Leitender Veterinar to Wehrmacht Befehlshaber Ostland (Eastern Territories) 1942, retired 08.1943. Awards: War Merit Cross 1st and 2nd Class with Swords, 1914 Iron Cross 1st and 2nd Class, Cross of Honor.

Buechs, Fritz: Generalleutnant (01.10.39), (Heer); born 09.03.85 in Neuruppin, died 03.03.59 in Detmold. WWI: Hauptmann and Adjutant to 328. Infanterie Brigade. Promotion to Generalmajor 01.04.37. Commander of Infanterie Regiment at Kolberg 10.1934–10.1935, Commander of Infanterie Regiment 4, 10.1935–03.1937, Commander of Heeres Service Office 1, 04.1937–11.1938. WWII: Commander of Fortifications at Neustettin 11.1938–08.1939, Commander of Grenschuetz Kommando 2, 08.1939–10.1939, attached to Hoehere Kommando XXXIII 09.1939–12.1939, Military Replacement Inspector for Dortmund 01.1940–04.1945. Awards: War Merit Cross 1st and 2nd Class with Swords, 1914 Iron Cross 1st and 2nd Class, 1914 Wound Badge in Silver, Cross of Honor.

Buechs, Walter: Generalleutnant z.V. (01.08.41), (Heer); born 09.11.81 in Cosel, died 23.07.70 in Hannover. WWI: Hauptmann and Ia in Section Kommando "Walk." Promotion to Generalmajor 01.09.35. Commander of Artillerie 16, 10.1935–10.1936. No assignment 10.1936–08.1939. WWII: Commander of Artillerie 22, 08.1939–01.1942, Senior Commander of Artillerie 315, 04.1942–06.1942, retired 01.1943. Awards: 1939 Clasps to the 1914 Iron Cross 1st and 2nd Class, General Assault Badge, 1914 Iron Cross 1st and 2nd Class, Cross of Honor.

Buechting, Andreas: Generalmajor (01.10.42), (Heer); born 17.01.96 in Danzig, died 24.10.42 in action at El Alamein. WWI: Leutnant in 3. Telegraph Bataillon. WWII: Commander of Signals Bataillon 46, 12.1935–01.1940, attached to Staff Signals Bataillon 222, 06.1940–04.1941, Hoehere Nachrichten Fuehrer 580, 04.1941–10.1942. Awards: German Cross in Silver 09.08.42, War Merit Cross 1st and 2nd Class with Swords, 1939 Wound Badge in Gold, 1914 Iron Cross 1st and 2nd Class, Cross of Honor.

Buehrmann, Robert: Generalmajor z.V. (01.10.40), (Heer); born 08.03.79 in Braunschweig, died 01.10.40 of natural causes in Brussels. WWI: Major on General Staff of A.O.K. Mackensen. WWII: recalled to military service 09.1939, Representative and later Inspector for Raw Materials Detection in Poland and then France 1939–1940. Awards: RK-Hohenzollern, 1914 Iron Cross 1st and 2nd Class, 1914 Wound Badge in Silver, Cross of Honor.

Buelow, Cord von: Generalmajor (01.02.42), (Heer); born 29.06.92 in Neubrandenburg, died 01.03.42 in action near Vitebsk. WWI: Oberleutnant in Hussar Regiment 2. Commander of II. Abteilung, Reiter Regiment 11, 10.1934–05.1935, Commander of Aufklarungs Abteilung 2, 05.1935–10.1937, Commander of Aufklarungs Abteilung 6, 10.1937–11.1938. WWII: Commander of Kavallerie Schule 11.1938–09.1939, Commander of Schuetzen Regiment 12, 10.1939–07.1940, Commander of Schuetzen Ersatz Regiment 83, 07.1940–04.1941, Commander of Schuetzen Regiment 69, 04.1941–08.1941, Commander of 10. Schuetzen Brigade 08.1941–03.1942. Awards: 1939 Clasps to the 1914 Iron Cross 1st and 2nd Class, Infantry Assault Badge in Silver, 1939 Wound Badge in Gold, 1914 Iron Cross 1st and 2nd Class, Cross of Honor, German Horseman's Badge in Silver.

Buelow, Hilmar Freiherr von: Generalleutnant (01.04.41), (Luftwaffe); born 26.07.83 in Bueckeburg, died 07.01.66 in Celle. WWI: in G.A.S. as Hauptmann and Commander of Flieger Abteilung 223. Promotion to Generalmajor 01.04.39. Chief of Abteilung "Fremde Luftstreitkraefte" in R.L.M. 06.1934–05.1938. WWII: Luftwaffe Attaché to German embassies in Rome and later Madrid 06.1938–03.1942, Chief of Kriegswissenschaftliche Abteilung of Luftwaffe 04.1942–08.1943, retired from Luftwaffe 10.1943. Awards: War Merit Cross 1st and 2nd Class with Swords, 1939 Observer's Badge, Pilot's Commemorative Badge, RK-Hohenzollern, 1914 Iron Cross 1st and 2nd Class, 1914 Observer's Badge, Cross of Honor.

Buelow, Werner von: Generalmajor (01.08.43), (Heer); born 04.07.98 in Korchow, died 30.08.43 in action near Obrodnoya. WWI: Leutnant in Instruction Infanterie Regiment. Regimental Signals Officer on Staff of Infanterie Regiment at Doeberitz 12.1934–10.1935, Kompanie Chef in Infanterie Regiment 48, 10.1935–11.1938. WWII: Commander of I. Bataillon, Infanterie Regiment 27, 11.1938–09.1940, Commander of Infanterie Regiment 252, 12.1940–02.1942, Commander of Infanterie Regiment 686, 03.1942–08.1943, Commander of 111. Infanterie Division 08.1943. Awards: German Cross in Gold 19.12.41, 1939 Iron Cross 1st Class, 1939 Clasp to the 1914 Iron Cross 2nd Class, Infantry Assault Badge in Silver, Eastern Front Medal, 1914 Iron Cross 2nd Class, Cross of Honor.

Buelowius, Alfred: General der Flieger (01.12.44), (Luftwaffe); born 14.01.92 in Koenigsberg, died 09.08.68 in Detmold. WWI: in G.A.S. as Oberleutnant in Bombengeschwader 3. Promotions to Generalmajor 01.06.41, Generalleutnant

01.03.43. Advisor in R.L.M. 09.1934–1935, Staffelkapitan in Fliegergruppe Merseburg 1935–1936, Gruppen Commander in K.G. "General Wever" 1936–1937. WWII: Commander of Grosse Kampfflieger Schule at Tutow 1937–04.1940, Commander of Lehr Geschwader 1, 05.1940–10.1940, Hoehere Flieger Ausbildungs Commander 7, 10.1940–01.1941, Higher Commander of Kampf- und Sturzkampf-Fliegerschulen 01.1941–08.1942, Commander of 1. Flieger Division 11.1942–06.1943, Commander of II. Flieger Korps (later Jagd Korps) 06.1943–10.1944, Commander of Luftgau Kommando XV 01.1945–02.1945. Awards: Knight's Cross 04.07.40, German Cross in Gold 21.12.42, 1939 Clasps to the 1914 Iron Cross 1st and 2nd Class, 1939 Wound Badge in Silver, Combined Pilot-Observer's Badge, Pilot's Commemorative Badge, 1914 Iron Cross 1st and 2nd Class, 1914 Wound Badge in Black, 1914 Observer's Badge, Cross of Honor.

General der Flieger Alfred Buelowius. (Bundesarchiv)

Buelowius, Karl: Generalleutnant (01.04.43), (Heer); born 02.03.90 in Koenigsberg, died 27.03.45 (suicide) at Camp Forrest P.O.W. Camp, TN, USA. WWI: Hauptmann in 14. Pionier Bataillon. Promotion to Generalmajor 01.04.42. Commander of Pionier Bataillon at Lyck 10.1934–10.1935, Commander of Pionier Bataillon 11, 10.1936–09.1936, Commander of Festung Pionier Stab 6, 10.1936–01.1939. WWII: Festung Pionier Inspector X 02.1939–09.1939, Pionier Leader of 8. Armee 10.1939–05.1940, Pionier Leader of 9. Armee 05.1940–10.1942, Pionier Leader of Panzer Armee "Afrika" 10.1942–05.1943, captured 05.1943. Awards: German Cross in Silver 30.11.42, War Merit Cross 1st and 2nd Class with Swords, Eastern Front Medal, 1914 Iron Cross 1st and 2nd Class, Cross of Honor.

Buelowius, Stephan: Generalmajor (01.04.44), (Heer); born 01.08.95 in Koenigsberg, died 26.04.79 in Westerland. WWI: Leutnant and Adjutant to 1. Pionier Bataillon. Pionier Staff Officer attached to Wehrkreis Kommando VI 10.1934–10.1935. WWII: Advisor on Inspection Staff of Pionier and Fortresses in Reich War Ministry (later O.K.H.) 10.1935–09.1939, Fortress Pionier Advisor to O.B. of Heeres 10.1939–06.1941, Commander of Pionier Regiment 413, 06.1941–01.1942, Fortress Pionier Leader in Norway and later Greece 05.1942–06.1944, attached to Staff then appointed Inspector of Land Fortifications for Italy 06.1944–05.1945. Awards: German Cross in Silver 20.04.45, 1939 Clasps to the 1914 Iron Cross 1st and 2nd Class, War Merit Cross 1st and 2nd Class with Swords, 1914 Iron Cross 1st and 2nd Class, Cross of Honor.

Buenau, Rudolf von: General der Infanterie (01.05.44), (Heer); born 19.08.90 in Stuttgart, died 14.01.62 in Kirchheim. WWI: Hauptmann and Adjutant to 407. Infanterie Brigade. Promotions to Generalmajor 01.09.40, Generalleutnant 01.09.42. Commander of III. Bataillon, Infanterie Regiment at Tuebingen 10.1934–10.1935, Instruction Group Leader A at Kriegsschule Dresden 10.1935–11.1938. WWII: Commander of Infanterie Regiment 133, 11.1938–10.1940, Commander of 73. Infanterie Division 11.1941–09.1943, Commander of XI. Armee Korps 03.1944–03.1945. Awards: Oak Leaves 05.03.45 (766), Knight's Cross 15.08.40, German Cross in Gold 23.01.43, 1939 Clasps to the 1914 Iron Cross 1st and 2nd Class, Infantry Assault Badge in Silver, Eastern Front Medal, Crimea Shield, Kuban Shield, 1914 Iron Cross 1st and 2nd Class, Cross of Honor.

Buercky, Heinrich: Generalmajor (01.12.43), (Heer); born 23.07.95 in Frankenthal, died 04.08.73 in Frankenthal. WWI: Leutnant in 3. M.G. Kompanie, Bavarian Infanterie Regiment 18. Kompanie Chef in II. Bataillon, Infanterie Regiment at Nuremberg 10.1934–10.1935, Tactics Instructor at Kriegsschule Hannover 10.1935–11.1938. WWII: Commander 7 Munich 12.1938–01.1940, Commander of Infanterie Regiment 528, 02.1940–09.1942, Commander of Schule VII for Infanterie Offizier Anwaerter 10.1942–03.1944, Commander of Infanterie Fahnenjunkerschulen 03.1944–10.1944, Commander of 159. Infanterie Division 12.1944–04.1945. Awards: German Cross in Gold 19.12.41, 1939 Clasps to the 1914 Iron Cross 1st and 2nd Class, Infantry Assault Badge in Silver, Eastern Front Medal, 1914 Iron Cross 1st and 2nd Class, 1914 Wound Badge in Black, Cross of Honor.

Buerkle de la Camp, Prof. Dr. Heinrich: General-Arzt der Res. (01.10.44), (Luftwaffe); born 03.09.65 in Bonndorf, died 02.05.74 in Doettingen. Medical doctor by profession. WWI: Leutnant in Bavarian Infanterie Regiment 113. WWII: Consultant Surgeon to Luftwaffen Kommando 2, 06.1940–09.1944, Consultant Surgeon to Armee Gruppen Kommando Sud-West 09.1944–05.1945. Awards: Knight's Cross of the War Merit Cross with Swords 01.02.45, German Cross in Gold 26.10.44, 1939 Clasps to the 1914 Iron Cross 1st and 2nd Class, 1914 Iron Cross 1st and 2nd Class, Cross of Honor.

General-Arzt der Res. Prof. Dr. Heinrich Buerkle de la Camp. (Josef Charita)

Buerkner, Leopold: Vizeadmiral (01.10.43), (Kriegsmarine); born 29.01.94 in Zerbst, died 15.07.75 in Frankfurt am Main. WWI: Oberleutnant zur See and Watch Officer on torpedo boat *G-39*. Promotion to Konteradmiral 01.04.42. Naval Liaison Officer between Marine attachés and Marineleitung 10.1933–09.1935, First Officer on battleship *Admiral Scheer* 10.1935–07.1937, Commandant of schule cruiser *Emden* 07.1937–06.1938. WWII: Chief of Abwehr of Foreign Department and later Gruppe in O.K.W. 06.1938–06.1944, Chief of Foreign Office of Wehrmacht Operations Staff of O.K.W. 07.1944–05.1945. Awards: Knight's Cross of the War Merit Cross with Swords 02.05.45, War Merit Cross 1st and 2nd Class with Swords, Spanish Cross in Silver with Swords, Officer's Cross of the Italian Order of the Crown, Commander's Cross of the Hungarian Service Order with Breast Star, Commander's Cross of the Romanian Order of the Star with Swords, Finnish Freedom Cross 1st Class with Swords, Spanish King's Service Order of the Sea 2nd Class, 1914 Iron Cross 1st and 2nd Class, Cross of Honor.

Vizeadmiral Leopold Buerkner. (Josef Charita)

Buescher, Erich: Generalmajor (01.12.44), (Heer); born 17.07.92 in Trier, died 30.04.82 in Bad Oldesloe. WWI: Leutnant in Infanterie Regiment 148. Tactics Instructor at Kriegsschule Hannover 10.1935–11.1936. WWII: attached to Reichs War Court 12.1936–02.1940, Commander of Infanterie Regiment 509, 02.1940–11.1940, Commander of Infanterie Regiment 571, 11.1940–02.1942, Commander of Kriegsschule VI 02.1942–04.1943, Commander of Grenadier Regiment 861, 09.1943–10.1944. Awards: 1939 Clasps to the 1914 Iron Cross 1st and 2nd Class, Infantry Assault Badge in Silver, Eastern Front Medal, 1914 Iron Cross 1st and 2nd Class, 1914 Wound Badge in Black, Cross of Honor.

Buesing, Otto: Generalmajor (01.03.44), (Heer); born 22.08.96 in Kiel, died 08.03.44 in action in Rownoje. WWI: Leutnant in Jaeger Regiment zu Pferde 1. Schwadron Chef in Reiter Regiment 10, 09.1934–11.1938. WWII: Adjutant to 5. Panzer Division 11.1938–12.1939, Commander of Aufklarungs Abteilung 8, 12.1939–10.1940, Commander of Panzer Regiment 39, 01.1941–02.1942, Commander of Panzer Regiment "Grossdeutschland" 02.1942–03.1944. Awards: Knight's Cross 21.11.42, Honor Roll Clasp 16.10.42, 1939 Clasps to the 1914 Iron Cross 1st and 2nd Class, Tank Assault Badge in Silver, Eastern Front Medal, 1939 Wound Badge in Gold, 1914 Iron Cross 1st and 2nd Class, Cross of Honor.

Buetow, Hans: Konteradmiral (01.01.43), (Kriegsmarine); born 28.12.94 in Volpersdorf, died 09.05.74 in Hamburg. WWI: Leutnant zur See on small cruiser *Augsburg*. Chief of 1. Torpedoboots Halbflotille 09.1932–09.1934, Staff Officer attached to Befehlshaber of Torpedo Boats 09.1934–10.1936, First Adjutant to

Commando of Naval Station Eastern Sea 10.1936–10.1938. WWII: Chief of Donau Naval Flottilla 11.1938–11.1939, Commander of Torpedo Boats 11.1939–04.1942, Chief of Staff to Marine Befehlshaber of Baltic Sea Naval Station 05.1942–05.1944, Chief of Security for Baltic Sea 06.1944–11.1944, Commander of 10. Security Division 12.1944–02.1945. Awards: Knight's Cross 12.03.41, 1939 Clasps to the 1914 Iron Cross 1st and 2nd Class, Destroyer's War Badge, Finnish Freedom Cross 1st Class with Swords, Baltic Cross 1st and 2nd Class, 1914 Iron Cross 1st and 2nd Class, Cross of Honor.

Buffa, Ernst: Generalleutnant (01.02.43), (Luftwaffe); born 14.02.93 in Oppeln, died 19.09.71 in Traben. WWI: Oberleutnant in Fuss Artillerie Regiment 5. Promotion to Generalmajor 01.08.40. Commander of I. Abteilung Flak Regiment 13, 04.1935–09.1937, Commander of Flak Regiment 3, 10.1937–06.1939. WWII: Commander of Flak Regiment 11, 06.1939–10.1939, Commander of Flak Regiment 104, 11.1939–07.1940, Inspector of Flak Artillerie for Holland 08.1940–03.1942, Commander of 12. Flak Division (mot.) 12.1942–04.1944, Commander of 21. Flak Division 06.1944–11.1944, attached to Reichs War Court 01.1945–05.1945. Awards: Knight's Cross 05.09.44, German Cross in Gold 09.11.43, 1939 Clasps to the 1914 Iron Cross 1st and 2nd Class, Flak War Badge, 1914 Iron Cross 1st and 2nd Class, Cross of Honor.

General der Infanterie Walter Buhle. (Bundesarchiv)

Buhle, Walter: General der Infanterie (01.04.44), (Heer); born 26.10.94 in Heilbronn, died 28.12.59 in Stuttgart. WWI: Oberleutnant in IV. Motor Bataillon. Promotions to Generalmajor 01.08.40, Generalleutnant 01.04.42. Advisor in Abteilung 2 of General Staff of Heeres in O.K.H. 07.1935–09.1936, Commander of II. Bataillon, Infanterie Regiment 87, 10.1936–10.1937, Ia to V. Armee Korps 10.1937–11.1938. WWII: Chief of Abteilung 2 in General Staff of Heeres in O.K.H. 11.1938–08.1939, Chief of Organization Department of Heeres General Staff 08.1939–01.1942, Chief of Heeres Staff in O.K.W. 01.1942–01.1945, Chief of Wehrmacht Armaments 02.1945–05.1945. Awards: 1939 Clasps to the 1914 Iron Cross 1st and 2nd Class, War Merit Cross 1st and 2nd Class with Swords, 20.07.44 Wound Badge in Black, RK-Hohenzollern, 1914 Iron Cross 1st and 2nd Class, Cross of Honor.

Bulcke, Richard: Generalmajor (20.04.45), (Heer); born 26.08.80 in Guettland, died 31.05.48 in Weingarten. WWI: Hauptmann and Ia to 11. Landwehr Division. Attached to Ersatz Bataillon, Infanterie Regiment at Weingarten 11.1934–10.1936.

WWII: Commander of Ersatz Bataillon, Infanterie Regiment 14, 11.1936–08.1939, Commander of Infanterie Ersatz Regiment 14, 09.1939–02.1940, Commander of Infanterie Regiment 390, 02.1940–03.1942, Commandant of Feldkommandantur 723, 08.1942–05.1943, delegated to care of military hospitals in Greater Reich 05.1943–05.1945. Awards: 1939 Clasps to the 1914 Iron Cross 1st and 2nd Class, Infantry Assault Badge in Silver, Eastern Front Medal, RK-Hohenzollern, RK-Sachsen Albrecht Order 1st Class with Swords, RK-Wuerttemberg Friedrich Order 1st Class with Swords, 1914 Iron Cross 1st and 2nd Class, 1914 Wound Badge in Black, Turkish Silver Liakat Medal with Sabre, Bavarian Military Service Order IV. Class with Swords, Austro-Hungarian Military Service Cross 3rd Class with War Decoration, Oldenburg Friedrich August Cross 1st and 2nd Class, Cross of Honor.

Bullinger, Richard: General-Ingenieur (01.09.41), (Luftwaffe); born 05.08.78 in Dischingen, died 03.09.46 in Schoengau. Engineer by profession. WWI: in G.A.S. as Lead Engineer attached to Staff of Inspectorate of Flieger. Group Leader LC III 2 in R.L.M. 03.1933–03.1936, Subordinate Department Leader LC III Fl. in R.L.M. 04.1936–12.1936, Department Leader LC III Fl. in R.L.M. 01.1937–06.1938. WWII: Department Director in LC B.f.S. of R.L.M. 07.1938–10.1941, Department Chief of B.f.S. in R.L.M. 10.1941–06.1944, attached to Luftwaffe Liaison Office of Reich Ministry for Armaments and War Production 09.1944–05.1945. Awards: War Merit Cross 1st and 2nd Class with Swords, Cross of Honor.

Bullion, Konrad Graf von: General-Ingenieur (01.08.42), (Luftwaffe); born 16.10.93 in Wuerzburg, died 26.08.76 in Munich. Engineer by profession. WWI: Oberleutnant and Adjutant in Bavarian Res. Feld Artillerie Regiment 8. Advisor, Group Leader and later Department Leader in R.L.M. 1933–date unknown, attached to Staff of Armaments Inspection III. Awards: War Merit Cross 1st and 2nd Class with Swords, 1914 Iron Cross 1st and 2nd Class, 1914 Wound Badge in Black, Bavarian Military Service Order IV. Class with Swords, Cross of Honor.

Bundsmann, Dr. Otto: General-Arzt (01.04.39), (Heer); born 30.05.75 in Innsbrueck, died 03.11.51 in Innsbrueck. Medical doctor by profession. WWI: Stabs-Arzt to Austrian Armee Gruppe "Conrad Erzherzog Josef." Transferred to German Wehrmacht 03.1938. WWII: Commander of Sanitats Abteilung at Innsbrueck 08.1939–02.1940, attached to Wehrkreis Kommando XVIII 02.1940–06.1943, retired 11.1943. Awards: War Merit Cross 1st and 2nd Class without Swords, Cross of Honor.

Burchard, Heinrich: General der Flak Artillerie (01.09.44), (Luftwaffe); born 05.10.94 in Fulda, died 11.04.45 (suicide) in Quassel. WWI: Leutnant in Fuss Artillerie Regiment 13. Promotions to Generalmajor 01.11.40, Generalleutnant

01.08.42. Commander of Fahr Abteilung in Wolfenbuettel 07.1934–03.1935, Commander of Flak Abteilung 6, 04.1935–09.1935, Abteilungs Commander in Flak Regiment 7, 10.1935–03.1937, Instructor at Luftwaffe Technical Academy in Berlin 04.1937–01.1938, Ia on Staff of Luftkreis Schule in Berlin 02.1938–06.1938. WWII: Chief of Staff to Luftgau Kommando XII 07.1938–08.1940, Commander of 7. Flak Division 09.1941–02.1942, Commander of Special Purpose Staff Air Region "Afrika" 02.1942–08.1942, Commander of 19. Flak Division 08.1942–12.1942, Commander of 7. Flak Division 03.1943–07.1944, General with Special Duties of Flak Artillerie with Reichsmarschall 07.1944–04.1945. Awards: German Cross in Gold 15.03.43, 1939 Clasps to the 1914 Iron Cross 1st and 2nd Class, Flak War Badge, Afrika Cuff Band, 1914 Iron Cross 1st and 2nd Class, 1914 Wound Badge in Black, Cross of Honor.

Burchardi, Theodor: Admiral (01.01.45), (Kriegsmarine); born 14.05.92 in Homburg, died 12.08.83 in Gluecksburg. WWI: Oberleutnant zur See and Commander of torpedo boat *G-39*. Promotions to Konteradmiral 01.01.41, Vizeadmiral 01.02.43. Commander of II. Schiff Stamm Abteilung Ost-See 10.1934–10.1936, attached to Marine Weapons Arsenal at Kiel 10.1936–10.1937. WWII: Commander of light cruiser *Koeln* 10.1937–01.1940, Chief of Central Department at Naval Shipyard at Kiel 01.1940–02.1941, Chief of Staff to Naval Shipyard at Kiel 02.1941–05.1941, Naval Commander "D" 05.1941–11.1941, Marine Befehlshaber of Eastern Territories 11.1941–06.1944, Marine Befehlshaber of Eastern Baltic Sea 06.1944–04.1945. Awards: Oak Leaves 08.04.45 (823), Knight's Cross 29.09.44, German Cross in Gold 31.03.44, 1939 Clasps to the 1914 Iron Cross 1st and 2nd Class, High Seas Fleet War Badge, Finnish Freedom Cross 1st Class with Swords, 1914 Iron Cross 1st and 2nd Class, Cross of Honor.

Admiral Theodor Burchardi. (Bundesarchiv)

Burckhardt, Karl: Generalleutnant (01.03.42), (Heer); born 13.03.89 in Reutlingen, died 30.01.46 (executed) in Kiev. WWI: Hauptmann on Staff of 26. Landwehr Division. Promotion to Generalmajor 01.03.40. Commander of Nachrichten Abteilung at Hannover 10.1934–10.1935. WWII: Commander of Nachrichtentruppen for VI. Armee Korps 10.1935–08.1939, Armee Signals Leader 5, 08.1939–10.1939, Signals Leader for O.B. Ost (occupied Poland) 10.1939–05.1940, Signals Leader to 9. Armee 05.1940–11.1940, Signals Leader to Heeresgruppe D 11.1940–08.1942, Commandant of Feldkommandantur 593, 02.1943–09.1944, captured 09.1944.

Awards: 1939 Clasps to the 1914 Iron Cross 1st and 2nd Class, 1914 Iron Cross 1st and 2nd Class, Cross of Honor.

Burdach, Karl: Generalleutnant (01.11.42), (Heer); born 28.07.91 in Chemnitz, died 30.12.76 in Freiburg. WWI: Oberleutnant and Adjutant to Commander of Artillerie 23. Promotion to Generalmajor 01.06.41. Commander of II. Abteilung, Artillerie Regiment 50, 10.1935–09.1937. WWII: Chief of Replacements Department in Reich War Ministry (later O.K.H.) 10.1937–09.1939, Commander of Artillerie Regiment 194, 09.1939–04.1940, Commander of Artillerie 123, 04.1940–08.1941, Commander of 251. Infanterie Division 08.1941–12.1942, Commander of 11. Infanterie Division 09.1943–05.1944, Senior Commander of Artillerie 320, 09.1944–04.1945. Awards: Knight's Cross 23.02.44, German Cross in Gold 26.12.41, 1939 Clasps to the 1914 Iron Cross 1st and 2nd Class, General Assault Badge, Eastern Front Medal, German Red Cross Decoration 1st Class, RK-Sachsen Military St. Heinrich's Order 29.04.18, 1914 Iron Cross 1st and 2nd Class, 1914 Wound Badge in Silver, Cross of Honor.

Burgdorf, Wilhelm: General der Infanterie (01.11.44), (Heer); born 15.02.95 in Furstenwalde, died 01.05.45 (suicide) in Berlin bunker. WWI: Leutnant and Adjutant to Grenadier Regiment 12. Promotions to Generalmajor 01.10.42, Generalleutnant 01.10.43. Instructor at Infanterie Schule Dresden (later Kriegsschule) 09.1934–10.1936. WWII: Adjutant to IX. Armee Korps 11.1936–05.1940, Commander of Infanterie Regiment 529, 05.1940–04.1942, Deputy Chief of Heeres Personnel Department in O.K.H. 05.1942–10.1944, Chief of Heeres Personnel Department in O.K.H. and Chief Wehrmacht Adjutant of the Fuehrer 10.1944–05.1945. Awards: Knight's Cross 29.09.41, 1939 Clasps to the 1914 Iron Cross 1st and 2nd Class, Infantry Assault Badge in Silver, Eastern Front Medal, RK-Hohenzollern, 1914 Iron Cross 1st and 2nd Class, Cross of Honor.

Burk, Karl: SS-Brigadefuehrer und Generalmajor der Waffen-SS (20.04.45); born 14.03.98 in Buchenau, died 23.09.63 in Fritzlar. P-1848222, SS-68910. WWI: Unteroffizier attached to Infanterie Regiment 132. Joined N.S.D.A.P. and S.S. in 1933. Attached to Staff of SS-Abschnitte XXX 01.07.35, attached to Staff of SS-Abschnitte XXIV 01.12.36, Leader of SS-Fuss Standarte 70, 01.12.38. WWII: Commander of SS-Flak Abteilung Ost 30.01.42, Stabsfuehrer to SS-Oberabschnitte Sudost and at same time Commander of SS-Flak Ersatz Regiment 15.05.43, Leader on Staff of H.S.S.P.F. Krakau 30.01.44, attached to SS-Fuehrungshauptamt 09.11.44, Commander of 5. SS-Freiwilligen Sturmbrigade "Wallonien," Commander of 15. Waffen Grenadier Division der SS (Lettische Nr. 1). Awards: German Cross in Gold 15.11.42, 1939 Clasps to the 1914 Iron Cross 1st and 2nd Class, War Merit Cross 1st and 2nd Class with Swords, General Assault Badge, Heer Flak Badge, Infantry Assault Badge in Bronze, 1914 Iron Cross 1st and 2nd Class, Cross of Honor, Reich Sports Badge in Gold, SA-Sports Badge in Gold, Degen, Ring.

Burkhardt, Prof. Hermann: Naval Senior Construction Director (06.03.39), (Kriegsmarine); born 23.06.81 in Glashuette, died 20.04.69 in Wattenscheid-Eppendorf. Engineer by profession. WWI: Director of Dock and Repair Operations for Imperial Shipyard at Wilhelmshaven. WWII: Chief of Naval Operations and Planning Office at Wilhelmshaven Shipyard 07.1940–10.1941, retired 10.1941. Awards: War Merit Cross 1st and 2nd Class with Swords, Cross of Honor.

Burmeister, Arnold: Generalleutnant (20.04.45), (Heer); born 28.02.99 in Norburg, died 02.07.88 in Stuehlingen. WWI: Fahnrich in Infanterie Regiment 24. Promotion to Generalmajor 01.01.45. Schwadron Chef in Reiter Regiment at Ludwigslust 10.1934–10.1935, Chief of 3. Schwadron, Reiter (later Kavallerie) Regiment 14, 10.1935–10.1937, Commander of II. Bataillon, Kavallerie Regiment 14, 10.1937–02.1939. WWII: attached to Staff of Panzer Regiment 6, 02.1939–08.1939, Commander of II. Abteilung, Panzer Regiment 6, 09.1939–05.1941, Group Director on Staff of Heeresgruppe K, In 6, 10.1941–07.1942, Commander of 21. Panzer Brigade 03.1943–07.1943, Department Chief in General Inspector of Panzertruppen 03.1944–10.1944, Commander of 25. Panzer Grenadier Division 10.1944–05.1945. Awards: Knight's Cross 14.01.45, German Cross in Gold 09.04.43, 1939 Clasps to the 1914 Iron Cross 1st and 2nd Class, Tank Assault Badge in Silver, 1939 Wound Badge in Black, 1914 Iron Cross 1st and 2nd Class, Cross of Honor.

Burmeister, Fritz: Admiral-Stabsintendant (01.05.44), (Kriegsmarine); born 21.06.84 in Danzig, died 11.07.56 in Kiel. Administrative Officer by profession. WWI: Marine Feld-Intendant to 3. Naval Division in Flanders. Promotion to Admiral-Intendant 17.11.41. Service unknown 1919–09.1934. WWII: Naval Chief Intendant to Baltic Sea Naval Station 10.1934–06.1943, Chief of Senior Administration Staff to Marine Befehlshaber of Baltic Sea 06.1943–05.1945. Awards: War Merit Cross 1st and 2nd Class with Swords, 1914 Iron Cross 1st and 2nd Class, Cross of Honor.

Generalfeldmarschall Ernst Busch. (Michael Miller)

Busch, Ernst: Generalfeldmarschall (01.02.43), (Heer); born 06.07.85 in Essen, died 17.07.45 at Camp Aldershot near London. WWI: Hauptmann and Commander of II. Bataillon, Infanterie Regiment 16. Promotions to Generalmajor 01.09.35, Generalleutnant 01.10.37, General der Infanterie 01.02.38, Generaloberst 19.07.40. Commander of Infanterie Regiment at Potsdam 10.1934–10.1935, Commander of 23. Division 10.1935–01.1938. WWII: Commander of VIII. Armee Korps 02.1938–02.1940, O.B. of 16.

Armee 02.1940–11.1943, O.B. of Heeresgruppe Mitte 10.1943–06.1944, Fuehrer Res. in O.K.H. 07.1944–03.1945, O.B. of German Forces North-West 03.1945–05.1945. Awards: Oak Leaves 21.08.43 (274), Knight's Cross 26.05.40, 1939 Clasps to the 1914 Iron Cross 1st and 2nd Class, Demjansk Shield, Eastern Front Medal, Finnish Freedom Cross 1st Class with Breast Star and Swords, Pour le Mérite 04.10.18, RK-Hohenzollern, 1914 Iron Cross 1st and 2nd Class, 1914 Wound Badge in Silver, Cross of Honor.

Busch, Hans: Generalmajor (01.08.44), (Luftwaffe); born 25.03.87 in Giessen, died 17.07.51 at Voikovo P.O.W. Camp. WWI: in G.A.S. as Hauptmann and Fuehrer of Flieger Abteilung A 202. Advisor in R.L.M. 07.1933–03.1934, Group Leader in Abwehr Abteilung of R.L.M. 04.1934–06.1938, attached to Staff of Luftgau Kommando XII 07.1938–03.1939. WWII: Luftwaffe Attaché to German Embassy in Lima 06.1939–05.1942, Department Chief in R.L.M. 06.1942–02.1943, Economic Officer in Romania 03.1943–08.1944, captured 08.1944. Awards: War Merit Cross 1st and 2nd Class with Swords, Pilot's Commemorative Badge, 1914 Iron Cross 1st and 2nd Class, 1914 Pilot's Badge, Cross of Honor.

Buschenhagen, Erich: General der Infanterie (01.01.44), (Heer); born 08.12.95 in Strassburg, died 13.09.94 in Kronberg. WWI: Oberleutnant and Liaison Officer of Signals Chief to Austrian Feld Armee. Promotions to Generalmajor 01.08.41, Generalleutnant 01.05.43. Advisor in Reichswehr (later Reich War Ministry) 08.1934–06.1935, Advisor in Abteilung 4 of General Staff of Heeres 07.1935–10.1936, Commander of Nachrichtentruppen III 10.1936–10.1937, attached to Staff of Infanterie Regiment 67, 10.1937–02.1938. WWII: Commander of Infanterie Regiment 5 (mot.) 03.1938–08.1939, Chief of Staff to XXI. Armee Korps 08.1939–12.1940, Chief of General Staff to A.O.K. Norway 12.1940–04.1942, Commander of 15. Infanterie Division 06.1942–11.1943, Commander of LII. Armee Korps 11.1943–09.1944, captured 09.1944. Awards: Oak Leaves 04.07.44 (521), Knight's Cross 05.12.43, German Cross in Gold 19.07.42, 1939 Clasps to the 1914 Iron Cross 1st and 2nd Class, Finnish Freedom Cross 1st Class with Swords, 1914 Iron Cross 1st and 2nd Class, Cross of Honor.

General der Infanterie Erich Buschenhagen. (Bundesarchiv)

Buschenhagen, Dr. Walther: General-Intendant (01.12.43), (Heer); born 19.04.90 in Karlsruhe, died 23.09.86 in Berlin. Administrative Officer by profession. WWI: service unknown. Ministerialrat in Administration Amt of Wehrkreis Kommando

III 10.1934–09.1936, Advisor in V 2 of Reich War Ministry 10.1936–1937. WWII: Advisor in V 2 of Reich War Ministry (later O.K.H.) 1937–1941, attached to Academy for Higher Intendant Service 1941–12.1943, Chief Intendant to Wehrkreis XX 12.1943–05.1945. Awards: War Merit Cross 1st and 2nd Class with Swords, Cross of Honor.

Buschmann, Friedrich: Generalleutnant (01.11.41), (Heer); born 24.01.85 in Wiesbaden, died 11.03.54 in Berlin. WWI: Hauptmann and Commander of Schwere Artillerie Abteilung 138. Promotion to Generalmajor 01.01.39. Commander of III. Abteilung, Artillerie Regiment at Schwerin 10.1934–09.1935, Commander of Artillerie Regiment 56, 10.1935–11.1938. WWII: Commander of Artillerie 4, 11.1938–1940, Commander of Artillerie 24, 1940–04.1942, retired 04.1942. Awards: German Cross in Gold 11.06.42, 1939 Clasps to the 1914 Iron Cross 1st and 2nd Class, General Assault Badge, 1914 Iron Cross 1st and 2nd Class, Cross of Honor.

Busich, Rudolf: Generalleutnant (01.12.43), (Heer); born 17.01.89 in Triest, died 24.02.46 in Gartenau. WWI: Hauptmann and Kompanie Chef in Austrian Eisenbahn Regiment. Promotion to Generalmajor 01.08.42. Transferred to German Wehrmacht 03.1938, Commander of Pionier Bataillon 85, 07.1938–11.1938. WWII: Commander of II. Bataillon, Pionier Regiment 68, 11.1938–08.1939, Commander of Eisenbahn Pionier Regiment 1, 09.1939–06.1942, Commander of 707. Infanterie Division 06.1943–04.1944, Commander of Processing Office "Stalingrad" in O.K.H. 10.1944–05.1945. Awards: German Cross in Gold 29.10.43, 1939 Iron Cross 1st Class, 1939 Clasp to the 1914 Iron Cross 2nd Class, General Assault Badge, 1914 Iron Cross 2nd Class, Cross of Honor.

Busse, Theodor: General der Infanterie (01.11.44), (Heer); born 15.12.97 in Frankfurt-Oder, died 21.10.86 in Wallerstein. WWI: Leutnant in Infanterie Regiment 396. Promotions to Generalmajor 01.03.43, Generalleutnant 01.09.43. Group Leader in Abteilung 6 of Heeres General Staff 07.1935–09.1936, Kompanie Chief in Infanterie Regiment 83, 10.1936–06.1937, Ia to 22. Division 07.1937–02.1939. WWII: attached to Abteilung 4 of Heeres General Staff 03.1939–10.1940, Ia to 11. Armee 10.1940–11.1942, Ia to Heeresgruppe Don and later Heeresgruppe Sud 11.1942–03.1943, Chief of General Staff to Heeresgruppe Sud 03.1943–03.1944, Commander of I. Armee Korps 09.1944–01.1945, Oberbefehlshaber of 9. Armee 01.1945–05.1945. Awards: Knight's

General der Infanterie Theodor Busse. (Bundesarchiv)

Cross 30.01.44, German Cross in Gold 24.05.42, 1939 Clasps to the 1914 Iron Cross 1st and 2nd Class, Eastern Front Medal, Crimea Shield, Kurland Cuff Band, RK-Hohenzollern, 1914 Iron Cross 1st and 2nd Class, 1914 Wound Badge in Black, Cross of Honor.

Busse, Wilhelm: Konteradmiral z.V. (01.09.44), (Kriegsmarine); born 20.03.78 in Berlin, died 09.12.65 in Kiel. WWI: Korvettenkapitan and Department Chief in Admiralty. Member of N.S.D.A.P. Not in service 08.1920–07.1939. WWII: Director of Reichs Union and German Seamen 10.1940–05.1945, RAD-Obergeneralarbeitsfuehrer. Awards: Golden Party Badge, War Merit Cross 1st and 2nd Class with Swords, Anhalt Commemorative Badge in Silver, Grand Officer's Cross of the Bulgarian St. Alexander Order, Commander's Cross of the Bulgarian Military Service Order, Red Eagle Order IV. Class with Crown, RK-Hohenzollern, 1914 Iron Cross 1st and 2nd Class, Turkish Silver Imtiaz Medal with Sabre, Cross of Honor.

Buttlar, Edgar von: Generalmajor (01.10.43), (Heer); born 19.02.89 in Wolfenhagen, died 08.05.55 in Bad Pyrmont. WWI: Oberleutnant in Dragoon Regiment 5. Attached to Staff of Nachrichten Abteilung at Potsdam 10.1934–03.1935, attached to Staff of Nachrichten Abteilung at Magdeburg 04.1935–10.1935. WWII: Commander of Nachrichten Abteilung 49, 10.1935–04.1940, Commander of Nachrichtentruppen VI 08.1940–09.1941, Wehrmacht Signals Leader in Boehmen-Maehren 09.1941–09.1942, Special Purpose Higher Signals Leader 515, 09.1942–11.1943, Fuehrer Res. in O.K.H. 11.1943–10.1944, Commandant of Feldkommandantur 677, 11.1944–05.1945. Awards: War Merit Cross 1st and 2nd Class with Swords, RK-Sachsen Order of the White Falcon 2nd Class with Swords, 1914 Iron Cross 1st and 2nd Class, Cross of Honor.

Butze, Otto: Generalleutnant (01.01.43), (Heer); born 05.07.91 in Arolsen, died 18.05.78 in Lingen. WWI: Oberleutnant and Chief of 1. M.G. Kompanie, 9. Res. Jaeger Bataillon. Promotion to Generalmajor 01.10.41. Adjutant to Wehrkreis Kommando VI 10.1934–10.1935. WWII: Adjutant to VI. Armee Korps 10.1935–08.1939 and at same time attached to Command Staff of Infanterie Regiment 39, 02.1938–03.1938, Adjutant to Deputy Commander of VI. Armee Korps 08.1939–07.1940, Commander of Infanterie Regiment 78, 08.1940–09.1941, Commander of 340. Infanterie Division 03.1942–01.1943, Fuehrer Res. in O.K.H. 02.1943–01.1945. Awards: 1939 Clasps to the 1914 Iron Cross 1st and 2nd Class, Infantry Assault Badge in Silver, 1914 Iron Cross 1st and 2nd Class, 1914 Wound Badge in Black, Cross of Honor.

C

Caanitz, Dr. Hugo: Admiral-Arzt (01.02.44), (Kriegsmarine); born 09.05.95 in Artern, died 28.02.68 in Berlin. Medical doctor by profession. WWI: service unknown. Chief Physician at Naval Hospital in Kiel 09.1932–04.1937. WWII: Medical Staff Officer attached to Marine Station Eastern Sea 04.1937–01.1940, Chief of Medical Science Department in O.K.M. 01.1940–02.1944, Chief Medic at Naval Hospital in Stralsung 01.1944–05.1945. Awards: War Merit Cross 1st and 2nd Class with Swords, Cross of Honor.

Cabanis, Ernst: Generalleutnant (01.05.43), (Luftwaffe); born 12.10.90 in Berlin, died 07.03.68 in Celle. WWI: Rittmeister in Dragoon Regiment 6. Promotion to Generalmajor 01.04.40. Advisor in Personalamt of R.L.M. 03.1934–08.1935, Group Leader in the Personalamt of R.L.M. 09.1935–09.1937, attached to Reichs War Court 10.1937–09.1938. WWII: Department Chief (LP 5) in Luftwaffe Personnel Office of R.L.M. 09.1939–05.1943, retired 05.1943, Honorary Member of People's Court 12.1938–06.1943. Awards: War Merit Cross 1st and 2nd Class with Swords, RK-Hohenzollern, 1914 Iron Cross 1st and 2nd Class, Cross of Honor.

Cabanis, Hans: Generalmajor (01.01.43), (Heer); born 16.05.86 in Berlin, died 18.08.64 in Bebenhausen. WWI: Hauptmann and Ia to 14. Landwehr Division. Official in Central Office of the Reichswehr 10.1934–06.1935. WWII: Leader on Staff of Military Replacement Inspection in Berlin 07.1935–10.1939, Ib to XXI. Armee Korps 11.1939–09.1940, Chief of Staff to Higher Kommando LX 09.1940–03.1941, Chief of Staff to Higher Kommando XXXIV. Korps 03.1941–02.1942, Chief of Staff to XXI. Armee Korps 02.1942–11.1943, Fuehrer Res. in O.K.H. 11.1943–08.1944, Wehrmacht Commander of Magdeburg 08.1944–04.1945. Awards: 1939 Clasps to the 1914 Iron Cross 1st and 2nd Class, Eastern Front Medal, German Red Cross Merit Cross, RK-Hohenzollern, 1914 Iron Cross 1st and 2nd Class, Cross of Honor.

Canaris, Wilhelm: Admiral (01.01.40), (Kriegsmarine); born 01.01.87 in Aplerbek, died 09.04.45 (executed by SS) at K.L. Flossenburg. WWI: U-boat service as Kapitanleutnant and Commandant of *U-128*. Promotions to Konteradmiral 01.05.35, Vizeadmiral 01.04.38. Commandant of line ship *Schlesien* 10.1932–09.1934, Naval Commandant of Swinemuende 09.1934–01.1935, Chief of Abwehr Abteilung in Reich War Ministry 04.1935–02.1938. WWII: Chief of Amtsgruppe Ausland/Abwehr in O.K.W. 06.1938–11.1939, Chief of Abwehr 11.1939–02.1944, placed in reserve 07.1944 then dismissed for part in 20.07.44 plot against Hitler's life. Awards: German Cross in Silver 11.11.43, 1939 Clasps to the 1914 Iron Cross 1st and 2nd Class, War Merit Cross 1st and 2nd Class with Swords, Grand Cross of the Italian Order of the Crown, Grand Cross of the Hungarian Service Order, Grand Cross of the Romanian Order of the Crown, Grand Cross of the Romanian Order of the Star with Swords, Commander's Cross 1st Class of the Finnish Order of the White Rose, Finnish Freedom Cross 1st Class with Breast Star and Swords, Grand Officer's Cross of the Bulgarian Military Service Order, Spanish Cross in Gold with Swords, Commander's Cross 1st Class of the Sachsen Ernestine House Order with Swords and Ring (post-war award), 1914 Iron Cross 1st and 2nd Class, Prussian Crown Order IV. Class with Swords, Austro-Hungarian Military Service Cross 3rd Class with War Decoration, 1914 Submarine Badge, Cross of Honor, German Horseman's Badge in Silver.

Cantzler, Oskar: Generalleutnant (01.08.42), (Heer); born 14.06.90 in Zell, died 03.02.60 in Munich. WWI: Oberleutnant on Staff of 6. Bavarian Infanterie Brigade. Promotion to Generalmajor 01.08.40. Commander of Pionier Bataillon at Stettin 10.1934–10.1935. WWII: Pionier Leader to II. Armee Korps 10.1935–08.1939, Pionier Leader to 2. Armee 10.1939–07.1940, Pionier Leader to 11. Armee 10.1940–04.1941, General of Pioniers attached to Heeresgruppe B followed by Heeresgruppe Sud 07.1941–12.1942, General of Pioniers to Heeresgruppe D 01.1943–05.1944, General of Pioniers to Heeresgruppe G 05.1944–08.1944, Inspector of Pioniers 08.1944–01.1945. Awards: 1939 Clasps to the 1914 Iron Cross 1st and 2nd Class, War Merit Cross 1st and 2nd Class with Swords, Eastern Front Medal, 1914 Iron Cross 1st and 2nd Class, Cross of Honor.

Carganico, Viktor: Generalmajor (01.12.41), (Luftwaffe); born 15.07.87 in Weenzen, died 27.05.45 (shot by Russians) at Gut Neugrimnitz. WWI: in G.A.S. as Oberleutnant in Feld Flieger Abteilung. Flughafen Commandant of Tempelhof 10.1934–01.1939. WWII: Fliegerhorst Commandant of Okzie 09.1939–1940, Fliegerhorst Commandant of Schwerin-Goerries 1940–06.1941, Flughafenbereichs Commandant of Baranowicze 06.1941–03.1942, Flughafenbereichs Commandant of Hagenow 03.1942–09.1942, Flughafenbereichs Commandant of 1-VI then Flughafenbereichs 7-XI 11.1942–03.1943, Flughafenbereichs Commandant of 1-IV 03.1943–10.1944, retired 01.1945. Awards: War Merit Cross 1st and 2nd Class with Swords, Pilot's Commemorative Badge, 1914 Iron Cross 1st and 2nd Class,

Prussian Crown Order IV. Class, 1914 Pilot's Badge, Austro-Hungarian Pilot's Badge, Cross of Honor.

Carls, Rolf: Generaladmiral (19.07.40), (Kriegsmarine); born 29.05.85 in Rostock, died 15.04.45 (killed) in Bad Oldesloe. WWI: U-boat service as Kapitanleutnant and Commandant of *U-124*. Promotions to Reichsmarine Konteradmiral 01.04.34, Vizeadmiral 01.01.37, Admiral 01.06.37. Commandant of line ship *Hessen* 10.1932–10.1933, Chief of Staff to Flottenkommando 10.1933–09.1934, Befehlshaber of all line ships 09.1934–09.1936 and at same time Befehlshaber of all line ships in Spain 07.1936–11.1936, Flottenchef 01.1937–10.1938. WWII: Marine Befehlshaber of Baltic Sea Naval Station 11.1938–09.1940, Oberbefehlshaber of Marine Gruppen Kommando Nord 09.1940–03.1943, retired 05.1943. Awards: Knight's Cross 16.04.40, German Cross in Gold 28.02.43, 1939 Clasps to the 1914 Iron Cross 1st and 2nd Class, Spanish Cross in Gold with Swords, Grand Cross of the Italian Order of the Crown, Grand Cross of the Order of the White Rose of Finland with Breast Star and Swords, Grand Cross of the Bulgarian Military Service Order, Grand Cross of the Hungarian Service Order, Grand Cross of the Spanish Order for Service, Finnish Freedom Cross 1st Class with Oak Leaves and Swords, Spanish War Cross (Spain), Silesian Eagle 1st and 2nd Class, 1914 Iron Cross 1st and 2nd Class, Mecklenburg-Schwerin Military Service Cross 1st and 2nd Class, Turkish Osmanje Order IV. Class with Sabre, 1914 Submarine Badge, Cross of Honor.

Generaladmiral Rolf Carls. (Roger James Bender)

Carlsen, Robert: Generalleutnant (01.10.40), (Luftwaffe); born 13.02.79 in Ranten, died 07.03.59 in Hamburg. WWI: Major attached to Grand General Staff. Promotion to Generalmajor 01.01.39. Ia and Quartermaster to Luftkreis Kommando I 06.1934–06.1937. WWII: Commander of Luftzeuggruppe 7, 07.1937–11.1942, Industry Representative for Luftgau Kommando XI 06.1943–04.1945. Awards: War Merit Cross 1st and 2nd Class with Swords, RK-Hohenzollern, RK-Sachsen Albrecht Order 1st Class with Swords, 1914 Iron Cross 1st and 2nd Class, Cross of Honor.

Carp, Georg: Generalleutnant (01.04.42), (Heer); born 16.05.86 in Neisse, died 06.05.83 in Tuebingen. WWI: Oberleutnant on Staff of 1.Finnish Division. Promotion to Generalmajor 01.04.38. Department Leader in In 3 of Reich War Ministry 02.1935–01.1938, Department Chief in In 8 of O.K.H. 02.1938–11.1938,

Inspector of Fahrtruppen for In 8 in O.K.H. 11.1938–06.1939. WWII: Military Replacement Inspector for Oppeln 07.1939–03.1940, Military Replacement Inspector for Kattowitz 03.1940–05.1942, Commandant of Feldkommandantur 559, 05.1942–04.1943, Fuehrer Res. in O.K.H. 04.1943–06.1944, retired 06.1944. Awards: 1939 Clasps to the 1914 Iron Cross 1st and 2nd Class, War Merit Cross 1st and 2nd Class with Swords, 1914 Iron Cross 1st and 2nd Class, Cross of Honor.

Casper, Karl: Generalleutnant (01.07.43), (Heer); born 22.02.93 in Rehden, died 25.08.70 in Munich. WWI: Leutnant on Staff of Infanterie Regiment 61. Promotion to Generalmajor 01.10.42. Attached to Staff of Infanterie Regiment 35, 10.1935–09.1936. WWII: Commander of I. Bataillon, Jaeger Regiment 13, 10.1936–02.1940, Commander of Infanterie Regiment 118 (mot.) 02.1940–10.1942, Commander of 335. Infanterie Division 10.1942–09.1943, Commander of 171. Infanterie Division 01.1944–10.1944, Commander of 48. Infanterie Division 12.1944–05.1945. Awards: Knight's Cross 22.09.41, Honor Roll Clasp 22.07.41, 1939 Clasps to the 1914 Iron Cross 1st and 2nd Class, German Army High Command Commendation Certificate 20.07.41, Infantry Assault Badge in Bronze, Eastern Front Medal, 1939 Wound Badge in Silver, West Wall Medal, 1914 Iron Cross 1st and 2nd Class, 1914 Wound Badge in Black, Cross of Honor.

Castorf, Helmuth: Generalleutnant (01.07.43), (Heer); born 26.01.92 in Penig, died 28.03.57 in Bielefeld. WWI: Hauptmann on Staff of 220. Infanterie Division. Promotion to Generalmajor 01.10.42. Advisor in Reichswehr Ministry (later Reich War Ministry) 08.1934–06.1935, Advisor in Abteilung 4 of General Staff of Heeres 07.1935–11.1938. WWII: Commander of II. Bataillon, Infanterie Regiment 64, 11.1938–08.1939, Commander of Infanterie Regiment 454, 08.1939–12.1940, Commander of Infanterie Regiment 586, 12.1940–12.1941, Commander of 329. Infanterie Division 12.1941–03.1942, Commander of Division 151, 04.1942–06.1942, Commander of Division 166, 06.1942–07.1944, Commander of Division 172, 07.1944–05.1945. Awards: 1939 Clasps to the 1914 Iron Cross 1st and 2nd Class, Infantry Assault Badge in Silver, 1914 Iron Cross 1st and 2nd Class, 1914 Wound Badge in Silver, Cross of Honor.

Cejka, Alois: Ministerialdirektor (01.04.40), (Luftwaffe); born 05.09.86 in Augsburg, died 21.08.47 in Bamberg. Civil Servant and Administrative Officer by profession. WWI: Leutnant der Res. in 18. Bavarian Fuss Artillerie Bataillon. Intendant to Luftkreis Kommando V 06.1934–11.1936, Chief of Abteilung L.D. I in R.L.M. 01.1937–01.1939. WWII: Office Group Chief of GL/F in R.L.M. 02.1939–10.1941, Chief of GL/F in R.L.M. 10.1941–05.1945. Awards: War Merit Cross 1st and 2nd Class with Swords, 1914 Iron Cross 1st and 2nd Class, Bavarian Military Service Order IV. Class with Swords, Cross of Honor.

Chales de Beaulieu, Walter: Generalleutnant (01.05.44), (Heer); born 14.06.98 in Saalfeld, died 26.08.74 in Kressbronn. WWI: Leutnant and Adjutant of II. Bataillon, Feld Artillerie Regiment 93. Promotion to Generalmajor 01.06.43. Kompanie Chef in Kraftfahr Abteilung at Koenigsberg 10.1934–10.1935, Ia to 2. Panzer Division 10.1935–07.1937. WWII: Tactics Instructor at Kriegsschule 08.1937–08.1939, Ia to XVI. Armee Korps 09.1939–02.1940, Chief of Staff to XVI. Armee Korps 02.1940–02.1941, Chief of General Staff to 4. Panzer Armee 02.1941–01.1942, Commander of Panzer Grenadier Regiment 394, 01.1942–07.1942, Commander of 168. Infanterie Division 03.1943–11.1943, Commander of 23. Infanterie Division 02.1944–09.1944. Awards: German Cross in Gold 07.08.43, 1939 Clasps to the 1914 Iron Cross 1st and 2nd Class, Infantry Assault Badge in Silver, 1914 Iron Cross 1st and 2nd Class, Cross of Honor.

Chamier-Glisczinski, Wolfgang von: Generalleutnant (25.10.43), (Luftwaffe); born 16.04.94 in Hagen. died 12.08.43 (killed by partisans) in Sissak. WWI: in G.A.S. as Leutnant in Flieger Abteilungen 12 and later 23. Promotion to Generalmajor 01.11.41. Staffelkapitan in Gotha 06.1934–03.1935, Flughafen Commandant of Cottbus 04.1935–01.1936, Commander of Flieger Langstreckenschule 02.1936–03.1939. WWII: Commander of K.G. 3, 04.1939–11.1941, Commander of Greater Kampfflieger Schule at Tutow 12.1941–03.1943, Flieger Fuehrer of South-East Croatia 04.1943–08.1943. Awards: Knight's Cross 06.10.40, 1939 Clasps to the 1914 Iron Cross 1st and 2nd Class, Bomber's Flight Clasp in Gold, Combined Pilot-Observer's Badge, 1939 Wound Badge in Gold, Pilot's Commemorative Badge, 1914 Iron Cross 1st and 2nd Class, 1914 Wound Badge in Silver, 1914 Observer's Badge, Cross of Honor.

Chappuis, Friedrich-Wilhelm von: General der Infanterie (01.04.41), (Heer); born 13.09.86 in Schubin, died 27.08.42 (suicide) in Magdeburg. WWI: Hauptmann on Staff of 206. Infanterie Division. Promotions to Generalmajor 01.04.38, Generalleutnant 01.04.41. Commander of Infanterie Regiment 5, 10.1934–02.1938. WWII: Chief of Staff to XIV. Armee Korps 04.1938–01.1940, Commander of 15. Infanterie Division 01.1940–08.1940, Commander of 16. Infanterie Division 08.1940–03.1941, Commander of XXXVIII. Armee Korps 03.1941–05.1942. Awards: Knight's Cross 15.08.40, 1939 Clasps to the 1914 Iron Cross 1st and 2nd Class, RK-Hohenzollern, 1914 Iron Cross 1st and 2nd Class, 1914 Wound Badge in Black, Cross of Honor.

Chaulin-Egersberg, Gaston von: Generalleutnant (01.12.43), (Luftwaffe); born 20.11.93 in Worms, died 30.12.74 in Herford. WWI: Oberleutnant and Adjutant to Flak Commander of 19. Armee. Promotion to Generalmajor 01.12.41. Battery Chef in Flak Regiment 4, 10.1935–09.1936, Commander of II. Abteilung, Flak Regiment

24, 10.1936–11.1938. WWII: Commander of Flak Regiment 24, 11.1938–08.1939, Commander of Flak Gruppe Duesseldorf 09.1939–11.1941, Commander of 13. Flak Division 02.1942–07.1942, Inspector and later Chief of Landing Gear of Luftwaffe 07.1942–11.1944, attached to Luftflotte Reich 02.1945–04.1945. Awards: 1939 Clasps to the 1914 Iron Cross 1st and 2nd Class, War Merit Cross 1st and 2nd Class with Swords, Flak War Badge, RK-Sachsen Order of the White Falcon 2nd Class with Swords, 1914 Iron Cross 1st and 2nd Class, Austro-Hungarian Military Service Cross 3rd Class with War Decoration, Cross of Honor.

Chevallerie Hellmuth von der: Generalleutnant (01.05.43), (Heer); born 09.11.96 in Berlin, died 01.06.65 in Wiesbaden. WWI: Leutnant in Guards Grenadier Regiment 5. Promotion to Generalmajor 01.11.42. Schwadron Chef in Reiter Regiment at Rathenow 10.1934–02.1935, attached to Staff of Wehrkreis Kommando X (later X. Armee Korps) 05.1935–09.1936. WWII: Adjutant on Staff of XII. Armee Korps 10.1936–01.1940, Commander of Schuetzen Regiment 86, 07.1940–03.1942, Commander of 10. Schuetzen Brigade 03.1942–09.1942, Commander of 13. Panzer Division 11.1942–10.1943, Commander of 273. Res. Panzer Division 11.1943–05.1944, Commander of Panzer Training Grounds at Bergen 11.1944–02.1945. Awards: Knight's Cross 30.04.43, German Cross in Gold 19.04.42, 1939 Clasps to the 1914 Iron Cross 1st and 2nd Class, Tank Assault Badge in Silver, Eastern Front Medal, 1939 Wound Badge in Gold, West Wall Medal, 1914 Iron Cross 1st and 2nd Class, 1914 Wound Badge in Black, Cross of Honor.

Chevallerie, Kurt von der: General der Infanterie (01.02.42), (Heer); born 23.12.91 in Berlin, died 18.04.45 near Kolberg. Older brother of Generalleutnant Hellmuth von der Chevallerie. WWI: Hauptmann and Adjutant to 34. Landwehr Infanterie Brigade. Promotions to Generalmajor 01.03.39, Generalleutnant 01.01.41. Commander of Infanterie Regiment 38, 10.1935–09.1936, Commander of Infanterie Regiment 87, 10.1936–10.1937, Chief of Abteilung 10 in General Staff of Heeres 10.1937–08.1938. WWII: Chief of Zentral Abteilung in Heeres General Staff 08.1938–11.1939, Commander of 83. Infanterie Division 12.1939–12.1940, Commander of 99. Light Division 12.1940–11.1941, Commander of LIX. Armee Korps 12.1941–02.1943, Oberbefehlshaber of 1. Panzer Armee 04.1944–09.1944, Fuehrer Res. in O.K.H. 09.1944–05.1945. Awards: Oak Leaves 19.12.43 (357), Knight's Cross 23.10.41, 1939 Clasps to the 1914 Iron Cross 1st and 2nd Class, Infantry Assault Badge in Silver, Eastern Front Medal, 1939 Wound Badge in Black, 1914 Iron Cross 1st and 2nd Class, 1914 Wound Badge in Black, Cross of Honor.

Chill, Kurt: Generalleutnant (01.06.43), (Heer); born 01.05.95 in Thorn, died 05.07.76 in Groenitz. WWI: in G.A.S. as Leutnant in Flieger Abteilung 12. Promotion to Generalmajor 01.12.42. Kompanie Chef in Infanterie Regiment 65,

10.1935–09.1936, attached to Staff of 30. Division 10.1936–03.1937. WWII: Commander of I. Bataillon, Infanterie Regiment 1, 04.1937–02.1940, Commander of Infanterie Regiment 45, 12.1940–09.1942, Commander of 122. Infanterie Division 12.1942–02.1944, Commander of 85. Infanterie Division 02.1944–12.1944. Awards: Knight's Cross 25.10.43, German Cross in Gold 01.12.41, 1939 Iron Cross 1st Class, 1939 Clasp to the 1914 Iron Cross 2nd Class, Infantry Assault Badge in Silver, Eastern Front Medal, Pilot's Commemorative Badge, 1914 Iron Cross 2nd Class, 1914 Observer's Badge, Cross of Honor.

General der Infanterie Dietrich von Choltitz. (Bundesarchiv)

Choltitz, Dietrich von: General der Infanterie (01.08.44), (Heer); born 09.09.94 in Neustadt, died 04.11.66 in Baden-Baden. WWI: Leutnant and Adjutant of Ersatz Bataillon, Infanterie Regiment 107. Promotions to Generalmajor 01.09.42, Generalleutnant 01.02.43. Kompanie Chef in Infanterie Regiment at Tuebingen 10.1934–04.1935, Kompanie Chef in Infanterie Regiment at Flensburg 05.1935–10.1935, Kompanie Chef in Infanterie Regiment 26, 10.1935–01.1937. WWII: Commander of III. Bataillon, Infanterie Regiment 16, 02.1937–09.1940, Commander of Infanterie Regiment 16, 09.1940–08.1942, Commander of 11. Panzer Division 03.1943–10.1943, Wehrmacht Commander for Paris 08.1944, captured 08.1944. Awards: Knight's Cross 29.05.40, German Cross in Gold 08.02.42, 1939 Clasps to the 1914 Iron Cross 1st and 2nd Class, German Army High Command Commendation Certificate 03.10.41, Infantry Assault Badge in Silver, Eastern Front Medal, Crimea Shield, 1939 Wound Badge in Gold, RK-Sachsen Military St. Heinrich's Order 26.12.17, 1914 Iron Cross 1st and 2nd Class, 1914 Wound Badge in Silver, Cross of Honor.

Christian, Eckhard: Generalmajor (01.09.44), (Luftwaffe); born 01.12.07 Berlin, died 03.01.85 in Bad Kreuznach. Attached to Fliegerschule Warnemuende 10.1934–09.1935, Observer attached to Fliegerstaffel M on battleship *Admiral Scheer* 10.1935–05.1936, attached to Staff of L.G. "Greifswald" 10.1936–02.1938, attached to Luftwaffe Kriegsschule at Gatow 02.1938–06.1938, Advisor 1 attached to General Staff of Luftwaffe 07.1938–01.1939. WWII: Chief of Staff for General Staff of Luftwaffe 01.1939–03.1940, Ia to X. Flieger Korps 03.1940–06.1940, Gruppe Commander in K.G. 26, 06.1940–01.1941, General Staff Officer attached to Luftwaffe Operations Staff of O.K.L. 01.1941–08.1943, Ia to Luftwaffe Operational Staff 08.1943–08.1944, Chief of Luftwaffe Operational Staff 09.1944–04.1945.

Awards: German Cross in Silver 10.05.45, 1939 Iron Cross 1st and 2nd Class, War Merit Cross 1st and 2nd Class with Swords, 1939 Combined Pilot/Observer's Badge in Gold with Diamonds, Finnish Freedom Cross 2nd Class with Swords.

Christiani, Horst: Generalmajor (01.11.42), (Heer); born 13.08.93, died 19.11.42 in action on Channel Islands. WWI: Oberleutnant on Staff of 35. Res. Infanterie Division. Commander of Ersatz Bataillon, Infanterie Regiment 3, 10.1934–12.1938. WWII: Commander of II. Ersatz Bataillon, Infanterie Regiment 103, 01.1939–08.1939, Commander of I. Bataillon, Infanterie Regiment 154, 08.1939–1940, Commander of Infanterie Regiment 585 then Infanterie Regiment 583, 1941–11.1942. Awards: German Cross in Gold 27.10.41, 1939 Clasps to the 1914 Iron Cross 1st and 2nd Class, Infantry Assault Badge in Silver, 1939 Wound Badge in Gold, 1914 Iron Cross 1st and 2nd Class, 1914 Wound Badge in Black, Cross of Honor.

Christiansen, Friedrich: General der Flieger (01.01.39), (Luftwaffe); born 12.12.79 in Wyk, died 03.12.72 in Innien. P-800471. WWI: in Naval G.A.S. as Kapitanleutnant der Res. in II. Seeflieger Abteilung. Promotions to Generalmajor 01.12.35, Generalleutnant 01.08.37. Inspector of Luftwaffe Schulen in R.L.M. 01.1934–03.1935, Commander of Fliegerschulen Kommando 04.1935–02.1937. WWII: N.S.F.K.-Korpsfuehrer 04.1937–06.1943, Wehrmacht Befehlshaber of Netherlands 05.1940–04.1945. Awards: Golden Party Badge (honorary), German Cross in Silver (date unknown), War Merit Cross 1st and 2nd Class with Swords, Combined Pilot/Observer's Badge in Gold with Diamonds, Marine Pilot's Commemorative Badge, Pour le Mérite 11.12.17, RK-Hohenzollern, 1914 Iron Cross 1st and 2nd Class, 1914 Marine Pilot's Badge, Cross of Honor.

Chrobeck, Bruno: Generalmajor (01.12.42), (Heer); born 09.10.95 in Pless, died 10.12.42 in action near Dimitriyevka. WWI: Unteroffizier in Kavallerie Jaeger Regiment 3. Company Chef in Infanterie Regiment 38, 10.1935–11.1938. WWII: Commander of I. Bataillon, Infanterie Regiment 54, 11.1938–11.1940, Commander of III. Bataillon, Infanterie Regiment 51 (mot.) and later Commander of regiment itself 1941–03.1942, Commander of Infanterie Regiment 672, 03.1942–12.1942. Awards: Knight's Cross 04.07.40, German Cross in Gold 08.02.42, 1939 Iron Cross 1st Class, 1939 Clasp to the 1914 Iron Cross 2nd Class, German Army High Command Commendation Certificate 30.07.41, Infantry Assault Badge in Silver, 1939 Wound Badge in Gold, 1914 Iron Cross 2nd Class, Cross of Honor.

Ciliax, Otto: Admiral (01.02.43), (Kriegsmarine); born 30.10.91 in Neudietedorf, died 12.12.64 in Luebeck. WWI: U-boat service as Oberleutnant zur See and Commandant of *U-27*. Promotions to Konteradmiral 01.11.39, Vizeadmiral 01.06.41. Advisor attached to Marineleitung 09.1931–09.1934, Chief of Fleet Operations Abteilung in Marineleitung 09.1934–09.1936, Commandant of battleship *Admiral*

Scheer 09.1936–10.1938. WWII: Commandant of battleship *Scharnhorst* 01.1939–09.1939, Chief of Staff to Marine Gruppen Kommando West 12.1939–06.1941, Befehlshaber of Battleships 06.1941–06.1942, Inspector of Torpedo Affairs in O.K.M. 06.1942–03.1943, Marine Befehlshaber of Norway 03.1943–05.1945. Awards: Knight's Cross 21.03.42, German Cross in Gold 20.11.41, 1939 Clasps to the 1914 Iron Cross 1st and 2nd Class, High Seas Fleet War Badge, Spanish Cross in Gold with Swords, Commander's Cross of the Italian Order of the Crown, Spanish War Cross (Spain), RK-Sachsen Ernestine House Order 2nd Class with Swords, 1914 Iron Cross 1st and 2nd Class, Austro-Hungarian Military Service Cross 3rd Class with War Decoration, 1914 Submarine Badge, Cross of Honor.

Admiral Otto Ciliax. (Roger James Bender)

Claassen, Franz: Konteradmiral z.V. (01.01.42), (Kriegsmarine); born 15.11.81 in Goldbeck, died 02.05.45 (missing in action) at Pomerania. P-1289757, SS-288638. WWI: Korvettenkapitan and First Torpedo Officer on liner *Bayern*. Joined N.S.D.A.P. and S.S., SS-Brigadefuehrer attached to SS-Oberabschnitte Ostsee. WWII: Commandant of Naval Abschnitt Kolberg 08.1939–04.1941, placed at disposal of Naval Station Baltic Sea 04.1941–02.1942, Naval Commander "C" 05.1941–11.1941, retired 02.1942. Awards: 1939 Clasps to the 1914 Iron Cross 1st and 2nd Class, War Merit Cross 1st and 2nd Class with Swords, 1914 Iron Cross 1st and 2nd Class, 1914 Naval Wound Badge in Black, Cross of Honor, Degen, Ring.

Claassen, Siegfried: Konteradmiral z.V. (01.01.43), (Kriegsmarine); born 05.12.84 in Thiegenhof, died 07.06.51 in Hamburg. WWI: Kapitanleutnant assigned to Submarine Construction. Chief of Staff to Werft Abteilung in Marineleitung 10.1930–06.1933. No service 06.1933–09.1939. WWII: Judge at Prize Court Hamburg 09.1939–12.1942, retired 01.1943. Awards: War Merit Cross 1st and 2nd Class with Swords, 1914 Iron Cross 1st and 2nd Class, Cross of Honor.

Claer, Bernhard von: Generalleutnant (01.10.44), (Heer); born 07.12.88 in Berlin, died 29.03.53 in Goettingen. WWI: Hauptmann on Staff of XX. Armee Korps. Promotion to Generalmajor 01.04.42. Training Leader at Stolp 12.1934–08.1937, Commander of III. Bataillon, Infanterie Regiment 4, 10.1937–11.1938. WWII: Commander of Infanterie Regiment 4, 11.1938–03.1940, Senior Commandant of Feldkommandantur 591, 04.1940–06.1940, Senior Commandant of Feldkommandantur 570, 07.1940–06.1942, Senior Commandant of Feldkommandantur 397, 06.1942–03.1943, Senior Commandant of Feldkommandantur 589, 06.1943–09.1944, Commander of Staff z.b.V. von Claer 09.1944–04.1945. Awards: 1939

Clasps to the 1914 Iron Cross 1st and 2nd Class, 1939 Wound Badge in Black, 1914 Iron Cross 1st and 2nd Class, Cross of Honor.

Claes, Heinrich: Generalmajor (01.03.44), (Luftwaffe); born 01.01.84 in Muehlhausen, died 31.07.69 in Bad Godesberg. WWI: in G.A.S. as Hauptmann and Commander of Flieger FT Abteilung. Advisor for Radio Navigation attached to General Staff of Luftwaffe 11.1934–12.1938. WWII: Instructor at Luftwaffe Schule in Berlin-Gatow 01.1939–09.1939, Signals Leader to Luftgau Kommando III 10.1939–08.1940, Signals Leader to Luftgau Kommando VI 12.1940–12.1942, Wehrmacht Signals Leader to Wehrmacht Befehlshaber of Netherlands 01.1943–05.1945. Awards: War Merit Cross 1st and 2nd Class with Swords, Pilot's Commemorative Badge, RK-Hohenzollern, 1914 Iron Cross 1st and 2nd Class, 1914 Wound Badge in Black, 1914 Observer's Badge, Cross of Honor.

Claussen, Carl-August: Konteradmiral z.V. (01.09.41), (Kriegsmarine); born 10.03.81 in Altengamme, died 01.09.68 in Hamburg. WWI: Korvettenkapitan and Chief of III.Torpedobootsflotille. Administrative Leader for Wehrkreis Kommando X 10.1933–03.1935, Administrative Inspector for District X 04.1935–09.1937, no service 09.1937–01.1939. WWII: placed at disposal of Kriegsmarine 01.1939–06.1941, Shipyard Representative in Romania 06.1941–01.1942, Shipyard Representative with Admiral Staff of Black Sea 01.1942–02.1943, retired 06.1943. Awards: War Merit Cross 1st and 2nd Class with Swords, Commander's Cross of the Romanian Order of the Star with Swords, RK-Hohenzollern, 1914 Iron Cross 1st and 2nd Class, Oldenburg Friedrich-August Cross 1st and 2nd Class, Austro-Hungarian Military Service Cross 3rd Class with War Decoration, Turkish Medschidie Order IV, Class, Cross of Honor.

Cloessner, Erich: General der Infanterie (01.01.42), (Heer); born 17.09.88 in Giessen, died 28.03.76 in Konstanz. WWI: Hauptmann on Staff of XXV. Reserve Korps. Promotions to Generalmajor 01.10.37, Generalleutnant 01.10.39. Commander of Infanterie Regiment at Konstanz 10.1934–10.1935, Commander of Infanterie Regiment 14, 10.1935–05.1938. WWII: Military Replacement Inspector for Innsbrueck 06.1938–10.1939, Commander of 25. Jaeger Division 10.1939–01.1942, Commander of LIII. Armee Korps 01.1942–08.1943, Commander of Special Staff I in O.K.H. 06.1944–12.1944. Awards: Knight's Cross 29.09.40, German Cross in Gold 15.07.42, 1939 Clasps to the 1914 Iron Cross 1st and 2nd Class, Eastern Front Medal, 1914 Iron Cross 1st and 2nd Class, 1914 Wound Badge in Black, Cross of Honor.

Cochenhausen, Conrad von: Generalleutnant (01.10.38), (Heer); born 14.07.79 in Marburg, died 13.12.41 (suicide) near Lyubovska. WWI: Hauptmann and Adjutant to 9. Territorial Brigade. Promotion to Generalmajor 01.01.37.

Commander of Kriegsschule at Munich 10.1934–02.1938. WWII: Commander of 10. Infanterie Division 03.1938–09.1940, Commander of 134. Infanterie Division 10.1940–12.1941. Awards: Honor Roll Clasp 09.09.41, 1939 Clasps to the 1914 Iron Cross 1st and 2nd Class, Infantry Assault Badge in Silver, 1939 Wound Badge in Gold, 1914 Iron Cross 1st and 2nd Class, Cross of Honor.

Cochenhausen, Friedrich von: General der Artillerie (01.12.40), (Luftwaffe and Heer); born 14.07.79 in Marburg, died 20.07.46 in Hochstadt. WWI: Major and General Staff Officer (unit unknown). Promotions to Reichswehr Generalmajor 01.03.30, Generalleutnant 01.10.35. Joined Luftwaffe 10.1935, Tactics Instructor at Luftwaffe Kriegsschule in Berlin 10.1935–02.1938, retired 02.1938. WWII: recalled to Heer 08.1939, Commander of Wehrkreis Kommando XIII 08.1939–05.1942, retired 05.1942. Awards: War Merit Cross 1st and 2nd Class with Swords, Red Eagle Order IV. Class with Swords, RK-Hohenzollern, 1914 Iron Cross 1st and 2nd Class, Cross of Honor.

Coeler, Joachim: General der Flieger (01.01.42), (Luftwaffe); born 01.06.91 in Posen, died 14.05.55 in Garmisch-Partenkirchen. WWI: in Naval G.A.S. as Oberleutnant zur See in I. Seeflieger Abteilung. Promotions to Generalmajor 01.01.39, Generalleutnant 19.07.40. Leader of Luftwaffe Sea Office at Wilhelmshaven 10.1934–03.1935, attached to Staff of Seeflieger for Luftkreis Kommando VI 04.1935–03.1936, Inspector of Seeflieger for Luftkreis Kommando VI in Kiel 04.1936–01.1939, Leader of Marine Aircraft 04.1939–06.1939. WWII: Commander of Naval Luftwaffe West 06.1939–04.1940, Commander of 9. Flieger Division 02.1940–10.1940, Commander of IX. Flieger Korps 10.1940–12.1942, Commander of XIV. Flieger Korps 04.1943–08.1944, General of Transportflieger 08.1944–02.1945. Awards: Knight's Cross 12.07.40, 1939 Clasps to the 1914 Iron Cross 1st and 2nd Class, 1939 Pilot's Badge, Naval Pilot's Commemorative Badge, 1914 Iron Cross 1st and 2nd Class, 1914 Naval Pilot's Badge, Cross of Honor.

Collani, Ingo von: Generalmajor (01.11.44), (Heer); born 24.09.00 in Kolberg, died 14.12.69 in Lueneburg. Attached to Staff of Fortress at Loetzen 09.1935–02.1937, attached to General Staff of Heeres 03.1937–10.1937, Schwadron Chef in Kavallerie Regiment 13, 10.1937–11.1938. WWII: Ia to 1. Kavallerie Brigade 11.1938–11.1940, Ia to 12. Infanterie Division 11.1940–12.1942, Chief of General Staff to Wehrmacht Befehlshaber of Denmark 02.1943–11.1944, Commander of 218. Infanterie Division 12.1944–5.1945. Awards: German Cross in Silver (date unknown), 1939 Iron Cross 1st and 2nd Class, War Merit Cross 1st and 2nd Class with Swords, Eastern Front Medal, Kurland Cuff Band.

Conrad, Fritz: Konteradmiral z.V. (01.02.41), (Kriegsmarine); born 18.04.83 in Schwedt, died 01.01.44 of natural causes in Griefswald. WWI: Kapitanleutnant and Pionier Commander in Naval Korps. WWII: Advisor in Nautical Department of Marineleitung 10.1933–11.1939, Chief of Nautical Science Department in O.K.M. 11.1939–01.1944. Awards: War Merit Cross 1st and 2nd Class with Swords, RK-Hohenzollern, 1914 Iron Cross 1st and 2nd Class, Prussian Crown Order IV. Class with Swords, Oldenburg Friedrich-August Cross 1st and 2nd Class, 1914 Naval Wound Badge in Black, Cross of Honor.

Conrad, Gerhard: Generalleutnant (01.04.43), (Luftwaffe); born 21.04.95 in Pregelmuehle, died 28.05.82 in Ruhpolding. WWI: Leutnant in Infanterie Regiment 93. Promotion to Generalmajor 01.04.41. Instructor at Fliegerschule Fassberg 01.1935–03.1936, Staffelkapitan in K.G. 1 "Hindenburg" 04.1936–02.1937, Commander of K.G. I/257, 03.1937–03.1939. WWII: Commander of Flugkommandos Berlin 04.1939–08.1939, Commander of Special Purpose Air Landing Wing 2, 09.1939–06.1940, Commander of K.G. 27 "Boelcke" 06.1940–10.1940, Fliegerfuehrer of IX. Flieger Korps 12.1940–01.1943, Troop Commander of Luftflotte 4, 02.1943–03.1945. Awards: Knight's Cross 24.05.40, 1939 Clasps to the 1914 Iron Cross 1st and 2nd Class, Kreta Cuff Band, Air-to-Ground Assault Flight Clasp, 1939 Pilot's Badge, Pilot's Commemorative Badge, RK-Hohenzollern, RK-Anhalt Albrecht Order of the Bear 2nd Class with Swords, 1914 Iron Cross 1st and 2nd Class, 1914 Wound Badge in Silver, 1914 Pilot's Badge, Cross of Honor.

Conrad, Dr. Johannes: General-Richter (01.05.44), (Heer); born 22.03.88 in Lomitz, died 06.03.67 in Hannover. Jurist by profession. WWI: Leutnant der Res. on Staff of 6. Landwehr Brigade. Judge attached to Wehrkreis Kommando I 01.1934–12.1934, Judge attached to VI. Armee Korps 01.1935–09.1937. WWII: Judge attached to XI. Armee Korps 10.1937–08.1939, Judge with Staff of 4. Armee 08.1939–04.1940, Judge with Chief of Heeres Armaments and Befehlshaber of Ersatz Armee in O.K.H. 04.1940–10.1942, Chief Judge to Heeresgruppe B 10.1942–03.1943, Chief Judge to Heeresgruppe Mitte 03.1943–05.1945. Awards: War Merit Cross 1st and 2nd Class with Swords, 1914 Iron Cross 1st and 2nd Class, Cross of Honor.

Conradi, Siegfried: Generalmajor (01.01.40), (Heer); born 26.01.87 in Limbach, died 15.04.74 in Augsburg. WWI: Hauptmann on Staff of XIX. Armee Korps. Commander attached to Staff of Artillerie Regiment 4, 10.1935–06.1936, Commander of II. Abteilung, Artillerie Regiment 4, 06.1936–10.1937. WWII: Commander of Artillerie Regiment 11, 10.1937–10.1939, Commander of Artillerie 6, 11.1939–11.1942, Commandant of Feldkommandantur 1036, 08.1943–11.1943, Commandant of Feldkommandantur 517, 01.1945–04.1945. Awards: German Cross in Gold 24.11.42, 1939 Clasps to the 1914 Iron Cross 1st and 2nd Class, General Assault Badge, Eastern Front Medal, RK-Sachsen Military St. Heinrich's Order 30.07.17, 1914 Iron Cross 1st and 2nd Class, Cross of Honor.

Conrady, Alexander von: Generalmajor (01.05.44), (Heer); born 16.07.03 in Neu-Ulm, died 21.12.83 in Augsburg. Attached to Kriegsschule 10.1934–09.1936, Kompanie Chef in Infanterie Regiment 40, 10.1936–03.1938. WWII: Ordnance Officer I with 27. Infanterie Division 03.1938–07.1940, Commander of I. Bataillon, Infanterie Regiment 118, 07.1941–09.1942, Commander of Infanterie Regiment 118, 10.1942–02.1944, Commander of 36. Infanterie Division 04.1944–07.1944, captured 07.1944. Awards: Oak Leaves 22.08.43 (279), Knight's Cross 17.10.42, German Cross in Gold 24.12.41, 1939 Iron Cross 1st and 2nd Class, Infantry Assault Badge in Bronze, Eastern Front Medal, 1939 Wound Badge in Black, West Wall Medal.

Conrath, Paul: General der Fallschirmtruppe (01.01.45), (Luftwaffe); born 21.11.96 in Berlin, died 15.01.79 in Hamburg. WWI: Leutnant in Feld Artillerie Regiment 66. Promotions to Generalmajor 15.06.42, Generalleutnant 01.09.43. IIa attached to Staff of Prussian Minister President Hermann Goering 06.1934–03.1935, Adjutant to O.B. of Luftwaffe Hermann Goering 04.1935–09.1936, Batterie Chef in Flak Regiment 12, 10.1936–09.1937. WWII: Chief Adjutant to O.B. of Luftwaffe 01.1938–05.1940, Commander of Luftwaffe Regiment "General Goering" and later Brigade "Hermann Goering" 06.1940–10.1942, Commander of Fallschirm Panzer Division "Hermann Goering" 10.1942–04.1944, Commander of Training Fallschirmjaeger as well as its Inspector in R.L.M. 04.1944–05.1945. Awards: Oak Leaves 22.08.43 (276), Knight's Cross 04.09.41, German Cross in Gold 18.05.44, 1939 Clasps to the 1914 Iron Cross 1st and 2nd Class, Afrika Cuff Band, 1914 Iron Cross 1st and 2nd Class, Cross of Honor.

General der Fallschirmtruppe Paul Conrath. (Bundesarchiv)

Conze, Wilhelm: Generalmajor (30.01.45), (Heer); born 07.02.96 in Schoenemoor, died 31.03.78 in Oldenburg. WWI: Leutnant in Infanterie Regiment 91. Instructor at Heeres Kraftfahr Schule 04.1935–03.1936, attached to Panzer Regiment 5, 04.1936–09.1936, Commander of II. Abteilung, Panzer Regiment 8, 10.1936–04.1939. WWII: Commander of Panzer Lehr Regiment 04.1939–01.1940 and at same time Commander of Panzer Regiment 5, 09.1939–10.1939, Commander of Panzer Regiment 33, 02.1940–08.1940, Commander of Panzer Regiment 201, 11.1940–02.1941, attached to Kriegswissenschaftliche Abteilung in O.K.H. 09.1941–01.1943, Chief of Instructions Office of Panzertruppen 06.1944–09.1944, Fuehrer Res. in O.K.H. 09.1944–02.1945. Awards: 1939 Clasps to the 1914 Iron

Cross 1st and 2nd Class, War Merit Cross 1st and 2nd Class with Swords, Tank Assault Badge in Silver, RK-Hohenzollern, 1914 Iron Cross 1st and 2nd Class, Oldenburg Friedrich-August Cross 1st and 2nd Class, Austro-Hungarian Military Service Cross 3rd Class with War Decoration, 1914 Wound Badge in Silver, Cross of Honor.

Cordes, Ludwig: Ministerialdirigent (03.17.44), (Kriegsmarine); born 25.10.96 in Hasbergen, died 30.03.58 in Bonn. Civil Servant by profession. WWI: service unknown. WWII: General Advisor in Naval Weapons Office of O.K.M. 12.1939–10.1942, Office Group Chief in Weapons Construction in O.K.M. 11.1942–05.1945. Awards: War Merit Cross 1st and 2nd Class with Swords, Cross of Honor.

Coretti, Julius: Generalmajor (30.01.45), (Heer); born 11.02.92 in Luttenberg, died 08.08.70 in Graz. WWI: Oberleutnant and Adjutant to Austrian Infanterie Regiment 87. Transferred to German Wehrmacht 03.1938, attached to Archive Staff of Heeresgruppe 5, 03.1938–11.1938. WWII: attached to Staff of Infanterie Regiment 110, 11.1938–08.1939, Commander of II. Bataillon, Security Regiment 2, 08.1939–03.1941, Commander of Security Regiment 4, 03.1941–07.1942, Fuehrer Res. in O.K.H. 11.1942–11.1943, Commander of Special Purpose Ost Truppen 700, 11.1943–10.1944, Course Commander for Heeresgruppe G 01.1945–05.1945. Awards: German Cross in Gold 03.01.1944, 1939 Iron Cross 1st Class, 1939 Clasp to the 1914 Iron Cross 2nd Class, 1914 Iron Cross 2nd Class, Cross of Honor.

Crailsheim, Hanns Freiherr von: Generalmajor (01.09.44), (Luftwaffe); born 08.10.88 in Augsburg, died 14.07.75 in Bad Windshiem. WWI: in G.A.S. as Oberleutnant and Leader of Bombenstaffel 25. Luftwaffe Representative to B.M.W. and Messerschmitt 07.1934–09.1937. WWII: Group Director and later Department Chief of GL/2 in R.L.M. 09.1937–04.1941, Armaments Inspector of Luftgau Kommando XIII 04.1941–04.1944, retired 09.1944. Awards: War Merit Cross 1st and 2nd Class with Swords, Pilot's Commemorative Badge, RK-Hohenzollern, 1914 Iron Cross 1st and 2nd Class, Bavarian Military Service Order IV. Class with Swords, 1914 Wound Badge in Black, 1914 Pilot's Badge, Cross of Honor.

Cramer, Hans: General der Panzertruppe (01.05.43), (Heer); born 13.07.96 in Minden, died 28.10.68 in Hausberge. WWI: Leutnant and Bataillon Adjutant in Infanterie Regiment 15. Promotions to Generalmajor 01.11.42, Generalleutnant 20.01.43. Instructor at Kavallerie Schule 07.1934–11.1938. WWII: Commander of Kavallerie Ausbildungs Abteilung 11.1938–08.1939, Commander of Aufklarungs Ausbildungs Abteilung 08.1939–11.1940, Commander of Panzer Regiment 8, 03.1941–04.1942, Chief of Staff to General of Schnelltruppen in O.K.H. 04.1942–08.1942, General of Schnelltruppen in O.K.H. 11.1942–01.1943, attached to German Afrika Korps

03.1943–04.1943, Commanding General of Afrika Korps 05.1943–05.1943, captured 05.1943, released as P.O.W. 05.1944, Fuehrer Res. in O.K.H. with rank of General with Special Duties 05.1944–07.1944, retired 07.1944. Awards: Knight's Cross 27.06.41, German Cross in Gold 05.03.42, 1939 Clasps to the 1914 Iron Cross 1st and 2nd Class, Tank Assault Badge in Silver, Afrika Cuff Band, 1914 Iron Cross 1st and 2nd Class, Cross of Honor.

General der Panzertruppe Hans Cramer. (Bundesarchiv)

Cramolini, Ludwig: Generalmajor (01.06.41), (Heer); born 08.10.79 in Darmstadt, died 01.12.57 in Hausham. WWI: Hauptmann and Commander of III. Bataillon, Res. Infanterie Regiment 240. WWII: Commander of Military District Kommando III 10.1933–08.1942, retired 08.1942. Awards: War Merit Cross 1st and 2nd Class with Swords, RK-Hohenzollern, 1914 Iron Cross 1st and 2nd Class, 1914 Wound Badge in Black, Cross of Honor.

Cranz, Friedrich: Generalleutnant (01.11.40), (Luftwaffe); born 03.01.90 in Memel, died 17.03.45 in Breslau. WWI: in G.A.S. as Hauptmann and Commander of Flieger Abteilung A 248 and later Lb 261. Promotion to Generalmajor 01.01.39. Department Leader for Air Photos in R.L.M. 05.1933–02.1936 and at same time Leader of Main Photo Office for R.L.M. 09.1933–02.1936, Fliegerhorst Commandant of Wuerzburg 03.1936–07.1937, attached to Staff of Luftgau Kommando 11, 08.1937–06.1938. WWII: Commander of Fliegerschule 11, 07.1938–08.1939, Commander of Luftwaffe Training Grounds at Dramburg 08.1939–05.1940, Defensive Replacement Inspector for Posen 10.1940–01.1945. Awards: War Merit Cross 1st and 2nd Class with Swords, Pilot's Commemorative Badge, RK-Hohenzollern, 1914 Iron Cross 1st and 2nd Class, 1914 Wound Badge in Black, 1914 Pilot's Badge, Cross of Honor.

Cranz, Friedrich-Karl: Generalleutnant (01.07.40), (Heer); born 14.11.86 in Kulm, died 24.03.41 from accident in Neuhammer. WWI: Hauptmann and Ia to 45. Res. Division. Promotion to Generalmajor 01.06.38. Adjutant to V. Armee Korps 10.1934–07.1936. WWII: Department Chief II in Heeres Personnel Office 08.1936–08.1939, Commander of 18. Infanterie Division 09.1939–03.1941. Awards: Knight's Cross 29.06.40, 1939 Clasps to the 1914 Iron Cross 1st and 2nd Class, 1939 Wound Badge in Gold, 1914 Iron Cross 1st and 2nd Class, Cross of Honor.

Crasemann, Eduard: General der Artillerie (20.04.45), (Heer); born 05.03.91 in Hamburg, died 28.04.50 at Werl Prison. WWI: Hauptmann and Staff Officer to 35. Infanterie Division. Promotions to Generalmajor 01.10.44, Generalleutnant 27.02.45. Hauptmann der Landwehr attached to Abteilung 1 of General Staff of Heeres 10.1936–10.1937, attached to Abteilung 10 of General Staff of Heeres 10.1937–11.1938, attached to Command Staff of II. Abteilung, Artillerie Regiment 20, 11.1938–03.1939. WWII: Batterie Chef in Artillerie Regiment 73, 04.1939–02.1940, Commander of II. Abteilung, Artillerie Regiment 78, 02.1940–05.1941, Commander of Artillerie Regiment 33, 05.1941–01.1943, Commander of 26. Panzer Division 07.1944–01.1945, Commander of XII. SS Panzer Korps 01.1945–05.1945. Awards: Oak Leaves 18.12.44 (683), Knight's Cross 26.12.41, German Cross in Gold 01.11.43, 1939 Clasps to the 1914 Iron Cross 1st and 2nd Class, General Assault Badge, Afrika Cuff Band, 1939 Wound Badge in Silver, 1914 Iron Cross 1st and 2nd Class, Cross of Honor.

Crato, Fritz: Generalmajor (01.06.42), (Heer); born 30.06.81 in Lueneburg, died 29.05.60 in Munich. WWI: Hauptmann and Ia to 19. Res. Division. WWII: Commander of Military District Kommando in Duesseldorf 04.1936–07.1942, captured 07.1942. Awards: War Merit Cross 1st and 2nd Class with Swords, RK-Hohenzollern, 1914 Iron Cross 1st and 2nd Class, Cross of Honor.

Criegern, Dietrich von: Generalleutnant (01.07.44), (Luftwaffe); born 02.12.86 in Dresden, died 06.11.52 in Hechendorf. WWI: Rittmeister on Staff of XII. Armee Korps. Promotion to Generalmajor 01.04.43. Attached to Staff of Luftkreis Kommando III 01.1936–05.1938, Quartermaster to Luftkreis Kommando 1, 06.1938–01.1939. WWII: Quartermaster to Luftflotte 1, 02.1939–04.1940, Senior Quartermaster to Luftflotte 1, 04.1940–08.1943, Chief of Supply Office in R.L.M. 08.1943–06.1944, General Quartermaster of Luftwaffe 07.1944–05.1945. Awards: German Cross in Silver. 03.11.42, 1939 Clasp to the 1914 Iron Cross 2nd Class, War Merit Cross 1st and 2nd Class with Swords, RK-Sachsen Military St. Heinrich's Order, RK-Sachsen Albrecht Order 2nd Class with Swords, 1914 Iron Cross 1st and 2nd Class, 1914 Wound Badge in Black, Cross of Honor.

Crisolli, Wilhelm: Generalleutnant (25.03.45), (Heer); born 20.01.95 in Berlin, died 12.09.44 in action near Modena. WWI: Leutnant in 15. Res. Jaeger Bataillon. Promotion to Generalmajor 01.02.44. Schwadron Chef in Reiter Regiment at Gera 10.1934–10.1935, Tactics Instructor at Kriegsschule Potsdam 10.1935–11.1938. WWII: Commander of I. Bataillon, Kavallerie Schuetzen Regiment 9, 11.1938–08.1939, Commander of III. Bataillon, Schuetzen Regiment 8, 09.1939–06.1940, Commander of Schuetzen Regiment 8, 01.1940–01.1942, Commander of 13. Schuetzen Brigade 05.1942–10.1942, Fuehrer Res. in O.K.H. 10.1942–11.1943, Commander of 20. Luftwaffe Feld Division 02.1944–09.1944. Awards: Knight's

Cross 15.07.41, 1939 Clasps to the 1914 Iron Cross 1st and 2nd Class, Tank Assault Badge in Bronze, Eastern Front Medal, 1939 Wound Badge in Gold, 1914 Iron Cross 1st and 2nd Class, Cross of Honor.

Cruewell, Ludwig: General der Panzertruppe (01.12.41), (Heer); born 20.03.92 in Dortmund, died 25.09.58 in Dortmund. WWI: Oberleutnant on Staff of 33. Infanterie Division. Promotions to Generalmajor 01.12.39, Generalleutnant 01.09.41. Ia to Wehrkreis Kommando VI 10.1934–10.1935, Ia to VI. Armee Korps 10.1935–03.1936, attached to O.B. des Heeres 04.1936–09.1936, Commander of Panzer Aufklarungs Truppen V 10.1936–01.1938, Commander of Panzer Regiment 6, 02.1938–03.1939, again attached to O.B. des Heeres 04.1939–05.1939. WWII: Chief of Abteilung 6 of Heeres General Staff of O.K.H. 06.1939–10.1939, Senior Quartermaster to 16. Armee 10.1939–06.1940, Commander of 11. Panzer Division 08.1940–08.1941, Commander of German Afrika Korps 09.1941–05.1942, captured 05.1942. Awards: Oak Leaves 01.09.41 (34), Knight's Cross 14.05.41, 1939 Clasps to the 1914 Iron Cross 1st and 2nd Class, Tank Assault Badge in Silver, Silesian Eagle 1st and 2nd Class, 1914 Iron Cross 1st and 2nd Class, Cross of Honor.

Cuno, Kurt: Generalleutnant (01.08.44), (Heer); born 27.0896 in Zweibruecken, died 14.07.61 in Munich. WWI: Leutnant and Adjutant to 9. Bavarian Pionier Bataillon. Promotion to Generalmajor 01.07.43. Tactics Instruction Leader at Panzertruppen Schule 10.1933–09.1937. WWII: Commander of I. Abteilung, Panzer Regiment 25, 10.1937–01.1940, Commander of Panzer Regiment 39, 10.1940–01.1942, Fuehrer Res. in O.K.H. 01.1942–12.1942, Commander of Schnelltruppen in Wehrkreis XIII 12.1942–08.1943, Commander of 233. Res. Panzer Division 08.1943–05.1944, General of Motor Transport Affairs 06.1944–05.1945. Awards: Knight's Cross 18.01.42, German Cross in Gold 14.01.42, 1939 Clasps to the 1914 Iron Cross 1st and 2nd Class, Tank Assault Badge in Silver, Eastern Front Medal, 1914 Iron Cross 1st and 2nd Class, 1914 Wound Badge in Silver, Cross of Honor.

Curtze, Heinrich: Generalleutnant z.V. (01.03.42), (Heer); born 22.07.76 in Worms, died 11.12.59 in Munich. WWI: Hauptmann and Commander of I. Abteilung, Bavarian Feld Artillerie Regiment 10. Promotion to Reichswehr Generalmajor 01.02.32. WWII: recalled to military service 06.1940, Commander of Truppenubungsplatz at Maria ter Heide 06.1940–03.1942, retired 04.1943. Awards: War Merit Cross 1st and 2nd Class with Swords, 1914 Iron Cross 1st and 2nd Class, 1914 Wound Badge in Black, Cross of Honor.

Czech, Hans-Armin: Generalleutnant (01.04.43), (Luftwaffe); born 28.06.98 in Oederan, died 04.01.70 in Poenitz am See. WWI: in Naval G.A.S. as Leutnant zur See in II. Seeflieger Abteilung. Promotion to Generalmajor 01.04.41. Leader of Kuesten Staffel 3/106, 10.1936–03.1937, Leader of Kuesten Flieger Gruppe 256 and Fliegerhorst Commandant of Norderney 04.1937–09.1937. WWII: Chief of Staff to Commander of Sea Luftwaffe Formations 11.1937–01.1940, Chief of Staff to 9. Flieger Division 02.1940–10.1940, Chief of Staff to IX. Flieger Korps 10.1940–08.1941, Higher Commander of Bomber Training 08.1941–05.1942, Aerial Mines Inspector in R.L.M. 05.1942–02.1944, General of Seacraft of Luftwaffe 03.1944–05.1945. Awards: War Merit Cross 1st and 2nd Class with Swords, Combined Pilot-Observer's Badge, Naval Pilot's Commemorative Badge, 1914 Iron Cross 2nd Class, 1914 Naval Pilot's Badge, Cross of Honor.

Czettritz und Neuhauss, Konrad von: Generalmajor (01.02.43), (Heer); born 30.11.80 in Berlin, died 05.02.46 at Osselede Hospital. WWI: Oberleutnant and Chief of 1 M.G. Kompanie, Fuss Guard Regiment 3. Attached to Staff of Reiter Regiment at Dresden 10.1934–05.1935, attached to Staff of Kommandantur Dresden 05.1935–10.1935, attached to Staff of Heeres Service Office 5, 10.1935–04.1936, attached to Schuetzen Regiment 2, 05.1936–03.1937, Commander of II. Abteilung, Schuetzen Regiment 2, 04.1937–11.1938. WWII: Commander of Schuetzen Regiment 12, 11.1938–11.1939, Commander of Truppenubungsplatz at Altengrabow 11.1939–05.1945. Awards: 1939 Clasps to the 1914 Iron Cross 1st and 2nd Class, RK-Hohenzollern, 1914 Iron Cross 1st and 2nd Class, 1914 Wound Badge in Silver, Cross of Honor.

D

Dahlmann, Hermann: Generalleutnant (01.12.43), (Luftwaffe); born 19.11.92 in Wanfried, died 21.01.78 in Rimsteig. WWI: in G.A.S. as Oberleutnant and Adjutant of Jagdgeschwader 3. Promotion to Generalmajor 01.12.41. Ministerialrat and Chief of Air Sovereignty of Reich in R.L.M. 05.1933–07.1939. WWII: Department Chief in R.L.M. 08.1939–11.1939, Fliegerhorst Commandant at Danzig 11.1939–03.1941, Flughafenbereichs Commandant of 13-XI (later 13-XL) 08.1941–05.1942, General with Special Duties attached to GFM Milch and Flight Operation Material Saving Commissioner 06.1942–11.1943, General of Flieger Ground Organization of Luftwaffe 12.1943–05.1945. Awards: War Merit Cross 1st and 2nd Class with Swords, 1939 Pilot's Badge, "Jagdstaffel Boelcke Nr. 2, 1916/18" Commemorative Cuff Band, Pilot's Commemorative Badge, 1914 Iron Cross 1st and 2nd Class, 1914 Pilot's Badge, Cross of Honor.

Dahlmann, Reinhold: Generalmajor (01.04.42), (Heer); born 12.12.89 in Bromberg, died 04.1945 (missing in action). WWI: Hauptmann and Adjutant to 13. Res. Infanterie Brigade. Commander of III. Bataillon, Infanterie Regiment 16, 08.1935–09.1936. WWII: Commander of Field Equipment Commando I 10.1936–06.1942, retired 06.1942. Awards: War Merit Cross 1st and 2nd Class with Swords, 1914 Iron Cross 1st and 2nd Class, Cross of Honor.

Dahme, Josef: Generalmajor (30.01.45), (Heer); born 24.06.94 in Mueschede, died 24.01.78 in Munich. WWI: in G.A.S. as Leutnant in Flieger Abteilung 199b. Kompanie Chef in Kraftfahr Abteilung 7, 08.1935–09.1936. WWII: Commander of Kraftfahr Abteilung 10, 10.1936–08.1939, Commander of Kraftfahr Regiment 602 (mot.) 09.1939–12.1940, Commander of Supply District North 1941–04.1942, High Supply Leader and later Army Group Supply Leader II 04.1942–10.1942, High Commander of Nachschubtruppe 2, 10.1942–05.1944, High Commander of Nachschubtruppe 6, 05.1944–11.1944, Fuehrer Res. in O.K.H. 11.1944–05.1945. Awards: German Cross in Silver 22.10.43, War Merit Cross 1st and 2nd Class with Swords, Pilot's Commemorative Badge, 1914 Iron Cross 1st and 2nd Class, Bavarian

Military Service Order IV. Class with Swords, 1914 Wound Badge in Black, 1914 Observer's Badge, Cross of Honor.

Dalwig zu Lichtenfels, Franz Freiherr von: General der Kavallerie (01.12.40), (Heer); born 21.04.76 in Duesseldorf, died 25.11.47 in Bad Wildungen. WWI: Rittmeister and Commander of II. Bataillon, Infanterie Regiment 93. Promotions to Reichswehr Generalmajor 01.02.33, Reichswehr Generalleutnant 01.10.34. Commander of Kavallerie Schule at Hannover 10.1931–03.1937. WWII: General z.b.V. attached to III. Armee Korps 04.1937–08.1939, Commander of Wehrkreis Kommando III 08.1939–03.1943, retired 05.1943. Awards: German Cross in Silver 31.05.43, War Merit Cross 1st and 2nd Class with Swords, RK-Hohenzollern, 1914 Iron Cross 1st and 2nd Class, 1914 Wound Badge in Black, Cross of Honor.

Damerau-Dambrowski, Joachim von der: Generalmajor (01.07.43), (Heer); born 07.08.96 in Kiel, died 22.07.43 in action near Orel. WWI: Leutnant and Adjutant to II. Bataillon, Grenadier Regiment 100. Kompanie Chef in Infanterie Regiment 10, 10.1934–11.1938. WWII: attached to Staff of 4. Infanterie Division 11.1938–01.1940, Commander of II. Bataillon, Infanterie Regiment 10, 01.1940–08.1940, Bataillon Commander in Schuetzen Regiment 108, 08.1940–06.1942, Commander of Panzer Grenadier Regiment 12, 07.1942–07.1943. Awards: German Cross in Gold 28.02.42, Honor Roll Clasp 27.05.43, 1939 Clasps to the 1914 Iron Cross 1st and 2nd Class, Infantry Assault Badge in Silver, Eastern Front Medal, 1939 Wound Badge in Gold, 1914 Iron Cross 1st and 2nd Class, Cross of Honor.

Danckelmann, Heinrich: General der Flieger (01.04.41), (Luftwaffe); born 02.08.87 in Hardenhausen, died 30.10.47 (executed) at Belgrade. WWI: Rittmeister on Staff of Armee Gruppe "Boehn." Promotions to Generalmajor 01.01.38, Generalleutnant 01.10.39. Special Purpose Officer attached to R.L.M. 10.1934–09.1935, Chief of Staff to Luftkreis Kommando III 1935–03.1938, Deputy Commander of Luftgau Kommando VIII 04.1938–01.1939. WWII: Military Replacement Inspector for Duesseldorf 05.1939–07.1941, Wehrmacht Befehlshaber of Serbia 07.1941–10.1941, attached to Luftgau Kommando VI 03.1942–05.1943, retired 05.1943. Awards: War Merit Cross 1st and 2nd Class with Swords, 1939 Observer's Badge, 1914 Iron Cross 1st and 2nd Class, 1914 Wound Badge in Black, Cross of Honor.

Danhauser, Paul: Generalleutnant (01.03.43), (Heer); born 02.08.92 in Regensburg, died 11.12.74 in Landshut. WWI: Oberleutnant in Bavarian Ersatz Infanterie Regiment 1. Promotion to Generalmajor 01.04.42. Attached to Infanterie Regiment at Flensbug 10.1934–03.1935, Group Leader in Feldzeug Inspection of Reich War Ministry 04.1935–10.1936, Commander of III. Bataillon, Infanterie Regiment 106, 10.1936–11.1938, Commander of Gebirgs Jaeger Regiment 139, 12.1938–03.1939.

WWII: Commander of Infanterie Ersatz Regiment 214, 08.1939–06.1940, Commander of Infanterie Regiment 427, 10.1940–02.1942, Commander of 256. Infanterie Division 02.1942–11.1943, Commander of 271. Infanterie Division 12.1943–09.1944, Heeres Feld Equipment Master in O.K.H. 11.1944–05.1945. Awards: Knight's Cross 10.02.42, German Cross in Gold 02.09.43, 1939 Clasps to the 1914 Iron Cross 1st and 2nd Class, Eastern Front Medal, West Wall Medal, 1914 Iron Cross 1st and 2nd Class, Cross of Honor.

Daniel, Richard: Generalmajor (01.10.44), (Heer); born 24.12.00 in Anspach, died 04.05.86 in Neumunster. WWI: attached to NCO Schule (rank unknown). Kompanie Chef in Infanterie Regiment 26, 10.1935–10.1937, Chief of 6. Kompanie, Infanterie Regiment 46, 10.1937–11.1938. WWII: Chief of 3. Kompanie, Infanterie Regiment 46, 11.1938–08.1939, Commander of Ersatz Bataillon, Infanterie Regiment 46, 09.1939–10.1939, Commander of I. Bataillon, Infanterie Regiment 401, 10.1939–01.1942, Commander of Infanterie Regiment 391, 04.1942–10.1943, Instructor for Regimental Commanders at Doberwitz 11.1943–07.1944, Commander of 45. Volks Grenadier Division 10.1944–03.1945. Awards: Oak Leaves 30.04.45 (857), Knight's Cross 25.07.42, German Cross in Gold 02.06.43, Honor Roll Clasp 25.02.45, 1939 Iron Cross 1st Class and 2nd Class, Infantry Assault Badge in Silver, Eastern Front Medal, Crimea Shield, 1939 Wound Badge in Silver.

Daniels, Alexander Edler von: Generalleutnant (01.12.42), (Heer); born 17.03.91 in Trier, died 06.01.60 in Bielefeld. WWI: Oberleutnant and Adjutant to Infanterie Regiment 143. Promotion to Generalmajor 01.01.42. Commander of II. Bataillon, Infanterie Regiment 1, 02.1934–09.1934, Commander of Ausbildungs Bataillion, Infanterie Regiment at Koenigsberg 10.1934–10.1935, Commander of M.G. Bataillon 9, 10.1935–09.1938. WWII: Commander of Infanterie Regiment 18, 11.1938–12.1940, Commander of Infanterie Regiment 239, 12.1940–03.1942, Commander of 376. Infanterie Division 04.1942–01.1943, captured at Stalingrad 01.1943. Awards: Knight's Cross 18.12.42, German Cross in Gold 15.12.41, 1939 Clasps to the 1914 Iron Cross 1st and 2nd Class, Infantry Assault Badge in Silver, Eastern Front Medal, RK-Hohenzollern, 1914 Iron Cross 1st and 2nd Class, Cross of Honor.

Daniels, Dr. Franz: General-Veterinar (01.10.43), (Heer); born 08.05.86 in Aachen, died 26.04.78 in Timmendorfer Strand. Medical veterinarian by profession. WWI: Veterinar in Kurassier Regiment 8. WWII: attached to Staff of Heeresgruppe Sud. Awards: War Merit Cross 1st and 2nd Class with Swords, Cross of Honor.

Danielsen, Dr. Ernst: General-Arzt (01.07.42), (Heer); born 18.11.91 in Bergedorf, died 01.06.80 in Bad Pyrmont. Medical doctor by profession. WWI: Assistenz-Arzt in Res. Infanterie Regiment 216. Attached to Wehrkreis Kommando IV in

Dresden 02.1934–06.1937, Standort-Arzt of Standort Dresden 07.1937–07.1938, Commander of Grenz Sanitats Abteilung 32, 07.1938–01.1939. WWII: Division Physician to 19. Infanterie Division 02.1939–10.1940, Corps Physician to Wehrkreis XX 10.1940–11.1942, Chief Physician to Wehrmacht Befehlshaber in Ostland (Riga) 11.1942–11.1943, Fuehrer Res. in O.K.H. 11.1943–05.1944, retired 05.1944. Awards: 1939 Clasp to the 1914 Iron Cross 2nd Class, War Merit Cross 1st and 2nd Class with Swords, Silesian Eagle 1st and 2nd Class, 1914 Iron Cross 2nd Class, Cross of Honor.

Danneel, Wilhelm: Generalmajor (01.02.43), (Heer); born 20.08.79 in Bruel, died 30.12.57 in Hamburg. WWI: Hauptmann and Commander of I. Bataillon, Infanterie Regiment 77. WWII: Director of Psychological Testing Office in Wehrkreis Kommando X 09.1935–07.1941, Commander of Schuetzen Regiment 22, 08.1941–08.1942, Commandant of Feldkommandantur 603, 08.1942–07.1943, retired 11.1943. Awards: 1939 Clasps to the 1914 Iron Cross 1st and 2nd Class, RK-Hohenzollern, 1914 Iron Cross 1st and 2nd Class, Cross of Honor.

Daser, Wilhelm: Generalleutnant (01.08.44), (Heer); born 31.08.84 in Germersheim, died 14.07.68 in Ingolstadt. WWI: Hauptmann and Adjutant to Bavarian Res. Infanterie Regiment 15. Promotion to Generalmajor 01.07.42. Training Leader at Regensburg 05.1935–10.1936. WWII: Training Leader at Aschaffenburg 10.1936–08.1939, Commander of Infanterie Regiment 388, 08.1939–09.1941, Commander of Infanterie Regiment 251, 12.1941–06.1942, Commandant of Feldkommandantur 580, 08.1942–12.1942, Commandant of Feldkommandantur 894, 12.1942–12.1942, Commandant of Feldkommandantur 670, 12.1942–06.1943, Commandant of Feldkommandantur 454, 06.1943–12.1943, Commander of 165. Res. Division 02.1944–05.1944, Commander of 70. Infanterie Division 05.1944–11.1944. Awards: 1939 Clasps to the 1914 Iron Cross 1st and 2nd Class, Infantry Assault Badge in Silver, 1914 Iron Cross 1st and 2nd Class, Cross of Honor.

Daube, Willi: Generalmajor (01.08.41), (Heer); born 01.05.83 at Hannoversch-Muenden, died 20.08.41 in action at Jerzwo. WWI: Hauptmann and Bataillon Commander in Infanterie Regiment 18. Landwehr Commander of Allenstein 10.1936–08.1937. WWII: Commander of Military District Kommando for Braunsberg 09.1937–09.1939, Commander of Military District Kommando for Allenstein 09.1939–12.1939, Commander of Infanterie Regiment 364, 12.1939–09.1940, Commander of Infanterie Regiment 371, 11.1940–08.1941. Awards: 1939 Clasps to the 1914 Iron Cross 1st and 2nd Class, Infantry Assault Badge in Silver, 1939 Wound Badge in Gold, 1914 Iron Cross 1st and 2nd Class, Cross of Honor.

Dauber, Julius: Generalmajor (01.07.42), (Heer); born 24.01.81 in Marburg, died 05.1946 at Tschechowetz P.O.W. Camp. WWI: Hauptmann and Commander of III. Abteilung, Res. Feld Artillerie Regiment 51. Commander of Military District Kommando Militzsch 10.1933–03.1938. WWII: Commander of Military District Remonteschule at Militzsch 04.1938–12.1940, Commander of Artillerie Regiment 12, 12.1940–04.1942, P.O.W. Commander for Wehrkreis Kommando XI 09.1942–12.1943, Fuehrer Res. in O.K.H. 12.1943–08.1944, retired 08.1944. Awards: 1939 Clasps to the 1914 Iron Cross 1st and 2nd Class, General Assault Badge, 1914 Iron Cross 1st and 2nd Class, Cross of Honor.

Daubert, Hans: Generalmajor (01.10.41), (Heer); born 30.12.92 in Weissenburg, died 08.10.41 in action at Vyasma. WWI: Oberleutnant and Adjutant to Infanterie Regiment 43. Commander of III. Bataillon, Infanterie Regiment 31, 10.1934–06.1937. WWII: Department Chief in Personnel Office of R.L.M. 07.1937–08.1939 (transferred to Luftwaffe in 1937 but returned to Heer in 1940), Commander of Infanterie Regiment 497, 08.1939–10.1941. Awards: 1939 Clasps to the 1914 Iron Cross 1st and 2nd Class, Infantry Assault Badge in Silver, 1939 Wound Badge in Gold, 1914 Iron Cross 1st and 2nd Class, 1914 Wound Badge in Black, Cross of Honor.

Dawans, Sigismund-Hellmut Ritter und Edler von: Generalmajor (01.02.44), (Heer); born 23.09.99 in Erfurt, died 11.06.44 in action near Caen. WWI: Leutnant and Bataillon Adjutant in Infanterie Regiment 110. Attached to Reichswehr Ministry 05.1934–03.1935, attached to General Staff of Heeres 04.1935–07.1936, Kompanie Chef in Infanterie Regiment 111, 10.1936–10.1937. WWII: Ic to I. Armee Korps 10.1936–08.1939, attached to Staff of Grenzabschnitt Kommando North 08.1939–10.1939, attached to Staff of 16. Armee 10.1939–12.1939, Ia to 19. Infanterie (later 19. Panzer Division) 01.1940–12.1941, Chief of Staff to XIII. Armee Korps 01.1942–05.1942, Chief of Staff to III. Armee Korps 01.1942–02.1943, Chief of General Staff to 4. Armee 05.1943–10.1943, Chief of Staff to Commander of Panzertruppen in O.B. West 12.1943–06.1944. Awards: German Cross in Gold 26.08.42, 1939 Clasps to the 1914 Iron Cross 1st and 2nd Class, 1939 Wound Badge in Gold, 1914 Iron Cross 1st and 2nd Class, Cross of Honor.

Debes, Lothar: SS-Gruppenfuehrer und Generalleutnant der Waffen-SS (30.01.44); born 21.06.90 in Eichstatt, died 14.07.60 in Bergisch-Gladbach. P-2401110, SS-278953. Joined N.S.D.A.P. in 1930, joined S.S. in 1937. WWI: Hauptmann attached to Staff of 23. Infanterie Division. Promotion to SS-Brigadefuehrer 21.06.42. Attached to SS-Fuehrer Schule Braunschweig 01.12.37–01.12.38. WWII: Leader of Verbaende "Debes" 30.01.42, Commander of SS-Panzer Grenadier Division "Karl de Gross" (later "Frundsberg") 15.05.43, Befehlshaber of Waffen-SS in Italy 30.01.44–05.1945. Awards: German Cross in Silver 07.02.45, 1939 Clasps to the 1914 Iron Cross 1st and 2nd Class, War Merit Cross 2nd Class with Swords,

Eastern Front Medal, 1914 Iron Cross 1st and 2nd Class, 1914 Wound Badge in Black, Cross of Honor, Degen, Ring.

SS-Gruppenfuehrer Lothar Debes. (Bundesarchiv)

Deboi, Heinrich-Anton: Generalleutnant (01.12.42), (Heer); born 06.04.93 in Landshut, died 05.07.55 in Kempten. WWI: Oberleutnant in Bavarian Infanterie Regiment 2. Promotion to Generalmajor 01.04.42. Tactics Instructor of Kriegsschule Munich 10.1935–09.1936. WWII: Commander of I. Bataillon, Infanterie Regiment 91, 10.1936–08.1939, Commander of Infanterie Regiment 191, 08.1939–01.1942, Commander of 44. Infanterie Division 01.1942–01.1943, captured at Stalingrad 01.1943. Awards: Knight's Cross 10.09.42, German Cross in Gold 21.02.42, 1939 Clasps to the 1914 Iron Cross 1st and 2nd Class, Infantry Assault Badge in Silver, Eastern Front Medal, 1914 Iron Cross 1st and 2nd Class, 1914 Wound Badge in Silver, Cross of Honor.

Generalleutnant Heinrich-Anton Deboi. (Bundesarchiv)

Decker, Karl: General der Panzertruppe (01.01.45), (Heer); born 30.11.97 in Borntia-Neustettin, died 21.04.45 (suicide) in Gross-Brunsrode. WWI: Leutnant in Infanterie Regiment 54. Promotions to Generalmajor 01.12.43, Generalleutnant 01.06.44. Schwadron Chef in Reiter Regiment at Schwedt 10.1934–10.1935, attached to Staff of Reiter Regiment 15, 10.1935–09.1936. WWII: Commander of Panzer Abwehr Bataillon 38, 10.1936–04.1940, Commander of I. Abteilung, Panzer Regiment 3, 04.1940–05.1941, Commander of Panzer Regiment 3, 05.1941–01.1943, Commander of 21. Panzer Brigade 06.1943–09.1943, Commander of 5. Panzer Division 10.1943–10.1944, Commander of XXXI. Panzer Korps 10.1944–04.1945. Awards: Swords 26.04.45 (149) (posthumously), Oak Leaves 04.05.44 (466), Knight's Cross 13.06.41, German Cross in Gold 01.08.42, 1939 Clasps to the 1914 Iron Cross 1st and 2nd Class, Tank Assault Badge Grade II (25), Eastern Front Medal, 1939 Wound Badge in Black, 1914 Iron Cross 1st and 2nd Class, Cross of Honor.

Deckert, Hans-Joachim: Generalmajor (30.01.45), (Heer); born 29.10.04 Tennrode, died 05.03.88 in Bielefeld. Adjutant to III. Abteilung, Artillerie Regiment at Dresden

10.1934–10.1935, Adjutant to III. Abteilung, Artillerie Regiment 4, 10.1935–04.1936, attached to Command Staff of Beobachter Abteilung 24, 05.1936–10.1936. WWII: Batterie Chef in Beobachter Abteilung 4, 10.1936–10.1939, Instructor at Artillerie Schule in Jueterbog 11.1939–05.1940, Ia to Commander of Artillerie 302, 05.1940–12.1940, Commander of Artillerie Beobachter Abteilung 35, 12.1940–01.1942, Instructor at Artillerie Schule 1, 01.1942–05.1943, Commander of II. Abteilung, Panzer Artillerie Regiment 76, 05.1943–09.1943, Commander of Panzer Artillerie Regiment 76, 09.1943–08.1944, attached to Formation Staff of 15. Panzer Grenadier Division 10.1944–01.1945, Commander of 19. Panzer Division 03.1945–05.1945. Awards: German Cross in Gold 29.10.44, 1939 Iron Cross 1st and 2nd Class, General Assault Badge, Eastern Front Medal.

Deckmann, Werner-Heinrich: Generalmajor (01.09.42), (Heer); born 12.07.92 in Danzig, died 27.02.45 at Neuruppin Hospital. WWI: Oberleutnant and Adjutant to Infanterie Regiment 44. Attached to Infanterie Regiment at Flensburg 10.1934–03.1935, Adjutant to Heeres Feldzeugmeisterei 04.1935–10.1936, Chief of Personnel and Training in Heeres Feldzeugmeisterei 10.1936–10.1937, Commander of II. Bataillon, Infanterie Regiment 5, 10.1937–12.1938. WWII: Commander of Truppenubungsplatz at Stablack 01.1939–12.1944. Awards: War Merit Cross 1st and 2nd Class, 1914 Iron Cross 1st and 2nd Class, 1914 Wound Badge in Black, Cross of Honor.

Dedek, Emil: Generalmajor (01.07.42), (Heer); born 17.08.88 in Laibach, died 04.10.79 in Graz. WWI: Hauptmann and Bataillon Commander in Austrian Schuetzen Regiment 23. Transferred to Geman Wehrmacht 03.1938, Officer z.b.V. attached to 2. Gebirgs Division 05.1938–07.1938, Commander of Pionier Bataillon 82, 08.1938–09.1938, Commander of Pionier Ersatz Bataillon at Sazlburg 09.1938–11.1938. WWII: Pionier Officer attached to Staff of XVII. Armee Korps 11.1938–01.1940, Commander of Senior Construction Staff 71, 01.1940–02.1942, Commander of Senior Construction Staff 22, 02.1942–12.1942, Fuehrer Res. in O.K.H. 12.1942–05.1945. Awards: War Merit Cross 1st and 2nd Class with Swords, Cross of Honor.

Degen, Hans: Generalleutnant (01.08.44), (Heer); born 18.02.99 in Rosenheim, died 08.11.71 in Bad Toelz. WWI: Leutnant in 2. Bavarian Jaeger Bataillon. Promotion to Generalmajor 01.01.44. Attached to Abteilung 4 of General Staff of Heeres 07.1935–03.1937, Kompanie Chef in Gebirgs Jaeger Regiment 100, 04.1937–11.1938. WWII: Ia to 2. Gebirgs Division 11.1938–01.1941, Chief of Staff to VI. Armee Korps 01.1941–07.1942, Chief of Staff to Gebirgs Korps in Norway 07.1942–10.1943, Commander of 2. Gebirgs Division 11.1943–02.1945. Awards: Knight's Cross 11.03.45, German Cross in Gold 12.03.42, Honor Roll Clasp 05.02.45, 1939 Iron Cross 1st Class, 1939 Clasp to the 1914 Iron Cross 2nd

Class, Eastern Front Medal, Finnish Freedom Cross 1st Class with Swords, Spanish Cross in Bronze without Swords, Heeres Bergfuehrer Badge, 1914 Iron Cross 2nd Class, 1914 Wound Badge in Black, Cross of Honor.

Degener, Joachim: Generalmajor (01.11.42), (Heer); born 28.11.93 in Metz, died 07.09.53 in Wuerzburg. WWI: Oberleutnant in Hussar Regiment 17. Attached to Reiter Regiment at Torgau 10.1934–12.1934, Tactics Instructor at Kriegsschule Munich 01.1935–10.1937, Commander of Kavallerie Ausbildungs Abteilung of Kavallerie Schule 10.1937–11.1938. WWII: Commander of Kavallerie Schuetzen Regiment 14, 11.1938–10.1939, Commander of 5. Schuetzen Brigade 10.1939–02.1941, Wehrmacht Commander of Wuerzburg 02.1941–01.1944, Fuehrer Res. in O.K.H. followed by several short assignments 01.1944–12.1944, Kampfgruppe Commander of Gyor 01.1945–05.1945. Awards: 1939 Clasps to the 1914 Iron Cross 1st and 2nd Class, Infantry Assault Badge in Silver, 1914 Iron Cross 1st and 2nd Class, Cross of Honor.

Dehmel, Martin: Generalleutnant (01.06.41), (Heer); born 06.02.86 in Waldau, died 26.08.64 in Minden. WWI: Hauptmann and Pionier Officer on Staff of V. Armee Korps. Promotion to Generalmajor 01.06.39. Commander of Pionier Bataillon at Minden 10.1934–10.1935, Pionier Commander for VI. Armee Korps 10.1935–03.1936, Higher Pionier Officer 1 in Berlin 04.1936–11.1938. WWII: Higher Pionier Officer 5 in Vienna 11.1938–08.1939, Pionier Leader to 14. Armee 09.1939–10.1939, General of Pioniers to Heeresgruppe A 10.1939–02.1940, Commander of 292. Infanterie Division 02.1940–09.1941, Commander of Fortifications for Upper Rhine 01.1942–10.1942, Inspector of Pioniers attached to O.B. of Ersatz Armee 10.1942–08.1944, General of Pioniers with Operational Staff of North Coast 10.1944–04.1945. Awards: German Cross in Silver 03.02.45, 1939 Clasps to the 1914 Iron Cross 1st and 2nd Class, War Merit Cross 1st and 2nd Class with Swords, Infantry Assault Badge in Silver, 1914 Iron Cross 1st and 2nd Class, 1914 Wound Badge in Black, Cross of Honor.

Dehner, Ernst: General der Infanterie (01.12.42), (Heer); born 05.03.89 in Hersbrueck, died 13.09.70 in Wiesbaden. WWI: Oberleutnant in Bavarian Infanterie Regiment 14. Promotions to Generalmajor 01.10.40, Generalleutnant 01.10.42. Commander of II. Bataillon, Infanterie Regiment at Muenster 10.1934–10.1935, Commander of II. Bataillon, Infanterie Regiment 39, 10.1935–10.1936. WWII: Commander of Infanterie Regiment 87, 11.1936–11.1940, Commander of 106. Infanterie Division 12.1940–11.1942, Commander of LXXXII. Armee Korps 12.1942–07.1943, Commander of LXIX. Armee Korps 07.1943–04.1944, attached to Heeresgruppe A for Special Duties 01.1945–05.1945. Awards: Knight's Cross 18.10.41, 1939 Clasps to the 1914 Iron Cross 1st and 2nd Class, Infantry Assault Badge in Silver, Eastern Front

Medal, West Wall Medal, 1914 Iron Cross 1st and 2nd Class, 1914 Wound Badge in Black, Cross of Honor.

Deichmann, Paul: General der Flieger (20.04.45), (Luftwaffe); born 27.08.98 in Fulda, died 10.01.81 in Hamburg. WWI: in G.A.S. as Leutnant in Flieger Abteilung 8. Promotions to Generalmajor 01.08.42, Generalleutnant 20.05.44. Advisor in Luftkommando Amt I in R.L.M. 10.1934–09.1935, Group Leader LA I in General Staff of Luftwaffe 10.1935–02.1937, Chief of Leadership Department in General Staff of Luftwaffe 03.1937–09.1937, Fliegerhorst Commandant of Gotha 10.1937–01.1939. WWII: Chief of Staff to Chief of Luftwaffe Training Affairs in R.L.M. 02.1939–06.1940, Chief of Staff of II. Flieger Korps 06.1940–08.1942, Chief of General Staff to Luftflotte 2, 08.1942–06.1943, Commander of 1. Flieger Division 06.1943–11.1943, Commander of I. Flieger Korps 11.1943–04.1945. Awards: Knight's Cross 26.03.44, German Cross in Gold 20.04.42, 1939 Clasps to the 1914 Iron Cross 1st and 2nd Class, 1939 Observer's Badge, Pilot's Commemorative Badge, 1914 Iron Cross 1st and 2nd Class, 1914 Wound Badge in Black, 1914 Observer's Badge, Cross of Honor.

Deindl, Otto: Generalmajor (01.02.42), (Heer); born 23.11.90 in Hundldorf, died 14.06.47 in an American P.O.W. camp. WWI: in G.A.S. as Oberleutnant and Commander of Fliegerschule 3. Commander of Panzer Abwehr Abteilung 7, 10.1935–10.1936, Commander of Panzer Abwehr Abteilung 27, 10.1936–02.1938. WWII: attached to Staff of General Kommando 4, 02.1938–10.1939, Anti-Tank Officer on Staff of XXV. Armee Korps 11.1939–10.1940, attached to Reichs War Court 10.1940–01.1942, Commander of Truppenubungsplatz at Bitsch 04.1943–08.1944, Fortress Commandant of Posen 08.1944–01.1945. Awards: 1939 Clasps to the 1914 Iron Cross 1st and 2nd Class, War Merit Cross 1st and 2nd Class with Swords, Pilot's Commemorative Badge, 1914 Iron Cross 1st and 2nd Class, Bavarian Military Service Order IV. Class with Swords, Austro-Hungarian Military Service Cross 3rd Class with War Decoration, 1914 Pilot's Badge, Cross of Honor.

Deinhardt, Karl: Generalleutnant (01.01.42), (Luftwaffe); born 13.01.87 in Heidelberg, died 03.03.66 in Kaufbeuren. WWI: in G.A.S. as Feldwebel-Leutnant in Kampfeinsitzer Staffel 1a. Promotion to Generalmajor 01.12.39. Attached to Flieger Gruppe 5 in Lechfeld 01.1934–08.1935, Fliegerhorst Commandant of Lechfeld 09.1935–03.1936, Fliegerhorst Commandant of Kaufbeuren 10.1936–01.1939. WWII: Senior Training Commander in Luftgau Kommando XIII 03.1939–01.1943, Higher Commander of Fliegerschulen A and B 02.1943–08.1943, retired 10.1943. Awards: War Merit Cross 1st and 2nd Class with Swords, Combined Pilot/Observer's Badge, Pilot's Commemorative Badge, 1914 Iron Cross 1st and 2nd Class, 1914 Pilot's Badge, Cross of Honor.

Deininger, Wolfgang: Generalmajor (01.08.41), (Heer); born 01.10.82 in Arolsen, died 04.11.46 in Kassel. WWI: Hauptmann attached to Protection Truppen in German South-West Africa. WWII: Director of Welfare and Provision Services in Wehrkreis Kommando IX 08.1939–01.1943, retired 01.1943. Awards: War Merit Cross 1st and 2nd Class with Swords, 1914 Iron Cross 1st and 2nd Class, Cross of Honor.

Demelhuber, Karl: SS-Obergruppenfuehrer und General der Waffen-SS (21.06.44); born 27.05.96 in Freising, died 18.03.88 in Seeshaupt. SS-252392. WWI: Leutnant attached to Bavarian Feld Artillerie Regiment 1. Joined S.S. in 1935, joined Bavarian Landespolizei in 1921. Promotions to SS-Brigadefuehrer 09.11.40, SS-Gruppenfuehrer 20.04.42. Leader of II. Sturmbann, SS-Standarte 1 "Deutschland" 01.07.35, Leader of SS-Standarte 2 "Germania" 01.12.36–01.12.38. WWII: Commander of SS-Gebirgs Division "Nord" 30.01.42, Befehlshaber of Waffen-SS for Netherlands 15.05.43–1945, Commander of SS-Fuehrungstab East Coast. Awards: German Cross in Silver 09.11.43, 1939 Clasps to the 1914 Iron Cross 1st and 2nd Class, Finnish Freedom Cross 1st Class with Swords, 1914 Iron Cross 1st and 2nd Class, Cross of Honor, 1929 Nuremberg Badge of Honor, SA-Sports Badge in Bronze, German Horseman's Badge in Silver, Degen, Ring.

Demme, Rudolf: Generalmajor (01.03.45), (Heer); born 03.06.94 in Muehlhausen, died 05.01.75 in Meckenheim. WWI: Leutnant der Res. in 402. Infanterie Division. WWII: attached to Staff of Commander of Fortifications for Lower Rhine 08.1939–04.1940, Commander of Pionier Ersatz Bataillon 208, 04.1940–07.1941, Commander of Panzer Pionier Bataillon 92, 07.1941–12.1941, Commander of Panzer Pionier Bataillon 58, 12.1941–10.1942, Commander of Panzer Grenadier Regiment 59, 01.1943–07.1944, Commander of 132. Infanterie Division 12.1944–05.1945. Awards: Oak Leaves 28.07.44 (537), Knight's Cross 14.08.43, German Cross in Gold 20.09.42, 1939 Clasps to the 1914 Iron Cross 1st and 2nd Class, General Assault Badge, Infantry Assault Badge in Silver, Eastern Front Medal, 1939 Wound Badge in Gold, Spanish Cross in Bronze with Swords, 1914 Iron Cross 1st and 2nd Class, 1914 Wound Badge in Black, Cross of Honor.

Demoll, Eugen: Generalleutnant (01.06.43), (Heer); born 20.08.81 in Kenzingen, died 28.12.69 in Poecking. WWI: Hauptmann and Department Commander in Feld Artillerie Regiment (unit unknown). Promotion to Generalmajor 01.06.41. WWII: Commander of Military District at Ludwigshafen 05.1936–03.1942, Commander of 201. Security Division 04.1942–09.1942, Commander of 463. Ersatz Division 09.1942–05.1943, retired 09.1943. Awards: 1939 Clasps to the 1914 Iron Cross 1st and 2nd Class, Eastern Front Medal, 1914 Iron Cross 1st and 2nd Class, Cross of Honor.

Dempwolff, Hugo: Generalmajor (01.03.45), (Heer); born 18.09.98 in Suderneuwald, died 09.12.84 in Hannover. WWI: Leutnant in Infanterie Regiment 92. Adjutant to Infanterie Regiment at Doeberitz 10.1934–10.1935, Adjutant to Infanterie Regiment 48, 10.1935–10.1936, Kompanie Chef in Infanterie Regiment 48, 10.1936–12.1937. WWII: Adjutant to 5. Infanterie Division 01.1938–06.1940, Adjutant on Staff of V. Armee Korps 09.1940–07.1942, Commander of Infanterie Regiment 489, 09.1942–01.1944, wounded then Fuehrer Res. in O.K.H. 03.1944–11.1944, Commander of 276. Volks Grenadier Division 12.1944–03.1945. Awards: 1939 Iron Cross 1st Class, 1939 Clasp to the 1914 Iron Cross 2nd Class, Infantry Assault Badge in Silver, 1939 Wound Badge in Black, 1914 Iron Cross 2nd Class, Cross of Honor.

Denecke, Erich: Generalleutnant (01.12.39), (Heer); born 18.10.85 in Dresden, died 07.03.63 in Darmstadt. WWI: Hauptmann on Staff of XIX. Armee Korps. Promotion to Generalmajor 01.10.37. Commander of Infanterie Regiment at Marienburg 10.1934–10.1935, Commander of Infanterie Regiment 45, 10.1935–05.1937, Commander of Heeres Service Office 2, 06.1937–11.1938, Commander of Heeres Service Office 6, 11.1938–05.1939. WWII: Landwehr Commander for Darmstadt 05.1939–08.1939, Commander of 246. Infanterie Division 08.1939–12.1941, Wehrmacht Commander of Smolensk 12.1941–07.1942, Commander of 471. Infanterie Division 09.1942–01.1945. Awards: 1939 Clasps to the 1914 Iron Cross 1st and 2nd Class, Infantry Assault Badge in Silver, Eastern Front Medal, RK-Sachsen Military St. Heinrich's Order 28.08.17, 1914 Iron Cross 1st and 2nd Class, Cross of Honor.

Denkert, Walter: Generalleutnant (20.04.45), (Heer); born 23.02.97 in Kiel, died 09.07.82 in Kiel. WWI: Leutnant der Res. in Fusilier Regiment 86. Promotion to Generalmajor 01.06.44. Kompanie Chef in Infanterie Regiment 65, 10.1935–10.1936, Commander of I. Bataillon, Infanterie Regiment 65, 10.1936–11.1938. WWII: Commander of M.G. Bataillon 52, 11.1938–08.1939, Commander of II. Bataillon, Infanterie Regiment 271, 08.1939–12.1940, Commander of Infanterie Regiment 8, 09.1941–09.1942, Fuehrer Res. in O.K.H. 09.1942–06.1943, Commander of Heer Waffen Schule for Panzertruppen at Kharkov 06.1943–01.1944, Deputy Commander of 19. Panzer Division 02.1944–09.1944, Commander of 3. Panzer Grenadier Division 10.1944–05.1945. Awards: Knight's Cross 14.05.44, German Cross in Gold 08.03.45, 1939 Clasps to the 1914 Iron Cross 1st and 2nd Class, Infantry Assault Badge in Bronze, Eastern Front Medal, 1914 Iron Cross 1st and 2nd Class, 1914 Wound Badge in Black, Cross of Honor.

Dennerlein, Max: Generalleutnant (01.03.40), (Heer); born 16.05.85 in Markteuthen, died 13.10.57 in Ortenburg. WWI: Hauptmann and Commander of

Pionier Bataillon, 5. Bavarian Infanterie Division. Promotion to Generalmajor 01.03.38. Higher Pionier Officer attached to Staff of Gruppen Kommando 2, 02.1934–12.1934, Commander of Pionier Inspection 2 at Kassel 01.1935–09.1935, Higher Pionier Officer 2, 10.1935–01.1939. WWII: Inspector of West Fortifications 02.1939–10.1939, Pionier Leader to Heeresgruppe C 10.1939–02.1940, Commander of 290. Infanterie Division 02.1940–06.1940, Commander of 335. Infanterie Division 11.1940–10.1942, Commander of 326. Infanterie Division 11.1942–05.1943, Commander of 433. Ersatz Division 06.1943–12.1944, Inspector of Fortresses in O.K.H. 01.1945–05.1945. Awards: 1939 Clasps to the 1914 Iron Cross 1st and 2nd Class, Infantry Assault Badge in Silver, 1914 Iron Cross 1st and 2nd Class, Cross of Honor.

Densch, Hermann: Admiral (01.01.40), (Kriegsmarine); born 15.06.87 in Koenigsberg, died 24.08.63 in Garmisch-Partenkirchen. WWI: Kapitanleutnant and Chief of 1. Torpedoboots Halbflotille at Flanders. Promotions to Konteradmiral 01.10.35, Vizeadmiral 01.04.38. Chief of Staff to Marineleitung (later O.K.M.) 09.1932–09.1936. WWII: Befehlshaber of Reconnaissance Surface Ships 10.1937–10.1939, Commander of North Sea Naval Station 11.1939–02.1943, Reich Commissioner of Upper Jury Court in Berlin 07.1943–04.1945. Awards: German Cross in Silver 19.02.43, 1939 Clasps to the 1914 Iron Cross 1st and 2nd Class, Commander's Cross of the Hungarian Service Order with Breast Star, RK-Hohenzollern, 1914 Iron Cross 1st and 2nd Class, Oldenburg Friedrich-August Cross 1st and 2nd Class, Cross of Honor.

Dermietzel, Dr. Friedrich Karl: SS-Brigadefuehrer und Generalmajor der Waffen-SS (20.04.42); born 07.02.99 in Lunow, died 07.07.81 in Koeln. P-1106473, SS-31115. Joined N.S.D.A.P. and S.S. in 1932. Medical doctor by profession. WWI: Leutnant attached to Pionier Ersatz Bataillon 1. Leader of SS-Sanitats Abt. Ost 01.10.34, attached to SS-Hauptamt 01.07.35, attached to Staff of RFSS 01.12.36, attached to Staff of SS-Hauptamt 01.12.37–01.12.38. WWII: Division Physician to SS-Verfugungstruppe (later "Reich" then "Das Reich") Division 30.01.42, Corps Physician to II. SS-Panzer Korps 15.05.43–30.01.44, Army Physician to 6. SS-Panzer Armee 09.11.44–05.1945. Awards: German Cross in Silver 02.06.44, 1939 Clasp to the 1914 Iron Cross 2nd Class, War Merit Cross 1st and 2nd Class with Swords, 1914 Iron Cross 1st and 2nd Class, Cross of Honor, SA-Sports Badge in Bronze, Degen, Ring.

Dernen, Friedrich-Wilhelm: Generalmajor der Res. (01.12.44), (Heer); born 15.02.84 in Koeln, died 15.02.67 in Bad Homburg. WWI: Leutnant der Res. in Grenadier Regiment 110. WWII: attached to Infanterie Regiment 26, 01.1936–08.1939, Commander of III. Bataillon, Infanterie Regiment 88, 10.1939–06.1940, Commander of I. Bataillon, Infanterie Regiment 550, 06.1940–07.1940, Training Leader for

Division 159, 08.1940–10.1940, Commander of III. Bataillon, Infanterie Regiment 36, 10.1940–01.1942, in hospital then Fuehrer Res. 01.1942–05.1942, Commander of Infanterie Ersatz Bataillon 9, 05.1942–09.1942, Commander of Grenadier Ersatz Regiment 9, 09.1942–05.1943, Commandant of Feldkommandantur in Belgium and Northern France 08.1943–02.1944, Commandant of Feldkommandantur 563, 02.1944–10.1944, attached to Formation Staff and later Commander of 159. Infanterie Division 10.1944–12.1944, in hospital 01.1945–05.1945. Awards: German Cross in Gold 10.01.42, 1939 Clasps to the 1914 Iron Cross 1st and 2nd Class, Infantry Assault Badge in Silver, Eastern Front Medal, Pour le Mérite 29.08.18, RK-Hohenzollern, 1914 Iron Cross 1st and 2nd Class, Cross of Honor.

Dessloch, Otto: Generaloberst (01.03.44), (Luftwaffe); born 11.06.89 in Bamberg, died 13.05.77 in Munich. WWI: in G.A.S. as Oberleutnant and Leader of Fliegerschule 1 and later 5. Promotions to Generalmajor 01.01.39, Generalleutnant 19.07.40, General der Flak Artillerie 01.01.42. Fliegerhorst Commandant of Cottbus 12.1933–03.1935, Commander of Flieger Gruppe 155 in Ansbach 10.1935–09.1936, Commander of K.G. 128, 10.1936–12.1938, Commander of Flieger Division 32, 02.1939–03.1939. WWII: Commander of 6. Flieger Division 04.1939–10.1939, Commander of II. Flak Korps 10.1939–03.1942, Commander of I. Flak Korps 04.1942–09.1943, Oberbefehlshaber of Luftflotte 4, 09.1943–04.1945. Awards: Oak Leaves 10.05.44 (470), Knight's Cross 24.06.40, 1939 Clasps to the 1914 Iron Cross 1st and 2nd Class, Combined Pilot/Observer's Badge in Gold with Diamonds, Eastern Front Medal, Kuban Shield, Pilot's Commemorative Badge, 1914 Iron Cross 1st and 2nd Class, 1914 Wound Badge in Black, 1914 Pilot's Badge, Cross of Honor.

Dethleffsen, Erich: Generalmajor (09.11.44), (Heer); born 02.08.04 in Kiel, died 04.07.80 in Munich. Adjutant to II. Bataillon, Infanterie Regiment at Koenigsberg 10.1934–05.1935, Adjutant to Fortress Commandant of Koenigsberg 06.1935–09.1935, attached to Staff of Kriegsschule 10.1935–07.1937, attached to Staff of Commandant of Glogau 08.1937–03.1939. WWII: attached to General Staff of Heeres 04.1939–08.1939, attached to Staff of XXXV. Armee Korps 08.1939–12.1939, Group Leader in Training Department of Heeres General Staff 12.1939–02.1941, Ia to LVI. Armee Korps 02.1941–11.1941, Tactics Instructor at Kriegsschule 08.1942–06.1943, Chief of Staff to XXXIX. Panzer Korps 06.1943–05.1944, Chief of General Staff to 4. Armee 05.1944–02.1945. Awards: Knight's Cross 23.12.43, German Cross in Gold 01.05.42, 1939 Iron Cross 1st and 2nd Class, 1939 Wound Badge in Black.

Detmering, Rolf: Generalleutnant (01.06.41), (Heer); born 02.19.89 in Pfalzburg, died 21.11.64 in Giessen. WWI: Hauptmann attached to Grand General Staff. Promotion to Generalmajor 01.04.38. Attached to Military Replacement Inspection

Generalleutnant Rolf Detmering. (Josef Charita)

of Kassel 05.1935–03.1936, Military Replacement Inspector of Kassel 03.1936–10.1936, Commander of Infanterie Regiment 17, 10.1936–03.1938, Military Replacement Inspector of Erfurt 04.1938–02.1939. WWII: Military Replacement Inspector of Frankfurt am Main 03.1939–05.1943, Commandant of Feldkommandantur 603, 07.1943–08.1944, P.O.W. Commander in several Wehrkreis 10.1944–05.1945. Awards: Knight's Cross of the War Merit Cross with Swords 16.03.45, War Merit Cross 1st and 2nd Class with Swords, 1914 Iron Cross 1st and 2nd Class, 1914 Wound Badge in Silver, Cross of Honor.

Detten, Gustav von: Generalmajor (01.11.41), (Heer); born 06.12.80 in Wesel, died 21.02.75 in Stuttgart. WWI: Hauptmann and Commander of II. Bataillon, Infanterie Regiment 20. WWII: Director of Psychological Test Office for Wehrkreis V 10.1933–09.1942, retired 09.1942. Awards: War Merit Cross 1st and 2nd Class with Swords, 1914 Iron Cross 1st and 2nd Class, Cross of Honor.

Dettling, August: Generalleutnant (01.01.43), (Heer); born 07.08.93 in Stuttgart, died 06.05.80 in Ulm. WWI: Oberleutnant on Staff of Infanterie Regiment 180. Promotion to Generalmajor 01.11.41. Adjutant on Staff of Artillerie Fuehrer V 10.1934–10.1935, Adjutant to 15. Division 10.1935–10.1936, Commander of I. Bataillon. WWII: Infanterie Regiment 56, 10.1936–09.1939, Commander of Infanterie Regiment 195, 09.1939–12.1940, Commander of Infanterie Regiment 523, 12.1940–01.1942, Commander of 183. Infanterie Division 01.1942–10.1943, Commander of 363. Infanterie Division 12.1943–02.1945. Awards: German Cross in Gold 07.03.42, 1939 Clasps to the 1914 Iron Cross 1st and 2nd Class, Infantry Assault Badge in Silver, Eastern Front Medal, 1914 Iron Cross 1st and 2nd Class, 1914 Wound Badge in Black, Cross of Honor.

Deutsch, Friedrich-Wilhelm: Generalleutnant (01.08.43), (Heer); born 19.02.82 Berlin, died 02.03.44 at Valona Hospital from automobile accident. WWI: Oberleutnant and Adjutant to Infanterie Regiment 418. Promotion to Generalmajor 01.07.42. Commander of I. Bataillon, Infanterie Regiment 15, 10.1935–04.1939. WWII: attached to Staff of Infanterie Regiment 15, 05.1939–08.1939, Commander of Infanterie Regiment 187, 08.1939–05.1941, Commander of Infanterie Regiment 522, 08.1941–07.1942, Commander of 711. Infanterie Division 07.1942–03.1943, Commander of 297. Infanterie Division 04.1943–02.1944. Awards: German Cross in Gold 30.05.42, 1939 Clasps to the 1914 Iron Cross 1st and 2nd Class, Infantry

Assault Badge in Silver, Eastern Front Medal, 1939 Wound Badge in Gold, 1914 Iron Cross 1st and 2nd Class, Cross of Honor.

Deutsch, Friedrich-Wilhelm: Generalmajor (01.07.44), (Luftwaffe); born 25.09.95 in Staltenhagen, died 27.03.45 in action in Wesel. WWI: Leutnant in Pionier Batail- lon 2. Batterie Chef in Fahr Abteilung 2, 1933–05.1935, Advisor in Heer Weapons Amt 06.1935–03.1936. WWII: Advisor and Group Director of Weapons Tests 10 in R.L.M. 04.1936–1943, Commander of Flak Regiment 25, 1943–01.1944, Commander of 16. (mot.) Flak Division 04.1944–02.1945. Awards: 1939 Clasps to the 1914 Iron Cross 1st and 2nd Class, Flak War Badge, 1939 Wound Badge in Gold, 1914 Iron Cross 1st and 2nd Class, Cross of Honor.

Dewald, Fritz: Generalmajor (01.10.43), (Heer); born 21.08.91 in Altfelde, died 07.05.73 in Buehl. WWI: Leutnant in Infanterie Regiment 138. Kompanie Chef in Infanterie Regiment 14, 10.1935–10.1936, Commander of II. Batail- lon, Infanterie Regiment 119, 10.1936–11.1938. WWII: attached to Staff of Infanterie Regiment 119, 11.1938–08.1939, Commander of Infanterie Ersatz Regiment 260, 09.1939–03.1940, Commander of Infanterie Ersatz Regiment 205, 12.1940–07.1941, Commander of Infanterie Regiment 358, 07.1941–06.1942, Commander of Truppenubungsplatz at Oksbol 10.1942–05.1945. Awards: 1939 Clasp to the 1914 Iron Cross 2nd Class, War Merit Cross 1st and 2nd Class with Swords, Infantry Assault Badge in Silver, Eastern Front Medal, 1914 Iron Cross 2nd Class, 1914 Wound Badge in Black, Cross of Honor.

Dewall, Job-Heinrich von: Generalleutnant (01.11.42), (Luftwaffe); born 13.07.80 in Salzwedel, died 19.09.45 at Neu-Rohlau P.O.W. Camp. WWI: in G.A.S. as Hauptmann and Commander of Kampfgeschwader 2. Promotion to Generalmajor 01.11.40. Leader of Luft Amt in Magdeburg 06.1934–07.1935, service unknown 08.1935–06.1938. WWII: Director of Air Office at Dresden 07.1938–08.1939, Flughafenbereichs Commandant of Radom 10.1939–02.1940, Flughafenbereichs Commandant of 7-IV 02.1940–11.1942, attached to Luftgau Kommando III 12.1942–05.1943, retired 05.1943, civil employee and member of Science Institute Department of Luftwaffe General Staff in Berlin 12.1942–05.1945. Awards: 1939 Clasp to the 1914 Iron Cross 2nd Class, War Merit Cross 1st and 2nd Class with Swords, 1939 Pilot's Badge, Pilot's Commemorative Badge, RK-Hohenzollern, RK-Sachsen Ernestine House Order 1st Class with Swords, 1914 Iron Cross 1st and 2nd Class, Prussian Crown Order IV. Class with Swords, Austro-Hungarian Military Service Cross 3rd Class with War Decoration, 1914 Pilot's Badge, Cross of Honor.

Dewitz, Kuno: Generalmajor (01.04.45), (Heer); born 17.10.97 in Soldau, died 03.01.60 in Kiel. WWI: Leutnant in Infanterie Regiment 128. Attached to Staff of II. Bataillon, Infanterie Regiment at Kolberg 10.1934–04.1935, Chief of 14. Kompanie, Infanterie Regiment 4, 05.1935–10.1937. WWII: Inspector and Tactics Instructor at Kriegsschule Potsdam 10.1937–09.1939, Commander of II. Bataillon, Infanterie Regiment 244, 10.1939–12.1941, Commander of Infanterie Regiment 9, 12.1941–01.1944, Commander of Fuehrer Schule for Fahnenjunker of Infanterie at Dresden 05.1944–01.1945. Awards: German Cross in Gold 09.07.42, 1939 Clasps to the 1914 Iron Cross 1st and 2nd Class, Infantry Assault Badge in Silver, 1914 Iron Cross 1st and 2nd Class, 1914 Wound Badge in Black, Cross of Honor.

Dewitz gen. von Krebs, Guenther von: Generalmajor (01.06.40), (Heer); born 06.12.85 in Berlin, died 05.06.40 in action near Tergnier. WWI: Hauptmann in Guards Fusilier Regiment. Training Leader at Saarbruecken 1935–08.1939, Commander of I. Bataillon, Infanterie Regiment 483, 08.1939–10.1939, Commander of Infanterie Regiment 483, 10.1939–06.1940. Awards: 1939 Clasps to the 1914 Iron Cross 1st and 2nd Class, 1939 Wound Badge in Gold, RK-Hohenzollern, 1914 Iron Cross 1st and 2nd Class, Cross of Honor.

Dewitz gen. von Krebs, Karl von: Generalmajor (01.08.41), (Heer); born 08.06.87 in Berlin, died 19.04.45 (shot by Hitler-Jugend for defeatism). WWI: Hauptmann on Staff of General Kommando 65. Attached to Grenz Abschnittes Kommando at Kuestrin 10.1934–10.1936. WWII: Training Leader of Berlin I 10.1936–08.1939, Commander of Infanterie Regiment 323, 08.1939–12.1941, Commander of 191. Infanterie Division 12.1941–03.1943, Commander of Truppenubungsplatz at Brod 08.1943–1944, Commander of 137. Infanterie Division 1944–10.1944. Awards: 1939 Clasps to the 1914 Iron Cross 1st and 2nd Class, Infantry Assault Badge in Silver, RK-Sachsen Albrecht Order 2nd Class with Swords, 1914 Iron Cross 1st and 2nd Class, Prussian Crown Order IV. Class with Swords, Austro-Hungarian Military Service Cross 3rd Class with War Decoration, 1914 Wound Badge in Black, Johann Ritter Order, Cross of Honor.

Dewitz gen. von Krebs, Stanislaus von: Generalmajor (01.07.42), (Heer); born 21.03.92 in Gross-Jauth, died 09.1948 (executed) in Vorkuta. WWI: Oberleutnant in Infanterie Regiment 14. Commander of II. Bataillon, Infanterie Regiment at Flensburg 10.1934–10.1935. WWII: Commander of II. Bataillon, Infanterie Regiment 26, 10.1935–08.1939, Commander of Infanterie Regiment 220, 08.1939–11.1941, Wehrmacht Commander of Frankfurt/Oder 05.1942–03.1944, Battle Commandant of Kishinev 07.1944–09.1944, captured 09.1944. Awards: German Cross in Gold 14.11.41, 1939 Clasps to the 1914 Iron Cross 1st and 2nd Class, Infantry Assault Badge in Silver, 1914 Iron Cross 1st and 2nd Class, Cross of Honor.

Deyrer, Dr. Adolf: General-Intendant (01.05.44), (Heer); born 30.12.97 in Zweibruecken, died 05.03.52 in Munich. Administrative Officer by profession. WWI:

in G.A.S. as Leutnant der Res. in Zeppelin Ersatz Abteilung "Muenchen." WWII: Chief Intendant to Wehrkreis Kommando XIII 1939–05.1945. Awards: War Merit Cross 1st and 2nd Class with Swords, 1920 Airship Commemorative Badge, 1914 Iron Cross 1st and 2nd Class, 1914 Wound Badge in Black, Cross of Honor.

Dickmann, Johann-Hugo: Generalmajor (01.06.42), (Heer); born 11.12.79 in Duesseldorf, died 03.08.53 in Dortmund. WWI: Hauptmann attached to German Protection Troops in Cameroon, P.O.W. 1915–1919. WWII: Commander of Military District Kommando I in Dortmund 10.1933–07.1942, retired 07.1942. Awards: 1939 Clasp to the 1914 Iron Cross 2nd Class, War Merit Cross 1st and 2nd Class with Swords, 1914 Iron Cross 1st and 2nd Class, Cross of Honor.

Dieckhoff, Gerhard: Generalmajor (01.09.44), (Luftwaffe); born 22.06.92 in Osterode, died 01.11.64 in Bernkastel-Kues. WWI: in G.A.S. as Turkish Oberleutnant and Commander of Turkish Flieger Abteilung 13. Advisor on Staff of Inspector of schools in R.L.M. 04.1934–01.1935, Special Purpose Officer attached to R.L.M. 02.1935–07.1935, Leader of Photo Observation attached to Luftwaffe Aufklarungs Schule in Hildesheim 08.1935–09.1936, Staffelkapitan in Fernaufklarungs Gruppe 25, 10.1936–03.1938, Instruction Group Leader at Luftwaffe Aufklarungs Schule in Braunschweig 04.1938–08.1938. WWII: Commander of Luftwaffe Aufklarungs Schulen at Grossenheim, Gotha and Perleberg 09.1938–03.1941, Luftwaffe Commander for 6. Armee 03.1941–04.1942, Flughafenbereichs Commandant of 8-III 04.1942–05.1945. Awards: 1939 Clasps to the 1914 Iron Cross 1st and 2nd Class, 1939 Observer's Badge, Pilot's Commemorative Badge, 1914 Iron Cross 1st and 2nd Class, 1914 Observer's Badge, Turkish Half Moon, Cross of Honor.

Diehm, Christoph: SS-Brigadefuehrer und Generalmajor der Waffen-SS und Polizei (21.03.34); born 01.03.92 in Rottenacker, died 21.02.60 in Rottenacker. P-212531, SS-28461. WWI: Vizefeldwebel attached to Infanterie Regiment 247. Joined N.S.D.A.P. in 1930, joined S.A. in 1928, SA-Oberfuehrer and Leader of SA-Untergruppe located at Wuerttemberg, Polizei President of Metz, joined S.S. Leader of SS-Abschnitte XIX 01.10.34–01.07.35, Leader of SS-Abschnitte I 01.12.36–01.12.38. WWII: Leader on Staff of RFSS 30.01.42, attached to R.u.S.H.A. 15.05.43, S.S.P.F. of Lemberg 30.01.44, Deputy H.S.S.P.F. of Belgium and Northern France, attached to SS-Hauptamt 09.11.44, Heer Hauptmann der Res., Member of Reichstag (WK 32 Baden). Awards: Golden Party Badge (honorary), 1939 Clasp to the 1914 Iron Cross 2nd Class, War Merit Cross 1st and 2nd Class with Swords, 1939 Wound Badge in Gold, 1914 Iron Cross 1st and 2nd Class, 1914 Wound Badge in Silver, Cross of Honor, 1929 Nuremberg Badge of Honor, SA-Rally at Braunschweig Badge of Honor, Reich Sports Badge in Bronze, SA-Sports Badge in Gold, Degen, Ring.

Diesener, Paul: Generalmajor (01.04.45), (Heer); born 27.04.82 in Berlin, died 22.05.70 in Hildesheim. WWI: Hauptmann and Adjutant on Staff of XIV. Armee Korps. WWII: Training Leader at German Krone 09.1934–08.1939, Commander of Border Protection Regiment 52, 08.1939–11.1939, Commander of Infanterie Ersatz Regiment 75, 11.1939–04.1940, Commander of Military District Kommando at Woldenberg 09.1940–06.1941, attached to Staff of German Afrika Korps 08.1941–05.1942, Commander of Liaison Staff of 2. Italian Armee 05.1942–06.1943, Commander of Railroad Security Section Staff 5, 06.1943–10.1944, Fuehrer Res. in O.K.H. 10.1944–05.1945. Awards: 1939 Clasps to the 1914 Iron Cross 1st and 2nd Class, Afrika Cuff Band, Italian Commander's Cross of the Colonial Order with Breast Star, Princely House Order of Hohenzollern 3rd Class Honor Cross, 1914 Iron Cross 1st and 2nd Class, Prussian Crown Order IV. Class with Swords, Turkish Half Moon, Cross of Honor.

Diesing, Ulrich: Generalmajor (01.11.44), (Luftwaffe); born 12.03.11 in Trebschen, died 17.04.45 from accident in Boizenburg. Training at Fliegerschule in Cottbus 02.1935–06.1935, Flugzeugfuehrer attached to Fluggenkommando Berlin 07.1935–01.1937, Flugzeugfuehrer in L.G. Griefswald 01.1937–04.1938. WWII: Advisor in R.L.M. 04.1938–08.1939, Ia to Luftwaffe Operational Staff in R.L.M. 08.1939–04.1940, attached to General Staff of Quartermaster of Luftwaffe in R.L.M. 04.1940–09.1941, Gruppe Commander in K.G. 210 and Z.G. 109.1941–03.1942, Commander of Z.G. 1, 03.1942–09.1942, Ia on Staff of Luftwaffe Operations in R.L.M. 09.1942–02.1944, Chief of Luftwaffe Technical Armaments Office in R.L.M. 08.1944–04.1945. Awards: Knight's Cross 06.09.42, 1939 Iron Cross 1st and 2nd Class, Spanish Cross in Silver with Swords, 1939 Pilot's Badge.

Diestel, Erich: Generalleutnant (01.08.43), (Heer); born 08.11.92 in Deutsch-Eylau, died 03.08.73 in Bad Wiessee. WWI: Leutnant and Adjutant to Infanterie Regiment 422. Promotion to Generalmajor 01.08.42. Instructor at Kriegsschule Dresden 01.1935–10.1937. WWII: Commander of I. Bataillon, Infanterie Regiment 68, 10.1937–01.1940, Commander of Infanterie Regiment 188, 01.1940–04.1942, Commander of 101. Light Infanterie Division 04.1942–09.1942, Commander of 346. Infanterie Division 09.1942–10.1944, Commander of Special Purposes Staff 331, 11.1944–03.1945. Awards: Knight's Cross 08.10.44, German Cross in Gold 02.01.42, 1939 Clasps to the 1914 Iron Cross 1st and 2nd Class, Infantry Assault Badge in Silver, Eastern Front Medal, 1914 Iron Cross 1st and 2nd Class, 1914 Wound Badge in Black, Cross of Honor.

Diesterweg, Gustav: SS-Brigadefuehrer und Generalmajor der Waffen-SS (30.01.44); born 02.06.75 in Berlin, died 04.01.53 in Munich. P-3958887, SS-259554.

WWI: Major and Bataillon Commander (unit unknown). Joined N.S.D.A.P. in 1937, joined S.S. in 1935, attached to SS-Hauptamt 01.07.35. Attached to Staff of SS-Hauptamt 01.12.36–01.12.38. WWII: Commander of SS-Waffen Meister Schule at Dachau 30.01.42–15.05.43, Commander of SS-Waffen Lehr Anst. 09.11.44. Awards: War Merit Cross 1st and 2nd Class with Swords, 1914 Iron Cross 1st and 2nd Class, 1914 Wound Badge in Black, Austro-Hungarian Military Service Cross 3rd Class with War Decoration, Cross of Honor, Degen, Ring.

Generaloberst Eduard Dietl. (Bundesarchiv)

Dietl, Eduard: Generaloberst (01.06.42), (Heer); born 21.07.90 in Bad Aibling, died 23.06.44 from air accident near Hartberg. WWI: Oberleutnant and Adjutant to 7. Bavarian Infanterie Brigade. Promotions to Generalmajor 01.04.38, Generalleutnant 01.04.40, General der Gebirgstruppe 19.07.40. Commander of Infanterie Regiment at Amberg 10.1934–10.1934, Commander of Infanterie Regiment at Regensburg 11.1934–10.1935, Commander of Gebirgs Jaeger Regiment 99, 10.1935–04.1938. WWII: Commander of 3. Gebirgs Division 05.1938–04.1940, Commander of Gruppe "Narvik" 04.1940–06.1940, Commander of Gebirgs Korps Norway 06.1940–01.1942, Oberbefehlshaber of Heeresgruppe Lapland 01.1942–06.1942, Oberbefehlshaber of 20. Gebirgs Armee 06.1942–06.1944. Awards: Golden Party Badge (honorary), Swords 01.07.44 (72), Oak Leaves 19.07.40 (1), Knight's Cross 09.05.40, 1939 Clasps to the 1914 Iron Cross 1st and 2nd Class, Narvik Shield, Destroyer's War Badge, Eastern Front Medal, 1939 Wound Badge in Gold, Heer Bergfuehrer Badge, Combined Pilot/Observer's Badge in Gold with Diamonds, German Olympic Games Decoration 1st Class, Grand Cross of the Order of the White Rose of Finland with Breast Star and Swords, Grand Cross of the Finnish Cross of Freedom with Breast Star and Swords, 1914 Iron Cross 1st and 2nd Class, 1914 Wound Badge in Silver, Cross of Honor.

Dietrich, Josef: SS-Oberst-Gruppenfuehrer und Generaloberst der Waffen-SS (20.04.42); born 28.05.92 in Hawangen, died 21.04.66 in Ludwigsburg. P-89015, SS-1177. WWI: Vizewachtmeister attached to Tank Bataillon 13. Served in Freikorps "Oberland," joined N.S.D.A.P. and S.S. in 1928. Promotions to SS-Brigadefuehrer (skipped), SS-Gruppenfuehrer 18.12.31, SS-Obergruppenfuehrer 01.07.34. Commander of Stabswache Berlin 1933, Leader of SS-Oberabschnitte Ost 01.10.34–01.07.35, Leader of SS-Oberabschnitte Ost and at same time Leader of "Leibstandarte-SS Adolf Hitler" 01.12.36–01.12.38. WWII: Commander of

SS-Infanterie Regiment (mot.) "LSSAH," Commander of SS-Division "LSSAH" 30.01.42, Commander of Panzer Grenadier Division "LSSAH" and at same time Leader of SS-Oberabschnitte Spree 15.05.43, Commander of I. SS-Panzer Korps "Leibstandarte" and at same time Leader of SS-Oberabschnitte Spree 30.01.44, Oberbefehlshaber of 6. SS-Panzer Armee and at same time Leader of SS-Oberabschnitte Spree 09.11.44, Prussian State Councilor, Member of Reichstag (WK 5 Frankfurt-Oder). Awards: Golden Party Badge, Blood Order (Bund Oberland Stab), Diamonds 06.08.44 (16), Swords 14.03.43 (26), Oak Leaves 31.12.41 (41), Knight's Cross 04.07.40, 1939 Clasps to the 1914 Iron Cross 1st and 2nd Class, Eastern Front Medal, Crimea Shield, Combined Pilot/Observer's Badge in Gold with Diamonds, Silesian Eagle 1st and 2nd Class, 1914 Iron Cross 1st and 2nd Class, 1921 Panzer Badge, Cross of Honor, German Olympic Games Decoration 1st Class, Reich Sports Badge in Gold, SA-Sports Badge in Gold, German Motor Sports Badge in Gold, Degen, Himmler Dedication Dagger, Ring.

SS-Oberst-Gruppenfuehrer Josef Dietrich. (Roger James Bender)

Dietrich, Dr. Wilhelm: General-Arzt (01.02.41), (Heer); born 24.09.79 in Schwebda, died 05.02.41 of natural causes in Brussels. Medical doctor by profession. WWI: Stabs-Arzt (unit unknown). WWII: attached to Higher Kommando XXXVI 02.1940–05.1940, Leitender Medical Officer attached to Military Befehlshaber of Belgium and Northern France 06.1940–02.1941. Awards: 1914 Iron Cross 2nd Class, Cross of Honor.

Dietz, Dr. Heinrich: General-Richter z.V. (01.05.44), (Heer); born 14.04.74 in Alzey, died 11.08.46 in Alzey. Jurist by profession. WWI: Oberkriegsgerichtsrat (Senior War Legal Official) with Military Government in Litauen. Attached to Gericht of Panzertruppen in Berlin and at same time attached to Reich War Ministry 11.1935–10.1938. WWII: attached to O.B. des Heeres 11.1938–07.1944, attached to Wehrkreis Kommando III 07.1944–10.1944. Awards: War Merit Cross 2nd Class with Swords, Cross of Honor.

Digeon von Monteton, Albrecht Freiherr: Generalleutnant (01.06.43), (Heer); born 08.12.87 in Bernburg, died 03.02.46 (executed) in Riga. WWI: Oberleutnant on Staff of 20. Infanterie Division. Promotion to Generalmajor 01.04.42. Attached to Staff of Heeres Service Office at Kassel 10.1934–04.1935, attached to Staff of IX. Armee Korps 05.1935–10.1936, Commander of I. Abteilung, Kavallerie Regiment 15, 10.1936–02.1938. WWII: Commander of Kavallerie Regiment 15,

03.1938–08.1939, Commander of Infanterie Regiment 167, 09.1939–05.1942, Commander of 391. Feld Aubildsdung Division 09.1942–09.1944, Wehrmacht Commander of Libau 10.1944–05.1945. Awards: German Cross in Gold 02.01.42, 1939 Clasps to the 1914 Iron Cross 1st and 2nd Class, Infantry Assault Badge in Silver, Eastern Front Medal, 1914 Iron Cross 1st and 2nd Class, 1914 Wound Badge in Black, Cross of Honor, German Horseman's Badge in Bronze.

Digeon von Monteton, Constantin Freiherr: Generalmajor (01.07.44), (Heer); born 28.02.86 in Bernburg, died 20.06.44 in action near Gorodey. WWI: Hauptmann on Staff of Chief to Armee General Staff. WWII: Training Director at Bartenstein 10.1933–09.1939, Commander of Infanterie Regiment 311, 09.1939–1943, Commander of Waffen Schule for 3. Panzer Armee 05.1943–06.1944. Awards: Knight's Cross 14.08.44, German Cross in Gold 09.07.42, 1939 Clasps to the 1914 Iron Cross 1st and 2nd Class, Infantry Assault Badge in Silver, Eastern Front Medal, 1939 Wound Badge in Gold, 1914 Iron Cross 1st and 2nd Class, 1914 Wound Badge in Black, Cross of Honor.

Dihm, Friedrich: Generalleutnant (01.10.42), (Heer); born 06.01.80 in Munich, died 11.08.56 in Sternberg. WWI: Hauptmann on Staff of Generalkommando z.b.V. 64. Promotion to Generalmajor 01.10.40. Commander of Heeres Feldzeug Kommando V 01.1935–12.1937. WWII: Commander of Heeres Feldzeug Kommando VII 01.1938–10.1939, Commander of Artillerie 104, 05.1940–07.1940, Heeres Supply Leader in O.K.H 12.1940–03.1942, Commander of Artillerie 115, 06.1942–03.1944, General with Special Duties with Heeresgruppe B 03.1944–08.1944, retired 12.1944. Awards: 1939 Clasps to the 1914 Iron Cross 1st and 2nd Class, War Merit Cross 1st and 2nd Class with Swords, General Assault Badge, 1914 Iron Cross 1st and 2nd Class, Cross of Honor.

Dini, Alexander: Generalmajor (01.10.44), (Luftwaffe); born 21.01.95 in Vienna, died 17.04.44 in Vienna. WWI: Oberleutnant in Austrian Infanterie Regiment 136. Transferred to German Wehrmacht 03.1938, attached to Flak Artillerie Schule Wustrow 03.1938–07.1938, attached to Staff of II. Abteilung, Flak Regiment 13, 07.1938–11.1938. WWII: Batterie Chef in Leicht Flak Bataillon 86, 11.1938–08.1939, Commander of Leicht Flak Bataillon 86, 09.1939–01.1940, Commander of Res. Flak Bataillon 266, 01.1940–03.1940, Commander of Flak Regiment 60, 03.1940–01.1943, Commander of Flak Regiment 136, 09.1943–12.1943, Commander of Der Dienststelle "General der Luftwaffe Kanalinseln" (Office of Luftwaffe Channel Islands) 01.1944–05.1945. Awards: 1939 Iron Cross 1st and 2nd Class, Flak War Badge, Cross of Honor.

Dinkel, Dr. Oskar: General-Intendant (01.05.44), (Heer); born 19.06.97 in Zapfendorf, died 10.01.69 in Munich. Administrative officer by profession. WWI: service unknown. WWII: Chief Intendant to Wehrkreis Kommando VII 1939–05.1945. Awards: War Merit Cross 1st and 2nd Class with Swords, Cross of Honor.

Dinort, Oskar: Generalmajor (01.04.45), (Luftwaffe); born 23.06.01 in Berlin, died 29.05.65 in Koeln-Riehl. Attached to Staff of I. Gruppe, J.G. "Richthofen" 05.1934–02.1935, Ia on Staff of Inspector of Day and Ground Assault Fighters in R.L.M. 03.1935–02.1936, Commander of I. Gruppe, J.G. 234, 03.1936–03.1937, Ia to Kommando of Flugzeugfuehrer Schulen 03.1937–08.1937, Commander of I. Gruppe, S.G. 165, 09.1937–01.1939. WWII: Commander of I. Gruppe, S.G. 2 "Immelmann" 02.1939–09.1939, Commander of S.G. 2 "Immelmann" 10.1939–10.1941, Advisor for Bombing Tactics on Staff of GFM Milch 02.1942–08.1943, Commander of Flieger Ziel Geschwader 08.1942–08.1943, Commander of Flieger Ziel Division 09.1943–08.1944, Commander of 3. Fliegerschule Division 09.1944–05.1945. Awards: Oak Leaves 14.07.41 (21), Knight's Cross 20.06.40, 1939 Iron Cross 1st and 2nd Class, Air to Ground Assault Clasp in Gold, 1939 Pilot's Badge.

Dinter, Rudolf: Generalleutnant (01.04.44), (Heer); born 19.01.93 in Wilkau, died 04.04.65 in Mehlbergern. WWI: Oberleutnant and Chief of 2. Kompanie, 12. Pionier Bataillon. Promotion to Generalmajor 01.02.43. Instructor at Pionier Schule (later Pionier Schule I) 10.1934–10.1936. WWII: Commander of Pionier Bataillon 22, 10.1936–01.1940, Commander of Pionier Regiment Staff 614, 05.1940–02.1941, Pionier Leader to Panzer Gruppe 4, 02.1941–12.1942, Commander of 295. Infanterie Division 04.1943–07.1944, Fuehrer Res. in O.K.H. 07.1944–01.1945, General of Pioniers to Heeresgruppe Vistula. Awards: 1939 Clasps to the 1914 Iron Cross 1st and 2nd Class, General Assault Badge, Eastern Front Medal, 1914 Iron Cross 1st and 2nd Class, Cross of Honor.

Dippold, Benignus: Generalleutnant (01.10.41), (Heer); born 04.07.89 in Sisslach, died 18.10.67 in Bamberg. WWI: Oberleutnant in Replacement Bataillon of Bavarian Infanterie Regiment 19. Promotion to Generalmajor 01.10.39. Commander of III. Bataillon, Infanterie Regiment at Regensburg 10.1934–10.1935, Commander of Infanterie Regiment 21, 10.1935–10.1936. WWII: Commander of Infanterie Regiment 104, 10.1936–12.1939, Commander of 183. Infanterie Division 12.1939–10.1941, in hospital followed by Fuehrer Res. in O.K.H. 10.1941–10.1942, Commander of 717. Infanterie Division 10.1942–03.1943, Commander of z.b.V. Division 540, 10.1943–03.1944, P.O.W. Commander for Wehrkreis Kommando VI 09.1944–04.1945. Awards: 1939 Clasps to the 1914 Iron Cross 1st and 2nd Class, Infantry Assault Badge in Silver, 1939 Wound Badge in Black, 1914 Iron Cross 1st and 2nd Class, 1914 Wound Badge in Black, Cross of Honor.

Diringshofen, Max von: Generalleutnant (01.03.43), (Heer); born 19.06.76 in Koeln, died 27.05.59 in Mainz. WWI: Major and Commander of I. Bataillon, Res. Infanterie Regiment 48. Promotion to Generalmajor 01.08.41. WWII: Training Leader at German Eylau 10.1933–08.1939, Commander of Infanterie Replacement Regiment 206, 08.1939–01.1942, Commander of 401. Infanterie Division 01.1942–09.1942, Fuehrer Res. in O.K.H. 09.1942–03.1943, retired 03.1943. Awards: 1939 Clasps to the 1914 Iron Cross 1st and 2nd Class, Infantry Assault Badge in Silver, 1914 Iron Cross 1st and 2nd Class, Cross of Honor.

Ditfurth, Wilhelm von: Generalmajor (01.04.43), (Heer); born 07.08.74 in Minden, died 20.05.49 in Lemmie. WWI: Major and Chief of Staff to I. Res. Korps. WWII: recalled to military service 02.1940, P.O.W. Commander for several Wehrkreis Kommandos 03.1940–12.1940, Chief of Staff to Higher Kommando XXXVII 02.1941–02.1943, retired 04.1943. Awards: 1939 Clasps to the 1914 Iron Cross 1st and 2nd Class, Pour le Mérite 21.04.18, RK-Hohenzollern, 1914 Iron Cross 1st and 2nd Class, Cross of Honor.

Ditfurth, Wolfgang von: Generalleutnant (01.10.41), (Heer); born 28.02.79 in Berlin, died 02.03.46 (executed) in Riga. WWI: Hauptmann and Signals Leader to Heeresgruppe "Scholtz." Promotion to Generalmajor 01.09.40. Advisor in Reichswehr Ministry and at same time Senior Quartermaster IV 10.1934–03.1939, retired 03.1939. WWII: recalled to military service 08.1939, Commander of 403. Sicherungs Division 10.1939–05.1942, attached to War Historical Research Institute 08.1942–02.1945. Awards: 1939 Clasps to the 1914 Iron Cross 1st and 2nd Class, 1914 Iron Cross 1st and 2nd Class, Cross of Honor.

Dittmar, Kurt: Generalleutnant (01.04.42), (Heer); born 05.01.91 in Magdeburg, died 26.04.59 in Stadtoldendorf. WWI: Hauptmann and Commander of III. Bataillon, Infanterie Regiment 165. Promotion to Generalmajor 01.04.40. Commander of Pionier Bataillon at Koenigsberg 10.1934–10.1935, Commander of Pioniere I 10.1935–04.1937. WWII: Commander of Pionier Schule I 04.1937–08.1939, Commander of Pionier Schule II 08.1939–10.1939, attached to Staff of General of Pioniers in O.K.H. 10.1939–03.1940, Pionier Leader to 1. Armee 03.1940–02.1941, Commander of 169. Infanterie Division 02.1941–10.1941, General with Special Duties in Broadcasting Department of O.K.H. 04.1942–04.1945. Awards: German Cross in Gold 19.12.41, 1939 Clasps to the 1914 Iron Cross 1st and 2nd Class, General Assault Badge, Finnish Freedom Cross 1st Class with Swords, 1914 Iron Cross 1st and 2nd Class, Cross of Honor.

Dittmeyer, Ludwig: Generalmajor (01.05.43), (Heer); born 13.03.93 in Wuerzburg, died 01.11.72 in Bad Kissingen. WWI: Oberleutnant and Chief of Flak Batterie

751b. WWII: Commander of Panzer Abwehr Abteilung 14, 10.1935–04.1940, Anti-Tank Officer attached to Staff of 16. Armee 04.1940–08.1944, Commander of Motor Vehicle Park Troops in Wehrkreis Kommando VI 08.1944–05.1945. Awards: 1939 Clasps to the 1914 Iron Cross 2nd Class, War Merit Cross 1st and 2nd Class with Swords, Eastern Front Medal, Silesian Eagle 1st and 2nd Class, RK-Sachsen Albrecht Order 2nd Class with Swords, 1914 Iron Cross 1st and 2nd Class, Bavarian Military Service Order IV. Class with Swords, Cross of Honor.

Doehla, Heinrich: Generalleutnant (01.02.41), (Heer); born 03.11.81 in Munich, died 14.07.46 in Stuttgart. WWI: Hauptmann and Bataillon Commander in Bavarian Infanterie Regiment 20. Promotion to Generalmajor 01.11.35. Commander of Heeres Service Office at Munich 11.1935–05.1938. WWII: Commander of Heeres Service Office at Innsbrueck 06.1938–12.1939, Commander of 537. Infanterie Division 12.1939–01.1941, Commandant of Feldkommandantur 553, 01.1941–07.1943, Fuehrer Res. in O.K.H. 07.1943–03.1944, retired 03.1944. Awards: 1939 Clasps to the 1914 Iron Cross 1st and 2nd Class, Infantry Assault Badge in Silver, 1914 Iron Cross 1st and 2nd Class, Cross of Honor.

Doehren, Georg von: Generalmajor (01.07.41), (Heer); born 23.05.84 in Hamburg, died 20.01.65 in Stuttgart. WWI: Hauptmann and Bataillon Commander in Infanterie Regiment 49. Commander of Infanterie Regiment 58, 10.1935–01.1937. WWII: Commander of Infanterie Regiment 58, 02.1937–08.1939, Commander of Infanterie Regiment 313, 08.1939–04.1941, Commander of 712. Infanterie Division 05.1941–04.1942, P.O.W. Commander for Wehrkreis Kommando VI 06.1942–04.1944, Fuehrer Res. in O.K.H. 04.1944–01.1945. Awards: 1939 Clasps to the 1914 Iron Cross 1st and 2nd Class, Infantry Assault Badge in Silver, RK-Hohenzollern, 1914 Iron Cross 1st and 2nd Class, 1914 Wound Badge in Silver, Cross of Honor.

Doenitz, Karl: Grossadmiral (30.01.43), (Kriegsmarine); born 16.09.91 in Grunau, died 24.12.80 in Aumuhle. WWI: U-boat service as Oberleutnant zur See and Kommandant of *U-28*. Promotions to Konteradmiral 01.10.39, Vizeadmiral 01.09.40, Admiral 14.03.42, Generaladmiral (skipped). WWII: First Admiral Staff Officer for Marine Station North Sea 09.1930–09.1934, Commandant of cruiser *Emden* 09.1934–09.1935, Chief of U-Boat Flottille *Weddigen* 09.1935–10.1936, Leader of U-Boats 01.1936–10.1939, Befehlshaber of Submarines 10.1939–01.1943, Oberbefehlshaber of Kriegsmarine 01.1943–04.1945, Reich President of Germany 05.1945. Awards: Golden Party Badge

Grossadmiral Karl Doenitz. (Roger James Bender)

(honorary), Oak Leaves 06.04.43 (223), Knight's Cross 21.04.40, 1939 Clasps to the 1914 Iron Cross 1st and 2nd Class, 1939 Submarine War Badge with Diamonds, Combined Pilot-Observer's Badge in Gold with Diamonds, Grand Cross of the Finnish Cross of Freedom with Breast Star and Swords, Commander's Cross of the Hungarian Service Order, RK-Italian Military House Order of Savoy, Romanian Order of Michael the Brave 2nd Class, RK-Hohenzollern, 1914 Iron Cross 1st and 2nd Class, Austro-Hungarian Military Service Cross 3rd Class with War Decoration, Turkish Silver Liakat Medal with Sabre, Turkish Half Moon, 1914 Submarine Badge, Cross of Honor.

Doepping, Oscar: Generalmajor (01.07.43), (Heer); born 08.08.93 in Amsbach, died 31.07.74 in Erlangen. WWI: Oberleutnant in Bavarian Infanterie Regiment 14. Instructor at Kriegsschule Dresden 01.1935–11.1938. WWII: Commander of III. Bataillon, Infanterie Regiment 42, 11.1938–08.1939, Commander of Infanterie Regiment 97, 09.1939–12.1941, Wehrmacht Commander of Regensburg 06.1942–05.1944, Commandant of Feldkommandantur 747, 07.1944–09.1944, Fuehrer Res. in O.K.H. 09.1944–03.1945. Awards: 1939 Clasps to the 1914 Iron Cross 1st and 2nd Class, Infantry Assault Badge in Silver, Crimea Shield, 1914 Iron Cross 1st and 2nd Class, Bavarian Military Service Order IV. Class with Swords, Cross of Honor.

Doerffler, Ernst: Generalleutnant (20.04.42), (Luftwaffe); born 03.10.90 in Eschwege, died 12.08.70 in Bochrum. WWI: in G.A.S. as Hauptmann and Leader of Flieger Abteilung A 249. Promotion to Generalmajor 01.11.40. Special Purpose Officer attached to R.L.M. 10.1937–03.1938, Deputy Commander of Luftzeugamtes in Schwerin 04.1938–06.1938. WWII: Commander of Luftzeuggruppe for Luftgau Kommando XII 07.1938–10.1939, Commander of Luftzeuggruppe VIII 10.1939–05.1940, Commander of Luftzeuggruppen in Holland, Norway and Kiev 05.1940–09.1942, Commander of Luftzeuggruppe for Kharkov 09.1942–05.1943, Commander of Luftzeuggruppe for Western France 07.1943–1944, Director of various minor offices 1944–05.1945. Awards: War Merit Cross 1st and 2nd Class with Swords, Pilot's Commemorative Badge, 1914 Iron Cross 1st and 2nd Class, Prussian Crown Order IV. Class with Swords, 1914 Pilot's Badge, Cross of Honor.

Doerffler-Schuband, Werner: SS-Brigadefuehrer und Generalmajor der Waffen-SS (01.09.43); born 15.12.92 in Zeitz, died 27.09.59 in Bad Toelz. P-1427198, SS-112955. WWI: Oberleutnant attached to Flieger Abteilung 280. Worked in industry after WWI, joined N.S.D.A.P. in 1932, joined S.S. in 1933. Attached to SS-Fuehrer Schule at Bad Toelz 01.07.35–01.12.36, attached to SS-Standarte 2 "Germania" 01.12.37, Leader of I. Sturmbann, SS-Standarte 2 "Germania" 01.12.38. WWII: Commander of SS-Junkerschule at Bad Toelz 30.01.42, attached to SS-Fuehrungshauptamt 15.05.43, Chief Amt XI of SS-Fuehrungshauptamt 30.01.44–09.11.44, Chief Amt II, Amtsgruppe A, SS-Personalhauptamt. Awards: 1939 Iron Cross 1st Class, 1939 Clasp to the 1914 Iron Cross 2nd Class, War Merit Cross 1st and 2nd Class with Swords, Pilot's Commemorative Badge, 1914 Iron Cross 2nd Class, 1914 Wound Badge in Black, 1914 Observer's Badge, Cross of Honor, Turkish Half Moon, Reich Sports Badge in Gold, SA-Sports Badge in Bronze, Degen, Ring.

Doering, Berndt von: Generalmajor (01.07.44), (Heer); born 16.01.03 in Smachowo, died 07.07.44 in action south of Florence. Kompanie Chef in Infanterie Regiment 60 and later Kompanie Chef in Infanterie Regiment 79, 1935–10.1937. WWII: Adjutant to 16. Infanterie Division 10.1937–03.1940, Commander of III. Bataillon, Schuetzen Regiment 79, 03.1940–08.1940, Commander of II. Bataillon, Schuetzen Regiment 79, 08.1940–12.1941, attached to and later Department Chief in Heeres Personnel Department of O.K.H. 02.1942–03.1943, Commander of Panzer Grenadier Regiment 79, 03.1943–11.1943, First Adjutant to O.B. Sud-West 11.1943–07.1944. Awards: Knight's Cross 30.11.40, 1939 Iron Cross 1st and 2nd Class, Infantry Assault Badge in Silver, 1939 Wound Badge in Gold.

Doering, Kurt-Bertram von: Generalleutnant (01.11.41), (Luftwaffe); born 18.02.89 in Ribbekardt, died 09.07.60 in Kloster-Medingen WWI: in G.A.S. as Rittmeister and Commander of Jagdgruppe 4. Promotion to Generalmajor 19.07.40. Commander of Fliegerschule Celle 06.1934–02.1936, Gruppen Commander in J.G. "Richthofen" 03.1936–04.1936. WWII: Commander of J.G. 134 "Horst Wessel" 04.1936–12.1939, Flieger Fuehrer 2, 12.1939–12.1940, Inspector of Fighters 12.1940–08.1941, Flieger Fuehrer Centre 08.1941–01.1942, Commander of 1. Jagd Division 05.1942–10.1943, General Officer with Special Duties in R.L.M. 11.1943–07.1944, Chief of Central Office Group in R.L.M. 07.1944–05.1945. Awards: German Cross in Gold 01.12.42, 1939 Clasps to the 1914 Iron Cross 1st and 2nd Class, 1939 Pilot's Badge, "J.G. Freiherr von Richthofen Nr. 1, 1917/18" Commemorative Cuff Band, Pilot's Commemorative Badge, RK-Hohenzollern, 1914 Iron Cross 1st and 2nd Class, Mecklenburg-Schweerin Military Service Cross 1st and 2nd Class, 1914 Wound Badge in Black, 1914 Pilot's Badge, Austro-Hungarian Military Service Cross 3rd Class with War Decoration, Austro-Hungarian Pilot's Badge, Cross of Honor.

Doering-Manteuffel, Johann-Wilhelm: Generalmajor (20.04.45); (Luftwaffe), born 17.07.98 in Heidersdorf, died 21.01.63 in Stuttgart. WWI: Leutnant in Feld Artillerie Regiment 64. Attached to Fahr Abteilung 5 in Ludwigsburg 04.1933–03.1935, Batterie Chef in Flak Abteilung Ludwigshafen 04.1935–09.1935, Batterie Chef in Flak Abteilung Stettin 10.1935–09.1936, Department Commander in Flak Regiment 24, 10.1936–10.1938. WWII: Commander of Training Staff at Rerik 11.1938–10.1939,

Commander of Flak Artillerie Schule I at Rerik and Flak Artillerie Firing Grounds at Rerik 10.1939–07.1940, Commander of Flak Regiment 101, 07.1940–04.1942, attached to General of Flak Weapons in R.L.M. 06.1942–05.1943, Flak Officer with German military mission in Romania 1943–03.1944, Commander of Flak Regiment 10, 03.1944–07.1944, Commander of 20. Flak Division 10.1944–01.1945, Commander of 15. Flak Division 01.1945–05.1945. Awards: Knight's Cross 10.09.44, German Cross in Gold 27.04.42, 1939 Iron Cross 1st Class, 1939 Clasp to the 1914 Iron Cross 2nd Class, Flak War Badge, 1939 Wound Badge in Black, Silesian Eagle 1st and 2nd Class, RK-Sachsen Albrecht Order 2nd Class with Swords, 1914 Iron Cross 2nd Class, Cross of Honor.

Doerr, Hans: Generalmajor (01.01.44), (Heer); born 14.07.97 in Wilhelmshaven, died 16.09.60 in Gross-Karolinenfeld. WWI: Leutnant in 151. Fuss Artillerie Bataillon. Attached to Wehrkreis Kommando VII (later VII. Armee Korps) 10.1934–10.1936, Batterie Chef in Artillerie Regiment 13, 10.1936–08.1937. WWII: Instructor at Kriegsschule 09.1937–08.1939, Plenipotentiary Commissioner for War Transport 09.1939–11.1939, Ia to 44. Infanterie Division 12.1939–09.1940, Tactics Instructor in Berlin for General Staff Courses 10.1940–04.1941, Chief of Staff to LII. Armee Korps 06.1941–09.1942, Chief of German Liaison Staff to 4. Romanian Armee 10.1942–03.1943, Chief of Staff to XVII. Armee Korps 03.1943–08.1943, Military Attaché in Madrid 08.1943–05.1945. Awards: German Cross in Gold 08.10.42, 1939 Clasps to the 1914 Iron Cross 1st and 2nd Class, Eastern Front Medal, 1914 Iron Cross 1st and 2nd Class, 1914 Wound Badge in Black, Cross of Honor.

Doerstling, Egon: General der Flieger (01.06.42), (Luftwaffe); born 28.01.90 in Chemnitz, died 09.11.65 in Garmisch-Partenkirchen. WWI: in G.A.S. as Hauptmann and Staffelfuehrer in Bombengeschwader 5. Promotions to Generalmajor 01.01.39, Generalleutnant 01.12.40. Fliegerhorst Commandant of Schleissheim 10.1933–12.1934, Department Chief LA II in R.L.M. 01.1935–03.1936, Chief of 2. Abteilung in General Staff of Luftwaffe 04.1936–09.1937, Commander of K.G. 253 "General Wever" 10.1937–06.1938. WWII: Chief of Supply Office in R.L.M. 07.1938–08.1943, Commander of Feld Luftgau Kommando in Holland 08.1943–01.1944, Commander of Luftgau Kommando XVIII 02.1944–05.1945. Awards: 1939 Clasps to the 1914 Iron Cross 1st and 2nd Class, War Merit Cross 1st and 2nd Class with Swords, 1939 Observer's Badge, Croatian Grand Cross of the Crown of King Zvonimir with Swords and Breast Star, Pilot's Commemorative Badge, RK-Sachsen Military St. Heinrich's Order 01.05.18, RK-Sachsen Albrecht Order 2nd Class with Swords, RK-Sachsen Service Order 2nd Class with Swords, 1914 Iron Cross 1st and 2nd Class, 1914 Wound Badge in Black, 1914 Observer's Badge, Cross of Honor.

Dohna-Schlobitten, Heinrich Burggraf und Graf zu: Generalmajor (01.06.42); (Heer), born 15.10.82 in Waldburg, died 14.09.44 (executed) at Plotzensee Prison for involvement in attempt on Hitler's life. WWI: Rittmeister and Ia to 240. Infanterie Division. WWII: recalled to military service 08.1939, Chief of Staff to XXXVI. Armee Korps 10.1939–10.1941, Chief of Staff to Wehrkreis XX 12.1941–06.1943, retired 09.1943. Awards: 1939 Clasps to the 1914 Iron Cross 1st and 2nd Class, Finnish Freedom Cross 2nd Class with Swords, Baltic Cross 1st and 2nd Class, RK-Hohenzollern, RK-Sachsen Albrecht Order 2nd Class with Swords, 1914 Iron Cross 1st and 2nd Class, 1914 Wound Badge in Black, Prussian Crown Order IV. Class with Swords, Cross of Honor.

Dollmann, Friedrich: Generaloberst (19.07.40), (Heer); born 02.02.82 in Wuerzburg, died 28.06.44 from heart attack at Le Mans. WWI: Hauptmann and General Staff Officer attached to 6. Armee. Promotions to Reichswehr Generalmajor 01.10.32, Reichswehr Generalleutnant 01.10.33, General der Artillerie 01.04.36. Commander of Heeres Service Office at Kassel 10.1934–04.1935. WWII: Commander of IX. Armee Korps and Befehlshaber of Wehrkreis Kommando IX 06.1935–10.1939, Oberbefehlshaber of 7. Armee 10.1939–06.1944. Awards: Oak Leaves 01.07.44 (518), Knight's Cross 24.06.40, 1939 Clasps to the 1914 Iron Cross 1st and 2nd Class, 1939 Wound Badge in Gold, 1914 Iron Cross 1st and 2nd Class, Cross of Honor.

Generaloberst Friedrich Dollmann. (Bundesarchiv)

Domansky, Heinrich: Generalmajor (09.11.44), (Heer); born 13.06.92 in Danzig, died 28.04.45 in action in Stutthof. WWI: Oberleutnant in Feld Artillerie Regiment 79. Batterie Chef in Artillerie Regiment at Allenstein 10.1934–03.1935, Commander of III. Abteilung, Artillerie Regiment at Allenstein 04.1935–10.1935, Commander of III. Abteilung, Artillerie Regiment 11, 10.1935–07.1938. WWII: Commander of II. Abteilung, Artillerie Regiment 98, 07.1938–01.1940, Commander of Artillerie Regiment 122, 01.1940–03.1944, Commander of Artillerie 401, 03.1944–09.1944, Commander of 50. Infanterie Division 10.1944–04.1945. Awards: 1939 Clasps to the 1914 Iron Cross 1st and 2nd Class, General Assault Badge, 1914 Iron Cross 1st and 2nd Class, Cross of Honor.

Dommenget, Erich: Generalmajor (01.08.43), (Luftwaffe); born 24.05.84 in Cummerow, died 14.07.65 in Stuttgart. WWI: in G.A.S. as Hauptmann and Commander of Flieger South. Leader of Verbindungs Office in Stuttgart for Luftkreis

Kommando V 04.1934–03.1936, Luftwaffe Officer attached to V. Armee Korps 04.1936–11.1936, Deputy to Commander of Luftgau 15, 04.1936–09.1936, Luftwaffe Attaché in Spain 12.1936–06.1938, Group Leader of Luftwaffe Inspection for Nuremberg 08.1938–02.1939. WWII: Military District Commander of Ingolstadt 03.1939–04.1942, Flughafenbereichs Commandant of 3-I 04.1942–02.1943, Officer with Special Duties attached to R.L.M. 02.1943–08.1943, retired 08.1943. Awards: War Merit Cross 1st and 2nd Class with Swords, Spanish Cross in Silver with Swords, Pilot's Commemorative Badge, RK-Hohenzollern, 1914 Iron Cross 1st and 2nd Class, Bavarian Military Service Order IV. Class with Swords, Austro-Hungarian Military Service Cross 3rd Class with War Decoration, 1914 Pilot's Badge, Austro-Hungarian Pilot's Badge, Cross of Honor.

Dommernicht, Friedrich: General-Intendant (01.01.40), (Luftwaffe); born 28.06.94 in Nienburg, died 08.06.79 in Kiel. Administrative Officer by profession. WWI: Leutnant der Res. in Fuss Artillerie Regiment 20. Regierungsrat for Luftkreis Kommando VI 02.1935–10.1936. WWII: Chief Intendant to Luftkreis (later Luftgau Kommando) I in Koenigsberg 10.1936–03.1943, Luftgau Intendant for Norway 03.1943–10.1943, Chief Intendant to Feld Luftgau Kommando XXV 10.1943–04.1944, Chief Intendant to Luftflotte 2, 05.1944–08.1944, Chief Intendant to Luftflotte 5, 08.1944–05.1945. Awards: War Merit Cross 1st and 2nd Class with Swords, 1914 Iron Cross 1st and 2nd Class, Cross of Honor.

Donat, Hans von: Generalleutnant (01.01.44), (Heer); born 06.07.91 in Stuttgart, died 11.06.92 in Stuttgart. WWI: Oberleutnant on Staff of Inspection of Railway Troops. Promotion to Generalmajor 01.11.41. Commander of Pionier Bataillon at Holzminden 10.1934–10.1935, Commander of Pionier Bataillon 19, 10.1935–03.1936, Commander of Pioniere VI, 04.1936–11.1938. WWII: Commander of Eisenbahn Pionier Regiment 68, 11.1938–10.1939, Higher Railway Pionier Leader to Heeresgruppe B 10.1939–11.1940, Higher Railway Pionier Leader to Heeresgruppe Nord 05.1941–02.1942, Commander of Eisenbahn Pionier Schule and Truppenubungsplatz at Rehagen 07.1942–05.1945. Awards: 1939 Clasps to the 1914 Iron Cross 1st and 2nd Class, General Assault Badge, Eastern Front Medal, Baltic Cross 1st and 2nd Class, 1914 Iron Cross 1st and 2nd Class, Cross of Honor.

Donner, Peter-Christian: Konteradmiral (01.01.41), (Kriegsmarine); born 31.03.81 in Stettin, died 12.06.44 of natural causes in Malente. WWI: Korvettenkapitan and First Adjutant to Marine Befehlshaber of Marine Korps Flanders. Naval History Instructor and Director of Instruction Staff on Inspectorate of Training in O.K.M. 10.1934–06.1944. Awards: War Merit Cross 1st and 2nd Class with Swords, RK-Baden Order of the Zaehringer Lion 1st Class with Swords, 1914 Iron Cross 1st and 2nd Class, Oldenburg Friedrich-August Cross 1st and 2nd Class, Cross of Honor.

Dormagen, Karl-Hans: Generalmajor (01.04.43), (Heer); born 17.01.90 Muelheim, died 14.01.69 in Offenburg. WWI: Hauptmann and Adjutant to Infanterie Regiment 131. Commander of III. Bataillon, Infanterie Regiment at Marienburg 10.1934–10.1935, attached to Staff of Heeres Service Office 3, 11.1935–07.1936. WWII: Training Director at Offenburg 08.1936–08.1939, Commander of Landwehr Regiment 40, 08.1939–01.1940, Commander of Infanterie Regiment 335, 01.1940–09.1942, Commandant of Feld Section 181, 12.1942–10.1943, Commandant of Feld Section 813, 10.1943–04.1945. Awards: German Cross in Gold 06.09.42, 1939 Clasps to the 1914 Iron Cross 1st and 2nd Class, Infantry Assault Badge in Silver, 1914 Iron Cross 1st and 2nd Class, Cross of Honor.

Dorn, Hellmuth: Generalmajor (20.04.45), (Heer); born 30.04.95 in Merseburg, died 22.03.61 in Farchant. WWI: Leutnant and Adjutant to 227. Pionier Bataillon. Instructor at Infanterie Schule in Dresden 10.1932–07.1936. WWII: Advisor in Abteilung 5 of Heeres General Staff 08.1936–03.1940, Commander of Pionier Bataillon 47, 03.1940–01.1941, attached to Staff of Heeresgruppe A and later O.B. West 06.1941–07.1942, Department Chief in Pionier Staff of O.K.H. 11.1942–04.1945. Awards: 1939 Clasps to the 1914 Iron Cross 1st and 2nd Class, General Assault Badge, 1914 Iron Cross 1st and 2nd Class, Cross of Honor.

Dornberger, Dr. Walter: Generalmajor (01.06.43), (Heer); born 06.09.95 in Giessen, died 27.06.80 in Obersasbach. WWI: Leutnant and Adjutant to 26. Fuss Artillerie Abteilung. Batterie Chef in Artillerie Abteilung at Koenigsbrueck 10.1934–10.1935, Kompanie Chef in Nebel Abteilung 1, 10.1935–01.1936, attached to Heeres Weapons Office 02.1936–07.1936, Department Chief in Heeres Weapons Office 07.1936–11.1938. WWII: Department Chief in Heeres Weapons Office and at same time Heeres Representative at Peenemuende for V-1 and V-2 Program 11.1938–10.1944, Senior Commander of Artillerie 191, 09.1943–10.1944, Inspector of Long Range Rocket Troops 10.1944–05.1945. Awards: Knight's Cross of the War Merit Cross with Swords 28.10.44, War Merit Cross 1st and 2nd Class with Swords, RK-Sachsen Order of the White Falcon 2nd Class with Swords, 1914 Iron Cross 1st and 2nd Class, 1914 Wound Badge in Black, Cross of Honor.

Generalmajor Walter Dornberger. (Josef Charita)

Dorsch, Xaver: Vizeadmiral (02.1940), (Kriegsmarine); born 24.12.99 in Illertissen, died 08.11.86 in Munich. P-number unknown. Joined N.S.D.A.P. WWII: Director of Central Bureau in Org Todt 02.1940–05.1945, Chief of Naval Construction

Affairs in O.K.M. 07.1944–05.1945. Awards: Golden Party Badge, Blood Order, Knight's Cross of the War Merit Cross with Swords 13.05.43, War Merit Cross 1st and 2nd Class with Swords.

Dose, Walter: Konteradmiral (01.10.42), (Kriegsmarine); born 14.06.86 in Hannover, died 10.11.70 in Hamburg. WWI: Naval Air Service as Kapitanleutnant and Naval Airship Commander. Attached to Admiral's Staff in Hamburg 09.1933–03.1935, Leader of Economic Office in Bremen 04.1935–03.1938. WWII: Group Director in Military Economic Staff of O.K.W. 04.1938–12.1939, Department Chief for General Military Economic Queries in O.K.M. 01.1940–08.1942, Defensive Inspector for Hamburg 09.1942–05.1945. Awards: War Merit Cross 1st and 2nd Class with Swords, 1914 Iron Cross 1st and 2nd Class, 1920 Airship Commemorative Badge, Cross of Honor.

Doser, Robert Ritter von: Generalmajor (01.09.43), (Heer); born 14.03.89 in Neuhofen, died 19.09.43 in action near Belyanskaya. WWI: Oberleutnant der Res. and Ordinance Officer in 53. Res. Infanterie Brigade. WWII: attached to Staff of Armaments Inspector for Wehrkreis Kommando XIII 03.1939–12.1939, Commander of 4. Fortress Bataillon 12.1939–06.1940, Commander of I. then II. Bataillon of Infanterie Regiment 117, 11.1940–01.942, Commander of Infanterie Regiment 556, 02.1942–04.1943, Commandant of Welizh 06.1943–09.1943. Awards: German Cross in Gold 19.01.42, 1939 Clasps to the 1914 Iron Cross 1st and 2nd Class, Close Combat Clasp in Bronze, Infantry Assault Badge in Silver, Eastern Front Medal, 1939 Wound Badge in Gold, RK-Bavarian Military Max Joseph Order 20.03.15, 1914 Iron Cross 1st and 2nd Class, Bavarian Military Service Order IV. Class with Swords, Cross of Honor.

Dostler, Anton: General der Infanterie (01.08.43), (Heer); born 10.05.91 in Munich, died 01.12.45 (executed) in Caserta. WWI: Oberleutnant and First Ordnance Officer of XV. Bavarian Res. Korps. Promotions to Generalmajor 01.09.41, Generalleutnant 01.01.43. Ia to 15. Division 10.1935–03.1937, Ia to Gruppen Kommando 4, 04.1937–11.1938. WWII: Commander of Infanterie Regiment 42, 11.1938–08.1939, Ia to 7. Armee 09.1939–02.1940, Chief of Staff to XXV. Armee Korps 02.1940–09.1941, Commander of 163. Infanterie Division 07.1942–12.1942, Fuehrer Res. in O.K.H. 12.1942–06.1943, Commander of XXXXII. Armee Korps 06.1943–10.1943, Commander of LXXV. Armee Korps

General der Infanterie Anton Dostler. (Bundesarchiv)

01.1944–12.1944, Commander of LXXIII. Armee Korps 12.1944–05.1945. Awards: 1939 Clasps to the 1914 Iron Cross 1st and 2nd Class, Infantry Assault Badge in Silver, Eastern Front Medal, 1914 Iron Cross 1st and 2nd Class, Cross of Honor.

Drabich-Waechter, Viktor von: Generalleutnant (01.08.42), (Heer); born 8.08.89 in Strassburg, died 02.08.44 in action in Le Mesnil. WWI: Hauptmann and Kompanie Chef in Grenadier Regiment 7. Promotion to Generalmajor 01.08.40. Advisor in Heeres Personnel Office of Reichswehr Ministry (later Reich War Ministry) 04.1933–03.1939. WWII: Chief of Abteilung 7 in Heeres Personnel Office of O.K.H. 04.1939–10.1940, Office Group Chief of Heeres Personnel Office of O.K.H. 10.1940–10.1942, Commander of 326. Infanterie Division 06.1943–08.1944. Awards: 1939 Clasps to the 1914 Iron Cross 1st and 2nd Class, War Merit Cross 1st and 2nd Class with Swords, Infantry Assault Badge in Silver, 1939 Wound Badge in Gold, 1914 Iron Cross 1st and 2nd Class, 1914 Wound Badge in Black, Cross of Honor.

Dransfeld, Eduard: General der Flieger (01.10.40), (Luftwaffe); born 06.11.83 in Bestnig, died 22.01.64 in Grose-Rohrheim. WWI: in G.A.S. as Hauptmann and Commander of Armee Flugparks 2. Promotions to Generalmajor 01.10.36, Generalleutnant 01.10.38. WWII: Inspector of Auto-Engineering of Luftwaffe in R.L.M. 04.1935–09.1941, inactive 10.1941–05.1943, retired 05.1943. Awards: War Merit Cross 1st and 2nd Class with Swords, Pilot's Commemorative Badge, RK-Sachsen Albrecht Order 2nd Class with Swords, 1914 Iron Cross 1st and 2nd Class, Austro-Hungarian Military Service Cross 3rd Class with War Decoration, 1914 Observer's Badge, Turkish Half Moon, Cross of Honor.

Drebber, Moritz von: Generalmajor (01.01.43), (Heer); born 12.02.92 in Oldenburg, died 30.05.68 in Oldenburg. WWI: Oberleutnant and Ordnance Officer with 19. Infanterie Division. Kompanie Chef in Infanterie Regiment at Osnabrueck 10.1934–10.1935, Commander of II. Bataillon, Infanterie Regiment 58, 10.1935–12.1937. WWII: Training Leader at Cosel 01.1938–08.1939, Commander of Infanterie Regiment 327, 08.1939–08.1941, Commander of Infanterie Regiment 523, 01.1942–01.1943, Commander of 297. Infanterie Division 01.1943, captured at Stalingrad 01.1943. Awards: Knight's Cross 30.06.42, German Cross in Gold 26.12.41, 1939 Clasps to the 1914 Iron Cross 1st and 2nd Class, Infantry Assault Badge in Silver, Eastern Front Medal, 1939 Wound Badge in Black, Romanian Commander's Cross with Swords and Breast Star, 1914 Iron Cross 1st and 2nd Class, Oldenburg Friedrich-August Cross 1st and 2nd Class, 1914 Wound Badge in Black, Cross of Honor.

Drechsel, Ernst: Generalmajor (01.02.42), (Luftwaffe); born 29.06.82 in Augsburg, died 13.02.65 in Oberalting-Seefeld. WWI: in G.A.S. as Hauptmann and

Commander of Flieger 3. Advisor attached to Photo Office in R.L.M. 04.1934–1936. WWII: Group Director for Organization and Testing for Mapping Affairs in R.L.M. 1936–01.1942, Chief of Abteilung 7 in General Staff of Luftwaffe 02.1942–10.1943, retired 10.1943. Awards: War Merit Cross 1st and 2nd Class with Swords, Pilot's Commemorative Badge, RK-Hohenzollern, 1914 Iron Cross 1st and 2nd Class, Prussian Crown Order IV. Class with Swords, 1914 Observer's Badge, Cross of Honor.

Drechsler, Julius: Generalmajor (01.12.43), (Luftwaffe); born 08.06.83 in Nuremberg, died 27.10.72 in Munich. WWI: Hauptmann on Staff of Feld Motor Vehicles Commander Sudost. WWII: Military District Commander of Munich II 07.1938–10.1941, Commander of Luftwaffe Construction Regiment 4, 11.1941–10.1942, Staff Officer of Luftwaffe Construction Troops in Feld Luftgau Kommando Moscow 10.1942–07.1943, retired 12.1943. Awards: War Merit Cross 1st and 2nd Class with Swords, 1914 Iron Cross 1st and 2nd Class, Bavarian Military Service Order IV. Class with Swords, 1914 Wound Badge in Black, Cross of Honor.

Dreckmann, Paul: Generalleutnant (01.05.44), (Heer); born 13.11.93 in Harburg, died 09.03.60 in Muelheim. WWI: Leutnant and Adjutant to III. Bataillon, Infanterie Regiment 160. Promotion to Generalmajor 01.10.43. Attached to Staff of Ausbildungs Bataillon of Infanterie Regiment at Tuebingen 10.1934–10.1935, Commander of I. Bataillon, Infanterie Regiment 75, 10.1935–09.1936. WWII: Group Director in Heeres Weapons Office of O.K.H. 10.1936–11.1940, Department Chief in Heeres Weapons Office of O.K.H. 11.1940–04.1942, Commander of Infanterie Regiment 34, 04.1942–03.1943, Commander of 161. Infanterie Division 08.1943–09.1944, Commander of 252. Infanterie Division 10.1944–05.1945. Awards: Knight's Cross 28.03.45, German Cross in Gold 15.04.44, Honor Roll Clasp 07.10.43, 1939 Clasps to the 1914 Iron Cross 1st and 2nd Class, War Merit Cross 1st and 2nd Class with Swords, 1939 Wound Badge in Silver, Spanish Cross in Bronze without Swords, 1914 Iron Cross 1st and 2nd Class, 1914 Wound Badge in Black, Cross of Honor.

Drees, Ludwig: Generalmajor (01.07.41), (Heer); born 20.12.77 in Deutz, died 12.08.45 at Eberswalde P.O.W. Camp. WWI: Rittmeister with Artillerie Testing Commission. WWII: Department Chief in Provisions Office of Reichswehr Ministry (later Reich War Ministry and O.K.H.) 10.1932–08.1942, retired 04.1943. Awards: War Merit Cross 1st and 2nd Class with Swords, RK-Sachsen Albrecht Order 2nd Class with Swords, 1914 Iron Cross 1st and 2nd Class, Oldenburg Friedrich-August Cross 1st and 2nd Class, Cross of Honor.

Drescher, Curt: General-Stabsintendant (01.10.41), (Heer); born 06.09.84 in Froehndorf, died 12.12.47 in Lauheide. Administrative Officer by profession. WWI: service unknown. Promotion to General-Intendant (date unknown). WWII: Chief

Intendant to Wehrkreis Kommando VI (dates unknown). Awards: War Merit Cross 1st and 2nd Class with Swords, Cross of Honor.

Drescher, Friedrich: Generalmajor (20.04.45), (Heer); born 19.03.06 in Nuremberg, died 09.04.84 in Nuremberg. Chief of 1. Kompanie, Infanterie Regiment 21, 10.1935–05.1936, attached to Staff of Infanterie Regiment 110, 05.1936–11.1937, attached to Staff of 33. Division 12.1937–03.1938. WWII: Chief of 6. Kompanie, Infanterie Regiment 110, 04.1938–08.1939, attached to Staff of 33. Infanterie Division 08.1939–01.1940, Ib to 208. Infanterie Division 05.1940–01.1941, Quartermaster on Staff of Branch Office Centre 04.1941–10.1941, attached to Heeres General Staff 10.1941–03.1943, Ia to 356. Res. Division 03.1943–11.1943, Instructor at Kriegsschule 11.1943–06.1944, Senior Quartermaster to Heeresgruppe Nord Ukraine and later Heeresgruppe A 06.1944–11.1944, Chief of Staff to General Quartermaster of Heeres 12.1944–05.1945. Awards: German Cross in Silver 30.03.43, War Merit Cross 1st and 2nd Class with Swords.

Drescher, Otto: Generalleutnant (01.12.43), (Heer); born 05.10.95 in Nickl, died 13.08.44 in action near Facelli. WWI: Oberleutnant and Adjutant to Jaeger Regiment 1. Promotion to Generalmajor 01.06.43. Attached to Staff of Infanterie Regiment 59, 05.1936–09.1936, Kompanie Chef in Infanterie Regiment 59, 10.1936–03.1937, Kompanie Chef in Infanterie Regiment 73, 04.1937–10.1937. WWII: Commander of II. Bataillon, Infanterie Regiment 74, 10.1937–10.1940, Commander of Infanterie Regiment 434, 10.1940–09.1942, Fuehrer Res. in O.K.H. 09.1942–04.1943, Commander of 267. Infanterie Division 06.1943–08.1944. Awards: Knight's Cross 06.04.44, German Cross in Gold 29.01.42, Honor Roll Clasp 21.06.42, 1939 Clasps to the 1914 Iron Cross 1st and 2nd Class, Infantry Assault Badge in Silver, Eastern Front Medal, 1939 Wound Badge in Gold, 1914 Iron Cross 1st and 2nd Class, 1914 Wound Badge in Black, Cross of Honor.

Dressler, Rudolf: Generalmajor (01.01.43), (Heer); born 11.02.81 in Wurzburg, died 11.02.53 in Trauenstein. WWI: Hauptmann and Adjutant to Commander of Artillerie 23. Attached to Reichswehr Central Office I in Stuttgart 12.1934–04.1935, attached to Military Replacement Inspection at Stuttgart 05.1935–06.1936. WWII: Welfare Advisor and later Leader to General Kommando of V. Armee Korps 07.1936–11.1939, Commander of Ersatz Artillerie Regiment 19, 11.1939–06.1940, Commander of Ersatz Artillerie Regiment 11, 07.1940–09.1942, Fuehrer Res. in O.K.H. 09.1942–02.1943, retired 02.1943. Awards: 1939 Clasps to the 1914 Iron Cross 1st and 2nd Class, General Assault Badge, 1914 Iron Cross 1st and 2nd Class, Bavarian Military Service Order IV. Class with Swords, Cross of Honor.

Drewes, Karl: Generalmajor (01.10.44), (Luftwaffe); born 15.08.95 in Wilhelmshaven, died 30.08.58 in Oldenburg. WWI: in G.A.S. as Leutnant (unit unknown).

Instructor at Kampfflieger Schule Jueterbog and Tutow 11.1933–10.1935, Chief of Airport Operations Kompanie for Fliegerschule Dresden 11.1935–1938. WWII: attached to Special Purpose Geschwader 1, 08.1939–1940, Advisor in R.L.M. 1940–1941, Commander of Kampfflieger Schule at Jessau-Posen 1941–12.1942, Commander of Luftwaffe Feld Jaeger Regiment 35, 12.1942–10.1943, Commander of 1. Special Kampfgeschwader 10.1943–1944, Flughafenbereichs Commandant in Italy and later Magdeburg 1944–05.1945. Awards: 1939 Clasps to the 1914 Iron Cross 1st and 2nd Class, Eastern Front Medal, 1939 Pilot's Badge, German West Wall Medal, Pilot's Commemorative Badge, 1914 Iron Cross 1st and 2nd Class, 1914 Observer's Badge, Cross of Honor.

Drobnig, Walter: Generalmajor (01.07.41), (Heer); born 22.07.88 in Anklam, died 02.11.57 in Munich. WWI: Hauptmann on Staff of Special Purpose General Commando 52. Commander of Military District Kommando at Kreuzberg 10.1935–01.1936, Commander of Military District Kommando at Waldenburg 02.1936–03.1939. WWII: Training Leader at Liegnitz 05.1939–08.1939, Commander of Infanterie Regiment 354, 08.1939–05.1941, Commander of 708. Infanterie Division 07.1941–03.1942, P.O.W. Commander for Operations Area IV 07.1942–06.1944, attached to Wehrkreis Kommando III then Wehrkreis Kommando II 10.1944–05.1945. Awards: 1939 Clasps to the 1914 Iron Cross 1st and 2nd Class, War Merit Cross 1st and 2nd Class with Swords, Infantry Assault Badge in Silver, 1914 Iron Cross 1st and 2nd Class, Oldenburg Friedrich-August Cross 1st and 2nd Class, 1914 Wound Badge in Black, Cross of Honor.

Drogand, Wilhelm: Generalleutnant (01.07.41), (Heer); born 09.12.81 in Graudenz, died 31.07.47 in Tegernsee. WWI: Hauptmann attached to War Ministry. Promotion to Generalmajor 01.06.39. Military Replacement Inspector of Hamburg 05.1935–08.1935, Commander of Military District Kommando II in Berlin 10.1935–03.1938. WWII: attached to Staff and later Deputy President of Reichs Welfare and Supply Court 05.1938–09.1939, attached to O.K.W. 09.1939–12.1939, Leader of Staff Division in O.K.H. 12.1939–06.1940, President of Military Orphanages at Potsdam 06.1940–03.1941, Inspector of Welfare and Supply Services in O.K.W. 03.1941–04.1945. Awards: War Merit Cross 1st and 2nd Class with Swords, 1914 Iron Cross 1st and 2nd Class, Austro-Hungarian Military Service Cross 3rd Class with War Decoration, Cross of Honor.

Drum, Karl: General der Flieger (01.07.44), (Luftwaffe); born 31.7.93 in Diemeringen, died 02.04.68 in Meersberg. WWI: in G.A.S. as Oberleutnant in Flieger Abteilung 23. Promotions to Generalmajor 01.01.41, Generalleutnant 01.01.43. Advisor attached to Chief of Technical Office in R.L.M. 04.1933–04.1934, Tactical Leader at Fliegerschule Hildesheim 05.1934–05.1935, Instruction Group Leader at Fliegerschule Hildesheim 05.1935–03.1936, Commander of Fliegerschule Braunschweig

04.1936–01.1938, Ia to Inspection of Fernaufklarungs in R.L.M. 04.1938–03.1939. WWII: Chief of Staff to General of Luftwaffe attached to O.B. of the Wehrmacht 04.1939–02.1941, Luftwaffe Commander for Heeresgruppe Sud 03.1941–10.1941, Chief of Staff to Wehrmacht Befehlshaber of Netherlands 10.1941–10.1942, Commander of 11. Luftwaffe Feld Division 10.1942–11.1943, attached to Feld Luftgau Kommando for Belgium and Northern France 01.1944–09.1944, Fuehrer Res. in O.K.L. 09.1944–02.1945, retired 02.1945. Awards: German Cross in Silver 13.04.44, 1939 Clasps to the 1914 Iron Cross 1st and 2nd Class, Combined Pilot-Observer's Badge, Pilot's Commemorative Badge, RK-Hohenzollern, RK-Baden Order of the Zaehringer Lion 2nd Class with Swords, RK-Sachsen Albrecht Order 2nd Class with Swords, 1914 Iron Cross 1st and 2nd Class, 1914 Wound Badge in Black, 1914 Observer's Badge, Cross of Honor.

Duemlein, Friedrich: Generalleutnant z.V. (01.12.41), (Heer); born 26.12.75 in Lindau, died 10.04.48 in Tutzing. WWI: Major on Staff of I. Bavarian Armee Korps. Promotion to Generalmajor z.V. 01.09.40. Recalled to military service 07.1938. WWII: Commander of Replacement Infanterie Regiment 44, 08.1939–04.1940, Commander of Special Purpose Division 407, 10.1940–05.1942, retired 04.1943. Awards: 1939 Clasps to the 1914 Iron Cross 1st and 2nd Class, RK-Hohenzollern, 1914 Iron Cross 1st and 2nd Class, 1914 Wound Badge in Black, Cross of Honor.

Duerking, Werner: Generalleutnant (01.09.44), (Heer); born 26.01.96 in Furstenberg, died 12.09.44 of wounds at Humenne Hospital. WWI: Leutnant and M.G. Officer on Staff of Infanterie Regiment 164. Promotion to Generalmajor 01.08.44. Kompanie Chef in Infanterie Regiment at Crossen 10.1934–10.1935, Kompanie Chef in Infanterie Regiment 29, 10.1935–10.1936. WWII: Tactics Instructor at Kriegsschule Hannover 10.1936–08.1939, Commander of I. Bataillon, Infanterie Regiment 471, 08.1939–10.1940, Commander of Infanterie Regiment 451, 10.1940–07.1941, attached to then Gruppe Commander of Infanterie Schule for Officer Aspirants at Dresden 01.1942–06.1942, Commander of Infanterie Schule for Officer Aspirants at Ohrdruf 06.1942–04.1944, attached to Heeresgruppe Nord as Division Commander 07.1944–09.1944. Awards: 1939 Clasps to the 1914 Iron Cross 1st and 2nd Class, War Merit Cross 1st and 2nd Class with Swords, Infantry Assault Badge in Silver, 1939 Wound Badge in Gold, 1914 Iron Cross 1st and 2nd Class, Cross of Honor.

Duerr, Alfred: Generalmajor (01.11.44), (Luftwaffe); born 11.02.88 in Ulm, died 30.05.52 in Karlsruhe. WWI: in G.A.S. as Hauptmann and Commander of Flieger Abteilung 39. Instructor at Luftwaffe Nachrichtenschule Halle-Saale 02.1935–04.1935, Luftwaffe Communications Officer attached to Staff of Reich Post Minister 04.1935–02.1938. WWII: Commander of Air Signals Construction Staff with Chief of Communication Affairs in R.L.M. 03.1938–04.1940, Signals Leader to Feld Luftgau Kommando in Norway 05.1940–12.1940, Signals Leader to Luftgau Kommando VII 12.1940–05.1941, Air Signals Equipment Inspector in R.L.M. 03.1941–03.1944, Signals Equipment Inspector with General Signals Commander in R.L.M. 04.1944–05.1945. Awards: 1939 Clasp to the 1914 Iron Cross 2nd Class, War Merit Cross 1st and 2nd Class with Swords, Pilot's Commemorative Badge, RK-Wuerttemberg Friedrich Order 2nd Class with Swords, 1914 Iron Cross 1st and 2nd Class, 1914 Observer's Badge, Cross of Honor.

Duerrstein, Gustav: Generalmajor (01.03.45), (Heer); born 31.08.89 in Frankfurt am Main, died 05.1945 (missing in action). WWI: Oberleutnant in Infanterie Regiment 113. Attached to Staff of Ausbildungs Bataillon of Infanterie Regiment at Konstanz 10.1934–10.1935, Commander of I. Bataillon, Infanterie Regiment 14, 10.1935–10.1936. WWII: Commander of II. Bataillon, Infanterie Regiment 14, 10.1936–08.1939, Commander of Infanterie Regiment 13, 10.1939–08.1940, Wehrmacht Commander of Oberhofen 08.1940–05.1944, Commandant of Feldkommandantur 581, 09.1944–05.1945. Awards: 1939 Clasps to the 1914 Iron Cross 1st and 2nd Class, Infantry Assault Badge in Silver, RK-Baden Order of the Zaehringer Lion 2nd Class with Swords, 1914 Iron Cross 1st and 2nd Class, 1914 Wound Badge in Black, Cross of Honor.

Duetschke, Dr. Kurt: Admiral-Arzt (01.01.41), (Kriegsmarine); born 15.10.92 in Aurich, died 21.05.55 in Luebeck. Medical doctor by profession. WWI: Marinefeldhilfsarzt der Res. on light cruiser *Koenigsberg*. Attached to Marine Hospital and Schule at Flensburg-Muerwik 03.1931–06.1936. WWII: Chief Physician at Marine Hospital in Kiel-Wik and at same time Chief of Sanitats Amt Eastern Sea 06.1936–12.1939, Medical Physician attached to Fleet Kommando 12.1939–12.1940, Chief of Medical Office for Naval Station Baltic Sea 12.1940–06.1943, Chief Physician for Naval Hospital at Bedburg-Hau 02.1944–01.1945. Awards: War Merit Cross 1st and 2nd Class with Swords, 1914 Iron Cross 2nd Class, Cross of Honor.

Duevert, Walther: Generalleutnant (01.01.43), (Heer); born 02.10.93 in Goerlitz, died 04.03.72 in Duesseldorf. WWI: Oberleutnant and Adjutant to Commander of Artillerie 232. Promotion to Generalmajor 01.01.41. Ia to Heeres Service Office at Kassel 10.1934–10.1935, Ia to IX. Armee Korps 10.1935–10.1936, General Staff Officer attached to Wehrmacht Academy 10.1936–10.1937, Commander of Artillerie Regiment 28, 10.1937–11.1938. WWII: Chief of Staff to VI. Armee Korps 12.1938–01.1941, Commander of 13. Panzer Division 06.1941–02.1942, Commander of 20. Panzer Division 07.1942–10.1942, Fuehrer Res. in O.K.H. 10.1942–04.1943, attached to Heeres Armaments followed by General Heeres Abteilung in O.K.H. 01.943–06.1943, Commander of 256. Infanterie Division

06.1943–07.1944, retired 11.1944. Awards: Knight's Cross 30.07.41, 1939 Clasps to the 1914 Iron Cross 1st and 2nd Class, Tank Assault Badge in Silver, Eastern Front Medal, West Wall Medal, 1914 Iron Cross 1st and 2nd Class, Cross of Honor.

Dufais, Wilhelm von: SS-Brigadefuehrer und Generalmajor der Waffen-SS (21.06.43); born 08.07.88 in Berlin, died 01.09.63 in Stuttgart. P-5276395, SS-283028. WWI: Rittmeister and Signals Commander (unit unknown). Remained in Reichswehr after WWI and retired as Oberst. Joined N.S.D.A.P. and S.S. in 1937. Attached to Staff of SS-Hauptamt 01.12.37–01.12.38. WWII: Hauptabteilungsleiter on Staff of Chief of SS-Fernmeldewesens 30.01.42, Commander of SS-Nachrichten Schule in Nuremberg 15.05.43, Leader on Staff of Chief of SS-Fernmeldewesen 30.01.44–09.11.44. Awards: War Merit Cross 1st and 2nd Class with Swords, 1914 Iron Cross 1st and 2nd Class, 1914 Wound Badge in Black, Cross of Honor, Degen, Ring.

Dufay, Wilhelm von: Generalmajor (01.04.36), (Heer); born 28.08.83 in Berlin, died 09.03.43 in Berlin. WWI: Rittmeister and Bataillon Commander in Infanterie Regiment 447. Commander of Truppenubungsplatz at Doeberitz 02.1934–09.1936, Higher Kavallerie Officer 4, 10.1936–09.1937, retired 09.1937. Awards: RK-Hohenzollern, 1914 Iron Cross 1st and 2nd Class, Cross of Honor.

Dutzmann, Dr. Max: General-Intendant (01.04.40), (Heer); born 11.13.89 in Potsdam, died 17.02.49 at Vorkuta P.O.W. Camp. Administrative Officer by profession. WWI: service unknown. WWII: Chief Intendant to 7. Armee (dates unknown). Awards: War Merit Cross 1st and 2nd Class with Swords, Cross of Honor.

Dybilasz, Walther: Generalmajor (01.08.42), (Heer); born 01.10.92 in Altona, died 31.01.50 at Stalino P.O.W. Camp. WWI: Oberleutnant in Railway Department West. Advisor in Heer Weapons Office of Reichswehr Ministry (later Reich War Ministry) 09.1934–02.1937, Group Leader in Reich War Ministry 03.1937–06.1938, Commander of Pionier Ausbildungs Bataillon 2, 07.1938–11.1938. WWII: Commander of Eisenbahn Pionier Ausbildungs Bataillon 11.1938–08.1939, Commander of III. Bataillon, Eisenbahn Pionier Regiment 68, 08.1939–04.1940, Commander of Railway Pionier Regiment 4, 04.1940–06.1940, Commander of Eisenbahn Pionier Regiment 3, 06.1940–01.1943, Commander of 1. Eisenbahn Pionier Brigade 01.1943–05.1945. Awards: German Cross in Silver 29.01.45, 1939 Clasp to the 1914 Iron Cross 2nd Class, War Merit Cross 1st and 2nd Class with Swords, General Assault Badge, 1914 Iron Cross 1st and 2nd Class, Cross of Honor.

E

Ebbert, Dr. Josef: General-Arzt (01.06.42), (Heer); born 04.04.86 in Nottuln, died 29.12.42 (suicide) in Forschstadt. Medical doctor by profession. WWI: Physician (unit unknown). Commander of Sanitats Abteilung 16, 1936–1938. WWII: Division Physician to Infanterie Division 33, 1938–05.1940, Corps Physician to XXIX. Armee Korps 05.1940–12.1942. Awards: War Merit Cross 1st and 2nd Class with Swords, Eastern Front Medal, 1914 Iron Cross 2nd Class, Cross of Honor.

Ebeling, Curt: Generalleutnant (01.04.44), (Heer); born 06.06.92 in Zehlendorf, died 04.05.66 in Freiburg. WWI: Oberleutnant and Chief of 2. Batterie, Feld Artillerie Regiment 102. Promotion to Generalmajor 01.04.42. Commander of II. Abteilung, Artillerie Regiment at Minden 10.1934–10.1935, Commander of II. Abteilung, Artillerie Regiment 6, 10.1935–10.1936, Commander of Instruction Staff at Artillerie Schule II Jueterbog 10.1936–10.1937. WWII: Commander of Instruction Staff A at Artillerie Schule 10.1937–08.1939, Commander of Weapons Artillerie Schule 08.1939–02.1940, Commander of Instruction Staff A at Artillerie Schule 02.1940–06.1940, Commander of Artillerie 19, 06.1940–04.1942, Commander of Artillerie Schule at Thorn 06.1942–01.1943, Commander of Artillerie Schule for Officer Aspirants 05.1943–01.1944, Commander of 210. Infanterie Division 02.1944–03.1945. Awards: 1939 Clasps to the 1914 Iron Cross 1st and 2nd Class, General Assault Badge, Eastern Front Medal, 1914 Iron Cross 1st and 2nd Class, Cross of Honor.

Ebeling, Fritz: Generalmajor (01.06.41), (Heer); born 28.04.87 in Stettin, died 27.01.70 in Bad Homburg. WWI: Hauptmann and Commander of III. Bataillon, Infanterie Regiment 74. WWII: Military District Commander for Celle 04.1937–02.1940, Fuehrer Res. in O.K.H. 07.1940–01.1941, Commander of Military District Commando at Potsdam I 01.1941–05.1943, Commandant of Feldkommandantur 1021, 08.1943–10.1944, Commandant of Feldkommandantur 1016, 10.1944–05.1945. Awards: 1939 Clasp to the 1914 Iron Cross 2nd Class,

War Merit Cross 1st and 2nd Class with Swords, RK-Hohenzollern, 1914 Iron Cross 1st and 2nd Class, 1914 Wound Badge in Black, Cross of Honor.

Ebeling, Werner: Ministerialdirigent (01.04.45), (Luftwaffe); born 23.12.97 in Berlin, died 17.01.80 in Bonn. Civil Servant by profession. WWI: Leutnant der Res. in Garde Grenadier Regiment 3. WWII: attached to R.L.M. 04.1934–05.1945. Awards: War Merit Cross 1st and 2nd Class with Swords, 1914 Iron Cross 2nd Class, Cross of Honor.

Eberbach, Heinrich: General der Panzertruppe (01.08.43), (Heer); born 24.11.95 in Stuttgart, died 13.07.92 in Notzingen. WWI: Oberleutnant in Infanterie Regiment 146. Promotions to Generalmajor 01.02.42, Generalleutnant 01.01.43. Commander of Panzer Abwehr Abteilung 12, 10.1935–07.1938, attached to Command Staff of Panzer Regiment 6, 08.1938–11.1938. WWII: Commander of Panzer Regiment 35, 11.1938–07.1941, Commander of 5. Panzer Brigade 07.1941–01.942, Commander of 4. Panzer Division 01.942–11.1942, Inspector of Panzertruppen 02.1943–06.1944, Commander of Panzer Gruppe West 08.1944, captured 08.1944. Awards: Oak Leaves 31.12.41 (42), Knight's Cross 04.07.40, Honor Roll Clasp 08.12.41, 1939 Clasps to the 1914 Iron Cross 1st and 2nd Class, Tank Assault Badge in Silver, Eastern Front Medal, 1939 Wound Badge in Silver, 1914 Iron Cross 1st and 2nd Class, 1914 Wound Badge in Black, Cross of Honor.

General der Panzertruppe Heinrich Eberbach. (Bundesarchiv)

Eberbeck, Prof. Dr. Erich: General-Veterinar (09.11.44), (Heer); born 10.10.82 in Christburg, died 23.09.62 in Koeln. Medical veterinarian by profession. WWI: Stabs-Veterinar for Feldlazarett 180. WWII: service unknown. Awards: 1914 Iron Cross 1st and 2nd Class, Cross of Honor.

Eberding, Knut: Generalmajor (01.09.43), (Heer); born 18.12.95 in Reppline, died 28.06.78 in Erlangen. WWI: Leutnant in 22. Res. Jaeger Bataillon. WWII: attached to Staff and later Commander of II. Bataillon, Infanterie Regiment 11, 02.1938–10.1941, Commander of Infanterie Regiment 53, 10.1941–01.1943, Commander of 38. Infanterie Division 03.1943–10.1943, Fuehrer Res. in O.K.H. 11.1943–04.1944, Commander of 64. Infanterie Division 07.1944–11.1944, captured 11.1944. Awards: German Cross in Gold 14.02.42, Honor Roll Clasp

26.01.43, 1939 Clasps to the 1914 Iron Cross 1st and 2nd Class, Close Combat Clasp in Bronze, Infantry Assault Badge in Silver, Eastern Front Medal, 1914 Iron Cross 1st and 2nd Class, Cross of Honor.

Eberhard, Kurt: Generalmajor z.V. (01.02.41), (Heer); born 22.09.84 in Rottweil, died 08.09.47 (suicide) in Stuttgart. WWI: Major and Commander of Feld Artillerie Regiment 501. WWII: recalled to military service 08.1939, attached to Feldkommandantur 550, 1940–05.1941, Commandant of Feldkommandantur 195, 05.1941–07.1942, retired 11.1942. Awards: War Merit Cross 1st and 2nd Class with Swords, 1914 Iron Cross 1st and 2nd Class, Cross of Honor.

Eberhardt, Friedrich-Georg: Generalleutnant (01.02.41), (Heer); born 15.01.92 in Strassburg, died 09.09.64 in Wiesbaden. WWI: Rittmeister and Ordnance Officer to 220. Infanterie Division. Promotion to Generalmajor 01.04.39. WWII: Commander of Infanterie Regiment 44, 10.1935–08.1939, Commander of 60. Infanterie Division 09.1939–05.1942, Commander of 38. Infanterie Division 07.1942–08.1943, Commander of 174. Res. Division 09.1943–08.1944, Officer Judge at Reichs War Court 09.1944–05.1945. Awards: Knight's Cross 31.12.41, 1939 Clasps to the 1914 Iron Cross 1st and 2nd Class, Infantry Assault Badge in Silver, Eastern Front Medal, Danzig Cross 1st Class, 1914 Iron Cross 1st and 2nd Class, 1914 Wound Badge in Black, Cross of Honor.

Eberle, Rene: Generalleutnant (01.09.43), (Heer); born 08.11.91 in Linz, died 21.03.45 in action in the West. WWI: Hauptmann and Kompanie Chef in Austrian 2. Sapper Bataillon. Promotion to Generalmajor 01.04.41. Transferred to German Wehrmacht 03.1938, attached to Military Replacement Inspection Staff in Vienna 08.1938–11.1938, attached to Staff of Inspection East 11.1938–03.1939. WWII: Higher Pionier Officer of Land Fortifications East 03.1939–08.1939, Chief of Staff to XXIV. Armee Korps 08.1939–12.1940, Commander of Senior Construction Staff 17, 03.1941–12.1941, Fortress Pionier Commander 1, 06.1942–12.1943, Inspector of Land Fortifications West 02.1944–03.1945. Awards: German Cross in Silver 10.03.44, War Merit Cross 1st and 2nd Class with Swords, 1939 Wound Badge in Gold, 1914 Iron Cross 2nd Class, Cross of Honor.

Eberstein, Karl Freiherr von: SS-Obergruppenfuehrer und General der Waffen-SS und Polizei (30.01.36); born 14.01.94 in Halle, died 10.02.79 in Tegernsee. P-15067, SS-1386. WWI: Leutnant der Res. attached to Feld Artillerie Regiment 17. Joined Polizei, joined N.S.D.A.P. and S.A. in 1925, reached rank of SA-Gruppenfuehrer and Leader of SA-Gruppe Hochland, joined S.S. in 1929. Promotions to SS-Brigadefuehrer (skipped), SS-Gruppenfuehrer 01.09.32. Leader of SS-Oberabschitte Mitte 01.10.34–01.07.35, Leader of SS-Oberabschnitte South

01.12.36–01.12.38. WWII: Leader of SS-Oberabschnitte South and H.S.S.P.F. 30.01.42–09.11.44, Regierungsprasident, Polizei President, Member of Reichstag (WK 24 Oberbayern-Schwaben). Awards: Golden Party Badge, War Merit Cross 1st and 2nd Class with Swords, 1929 Nuremberg Badge of Honor, SA-Rally at Braunschweig Badge of Honor, Gau Thuringen Commemorative Badge, Luftschutz Ehrenzeichen 2nd Class, German Social Welfare Decoration 1st Class, Grand Officer's Cross of the Italian Order of the Crown, Commander's Cross of the Saxon Ernestine House Order with Swords (Post-WWI), 1914 Iron Cross 1st and 2nd Class, Cross of Honor, Degen, Ring.

Eberth, Anton: Generalmajor (30.01.45), (Heer); born 19.03.88 in Bamberg, died 05.09.55 at Voikovo P.O.W. Camp. WWI: Senior N.C.O. in 306. Motorized Kompanie. Kompanie Chef in Infanterie Regiment at Augsburg 10.1934–10.1935, Kompanie Chef in Infanterie Regiment 40, 10.1935–06.1936, Adjutant to Commander of Truppenubungsplatz at Hammelburg 07.1936–05.1938. WWII: attached to Staff of Military Commander of Wurzburg 06.1938–11.1939, Commander of Replacement Infanterie Bataillon 55, 11.1939–08.1940, Commander of II. Bataillon, Infanterie Regiment 330, 08.1940–02.1941, Commander of Infanterie Regiment 343, 03.1941–06.1942, Commander of N.C.O. courses in Wehrkreis Kommando XIII 07.1942–03.1943, Commander of Res. Grenadier Regiment 231, 03.1943–02.1944, Commander of Waffen Schule at Narva 04.1944–10.1944, Commander of Special Purpose Division Staff 300, 01.1945–05.1945. Awards: German Cross in Gold 03.02.42, 1939 Iron Cross 1st Class, 1939 Clasp to the 1914 Iron Cross 2nd Class, Infantry Assault Badge in Silver, Eastern Front Medal, 1914 Iron Cross 2nd Class, Cross of Honor.

Eberth, Karl: General der Artillerie z.V. (01.12.42), (Luftwaffe and Heer); born 12.11.77 in Munich, died 13.04.52 in Steingaden. WWI: Major and Ia to Special Purpose General Kommando 57. Promotions to Reichswehr Generalmajor 01.04.29, Generalleutnant 01.04.35, General der Flieger in Luftwaffe 31.08.35. President of Higher Luftwaffe Office in Munich 04.1934–03.1935, Befehlshaber of Luftkreis Kommando V 04.1935–08.1935, retired 09.1935–08.1938, transferred from Luftwaffe to Heer 07.1938. WWII: at disposal of Heeres 07.1938–05.1940, Higher Commander of Artillerie 301, 05.1940–11.1942, retired 01.1943. Awards: 1939 Clasps to the 1914 Iron Cross 1st and 2nd Class, General Assault Badge, Eastern Front Medal, 1914 Iron Cross 1st and 2nd Class, Bavarian Military Service Order IV. Class with Swords, 1914 Wound Badge in Black, Cross of Honor.

Eberts, Kurt: Generalmajor z.V. (01.07.41), (Heer); born 11.08.83 in Kassel, died 13.05.67 in Dueren. WWI: Hauptmann and Commander of 234. Pionier Bataillon. Inspector of Fortress Inspection I 10.1934–03.1937, retired 03.1937. WWII: recalled to military service 08.1939, Commander of Senior Construction

Staff 32, 08.1939–08.1943, Higher Pionier Leader 32, 08.1943–02.1944, retired 05.1944. Awards: 1939 Clasps to the 1914 Iron Cross 1st and 2nd Class, General Assault Badge, 1914 Iron Cross 1st and 2nd Class, Cross of Honor.

Ebner, Dr. Peter-Josef: General-Veterinar (01.08.43), (Heer); born 29.06.88 in Hechweil, died 28.08.62 in Frankfurt am Main. Medical veterinarian by profession. WWI: Veterinar (unit unknown). WWII: Commander of Lehrgruppe I at Heeres Veterinar Academy 1939–12.1940, Korps Veterinar to XX. Armee Korps 12.1940–02.1942, Leitender Veterinar to Senior Quartermaster of Black Sea 02.1942–09.1942. Awards: 1939 Clasp to the 1914 Iron Cross 2nd Class, War Merit Cross 1st and 2nd Class with Swords, 1914 Iron Cross 2nd Class, Cross of Honor.

Eckerle, Dr. Karl: General-Richter (01.05.44), (Luftwaffe); born 04.06.98 in Lemberg, died 15.03.76 in Mindelheim. Jurist by profession. WWI: Leutnant der Res. in Bavarian Fuss Artillerie Regiment 3. WWII: Judge in Luftgau Kommando V 02.1936–09.1940, Chief Judge to Luftflotte 3, 10.1940–10.1944, Chief Judge to Luftflotte 6, 10.1944–05.1945. Awards: German Cross in Silver (date unknown), War Merit Cross 1st and 2nd Class with Swords, 1914 Iron Cross 2nd Class, Bavarian Military Service Cross 3rd Class, Cross of Honor.

Eckert, Dr. Julius: Generalstabs-Veterinar (01.06.41), (Heer); born 02.09.84 in Biebrich, died 20.12.43 of natural causes in Mainz. Medical veterinarian by profession. WWI: Veterinar (unit unknown). Promotion to General-Veterinar 01.10.37. WWII: Heeres Gruppen Veterinar 2, 10.1937–08.1939, Armee Veterinar to 7. Armee then Fuehrer Res. in O.K.H. (dates unknown), retired 09.1943. Awards: War Merit Cross 1st and 2nd Class with Swords, 1914 Iron Cross 1st and 2nd Class, Cross of Honor.

Eckhardt, Alfred: Ministerialdirektor (20.04.42), (Kriegsmarine); born 30.05.72 in Kassel, died 10.02.60 in Wiessee. Civil Servant by profession. WWII: Chief of Office Group for Shipyards, Ports and River Affairs in O.K.M. 11.1939–03.1943, Chief of Naval Construction Affairs in O.K.M. 04.1943–07.1944, placed at disposal of O.K.M. 07.1944–05.1945. Awards: Knight's Cross of the War Merit Cross without Swords 07.12.44, German Cross in Silver 02.08.44, War Merit Cross 1st and 2nd Class with Swords.

Eckhardt, Eduard: Generalmajor (01.04.41), (Heer); born 29.01.75 in Kolberg, died 15.06.59 in Berlin. WWI: Hauptmann and Adjutant to Heeresgruppe "Linsingen." Welfare and Supply Officer of Ersatz Kommando III. Armee Korps 10.1937–07.1942, retired 07.1942. Awards: War Merit Cross 1st and 2nd Class with Swords, 1914 Iron Cross 1st and 2nd Class, 1914 Wound Badge in Black, Cross of Honor.

Eckhardt, Johann-Heinrich: Generalleutnant (01.04.44), (Heer); born 03.11.96 in Boeddiger, died 15.05.45 in Winterberg. WWI: Leutnant der Res. in Infanterie Regiment 54. Promotion to Generalmajor 01.10.43. Attached to Staff of Heeres Service Office at Breslau 10.1934–04.1935, attached to Staff of VIII. Armee Korps 05.1935–10.1937. WWII: Commander of II. Bataillon, Infanterie Regiment 38, 10.1937–02.1940, Commander of Infanterie Regiment 38, 02.1940–04.1943, Fuehrer Res. in O.K.H. 04.1943–07.1943, Commander of Formation Staff 211 and later Commander of 211. Infanterie Division 07.1943–05.1945. Awards: Oak Leaves 03.11.44 (644), Knight's Cross 20.05.42, German Cross in Gold 25.01.42, 1939 Clasps to the 1914 Iron Cross 1st and 2nd Class, Infantry Assault Badge in Silver, Demjansk Shield, Eastern Front Medal, RK-Hohenzollern, 1914 Iron Cross 1st and 2nd Class, 1914 Wound Badge in Silver, Cross of Honor.

Eckhardt, Dr. Kurt: Admiral-Richter (01.05.44), (Kriegsmarine); born 08.08.87 in Berlin, died 28.02.48 at Ostende P.O.W. Camp. Jurist by profession. WWI: service unknown. WWII: Advisor for International Law in Operations Department of O.K.M. 08.1936–05.1945. Awards: War Merit Cross 1st and 2nd Class with Swords, Cross of Honor.

Eckholt, Oskar: Generalmajor (01.04.44), (Heer); born 04.11.94 in Freisenbruch, died 12.08.82 in Theesen. WWI: Oberleutnant in Fuss Artillerie Regiment 18. Batterie Chef in Artillerie Regiment at Minden 10.1934–10.1935, Batterie Chef in Artillerie Regiment 6, 10.1935–10.1936, Batterie Chef in Artillerie Regiment 26, 10.1936–11.1938. WWII: Commander of IV. Abteilung, Artillerie Regiment 211, 11.1938–08.1939, Commander of IV. Abteilung, Artillerie Regiment 236, 08.1939–01.942, Commander of IV. Abteilung, Artillerie Regiment 251, 01.1942–02.1943, Commander of Artillerie Regiment 178, 02.1943–11.1943, Commander of 291. Infanterie Division 01.1944–07.1944, hospitalized due to severe wounds 07.1944–05.1945. Awards: Knight's Cross 09.04.43, German Cross in Gold 18.05.42, Honor Roll Clasp 26.01.43, 1939 Clasps to the 1914 Iron Cross 1st and 2nd Class, General Assault Badge, Eastern Front Medal, 1939 Wound Badge in Silver, 1914 Iron Cross 1st and 2nd Class, Cross of Honor.

Eckl, Dr. Richard: General-Arzt (01.01.41), (Heer); born 28.07.86 in Neustadt, died 08.04.59 in Munich. Medical doctor by profession. WWI: Assistenz-Arzt (unit unknown). WWII: Division Physician to 27. Division 1938–08.1939, Corps Physician to XXVII. Armee Korps 08.1939–01.1941, Corps Physician to XXXXIX Armee Korps 01.1941–08.194, Corps Physician to XI. Armee Korps 08.1941–01.1942, Chief Physician to Wehrmacht Befehlshaber in Serbia 08.1942–08.1943, Chief Physician to Wehrmacht Befehlshaber in Denmark 08.1943–02.1945. Awards: War Merit Cross 1st and 2nd Class with Swords, Cross of Honor.

Eckstein, Walter: Generalleutnant (01.06.42), (Heer); born 16.02.88 in Weimar, died 25.02.66 in Baden-Baden. WWI: Hauptmann on Staff of XVIII. Armee Korps. Promotion to Generalmajor 01.12.39. Fortress Inspector IV at Glogau 10.1934–07.1936, Officer z.b.V. attached to O.B. des Heeres 08.1936–12.1936, Fortress Inspector to Wehrkeis Kommando VII 01.1937–03.1939. WWII: Fortress Pionier Commander VII 03.1939–08.1939, Commander of Senior Construction Staff 7, 09.1939–10.1939, Pionier Leader to 7. Armee 10.1939–08.1940, Commander of Fortifications Upper Rhine 08.1940–12.1941, Fortress Pionier Leader XIX 12.1941–08.1943, Commander of Fortifications Lower Rhine 09.1943–10.1944, Commander of Fortifications Upper Rhine 10.1944–03.1945. Awards: 1939 Clasps to the 1914 Iron Cross 1st and 2nd Class, General Assault Badge, 1914 Iron Cross 1st and 2nd Class, 1914 Wound Badge in Black, Cross of Honor.

Edelmann, Karl: Generalleutnant (01.10.43), (Heer); born 05.07.91 in Dresden, died 25.01.71 in Wiesbaden. WWI: Oberleutnant on Staff of 45. Landwehr Division. Promotion to Generalmajor 01.10.41. Group Leader in Reichswehr Ministry (later Reich War Ministry and O.K.H.) 01.1934–11.1938. WWII: attached to Staff of Infanterie Regiment 103, 11.1938–08.1939, Commander of Infanterie Regiment 103, 09.1939–12.1939, Office Group Chief for Replacement Army Officers in O.K.H. 01.1940–09.1943, Commander of 702. Infanterie Division 10.1943–01.1945. Awards: German Cross in Silver 09.11.43, 1939 Clasps to the 1914 Iron Cross 1st and 2nd Class, War Merit Cross 1st and 2nd Class with Swords, Infantry Assault Badge in Silver, RK-Sachsen Military St. Heinrich's Order 27.07.15, 1914 Iron Cross 1st and 2nd Class, 1914 Wound Badge in Black, Cross of Honor.

Edelsheim, Maximilian Reichsfreiherr von: General der Panzertruppe (01.12.44), (Heer); born 06.07.97 in Berlin, died 26.04.94 in Konstanz. WWI: Leutnant in Res. Infanterie Regiment 59. Promotions to Generalmajor 01.06.43, Generalleutnant 01.03.44. Squadron Chief in Reiter Regiment at Potsdam 10.1934–05.1935, attached to Staff of Kavallerie Kommando Potsdam 05.1935–10.1935, Adjutant to 4. Reiter Brigade 10.1935–03.1936, attached to Staff of Higher Kavallerie Officer 4, 04.1936–10.1937, Higher Kavallerie Officer 2, 10.1937–11.1938. WWII: Commander of Radfahrer (later Kradschuetzen) Bataillon 1, 11.1938–09.1941, Commander of Schuetzen Regiment 26, 12.1941–10.1942, Commander of 24. Panzer Division 03.1943–09.1944, Commander of XXXXVIII. Panzer Korps 09.1944–05.1945. Awards: Swords 23.10.44 (105), Oak Leaves 23.12.42 (162), Knight's Cross 30.07.41, 1939 Clasps to the 1914 Iron Cross 1st and 2nd Class, Infantry Assault Badge in Bronze, Tank Assault Badge in Silver, 1914 Iron Cross 1st and 2nd Class, Cross of Honor.

Eder, Dr. Friedrich: General-Intendant (01.06.40), (Luftwaffe); born 22.07.88 in Neu-Ulm, died 05.09.58 in Munich. Administrator by profession. WWI: Oberleutnant der Res. and Batterie Fuehrer in Bavarian Feld Artillerie Regiment 20. Member of N.S.D.A.P. Attached to District Office in Mindelheim 11.1933–07.1935, Oberregierungsrat attached to Luftkreis Kommando V in Munich 07.1935–12.1937, attached to R.L.M. and R.K.M. 01.1938–03.1938, attached to Luftwaffe Staff in Austria 03.1938–05.1938. WWII: attached to LD 3 in R.L.M. 05.1938–12.1939, attached to Department V in O.K.H. 12.1939–05.1940, Intendant to Feld Luftgau Belgium and Northern France 09.1940–09.1942, Chief Intendant to Luftflotte 3, 09.1943–09.1944, Chief Intendant to Luftgau Kommando VIII 12.1944–05.1945, Awards: 1939 Clasp to the 1914 Iron Cross 2nd Class, War Merit Cross 1st and 2nd Class with Swords, 1914 Iron Cross 1st and 2nd Class, Bavarian Military Service Order IV. Class with Swords, Cross of Honor.

Egan-Krieger, Jeno von: Generalleutnant (01.12.42), (Luftwaffe); born 10.07.86 in Schloss Bernstein, died 22.02.65 in Koeln. WWI: Hauptmann i.G. and Bataillon Commander in Infanterie Regiment 51. Promotion to Generalmajor 01.11.40. Ia to Staff of Generalluftzeugmeister in R.L.M. 11.1934–07.1936, Chief of Supply Department (LE 1) in R.L.M. 08.1936–11.1937, Quartermaster on Staff of "Legion Condor" 11.1937–07.1938, Quartermaster to Luftgau Kommando VIII 08.1938–07.1939. WWII: Quartermaster for Luftgau Kommando III 07.1939–03.1941, Senior Quartermaster with Luftwaffe Commander Centre 03.1941–11.1941, Savings Commissioner for Greater German Reich 01.1944–09.1944, Defensive Replacement Inspector for Magdeburg 05.1942–12.1943, retired 09.1944. Awards: War Merit Cross 1st and 2nd Class with Swords, Spanish Cross in Bronze with Swords, German West Wall Medal, RK-Hohenzollern, 1914 Iron Cross 1st and 2nd Class, 1914 Wound Badge in Silver, Prussian Crown Order IV. Class with Swords, Johann Ritter Order, Cross of Honor.

Eggert, Dr. Curt: General-Intendant (20.02.40), (Luftwaffe); born 04.09.85 in Stralsund, died 30.08.65 in Muenster. Administrative Officer by profession. WWI: Marine Intendant Assessor in Wilhelmshaven. Advisor in R.L.M. 02.1936–05.1939. WWII: Intendant for Luftgau Kommando IV 06.1939–09.1941, Chief Intendant to Luftgau Kommando II 09.1941–06.1942, Chief of Department V 5 in R.L.M. 06.1942–03.1943, Chief Intendant to Luftgau Kommando I 03.1943–02.1945. Awards: War Merit Cross 1st and 2nd Class with Swords, 1914 Iron Cross 2nd Class, 1914 Wound Badge in Black, Cross of Honor.

Eglseer, Karl: General der Gebirgstruppe (01.03.44), (Heer); born 05.07.90 in Bad Ischl, died 23.06.44 from air accident near Hartberg. WWI: Hauptmann and Director of Training in Austrian Infanterie Regiment 87, P.O.W. 12.1914–03.1918.

Promotions to Generalmajor 01.11.40, Generalleutnant 01.02.43. Transferred to German Wehrmacht 03.1938. WWII: Commander of Gebirgs Jaeger Regiment 136, 08.1938–08.1939, Chief of Staff to XVIII. Armee Replacement Korps 08.1939–11.1940, Commander of 4. Gebirgs Division 11.1940–10.1942, Commander of 114. Jaeger Division 03.1943–12.1943, Commander of XVIII. Gebirgs Korps 12.1943–06.1944. Awards: Knight's Cross 23.10.41, 1939 Iron Cross 1st and 2nd Class, Infantry Assault Badge in Silver, Eastern Front Medal, Crimea Shield, 1939 Wound Badge in Gold, Heeres Bergfuehrer Badge, Cross of Honor.

Ehlert, Hans-Joachim: Generalmajor (01.12.44), (Heer); born 12.02.98 in Charlottenthal, died 04.04.66 in Schoenkirchen. WWI: Leutnant in Feld Artillerie Regiment 71. Attached to Central Office of Reichswehr 10.1934–04.1935, attached to Staff of Military Replacement Inspection at Allenstein 05.1935–10.1936, Batterie Chef in I. Abteilung, Artillerie Regiment 65, 10.1936–10.1937, Ia to 16. Division 10.1937–07.1938. WWII: attached to Staff of Abteilung 5 in Heeres General Staff 07.1938–08.1939, Department Commander in Artillerie Regiment 293, 09.1939–09.1940, Commander of Artillerie Regiment 269, 10.1940–04.1942, Commander of Artillerie Regiment 377, 04.1942–01.1943, Commander of Artillerie Regiment 334, 06.1943–05.1944, Commander of 114. Jaeger Division 09.1944–02.1945. Awards: 1939 Iron Cross 1st Class, 1939 Clasp to the 1914 Iron Cross 2nd Class, General Assault Badge, 1914 Iron Cross 2nd Class, 1914 Wound Badge in Black, Cross of Honor.

Ehrenberg, Hans: Generalmajor (01.08.41), (Heer); born 18.09.88 in Dresden, died 12.10.47 in Eschwege. WWI: Hauptmann and Bataillon Commander in Res. Infanterie Regiment 241. Commander of I. Bataillon, Infanterie Regiment at Plauen 10.1934–10.1935, Commander of II. Bataillon, Infanterie Regiment 31, 10.1935–10.1936. WWII: Commander of Infanterie Regiment 86, 10.1936–10.1939, Commander of Special Purpose Division 409, 10.1939–04.1943, Commandant of Feldkommandantur 248, 06.1943–09.1943, Commandant of P.O.W. Camp Oflag XVII 11.1943–05.1945. Awards: 1939 Clasp to the 1914 Iron Cross 2nd Class, War Merit Cross 1st and 2nd Class with Swords, RK-Sachsen Military St. Heinrich's Order 04.1920, 1914 Iron Cross 1st and 2nd Class, 1914 Wound Badge in Black, Cross of Honor.

Ehrhardt, Werner: Konteradmiral (01.08.44), (Kriegsmarine); born 25.05.89 in Liebstadt, died 23.09.67 in Kiel. WWI: Leutnant zur See on liner *Kronprinz*. Third Admiral Staff Officer for Marine Station Eastern Sea 09.1933–11.1936, Navigations Officer for battleship *Admiral Graf Spee* 11.1936–10.1938. WWII: Advisor in Personnel Office of O.K.M. 11.1938–11.1939, Department Chief in Personnel Office of O.K.M. 11.1939–01.1943, Commander of heavy cruiser

Prinz Eugen 03.1943–01.1944, Commandant of Marine Kriegsschule at Schleswig 01.1944–05.1945. Awards: War Merit Cross 1st and 2nd Class with Swords, High Seas Fleet War Badge, Spanish Cross in Bronze without Swords, 1914 Iron Cross 2nd Class, Cross of Honor.

Ehrig, Richard: Generalmajor (01.06.41), (Heer); born 24.06.82 in Dresden, died 04.07.68 in Bad Homburg. WWI: Hauptmann and Commander of 26. Res. Jaeger Bataillon. WWII: Director of Wehrkreis-Fursorge-und Versorgungs Abteilung in Wehrkreis Kommando IV 04.1933–03.1943, retired 08.1943. Awards: War Merit Cross 1st and 2nd Class with Swords, RK-Hohenzollern, RK-Sachsen Military St. Heinrich's Order 02.06.15, 1914 Iron Cross 1st and 2nd Class, 1914 Wound Badge in Black, Cross of Honor.

Ehrig, Werner: Generalleutnant (09.11.44), (Heer); born 22.04.97 in Eibenstock, died 31.01.81 in Oldenburg. WWI: Leutnant in Schuetzen Regiment 108. Promotion to Generalmajor 01.01.44. Attached to Staff of Reichswehr Central Office at Stettin 10.1934–04.1935, attached to Staff of Military Replacement Inspection at Stettin 05.1935–10.1936, Kompanie Chef in Infanterie Regiment 116, 10.1936–08.1937, attached to Staff of XIII. Armee Korps 10.1937–02.1939. WWII: Ia to 22. Infanterie Division 03.1939–08.1939, Commander of II. Bataillon, Infanterie Regiment 216, 10.1939–03.1940, Ia to 164. Infanterie Division 03.1940–01.1941, Ia to 15. Armee 01.1941–11.1942, Chief of Staff to LXXXVII. Armee Korps 11.1942–06.1943, Commander of 340. Infanterie Division 10.1943–06.1944, Commander of 544. Volks Grenadier Division 07.1944–05.1945. Awards: Knight's Cross 26.05.40, German Cross in Gold 14.07.44, 1939 Clasps to the 1914 Iron Cross 1st and 2nd Class, Infantry Assault Badge in Silver, 1914 Iron Cross 1st and 2nd Class, 1914 Wound Badge in Black, Cross of Honor.

Eibenstein, Rudolf: Generalleutnant (01.08.43), (Luftwaffe); born 02.07.94 in Bischofswerda, died 18.01.84 in Gauting. WWI: Oberleutnant in Feld Artillerie Regiment 408. Promotion to Generalmajor 01.08.41. Attached to Staff of Fahr Abteilung 1 in Koenigsberg 04.1934–09.1934, Commander of Fahr (later Flak) Abteilung in Seerappen 10.1934–09.1936, attached to Luftwaffe Kriegsschule 01.1937–06.1938. WWII: Chief of Staff to Luftgau Kommando IV 07.1938–08.1939, Chief of Staff to Luftgau Kommando II 08.1939–03.1941, Commander of Flak Brigade IX 04.1941–09.1941, Commander of 7. Flak Division 02.1942–12.1942, Commander of 16. Flak Division 03.1943–04.1944, Commander of 26. Flak Division 05.1944–05.1945. Awards: German Cross in Gold 09.03.42, 1939 Clasps to the 1914 Iron Cross 1st and 2nd Class, Flak War Badge, Afrika Cuff Band, RK-Sachsen Military St. Heinrich's Order 29.10.15, RK-Sachsen Albrecht Order 2nd Class with Swords, 1914 Iron Cross 1st and 2nd Class, 1914 Wound Badge in Silver, Cross of Honor.

Eibl, Karl: General der Infanterie (01.01.43), (Heer); born 23.07.91 in Steeg, died 21.01.43 in action near Stalingrad. WWI: Oberleutnant and Adjutant to Austrian Schuetzen Regiment 21. Promotions to Generalmajor 01.02.42, Generalleutnant 19.12.42. Transferred to German Wehrmacht 03.1938. WWII: Commander of III. Bataillon, Infanterie Regiment 131, 04.1938–08.1939, Commander of I. Bataillon, Infanterie Regiment 132, 09.1939–06.1940, Commander of Infanterie Regiment 132, 06.1940–01.1942, Commander of 385. Infanterie Division 01.1942–12.1942, Commander of XXIV. Panzer Korps 01.1943. Awards: Swords 19.12.42 (21), Oak Leaves 31.12.41, Knight's Cross 15.08.40, Honor Roll Clasp 08.08.41, 1939 Iron Cross 1st and 2nd Class, Infantry Assault Badge in Silver, Eastern Front Medal, 1939 Wound Badge in Gold, Cross of Honor.

Eichel, Eduard: Vizeadmiral (01.08.41), (Kriegsmarine); born 21.12.80 in Gut Linow, died 03.05.56 in Kiel. WWI: Korvettenkapitan and Assistant in Polizei Gruppe Admiralty Staff of Navy. Promotion to Reichsmarine Konteradmiral 01.11.28. WWII: placed at disposal of Kriegsmarine 08.1939–05.1940, Senior Shipyard Director at Drontheim 08.1940–04.1943, retired 04.1943. Awards: War Merit Cross 1st and 2nd Class with Swords, Red Eagle Order IV. Class, 1914 Iron Cross 1st and 2nd Class, Austro-Hungarian Military Service Cross 3rd Class with War Decoration, Turkish Half Moon, Cross of Honor.

Eichler, Hermann: General-Richter (01.05.44), (Luftwaffe); born 24.07.85 in Berlin, died 02.10.68 in Wehrda. Jurist by profession. WWI: service unknown. WWII: Judge for Reichs War Court 1944–1945. Awards: War Merit Cross 1st and 2nd Class with Swords, Cross of Honor.

Eichstaedt, Max: Generalmajor (01.04.41), (Heer); born 29.11.93 in Schneidemuehl, died 16.04.41 in action near Island of Pantelleria. WWI: Oberleutnant and Member of Test Commission. WWII: Commander of I. Abteilung, Artillerie Regiment 73, 10.1935–11.1939, Commander of Panzer Artillerie Regiment 73, 11.1939–03.1941, Commander of Artillerie Regiment 33 (mot.) 03.1941–04.1941. Awards: 1939 Clasps to the 1914 Iron Cross 1st and 2nd Class, General Assault Badge, 1939 Wound Badge in Gold, 1914 Iron Cross 1st and 2nd Class, 1914 Wound Badge in Black, Cross of Honor.

Eichstaedt, Werner von: Generalmajor (01.03.44), (Heer); born 01.01.96 in Saerbeck, died 26.08.44 in action in Kishinew. WWI: Leutnant in Infanterie Regiment 13. Kompanie Chef in Infanterie Regiment at Breslau 10.1934–10.1935, Kompanie Chef in Infanterie Regiment 28, 10.1935–10.1936. WWII: Instructor at Kriegsschule Dresden 10.1936–08.1939, Commander of II. Bataillon, Infanterie Regiment 52, 08.1939–03.1940, Commander of Infanterie Regiment 4, 10.1940–04.1941, Commander of Infanterie Regiment 436, 10.1941–02.1943, Commander of 294. Infanterie Division 12.1943–08.1944. Awards: Knight's Cross 18.08.42, 1939 Clasps to the 1914 Iron Cross 1st and 2nd Class, Infantry Assault Badge in Silver, Eastern Front Medal, Crimea Shield, 1939 Wound Badge in Gold, 1914 Iron Cross 1st and 2nd Class, Cross of Honor.

SS-Obergruppenfuehrer Theodor Eicke. (Marc Rikmenspoel)

Eicke, Theodor: SS-Obergruppenfuehrer und General der Waffen-SS (20.04.42); born 17.10.92 in Kampont, died 26.02.43 in action during reconnaissance flight over Orelka. P-114901, SS-2921. WWI: Zahlmeister attached to 6. M.G. Kompanie. Joined N.S.D.A.P. and S.A in 1928, joined S.S. in 1930. Promotions to SS-Brigadefuehrer 30.01.34, SS-Gruppenfuehrer 11.07.34. Leader of SS-Fuss Standarte 10, Second Commandant of KL-Dachau, shot and killed SA-Stabschef Ernst Roehm 07.1934, z.b.V. RFSS 01.10.34, Inspector of K.L. 01.07.35, Leader of SS-Totenkopfverbaende 01.12.36, Leader of SS-Totenkopfverbaende and K.L. 01.12.37–01.12.38. WWII: gave up control of camp system to become Commander of SS-Division "Totenkopf" 1939, Commander of SS-Division "Totenkopf" 30.01.42, Commander of SS-Panzer Grenadier Division "Totenkopf," Member of Reichstag (WK 30 Chemnitz-Zwikau). Awards: Golden Party Badge (honorary), Oak Leaves 20.04.42 (88), Knight's Cross 26.12.41, 1939 Iron Cross 1st Class, 1939 Clasp to the 1914 Iron Cross 2nd Class, Eastern Front Medal, 1939 Wound Badge in Gold, Danzig Cross 1st Class, 1914 Iron Cross 2nd Class, 1914 Wound Badge in Silver, Cross of Honor, SA-Sports Badge in Bronze, Degen, Himmler Dedication Dagger, Ring.

Eicken, Prof. Dr. Carl von: General-Arzt der Res. (01.09.44), (Heer); born 31.12.73 in Muelheim, died 29.06.60 in Heilbronn. Medical doctor by profession. WWI: Stabs-Arzt der Res. with XVIII. Armee Korps. WWII: consultant ontologist with Heeres Medical Inspection in O.K.H. 08.1939–05.1945. Awards: 1914 Iron Cross 1st and 2nd Class, War Merit Cross 1st and 2nd Class with Swords, Cross of Honor.

Eimler, Robert: Generalmajor (09.11.44), (Heer); born 06.04.91 in Helbra, died 03.02.60 in Ulm. WWI: Leutnant in 4. Pionier Bataillon. Leader of Fortress Pionier Gruppe (later Pionier Staff 1) at Koenigsberg 10.1934–09.1938. WWII: attached to Staff of Fortress Inspection II 11.1938–08.1939, Commander of Festung Pionier Stab 22, 09.1939–06.1941, Commander of Festung Pionier Stab 14, 06.1941–08.1943, Higher Pionier Leader 17, 08.1943–08.1944, Fortress Pionier Commander XXI 11.1944–04.1945. Awards: 1939 Clasps to the 1914 Iron Cross

1st and 2nd Class, General Assault Badge, 1914 Iron Cross 1st and 2nd Class, 1914 Wound Badge in Black, Cross of Honor.

Eisenbach, Erich: Generalmajor (01.10.43), (Heer); born 24.02.82 in Ulm, died 07.07.64 in Ulm. WWI: German Airship Service as Oberleutnant in 3. Airship Bataillon. Commander of I. Bataillon, Infanterie Regiment 110, 05.1936–10.1936. WWII: Commander of II. Bataillon, Infanterie Regiment 104, 10.1936–11.1939, Military Replacement Inspector of Mannheim, Musterungs and Zweibruecken 12.1939–07.1941, Commander of Infanterie Regiment 352, 07.1941–07.1942, Commander of Fortress Infanterie Regiment 861, 10.1942–09.1943, Field Commandant of Sections 1042, 817 followed by 641, 12.1943–05.1945. Awards: 1939 Clasps to the 1914 Iron Cross 1st and 2nd Class, Infantry Assault Badge in Silver, Eastern Front Medal, 1920 Airship Commemorative Badge, RK-Wuerttemberg Military Service Order, 1914 Iron Cross 1st and 2nd Class, Cross of Honor.

Eisenhart-Rothe, Ernst-Georg von: Generalmajor (01.04.42), (Heer); born 25.09.90 in Lietzow, died 24.05.87 in Bremen. WWI: Oberleutnant in Hussar Regiment 2. Attached to Staff of Reiter Regiment at Paderborn 10.1934–10.1935, Commander of Panzer Abwehr Abteilung 23, 10.1935–11.1938. WWII: Adjutant to Heeres Gruppen Kommando 3, 11.1938–08.1939, Wehrmacht Commandant of Potsdam 08.1939–08.1939, Commander of Panzer Abwehr Troop XII 10.1939–05.1940, Commander of Truppenubungsplatz at Doeberitz 05.1940–11.1941, Commander of Infanterie Regiment 685, 11.1941–04.1942, Commandant of Feldkommandantur 602, 05.1942–08.1943, Commandant of Feldkommandantur 608, 08.1943–05.1945. Awards: 1939 Clasps to the 1914 Iron Cross 1st and 2nd Class, 1914 Iron Cross 1st and 2nd Class, 1914 Wound Badge in Black, Cross of Honor.

Eisenlohr, Wolfram: General-Ingenieur (01.11.41), (Luftwaffe); born 25.02.93 in Freiburg, died 05.01.91 in Weinheim. Engineer by profession. WWI: in Naval G.A.S. as Leutnant zur See der Res. in I. Seeflieger Abteilung. Advisor in R.L.M. 04.1933–03.1934. WWII: Group Leader and later Department Director for Engines and Accessories in Technical Department of R.L.M. 04.1934–01.1944, retired 04.1944. Awards: War Merit Cross 1st and 2nd Class with Swords, German West Wall Medal, Naval Pilot's Commemorative Badge, 1914 Iron Cross 1st and 2nd Class, 1914 Naval Pilot's Badge, Cross of Honor.

Eisenstuck, Hellmuth: Generalmajor (01.09.42), (Heer); born 27.06.92 in Hamburg, died 01.05.59 in Heilbronn. WWI: Oberleutnant in Infanterie Regiment 391. Attached to Heer Weapons Office in Reichswehr (later Reich War Ministry) 04.1931–04.1937, Commander of III. Bataillon, Infanterie Regiment 14, 05.1937–11.1937, attached to Staff of Infanterie Regiment 34, 12.1937–11.1938. WWII: Commander of II. Bataillon, Infanterie Regiment 132, 11.1938–08.1939, Commander of

Infanterie Regiment 462, 09.1939–10.1940, Commander of Infanterie Regiment 449, 10.1940–04.1941, Commander of Infanterie Replacement Regiment 45, 06.1941–07.1942, Commander of 381. Feld Training Division 09.1942–07.1943, attached to Heeresgruppe A 07.1943–02.1944, Fortress Commander of Royan 02.1944–06.1944, Commander of Fortress Warsaw 10.1944–01.1945, attached to Construction Staff of 1. Panzer Armee 01.1945–05.1945. Awards: 1939 Clasps to the 1914 Iron Cross 1st and 2nd Class, Infantry Assault Badge in Silver, German West Wall Medal, RK-Sachsen Albrecht Order 2nd Class with Swords, 1914 Iron Cross 1st and 2nd Class, Cross of Honor.

Elfeldt, Otto: Generalleutnant (08.08.43), (Heer); born 10.10.95 in Suelze, died 23.10.82 in Bad Schwastau. WWI: Leutnant and Adjutant to Fuss Artillerie Regiment 20. Promotion to Generalmajor 01.01.43. Commander of II. Abteilung, Artillerie Regiment at Schwerin 10.1934–10.1935, Commander of II. Abteilung, Artillerie Regiment 56, 10.1935–05.1939. WWII: attached to Staff of Inspector 4 in O.K.H. 06.1939–08.1939, Commander of Artillerie Regiment Staff 619, 08.1939–10.1939, Artillerie Officer with General Staff of Heeresgruppe A 10.1939–09.1940, Artillerie Officer on General Staff of O.B. of Heeres 09.1940–10.1942, Commander of 302. Infanterie Division 11.1942–11.1943, Commander of 47. Infanterie Division 12.1943–08.1944, captured 08.1944. Awards: German Cross in Gold 17.11.43, 1939 Clasps to the 1914 Iron Cross 1st and 2nd Class, General Assault Badge, 1914 Iron Cross 1st and 2nd Class, 1914 Wound Badge in Black, Cross of Honor.

Elster, Botho: Generalmajor (01.03.43), (Heer); born 17.05.94 in Berlin, died 24.06.52 in Boeblingen. WWI: Oberleutnant and Brigade Adjutant in 213. Infanterie Division. Commander of Panzer Abwehr Abteilung 3, 10.1935–11.1938. WWII: Commander of Panzer Regiment 8, 11.1938–03.1941, Commander of 101. Panzer Brigade 07.1941–02.1943, Commandant of Feldkommandantur 541, 04.1944–09.1944, captured 09.1944. Awards: 1939 Clasps to the 1914 Iron Cross 1st and 2nd Class, Tank Assault Badge in Silver, RK-Hohenzollern, 1914 Iron Cross 1st and 2nd Class, 1914 Wound Badge in Black, Cross of Honor.

Elster, Wolfgang: Generalmajor (01.02.44), (Heer); born: 05.04.97 Leipzig, died 15.02.44 in action at Nikopol Bridgehead. WWI: Leutnant in Feld Artillerie Regiment 47. WWII: Commander of II. Abteilung, Artillerie Regiment 71, 10.1937–09.1939, Group Director in (Inspector 4) of O.K.H. 10.1939–04.1941, Commander of Panzer Artillerie Regiment 27, 04.1941–04.1943, Fuehrer Res. in O.K.H. 04.1943–10.1943, Commander of Artillerie 128, 09.1943–02.1944. Awards: German Cross in Gold 23.10.42, Honor Roll Clasp 27.03.44, 1939 Clasps to the 1914 Iron Cross 1st and 2nd Class, General Assault Badge, Eastern Front Medal, 1939 Wound Badge in Gold, 1914 Iron Cross 1st and 2nd Class, Cross of Honor.

Elverfeldt, Harald Freiherr von: Generalleutnant (01.03.45), (Heer); born 06.02.00 in Hildesheim, died 06.03.45 in action in Koeln. WWI: Fahnrich in 1. Guards Division. Promotion to Generalmajor 01.09.43. Attached to Abteilung 5 of Reichswehr Ministry 05.1934–05.1935, attached to Abteilung 3 of General Staff of Heeres 07.1935–10.1937, Kompanie Chef in Infanterie Regiment 83, 10.1937–11.1938. WWII: Ia to 3. Light Infanterie Division 11.1938–09.1939, Ia to 8. Panzer Division 10.1939–02.1940, Ia to XV. Armee Korps 02.1940–11.1940, Ia to Panzer Gruppe 3, 11.1940–02.1941, Chief of Staff to VI. Panzer Korps 02.1941–01.1943, Chief of General Staff to 9. Armee 01.1943–10.1943, Commander of 9. Panzer Division 09.1944–03.1945. Awards: Oak Leaves 23.03.45 (801), Knight's Cross 09.12.44, German Cross in Gold 16.03.42, 1939 Iron Cross 1st Class, 1939 Clasp to the 1914 Iron Cross 2nd Class, Eastern Front Medal, 1939 Wound Badge in Gold, 1914 Iron Cross 2nd Class, Cross of Honor.

Emshoff, Dr. Ernst: General-Veterinar z.V. (01.11.42), (Heer); born 31.03.75 in Leipzig, died 31.05.65 in Dresden. Medical veterinarian by profession. WWI: Veterinar (unit unknown). WWII: Korps Veterinar to Wehrkreis IV 1939–12.1942, retired 08.1943. Awards: War Merit Cross 1st and 2nd Class with Swords, 1914 Iron Cross 1st and 2nd Class, Cross of Honor.

Enckevort, Gerhard von: Generalmajor (01.08.41), (Heer); born 15.08.68 in Gratz, died 16.12.45 at Sachsenhausen P.O.W. Camp. WWI: Oberst and Commander of Landwehr Infanterie Regiment 60. WWII: recalled to military service 08.1939, Commandant of P.O.W. Camp III B 09.1939–08.1940, Commandant of P.O.W. Camp III D 08.1940–04.1942, retired 04.1943. Awards: War Merit Cross 1st and 2nd Class with Swords, RK-Hohenzollern, 1914 Iron Cross 1st and 2nd Class, Cross of Honor.

Endres, Theodor: General der Artillerie z.V. (01.01.43), (Heer); born 25.09.76 in Ansbach, died 19.01.56 in Traunstein. WWI: Major and Ia to 5. Bavarian Infanterie Division. Promotions to Reichswehr Generalmajor 01.02.30, Generalleutnant 01.09.40. WWII: recalled to military service 08.1939, Commander of 212. Infanterie Division 08.1939–02.1942, Fuehrer Res. in O.K.H. 10.1942–01.1943, retired 04.1943. Awards: Knight's Cross 13.07.40, 1939 Clasps to the 1914 Iron Cross 1st and 2nd Class, Infanterie Assault Badge in Silver, Eastern Front Medal, RK-Hohenzollern, 1914 Iron Cross 1st and 2nd Class, Cross of Honor.

Engel, Franz: Generalmajor (01.10.44), (Luftwaffe); born 06.11.95 in Neusalz, died 12.05.65 in Munich. WWI: Leutnant in Infanterie Regiment 154. Department Leader in Prussian Ministry of Interior 11.1933–07.1935, Batterie Chef in Flak Regiment 23, 10.1935–03.1936, Batterie Chef in Flak Regiment 3, 04.1936–09.1936, Department Commander in Flak Regiment 3, 10.1936–11.1938. WWII:

Instructor at Wildpark-Werder Luftwaffe Kriegsschule for Officer Aspirants 11.1938–06.1940, Commander of Flak Regiment 100, 06.1940–01.1942, Commander of Luftwaffe Kriegsschule 6 at Bernau 01.1942–06.1943, Commander of 10. Flak Division 06.1943–05.1945. Awards: German Cross in Gold 01.01.45, 1939 Clasps to the 1914 Iron Cross 1st and 2nd Class, Flak War Badge, 1914 Iron Cross 1st and 2nd Class, Cross of Honor.

Engel, Gerhard: Generalleutnant (01.04.45), (Heer); born 13.04.06 in Guben, died 09.12.76 in Munich. Promotion to Generalmajor 01.11.44. Wehrmacht Heeres Adjutant to III. Bataillon, Infanterie Regiment at Rostock 10.1934–12.1934, Adjutant to Halb Regiment at Rostock 01.1935–10.1935, Adjutant to Infanterie Regiment 27, 10.1935–10.1937, Chief of 11. Kompanie, Infanterie Regiment 27, 10.1937–12.1937, attached to Infanterie Schule at Doeberitz 01.1938–03.1938. WWII: Adjutant to the Fuehrer 03.1938–02.1944, Commander of Fusilier Regiment 27, 02.1944–07.1944, Commander of 12. Infanterie Division 07.1944–04.1945. Awards: Oak Leaves 11.12.44 (679), Knight's Cross 04.0744, German Cross in Silver 16.10.43, 1939 Iron Cross 1st and 2nd Class, War Merit Cross 1st and 2nd Class with Swords, Infantry Assault Badge in Silver, 1939 Wound Badge in Gold, Reich Sports Badge in Bronze.

Generalleutnant Gerhard Engel. (Bundesarchiv)

Engel, Joachim: Generalmajor (01.06.44), (Heer); born 25.05.97 in Wandsbek, died 03.06.48 in a Soviet P.O.W. camp. WWI: Leutnant der Res. in Infanterie Regiment 31. Schwadron Chef in Reiter Regiment at Hannover 10.1934–10.1935, Chief of 5. Schwadron, Reiter Regiment 13, 10.1935–02.1936, attached to I. Abteilung, Artillerie Regiment 22, 03.1936–11.1938. WWII: Commander of II. Abteilung, Artillerie Regiment 22, 11.1938–08.1939, Commander of Artillerie Regiment 158, 09.1939–1942, Personnel Officer for XX. Armee Korps 05.1942–11.1943, Commander of 45. Infanterie Division 12.1943–07.1944, captured 07.1944. Awards: 1939 Clasps to the 1914 Iron Cross 1st and 2nd Class, General Assault Badge, 1914 Iron Cross 1st and 2nd Class, 1914 Wound Badge in Black, Cross of Honor.

Engel, Siegfried: Konteradmiral (01.04.43), (Kriegsmarine); born 10.05.92 in Berlin, died 12.07.76 in Hamburg. WWI: Oberleutnant zur See and Watch Officer on liner *Oldenburg*. First Officer for cruiser *Koeln* 03.1934–03.1936, Leader of Gruppe Fremde Marinen in O.K.M. 03.1936–05.1938. WWII: Chief of Staff to Second Admiral of North Sea 05.1938–04.1943, Second Admiral of North Sea 04.1943–04.1945.

Awards: 1939 Clasps to the 1914 Iron Cross 1st and 2nd Class, High Seas Fleet War Badge, 1914 Iron Cross 1st and 2nd Class, Cross of Honor.

Engelbrecht, Erwin: General der Artillerie (01.09.42), (Heer); born 12.11.91 in Wildpark, died 08.04.64 in Munich. WWI: Hauptmann on Staff of 14. Res. Division. Promotions to Generalmajor 01.01.39, Generalleutnant 01.10.40. Advisor in Reichswehr Ministry (later Reich War Ministry) 01.1935–04.1937, Commander of Heeres Service Office 11, 05.1937–11.1938. WWII: Commander of Heeres Service Office 30, 11.1938–10.1939, Commander of 163. Infanterie Division 11.1939–06.1942, Commander of Special Purpose Kommando XXXIII 06.1942–12.1943, Fuehrer Res. in O.K.H. 12.1943–09.1944, Commander of High Kommando Saarpfalz 09.1944–05.1945. Awards: Knight's Cross 09.05.40, 1939 Clasps to the 1914 Iron Cross 1st and 2nd Class, Infantry Assault Badge in Silver, Eastern Front Medal, Finnish Freedom Cross 1st Class with Swords, Silesian Eagle 1st and 2nd Class, RK-Hohenzollern, 1914 Iron Cross 1st and 2nd Class, Cross of Honor.

General der Artillerie Erwin Engelbrecht. (Bundesarchiv)

Engelbrecht, Dr. Georg: General-Arzt (01.10.43), (Luftwaffe); born 10.02.92 in Murnau, died 08.11.76 in Murnau. Medical doctor by profession. WWI: Physician for Bavarian Res. Infanterie Regiment 23. Advisor to Luftgau Kommando V in Munich 07.1936–06.1938. WWII: Physician for Luftgau Kommando VII 06.1938–05.1940, Physician for Feld Luftgau Kommando Belgium and Northern France 06.1940–05.1942, Chief Physician for Luftflotte 3, 06.1942–09.1944, Chief Physician to Luftwaffe Kommando West 09.1944–03.1945. Awards: War Merit Cross 1st and 2nd Class with Swords, 1914 Iron Cross 2nd Class, Cross of Honor.

Engelhardt, Alfred: Generalmajor (01.11.42), (Heer); born 09.10.91 in Kitzingen, died 29.11.74 in Wurzburg. WWI: Oberleutnant and Adjutant to Infanterie Regiment 437. Attached to Staff of Commander of Regensburg 10.1934–10.1935, attached to Staff of 10. Division and Commandant of Transport at Regensburg 10.1935–03.1938, Transport Commandant of Regensburg 04.1938–11.1938, Commander of II. Bataillon, Infanterie Regiment 24, 11.1938–07.1939. WWII: Transport Officer attached to Armee Oberkommando 14, 08.1939–12.1939, Fuehrer Res. in O.K.H. 12.1939–04.1940, Commander of Eisenbahn Transport Bataillon Ost 04.1940–11.1940, Commander of Infanterie Regiment 107, 11.1940–07.1941, attached to Wehrmacht Transport Kommando Paris 08.1941–10.1942, Fuehrer Res. in O.K.H. 10.1942–05.1943, Wehrmacht Commander of Muenster

05.1943–05.1945. Awards: 1939 Clasps to the 1914 Iron Cross 1st and 2nd Class, 1914 Iron Cross 1st and 2nd Class, Cross of Honor.

Engelhardt, Conrad: Konteradmiral (16.09.44), (Kriegsmarine); born 03.26.98 in Lueneburg, died 10.28.73 in Lueneburg. WWI: Leutnant zur See on liner *Ostfriesland.* Roll Officer for line ship *Hessen* 09.1932–09.1934, Commandant of torpedo boat *Kondor* 09.1934–09.1936, Kompanie Chef in II. Marine Artillerie Abteilung 10.1936–10.1937, First Artillerie Officer for battleship *Admiral Scheer* 10.1937–11.1938. WWII: Artillerie Director at Schiff Artillerie Schule 11.1938–09.1939, Naval Flak Gruppe and later Section Commander Brunsbuettel 12.1939–05.1940, First Admiral of Staff to Naval Commander Channel Coast 07.1940–12.1940, Chief of Staff to Naval Commander of Occupied Eastern Territories 05.1941–03.1943, German Sea Transport Chief for Italy 05.1943–12.1943, Chief of Shipping Department in O.K.M. and Sea Transport Chief for Wehrmacht 01.1944–05.1945. Awards: Knight's Cross of the War Merit Cross with Swords 02.24.45, German Cross in Gold 11.09.43, 1939 Iron Cross 1st Class, 1939 Clasp to the 1914 Iron Cross 2nd Class, War Merit Cross 1st and 2nd Class with Swords, 1914 Iron Cross 2nd Class, Cross of Honor.

Engwitz, Dr. Walter: General-Veterinar (01.01.45), (Heer); born 02.01.91 in Wilhelmsfelde, died 18.02.70 in Munich. Medical veterinarian by profession. WWI: Veterinar (unit unknown). WWII: Brigade then Division Veterinar to 1. Kavallerie Division 04.1936–01.1940, Korps Veterinar to XXXXIII. Armee Korps 10.1940–date unknown, Armee Veterinar to 19. Armee (dates unknown). Awards: 1939 Clasp to the 1914 Iron Cross 2nd Class, War Merit Cross 1st and 2nd Class with Swords, 1914 Iron Cross 1st and 2nd Class, Cross of Honor.

Enke, Gustav: Generalmajor (20.04.45), (Heer); born 21.06.89 in Siebigerode, died 13.02.54 in Luebeck. WWI: Senior N.C.O. in Bicycle Kompanie 52. Kompanie Chef in Infanterie Regiment at Crossen 10.1934–05.1935, attached to Staff of Infanterie Regiment at Crossen 05.1935–10.1935, Commander of I. Bataillon, Infanterie Regiment 50, 10.1935–07.1939. WWII: attached to Heeres Unteroffizier Schule in Potsdam 07.1939–02.1940, Commander of Unteroffizier Schule at Treptow 02.1940–07.1943, Commander of Luftwaffe Jaeger Regiment 21, 10.1943–09.1944, in military hospital due to malaria 09.1944–05.1945. Awards: War Merit Cross 1st and 2nd Class with Swords, 1914 Iron Cross 1st and 2nd Class, Cross of Honor.

Enzmann, August: General-Intendant (01.05.44), (Luftwaffe); born 27.08.82 in Vienna, died 21.06.60 in Vienna. Administrative Officer by profession. WWI: Military Unter-Intendant in Austrian 35. Infanterie Division. Transferred to German Wehrmacht 03.1938, Ministerialrat attached to Luftgau Kommando

XVII in Vienna 08.1938–01.1939, Ministerialrat attached to Luftgau Kommando VII in Munich 01.1939–04.1939. WWII: attached to Luftflotte Kommando 3, 05.1939–08.1939, Advisor in Office Group for Administration in R.L.M. 09.1939–04.1940, Intendant for Luftgau Kommando VIII. IV, Moscow, XXX, XXVI and again VIII 08.1940–08.1944, Officer with Special Duties in O.K.L. 08.1944–02.1945. Awards: German Cross in Silver 31.03.45, War Merit Cross 1st and 2nd Class with Swords.

Erban, Dr. Kurt: General-Veterinar (01.04.42), (Heer); born 29.06.89 in Danzig, died 03.01.66 in Stuttgart. Medical veterinarian by profession. WWI: Ober-Veterinar in Feld Regiment 35. Division Veterinar to 19. Division 08.1935–1939. WWII: Korps Veterinar to Wehrkreis I 1939–02.1942, Armee Veterinar to 18. Armee 02.1942–1945. Awards: 1939 Clasp to the 1914 Iron Cross 2nd Class, War Merit Cross 1st and 2nd Class with Swords, 1914 Iron Cross 1st and 2nd Class, Cross of Honor.

Erdmann, Hans: Generalmajor (01.04.43), (Luftwaffe); born 18.02.95 in Loechnitz, died 23.04.91 in Duisburg. WWI: in G.A.S. as Leutnant der Res. in Flieger Abteilung A 210. Chief of Staff to Commander of Luftgau Res. 4 in Berlin 06.1935–09.1936, Kompanie Chef in Flieger Ersatz Abteilung 37, 10.1936–08.1937. WWII: Commander of Flieger Regiment 61, 09.1937–10.1942, Commander of 9. Luftwaffe Feld Division 10.1942–08.1943, Flughafenbereichs Commandant of 11-VII 08.1943–02.1945. Awards: 1939 Clasps to the 1914 Iron Cross 1st and 2nd Class, 2 Tank Destruction Badges, Pilot's Commemorative Badge, RK-Baden Order of the Zaehringer Lion 2nd Class with Swords, 1914 Iron Cross 1st and 2nd Class, 1914 Observer's Badge, Cross of Honor.

Erdmann, Kurt: Generalmajor (01.01.43), (Heer); born 23.09.88 in Insterburg, died 10.11.66 in Muenster. WWI: Hauptmann on Staff of XXI. Armee Korps. WWII: Economic Inspector VI in Muenster 04.1935–11.1939, Armaments Inspector for Wehrkreis Kommando VI 11.1939–04.1945. Awards: Knight's Cross of the War Merit Cross with Swords 24.06.44, War Merit Cross 1st and 2nd Class with Swords, 1914 Iron Cross 1st and 2nd Class, Oldenburg Friedrich-August Cross 1st and 2nd Class, Bavarian Military Service Order IV. Class with Swords, Cross of Honor.

Generalmajor Kurt Erdmann. (Josef Charita)

Erdmann, Wolfgang: Generalleutnant (01.07.44), (Luftwaffe); born 13.11.98 in Koenigsberg, died

05.09.46 (suicide) at Muenster P.O.W. Camp. WWI: Leutnant in Fuss Artillerie Regiment 26. Promotion to Generalmajor 01.03.43. Attached to Training General Staff of Luftwaffe 04.1935–06.1937, attached to Organization Department of Luftwaffe General Staff 07.1937–07.1938, Ia on Staff of Luftgau Kommando XVII in Vienna 07.1938–02.1939, Commander of II. Gruppe, K.G. 4 "General Wever" 03.1939–01.1940, Chief of Department 2 of General Quartermaster in R.L.M. 01.1940–03.1943, Flieger Fuehrer of Croatia 08.1943–04.1944, Chief of General Staff to Fallschirm Armee 05.1944–09.1944, Commander of 7. Fallschirmjaeger Division 10.1944–05.1945. Awards: Knight's Cross 08.02.45, German Cross in Gold 28.12.43, 1939 Clasps to the 1914 Iron Cross 1st and 2nd Class, 1939 Pilot's Badge, 1914 Iron Cross 1st and 2nd Class, 1914 Wound Badge in Black, Cross of Honor.

Erdmannsdorff, Gottfried von: Generalmajor (01.12.42), (Heer); born 25.04.93 in Kamenz, died 30.10.46 (executed) in Minsk. WWI: Oberleutnant and Adjutant to Jaeger Regiment 7. Commander of III. Bataillon, Infanterie Regiment at Kolberg 10.1934–10.1935, Commander of III. Bataillon, Infanterie Regiment 4, 10.1935–11.1938. WWII: Wehrmacht Commander of Erfurt 11.1938–08.1939, attached to Staff of 12. Armee 09.1939–10.1939, Commander of Infanterie Regiment 171, 11.1939–10.1942, Commander of Division 465, 12.1942–03.1944, Fortress Commander of Mogilov 04.1944–08.1944, captured 08.1944. Awards: Knight's Cross 20.03.42, German Cross in Gold 14.02.42, 1939 Clasps to the 1914 Iron Cross 1st and 2nd Class, Infantry Assault Badge in Silver, Eastern Front Medal, 1914 Iron Cross 1st and 2nd Class, 1914 Wound Badge in Silver, Cross of Honor.

Erdmannsdorff, Werner von: General der Infanterie (30.01.45), (Heer); born 26.07.91 in Bautzen, died 05.06.45 (shot by partisans) at Laibach. WWI: Oberleutnant on Staff of 241. Infanterie Division. Promotions to Generalmajor 01.03.42, Generalleutnant 01.01.43. Commander of I. Bataillon, Infanterie Regiment at Breslau 10.1934–10.1935, Commander of I. Bataillon, Infanterie Regiment 49, 10.1935–10.1936, Commander of I. Bataillon, Infanterie Regiment 51, 10.1936–10.1937, attached to Staff of Infanterie Regiment 30, 10.1937–10.1938. WWII: Commander of Infanterie Regiment 30, 11.1938–12.1941, Commander of 18. Infanterie Division (mot.) 12.1941–08.1943, Military Replacement Inspector for Dresden 12.1943–05.1944, Fuehrer Res. in O.K.H. 05.1944–10.1944, Commander of LXXXXI. Armee Korps 10.1944–05.1945. Awards: Knight's Cross 08.03.42, German Cross in Gold 16.11.41, 1939 Clasps to the 1914 Iron Cross

General der Infanterie Werner von Erdmannsdorff. (Bundesarchiv)

1st and 2nd Class, Infantry Assault Badge in Silver, Eastern Front Medal, RK-Sachsen Military St. Heinrich's Order 26.08.17, 1914 Iron Cross 1st and 2nd Class, 1914 Wound Badge in Silver, Cross of Honor.

General der Infanterie Waldemar Erfurth. (Josef Charita)

Erfurth, Dr. Waldemar: General der Infanterie (01.04.40), (Heer); born 04.08.79 in Berlin, died 02.05.71 in Tubingen. WWI: Major and Chief of Staff to V. Res. Korps. Promotions to Reichswehr Generalmajor 01.10.29, Reichswehr Generalleutnant 01.05.31. Attached to Troops Office in Reichswehr Ministry 09.1934–10.1935, Chief of Abteilung 7 in Heeres General Staff 11.1935–11.1938. WWII: Senior Quartermaster V in Heeres General Staff 11.1938–06.1941, Commander of Liaison Staff North 06.1941–11.1942, attached to Finnish Oberkommando 11.1942–09.1944, attached to O.K.H. 12.1944–05.1945. Awards: Knight's Cross of the War Merit Cross with Swords 08.11.44, War Merit Cross 1st and 2nd Class with Swords, Finnish Gold Medal of Merit (only recipient), Finnish Freedom Cross 1st Class with Breast Star and Swords, RK-Hohenzollern, 1914 Iron Cross 1st and 2nd Class, Cross of Honor.

Erhard, Alfred: Generalmajor (01.01.45), (Luftwaffe); born 15.04.99 Aschaffenburg, died 17.04.45 (suicide) in Duesseldorf. WWI: Leutnant in Bavarian Infanterie Regiment 2. On Staff of I. Abteilung, Flak Regiment 5, 09.1935–09.1936, attached to Training Staff of Luftwaffe Kriegsschule in Berlin 12.1936–12.1937. WWII: Gruppe Commander in K.G. 23, 12.1937–08.1939 and at same time Group Director III with General Quartermaster 2 in R.L.M. 02.1939–07.1940, Chief of Staff to Luftgau Kommando Western France 12.1940–11.1943, Commander of Flak Brigade V (mot.) 12.1943–07.1944, Commander of 7. Flak Division 08.1944–04.1945. Awards: 1939 Clasps to the 1914 Iron Cross 1st and 2nd Class, War Merit Cross 1st and 2nd Class with Swords, Flak War Badge, 1914 Iron Cross 1st and 2nd Class, Bavarian Military Service Order IV. Class with Swords, Cross of Honor.

Erler, Heinrich: Generalmajor (01.06.42), (Heer); born 28.05.77 in Berlin, died 18.03.46 in Berlin. WWI: Hauptmann in Operations Department of Railway Troops. WWII: Commander of P.O.W. District 4 in Wehrkreis Kommando III 08.1939–07.1942, retired 07.1942. Awards: War Merit Cross 1st and 2nd Class with Swords, 1914 Iron Cross 1st and 2nd Class, Cross of Honor.

Ernst, Dr. Franz: General-Richter (01.05.44), (Luftwaffe); born 09.08.91 in Grevenbroich, died 29.08.72 in Koeln. Jurist by profession. WWI: Leutnant der Res. in Feld Artillerie Regiment 61. Judge attached to Luftwaffe Gericht III in Dresden 01.1937–09.1937, Judge in Luftwaffe Obergericht VII in Braunschweig 10.1937–08.1938. WWII: Assistant Judge at Reichs War Court 08.1938–06.1940, Chief Judge to Luftflotte 5, 07.1940–01.1941, Group Director in Legal Department of R.L.M. 01.1941–04.1942, War Official in Reichs War Court 10.1942–05.1945. Awards: War Merit Cross 1st and 2nd Class with Swords, 1914 Iron Cross 1st and 2nd Class, 1914 Wound Badge in Black, Cross of Honor.

Ertel, Theodor: Generalmajor (15.10.41), (Heer); born 04.12.74 in Woerth, died 13.04.61 in Munich. WWI: Major and Commander of Bavarian Fuss Artillerie Regiment 2, Leader of Feldzeug Administration VII 01.1935–12.1937 and at same time Leader of Heeres Feldzeuggruppe 3, 01.1935–10.1935, retired 12.1937, recalled to military service 11.1938. WWII: Commander of Feld Equipment in Wehrkreis Kommando VII 10.1939–01.1943, retired 03.1943. Awards: War Merit Cross 1st and 2nd Class with Swords, RK-Hohenzollern, 1914 Iron Cross 1st and 2nd Class, Cross of Honor.

Erxleben, Johannes: Generalmajor (01.10.43), (Heer); born 01.04.93 in Vierraden, died 02.11.72 in Biefeld. WWI: Oberleutnant and Adjutant in War Telegraph Department. Staff Officer of Nachrichtentruppen for Wehrkreis Kommando II 10.1934–10.1935, Commander of Nachrichten Abteilung 6, 10.1935–11.1938. WWII: Commander of Nachrichtentruppen XIII 11.1938–08.1939, Signals Leader of Posen 10.1939–02.1940, Commander of Signals Regiment 549, 02.1940–10.1940, Signals Leader to 11. Armee 10.1940–03.1942, Signals Leader to 12. Armee 03.1942–01.1943, Signals Leader to Southern France 02.1943–11.1943, Higher Signals Leader 513, 11.1943–06.1944, Wehrmacht Commander of Kassel 08.1944–04.1945. Awards: 1939 Clasps to the 1914 Iron Cross and 2nd Class, War Merit Cross 1st and 2nd Class with Swords, 1914 Iron Cross 1st and 2nd Class, Cross of Honor.

Esebeck, Hans-Karl Freiherr von: General der Panzertruppe (01.02.44), (Heer); born 10.07.92 in Potsdam, died 05.01.55 in Dortmund. WWI: Oberleutnant and Adjutant to 3. Guards Kavallerie Brigade. Promotions to Generalmajor 15.04.41, Generalleutnant 01.02.42. Instructor at Infanterie Schule 04.1934–12.1934, Instructor at Kriegsschule Hannover 01.1935–10.1936, Commander of Reiter Regiment 1, 10.1936–03.1939. WWII: Commander of 6. Schuetzen Brigade 04.1939–03.1941, Commander of 11. Panzer Division 08.1941–12.1941, Commander of 2. Panzer Division 02.1942–10.1942, Fuehrer Res. in O.K.H. 10.1942–06.1943, attached to Heeresgruppe Mitte 06.1943–12.1943, arrested and imprisoned for 20.07.44 attempt on Hitler's life 07.1944–05.1945.

Awards: Knight's Cross 04.07.40, German Cross in Gold 23.08.42, 1939 Clasps to the 1914 Iron Cross 1st and 2nd Class, Tank Assault Badge in Silver, 1939 Wound Badge in Silver, 1914 Iron Cross 1st and 2nd Class, Cross of Honor.

Estorff, Detlev von: Generalmajor z.V. (01.06.42), (Heer); born 13.12.71 in Leipzig, died 31.05.54 in Veersen. WWI: Major attached to Prussian War Ministry. Retired 09.1936. WWII: recalled to military service 08.1939, Commander of Wehrmacht Clothing Office in Hannover 08.1939–07.1942, retired 07.1942. Awards: War Merit Cross 1st and 2nd Class with Swords, 1914 Iron Cross 1st and 2nd Class, Turkish Half Moon, Cross of Honor.

Evers, Dr. Alois: Admiral-Arzt (01.06.44), (Kriegsmarine); born 13.03.93 in Muenster, died 31.03.65 in Freiburg. Medical doctor by profession. WWI: Leutnant der Res. in the Army (unit unknown). Attached to Sanitats Amt for Marine Station North Sea 04.1931–09.1936, Ship Physician for line ship *Schlesien* 09.1936–04.1937. WWII: Chief Physician for Marine Hospital at Swinemuende 09.1937–12.1939, Commander of Naval Medical Academy 01.1940–03.1941, Chief Medical Officer with Staff of Marine Gruppen Kommando South 06.1941–08.1942, Chief Physician of Naval Hospital at Stralsund 11.1942–02.1944, Physician attached to Fleet Kommando 02.1944–05.1945. Awards: War Merit Cross 1st and 2nd Class with Swords, 1914 Iron Cross 2nd Class, Cross of Honor.

Ewert, Wolf: Generalmajor (01.03.45), (Heer); born 31.07.05 in Stralsund, died 16.03.94 in Bad Nauheim. Adjutant to II. Bataillon, Infanterie Regiment at Doeberitz 10.1934–10.1935, Adjutant to II. Bataillon, Infanterie Regiment 48, 10.1935–10.1936, Chief of 8. Kompanie, Wachtruppe (later Wach-Regiment) Berlin 10.1936–04.1939. WWII: Kompanie Chef in Infanterie Regiment "Grossdeutschland" 04.1939–01.1940, Chief of 1. Kompanie, Infanterie Replacement Bataillon 99, 01.1940–06.1940, Commander of I. Bataillon, Infanterie Regiment 196, 06.1940–12.1942, Commander of Grenadier Regiment 196, 12.1942–10.1943, Commander of Grenadier Regiment 274, 02.1944–09.1944, Commander of 338. Infanterie Division 01.1945–04.1945. Awards: Knight's Cross 18.07.44, German Cross in Gold 01.11.43, 1939 Iron Cross 1st and 2nd Class, Infantry Assault Badge in Silver, Eastern Front Medal.

Exss, Ernst: Generalmajor (01.04.42), (Luftwaffe); born 22.09.96 in Lindenberg, died 28.01.65 in Recklinghausen. WWI: in G.A.S. as Leutnant in Flieger Abteilung A 22. Attached to R.L.M. and O.B. der Luftwaffe 07.1935–03.1936, Training Observer for Flieger Gruppe Tutow 04.1936–06.1936, attached to Staff of Flieger Gruppe I-155 in Giebelstadt 07.1936–02.1937, Commander of II. Gruppe, K.G. 153, 03.1937–11.1938. WWII: Tactics Instructor at Hoehere Luftwaffe Schule in Berlin-Gatow 12.1938–08.1939, Advisor in Department for National Defense in

O.K.W. 08.1939–12.1939, Commander of K.G. 1 "Hindenburg" 12.1939–07.1940, Chief of Luftwaffe Control Commission V 10.1940–03.1943, Flughafenbereichs Commandant of 6-III 05.1943–1945. Awards: 1939 Clasps to the 1914 Iron Cross 1st and 2nd Class, War Merit Cross 1st and 2nd Class with Swords, 1939 Pilot's Badge, Pilot's Commemorative Badge, RK-Hohenzollern, 1914 Iron Cross 1st and 2nd Class, 1914 Wound Badge in Black, 1914 Observer's Badge, Cross of Honor.

Eyerich, Dr. Karl: Admiral-Arzt (01.01.37), (Kriegsmarine); born 05.02.86 in Wurzburg, died 17.07.71 in Wurzburg. Medical doctor by profession. WWI: Marinestabsarzt and Chief Medic in field hospital. Chief of Sanitats Amt for Marine Station North Sea 10.1931–10.1938. WWII: attached to Naval Medical and Personnel Office of O.K.M. 11.1938–05.1941, Chief Physician of Naval Hospital at Bergen 05.1941–02.1944, Chief Physician of Naval Hospital at Marseille 02.1944–08.1944, captured 08.1944. Awards: War Merit Cross 1st and 2nd Class with Swords, 1914 Iron Cross 2nd Class, Cross of Honor.

Eyssen, Robert: Konteradmiral (01.01.41), (Kriegsmarine); born 02.04.92 in Frankfurt am Main, died 31.03.60 in Baden-Baden. WWI: Oberleutnant zur See and Kdt. of torpedo boat *V-130*. Advisor in Nautical Department of Marineleitung 10.1931–09.1935, Commandant of survey ship *Meteor* 09.1935–10.1937. WWII: Chief of Military Department in Naval Defense Office of O.K.M. 10.1937–11.1939, Commander of auxiliary cruiser *Komet* 12.1939–02.1942, Chief of Kriegsmarine Service Office in Oslo 08.1942–07.1944, Commander in Naval District III 07.1944–01.1945, placed at disposal of Kriegsmarine 01.1945–05.1945. Awards: Knight's Cross 29.11.41, 1939 Clasps to the 1914 Iron Cross 1st and 2nd Class, Auxiliary Cruisers War Badge, RK-Baden Order of the Zaehringer Lion 2nd Class with Swords, 1914 Iron Cross 1st and 2nd Class, Cross of Honor.

F

Faber du Faur, Moritz von: Generalleutnant (01.04.39), (Heer); born 01.09.86 in Stuttgart, died 04.03.71 in Graefelfing. WWI: Rittmeister and Adjutant to 26. Kavallerie Brigade. Promotion to Generalmajor 01.04.37. Commander of Reiter Regiment at Brieg 10.1934–08.1935, Military Attaché to Belgrade 10.1935–07.1939. WWII: Commandant of Feldkommandantur 588, 09.1939–09.1940, Chief of Military Administration District in Bordeaux 09.1940–01.1942, Commandant of Feldkommandantur 593, 01.1942–10.1942, Military Replacement Inspector for Innsbrueck 05.1943–10.1944, Fuehrer Res. in O.K.H. 10.1944–05.1945. Awards: 1939 Clasps to the 1914 Iron Cross 1st and 2nd Class, 1914 Iron Cross 1st and 2nd Class, Cross of Honor.

Fabiunke, Karl: Generalmajor (01.12.43), (Heer); born 05.06.93 in Goerchen, died 30.12.80 in Wohltorf. WWI: Senior NCO at Artillerie Depot in Spandau. Attached to Fahr Abteilung at Ponath 10.1934–10.1935, Artillerie Advisor in China 10.1935–09.1936 and at same time attached to Staff of Beobachter Abteilung 1, 10.1935–10.1936, Commander of Beobachter Abteilung 2, 10.1936–03.1939. WWII: Commander of I. Abteilung, Artillerie Regiment 74, 05.1939–08.1939, Commander of Artillerie (later Panzer Artillerie) Regiment 74, 03.1939–04.1943, Fuehrer Res. in O.K.H. 04.1943–09.1943, Commander of 129. Infanterie Division 09.1943–02.1944, Commander of Artillerie 144, 03.1944–08.1944, wounded and placed in Fuehrer Res. of O.K.H. 08.1944–05.1945. Awards: German Cross in Gold 14.02.42, 1939 Iron Cross 1st Class, 1939 Clasp to the 1914 Iron Cross 2nd Class, General Assault Badge Eastern Front Medal, 1939 Wound Badge in Black, 1914 Iron Cross 2nd Class, Cross of Honor.

Fabrice-Falk, Eberhard von: Generalleutnant (01.03.44), (Heer); born 31.01.92 in Berlin, died 02.09.64 in Lueneburg. WWI: Oberleutnant and Adjutant to Commander of Artillerie of 234. Infanterie Division. Promotion to Reichswehr Generalmajor 01.03.42. Commander of I. Bataillon, Infanterie Regiment 47, 10.1935–05.1939. WWII: attached to Staff of Infanterie Regiment 47,

06.1939–08.1939, Commander of Infanterie Regiment 490, 09.1939–02.1942, Commander of 383. Infanterie Division 02.1942–11.1942, Commander of Division 172, 12.1942–07.1944, Commander of 166. Res. Division 07.1944–05.1945. Awards: German Cross in Silver 26.04.45, 1939 Clasps to the 1914 Iron Cross 1st and 2nd Class, War Merit Cross 1st and 2nd Class with Swords, Infantry Assault Badge in Silver, RK-Hohenzollern, 1914 Iron Cross 1st and 2nd Class, Cross of Honor.

Faeckenstedt, Ernst-Felix: Generalleutnant (01.09.43), (Heer); born 17.12.96 in Dresden, died 06.04.61 in Hoexter. WWI: Leutnant and Ordnance Officer with 3. Infanterie Division. Promotion to Generalmajor 01.07.42. Attached to Military Replacement Inspection at Liegnitz 10.1935–07.1935, Ia to 5. Reiter Brigade 10.1935–10.1936, Ia to 1. Kavallerie Brigade 10.1936–11.1938. WWII: Ia to III. Armee Korps 11.1938–05.1940, Chief of Staff to III. Armee Korps 05.1940–04.1942, Chief of General Staff to 1. Panzer Armee 04.1942–03.1943, Commander of 5. Panzer Division 05.1943–10.1943, Chief of Staff to Wehrkreis VI then later Wehrkreis XII 12.1943–05.1945. Awards: German Cross in Gold 26.01.42, 1939 Clasps to the 1914 Iron Cross 1st and 2nd Class, Eastern Front Medal, 1914 Iron Cross 1st and 2nd Class, 1914 Wound Badge in Black, Cross of Honor.

Faessig, Wilhelm: Generalmajor z.V. (01.06.42), (Heer); born 06.09.74 in Erfurt, died 11.10.45 in Berlin. WWI: Major and General Staff Officer (unit unknown). WWII: civil engineer attached to Reich War Ministry (later O.K.H.) 10.1936–08.1939, recalled to military service 09.1939, attached to General Staff of O.K.H. 09.1939–01.1943, retired 01.1943. Awards: 1939 Clasps to the 1914 Iron Cross 1st and 2nd Class, 1914 Iron Cross 1st and 2nd Class, Cross of Honor.

Fahnert, Friedrich: General der Luftnachrichtentruppe (01.02.44), (Luftwaffe); born 18.01.79 in Limbach, died 10.06.64 in Baden-Baden. WWI: in G.A.S. as Hauptmann and Abteilungs Commander in Armee Flugpark 11. Promotions to Generalmajor 01.04.38, Generalleutnant 01.04.40. Signals Instructor at Luftwaffe Kriegsschule in Berlin 08.1936–09.1938, Higher Commander of Luftwaffe Nachrichtenschule in Berlin 10.1938–04.1939. WWII: Higher Commander of Luftwaffe Nachrichten Ausbildungs Regiments in Berlin 05.1939–09.1940, Higher Signals Leader to Luftflotte 1, 10.1940–09.1942, Commander of Luftwaffe Nachrichten Ausbildungs Division in France 10.1942–09.1944, Commander of Luftwaffe Nachrichten Ausbildungs Division in Berlin 09.1944–01.1945. Awards: German Cross in Silver 03.11.42, 1939 Clasps to the 1914 Iron Cross 1st and 2nd Class, War Merit Cross 1st and 2nd Class with Swords, Pilot's Commemorative Badge, 1914 Iron Cross 1st and 2nd Class, 1914 Pilot's Badge, Cross of Honor.

Fahrig, Hermann: Generalmajor (01.02.44), (Luftwaffe); born 11.07.90 in Bad Liebenstein, died 13.02.47 in Wurzburg. WWI: in G.A.S. as Rittmeister in Flieger

Abteilung A 244. Advisor to Luftkreis Kommando III 04.1934–08.1934, Commander of the Luftwaffe Processing Office in Kassel 09.1934–03.1936, attached to Staff of Luftkreis Kommando VII 03.1936–06.1938. WWII: Commander of Luftwaffe Nachrichten Kommando at Wuerzburg 07.1938–03.1940, Signals Leader to Luftgau Kommando IV 03.1940–04.1941, Signals Leader of Luftgau Kommando XII and later Luftgau Kommando XIII 11.1941–11.1943, retired 02.1944. Awards: War Merit Cross 1st and 2nd Class with Swords, Pilot's Commemorative Badge, RK-Sachsen Military St. Heinrich's Order 02.06.17, 1914 Iron Cross 1st and 2nd Class, 1914 Wound Badge in Black, 1914 Observer's Badge, Cross of Honor.

Fahrmbacher, Wilhelm: General der Artillerie (01.10.40), (Heer); born 19.09.88 in Zweibruecken, died 27.04.70 in Garmisch-Partenkirchen. WWI: Hauptmann and Adjutant to Commander of Bavarian Artillerie 5. Promotions to Generalmajor 01.08.37, Generalleutnant 01.06.39. Department Chief in Weapons Amt of Reichswehr Ministry (later Reich War Ministry) 04.1934–02.1938, Commander of Artillerie 35, 03.1938–08.1938. WWII: Commander of 5. Infanterie Division 08.1938–10.1940, Commander of VII. Armee Korps 10.1940–03.1942, Commander of XXV. Armee Korps 05.1942–06.1944, Commander of Heeresgruppe "Normandy" 06.1944–08.1944, Wehrmacht Commander in Brittany 08.1944–05.1945. Awards: Knight's Cross 24.06.40, German Cross in Silver 30.10.43, 1939 Clasps to the 1914 Iron Cross 1st and 2nd Class, War Merit Cross 1st and 2nd Class with Swords, Eastern Front Medal, Heer Bergfuehrer Badge, 1914 Iron Cross 1st and 2nd Class, 1914 Wound Badge in Black, Cross of Honor.

Falb, Dr. Walter: General-Arzt (01.04.36), (Heer); born 17.01.84 in Obdach, died 30.12.50 in Bremen. WWI: Stabs-Arzt (unit unknown). Division Physician to 1. Kavallerie Division 1933–10.1935, Division Physician to 23. Division 10.1935–12.1936, retired 12.1936. Awards: 1914 Iron Cross 1st and 2nd Class, Cross of Honor.

Falkenhausen, Alexander von: General der Infanterie z.V. (01.09.40), (Heer); born 29.10.78 in Blumenthal, died 31.07.66 in Nassau. WWI: Major and Chief of General Staff to 7. Turkish Armee. Promotions to Reichswehr Generalmajor 01.04.28, Reichsswehr Generalleutnant 01.11.29. Military Official and Advisor attached to Armee of General Chiang Kai-shek 04.1934–07.1938. WWII: without assignment 07.1938–08.1939, Commander of Wehrkreis Kommando IV 08.1939–05.1940, Military Befehlshaber of Belgium and Northern France 05.1940–07.1944, Fuehrer Res. in O.K.H. 07.1944–05.1945. Awards: German Cross in Silver 20.04.43, War Merit Cross 1st and 2nd Class with

General der Infanterie Alexander von Falkenhausen. (Bundesarchiv)

Swords, Pour le Mérite 07.05.18, RK-Hohenzollern, 1914 Iron Cross 1st and 2nd Class, 1194 Wound Badge in Black, Cross of Honor.

Falkenhayn, Erich von: Generalmajor (01.11.41), (Luftwaffe); born 03.06.81 in Kuestrin, died 27.04.50 in Tiefenbronn. WWI: in G.A.S. as Hauptmann and Luftwaffe Processing Officer attached to VIII. Armee Korps 10.1933–12.1937. Luftwaffe Processing Officer attached to XII. Armee Korps 01.1938–01.1939. WWII: Commander of Military District Pforzheim 01.1939–03.1941, Commander of Luftwaffe Construction Brigade II 04.1941–07.1942, retired 11.1942. Awards: War Merit Cross 1st and 2nd Class with Swords, Pilot's Commemorative Badge, 1914 Iron Cross 1st and 2nd Class, 1914 Pilot's Badge, Cross of Honor.

Falkenhorst, Nikolaus von: Generaloberst (19.07.40), (Heer); born 17.01.85 in Breslau, died 18.06.68 in Holzminden. WWI: Hauptmann and Ia to German General Staff in Finland. Promotions to Generalmajor 01.08.35, Generalleutnant 01.08.37, General der Infanterie 01.10.39. Chief of Staff to Heeres Service Office at Dresden 04.1935–10.1935, Chief of Staff to Gruppenkommando 3, 10.1935–10.1936. WWII: Commander of 32. Division 10.1936–08.1939, Commander of XXI. Armee Korps 08.1939–12.1940, O.B. of Norway 12.1940–01.1945. Awards: Knight's Cross 30.04.40, German Cross in Silver 20.01.45, 1939 Clasps to the 1914 Iron Cross 1st and 2nd Class, War Merit Cross 1st and 2nd Class with Swords, Grand Cross of the Order of the White Rose of Finland with Breast Star and Swords, 1914 Iron Cross 1st and 2nd Class, 1914 Wound Badge in Black, Cross of Honor.

Generaloberst Nikolaus von Falkenhorst. (Bundesarchiv)

Falkenstein, Erich Freiherr von: Generalmajor (01.04.41), (Heer); born 13.04.77 in Koenigsberg, died 17.11.45 in Ludinghausen. WWI: Major and Bataillon Commander (unit unknown). WWII: Commander of Field Equipment for Wehrkreis Kommando VI 10.1935–04.1943, retired 04.1943. Awards: War Merit Cross 1st and 2nd Class with Swords, RK-Hohenzollern, 1914 Iron Cross 1st and 2nd Class, Cross of Honor.

Falkenstein, Hans Freiherr von: Generalleutnant (01.11.43), (Heer); born 12.09.93 in Dresden, died 30.10.80 in Hannover. WWI: Leutnant in Grenadier Regiment 100. Promotion to Generalmajor 01.05.43. Attached to Reich War Ministry 05.1935–10.1937. WWII: Commander of M.G. Bataillon 7, 10.1937–01.1940, Commander of Infanterie Regiment 103, 01.1940–12.1941, Commander of 14.

Schuetzen Brigade 12.1941–11.1942, Commander of 45. Infanterie Division 04.1943–12.1943, Commander of 24. Infanterie Division 02.1944–06.1944, Military Replacement Inspector for Dresden 08.1944–05.1945. Awards: German Cross in Gold 15.11.41, 1939 Clasps to the 1914 Iron Cross 1st and 2nd Class, Infantry Assault Badge in Silver, Eastern Front Medal, RK-Sachsen Military St. Heinrich's Order 02.12.17, 1914 Iron Cross 1st and 2nd Class, Cross of Honor.

Falkenstein, Sigismund Freiherr von: Generalmajor (01.10.43), (Luftwaffe); born 14.09.03 in Muenster, died 02.06.72 in Bueckeburg. Advisor and Group Leader attached to Training Department of General Staff and at same time attached to Inspector of Kampfflieger 01.1936–03.1938, Staffelkapitan in Kampfflieger Gruppe Giebelstadt 04.1938–10.1938. WWII: Leader in Training Department of R.L.M. 02.1939–09.1939, Group Commander in K.G. 27 "Boelcke" 10.1939–05.1940, Staff Officer attached to Department of State Defense in O.K.W. 06.1940–03.1942, Chief of Staff to X. Flieger Korps 04.1942–04.1943, Chief of General Staff to Luftflotte Reich 02.1944–05.1944, Commander of 3. Flieger Division 06.1944–05.1945. Awards: German Cross in Gold 12.07.43, 1939 Iron Cross 1st and 2nd Class, 1939 Pilot's Badge.

Falkowski, Kurt von: Generalmajor (01.11.41), (Luftwaffe); born 03.11.86 in Metz, died 01.04.53 in Einbeck. WWI: Hauptmann and Commander of Fuss Artillerie Bataillon 61. Attached to Staff of Generalluftzeugmeister of R.L.M. 08.1935–12.1935, Commander of Luftzeuggruppe V in Munich 01.1936–11.1936. WWII: Military District Commander for Passau 12.1936–03.1941, Commander of Luftwaffe Construction Brigade I 03.1941–11.1942, retired 11.1942. Awards: War Merit Cross 1st and 2nd Class with Swords, RK-Hohenzollern, 1914 Iron Cross 1st and 2nd Class, Cross of Honor.

Falley, Wilhelm: Generalleutnant (01.05.44), (Heer); born 25.09.97 in Metz, died 06.06.44 in action near Sainte-Mère-Église, France. WWI: Leutnant der Res. in Guards Infanterie Regiment 7. Promotion to Generalmajor 01.12.43. Attached to Staff of II. Bataillon, Infanterie Regiment at Stettin 10.1934–10.1935, Chief of 18. Kompanie, Infanterie Regiment 5, 10.1935–10.1936. WWII: Tactics Instructor at Kriegsschule Munich 10.1936–08.1939, Commander of III. Bataillon, Infanterie Regiment 238, 08.1939–01.1940, Commander of II. Bataillon, Infanterie Regiment 433, 01.1940–04.1941, Commander of Infanterie Regiment 4, 04.1941–06.1942, Commander of Infanterie Schule V for Fahnenjunker 08.1942–06.1943, Commander of 246. Infanterie Division 12.1943–04.1944, Commander of 91. Air Landing Division 04.1944–06.1944. Awards: Knight's Cross 26.11.41, German Cross in Gold 20.01.44, 1939 Clasps to the 1914 Iron Cross 1st and 2nd Class, Infantry Assault Badge in Silver, Eastern Front Medal, Demjansk Shield, 1939

Wound Badge in Gold, 1914 Iron Cross 1st and 2nd Class, 1914 Wound Badge in Black, Cross of Honor.

Fanger, Paul: Admiral (01.12.42), (Kriegsmarine); born 11.04.89 in Schoeningen, died 5.04.45 in action in Schoeningen. WWI: Kapitanleutnant and Watch Officer on heavy cruiser *Moltke*. Promotions to Konteradmiral 01.10.38, Vizeadmiral 01.12.40. Commandant of Artillerie Schule ship *Bremse* 07.1932–03.1933, Commander of all Artillerie Schule Ships 03.1933–09.1935, Commandant of battleship *Deutschland* 09.1935–09.1937. WWII: Commander of Fortifications at Ostfriesland 09.1937–01.1940, Chief of Marine Artillerie Office in O.K.M. 01.1940–03.1943, Inspector of Coastal and Ship Artillery in Norway 08.1944–04.1945. Awards: Knight's Cross of the War Merit Cross with Swords 30.04.45, German Cross in Silver 05.03.43, 1939 Clasp to the 1914 Iron Cross 2nd Class, War Merit Cross 1st and 2nd Class with Swords, 1939 Wound Badge in Gold, Spanish Cross in Silver with Swords, Grand Officer's Cross of the Italian Order of the Crown, Commander's Cross of the Hungarian Service Order, 1914 Iron Cross 2nd Class, Cross of Honor.

Admiral Paul Fanger. (Josef Charita)

Fangohr, Friedrich: General der Infanterie (16.03.45), (Heer); born 12.08.99 Hannover, died 17.04.56 in Munich. WWI: Leutnant in Infanterie Regiment 477. Promotions to Generalmajor 01.02.43, Generalleutnant 01.02.44. Attached to Staff of Grenz Abschnitte Kommando at Dresden 10.1934–10.1935, attached to Staff of Heeres Service Office 5, 10.1935–10.1936, Kompanie Chef in Infanterie Regiment 103, 10.1936–06.1937, attached to Staff of Gruppen Kommando 3, 06.1937–10.1937. WWII: Ia to 13. Infanterie Division 10.1937–02.1940, Ia to XXXXI. Armee Korps 02.1940–02.1941, Chief of Staff to LVII. Panzer Korps 02.1941–07.1942, Chief of General Staff to 4. Panzer Armee 07.1942–06.1944, Commander of 122. Infanterie Division 08.1944–02.1945, Commander of I. Armee Korps 02.1945–04.1945. Awards: Knight's Cross 09.06.44, German Cross in Gold 25.03.42, 1939 Clasps to the 1914 Iron Cross 1st and 2nd Class, Infantry Assault Badge in Silver, Eastern Front Medal, Kurland Cuff Band, 1914 Iron Cross 1st and 2nd Class, Cross of Honor.

Fanslau, Heinz: SS-Brigadefuehrer und Generalmajor der Waffen-SS (09.11.44), born 06.06.09 in Duringhof, died 10.03.87 in Munich. P-581867, SS-13200. Joined N.S.D.A.P. and S.S. in 1931. Attached to Staff of SS-Oberabschnitte Mitte 01.10.34–01.07.35, attached to Staff of SS-Oberabschnitte Elbe 01.12.36–01.12.37, attached to Staff Inspectorate of SS-V.T. 01.12.38. WWII: attached to W.V.H.A. 30.01.42–15.05.43, Chief of Amt A V (Personnel) of W.V.H.A. 30.01.44, Chief of Amtsgruppe A (Troop Administration) of W.V.H.A. 09.11.44. Awards: 1939 Iron Cross 2nd Class, War Merit Cross 1st and 2nd Class with Swords, SA-Sports Badge in Bronze, Degen, Ring.

Faulenbach, Karl: Generalleutnant (01.01.43), (Heer); born 03.10.93 in Hanau, died 22.11.71 in Stuttgart. WWI: Oberleutnant and First Ordnance Officer on Staff of 12. Infanterie Division. Promotion to Generalmajor 01.04.42. Commander of Ausbildungs Bataillon of Infanterie Regiment at Tuebingen 10.1934–10.1935, Commander of II. Bataillon, Infanterie Regiment 56, 10.1935–05.1939. WWII: Commander of Infanterie Regiment 14, 06.1939–10.1940, Commander of Infanterie Regiment 419, 10.1940–03.1942, Commander of 296. Infanterie Division 04.1942–01.1943, Commander of 356. Infanterie Division 05.1943–12.1944, Commander of Division 401, 12.1944–02.1945. Awards: German Cross in Gold 13.09.42, 1939 Clasps to the 1914 Iron Cross 1st and 2nd Class, Infantry Assault Badge in Silver, Eastern Front Medal, 1914 Iron Cross 1st and 2nd Class, Cross of Honor.

Fechter, Hans: Vizeadmiral (01.11.37), (Kriegsmarine); born 26.05.85 in Elbing, died 04.07.55 in Berlin. WWI: U-boat service as Marine-Oberingenieur and Chief Engineer of *U-139*. Promotion to Konteradmiral 01.10.35. Chief Station Engineer for Marine Station North Sea 06.1931–09.1933, Fleet Engineer for Flottenkommando 09.1933–09.1935. WWII: Ship Machine Inspector 10.1935–12.1939, retired 12.1939. Awards: RK-Hohenzollern, 1914 Iron Cross 1st and 2nd Class, Turkish Silver Liakat Medal with Sabre, Turkish Half Moon, 1914 Submarine Badge, Cross of Honor.

Fegelein, Hermann: SS-Gruppenfuehrer und Generalleutnant der Waffen-SS (21.06.44); born 30.10.06 in Ansbach, died 29.04.45 (executed) at Reich Chancellery in Berlin. P-1200158, SS-66680. Joined N.S.D.A.P. in 1932, joined S.S. in 1933. Promotion to SS-Brigadefuehrer 01.05.43. Attached to Staff of SS-Oberabschnitte Sud 01.10.34–01.07.35, Leader of SS-Hauptreitschule Muenchen 01.12.36–01.12.38. WWII: Commander of 1. SS-Totenkopf Reiter Standarte (later SS-Kavallerie Standarte 1), Commander of SS-Kavallerie Brigade 30.01.42, Commander of SS-Kampfgruppe "Fegelein," Chief Amt VI (Reit und Fehrwesen) of SS-Fuehrungshauptamt, Commander of SS-Kavallerie Division 15.05.43, attached to Kommando Staff of RFSS 30.01.44, Commander of 8.

SS-Gruppenfuehrer Hermann Fegelein. (Marc Rikmenspoel)

SS-Kavallerie Division "Florian Geyer," Waffen-SS Liaison at Fuehrer H.Q. and at same time Chief of Amt VI in SS-Fuehrungshauptamt 09.11.44. Awards: Swords 30.07.44 (83), Oak Leaves 22.12.42 (157), Knight's Cross 02.03.42, German Cross in Gold 01.11.43, 1939 Iron Cross 1st and 2nd Class, Close Combat Clasp in Silver, General Assault Badge, Infantry Assault Badge in Silver, 20.07.44 Wound Badge in Silver, Eastern Front Medal, German Social Welfare Decoration 2nd Class, German Olympic Games Decoration 1st Class, Reich Sports Badge in Bronze, SA-Sports Badge in Silver, German Horseman's Badge in Gold, Degen, Ring.

Fehn, Franz: Generalmajor (01.06.41), (Heer); born 09.03.83 in Bayreuth, died 22.10.72 in Bayreuth. WWI: Rittmeister and Commander of II. Bataillon, Bavarian Infanterie Regiment 31. WWII: Training Leader at Bayreuth 04.1934–08.1939, Commander of Infanterie Regiment 342, 08.1939–10.1939, Commander of Infanterie Replacement Regiment 296, 10.1939–05.1941, Commander of 713. Infanterie Division 05.1941–05.1942, Military Commander of Augsburg 06.1942–04.1945. Awards: 1939 Clasps to the 1914 Iron Cross 1st and 2nd Class, Infantry Assault Badge in Silver, 1914 Iron Cross 1st and 2nd Class, Bavarian Military Service Order IV. Class with Swords, Cross of Honor.

Fehn, Gustav: General der Panzertruppe (01.11.42), (Heer); born 21.02.92 in Nuremberg, died 05.06.45 (executed by Yugoslav Partisans) in Laibach. WWI: Oberleutnant and Adjutant to 89. Res. Infanterie Brigade. Promotions to Generalmajor 01.08.40, Generalleutnant 01.08.42. Instructor at Kavallerie Schule in Dresden 01.1935–11.1935, Commander of I. Bataillon, Infanterie Regiment 33, 12.1935–10.1937, attached to Staff of Infanterie Regiment 33, 10.1937–03.1939. WWII: Commander of Infanterie Regiment 33, 04.1939–07.1940, Commander of 5. Panzer Division 11.1940–10.1942, Commander of Afrika Korps 11.1942–01.1943, Commander of XXI. Armee Korps 10.1943–07.1944, Commander of XV. Gebirgs Korps 07.1944–05.1945. Awards: Knight's Cross 05.08.40, German Cross in Gold 07.07.42, 1939 Clasps to the 1914 Iron Cross 1st and 2nd Class, Tank Assault Badge in Silver, Eastern Front Medal, Afrika Cuff Band, 1939 Wound Badge in Black, 1914 Iron Cross 1st and 2nd Class, 1914 Wound Badge in Black, Cross of Honor.

Feichtmeier, Josef: Generalleutnant z.V. (01.01.42), (Heer); born 08.09.83 in Vienna, died 1945 (missing in action). WWI: Major and Bataillon Commander in Austrian Infanterie Regiment 76. Promotion to Generalmajor z.V. 01.04.39. Transferred to German Wehrmacht 03.1938. WWII: Commander of Landes Schuetzen Regiment 1, 08.1939–03.1940, Commander of Infanterie Regiment 664, 03.1940–08.1940, Commander of Section Staff South 08.1940–06.1941, P.O.W. Commander for Ukraine 1941–11.1942, retired 03.1943. Awards: War Merit Cross 1st and 2nd Class with Swords, Cross of Honor.

Feige, Hans: General der Infanterie (01.12.40), (Heer); born 10.11.80 in Koenigsberg, died 17.09.53 in Schussenried. WWI: Major on Staff of Guards Replacement Division. Promotions to Reichswehr Generalmajor 01.10.31, Reichswehr Generalleutnant 01.10.33. Commander of 1. Kavallerie Division 10.1933–09.1935, retired 09.1935. WWII: recalled to military service 08.1939, Commander of Wehrkreis II 08.1939–05.1940, Commander of A.O.K. XXXVI. 05.1940–11.1941, Fuehrer Res. in O.K.H. 06.1942–06.1943, retired 03.1943. Awards: German Cross in Gold 19.12.41, 1939 Clasps to the 1914 Iron Cross 1st and 2nd Class, Grand Cross of the Order of the White Rose of Finland with Breast Star and Swords, RK-Hohenzollern, 1914 Iron Cross 1st and 2nd Class, 1914 Wound Badge in Black, Cross of Honor.

General der Infanterie Hans Feige. (Bundesarchiv)

Feige, Otto: Admiral z.V. (01.09.41), (Kriegsmarine); born 21.09.82 in Neisse, died 02.01.51 in Kaufbeuren. WWI: Kapitanleutnant and Artillery Advisor to Submarines. Promotions to Reichsmarine Konteradmiral 01.01.33, Vizeadmiral 01.10.35. Inspector for Marine Artillerie 09.1932–09.1937. WWII: no posts held 09.1937–05.1940, placed at disposal of Naval Director of Coastal Administration in Leningrad 05.1940–06.1941, Senior Shipyard Director at Nikolayev 12.1941–09.1942, retired 12.1942. Awards: War Merit Cross 1st and 2nd Class with Swords, Commander's Cross of the Romanian Order of the Crown with Swords, 1914 Iron Cross 1st and 2nd Class, Oldenburg Friedrich-August Cross 1st and 2nd Class, Cross of Honor.

Fein, Otto: Konteradmiral (01.04.42), (Kriegsmarine); born 28.03.95 in Hamburg, died 09.01.53 in Hamburg. WWI: U-boat service as Leutnant zur See and Watch Officer on *U-140*. Navigations Officer for cruiser *Koeln* 09.1931–02.1934, First Admiral Staff Officer for Marine Station Eastern Sea 02.1934–09.1937, attached to Wehrmacht Academy and at same time Advisor in O.K.M. 10.1937–08.1938. WWII: First Admiral Staff Officer to Marine Gruppen Kommando East 11.1938–08.1940, Commander of battleship *Gneisenau* 08.1940–04.1942, Chief of Staff to Marine Befehlshaber Norway 05.1942–11.1944, Office Group Chief for Nautical Radio/Communication Services in O.K.M. 12.1944–05.1945. Awards: German Cross in Gold 02.02.42, 1939 Clasps to the 1914 Iron Cross 1st and 2nd Class, High Seas Fleet War Badge, 1914 Iron Cross 1st and 2nd Class, 1914 Submarine Badge, Cross of Honor.

Felber, Hans: General der Infanterie (01.08.40), (Heer); born 08.07.89 in Wiesbaden, died 08.03.62 in Frankfurt am Main. WWI: Hauptmann on Staff of A.O.K. 2. Promotions to Generalmajor 01.10.37, Generalleutnant 01.10.39. Attached to Staff of Kriegsschule 08.1934–04.1935, Commander of Kriegsschule 05.1935–06.1935, Chief of Staff to III. Armee Korps 07.1935–03.1938. WWII: Chief of Staff to Armee Oberkommando 3, 04.1938–08.1939, Chief of General Staff to 2. Armee 08.1939–02.1940, Chief of General Staff to Heeresgruppe C 02.1940–10.1940, Commander of XIII. Armee Korps 10.1940–01.1942, Commander of LXXXIII. Armee Korps 05.1942–08.1943, Wehrmacht Befehlshaber South-East and Serbia 08.1943–09.1944, Commander of XIII. Armee Korps 01.1945–02.1945. Awards: Knight's Cross 17.09.41, 1939 Clasps to the 1914 Iron Cross 1st and 2nd Class, Infantry Assault Badge in Silver, Eastern Front Medal, 1914 Iron Cross 1st and 2nd Class, Cross of Honor.

Felbert, Paul von: Generalmajor (01.10.43), (Heer); born 09.11.94 in Wiesbaden, died 03.02.73 in Wiesbaden. WWI: Oberleutnant in 14. Jaeger Bataillon. Commander of II. Abteilung, Kavallerie Schuetzen Regiment at Gera 04.1935–10.1935, Commander of I. Abteilung, Schuetzen Regiment 3, 10.1935–11.1938. WWII: attached to Staff of Kavallerie Schuetzen Regiment 9, 11.1938–08.1939, Commander of Replacement Bataillon, Schuetzen Regiment 8, 08.1939–10.1939, Commander of Schuetzen Regiment 8, 10.1939–06.1940, Commander of Infanterie Replacement Regiment for Wehrkreis Kommando VI 06.1940–06.1942, Wehrmacht Commander at Besancon 07.1942–09.1944, captured 09.1944. Awards: 1939 Clasps to the 1914 Iron Cross 1st and 2nd Class, 1914 Iron Cross 1st and 2nd Class, 1914 Wound Badge in Silver, Cross of Honor.

Feldbausch, Hans: Konteradmiral (01.06.40), (Kriegsmarine); born 05.10.91 in Edenkoben, died 20.10.85 in Hamburg. WWI: Oberleutnant zur See and Watch Officer on torpedo boats *V-44* and later *V-127*. First Officer on line ship *Schlesien* 09.1933–09.1935, Leader at Naval Service Office in Koenigsberg 09.1935–05.1937, Commandant of line ship *Schleswig-Holstein* 05.1937–06.1938. WWII: Chief of Naval Service Office in Bremen 08.1938–05.1940, Chief of Naval Service Office in Oslo 05.1940–08.1942, Director of Head Department for Nautic and Naval Observatory 1942–1945. Awards: War Merit Cross 1st and 2nd Class with Swords, 1914 Iron Cross 1st and 2nd Class, Oldenburg Friedrich-August Cross 1st and 2nd Class, Bavarian Military Service Order IV. Class with Swords, Turkish Silver Liakat Medal with Sabre, Turkish Half Moon, Cross of Honor.

Feldt, Kurt: General der Kavallerie (01.02.44), (Heer); born 22.11.87 in Schmentau, died 11.03.70 in Berlin. WWI: Rittmeister and Commander of II. Bataillon, Res. Infanterie Regiment 27. Promotions to Generalmajor 01.02.40, Generalleutnant 01.02.41. Commander of Reiter Regiment at Rathenow 10.1934–10.1935,

Commander of Reiter (later Kavallerie) Regiment 3, 10.1936–11.1938. WWII: Commander of 1. Kavallerie Brigade 11.1938–10.1939, Commander of 1. Kavallerie Division 10.1939–12.1941, Commander of 24. Panzer Division 12.1941–04.1942, Heeres Administrative Commander in France 07.1942–09.1944, Commander of Korps "Feldt" 09.1944–12.1944, attached to Wehrmacht Befehlshaber of Denmark 02.1945–05.1945. Awards: Knight's Cross. 23.08.41, 1939 Clasps to the 1914 Iron Cross 1st and 2nd Class, General Assault Badge, 1914 Iron Cross 1st and 2nd Class, Cross of Honor.

Feller, Gustav: Generalmajor (01.10.44), (Heer); born 16.06.96 in Stuttgart, died 13.04.45 in Landgrafrode. WWI: Leutnant and Ordnance Officer on Staff of Infanterie Regiment 125. Schwadron Chef in Reiter Regiment at Cannstatt 10.1934–10.1935, Schwadon Chief in Reiter Regiment 18, 10.1935–01.1936, Adjutant to 2. Reiter Brigade (later Higher Kavallerie Officer 2) 02.1936–10.1937. WWII: Advisor in General Office of Reich War Ministry (later O.K.H.) 10.1937–11.1940, Department Chief in O.K.H. 11.1940–08.1941, Fuehrer Res. in O.K.H. 08.1941–07.1942, attached to Panzertruppen Schule 07.1942–08.1943, Commander of Panzer Regiment 1, 08.1943–12.1943, Commander of Panzertruppen in Wehrkreis Kommando III and later Wehrkreis Kommando IX 06.1944–04.1945. Awards: 1939 Clasp to the 1914 Iron Cross 2nd Class, War Merit Cross 1st and 2nd Class with Swords, 1914 Iron Cross 1st and 2nd Class, Cross of Honor.

Fellgiebel, Erich: General der Nachrichtentruppe (01.08.40), (Heer); born 04.10.86 in Porpelwitz, died 04.09.44 (executed) at Plotzensee Prison for role in attempt on Hitler's life. WWI: Hauptmann on Staff of 6. Infanterie Division. Promotions to Generalmajor 01.03.38, Generalleutnant 01.02.40. WWII: Inspector of Nachrichten Truppen in Reichswehr Ministry (later Reich War Ministry and O.K.H.) 10.1934–08.1939, Chief of Heeres Signal Affairs and Chief of Communications in O.K.W. 08.1939–07.1944, dismissed and arrested. Awards: 1939 Clasps to the 1914 Iron Cross 1st and 2nd Class, War Merit Cross 1st and 2nd Class with Swords, Finnish Freedom Cross 1st Class with Oak Leaves and Swords, 1914 Iron Cross 1st and 2nd Class, Cross of Honor.

Felmy, Gerhard: Generalmajor (30.01.45), (Luftwaffe); born 12.12.91 in Berlin, died 08.12.55 in Dreicishenhain. WWI: in G.A.S. as Oberleutnant and Leader of Jasta 2. Commander of Fliegerschule Cottbus and Advisor in R.L.M. 04.1935–06.1938. WWII: attached to Staff of Luftgau Kommando XII 07.1938–1940, Flughafenbereichs Commandant of Thorn 1940–1944, Supply Troop Commander of Fallschirm Armee 1944–05.1945. Awards: War Merit Cross 1st and 2nd Class with Swords, Pilot's Commemorative Badge, RK-Hohenzollern, 1914 Iron Cross 1st and 2nd Class, Turkish Golden Liakat Medal with Sabre, Austro-Hungarian

Military Service Cross 3rd Class with War Decoration, Turkish Half Moon, 1914 Pilot's Badge, Turkish Pilot's Badge, Cross of Honor.

General der Flieger Hellmuth Felmy. (Bundesarchiv)

Felmy, Hellmuth: General der Flieger (04.02.38), (Luftwaffe and Heer); born 28.05.85 in Berlin, died 14.12.65 in Darmstadt. WWI: in G.A.S. as Hauptmann and Commander of Flieger Abteilung 300. Promotions to Generalmajor 01.01.36, Generalleutnant 20.04.37. Commander of Fliegerwaffen Schule and Chief of Staff to Commander of Luftwaffe Schulen 12.1933–03.1935, Hoehere Flieger Commander V 04.1935–09.1936, Commander of Luftkreis Kommando VII 10.1936–03.1938, Commander of Luftwaffen Gruppen Kommando 2, 04.1938–01.1939. WWII: O.B. of Luftflotte 2, 02.1939–01.1940, dismissed for Mechelen Affair 01.1940–04.1941, returned to Heer in 05.1941, Military Befehlshaber for Southern Greece 06.1941–09.1942, Commander of Special Purpose General Kommando "Felmy" 09.1942–03.1943, Commander of LXVIII. Armee Korps 03.1943–12.1944, Commander of XXXIV. Armee Korps 12.1944–05.1945. Awards: German Cross in Gold 16.01.45, 1939 Clasps to the 1914 Iron Cross 1st and 2nd Class, War Merit Cross 1st and 2nd Class with Swords 1939 Observer's Badge, Pilot's Commemorative Badge, RK-Hohenzollern, 1914 Iron Cross 1st and 2nd Class, Austro-Hungarian Military Service Cross 3rd Class with War Decoration, Turkish Silver Liakat Medal with Sabre, 1914 Observer's Badge, Austro-Hungarian Pilot's Badge, Cross of Honor.

General der Artillerie Maximilian Felzmann. (Bundesarchiv)

Felzmann, Maximilian: General der Artillerie (01.01.45), (Heer); born 22.04.94 in Zwittau, died 08.06.62 in Zurich. WWI: Oberleutnant in Austrian Schwere Artillerie Regiment 9. Promotions to Generalmajor 01.06.43, Generalleutnant 01.12.43. Transferred to German Wehrmacht 03.1938, Commander of II. Abteilung, Leichte Artillerie Regiment 6, 06.1938–07.1938, Commander of II. Abteilung, Gebirgs Artillerie Regiment 111, 08.1938–10.1938. WWII: attached to Staff of Artillerie Regiment 51, 11.1938–08.1939, Commander of Artillerie Regiment 251, 08.1939–12.1942, Commander of 251. Infanterie Division 03.1943–11.1943, Commander of Korps Abteilung E 11.1943–08.1944, Commander of XXVII. Armee Korps 10.1944–04.1945. Awards: Oak Leaves

03.11.44 (643), Knight's Cross 28.11.43, German Cross in Gold 29.01.42, 1939 Iron Cross 1st and 2nd Class, General Assault Badge, Eastern Front Medal, Cross of Honor.

Fessmann, Ernst: General der Panzertruppe z.V. (01.07.41), (Heer); born 06.01.81 in Pfersee, died 25.10.62 in Pullach. WWI: Rittmeister on Staff of Armee Attachment A. Promotions to Reichswehr Generalmajor 01.01.34, Generalleutnant 01.10.35. Commander of Staff for Transport Training Brigade 08.1934–10.1935, Commander of 3. Panzer Division 10.1935–09.1937, retired 09.1937, returned to service 10.1937 but without assignment until 08.1939. WWII: Commander of 267. Infanterie Division 08.1939–06.1941, Fuehrer Res. in O.K.H. 06.1941–04.1943, retired 04.1943. Awards: 1939 Clasps to the 1914 Iron Cross 1st and 2nd Class, Infantry Assault Badge in Silver, 1914 Iron Cross 1st and 2nd Class, Cross of Honor.

Fett, Albert: Generalleutnant z.V. (01.02.41), (Heer); born 01.11.72 in Rennerod, died 08.02.63 in Frankfurt am Main. WWI: Major and Commander of Infanterie Regiment 164. Promotion to Reichswehr Generalmajor 01.05.27. WWII: recalled to military service 08.1939, Commander of Division 159, 08.1939–08.1941, Commander of 328. Infanterie Division 08.1941–03.1942, Fuehrer Res. in O.K.H. 03.1942–09.1942, retired 09.1942. Awards: 1939 Clasps to the 1914 Iron Cross 1st and 2nd Class, Infanterie Assault Badge in Silver, Eastern Front Medal, 1914 Iron Cross 1st and 2nd Class, Cross of Honor.

Feuchtinger, Edgar: Generalleutnant (01.08.44), (Heer); born 09.11.94 in Metz, died 21.01.60 in Berlin. WWI: Leutnant in Fusilier Artillerie Regiment 212. Promotion to Generalmajor 01.08.43. Batterie Chef in Artillerie Regiment at Amberg 10.1934–12.1934, Instructor on Staff A at Artillerie Schule at Jueterbog 01.1935–10.1937, Commander of III. Abteilung. WWII: Artillerie Regiment 26, 10.1937–08.1939, Commander of Artillerie Regiment 227, 08.1939–08.1942, Commander of 21. Panzer Division 07.1943–01.945, court martialed for going AWOL 01.1945, avoided death sentence by serving as Kanonier in 20. Panzer Grenadier Division 03.1945–04.1945. Awards: Knight's Cross 06.08.44, German Cross in Silver 15.07.43, 1939 Clasps to the 1914 Iron Cross 1st and 2nd Class, War Merit Cross 1st and 2nd Class with Swords, 1914 Iron Cross 1st and 2nd Class, 1914 Wound Badge in Black, Cross of Honor.

Feurstein, Valentin: General der Gebirgstruppe (01.11.41), (Heer); born 18.01.85 in Bregenz, died 08.06.70 in Innsbrueck. WWI: Hauptmann on Staff of Section Kommando Riva. Promotions to Generalmajor 25.06.35, Generalleutnant 01.06.39. Transferred to Wehrmacht 03.1938. WWII: Commander of 2. Gebirgs Division 04.1938–03.1941, Commander of LXX. Armee Korps 05.1941–06.1943, Commander of LI. Gebirgs Korps 08.1943–03.1945. Awards: Knight's Cross 12.08.44,

1939 Iron Cross 1st and 2nd Class, Infantry Assault Badge in Silver, Heeres Bergfuehrer Badge, Cross of Honor.

Feyerabend, Gerhard: Generalleutnant (01.03.45), (Heer); born 29.04.98 in Dopsattel, died 06.11.65 in Rottach-Egern. WWI: Leutnant in Feld Artillerie Regiment 82. Promotion to Generalmajor 01.02.44. Ia to 1. Division 05.1934–10.1935, attached to Staff of Wehrkreis Kommando I 10.1935–10.1936, Chief of 4. Batterie, Artillerie Regiment 1, 10.1936–10.1937. WWII: Ia to 24. Infanterie Division 10.1937–10.1939, Ia to General of Artillerie in O.K.H. 10.1939–01.1940, Ia to XXXX. Armee Korps 02.1940–07.1940, Ia to 2. Armee 04.1941–08.1941, Chief of Staff to XXVII. Armee Korps 10.1941–07.1943, Chief of General Staff to 1. Armee 08.1943–08.1944, Commander of 11. Infanterie Division 11.1944–05.1945. Awards: Knight's Cross 05.04.45, German Cross in Gold 30.01.43, 1939 Clasps to the 1914 Iron Cross 1st and 2nd Class, Eastern Front Medal, Kurland Cuff Band, 1914 Iron Cross 1st and 2nd Class, Cross of Honor.

Feyerabend, Walter: Generalleutnant (01.04.41), (Luftwaffe); born 03.12.91 in Warten, died 15.04.62 in Detmold. WWI: Oberleutnant and Leader of Heavy Flak Batterie 149. Promotion to Generalmajor 20.04.39. Commander of Flak Abteilung 1 at Koenigsberg 04.1935–09.1935, Commander of I. Abteilung, Flak Regiment 1, 10.1935–09.1936, Commander of Flak Regiment 25, 10.1936–10.1937, Senior Commander of Flak Artillerie 1, 11.1937–09.1938, Commander of Luftverteidigungs Kommando Leipzig 09.1938–06.1939. WWII: Commander of Air Defense Kommando 2, 07.1939–04.1940, Flak Artillery Commander for Norway 04.1940–06.1941, Commander of 14. Flak Division 07.1941–11.1942, retired 11.1942. Awards: 1939 Clasps to the 1914 Iron Cross 1st and 2nd Class, Flak War Badge, 1914 Iron Cross 1st and 2nd Class, Bavarian Military Service Order IV. Class with Swords, 1914 Wound Badge in Black, Cross of Honor.

Fichte, Hans von: Generalmajor (01.04.44), (Luftwaffe); born 09.09.94 in Kassel, died 20.11.63 in Garmisch-Partenkirchen. WWI: in G.A.S. as Leutnant and Leader of Schlachtstaffel 16. Adjutant and IIa on Staff of Luftkreis Kommando II 05.1934–12.1935, attached to Fliegerstaffel Prenzlau and later Fliegergruppe 1/122, 01.1936–09.1936, Staffelkapitan to Fernaufklarungs Staffel 3/122, 10.1936–02.1937, Training Leader on Staff of Fliegerschulen 03.1937–08.1938. WWII: Adjutant and IIa to 7. Flieger Division 08.1938–12.1943, Commander of Staff Troops on Staff of Luftwaffe Kommando Northern Balkans 01.1944–11.1944. Awards: 1939 Iron Cross 1st Class, 1939 Clasp to the 1914 Iron Cross 2nd Class, War Merit Cross 1st and 2nd Class with Swords, Kreta Cuff Band, 1939 Observer's Badge, Pilot's Commemorative Badge, 1914 Iron Cross 2nd Class, Austro-Hungarian Military Service Cross 3rd Class with War Decoration, 1914 Wound Badge in Silver, 1914 Observer's Badge, Cross of Honor.

Fichtner, Sebastian: Generalleutnant (01.08.43), (Heer); born 17.06.94 in Pflugdorf, died 07.03.50 in Munich. WWI: Oberleutnant in 1. Bavarian Pionier Bataillon. Promotion to Generalmajor 01.08.42. Attached to Inspection of Transport Troops in Reichswehr Ministry (later Reich War Ministry) 08.1934–09.1937. WWII: Department Chief in Heeres Weapons Office of O.K.H. 10.1937–09.1942, Commander of 8. Panzer Division 01.1943–11.1943, Fuehrer Res. in O.K.H. 11.1943–04.1944, arrested and later released due to events stemming from 20.07.44. Awards: 1939 Clasps to the 1914 Iron Cross 1st and 2nd Class, War Merit Cross 1st and 2nd Class with Swords, Tank Assault Badge in Silver, 1914 Iron Cross 1st and 2nd Class, Cross of Honor.

Fick, Ernst: SS-Brigadefuehrer und Generalmajor der Waffen-SS (30.01.44); born 05.02.98 in Kirchdorf, died 29.04.45 in action in Berlin. P-124987, SS-2853. WWI: Vizewachtmeister attached to Gebirgs Batterie 10. Joined N.S.D.A.P. in 1929, joined S.S. in 1930. Attached to Hilfswerke "Dachau" 01.10.34, attached to R.u.S.H.A. 01.07.35, attached to Staff of R.u.S.H.A. 01.12.36, attached to SS-Fuehrer Schule at Bad Toelz 01.12.37–01.12.38. WWII: Commander of SS-Educational Training at "Sennheim" 30.01.42, Commander of SS-Schule at "Sennheim" 15.05.43, Commander of I. Abteilung, SS-Artillerie Regiment, "Wiking," Inspector of W.E. in SS-Hauptamt 30.01.44–09.11.44. Awards: 1939 Clasp to the 1914 Iron Cross 2nd Class, War Merit Cross 1st and 2nd Class with Swords, 1914 Iron Cross 2nd Class, Cross of Honor, Reich Sports Badge in Silver, SA-Sports Badge in Bronze, Degen, Ring.

Fiebig, Heinz: Generalmajor (01.12.44), (Heer); born 23.03.97 in Zaborze, died 30.03.64 in Seesen. WWI: Leutnant in Infanterie Regiment 156. Chief of 1. Kompanie, Wach Regiment Berlin 10.1934–10.1936. WWII: Instructor at Kriegsschule Dresden 11.1936–08.1939, Commander of I. Bataillon, Infanterie Regiment 192, 08.1939–11.1940, Commander of I. Bataillon, Infanterie Regiment 575, 11.1940–3.1941, Commander of Infanterie Regiment 448, 03.1941–06.1943, Commander of Waffen Schule for 4. Armee 10.1943–04.1944, Commander of 84. Infanterie Division 09.1944–05.1945. Awards: Knight's Cross 08.05.45, German Cross in Gold 28.02.42, 1939 Clasps to the 1914 Iron Cross 1st and 2nd Class, Infantry Assault Badge in Silver, Eastern Front Medal, 1914 Iron Cross 1st and 2nd Class, 1914 Wound Badge in Black, Cross of Honor.

Generalmajor Heinz Fiebig. (Bundesarchiv)

Fiebig, Martin: General der Flieger (01.03.43), (Luftwaffe); born 07.05.91 in Roesnitz, died 24.10.47 (executed) in Belgrade. WWI: in G.A.S. as Hauptmann and Staffelfuehrer in Bombengeschwader 3. Promotions to Generalmajor 01.04.41, Generalleutnant 01.04.42. Fliegerhorst Commandant of Greifswald 05.1934–1936, Commander of Kampfflieger Schule at Fassberg 1936–06.1938. WWII: Commander of K.G. 253 and later K.G. 4 "General Wever" 07.1938–05.1940, Chief of Flight Security in R.L.M. 08.1940–04.1941, Close Combat Leader with IV, II and later VIII Flieger Korps 04.1941–04.1942, Commander of VIII. Flieger Korps 07.1942–05.1943, Commander of X. Flieger Korps 05.1943–09.1944, Fuehrer Res. in O.K.L. 09.1944–01.1945, Commander of II. Flieger Korps 02.1945–04.1945. Awards: Oak Leaves 23.12.42 (168), Knight's Cross 08.05.40, German Cross in Gold 11.05.42, 1939 Clasps to the 1914 Iron Cross 1st and 2nd Class, Eastern Front Medal, Day Fighter Clasp in Gold, Combined Pilot-Observer's Badge, Pilot's Commemorative Badge, RK-Hohenzollern, 1914 Iron Cross 1st and 2nd Class, 1914 Wound Badge in Black, 1914 Observer's Badge, Cross of Honor.

Fiedler, Erich: Generalmajor (01.07.42), (Heer); born 31.03.85 in Kroeglitz, died 13.03.60 in Frankfurt am Main. WWI: Hauptmann and Commander of 142. Pionier Bataillon. Attached to Staff of Wehrkreis Kommando IV 10.1934–03.1935, attached to E-Officer Korps 03.1935–03.1939. WWII: Commander of Military District Kommando in Saarbruecken 04.1939–12.1942, Wehrmacht Commander of Koblenz 03.1943–07.1944, Fuehrer Res. in O.K.H. 07.1944–12.1944. Awards: War Merit Cross 1st and 2nd Class with Swords, 1914 Iron Cross 1st and 2nd Class, Cross of Honor.

Fiedler, Dr. Georg: General-Veterinar z.V. (01.11.42), (Heer); born 04.05.81 in Breslau, died 21.01.59 in Eckernfoerde. Medical veterinarian by profession. WWI: German Medical Service as Stabs-Veterinar in Ulan Regiment 8. WWII: Korps Veterinar to II. Armee Korps 08.1939–12.1942, retired 08.1943. Awards: War Merit Cross 1st and 2nd Class with Swords, 1914 Iron Cross 1st and 2nd Class, Cross of Honor.

Fikentscher, Prof. Dr. Alfred: Admiral-Oberststabsarzt (01.09.42), (Kriegsmarine); born 30.04.88 in Augsburg, died 10.01.79 in Kiel. Medical doctor by profession. WWI: German Medical Service as Marine Stabs-Arzt and Medic on heavy cruiser *Seydlitz*. Promotions to Admiral-Arzt 01.11.38, Admiral-Stabsarzt 0.11.39. Chief Physician at Marine Hospital in Kiel-Wik 03.1932–06.1936, Physician for Flottenkommando 06.1936–10.1938. WWII: Chief Physician to North Sea Naval Station 10.1938–11.1939, Chief of Naval Medical Office and Medical Chief of Kriegsmarine in O.K.M. 01.1940–11.1943, retired 11.1943. Awards: German Cross in Silver 21.09.43, War Merit Cross 1st and 2nd Class with Swords, 1914 Iron Cross 1st and 2nd Class, Cross of Honor.

Finger, Arthur: Generalmajor (01.10.44), (Heer); born 18.01.98 in Mocker, died 28.01.45 in action near Tschenstochau. WWI: Leutnant der Res. in Res. Feld

Artillerie Regiment 36. Attached to Staff of I. Abteilung, Artillerie Regiment at Glogau 04.1935–10.1935, Batterie Chef in Artillerie Regiment 18, 10.1935–05.1937. WWII: Instructor at Luftwaffe Kriegsschule Dresden 06.1937–09.1939, Commander of Schwere Abteilung 757, 09.1939–10.1940, Commander of Artillerie Regiment 214, 10.1940–12.1942, Commander of Artillerie Regiment 306, 02.1943–01.1944, Commander of 291. Infanterie Division 07.1944–01.1945. Awards: Knight's Cross 16.11.43, 1939 Clasps to the 1914 Iron Cross 1st and 2nd Class, General Assault Badge, 1939 Wound Badge in Black, 1914 Iron Cross 1st and 2nd Class, Cross of Honor.

Fink, Carl: Generalmajor (01.06.43), (Luftwaffe); born 16.12.86 in Berlin, died 04.04.69 in Karlsruhe. WWI: in G.A.S. as Hauptmann and Chief of Bild Abteilung in G.A.S. High Command. WWII: Advisor to Technische Amt in R.L.M. 02.1935–12.1939, Department Leader in Armaments Inspection III 12.1939–06.1941, Military Economics Commander for Oppeln and later Kharkov 06.1941–01.1942, Commander of Armaments Area Hannover 02.1942–02.1943, Armaments Inspector for Magdeburg-Dessau-Halle-Saale 03.1943–05.1945. Awards: War Merit Cross 1st and 2nd Class with Swords, Pilot's Commemorative Badge, RK-Hohenzollern, 1914 Iron Cross 1st and 2nd Class, Prussian Crown Order IV. Class with Swords, Bavarian Military Service Cross IV. Class with Swords, 1914 Observer's Badge, Cross of Honor.

Fink, Dr. Friedrich: General-Intendant (01.10.39), (Heer); born 18.04.82 in Koeslin, died 13.03.46 in Muehlberg. Administrative Officer by profession. WWI: service unknown. WWII: Chief Intendant to Wehrkreis Kommando IV (dates unknown). Awards: War Merit Cross 1st and 2nd Class with Swords, Cross of Honor.

Fink, Johannes: General der Flieger (01.04.44), (Luftwaffe); born 28.03.95 in Pfullingen, died 01.06.80 in Pfullingen. WWI: Oberleutnant and Adjutant to Infanterie Regiment 127. Promotions to Generalmajor 01.10.40, Generalleutnant 01.10.42. Staffelkapitan attached to Fliegerschule Fassberg 07.1934–03.1935, Commander of K.G. "Boelcke" 04.1935–03.1936, attached to Staff of Inspection for Flight Safety in R.L.M. 04.1936–03.1937, Inspector for Flight Safety in R.L.M. 04.1937–01.1938, assignments unknown 02.1938–10.1938. WWII: Commander of K.G. 2, 11.1938–10.1940, Inspector and General of Kampfflieger in O.K.L. 10.1940–10.1942, Commander of 2. Flieger Division 11.1942–02.1944, Commander of Luftwaffe in Greece 02.1944–09.1944, Commander

General der Flieger Johannes Fink. (Bundesarchiv)

of II. Flieger Korps 12.1944–02.1945. Awards: Knight's Cross 20.06.40, German Cross in Gold 01.10.44, 1939 Clasps to the 1914 Iron Cross 1st and 2nd Class, Bomber's Flight Clasp in Gold, 1939 Pilot's Badge, 1914 Iron Cross 1st and 2nd Class, 1914 Wound Badge in Black, Cross of Honor.

Fisch, Willy: Ministerialdirektor with the rank of General der Flieger (19.09.41); (Luftwaffe), born 12.09.86 in Berlin, died 26.07.63 in Rosenheim. Civil Servant by profession. WWI: in G.A.S. as Hauptmann and 1st Adjutant to Inspector of Fliegertruppen. WWII: Chief of General Office in R.L.M. 03.1933–05.1945. Awards: War Merit Cross 1st and 2nd Class with Swords, Pilot's Commemorative Badge, RK-Sachsen Ernestine House Order 1st Class with Swords, RK-Sachsen Albrecht Order 2nd Class with Swords, 1914 Iron Cross 1st and 2nd Class, Prussian Crown Order IV. Class with Swords, Bavarian Military Service Cross IV. Class with Swords, Austro-Hungarian Military Service Cross 3rd Class with War Decoration, 1914 Pilot's Badge, Cross of Honor.

Fischel, Hermann von: Admiral (01.09.41), (Kriegsmarine); born 13.01.87 in Kiel, died 13.05.50 at Budirka P.O.W. Camp in Moscow. WWI: U-boat service as Kapitanleutnant and Commandant of *U-65*. Promotions to Konteradmiral 01.10.35, Vizeadmiral 01.04.38. Commandant of battleship *Deutschland* 04.1933–09.1935, Chairman of Testing Kommando for Surface Ships 09.1935–09.1936, Befehlshaber of Battleships 11.1936–02.1938 and at same time Befehlshaber of Surface Ships in Spain 12.1936–03.1938. WWII: Chief of General Naval Office in O.K.M. 04.1938–10.1939, Chief of Test Command of Warship Construction in O.K.M. 01.1940–01.1941, Naval Commander for Channel Coast 02.1941–05.1943, Director of Luftwaffe Instruction Staff 06.1943–09.1944, retired 11.1944. Awards: German Cross in Gold 25.05.43, 1939 Clasps to the 1914 Iron Cross 1st and 2nd Class, Coastal Artillery War Badge, Spanish Cross in Gold with Swords, Grand Cross of the Spanish Order for Service, Spanish War Cross (Spain), Silesian Eagle 1st and 2nd Class, RK-Hohenzollern, 1914 Iron Cross 1st and 2nd Class, Oldenburg Friedrich-August Cross 1st and 2nd Class, Austro-Hungarian Military Service Cross 3rd Class with War Decoration, Turkish Half Moon, 1914 Submarine Badge, Cross of Honor.

Admiral Hermann von Fischel. (Bundesarchiv)

Fischer, Adolf: Generalmajor (01.07.44), (Heer); born 23.07.93 in Schwerte, died 23.10.47 (executed) in Belgrade. WWI: Leutnant der Res. in Landwehr Infanterie Regiment 110. WWII: Commander of I. Bataillon, Infanterie Regiment 88,

10.1936–06.1940, Commander of Infanterie Regiment 459, 06.1940–10.1943, Commander of 367. Infanterie Division 05.1944–08.1944, Commander of Kampfgruppe "Sud-Ost" 09.1944–05.1945. Awards: Knight's Cross 04.05.44, German Cross in Gold 19.01.42, 1939 Clasps to the 1914 Iron Cross 1st and 2nd Class, Infantry Assault Badge in Silver, Eastern Front Medal, 1939 Wound Badge in Black, 1914 Iron Cross 1st and 2nd Class, 1914 Wound Badge in Black, Cross of Honor.

Fischer, Eberhard: Generalmajor (01.06.42), (Luftwaffe); born 24.06.93 in Carolath, died 02.09.62. WWI: in G.A.S. as Oberleutnant in Flieger Abteilung A 218. Leader of Main Photo Office in R.L.M. 02.1934–06.1935, Commander of Flieger Bild Schule at Hildesheim 10.1935–02.1937, Fliegerhorst Commandant of Kassel-Rothwesten 03.1937–12.1938. WWII: Course Commander at Luftwaffe Kriegsschule in Berlin-Gatow 01.1939–01.1940, Commander of Flieger Bild Schule Hildesheim and Fliegerhorst Commandant 02.1940–12.1944. Awards: War Merit Cross 1st and 2nd Class with Swords, Silesian Eagle 2nd Class, Pilot's Commemorative Badge, 1914 Iron Cross 1st and 2nd Class, 1914 Wound Badge in Black, 1914 Observer's Badge, Cross of Honor.

Fischer, Gerhard: Generalmajor (01.06.44), (Heer); born 16.05.94 in Greifenberg, died 24.03.67 in Gielgen. WWI: Leutnant in Infanterie Regiment 42. Kompanie Chef in Infanterie Regiment at Stettin 10.1934–10.1935, Commander of I. Bataillon, Infanterie Regiment 18, 10.1935–10.1936. WWII: Commander of II. Bataillon, Infanterie Regiment 80, 10.1936–08.1939, Commander of Infanterie Replacement Regiment 34, 08.1939–04.1940, Commander of Infanterie Regiment 478, 04.1940–02.1941, Fuehrer Res. in O.K.H. 02.1941–09.1941, attached to Wehrkreis Kommando XII 01.1942–03.1945. Awards: 1939 Clasps to the 1914 Iron Cross 1st and 2nd Class, Infantry Assault Badge in Silver, 1914 Iron Cross 1st and 2nd Class, 1914 Wound Badge in Black, Cross of Honor.

Fischer, Gotthard: Generalleutnant (01.09.44), (Heer); born 10.01.91 in Goldap, died 27.07.69 in Flensburg. WWI: Hauptmann on Staff of 12. Res. Division. Promotion to Generalmajor 01.03.44. Commander of Military District Kommando at Angerburg 10.1934–09.1936, attached to Staff of I. Abteilung, Artillerie Regiment 37, 10.1936–09.1937, Batterie Chef in Artillerie Regiment 57, 10.1937–06.1938. WWII: Commander of I. Abteilung, Artillerie Regiment 47, 07.1938–04.1940, Commander of Artillerie Regiment 21, 04.1940–02.1942, Commander of Artillerie 123, 02.1942–08.1943, Commander of 126. Infanterie Division 12.1943–01.1945, Senior Commander of Artillerie 303, 01.1945–05.1945. Awards: Knight's Cross 07.02.44, German Cross in Gold 29.01.42, 1939 Clasps to the 1914 Iron Cross 1st and 2nd Class, General Assault Badge Eastern Front Medal, 1914 Iron Cross 1st and 2nd Class, Cross of Honor.

Fischer, Hans: General-Engineer (01.04.42), (Luftwaffe); born 31.01.95 in Regensburg, died 02.04.43 from air accident over Riga. Engineer by profession. WWI: in G.A.S. as Leutnant der Res. and later transferred to Infanterie. Technical Leader for Fliegerhorst Celle 03.1934–02.1935, First Advisor attached to Inspection of Seeflieger in Kiel 03.1935–09.1938, Chief Engineer to Luftgau Kommando VI 09.1938–07.1939. WWII: Engineer to Luftgau III 08.1939–02.1940, Engineer to Luftgau Kommando XI. 02.1940–11.1941, Chief Engineer to Luftflotte 1, 12.1941–04.1943. Awards: War Merit Cross 1st and 2nd Class with Swords, 1939 Wound Badge in Gold, Pilot's Commemorative Badge, 1914 Iron Cross 1st and 2nd Class, 1914 Pilot's Badge, Cross of Honor.

Fischer, Herbert: Generalleutnant (01.12.35), (Heer); born 12.10.82 in Stuttgart, died 23.10.39 in Berlin. WWI: Hauptmann attached to Turkish Armee. Promotion to Reichswehr Generalmajor 01.04.34. Military Attaché in Budapest 04.1933–10.1936, Commander of 31. Division 10.1936–04.1937, attached to O.B. des Heeres 04.1937, retired 10.1937. Awards: 1914 Iron Cross 1st and 2nd Class, Cross of Honor.

Fischer, Hermann: Generalleutnant (01.04.43), (Heer); born 19.02.94 in Ostheim, died 12.03.68 in Bonn. WWI: Oberleutnant in Infanterie Regiment 32. Promotion to Generalmajor 01.04.44. Commander of III. Bataillon, Infanterie Regiment 39, 10.1934–10.1936. WWII: Commander of III. Bataillon, Infanterie Regiment 77, 10.1936–12.1939, Commander of Infanterie Regiment 340, 12.1939–03.1942, Commander of 181. Infanterie Division 03.1942–10.1944, Commandant of Feldkommandantur for 16. Armee 11.1944–05.1945. Awards: Knight's Cross 09.05.40, 1939 Clasps to the 1914 Iron Cross 1st and 2nd Class, Infantry Assault Badge in Silver, Eastern Front Medal, Kurland Cuff Band, Baltic Cross 1st and 2nd Class, 1914 Iron Cross 1st and 2nd Class, 1914 Wound Badge in Black, Cross of Honor.

Fischer, Karl: Generalmajor (01.04.41), (Heer); born 21.09.76 in Nuremberg, died 04.12.57 in Jungen. WWI: Major and Adjutant to I. Bavarian Armee Korps. WWII: Director of Wehrkreis-Fursorge-und Versorgungs Abteilung for Wehrkreis Kommando VII 07.1933–04.1942, retired 07.1942. Awards: War Merit Cross 1st and 2nd Class with Swords, RK-Hohenzollern, 1914 Iron Cross 1st and 2nd Class, Cross of Honor.

Fischer, Karl: Generalmajor (01.03.42), (Heer); born 28.09.91 in Bornstadt, died 31.03.42 in action outside of Moscow. WWI: Oberleutnant in Fusilier Artillerie Regiment 15. Artillerie Department Commander at Braunsberg 10.1933–09.1935, Commander of Beobachter Abteilung 3, 10.1935–03.1937. WWII: Commander of Instruction Staff B at Artillerie Schule 04.1937–11.1939, Commander of Artillerie Regiment 76, 11.1939–02.1940, Commander of Artillerie Regiment Staff 677, 02.1940–10.1940, Commander of Artillerie 101, 10.1940–01.1942, Commander of 267. Infanterie Division 01.1942–03.1942. Awards: 1939 Clasps to the 1914 Iron Cross 1st and 2nd Class, General Assault Badge, 1939 Wound Badge in Gold, 1914 Iron Cross 1st and 2nd Class, Cross of Honor.

Fischer, Kurt: Generalleutnant z.V. (01.02.42), (Heer); born 16.08.77 in Berlin, died 08.01.47 in Wiesbaden. WWI: Major on Staff of 3. Guards Infanterie Division. Promotion to Reichswehr Generalmajor 01.04.29. Recalled to military service 07.1938. WWII: Commander of Supply Truppen XII 08.1939–11.1939, Commander of 172. Infanterie Division 11.1939–12.1942, retired 04.1943. Awards: 1939 Clasps to the 1914 Iron Cross 1st and 2nd Class, Infantry Assault Badge in Silver, RK-Hohenzollern, 1914 Iron Cross 1st and 2nd Class, Cross of Honor.

Fischer, Theodor: Generalmajor (01.8.42), (Heer); born19.12.88 in Stuhm, died 01.04.49 in hospital in Belgrade. WWI: Hauptmann and Commander of II. Bataillon, Infanterie Regiment 115. Attached to Staff of Infanterie Regiment 30, 10.1935–03.1936, Commander of I. Bataillon, Infanterie Regiment 1, 04.1936–03.1937, attached to Staff of Infanterie Regiment 57, 03.1937–05.1938, attached to Command Staff of Landwehr Commander of Muelheim 06.1938–11.1938. WWII: Training Leader for Rheydt 11.1938–08.1939, Commander of Infanterie Regiment 328, 08.1939–07.1942, Commandant of Feldkommandantur 610, 09.1942–01.1944, Commandant of Feldkommandantur 550, 05.1944–08.1944, attached to Staff of A.O.K. 8, 09.1944–05.1945. Awards: 1939 Clasps to the 1914 Iron Cross 1st and 2nd Class, Infantry Assault Badge in Silver, Eastern Front Medal, 1914 Iron Cross 1st and 2nd Class, Cross of Honor.

Fischer, Veit: General der Flieger (01.06.42), (Luftwaffe); born 18.05.90 in Landshut, died 30.10.66 (suicide) in Prien. WWI: in G.A.S. as Oberleutnant in Flieger Abteilung 304 b. Promotions to Generalmajor 01.01.39, Generalleutnant 01.12.40. Commander of Luftwaffe Fliegerschule at Perleberg und Gotha 04.1935–03.1936, Commander of Luftwaffe Fliegerschule at Neuruppin 04.1936–02.1937, Higher Training Commander III 03.1937–09.1937. WWII: Inspector of Luftwaffe Fliegerschulen in R.L.M. 10.1937–02.1941, Commander of Special Purpose Air Region Staff 1, 04.1941–10.1941, Commander of Luftgau Moscow 10.1941–03.1943, Commander of Feld Luftgau XXVII Minsk 04.1943–08.1944, Commander of Luftgau Kommando VIII, Breslau then Prague 08.1944–05.1945. Awards: Knight's Cross of the War Merit Cross with Swords 15.07.44, German Cross in Silver 03.12.42, War Merit Cross 1st and 2nd Class with Swords, Eastern Front Medal, Combined Pilot-Observer's Badge, Pilot's Commemorative Badge, RK-Hohenzollern, 1914 Iron Cross 1st and 2nd Class, Bavarian Military Service Order IV. Class with Swords, Turkish Silver Liakat Medal with Sabre, Turkish Half Moon, 1914 Wound Badge in Black, 1914 Observer's Badge, Cross of Honor.

Fischer, Dr. Walter: General-Richter (01.05.44), (Luftwaffe); born 17.07.90 in Mannheim, died 03.04.61 in Ulm. Jurist by profession. WWI: in G.A.S. and later Infanterie as Unteroffizier (units unknown). War Legal Official attached to Luftwaffe Kommando V in Munich 11.1935–02.1937, Assistant to Reich War Attorney's Office in Berlin 02.1937–03.1939. WWII: Senior War Legal Official in Reichs War Court 04.1939–03.1944, Attorney at Reichs War Court 03.1944–05.1945. Awards: War Merit Cross 1st and 2nd Class with Swords, 1914 Iron Cross 2nd Class, Cross of Honor.

Fischer, Dr. Walter: General-Veterinar (1945), (Heer); born 22.12.88 in Erfurt, died 27.01.46 in British P.O.W. camp. Medical veterinarian by profession. WWI: Ober-Veterinar (unit unknown). WWII: Division Veterinar to 28. Infanterie Division 05.1940–date unknown, Leitender Veterinar to Security District Alpenvorland (dates unknown). Awards: War Merit Cross 1st and 2nd Class with Swords, 1914 Iron Cross 1st and 2nd Class, Cross of Honor.

Fischer, Wolfgang: General der Panzertruppe (01.02.43), (Heer); born 11.12.88 in Carolath, died 05.02.43 in action in Tunisia. WWI: Hauptmann and Adjutant to 22. Landwehr Infanterie Brigade. Promotions to Generalmajor 01.08.41, Generalleutnant 01.11.42. Bataillon Commander in Infanterie Regiment 46, 10.1934–09.1937, attached to Staff of Infanterie Regiment 69, 10.1937–01.1938. WWII: Commander of Infanterie Regiment 69, 02.1938–10.1939, Commander of 10. Schuetzen Brigade 10.1939–08.1941, Commander of 10. Panzer Division 08.1941–02.1943. Awards: Oak Leaves 09.12.42 (152), Knight's Cross 03.06.40, German Cross in Gold 22.04.42, 1939 Clasps to the 1914 Iron Cross 1st and 2nd Class, Tank Assault Badge in Silver, Eastern Front Medal, 1939 Wound Badge in Gold, 1914 Iron Cross 1st and 2nd Class, Cross of Honor.

Fischer von Weikersthal, Walther: General der Infanterie (01.12.41), (Heer); born 15.09.90 in Stuttgart, died 11.02.53 in Stuttgart. WWI: Hauptmann and Adjutant to Grenadier Regiment 119. Promotions to Generalmajor 01.03.38, Generalleutnant 01.04.40. Commander of I. Bataillon, Infanterie Regiment at Ludwigsburg 10.1934–10.1935, Commander of Infanterie Regiment 9, 10.1935–10.1936. WWII: Chief of Staff to V. Armee Korps 10.1936–08.1939, Chief of General Staff to 7. Armee 08.1939–11.1940, Commander of 35. Infanterie Division 11.1940–12.1941, Fuehrer Res. in O.K.H. 03.1942–09.1942, Commander of LXVII. Armee Korps 09.1942–07.1944, Fuehrer Res. in O.K.H. 07.1944–03.1945. Awards: Knight's Cross 06.08.41, 1939 Clasps to the 1914 Iron Cross 1st and 2nd Class, Infantry Assault Badge in Silver, Eastern Front Medal, 1914 Iron Cross 1st and 2nd Class, 1914 Wound Badge in Black, Cross of Honor.

Fisser, Dr. Johann-Volkmar: Generalmajor (10.11.44), (Luftwaffe); born 02.07.93 in Dresden, died 12.08.40 in action over Isle of Wight. WWI: in G.A.S. as Oberleutnant in Flieger Abteilung 3. Adjutant on Staff of Jet Propelled Flieger Office Kommando 07.1934–01.1935, instructor at Beobachter Schule in Hildesheim 03.1935–06.1935, Staffelkapitan in K.G. 255, 06.1935–09.1936, Gruppen Commander in K.G. 255, 10.1936–01.1939. WWII: Commander of K.G. 255, 02.1939–08.1939, Commander of K.G. 51, 09.1939–08.1940, member of N.S.D.A.P. Awards: 1939 Clasps to the 1914 Iron Cross 1st and 2nd Class, 1939 Wound Badge in Gold, 1939 Pilot's Badge, Pilot's Commemorative Badge, RK-Hohenzollern, RK-Sachsen Order of the White Falcon 2nd Class with Swords, 1914 Iron Cross 1st and 2nd Class, Austro-Hungarian Military Service Cross 3rd Class with War Decoration, 1914 Observer's Badge, Cross of Honor.

Fitzau, Erich-Erdmann: Generalmajor (01.03.44), (Luftwaffe); born 31.05.96 in Koethen, died 07.10.53 in Ebersteinburg. WWI: in G.A.S. as Leutnant in Flieger Abteilung 261. Instructor at Luftwaffe Kriegsschule Eiche 08.1935–04.1936, Staffelkapitan in Fliegergruppe I/153 in Merseburg 07.1936–02.1937, Fliegerhorst Commandant of Merseburg 03.1937–03.1939. WWII: attached to Staff of 1. Flieger Division 04.1939–09.1939, attached to Staff of I. Flieger Korps 10.1939–08.1940, Commander of Acceptance Office 4 for Luftwaffe Officer Candidates 08.1940–11.1941, Advisor in L In 10 of R.L.M. 11.1941–1942, Commander of Luftwaffe Kriegsschule 9, 1942–11.1943, Flughafenbereichs Commandant in Finland 11.1943–03.1945. Awards: 1939 Clasps to the 1914 Iron Cross 1st and 2nd Class, 1939 Pilot's Badge, Pilot's Commemorative Badge, 1914 Iron Cross 1st and 2nd Class, 1914 Wound Badge in Black, 1914 Pilot's Badge, Cross of Honor.

Fitze, Georg: Generalmajor (30.01.45), (Luftwaffe); born 05.09.96 in Brostau, died 13.12.68 in Furstenfeldbruck. WWI: in G.A.S. as Leutnant der Res. (unit unknown). Attached to Staff of Luftkreis Kommando IV 08.1935–03.1938, IIb on Staff of Luftwaffen Kommando Osterreich 04.1938–03.1939. WWII: attached to O.B. der Luftwaffe 04.1939–08.1939, Gruppen Commander in S.G. 2, 10.1939–12.1939, Commandant of A-B Fliegerschule and Luftwaffe Kriegsschule 4, 12.1939–09.1940, Commander of Air Base at Neuhausen 10.1940–1942, Commander of Flieger Replacement Bataillon III 1942–03.1945. Awards: 1939 Clasps to the 1914 Iron Cross 1st and 2nd Class, 1939 Pilot's Badge, Pilot's Commemorative Badge, 1914 Iron Cross 1st and 2nd Class, 1914 Pilot's Badge, Cross of Honor.

Fitzlaff, Hans: Generalmajor (01.01.43), (Heer); born 02.09.92 in Thorn, died 22.04.80 in Forbach. WWI: Oberleutnant attached to Artillerie Beobachter Schule at Wahn. Commander of IV. Abteilung, Artillerie Regiment at Elbing 10.1934–10.1935, Commander of I. Abteilung, Artillerie Regiment 57, 10.1935–11.1938.

WWII: Commander of Artillerie Regiment 29 (mot.) 11.1938–03.1940, attached to Artillerie Staff of 9. Armee 05.1940–10.1941, Commander of Feld N.C.O. Artillerie Schule at Autun 04.1942–04.1943, Military Replacement Inspector for Kassel 06.1943–05.1945. Awards: 1939 Clasps to the 1914 Iron Cross 1st and 2nd Class, General Assault Badge, 1914 Iron Cross 1st and 2nd Class, Cross of Honor.

Fitzler, Dr. Ernst: Admiral-Intendant (01.05.44), (Kriegsmarine); born 16.08.93 in Elsterwerda, died 24.06.71 in Bad Neuenahr. Administrative Officer by profession. WWI: service unknown. WWII: Chief of Accommodation Settlement Department in O.K.M. 11.1939–06.1943, Chief of Upper Administration Staff to Marine Kommando North Sea 06.1943–05.1945. Awards: War Merit Cross 1st and 2nd Class with Swords, Cross of Honor.

Fitzthum, Josef: SS-Gruppenfuehrer und Generalleutnant der Waffen-SS und Polizei (01.08.44); born 14.09.96 in Loimersdorf, died 10.01.45 from automobile accident in Wien-Neudorf. P-363169, SS-41936. WWI: Air Service as Oberleutnant and Leader of Austrian Flieger Kompanie 17. Joined N.S.D.A.P. in 1930, joined S.S. in 1932. Promotion to SS-Brigadefuehrer 30.10.43. Leader on Staff of SS-Sammelstelle 01.12.36, attached to SD-Hauptamt 01.12.37–01.12.38. WWII: Commander of I. Bataillon, SS-Infanterie Regiment 4, Deputy Commander of 2. SS-Infanterie Brigade (mot.), attached to R.S.H.A. 30.01.42, Commander of SS-Freiwilligen Legion "Nederland" 15.05.43, H.S.S.P.F. for Albania 30.01.44–09.11.44, Member of Reichstag (Land Osterreich). Awards: Blood Order (honorary), German Cross in Gold 24.08.43, 1939 Iron Cross 1st and 2nd Class, War Merit Cross 2nd Class with Swords, 1914 Wound Badge in Black, 1914 Austrian Observer's Badge, Cross of Honor, SA-Sports Badge in Bronze, German Horseman's Badge in Bronze, Degen, Ring.

Flegel, Dr. Max: Vizeadmiral (30.09.42), (Kriegsmarine); born 24.03.78 in Jena, died 04.05.56 in Jenz. Jurist by profession. WWI: Court Official on Staff of II. Naval Division. Promotion to Konteradmiral (date unknown). WWII: Advisor with Reichs War Court in O.K.W. 10.1936–11.1942, retired 09.1942. Awards: War Merit Cross 1st and 2nd Class with Swords, 1914 Iron Cross 1st and 2nd Class, Cross of Honor.

Fleischer, Friedrich-Wilhelm: Admiral (01.09.42), (Kriegsmarine); born 14.09.90 in Hanua, died 13.02.52 in Norden. WWI: Oberleutnant zur See and torpedo boat Commandant. Promotions to Konteradmiral 01.04.39, Vizeadmiral 01.04.41. Advisor in Abwehr Abteilung of Reich War Ministry 06.1932–09.1934, Chief of Marine Organizational Department in Marineleitung (later O.K.M.) 09.1934–09.1937, Commandant of line ship *Schlesien* 10.1937–08.1938, Naval Fortress Commandant of Pillau 08.1938–04.1939. WWII: Coastal Commander for Eastern Baltic Sea 04.1939–01.1940, Admiral of Black Sea 07.1941–05.1942, Senior Shipyard Director at Wilhelmshaven 09.1942–10.1944, retired 12.1944. Awards: German Cross in Silver 29.09.44, 1939 Clasps to the 1914 Iron Cross 1st and 2nd Class, War Merit Cross 1st and 2nd Class with Swords, Grand Cross of the Romanian Order of the Crown with Swords, Romanian Order of Michael the Brave 3rd Class, 1914 Iron Cross 1st and 2nd Class, 1914 Naval Wound Badge in Black, Cross of Honor.

Floerke, Hermann: Generalleutnant (01.12.43), (Heer); born 23.10.93 in Hannover, died 19.08.79 in Giessen. WWI: Leutnant in Infanterie Regiment 74. Promotion to Generalmajor 01.06.43. Kompanie Chef in Infanterie Regiment at Breslau 10.1934–03.1935, attached to Inspection of Kriegsschulen in Reich War Ministry (later O.K.H.) 04.1935–02.1939. WWII: Commander of I. Bataillon, Infanterie Regiment 53, 03.1939–02.1940, Commander of Infanterie Regiment 53, 02.1940–03.1941, Commander of Infanterie Regiment 12, 01.1942–12.1942, Commander of 14. Infanterie Division 06.1943–12.1944, Fuehrer Res. in O.K.H. 12.1944–04.1945. Awards: Oak Leaves 02.09.44 (565), Knight's Cross 15.12.43, German Cross in Gold 23.10.42, 1939 Clasps to the 1914 Iron Cross 1st and 2nd Class, Infantry Assault Badge in Silver, Eastern Front Medal, RK-Hohenzollern, 1914 Iron Cross 1st and 2nd Class, 1914 Wound Badge in Black, Cross of Honor.

Foehrenbach, Max: General der Artillerie (01.09.40), (Heer); born 12.04.72 in Rastatt, died 26.06.42 of natural causes in Freiburg. WWI: Oberstleutnant and Commander of Feld Artillerie Regiment 107. Promotions to Reichswehr Generalmajor 01.01.25, Reichswehr Generalleutnant 01.05.27. WWII: recalled to military service 05.1940, Commander of Wehrkreis II 05.1940–04.1942, Fuehrer Res. in O.K.H. 05.1942–06.1942. Awards: War Merit Cross 1st and 2nd Class with Swords, RK-Hohenzollern, Prussian Red Eagle Order IV Class, 1914 Iron Cross 1st and 2nd Class, Cross of Honor.

Foelkersamb, Hans-Henning Freiherr von: Generalmajor (01.04.44), (Luftwaffe); born 25.11.89 in Metz, died 05.01.84 in Tutzing. WWI: Hauptman on Staff of Austrian Railway Line Kommando Intelligence Officer (Ic) attached to Senior Luftwaffe Office in Muenster 11.1934–03.1935, WWII: Ic attached to Staff of Luftkreis (later Luftgau) Kommando VI in Muenster 04.1935–11.1941, Ic for Luftgau II 12.1941–11.1942, Chief of Military Support in Abschnitten Norway, the West, North Africa, the Balkans and Eastern Front of R.L.M. 11.1942–05.1944, Department Chief in Personnel Armaments and N.S. Operations of R.L.M. 06.1944–11.1944, Fuehrer Res. in O.K.L. 11.1944–04.1945. Awards: 1939 Clasps to the 1914 Iron Cross 1st and 2nd Class, RK-Baden Order of the Zaehringer Lion 2nd Class with Swords, 1914 Iron Cross 1st and 2nd Class, Austro-Hungarian Military Service Cross 3rd Class with War Decoration, 1914 Wound Badge in Black, Cross of Honor.

Foelsch, Dr. Wilfried: General-Arzt (01.01.45), (Heer); born 24.12.97 in Berlin, died 08.02.67 in Luebeck. Medical doctor by profession. WWI: service unknown. WWII: Division Physician to 61. Infanterie Division 08.1939–12.1940, Chief of Personnel Department of Heeres Medical Inspection in O.K.H. 03.1941–10.1944, Army Physician to 4. Armee 10.1944–05.1945. Awards: War Merit Cross 1st and 2nd Class with Swords, 1914 Iron Cross 2nd Class, Cross of Honor.

Foerste, Erich: Admiral (01.03.43), (Kriegsmarine); born 11.02.92 in Magdeburg, died 10.07.63 in Kiel. WWI: U-boat service as Oberleutnant zur See and Kommandant of *U-34*. Promotions to Konteradmiral 01.11.39, Vizeadmiral 01.09.41. Advisor in Marine Household Department of Marineleitung 10.1931–09.1934, Chief of Marine Household Department in Marineleitung (later O.K.M.) 09.1934–09.1937, Commandant of cruiser *Karlsruhe* 09.1937–05.1938. WWII: Commander of battleship *Gneisenau* 05.1938–11.1939, Chief of Central Department at Kiel Shipyard 12.1939–02.1941, Chief of Shipyard at Wilhelmshaven 02.1941–09.1941, Admiral of Aegean Sea 09.1941–02.1943, Befehlshaber of Marine Gruppen Kommando North Sea 06.1943–05.1945. Awards: German Cross in Gold 25.05.43, 1939 Clasps to the 1914 Iron Cross 1st and 2nd Class, Silesian Eagle 2nd Class, RK-Sachsen Albrecht Order 2nd Class with Swords, 1914 Iron Cross 1st and 2nd Class, 1914 Naval Wound Badge in Black, 1914 Submarine Badge, Cross of Honor.

Foerster, Helmuth: General der Flieger (19.04.41), (Luftwaffe); born 19.04.89 in Gross-Strehlitz, died 07.04.65 in Lenggries. WWI: in G.A.S. as Hauptman on Staff of Befehshaber of G.A.S. Promotions to Generalmajor 01.02.38, Generalleutnant 01.01.40. Chief of Staff to Senior Luftwaffe Office in Koenigsberg 04.1934–03.1935, Chief of Staff to Luftkreis Kommando I in Koenigsberg 04.1935–07.1935, Commander of K.G. 253 "General Wever" 08.1935–1937, Commander of Lehr Truppen of Luftwaffe 1937–01.1938. WWII: Commander of Lehr Division of Luftwaffe 02.1938–09.1939, attached to State Secretary of Aviation and General Inspector of Luftwaffe Generaloberst Milch 10.1939–04.1940, Chief of General Staff to Luftflotte 5, 04.1940–06.1940, Commander of I. Flieger Korps 06.1941–08.1942, Chief of Air Defense in R.L.M. 08.1942–07.1944, Chief of Air Transport in R.L.M. 08.1944–05.1945. Awards: Knight's Cross 22.02.42, 1939 Clasps to the 1914 Iron Cross 1st and 2nd Class, Combined Pilot/Observer's Badge, Pilot's Commemorative Badge, RK-Hohenzollern, RK-Sachsen Order of the White Falcon 2nd Class with Swords, 1914 Iron Cross 1st and 2nd Class, Prussian Crown Order IV. Class with Swords, Austro-Hungarian Military Service Cross 3rd Class with War Decoration, 1914 Pilot's Badge, Cross of Honor.

Foerster, Otto-Wilhelm: General der Pioniere (01.04.38), (Heer); born 16.03.85 in Illmenau, died 24.06.66 in Walsrode. WWI: Hauptmann on Staff of 103. Infanterie

Division. Promotions to Reichswehr Generalmajor 01.10.34, Generalleutnant 01.01.37. Inspector of Pionier and Fortresses in Reichswehr Ministry (later Reich War Ministry) 02.1933–11.1938. WWII: Commander of VI. Armee Korps 11.1938–12.1941, Fuehrer Res. in O.K.H. 01.1942–1.1944, retired 01.1944. Awards: Knight's Cross 23.08.41, 1939 Clasps to the 1914 Iron Cross 1st and 2nd Class, Infantry Assault Badge in Silver, RK-Hohenzollern, 1914 Iron Cross 1st and 2nd Class, Cross of Honor.

Foerster, Richard: Admiral (01.12.35), (Kriegsmarine); born 31.03.79 in Stralsund, died 09.04.52 in Berlin. WWI: Korvettenkapitan and Department Chief in Weapons Office. Promotions to Reichsmarine Konteradmiral 01.12.28, Reichsmarine Vizeadmiral 01.10.32. Chief of Marine Station North Sea 09.1932–09.1933, Flottenchef 09.1933–12.1936. WWII: no service 01.1937–05.1945. Awards: Grand Cross of the Hungarian Service Order, 1914 Iron Cross 1st and 2nd Class, Oldenburg Friedrich-August Cross 1st and 2nd Class, Austro-Hungarian Military Service Cross 3rd Class with War Decoration, Cross of Honor.

Foerster, Sigismund von: General der Infanterie (01.05.43), (Heer); born 23.06.87 in Sonderburg, died 12.01.59 in Bremen. WWI: Hauptmann attached to Armee General Staff. Promotions to Generalmajor 01.08.36, Generalleutnant 01.04.38. Commander of Grenz Abschnitte Kommando Deutsch-Krone 10.1934–10.1935, Commander of Heeres Service Office 2 at Deutsch-Krone 10.1935–12.1935, Military Replacement Inspector of Erfurt 01.1936–03.1938, attached to Formation Staff of 24. Division 04.1938–11.1938. WWII: Commander of 26. Infanterie Division 11.1938–01.1941, Commander of 97. Light Division 01.1941–04.1941, attached to Staff of Heeresgruppe Sud 10.1941–11.1942, Wehrmacht Commander of West Taurida 05.1943–02.1944, Commander of LXXII. Special Purpose Armee Korps 02.1944–09.1944, Commander of A.O.K. Niederrhein (Northern Rhein) 09.1944–04.1945. Awards: German Cross in Gold 22.07.43, 1939 Clasps to the 1914 Iron Cross 1st and 2nd Class, Infantry Assault Badge in Silver, Eastern Front Medal, RK-Hohenzollern, 1914 Iron Cross 1st and 2nd Class, Cross of Honor.

Foerster, Prof. Wolfgang: Ministerialdirigent (01.04.37), (Heer); born 04.08.75 in Breslau, died 14.10.63 in Irschenahusen. Civil Servant by profession. WWI: Major and Chief of Staff to XI. Armee Korps. President of Heeres War History Research Institute 05.1937–05.1945. Awards: War Merit Cross 1st and 2nd Class with Swords, 1914 Iron Cross 1st and 2nd Class, Cross of Honor.

Foertsch, Friedrich: Generalleutnant (01.03.45), (Heer); born 19.05.00 in Drahnow, died 14.12.76 in Goslar. WWI: Fahnenjunker in Infanterie Regiment 175. Promotion to Generalmajor 01.06.44. Attached to Command Staff at Kriegsschule 10.1932–1935, attached to Command Staff of Commander of Koenigsberg

04.1935–09.1937, Kompanie Chef in Infanterie Regiment 81, 10.1937–09.1938. WWII: attached to Staff of III. Armee Korps 10.1938–10.1939, Ia to 60. Infanterie Division 10.1939–07.1940, Group Leader I in O.K.H. 10.1940–06.1942, Ia to 18. Armee 06.1942–12.1943, Chief of General Staff to 18. Armee 12.1943–01.1945, Chief of General Staff to Heeresgruppe Kurland 01.1945–05.1945. Awards: Knight's Cross 05.09.44, German Cross in Gold 10.05.43, 1939 Iron Cross 1st Class, 1939 Clasp to the 1914 Iron Cross 2nd Class, Kurland Cuff Band, 1914 Iron Cross 2nd Class, Cross of Honor.

Foertsch, Hermann: General der Infanterie (01.11.44), (Heer); born 04.04.95 in Drahnow, died 27.12.61 in Munich. Brother of Generalleutnant Friedrich Foertsch. WWI: Oberleutnant in 7. Assault Bataillon. Promotions to Generalmajor 01.02.42, Generalleutnant 01.01.43. Chief of the Home Intelligence Department of the Reichswehr Ministry (later Reich War Ministry) 08.1932–10.1935, Commander of IV. Bataillon, Infanterie Regiment 4, 10.1935–10.1936. WWII: Tactics Instructor at Kriegsschule 10.1936–08.1939, Chief of Staff to Wehrkreis VIII 08.1939–10.1939, Chief of Staff to XXVI. Armee Korps 10.1939–09.1940, Commander of General Staff Courses in Berlin 10.1940–05.1941, Chief of General Staff to 12. Armee 05.1941–12.1942, Chief of General Staff to Heeresgruppe E 01.1943–08.1943, Chief of General Staff to Heeresgruppe F 08.1943–03.1944, Commander of 21. Infanterie Division 03.1944–08.1944, Commander of X. Armee Korps 09.1944–12.1944. Awards: Knight's Cross 27.08.44, German Cross in Gold 10.07.43, 1939 Clasps to the 1914 Iron Cross 1st and 2nd Class, Infantry Assault Badge in Silver, RK-Hohenzollern, 1914 Iron Cross 1st and 2nd Class, 1914 Wound Badge in Black, Cross of Honor.

Folttmann, Josef: Generalleutnant (01.02.41), (Heer); born 18.01.87 in Breslau, died 11.04.58 in Aachen. WWI: Hauptmann on Staff of 5. Guards Infanterie Division. Promotion to Generalmajor 01.04.39. Commander of III. Bataillon, Infanterie Regiment at Goerlitz 10.1934–10.1935, Commander of Infanterie Regiment 52, 10.1935–11.1938, Commander of Infanterie Regiment 103, 11.1938–04.1939. WWII: Inspector of Personnel Test Affairs in O.K.H. 05.1939–09.1939, Commander of 256. Infanterie Division 09.1939–01.1940, Commander of 164. Infanterie Division 01.1940–01.1942, Commander of Fortress Division "Crete" 01.1942–08.1942, Commander of 338. Infanterie Division 11.1942–01.1944, Chief of Special Purpose Staff III in O.K.H. 01.1944–04.1945. Awards: German Cross in Silver 10.03.44, 1939 Clasps to the 1914 Iron Cross 1st and 2nd Class, War Merit Cross 1st and 2nd Class with Swords, Infantry Assault Badge in Silver, 1914 Iron Cross 1st and 2nd Class, Cross of Honor.

Fonck, Alfons: Generalmajor z.V. (01.06.42), (Heer); born 22.07.72 in Oberwesel, died 30.03.44 of natural causes in Hirschberg. WWI: Major and Department Chief in War Ministry. Without assignment 07.1935–03.1937, retired 03.1937.

WWII: recalled to military service 09.1939, attached to Foreign Office of O.K.W. 09.1939–06.1942, Fuehrer Res. in O.K.H. 07.1942–04.1943, retired 04.1943. Awards: War Merit Cross 1st and 2nd Class with Swords, 1914 Iron Cross 1st and 2nd Class, Cross of Honor.

Fontaine, Dr. Hans: Generalstabs-Veterinar (01.04.38), (Heer); born 07.04.80 in Guben, died 27.11.58 in Stuttgart. Medical veterinarian by profession. WWI: Stabs-Veterinar (unit unknown). Promotion to Reichswehr General-Veterinar 01.04.34. WWII: Commander of Heeres Veterinar Academy at Hannover 11.1935–09.1939, Heeres Veterinar 09.1939–1943 (assignments unknown), Commander of Heeres Veterinar Academy at Hannover 1943–1945. Awards: War Merit Cross 1st and 2nd Class with Swords, 1914 Iron Cross 1st and 2nd Class, Cross of Honor.

Forst, Guenther von der: Konteradmiral (01.04.44), (Kriegsmarine); born 17.12.97 in Bad Driburg, died 24.03.82 in Berchtesgaden. WWI: Leutnant zur See and Artillery Officer on torpedo boat *V-69*. Attached to Inspection of Education in Marineleitung 10.1933–03.1935, attached to Marineleitung 03.1935–10.1937, First Officer for aviso *Grille* 10.1937–05.1938. WWII: Commander of aviso *Grille* 05.1938–03.1940, Commander of Sea Defenses Stavanger 07.1940–05.1941, Senior Quartermaster to Marine Befehlshaber of Norway 12.1941–11.1942, Chief of Staff to Marine Befehlshaber of Aegean Sea 02.1943–11.1943, Chief of Staff to Marine Befehlshaber of Baltic Sea 05.1944–05.1945. Awards: 1939 Clasps to the 1914 Iron Cross 1st and 2nd Class, 1914 Iron Cross 1st and 2nd Class, Cross of Honor.

Forst, Werner: Generalleutnant (01.01.43), (Heer); born 21.12.92 in Magdeburg, died 03.02.71 in Wiesbaden. WWI: Oberleutnant and Adjutant to Feld Artillerie Regiment 15. Promotion to Generalmajor 01.02.42. Commander of II. Abteilung, Artillerie Regiment at Fulda 10.1934–03.1935, Commander of Reitenden Abteilung at Sagan 04.1935–03.1936, Commander of II. Abteilung, Artillerie Regiment 76, 04.1936–09.1936. WWII: Commander of Artillerie Regiment 76, 10.1936–11.1940, Fuehrer Res. in O.K.H. 11.1940–01.1941, Commander of Artillerie 146, 01.1941–12.1941, Commander of 293. Infanterie Division 12.1941–01.1943, Commander of 106. Infanterie Division 01.1943–02.1944, Inspector of Artillerie attached to O.B. of Replacement Armee 06.1944–05.1945. Awards: Oak Leaves 22.02.44 (407), Knight's Cross 29.08.43, German Cross in Gold 14.03.42, 1939 Clasps to the 1914 Iron Cross 1st and 2nd Class, General Assault Badge, Eastern Front Medal, RK-Hohenzollern, 1914 Iron Cross 1st and 2nd Class, 1914 Wound Badge in Silver, Cross of Honor.

Forster, Dr. Edgar: General-Arzt (01.03.42), (Heer); born 28.06.90 in Ulm, died 14.02.75 in Bruehl. Medical doctor by profession. WWI: Ober-Arzt and Chief Physician of field hospital. WWII: Corps Physician to I. Armee Korps 08.1939–12.1942,

Corps Physician to XX. Armee Korps 12.1942–03.1945. Awards: 1939 Clasp to the 1914 Iron Cross 2nd Class, War Merit Cross 1st and 2nd Class with Swords, 1914 Iron Cross 2nd Class, Cross of Honor.

Forster, Kurt: Generalmajor (01.07.42), (Heer); born 28.10.91 in Ulm, died 30.11.62 in Duisburg. WWI: Oberleutnant in Res. Fusilier Artillerie Regiment 3. Attached to Staff of Artillerie Regiment 24, 10.1935–10.1937, Commander of I. Abteilung, Artillerie Regiment 24, 10.1937–11.1938. WWII: Commander of Artillerie Regiment 75, 11.1938–01.1941, Commander of Artillerie 143, 01.1941–08.1941, wounded and placed in Fuehrer Res. in O.K.H. 08.1941–06.1942, Commander of Artillerie 117, 06.1942–08.1943, Wehrmacht Commander of Kolmar 03.1944–09.1944, Fuehrer Res. in O.K.H. 09.1944–04.1945. Awards: German Cross in Gold 01.02.42, 1939 Clasps to the 1914 Iron Cross 1st and 2nd Class, General Assault Badge, 1939 Wound Badge in Silver, 1914 Iron Cross 1st and 2nd Class, Cross of Honor.

Forstner, Hugo: General-Intendant (01.01.36), (Heer); born 08.10.79 in Judenburg, died 13.12.70 in Linz. Administrative Officer by profession. WWI: Intendant to Austrian 14. Armee Korps. Transferred to German Wehrmacht 03.1938, attached to Staff of Abteilung Iva of Heeres Gruppen Kommando 5, 07.1938–10.1938, retired 10.1938. WWII: recalled to military service 09.1939, Intendant to Wehrkreis Kommando XVII 09.1939–03.1944, retired 03.1944. Awards: War Merit Cross 1st and 2nd Class with Swords, Cross of Honor.

Fortner, Johann: Generalleutnant (01.11.42), (Heer); born 25.11.84 in Zweibruecken, died 26.02.47 (executed) in Belgrade. WWI: Hauptmann in Bavarian Infanterie Regiment 5. Promotion to Generalmajor 01.06.41. Commander of Military District Kommando I at Kassel 10.1935–06.1939. WWII: Training Leader at Landeck 07.1939–05.1941, Commander of 718. Infanterie Division 05.1941–03.1943, Fuehrer Res. in O.K.H. 03.1943–03.1944, retired 03.1944. Awards: 1939 Clasps to the 1914 Iron Cross 1st and 2nd Class, Infantry Assault Badge in Silver, 1914 Iron Cross 1st and 2nd Class, Cross of Honor.

Fouquet, Hans-Joachim: Generalmajor (01.02.44), (Heer); born 07.04.95 in Braunschweig, died 17.02.44 in action in Russia. WWI: Leutnant in Feld Artillerie Regiment 37. Batterie Chef in Artillerie Regiment 5, 10.1934–03.1936, Commander of II. Abteilung, Artillerie Regiment 36, 04.1936–03.1939. WWII: Commander of I. Bataillon, Artillerie Regiment 67, 04.1939–03.1940, Commander of Artillerie Regiment 233, 03.1940–12.1942, Commander of Artillerie 113, 12.1942–06.1943, Commander of Artillerie 107, 06.1943–11.1943, Commander of Division Gruppe 112, 11.1943–02.1944. Awards: German Cross in Gold 14.02.44,

1939 Clasps to the 1914 Iron Cross 1st and 2nd Class, General Assault Badge, Eastern Front Medal, 1939 Wound Badge in Gold, 1914 Iron Cross 1st and 2nd Class, Cross of Honor.

Fox, Wilhelm: Generalmajor (20.04.45), (Heer); born 15.07.95 in Graz, died 16.04.85 in Weinheim. WWI: Oberleutnant in Austrian Royal Field Howitzer Regiment 8. Retired from Czech Army 10.1938. WWII: transferred to German Wehrmacht 09.1939, attached to Staff of Artillerie Regiment 8, 09.1939–01.1940, Commander of II. Abteilung, Artillerie Regiment 8, 01.1940–11.1941, Commander of Artillerie Regiment 8, 11.1941–10.1943, Fuehrer Res. in O.K.H. 10.1943–09.1944, Commander of Artillerie 30, 09.1944–05.1945. Awards: German Cross in Gold 27.08.42, 1939 Iron Cross 1st and 2nd Class, General Assault Badge, Cross of Honor.

Franek, Dr. Fritz: Generalleutnant (01.04.43), (Heer); born 16.07.91 in Vienna, died 04.08.76 in Vienna. WWI: Hauptmann and Adjutant in Austrian Infanterie Regiment 63. Promotion to Generalmajor 01.04.42. Transferred to German Wehrmacht 03.1938, attached to Staff of Infanterie Regiment 32, 11.1938–03.1939. WWII: Commander of I. Bataillon, Gebirgs Jaeger Regiment 98, 04.1939–02.1940, Commander of Infanterie Regiment 634, 02.1940–08.1940, Commander of Infanterie Regiment 405, 10.1940–09.1941, Commander of 196. Infanterie Division 03.1942–12.1943, Commander of 73. Infanterie Division 06.1944–07.1944, captured 07.1944. Awards: Knight's Cross 04.11.41, 1939 Iron Cross 1st Class, 1939 Clasp to the 1914 Iron Cross 2nd Class, Infantry Assault Badge in Silver, Eastern Front Medal, RK-Military Maria Theresia Order 17.08.17, 1914 Iron Cross 2nd Class, Cross of Honor.

Frank, August: SS-Obergruppenfuehrer und General der Waffen-SS und Polizei (09.10.44); born 05.04.98 in Augsburg, died 21.03.84 in Karlsruhe. P-1471185, SS-56169. WWI: Wachtmeister attached to Bavarian Res. Feld Artillerie Regiment 1. Joined N.S.D.A.P. and S.S. in 1932. Promotions to SS-Brigadefuehrer 20.04.40, SS-Gruppenfuehrer 30.01.43. Attached to Staff of RFSS 01.10.34, attached to SS-Hauptamt 01.07.35, attached to Fuehrung Stab of the SS-V.T. 01.12.36, attached to Staff Inspectorate of SS-V.T. 01.12.37–01.12.38. WWII: Chief of Verwaltungs Amt of SS-Hauptamt, Chief of Amt VI (Administration) of SS-Fuehrungshauptamt, Chief of Amtsgruppe A (Troop Administration) of W.V.H.A. 30.01.42–15.05.43, Chief of W.V. Amt of Hauptamt Orpo 30.01.44–09.11.44. Awards: German Cross in Silver 13.12.44, War Merit Cross 1st and 2nd Class with Swords, 1914 Iron Cross 2nd Class, Bavarian Military Service Order 3rd Class with Swords, Cross of Honor, Reich Sports Badge in Gold, SA-Sports Badge in Bronze, German Horseman's Badge in Silver, Degen, Ring.

Frank, Karl-Hermann: SS-Obergruppenfuehrer und General der Waffen-SS und Polizei (21.06.43); born 24.01.98 in Karlsbad, died 22.05.46 (executed) in Prague. P-6600002, SS-310466. Deputy Leader and N.S.D.A.P.-Deputy Gauleiter of Sudeten German Party. Joined N.S.D.A.P. and S.S. in 1938. Promotions to SS-Brigadefuehrer 01.11.38, SS-Gruppenfuehrer 09.11.39. Attached to Staff of RFSS 01.12.38. WWII: H.S.S.P.F. of Boehmen-Maehren 30.01.42–15.05.43, Leader of SS-Oberabschnitte Boehmen-Maehren and H.S.S.P.F. 30.01.44–09.11.44, State Secretary for Reichsprotektorate of Boehmen-Maehren, State Minister for Boehmen-Maehren, Member of Reichstag (Sudeten Deutschen Gebiete). Awards: Golden Party Badge, Golden HJ Honor Badge with Oak Leaves, Knight's Cross of the War Merit Cross without Swords 20.04.45, War Merit Cross 1st and 2nd Class without Swords, Gau Sudetenland Commemorative Badge, German Social Welfare Decoration 2nd Class, Degen, Ring.

SS-Obergruppenfuehrer Karl-Hermann Frank. (Bundesarchiv)

Franke, Hermann: Generalleutnant z.V. (01.04.41), (Heer); born 14.05.78 in Wernigerode, died 30.03.56 in Gross-Buseck. WWI: Major and Ia to XVII. Armee Korps. Promotion to Reichswehr Generalmajor 01.02.31. WWII: recalled to military service 08.1939, Commander of 162. Infanterie Division 12.1939–01.1942, retired 06.1942. Awards: German Cross in Gold 16.01.42, 1939 Clasps to the 1914 Iron Cross 1st and 2nd Class, Infantry Assault Badge in Silver, RK-Hohenzollern, 1914 Iron Cross 1st and 2nd Class, Cross of Honor.

Frankewitz, Bruno: Generalleutnant (01.07.43), (Heer); born 08.12.97 in Tiefensee, died 11.08.82 in Straehlen. WWI: Leutnant der Res. and Artillerie Observer in 13. Balloon Platoon. Promotion to Generalmajor 01.01.43. Attached to Staff of Artillerie Regiment at Fulda 03.1935–10.1935, Batterie Chef in Artillerie Regiment 29, 10.1935–03.1937. WWII: Commander of I. Abteilung, Artillerie Regiment 37, 04.1937–08.1939, Commander of Artillerie Regiment 161, 08.1939–11.1942, Commander of 215. Infanterie Division 11.1942–04.1945. Awards: Oak Leaves 16.03.45 (790), Knight's Cross 29.02.44, German Cross in Gold 01.04.42, 1939 Clasps to the 1914 Iron Cross 1st and 2nd Class, General Assault Badge, Eastern Front Medal, Kurland Cuff Band, 1939 Wound Badge in Silver, 1914 Iron Cross 1st and 2nd Class, 1914 Wound Badge in Silver, Cross of Honor.

Franssen, Udo: Generalleutnant (01.08.42), (Luftwaffe); born 19.09.84 in Bad Godesberg, died 18.04.59 in Goettingen. WWI: Kapitanleutnant and Chief of II. Vorpostenflottille. Promotion to Generalmajor 01.08.1940. Advisor to Luftwaffe Industry of R.L.M. 01.1935–09.1937. WWII: Group Leader in Military Economics Office Group of O.K.W. 10.1937–06.1940, Armaments Inspector for Belgium and Northern France 06.1940–11.1944, attached to Luftgau Kommando III in Berlin 11.1944–01.1945, retired 01.1945. Awards: War Merit Cross 1st and 2nd Class with Swords, 1914 Iron Cross 1st and 2nd Class, Cross of Honor.

Frantz, Gotthard: Generalleutnant (01.04.43), (Heer and Luftwaffe); born 05.05.88 in Berlin, died 21.01.73 in Bad Homburg. WWI: Hauptmann and Adjutant to Feld Artillerie Regiment 56. Promotion to Generalmajor 01.09.41. Training Leader attached to Commandant of Berlin 11.1934–03.1936, Commander of Military District Kommando Landsberg/Warthe 04.1936–09.1936, transferred to Luftwaffe 12.1936, Batterie Leader in Flak Regiment 2, 02.1937–03.1937, Batterie Chef in Flak Lehr Regiment 04.1937–01.1938, Commander of I. Abteilung, Flak Regiment 20, 02.1938–11.1938, Commander of I. Abteilung, Flak Regiment 7, 11.1938–05.1939. WWII: Commander of Flak Regiment 7, 06.1939–09.1939, Commander of Flak Artillerie For Luftgau Kommando VIII 10.1939–06.1940, Commander of Flak Schule 6, 07.1940–11.1941, Commander of 12. Flak Division 12.1941–12.1942, Commander of 19. Flak Division (mot.) 12.1942–05.1943, captured 05.1943. Awards: Knight's Cross 18.05.43, German Cross in Gold 21.09.42, 1939 Clasps to the 1914 Iron Cross 1st and 2nd Class, Flak War Badge, Eastern Front Medal, Afrika Cuff Band, German Horseman's Badge in Bronze, 1914 Iron Cross 1st and 2nd Class, 1914 Wound Badge in Black, Cross of Honor.

Frantzius, Botho von: Generalmajor (01.12.42), (Heer); born 09.08.98 in Sawdin, died 10.12.42 in action near Nevel. WWI: Leutnant in Dragoon Regiment 10. Schwadron Chef in Reiter Regiment 10, 10.1934–10.1937. WWII: Instructor at Schnelltruppen Schule Krampnitz 10.1937–10.1939, Commander of Aufklarungs Abteilung 161, 10.1939–01.1942, Commander of Infanterie Regiment 504, 02.1942–12.1942. Awards: Knight's Cross 04.11.41, 1939 Iron Cross 1st Class, 1939 Clasp to the 1914 Iron Cross 2nd Class, General Assault Badge, Eastern Front Medal, 1939 Wound Badge in Gold, 1914 Iron Cross 2nd Class, Cross of Honor.

Franz, Prof. Dr. Carl: General-Oberstabsarzt z.V. (01.07.38), (Heer); born 27.09.70 in Koenigsberg, died 10.10.46 in Soemmerda. Medical doctor by profession. WWI: Oberfeld-Arzt at Kaiser Wilhelm Academy. Promotions to Reichswehr General-Arzt 01.04.25, Reichswehr General-Stabsarzt 01.11.27. WWII: attached to Heeres

Military Medical Academy 10.1934–06.1944. Awards: War Merit Cross 1st and 2nd Class with Swords, 1914 Iron Cross 1st and 2nd Class, Cross of Honor.

Franz, Gerhard: Generalmajor (01.12.44), (Heer); born 26.02.02 in Bobeck, died 24.12.75 in Bad Wildungen. Attached to Command Staff of Heeres Service Office 4, 10.1935–12.1936, attached to General Staff of Heeres 01.1937–11.1938, Chief of 9. Kompanie, Infanterie Regiment 5, 11.1938–06.1939. WWII: Ia to 29. Infanterie Division (mot.) 07.1939–12.1941, Chief of Staff to XXXX. Armee Korps 05.1942–07.1942, Chief of Staff to German Afrika Korps 12.1942–02.1943, Chief of Staff to XXXXII. Armee Korps 08.1943–08.1944, Commander of 256. Volks Grenadier Division 09.1944–04.1945. Awards: Knight's Cross 24.07.41, German Cross in Gold 14.02.44, 1939 Iron Cross 1st and 2nd Class, Infantry Assault Badge in Silver, Eastern Front Medal, Afrika Cuff Band.

Franz, Walther: Generalleutnant (01.06.43), (Luftwaffe); born 27.02.96 in Konitz, died 01.08.67 in Karlsruhe. WWI: Leutnant in Infanterie Regiment 21. Promotion to Generalmajor 01.06.41. Administrative Official attached to Signals Staff of Luftkreis Kommando II in Berlin 04.1934–10.1935, Commander of Luft Nachrichten Ersatz Abteilung II/12, 11.1935–12.1937, Commander of Luft Nachrichtenschule at Halle-Saale 01.1938–06.1939. WWII: attached to Luft Signals Inspection in R.L.M. 08.1939–10.1939, Signals Leader to Luftgau Kommando VI 10.1939–05.1940, Signals Leader to Feld Luftgau Belgium and Northern France 06.1940–11.1941, Signals Leader to I. Flieger Korps 07.1942–05.1943, attached to Signals Office of R.L.M. 06.1943–07.1944, Radio Inspector of General of Signals in R.L.M. 08.1944–05.1945. Awards: 1939 Clasps to the 1914 Iron Cross 1st and 2nd Class, Spanish Cross in Silver with Swords, 1914 Iron Cross 1st and 2nd Class, 1914 Wound Badge in Silver, Cross of Honor.

Frede, Georg: Naval Senior Construction Director (01.04.44), (Kriegsmarine); born 23.02.82 in Braunschweig, died 20.02.47 in Wilhelmshaven. Engineer by profession. WWI: Oberleutnant der Res. and Executive in Port Construction Department Shipyard at Brugge. WWII: Director of Port Construction Department at Wilhelmshaven 10.1939–10.1944, Higher Liaison Engineer with Marine Gruppen Kommando North Sea 10.1944–04.1945. Awards: War Merit Cross 1st and 2nd Class with Swords, Cross of Honor.

Freitag, Fritz: SS-Brigadefuehrer und Generalmajor der Waffen-SS und Polizei (20.04.44); born 28.04.94 in Allenstein, died 20.05.45 (suicide) at Graz P.O.W. Camp. P-3052501, SS-393266. WWI: Leutnant der Res. attached to Grenadier Regiment 4 "Kronprinz." Joined Schutzpolizei in 1921, reached rank of Oberstleutnant der Schupo, joined N.S.D.A.P. in 1933, Commander of Polizei Schule in Berlin-Koepnick, Commander of Polizei Schule at Fuerstenfeldbruck, joined S.S. in 1940. WWII: Ia to 1. SS-Infanterie Brigade (mot.), Commander of 2. SS-Infanterie

Brigade (mot.) 15.05.43 SS-DAL, Commander of 14. Waffen Grenadier Division der SS (Ukrainische Nr 1) 30.01.44, 09.11.44 SS-DALs. Awards: Knight's Cross 30.09.44, German Cross in Gold 30.04.43, 1939 Clasps to the 1914 Iron Cross 1st and 2nd Class, War Merit Cross 2nd Class with Swords, 1939 Wound Badge in Gold, RK-Hohenzollern, 1914 Iron Cross 1st and 2nd Class, 1914 Wound Badge in Silver, Cross of Honor, German Olympic Games Decoration 2nd Class, Ring.

SS-Brigadefuehrer Fritz Freitag. (Marc Rikmenspoel)

Fremerey, Max: Generalleutnant (01.06.43), (Heer); born 05.05.89 in Koeln, died 20.09.68 in Kruen. WWI: Rittmeister and 1. Ordnance Officer to 201. Infanterie Division. Promotion to Generalmajor 01.06.41. Commander of Reiter Regiment at Bamberg 10.1934–10.1935, Commander of Reiter (later Kavallerie) Regiment 17, 10.1935–04.1939. WWII: Higher Kavallerie Officer 3, 05.1939–08.1939, Commander of Infanterie Regiment 480, 08.1939–10.1940, Commander of 18. Schuetzen Brigade 10.1940–09.1941, Commander of 29. Infanterie Division (mot.), 09.1941–09.1942, Commander of Panzer Division 155, 10.1942–03.1944, Commander of 233. Panzer Division 05.1944–05.1945. Awards: Knight's Cross 28.07.42, German Cross in Gold 19.12.41, 1939 Clasps to the 1914 Iron Cross 1st and 2nd Class, Tank Assault Badge in Silver, Eastern Front Medal, 1914 Iron Cross 1st and 2nd Class, 1914 Wound Badge in Black, Cross of Honor.

Frenking, Hermann: Generalmajor (01.12.43), (Heer); born 16.09.94 in Hagen, died 13.05.56 in Muenster. WWI: Leutnant in Infanterie Regiment 158. Chief of 8. (M.G.) Kompanie, Infanterie Regiment at Muenster 10.1934–10.1935. WWII: Instruction Group Leader at Kriegsschule Potsdam 10.1935–08.1939, Commander of III. Bataillon, Infanterie Regiment 77, 10.1939–04.1940, Commander of Infanterie Regiment 123, 04.1940–01.1942, Fuehrer Res. in O.K.H. 01.1942–06.1942, Commander of Infanterie Regiment 512, 06.1942–04.1943, Commander of 282. Infanterie Division 08.1943–08.1944, captured 08.1944. Awards: German Cross in Gold 15.12.41, 1939 Clasps to the 1914 Iron Cross 1st and 2nd Class, Infantry Assault Badge in Silver, Eastern Front Medal, Crimea Shield, 1914 Iron Cross 1st and 2nd Class, Cross of Honor.

Fretter-Pico, Maximilian: General der Artillerie (01.06.42), (Heer); born 06.02.92 in Karlsruhe, died 04.04.84 in Kreuth. WWI: Hauptmann on Staff of 19. Res. Division. Promotions to Generalmajor 01.03.41, Generalleutnant 01.02.42. Attached to Staff of Military Commander at Frankfurt/Oder 10.1934–10.1935,

Leader of Advisors Ost (East) in Abteilung 3 of Heeres General Staff 10.1935–1938, attached to Turkish Army 1938–11.1938. WWII: Chief of Staff to Heeres General Kommando at Saarpfalz 11.1938–09.1939, Chief of Staff to XXIV. Armee Korps 09.1939–04.1941, Commander of 97. Light Division 04.1941–12.1941, Commander of XXX. Armee Korps 12.1941–07.1944, Oberbefehlshaber of 6. Armee 07.1944–12.1944, Fuehrer Res. in O.K.H. 12.1944–05.1945. Awards: Oak Leaves 16.01.44 (368), Knight's Cross 26.12.41, German Cross in Gold 19.09.42, 1939 Clasps to the 1914 Iron Cross 1st and 2nd Class, Infantry Assault Badge in Silver, Eastern Front Medal, Crimea Shield, 1914 Iron Cross 1st and 2nd Class, 1914 Wound Badge in Black, Cross of Honor.

Fretter-Pico, Otto: Generalleutnant (09.10.44), (Heer); born 02.02.93 in Karlsruhe, died 30.07.66 in Flins. WWI: Oberleutnant and Adjutant to II. Abteilung, Feld Artillerie Regiment 14. Promotion to Generalmajor 01.03.43. Attached to Inspection of Artillerie Observers in Reichswehr Ministry (later Reich War Ministry) 10.1934–11.1938. WWII: Commander of Beobachter Abteilung 7, 11.1938–02.1940, Commander of Artillerie Regiment 297, 02.1940–03.1942, Commander of Artillerie 102, 02.1942–12.1942, Commander of 57. Infanterie Division 02.1943–09.1943, Commander of 148. Infanterie Division 09.1943–04.1945. Awards: Knight's Cross 12.12.44, German Cross in Gold 11.12.41, 1939 Clasps to the 1914 Iron Cross 1st and 2nd Class, General Assault Badge, Eastern Front Medal, 1914 Iron Cross 1st and 2nd Class, 1914 Wound Badge in Black, Cross of Honor.

Generalleutnant Otto Fretter-Pico. (Bundesarchiv)

Freutel, Lothar: Generalmajor (01.02.44), (Heer); born 21.02.94 in Rosenberg, died 18.02.44 in action in Colomo. WWI: Leutnant der Res. in Feld Artillerie Regiment 35. Batterie Chef in Artillerie Regiment 20, 1.1936–10.1937. WWII: Commander of III. Abteilung, Artillerie Regiment 20, 10.1937–08.1939, Commander of Special Purpose Artillerie Regiment 707, 09.1939–03.1940, Commander of Artillerie Regiment 217, 03.1940–01.1943, Commander of Res. Artillerie Regiment 26, 01.1943–09.1943, Commander of Grenadier Regiment 503, 10.1943–02.1944. Awards: German Cross in Gold 25.03.44, 1939 Clasps to the 1914 Iron Cross 1st and 2nd Class, General Assault Badge, Eastern Front Medal, 1939 Wound Badge in Gold, 1914 Iron Cross 1st and 2nd Class, Cross of Honor.

Freyberg-Eisenberg-Allmendingen, Egloff Freiherr von: Generalmajor (01.04.39), (Luftwaffe); born 03.10.83 in Allmendingen, died 11.02.84 in Allmendingen.

WWI: in G.A.S. as Hauptmann and Fliegergruppenfuehrer 5. Fliegerhorst Commandant of Jueterbog 04.1934–03.1936, Commander of Luftgau Kommando 13, 04.1936–09.1936, Luftwaffe Attaché attached to German Embassy in Paris 10.1936–09.1937, attached to several Flieger Schulen 12.1937–07.1938, Commandant of Luftwaffe Training Grounds at Wildforth 08.1938–03.1939. WWII: Commandant of Luftwaffe Training Grounds at Dramburg 04.1939–08.1939, Flughafenbereichs Commandant of Kolberg 08.1939–10.1943, retired 10.1943. Awards: War Merit Cross 1st and 2nd Class with Swords, Pilot's Commemorative Badge, RK-Hohenzollern, RK-Wuerttemberg Friedrich Order 1st Class with Swords, 1914 Iron Cross 1st and 2nd Class, Bavarian Military Service Order IV. Class with Swords, Prussian Crown Order IV. Class with Swords, 1914 Pilot's Badge, Cross of Honor.

Freye, Johannes: Generalmajor (01.07.42), (Heer); born 16.12.78 in Magdeburg, died 28.10.52 in Ulm. WWI: Hauptmann and Commander of 214. Pionier Bataillon. WWII: attached to Field Equipment Inspection of Reichswehr Ministry (later Reich War Ministry and O.K.H.) 04.1932–07.1941, Commander of Heeres Waffenmeisterschule 07.1941–01.1943, Fuehrer Res. in O.K.H. 01.1943–06.1943, retired 06.1943. Awards: War Merit Cross 1st and 2nd Class with Swords, 1914 Iron Cross 1st and 2nd Class, Cross of Honor.

Freytag, Walter: Generalmajor (01.08.42), (Heer); born 02.07.92 in Rittergut, died 06.02.82 in Dresden. WWI: Oberleutnant and Adjutant to Res. Infanterie Regiment 263. Commander of Ausbildungs Bataillon of Infanterie Regiment at Halberstadt 10.1934–05.1935, Commander of Ausbildungs Bataillon of Infanterie Regiment at Dessau 06.1935–10.1935, Commander of III. Bataillon, Infanterie Regiment 33, 10.1935–12.1936, attached to Staff of Fortress Commander at Glogau 01.1937–11.1938, attached to Staff of Infanterie Regiment 54, 11.1938–03.1939. WWII: Wehrmacht Commander of Bruenn 04.1939–04.1941, Commander of Infanterie Regiment 240, 06.1941–01.1942, Commander of Infanterie Regiment 769, 03.1942–07.1942, Wehrmacht Commander of Smolensk 07.1942–11.1942, Commander of Ost Truppe 741 followed by 853, 03.1943–10.1943, Wehrmacht Commander of Danzig 12.1943–02.1945. Awards: Honor Roll Clasp 1945, 1939 Clasps to the 1914 Iron Cross 1st and 2nd Class, War Merit Cross 1st and 2nd Class with Swords, Infantry Assault Badge in Silver, Eastern Front Medal, RK-Hohenzollern, 1914 Iron Cross 1st and 2nd Class, Braunschweig War Service Cross 1st and 2nd Class, 1914 Wound Badge in Black, Cross of Honor.

Freytag, Wolfgang: Generalmajor (01.08.44), (Luftwaffe); born 04.08.93 in Hasselburg, died 16.01.79 in Goettingen. WWI: Leutnant in Infanterie Regiment 27. Batterie Chef in Flak Abteilung at Brandenburg 04.1935–09.1935, Batterie Chef in Flak Regiment 22, 10.1935–03.1936, Department Commander in Flak

Regiment 26, 04.1936–11.1938. WWII: Department Commander in Flak Regiment 43, 11.1938–10.1939, Commander of Flak Gruppe at Muenster 10.1938–11.1939, Commander of Flak Regiment 111, 12.1939–04.1940, Commander of Flak Gruppe for Amsterdam 05.1940–08.1940, Commander of Flak Regiment 143, 09.1940–06.1941, Commander of Flak Regiment 153, 06.1941–11.1942, Commander of Flak Brigade XIII (Finland) 12.1942–12.1944, Commander of Flak Firing Grounds at Buesum 12.1944–05.1945. Awards: German Cross in Gold 05.10.42, 1939 Clasps to the 1914 Iron Cross 1st and 2nd Class, Flak War Badge, RK-Hohenzollern, 1914 Iron Cross 1st and 2nd Class, 1914 Wound Badge in Silver, Cross of Honor.

Fricke, Hermann: Generalmajor (01.12.43), (Luftwaffe); born 17.06.90 in Wolfenbuettel, died 14.05.46 in hospital at Augsburg. WWI: in G.A.S. as Oberleutnant and Commander of Flieger Abteilung 3 LB. Adjutant to Luftkreis Schule II in Berlin 04.1934–04.1936, Training Staffelkapitan attached to Fernaufklarungs Gruppe 212, 05.1936–09.1936, Deputy Staffelkapitan and later Staffelkapitan to Fernaufklarungs Gruppe 212, 10.1936–09.1937, Staffelkapitan to Fernaufklarungs Gruppe 127, 10.1937–03.1938, Fliegerhorst Commandant of Goslar 04.1938–03.1939. WWII: Instructor at Luftwaffe Nachrichtenschule Halle-Saale 04.1939–08.1941, attached to Staff and later Commander of Luftwaffe Feld Regiment 1, 02.1942–05.1943, Flughafenbereichs Commandant of 6-VII 06.1943–05.1944, Flughafenbereichs Commandant of 4-VIII 05.1944–09.1944, retired 12.1944. Awards: 1939 Clasps to the 1914 Iron Cross 1st and 2nd Class, 1939 Observer's Badge, Pilot's Commemorative Badge, Pour le Mérite 23.12.17, RK-Hohenzollern, RK-Sachsen Ernestine House Order 2nd Class with Swords, 1914 Iron Cross 1st and 2nd Class, 1914 Observer's Badge, Cross of Honor.

Fricke, Kurt: Admiral (1.04.42), (Kriegsmarine); born 08.11.89 in Berlin, died 02.05.45 in Berlin. WWI: Oberleutnant zur See on heavy cruiser *Moltke*. Promotions to Konteradmiral 01.11.39, Vizeadmiral 01.06.41. Chief of 1. Torpedobootsflotille 09.1931–09.1933, Leader of Torpedo Boats 09.1933–10.1934, Chief of Staff to Inspection of Torpedo Boats and Mine Ships 10.1934–09.1936, Chief of Operations Department in O.K.M. 10.1936–06.1941, Chief of Staff of Naval Warfare Kommando in O.K.M. 06.1941–02.1943, Befehlshaber of Marine Gruppen Kommando Sud 03.1943–12.1944, Fuehrer Res. in O.K.M. 12.1944–05.1945.

Admiral Kurt Fricke (front center). (Bundesarchiv)

Awards: Knight's Cross 01.10.42, 1939 Clasps to the 1914 Iron Cross 1st and 2nd Class, Grand Cross of the Romanian Order of the Star with Swords, Grand Cross of the Bulgarian Military Service Order, Grand Cross of the Croatian Order of the Crown of King Zvonimir with Swords, Finnish Freedom Cross 1st Class with Breast Star and Swords, Romanian Order of Michael the Brave 3rd Class, Romanian Order of the Star 1st Class with Swords, RK-Hohenzollern, 1914 Iron Cross 1st and 2nd Class, Oldenburg Friedrich-August Cross 1st and 2nd Class, Cross of Honor.

Fricke, Ludwig: Generalmajor (01.06.44), (Heer); born 25.07.93 in Goerlitz, died 15.10.67 in Hamburg. WWI: Leutnant in Grenadier Regiment 4. Attached to Staff of Infanterie Regiment 22, 10.1935–11.1936, attached to Command Staff of Transport Kampf Truppen Schule 11.1936–03.1937, Commander of Panzer Abwehr Abteilung 1, 04.1937–10.1937. WWII: Commander of Panzer Abwehr Abteilung 20, 10.1937–08.1939, Commander of Schuetzen Regiment 4, 08.1939–08.1940, Fuehrer Res in Wehrkreis Kommando VI and Wehrkreis Kommando XIII 08.1940–06.1941, attached to Heeresgruppe Sud 06.1941–11.1941, Commander of Schuetzen Regiment 110, 1942–1943, Commander of 129. Panzer Grenadier Brigade 07.1943–10.1943, temporary Commander of Assault Division "Rhodes" 10.1943–04.1944, Wehrmacht Commander of Graudenz 08.1944–03.1945. Awards: German Cross in Gold 14.03.42, 1939 Clasps to the 1914 Iron Cross 1st and 2nd Class, Tank Assault Badge in Bronze, Eastern Front Medal, 1914 Iron Cross 1st and 2nd Class, 1914 Wound Badge in Gold, Cross of Honor.

Fricke, Otto: Konteradmiral (01.09.42), (Kriegsmarine); born 29.05.94 in Wennigsen, died 26.11.66 in Heidelberg. WWI: Leutnant zur See and Commandant of minesweeper *M-38*. Artillerie Officer for cruiser *Koenigsberg* 09.1932–09.1934, Instructor and Staff Officer for Ship Artillerie Schulen 09.1934–09.1937. WWII: Commander of Naval Artillerie Regiment 11 at West Wall and Inspector of Marine Artillerie 10.1937–04.1940, Chief of Staff to Marine Befehlshaber Channel Coast 07.1940–04.1942, Chief of Staff to Marine Befehlshaber France 04.1942–11.1942, Senior Quartermaster to Marine Gruppen Kommando West 11.1942–03.1943, Inspector of Marine Artillery in O.K.M. 04.1943–05.1945. Awards: 1939 Clasps to the 1914 Iron Cross 1st and 2nd Class, Coastal Artillery War Badge, German West Wall Medal, 1914 Iron Cross 1st and 2nd Class, Cross of Honor.

Friderici, Erich: General der Infanterie (01.04.39), (Heer); born 21.12.85 in Timmendorf, died 19.09.64 in Garmisch-Partenkirchen. WWI: Hauptmann on General Staff of Sachsen Armee. Promotions to Generalmajor 01.10.35, Generalleutnant

01.10.37. Commandant of Leipzig 10.1933–09.1935, Military Attaché in Budapest and Sofia 10.1935–10.1937, Commander of 17. Division 10.1937–03.1939. WWII: Wehrmacht Plenipotentiary in Reichsprotektorate of Boehmen-Maehren 04.1939–10.1941, Security Commander in Heeres Area South 10.1941–06.1942, placed at disposal of O.B. of Heeres 06.1942–07.1944, Chief of Special Staff IV in O.K.H. 07.1944–05.1945. Awards: German Cross in Silver 23.03.45, War Merit Cross 1st and 2nd Class with Swords, RK-Sachsen Military St. Heinrich's Order 07.01.15, 1914 Iron Cross 1st and 2nd Class, 1914 Wound Badge in Black, Cross of Honor.

Friebe, Helmut: Generalleutnant (01.09.43), (Heer); born 04.11.94 in Droschkau, died 14.01.70 in Friedrichshafen. WWI: Leutnant in Fusilier Regiment 38. Promotion to Generalmajor 01.03.43. Kompanie Chef in Infanterie Regiment at Koenigsberg 10.1934–10.1935. WWII: Commander of III. Bataillon, Infanterie Regiment 2, 10.1935–08.1939, Adjutant to Commander of XXI. Armee Korps 08.1939–09.1939, wounded and in hospital 09.1939–12.1939, Commander of Infanterie Replacement Regiment 1, 12.1939–05.1940, Commander of Infanterie Regiment 164, 05.1940–06.1941, wounded again and placed in Fuehrer Res. 06.1941–04.1942, Commander of Infanterie Regiment 419, 04.1942–12.1942, Commander of 125. Infanterie Division 12.1942–03.1944, Commander of 122. Infanterie (later V.G.D.) Division 05.1944–05.1945. Awards: Knight's Cross 13.08.41, German Cross in Gold 16.01.42, 1939 Clasps to the 1914 Iron Cross 1st and 2nd Class, Infantry Assault Badge in Silver, Eastern Front Medal, 1939 Wound Badge in Silver, RK-Hohenzollern, 1914 Iron Cross 1st and 2nd Class, 1914 Wound Badge in Silver, Cross of Honor.

Friebe, Werner: Generalmajor (01.06.44), (Heer); born 12.07.97 in Droschkau, died 08.03.62 in Stuttgart. Brother of Generalleutnant Helmut Friebe. WWI: Leutnant and Signals Leader to Fusilier Regiment 38. Attached to Truppe Amt in Reichswehr Ministry (later Reich War Ministry) 05.1934–06.1935, attached to Abteilung 5 in General Staff of Heeres 07.1935–10.1937, Chief of 1. Kompanie, Kradschuetzen Bataillon 3, 10.1937–05.1938. WWII: Ia to 20. Infanterie Division (mot.) 06.1938–01.1941, Chief of Staff to XXXXVIII. Armee (later Panzer Korps) 01.1941–11.1942, Fuehrer Res. in O.K.H. 01.1943–03.1944, Commander of 8. Panzer Division 04.1944–07.1944, Chief of Staff to Wehrkreis III 09.1944–05.1945. Awards: Knight's Cross 21.04.44, German Cross in Gold 30.05.42, 1939 Clasps to the 1914 Iron Cross 1st and 2nd Class, Eastern Front Medal, 1914 Iron Cross 1st and 2nd Class, 1914 Wound Badge in Black, Cross of Honor.

Friedeburg, Hans-Georg von: Generaladmiral (01.05.45), (Kriegsmarine) born 15.07.95 in Strassburg, died 23.05.45 (suicide) in Flensburg. WWI: Leutnant zur

Generaladmiral Hans-Georg von Friedeburg. (Josef Charita)

See on battleship *Kronprinz*. Promotions to Konteradmiral 01.09.42, Vizeadmiral 01.02.43, Admiral 01.04.43. Naval Adjutant to Reich War Ministry 02.1933–09.1936, First Officer on cruiser *Karlsruhe* 09.1936–03.1938, Staff Officer to Befehlshaber of Surface Ships in Spain 03.1938–11.1938. WWII: attached to Staff of Submarines 02.1939–09.1939, Chief of Organization Department on Staff of Submarine Kommando in O.K.M. 09.1939–09.1941, Second Admiral of Submarines 09.1941–01.1943, Befehlshaber of Submarines 02.1943–04.1945, appointed by Doenitz as Oberbefehlshaber of Kriegsmarine 05.1945–05.1945. Awards: Knight's Cross of the War Merit Cross with Swords 17.01.45, German Cross in Silver 06.06.42, 1939 Clasps to the 1914 Iron Cross 1st and 2nd Class, War Merit Cross 1st and 2nd Class with Swords, Spanish Cross in Silver without Swords, RK-Baden Order of the Zaehringer Lion 2nd Class with Swords, 1914 Iron Cross 1st and 2nd Class, Johann Ritter Order, Cross of Honor.

Friedensburg, Walter: Generalleutnant (01.12.41), (Luftwaffe); born 06.01.89 in Berlin, died 22.03.59 in Kassel. WWI: in G.A.S. as Kapitanleutnant in Seeflug-Versuchskommando. Promotion to Generalmajor 01.12.39. Commander of Seeflieger Gruppe at Neu-Kladow 06.1935–03.1936, Fliegerhorst Commandant of Travemuende 04.1936–09.1936, Fliegerhorst Commandant of Neuruppin 10.1936–09.1937, Fliegerhorst Commandant of Parow 01.1937–08.1938, member of International Board of Non-Intervention in Spain and London 08.1938–03.1939. WWII: Hoehere Flieger Ausbildungs Commander 17, 04.1939–03.1940, Officer with Special Duties attached to R.L.M. and O.B. der Luftwaffe 04.1940–09.1940, Armaments Inspector for Dresden 10.1940–08.1943, attached to Luftgau Kommando III 08.1943–05.1944, retired 05.1944. Awards: 1939 Clasps to the 1914 Iron Cross 1st and 2nd Class, War Merit Cross 1st and 2nd Class with Swords, Combined Pilot-Observer's Badge, Naval Pilot's Commemorative Badge, 1914 Iron Cross 1st and 2nd Class, 1914 Naval Pilot's Badge, Austro-Hungarian Pilot's Badge, 1914 Naval Wound Badge in Black, Cross of Honor.

Friedrich, Rudolf: Generalleutnant (01.04.41), (Heer); born 23.08.89 in Zwickau, died 09.05.45 in action near Prague. WWI: Hauptmann on Staff of 19. Replacement Division. Promotion to Generalmajor 01.04.40. Commander of III. Abteilung, Artillerie Regiment at Dresden 10.1934–10.1935, Commander of III. Abteilung, Artillerie Regiment 4, 10.1935–11.1938. WWII: Commander of Artillerie Regiment 4, 11.1938–11.1939, Commander of Artillerie 114, 11.1939–09.1941, Commander of 62. Infanterie Division 09.1941–10.1942, Commander of 327. Infanterie Division 10.1942–08.1943, Senior Commander of Artillerie 317, 11.1943–03.1944, Commander of Artillerie Division 312, 04.1944–05.1945. Awards: German Cross in Gold 18.06.42, 1939 Clasps to the 1914 Iron Cross 1st and 2nd Class, General Assault Badge, Eastern Front Medal, RK-Sachsen Military St. Heinrich's Order 29.04.18, 1914 Iron Cross 1st and 2nd Class, 1914 Wound Badge in Black, Cross of Honor.

Friedrichs, Walter: Generalmajor (01.04.39), (Heer); born 30.09.84 in Weiden, died 04.07.42 of natural causes in Munich. WWI: Hauptmann on Staff of 1. Bavarian Landwehr Division. Attached to Staff of Military Commander of Munich 01.1935–10.1935, Military Commander of Munich 11.1935–02.1937. WWII: Landwehr Commander of Munich 03.1937–08.1939, Commander of 212. Infanterie Division 08.1939–09.1939, Fuehrer Res. in O.K.H. 09.1939–05.1941, retired 05.1941. Awards: 1914 Iron Cross 1st and 2nd Class, Cross of Honor.

Friemel, Georg: Generalmajor (01.01.41), (Heer); born 21.02.91 in Magdeburg, died 14.10.77 in Konstanz. WWI: Hauptmann in Pionier Bataillon 14. Commander of I. Bataillon, Infanterie Regiment at Heilbronn 10.1934–10.1935, Commander of I. Bataillon, Infanterie Regiment 34, 10.1935–07.1937. WWII: Commander of Infanterie Regiment 65, 07.1937.05.1940, captured 05.1940. Awards: RK-Baden Order of the Zaehringer Lion 2nd Class with Swords, 1914 Iron Cross 1st and 2nd Class, Cross of Honor.

Fries, Walter: General der Panzertruppe (01.12.44), (Heer); born 22.04.94 in Gusternheim, died 06.08.82 in Weilburg an der Lahn. WWI: Leutnant der Res. in Infanterie Regiment 83. Promotions to Generalmajor 01.06.43, Generalleutnant 01.01.44. IIb on Staff of 34. Division 04.1936–10.1936. WWII: Commander of II. Bataillon, Infanterie Regiment 15 (mot.) 10.1936–11.1940, Commander of Infanterie Regiment 87 (mot.) 11.1940–12.1942, Commander of 29. Panzer Grenadier Division 03.1943–09.1944, Commander of XXXXVI. Panzer Korps 09.1944–01.1945. Awards: Swords 11.08.44 (87), Oak Leaves 29.01.44 (378), Knight's Cross 14.12.41, German Cross in Gold 09.10.42, 1939 Clasps to the 1914 Iron Cross 1st and 2nd Class, Infantry Assault Badge in Bronze, 1914 Iron Cross 1st and 2nd Class, Cross of Honor.

General der Panzertruppe Walter Fries. (Bundesarchiv)

Generaloberst Johannes Friessner. (Bundesarchiv)

Friessner, Johannes: Generaloberst (01.07.44), (Heer); born 22.03.92 in Chemnitz, died 26.06.71 in Bad Reichenhall. WWI: Oberleutnant and Ordnance Officer on Staff of 24. Infanterie Division. Promotions to Generalmajor 14.08.40, Generalleutnant 10.16.42, General der Infanterie 01.04.43. Commander of II. Bataillon, Infanterie Regiment 82, 10.1934–10.1935, Lehrer Gruppe Commander B at Kriegsschule Potsdam 10.1935–02.1938. WWII: Chief of Staff to Inspector of Kriegsschulen in O.K.H. 03.1938–08.1939, Chief of Staff to Inspector of Education and Training Affairs in O.K.H. 08.1939–05.1942, Commander of 102. Infanterie Division 05.1942–01.1943, Commander of XXIII. Armee Korps 01.943–01.1944, O.B. of Heeresgruppe "Narva" 02.1944–07.1944, O.B. of Heeresgruppe Sud 07.1944–12.1944, Fuehrer Res. in O.K.H. 12.1944–05.1945. Awards: Oak Leaves 09.04.44 (445), Knight's Cross 23.07.43, German Cross in Gold 09.06.43, 1939 Clasps to the 1914 Iron Cross 1st and 2nd Class, RK-Sachsen Military St. Heinrich's Order 27.11.16, 1914 Iron Cross 1st and 2nd Class, 1914 Wound Badge in Black, Cross of Honor.

Frisius, Friedrich: Vizeadmiral (30.09.44), (Kriegsmarine); born 17.01.75 in Bad Salzuflen, died 30.08.70 in Lingen. WWI: Leutnant zur See and Watch Officer with 18. Torpedoboots Halbflotille. Promotion to Konteradmiral 01.12.42. Navigations Officer for cruiser *Leipzig* 10.1931–09.1933, Instructor at Marine Schule Muerwik 09.1933–09.1934, Staff Officer at Marine Schule Muerwik 09.1934–09.1935, Advisor attached to Ausland Abwehr in Reich War Ministry 09.1935–12.1938. WWII: attached to Staff of Naval Service Office in Hamburg 12.1938–08.1940, Commander of Sea Fortifications at Boulogne 01.1941–12.1941, Commander of Sea Fortifications as Pas de Calais 12.1941–10.1944, Commander of Fortress Dunkirk 09.1944–05.1945. Awards: German Cross in Gold 16.09.44, 1939 Clasps to the 1914 Iron Cross 1st and 2nd Class, Coastal Artillery War Badge, Commander's Cross of the Spanish Imperial Order of the Yoke, 1914 Iron Cross 1st and 2nd Class, Cross of Honor.

Fritsch, Friedrich: General-Stabsintendant (01.10.41), (Heer); born 05.02.84 in Strasbourg, died 24.11.54 in Munich. Administrative Officer by profession. WWI: Hauptmann (unit unknown). Promotion to General-Intendant 01.03.38. WWII: Chief Intendant to Wehrmacht Befehlshaber of Belgium and Northern France (dates unknown), Chief Intendant to Heeresgruppe B (dates unknown).

Awards: German Cross in Silver 30.04.45, War Merit Cross 1st and 2nd Class with Swords, RK-Sachsen Albrecht Order 1st Class with Swords, RK-Wuerttemberg Friedrich Order 1st Class with Swords, 1914 Iron Cross 1st and 2nd Class, Cross of Honor.

Fritsch, Dr. Philipp: General-Stabsveterinar (01.04.42), (Heer); born 24.07.80 in Munich, died 10.04.45 of natural causes in Munich. Medical veterinarian by profession. WWI: Ober-Veterinar in Bavarian Feld Artillerie Regiment 12. Promotion to General-Veterinar 01.06.39. WWII: Korps Veterinar to VII. Armee Korps 04.1935–08.1939, Armee Veterinar to 6. Armee 10.1939–07.1942, Armee Veterinar to Heeresgruppe B 07.1942–02.1943, Armee Veterinar to Heeresgruppe Sud 02.1943–03.1944, Armee Veterinar to Heeresgruppe Sud Ukraine 03.1944–09.1944. Awards: German Cross in Silver 10.03.44, War Merit Cross 1st and 2nd Class with Swords, 1914 Iron Cross 1st and 2nd Class, Cross of Honor.

Fritsch, Werner Freiherr von: Generaloberst (20.04.36), (Heer); born 04.08.80 in Benrath, died 22.09.39 in action at Warsaw. P-3805227. WWI: Major and Ia to IV. Res. Korps. Promotions to Reichswehr Generalmajor 01.11.30, Reichswehr Generalleutnant 01.06.32, Reichswehr General der Artillerie 01.02.34. Oberbefehlshaber of German Heeres 01.1935–01.1938, dismissed after unfounded scandal 01.1938. WWII: honorary Chief of Artillerie Regiment 12, 06.1938–09.1939. Awards: Golden Party Badge (honorary), 1939 Wound Badge in Gold, Red Eagle Order 4th Class, RK-Hohenzollern, 1914 Iron Cross 1st and 2nd Class, 1914 Wound Badge in Black, Cross of Honor.

Generaloberst Werner Freiherr von Fritsch. (Bundesarchiv)

Froehlich, Stefan: General der Flieger (01.07.43), (Luftwaffe); born 07.10.89 in Orsova, died 02.10.78 in Duisburg. WWI: Hauptmann and Fuehrer of Austrian Sappeur Kompanie 13. Promotions to Generalmajor 01.07.40, Generalleutnant 01.01.42. Transferred to German Wehrmacht 03.1938, attached to Kampfflieger Gruppe Memmingen of German Luftwaffe 03.1938–12.1938. WWII: Fliegerhorst Commandant of Wiener-Neustadt 02.1939–11.1939, Commander of K.G. 76, 11.1939–02.1941, Flieger Fuehrer for Africa 02.1941–04.1942, Commander of 2. Flieger Division 04.1942–12.1942, Commander of IX. Flieger Korps 12.1942–09.1943, Commander of Luftgau Kommando XVII 09.1943–02.1944, attached to Staff of Luftflotte 3, 03.1944–08.1944, Fuehrer Res. in O.K.L. 11.1944–02.1945,

O.B. of Luftflotte 10, 02.1945–04.1945. Awards: Knight's Cross 04.07.40, German Cross in Gold 11.05.42, 1939 Iron Cross 1st Class, 1939 Clasp to the 1914 Iron Cross 2nd Class, Afrika Cuff Band, 1939 Observer's Badge, 1914 Iron Cross 2nd Class, Cross of Honor.

Froelich, Gottfried: Generalmajor (01.12.43), (Heer); born 03.06.94 in Dresden, died 30.07.59 in Heidenheim. WWI: Leutnant in Feld Artillerie Regiment 48. Commander of I. Abteilung, Artillerie Regiment at Naumburg 10.1934–10.1935, Commander of I. Abteilung, Artillerie Regiment 14, 10.1935–11.1938. WWII: Commander of II. Abteilung, Artillerie Regiment 76, 11.1938–10.1939, Commander of Panzer Artillerie Regiment 78, 10.1939–09.1943, Commander of 8. Panzer Division 09.1943–01.1945, Fuehrer Res. in O.K.H. 01.1945–03.1945. Awards: Knight's Cross 20.12.43, German Cross in Gold 02.01.42, 1939 Clasps to the 1914 Iron Cross 1st and 2nd Class, Tank Assault Badge in Silver, Eastern Front Medal, RK-Sachsen Military St. Heinrich's Order 15.04.18, 1914 Iron Cross 1st and 2nd Class, 1914 Wound Badge in Black, Cross of Honor.

Froelich, Walter: Vizeadmiral (01.04.43), (Kriegsmarine); born 05.08.93 in Berlin, died 12.12.69 in Baden-Baden. WWI: U-boat service as Marineingenieur-oberaspirant and Chief Engineer of *U-94*. Promotion to Konteradmiral 01.04.42. Lead Engineer for line ship *Schlesien* 09.1932–09.1934, Engineer Advisor in Marineleitung 09.1934–09.1936, Engineer Officer attached to Staff of Befehlshaber of Battleships 09.1936–11.1938. WWII: Chief of Staff to Ship Machine Inspection 11.1938–11.1939, Fleet Engineer attached to Fleet Kommando 12.1939–01.1941, Chief of Staff of Test Command for Warship Construction in O.K.M. 01.1941–03.1943, Ship Machine Inspector in O.K.M. 03.1943–05.1945. Awards: 1939 Clasp to the 1914 Iron Cross 2nd Class, War Merit Cross 1st and 2nd Class with Swords, 1914 Iron Cross 1st and 2nd Class, 1914 Submarine Badge, Cross of Honor.

Froemert, Werner: Generalmajor (01.07.44), (Heer); born 15.05.99 in Oppeln, died 28.07.44 in hospital in Danzig. WWI: Obermaatrose on liner *Bayern*. Chief of 4. Kompanie, Infanterie Regiment at Schweidnitz 10.1934–10.1935, Chief of 4. Kompanie, Infanterie Regiment 28, 10.1935–12.1935, Chief of 4. Kompanie, Infanterie Regiment 3, 01.1936–10.1937, Instructor at Kriegsschule Potsdam 10.1937–10.1938. WWII: attached to Command Staff of Kriegsschule Wiener-Neustadt 10.1938–08.1939, Commander of I. Bataillon, Infanterie Regiment 217, 08.1939–04.1941, O.K.H. Liaison to S.A. and N.S.K.K. Fuehrung 04.1941–09.1942, Wehrmacht Representative to Stabschef der SA 09.1942–08.1943, Commander of Replacement Brigade "Feldherrnhalle" 08.1943–07.1944. Awards: 1939 Iron Cross 1st and 2nd Class, War Merit Cross 1st and 2nd Class with Swords, Infantry Assault Badge in Silver, Cross of Honor.

Fromm, Friedrich: Generaloberst (19.07.40), (Heer); born 08.10.88 in Berlin, died 12.03.45 (executed at Brandenburg Prison for involvement in 20.07.44 attempt on Hitler's life). WWI: Hauptmann on Staff of 30. Infanterie Division. Promotions to Generalmajor 01.11.35, Generalleutnant 01.01.38, General der Artillerie 20.04.39. WWII: Chief of General Heeres Abteilung in Reichswehr Ministry (later Reich War Ministry and O.K.H.) 02.1934–09.1939, Chief of Heeres Armaments and O.B. of Replacement Armee 11.1939–07.1944. Awards: Knight's Cross 13.07.40, 1939 Clasps to the 1914 Iron Cross 1st and 2nd Class, 1914 Iron Cross 1st and 2nd Class, 1914 Wound Badge in Black, Cross of Honor.

Generaloberst Friedrich Fromm. (Bundesarchiv)

Frommherz, Hermann: Generalmajor (01.04.43), (Luftwaffe); born 10.08.91 in Waldshut, died 30.12.64 in Waldshut. WWI: in G.A.S. as Leutnant der Res. and Leader of Jasta 27. Training Leader on Inspection of Flieger Res. in R.L.M. 10.1934–09.1935, attached to Jagdflieger Schule Schleissheim 10.1935–03.1936, Staffelkapitan in J.G. "Horst Wessel" 04.1936–06.1938, Gruppen Commander in J.G. "Horst Wessel" 07.1938–01.1939. WWII: Commander of Jagdflieger Schule 2 at Schleissheim 02.1939–06.1941, Jagdfliegerfuehrer of Berlin and Central Germany 10.1941–03.1942, Jagdfliegerfuehrer of German Bay 04.1942–09.1942, Jagdfliegerfuehrer of Berlin and Central Germany 10.1942–09.1943, Commander of Flieger Ground Organization 10.1943–09.1944, Flughafenbereichs Commandant of 2-I 10.1944–03.1945. Awards: 1939 Clasps to the 1914 Iron Cross 1st and 2nd Class, 1939 Pilot's Badge, "Jagdstaffel Boelcke Nr. 2, 1916/18" Commemorative Cuff Band, Pilot's Commemorative Badge, RK-Hohenzollern, 1914 Iron Cross 1st and 2nd Class, 1914 Pilot's Badge, Cross of Honor.

Fronhoefer, Erich: Generalmajor (01.08.44), (Heer); born 27.12.95 in Ragaischen, died 12.01.70 in Dortmund. WWI: Leutnant and Adjutant to II. Bataillon, Fusilier Regiment 34. Adjutant to Inspector of Transport Troops 07.1934–10.1935, Adjutant on Kommando Staff of Panzertruppen 10.1935–09.1936, Commander of Transport Troops Training Department 10.1936–10.1937. WWII: Tactics Leader at Panzertruppen Schule 10.1937–06.1940, Commander of Panzer Regiment 10, 08.1940–02.1942, Head of Officer Aspirant Courses 11.1942–06.1944, Commander of 20. Luftwaffe Feld Division 09.1944–12.1944, Commander of 547. Volks Grenadier Division 04.1945–05.1945. Awards: Knight's Cross 24.07.41, 1939 Clasps to the 1914 Iron Cross 1st and 2nd Class, Tank Assault Badge in

Silver, 1914 Iron Cross 1st and 2nd Class, 1914 Wound Badge in Black, Cross of Honor.

Frotscher, Werner: Generalmajor (20.04.45), (Heer); born 31.12.94 in Croppenstedt, died 22.05.59 in Bandenweiler. WWI: Leutnant attached to Line Commandant L 2 at Kattowitz. Attached to Staff of III. Bataillon, Infanterie Regiment at Tuebingen 10.1934–12.1934, Chief of 10. Kompanie, Infanterie Regiment at Tuebingen 01.1935–10.1935, Chief of 2. Kompanie, Infanterie Regiment 56, 10.1935–10.1937, Chief of 2. Kompanie, Infanterie Regiment 109, 10.1937–11.1938. WWII: Chief of 5. Kompanie, Wach Regiment Berlin 11.1938–09.1939, Commander of II. Bataillon, Infanterie Regiment 29, 1939–12.1940, Commander of Wach Bataillon Berlin 12.1940–09.1942, Commander of Fusilier Regiment 270, 09.1942–12.1943, Commander of Grenadier Regiment 176, 03.1944–11.1944, Commander of Infanterie Regiment 422, 11.1944–05.1945. Awards: Knight's Cross 11.03.45, 1939 Clasps to the 1914 Iron Cross 1st and 2nd Class, Infantry Assault Badge in Silver, Silesian Eagle 1st and 2nd Class, RK-Sachsen Ernestine House Order 2nd Class with Swords, RK-Sachsen Order of the White Falcon 2nd Class with Swords, 1914 Iron Cross 1st and 2nd Class, 1914 Wound Badge in Black, Cross of Honor.

Fruhner, Otto: Generalmajor (01.05.44), (Luftwaffe); born 06.09.93 in Brieg, died 19.06.65 in Villach. WWI: in G.A.S. as Leutnant der Res. in Jasta 26. Commander of Flugzeugfuehrer Schule C in Ludwigslust 05.1935–09.1937. WWII: Fliegerhorst Commandant of Stade 10.1937–08.1939, Fliegerhorst Commandant of Burg 08.1939–11.1939, Fliegerhorst Commandant at Kolberg 11.1939–07.1940, Fliegerhorst Commandant of Brandenburg-Briest 08.1940–05.1945. Awards: War Merit Cross 1st and 2nd Class with Swords, 1939 Pilot's Badge, Pilot's Commemorative Badge, Golden Prussian Military Service Cross 03.06.18, 1914 Iron Cross 1st and 2nd Class, 1914 Pilot's Badge, Cross of Honor.

Frydag, Peter Freiherr von: Generalmajor z.V. (01.11.41), (Heer); born 01.02.81 in Oldenburg, died 05.04.61 in Freiburg. WWI: Rittmeister and Bataillon Commander in Infanterie Regiment 38. Military District Commander of Lueneburg 04.1935–09.1936, retired 09.1936. WWII: recalled to military service 08.1939, Military District Commander for Lueneburg 08.1939–06.1942, retired 06.1942. Awards: War Merit Cross 1st and 2nd Class with Swords, 1914 Iron Cross 1st and 2nd Class, Cross of Honor.

Fuchs, Egon: Generalmajor (01.06.40), (Heer); born 11.12.92 in Graudenz, died 19.06.40 in action near St. Aignan. WWI: Oberleutnant and Adjutant to Infanterie Regiment 156. Adjutant to 4. Division 04.1934–03.1937, Commander of III. Bataillon, Infanterie Regiment 102, 04.1937–11.1938. WWII: Commander of II. Bataillon, Infanterie Regiment 72, 11.1938–08.1939, Commander of Infanterie Replacement Regiment

102, 08.1939–12.1939, Commander of Infanterie Regiment 104, 12.1939–06.1940. Awards: 1939 Clasps to the 1914 Iron Cross 1st and 2nd Class, 1939 Wound Badge in Gold, 1914 Iron Cross 1st and 2nd Class, Cross of Honor.

Fuchs, Robert: Generalmajor: (01.09.43), (Luftwaffe); born 11.05.95 in Berlin, died 15.01.77. WWI: Leutnant in Fusilier Regiment 34. Advisor in Technical Office of R.L.M. 10.1933–09.1934, Instructor at Flieger Technische Schule at Jueterbog 10.1934–03.1935, attached to Fliegergruppe Finsterwalde 04.1935–03.1936, Fliegerhorst Commandant of Altenburg 03.1936–03.1938, attached to R.L.M. and O.B. der Luftwaffe 04.1938–01.1939. WWII: Inspector of Technical Troop Training in R.L.M. 02.1939–09.1939, Commander of K.G. 26, 09.1939–10.1940, Fuehrer Res. in O.K.L. and placed at disposal of Luftwaffe 10.1940–12.1942, Commander of Luftwaffe Jaeger Regiment 33, 12.1942–08.1943, Commander of 20. Luftwaffe Feld Division 08.1943–10.1943, Commander of 1. Flieger Division 11.1943–05.1945. Awards: Knight's Cross 06.04.40, 1939 Clasps to the 1914 Iron Cross 1st and 2nd Class, Narvik Shield, Spanish Cross in Gold with Swords, 1939 Pilot's Badge, 1914 Iron Cross 1st and 2nd Class, 1914 Wound Badge in Black, Cross of Honor.

Fuchs, Werner: Admiral (01.04.42), (Kriegsmarine); born 18.01.91 in Insterburg, died 30.06.76 in Kitzeberg. WWI: Oberleutnant zur See and Watch Officer on light cruiser *Regensburg*. Promotions to Konteradmiral 01.10.38, Vizeadmiral 01.12.40. First Admiral Staff Officer attached to Marine Station Eastern Sea 09.1931–02.1934, Commandant of cruiser *Koeln* 03.1934–09.1935, Chief of Marine Training Department in Marineleitung (later O.K.M.) 10.1935–03.1938, Chief of Flotten Abteilung in O.K.M. 03.1938–06.1939. WWII: Chief of Amt and later Main Office for Warship Construction in O.K.M. 06.1939–10.1944, Fuehrer Res. in O.K.M. 11.1944–05.1945. Awards: Knight's Cross of the War Merit Cross with Swords 30.12.44, German Cross in Silver 30.01.43, 1939 Clasps to the 1914 Iron Cross 1st and 2nd Class, War Merit Cross 1st and 2nd Class with Swords, 1914 Iron Cross 1st and 2nd Class, Bavarian Military Service Order IV. Class with Swords, Cross of Honor.

Admiral Werner Fuchs. (Josef Charita)

Fuchs, Willy von: Generalmajor z.V. (01.08.42), (Heer); born 07.05.68 in Graudenz, died 26.02.55 in Hamburg. WWI: Oberst and Commander of Artillerie 25. WWII:

Commander of P.O.W. Camp Xa 08.1939–09.1940, Commandant of P.O.W. Camp Xd 09.1940–11.1942, retired 04.1943. Awards: War Merit Cross 1st and 2nd Class with Swords, RK-Hohenzollern, 1914 Iron Cross 1st and 2nd Class, Cross of Honor.

Fucik, Karl: Generalmajor (01.07.41), (Heer); born 10.10.85 in Vienna, died 10.11.56 in Vienna. WWI: Hauptmann in Austrian Schuetzen Regiment 35. Transferred to German Wehrmacht 03.1938, Commander of I. Bataillon, Infanterie Regiment 134, 04.1938–06.1939. WWII: Commander of Infanterie Regiment 29, 06.1939–08.1939, Commander of Infanterie Regiment 457, 08.1939–10.1940, Commander of Infanterie Regiment 416, 10.1940–06.1941, retired 07.1941. Awards: 1939 Iron Cross 1st and 2nd Class, Infantry Assault Badge in Silver, Cross of Honor.

Fuechtbauer, Heinrich Ritter von: Generalmajor z.V. (01.09.41), (Heer); born 03.04.79 in Nuremberg, died 11.12.47 in Rosenheim. WWI: Major and Staff Officer to III. Bavarian Armee Korps. WWII: recalled to military service 08.1939, attached to XIII. Armee Korps 10.1939–05.1940, Commander of Administration Staff in Military District C (North-East France) 07.1940–05.1941, Commandant of Feldkommandantur 568, 06.1941–06.1942, Commandant of Feldkommandantur 669, 06.1942–12.1942, Commandant of Feldkommandantur 590, 12.1942–07.1943, retired 12.1943. Awards: War Merit Cross 1st and 2nd Class with Swords, RK-Bavarian Military Max Joseph Order 09.05.15, RK-Hohenzollern, 1914 Iron Cross 1st and 2nd Class, Bavarian Military Service Order IV. Class with Swords, Austro-Hungarian Military Service Cross 3rd Class with War Decoration, 1914 Wound Badge in Black, Cross of Honor.

Fuerbringer, Werner: Konteradmiral (01.12.42), (Kriegsmarine); born 02.10.88 in Braunschweig, died 08.02.82 in Braunschweig. WWI: U-Boat Service as Kapitanleutnant and Commandant of several U-boats. Advisor in U-Boot Schule 10.1933–02.1938, Chief of Statistics Department in O.K.M. 02.1938–11.1938. WWII: Chief of Export Abteilung in O.K.M. 11.1938–10.1939, Chief of Anti-Submarine Department in O.K.M. 11.1939–10.1942, Armaments Inspector for Occupied Eastern Territories 11.1942–06.1943, retired 06.1943. Awards: War Merit Cross 1st and 2nd Class with Swords, RK-Hohenzollern, 1914 Iron Cross 1st and 2nd Class, 1914 Submarine Badge, Cross of Honor.

Fuerst, Friedrich: Generalleutnant (01.10.42), (Heer); born 26.05.89 in Munich, died 10.04.56 in Ruhpolding. WWI: Oberleutnant in Bavarian Res. Infanterie Regiment 10. Promotion to Generalmajor 01.10.40. Commander of II. Bataillon, Infanterie Regiment at Nuremberg 10.1934–10.1935, Commander of II. Bataillon, Infanterie Regiment 21, 10.1935–04.1937, Commander of Infanterie Regiment 103, 05.1937–11.1938. WWII: Commander of Kavallerie Schuetzen Regiment

6, 11.1938–09.1939, Commander of 6. Schuetzen Brigade 09.1939–10.1939, Commander of 7. Schuetzen Brigade 10.1939–10.1940, Commander of 14. Infanterie Division (mot.) 10.1940–06.1941, Commander of 34. Infanterie Division 10.1941–09.1942, Commander of 171. Res. Division 09.1942–01.1944, Commander of z.b.V. Division 442, 02.1944–07.1944, P.O.W. Commander for Wehrkreis Kommando XI 12.1944–05.1945. Awards: German Cross in Silver 28.01.44, 1939 Clasps to the 1914 Iron Cross 1st and 2nd Class, War Merit Cross 1st and 2nd Class with Swords, Tank Assault Badge in Silver, Eastern Front Medal, 1914 Iron Cross 1st and 2nd Class, 1914 Wound Badge in Silver, Cross of Honor.

Fuetterer, Kuno Heribert: General der Flieger (20.04.45), (Luftwaffe); born 02.04.94 in Hettstedt, died 24.08.63 in Munich. WWI: in G.A.S. as Leutnant in Bombengeschwader 6. Promotions to Generalmajor 01.11.41, Generalleutnant 01.11.43. Commander of Flieger Langstrecken Schule in Berlin 10.1933–04.1936, Chief of Staff to Inspection of Luftwaffe Res. in R.L.M. 05.1936–02.1937, Commander of II. Gruppe, K.G. 157 "Boelcke" 03.1937–05.1938. WWII: Luftwaffe Attaché in Budapest 06.1938–12.1944, Commander of Luftgau Kommando XV 12.1944–04.1945. Awards: 1939 Clasp to the 1914 Iron Cross 2nd Class, War Merit Cross 1st and 2nd Class with Swords, 1939 Observer's Badge, Pilot's Commemorative Badge, 1914 Iron Cross 1st and 2nd Class, 1914 Wound Badge in Black, 1914 Observer's Badge, Cross of Honor.

Fugger von Rabenhausen, Leopold Graf: Generalmajor (30.01.45), (Luftwaffe); born 18.07.93 in Odenburg, died 08.07.66 in Hamburg. WWI: in G.A.S. as Leutnant (unit unknown). Photo Officer attached to Staff of Luftkreis Kommando III 01.1936–07.1937, attached to Staff of Legion Condor 07.1937–03.1939. WWII: Advisor to Zentral Abteilung of R.L.M. 04.1939–08.1939, attached to R.L.M. and O.B. of Luftwaffe 09.1939–01.1940, Chief Supply Officer to Quartermaster of Luftflotte 4, 01.1940–07.1942, Flughafenbereichs Commandant of 1-XVII 07.1942–01.1943, Flughafenbereichs Commandant of 1-VIII 01.1943–07.1943, Flughafenbereichs Commandant of 6-IV 07.1943–05.1945. Awards: War Merit Cross 1st and 2nd Class with Swords, Spanish Cross in Gold with Swords, Pilot's Commemorative Badge, Spanish War Cross (Spain), RK-Hohenzollern, RK-Wuerttember Friedrich Order 2nd Class with Swords, 1914 Iron Cross 1st and 2nd Class, Bavarian Military Service Cross IV. Class with Swords, Austro-Hungarian Military Service Cross 3rd Class with War Decoration, 1914 Observer's Badge, Cross of Honor.

Fuhrmann, Albert: Naval Senior Construction Director (23.12.41), (Kriegsmarine); born 28.02.87 in Bremen, died 07.12.41 in Berlin. Engineer by profession. WWI: Machine Construction Master in Navy. WWII: Director of Machine Construction Department at Kiel Shipyard 04.1939–02.1941, Chief of Department for Test and

Development in O.K.W. 03.1941–12.1941. Awards: War Merit Cross 1st and 2nd Class with Swords.

Full, Dr. Friedrich: General-Stabsarzt (01.11.41), (Heer); born 11.12.88 in Wurzburg, died 29.10.66 in Bad Kissingen. Medical doctor by profession. WWI: Assistenz-Arzt (unit unknown). Promotion to General-Arzt 01.10.39. Division Physician to 33. Division 1936–11.1938. WWII: Corps Physician to XVI Armee Korps (mot.) 11.1938–02.1941, Army Physician to Panzer Gruppe 4 (later 4. Panzer Armee) 02.1941–11.1942, Fuehrer Res. in O.K.H. 11.1942–11.1943, retired 11.1943. Awards: 1939 Clasp to the 1914 Iron Cross 2nd Class, War Merit Cross 1st and 2nd Class with Swords, 1914 Iron Cross 2nd Class, Cross of Honor.

Fullriede, Fritz: Generalmajor (20.04.45), (Heer); born 01.04.95 in Bremen, died 13.11.69 in Borstel. WWI: Leutnant der Res. in 10. Res. Jaeger Bataillon. Chief of 5. Kompanie, Infanterie Regiment 66, 04.1937–11.1938, Chief of 6. Kompanie, Infanterie Regiment 93, 11.1938–02.1939. WWII: Chief of 7. Kompanie, Infanterie Regiment 93, 03.1939–08.1939, Commander of Infanterie Replacement Bataillon 93, 08.1939–12.1939, Adjutant on Staff of Division 171, 12.1939–10.1940, Commander of I. Bataillon, Infanterie Regiment 642, 10.1940–07.1941, wounded and placed in Fuehrer Res. of O.K.H. 09.1941–02.1943, Commander of Panzer Grenadier Regiment 165, 02.1943–05.1943, Commander of Panzer Grenadier Regiment 129, 07.1943–09.1943, held several commands for short periods of time 09.1943–1944, Commandant of Fortress Kolberg 1945–1945. Awards: Oak Leaves 23.03.45 (803), Knight's Cross 11.04.43, 1939 Clasps to the 1914 Iron Cross 1st and 2nd Class, Infantry Assault Badge in Silver, Afrika Cuff Band, 1939 Wound Badge in Gold, 1914 Iron Cross 1st and 2nd Class, 1914 Iron Cross 1st and 2nd Class, Cross of Honor.

Funck, Hans Freiherr von: General der Panzertruppe (01.03.44), (Heer); born 23.12.91 in Aachen, died 14.02.79 in Viessen. WWI: Leutnant in Res. Dragoon Regiment 12. Promotions to Generalmajor 01.01.41, Generalleutnant 01.09.42. WWII: Military Attaché in Spain 11.1936–08.1939, Military Attaché in Lisbon 08.1939–10.1939, Commander of Panzer Regiment 5, 10.1939–11.1940, Commander of 3. Panzer Brigade 11.1940–01.1941, Commander of 7. Panzer Division 02.1941–08.1943, Commander of XXIII. Armee Korps 12.1943–02.1944, Commander of XXXXVII. Panzer Korps 03.1944–09.1944, Fuehrer Res. in O.K.H. 09.1944–05.1945. Awards: Oak Leaves 22.08.43 (278), Knight's Cross 15.07.41, German Cross in Gold 14.03.43, 1939 Clasps to the 1914 Iron Cross 1st and 2nd Class, Tank Assault Badge in Silver, Eastern Front Medal, Afrika Cuff Band, Spanish Cross in Gold with Swords, 1914 Iron Cross 1st and 2nd Class, 1914 Wound Badge in Silver, Cross of Honor.

Funck, Werner: Generalmajor (30.01.45), (Luftwaffe); born 18.09.85 in Posen, died 29.10.65 in Bad Kissingen. WWI: in G.A.S. as Hauptmann and Commander of Armeeflugparks 17. Attached to Luftkreis Kommando III in Berlin 03.1935–09.1936, Commander of Jet Propelled Office at Rechlin 10.1936–02.1937, Advisor to Quartermaster of Flieger in R.L.M. 03.1937–06.1938. WWII: Commander of Luftparks at Wiener-Neustadt 06.1938–03.1940, attached to Luftzeuggruppe XIII 04.1940–11.1940, Commander of Luftzeuggruppe Norway 12.1940–04.1941, Commander of Luftzeuggruppe Riga 10.1941–01.1943, Commander of Luftzeuggruppe Koenigsberg 01.1943–11.1943, assigned to special tasks in Florence 12.1943–06.1944, attached to Flieger Replacement Bataillon III 10.1944–02.1945. Awards: War Merit Cross 1st and 2nd Class with Swords, Pilot's Commemorative Badge, RK-Hohenzollern, RK-Sachsen Ernestine House Order 1st Class with Swords, RK-Sachsen Albrecht Order 1st Class with Swords, 1914 Iron Cross 1st and 2nd Class, Prussian Crown Order IV. Class with Swords, 1914 Pilot's Badge, Cross of Honor.

Funcke, Heinz: Generalleutnant (01.01.45), (Luftwaffe); born 21.12.92 in Hagen, died 16.06.69 in Muenster. WWI: in G.A.S. as Oberleutnant in Flieger Abteilung 256. Promotion to Generalmajor 01.10.41. IIa on Staff of Luft Amtes (later Luftkreis Kommando IV) in Muenster 04.1934–09.1935, Air Tactics Instructor at Kriegsschule Munich 01.1935–12.1938. WWII: Commander of Flieger Training Regiment 62, 01.1939–01.1940, Commander of Luftwaffe Kriegsschule 2 at Berlin-Gatow 02.1940–11.1943, Troop Commander for Luftflotte 2, 11.1943–05.1945. Awards: 1939 Clasps to the 1914 Iron Cross 1st and 2nd Class, War Merit Cross 1st and 2nd Class with Swords, 1939 Pilot's Badge, Pilot's Commemorative Badge, 1914 Iron Cross 1st and 2nd Class, 1914 Wound Badge in Black, 1914 Observer's Badge, Cross of Honor.

Furbach, Heinz: Generalmajor (01.03.44), (Heer); born 27.09.95 in Karlshof, died 23.10.68 in Munich. WWI: Leutnant in Guards Grenadier Regiment 5. Chief of 12. (M.G.) Kompanie, Infanterie Regiment at Kolberg 10.1934–10.1935. WWII: Tactics Instructor at Kriegsschule Munich 10.1935–10.1939, Commander of M.G. Bataillon 7, 01.1940–05.1940, Department Chief of Personnel in Field Equipment Inspectorate of O.K.H. 07.1940–05.1941, Specialist with Inspector of Education and Training Affairs in O.K.H. 05.1941–05.1942, Commander of Infanterie Regiment 58, 05.1942–03.1943, Commander of 331. Infanterie Division 11.1943–07.1944, Fuehrer Res. in O.K.H. 07.1944–02.1945. Awards: Knight's Cross 04.10.42, 1939 Clasps to the 1914 Iron Cross 1st and 2nd Class, Infantry Assault Badge in Silver, RK-Hohenzollern, 1914 Iron Cross 1st and 2nd Class, 1914 Wound Badge in Black, Cross of Honor.

G

Gabcke, Otto: Generalleutnant (01.02.41), (Heer); born 20.11.82 in Gardelagen, died 22.03.42 in action in Michailovka. WWI: Hauptmann and Commander of I. Bataillon, Infanterie Regiment 158. Promotion to Generalmajor 01.10.36. Commander of Infanterie Regiment 3, 02.1933–04.1935. WWII: Military Replacement Inspector for Leipzig 05.1935–02.1940, Commander of 29. Infanterie Division 02.1940–03.1942. Awards: German Cross in Gold 26.12.41, 1939 Clasps to the 1914 Iron Cross 1st and 2nd Class, Infantry Assault Badge in Silver, 1939 Wound Badge in Gold, Pour le Mérite 01.09.18, RK-Hohenzollern, 1914 Iron Cross 1st and 2nd Class, 1914 Wound Badge in Black, Cross of Honor.

Generalmajor Carl-August Freiherr von Gablenz. (Josef Charita)

Gablenz, Carl-August Freiherr von: Generalmajor (01.01.41), (Luftwaffe); born 13.10.93 in Erfurt, died 21.08.42 from air accident over Muehlberg. WWI: in G.A.S. as Leutnant in Bombengeschwader 7. Joined N.S.F.K., NSFK-Oberfuehrer, Member of Board of Directors for German Lufthansa 07.1933–08.1942. WWII: Commander of 172. Special Purpose Jagdgeschwader 08.1939–11.1939, Commander of Blindflug Schule of Luftwaffe 11.1939–09.1941, Chief of Planning Department assigned to GFM Milch in R.L.M. 10.1941–08.1942. Awards: Knight's Cross of the War Merit Cross with Swords 25.08.42 (posthumously), 1939 Clasps to the 1914 Iron Cross 1st and 2nd Class, War Merit Cross 1st and 2nd Class with Swords, Combined Pilot/Observer's Badge in Gold with Diamonds, Spanish Cross in Silver without Swords, 1939 Wound Badge in Gold, Pilot's Commemorative Badge, RK-Hohenzollern, 1914 Iron Cross 1st and 2nd Class, Austro-Hungarian Military Service Cross 3rd Class with War Decoration, 1914 Wound Badge in Silver, Turkish Half Moon, 1914 Pilot's Badge, Cross of Honor.

Gablenz, Eccard Freiherr von: Generalleutnant (01.08.40), (Heer); born 26.01.91 in Koenigsberg, died 17.12.78 in Rheinbach. WWI: Hauptmann attached to Chief of General Staff of Feld Armee. Promotion to Generalmajor 01.08.38. Commander of Infanterie Regiment at Crossen 10.1934–10.1935, Commander of Infanterie Regiment 29, 10.1935–12.1935, Commander of Infanterie Regiment 18, 12.1935–11.1938, Commander of Heeres Service Office 5, 11.1938–04.1939. WWII: Commander of Heeres Service Office 4, 05.1939–08.1939, attached to Staff of Border Protection Commando 2, 08.1939–12.1939, Commander of 7. Infanterie Division 12.1939–12.1941, Commander of 384. Infanterie Division 02.1942–01.1943, Commander of 404. Infanterie Division 03.1943–07.1944, Commander of 232. Infanterie Division 07.1944–05.1945. Awards: Knight's Cross 15.08.40, 1939 Clasps to the 1914 Iron Cross 1st and 2nd Class, Infantry Assault Badge in Silver, Eastern Front Medal, 1914 Iron Cross 1st and 2nd Class, Cross of Honor.

Gadow, Hans-Joachim: Konteradmiral (01.02.44), (Kriegsmarine); born 06.09.98 in Tillendorf, died 04.08.78 in Ruhpolding. WWI: Fahnrich zur See attached to Admiralty Staff. Torpedo Officer for cruiser *Karlsruhe* 09.1933–09.1934, attached to Training Department in Marineleitung (later O.K.M.) 09.1934–03.1937, Commandant of destroyer *Richard Beitzen* 05.1937–05.1938. WWII: First Admiral Staff Officer attached to torpedo boats 05.1938–10.1939, First Admiral Staff Officer attached to destroyers 10.1939–11.1939, Chief of 3. Zerstorer Flottilla 12.1939–04.1940, Naval Representative at Narvik 04.1940–08.1940, Transport Fleet Chief in France 11.1940–02.1941, Chief of Staff to Romanian Naval Forces and at same time Escort Chief of Black Sea 04.1941–03.1943, Chief of Staff to Marine Gruppen Kommando North Sea 06.1943–05.1945. Awards: German Cross in Gold 10.10.43, 1939 Iron Cross 1st Class, 1939 Clasp to the 1914 Iron Cross 2nd Class, High Seas Fleet War Badge, Narvik Shield, Commander's Cross of the Romanian Order of the Star with Swords, Silesian Eagle 1st and 2nd Class, 1914 Iron Cross 2nd Class, Cross of Honor.

Gadow, Reinhold: Konteradmiral z.V. (01.07.42), (Kriegsmarine); born 25.04.82 in Berlin, died 29.04.49 in Russian P.O.W. camp. WWI: Korvettenkapitan (unit unknown), P.O.W. 08.1914–11.1918. WWII: Director of Libraries in O.K.W. 09.1940–03.1945. Awards: War Merit Cross 1st and 2nd Class with Swords, Cross of Honor.

Gaedcke, Ludwig-Heinrich: Generalmajor (01.11.44), (Heer); born 16.01.05 in Guban, died 21.12.92 in Waldesch. Attached to Kriegsschule 10.1935–10.1937. WWII: attached to Kommando Staff of Operations Department of Heeres General Staff 10.1937–06.1940, Ia to 25. Infanterie Division 06.1940–02.1943,

Instructor at Kriegsschule 03.1943–10.1943, Chief of Staff to XXIV. Panzer Korps 10.1943–11.1943, Fuehrer Res. in O.K.H. 12.1943–04.1944, Chief of Staff to XI. Armee Korps 04.1944–06.1944, Chief of General Staff to 4. Armee 07.1944–08.1944, Chief of General Staff to 6. Armee 08.1944–05.1945. Awards: Knight's Cross 07.04.44, German Cross in Gold 07.03.42, 1939 Iron Cross 1st and 2nd Class, Eastern Front Medal.

Gaede, Heinrich: Generalmajor (20.05.44), (Heer); born 19.12.98 in Gut Rathmannsdorf, died 01.01.83 in Landau. WWI: Leutnant in Feld Artillerie Regiment 45. Ia on Staff of Grenz Abschnitte Kommando at Kuestrin 10.1934–04.1935, Ia on Staff of Commander of Kuestrin 05.1935–10.1936, Chief of 7. Batterie, Artillerie Regiment 30, 10.1936–10.1937. WWII: Ia to Inspector of Artillerie in Reich War Ministry (later O.K.H.) 10.1937–08.1939, Ia to 225. Infanterie Division 08.1939–11.1940, Ia to 110. Infanterie Division 12.1940–11.1941, Fuehrer Res. in O.K.H. 12.1941–06.1942, Chief of German Training Staff attached to Bulgarian Army High Command 06.1942–09.1944, Commander of 719. Infanterie Division 12.1944–03.1945. Awards: 1939 Clasps to the 1914 Iron Cross 1st and 2nd Class, War Merit Cross 1st and 2nd Class with Swords, Eastern Front Medal, 1914 Iron Cross 1st and 2nd Class, Cross of Honor.

Gaedicke, Fritz: Generalmajor (01.10.44), (Heer); born 16.02.96 in Berlin, died 26.03.70 in Berlin. WWI: Leutnant in 18. Pionier Bataillon. Attached to Pionier Schule (later Pionier Schule I) 10.1934–10.1936, Commander of Pionier Bataillon 21, 10.1936–08.1937. WWII: Ia to Inspector of Fortresses in Reich War Ministry (later O.K.H.) 09.1937–06.1940, Commander of z.b.V. Pionier Regiment 628, 06.1940–06.1942, Commander of Festung Pionier Schule 10.1942–01.1944, Commander of Grenadier Regiment 316, 02.1944–04.1944, placed in Fuehrer Res. in O.K.H. due to wounds 04.1944–12.1944, Commander of 203. Infanterie Division 12.1944–05.1945. Awards: Honor Roll Clasp 17.05.44, 1939 Clasps to the 1914 Iron Cross 1st and 2nd Class, General Assault Badge, 1939 Wound Badge in Black, 1914 Iron Cross 1st and 2nd Class, Cross of Honor.

Gaertner, Heinrich: SS-Brigadefuehrer und Generalmajor der Waffen-SS (30.01.44); born 27.02.97 in Nuremberg, died 05.05.63 in Attel. P-35359, SS-148903. WWI: Leutnant der Res. attached to 6. Foot Artillerie Regiment. Joined N.S.D.A.P. and S.A. in 1926, reached rank of SA-Sturmbannfuehrer, joined S.S. in 1934. Attached to Staff of RFSS 01.10.34, attached to SS-Hauptamt 01.07.35, attached to Staff of SS-Hauptamt 01.12.36–01.12.38. WWII: Chief of Amt IX of the SS-Hauptamt, Chief of Amt V of SS-Fuehrungshauptamt 30.01.42, Chief of Amt VIII (Weapons Office) of SS-Fuehrungshauptamt 15.05.43–30.01.44, attached to SS-Fuehrungshauptamt 09.11.44. Awards: Golden Party Badge, Blood Order (Bund

R.K.F., Fuehrer Abt. Schleissheim), War Merit Cross 1st and 2nd Class with Swords, Finnish Freedom Cross 1st Class with Swords, 1914 Iron Cross 2nd Class, Cross of Honor, Degen, Ring.

Gagern, Ernst Freiherr von: Admiral z.V. (01.09.42), (Kriegsmarine); born 06.07.78 in Neuenburg, died 14.09.54 in Neuenburg. WWI: Fregattenkapitan and Commandant of small cruiser *Emden*. Promotions to Reichsmarine Konteradmiral 01.04.21, Reichsmarine Vizeadmiral 01.10.24. WWII: Deputy Reich Commissioner of Upper Jury Court in Berlin 09.1939–10.1942, retired 10.1942. Awards: War Merit Cross 1st and 2nd Class with Swords, Red Eagle Order 4th Class with Swords, RK-Hohenzollern, 1914 Iron Cross 1st and 2nd Class, Bavarian Military Service Order IV. Class with Swords, Cross of Honor.

Gaissert, Victor: Generalleutnant z.V. (01.04.42), (Heer); born 05.01.79 in Stuttgart, died 21.03.45 of natural causes in Wiesbaden. WWI: German Airship Service as Major and Commander of 42. Feld Zeppelin Abteilung. Promotion to Generalmajor z.V. 01.12.40. WWII: recalled to military service 08.1939, Commander of P.O.W. Camps in Nuremberg, Hadamar, Limburg 08.1939–07.1940, P.O.W. Camp Commander in France 08.1939–06.1941, Wehrmacht P.O.W. Commander for Occupied Eastern Territories 06.1941–11.1942, retired 01.1943. Awards: War Merit Cross 1st and 2nd Class with Swords, Eastern Front Medal, RK-Sachsen Military St. Heinrich's Order 02.02.16, 1914 Iron Cross 1st and 2nd Class, 1914 Wound Badge in Black, 1920 Airship Commemorative Badge, Cross of Honor.

Gall, Franz: Generalleutnant (01.07.44), (Heer); born 02.09.84 in Trier, died 27.12.44 in action in Mestre. WWI: Hauptmann on Staff of 117. Infanterie Division. Promotion to Generalmajor 01.01.43. WWII: attached to E-Officer Korps 03.1935–09.1939, Commander of Landwehr Infanterie Regiment 161, 09.1939–12.1939, Ia to Wehrkreis XVII 12.1939–04.1940, Ia and later Chief of Staff to Wehrkreis I 04.1940–03.1941, assignments unknown 04.1941–07.1943, Fuehrer Res. in O.K.H. 07.1943–09.1943, Wehrmacht Commander of Defensive Sections Marseille, Elbe and later Venedig 09.1943–012.1944. Awards: Knight's Cross 19.06.44, 1939 Clasps to the 1914 Iron Cross 1st and 2nd Class, War Merit Cross 1st and 2nd Class with Swords, 1939 Wound Badge in Gold, 1914 Iron Cross 1st and 2nd Class, Cross of Honor.

Galland, Adolf: Generalleutnant (01.11.44), (Luftwaffe); born 19.03.12 in Westerholt, died 09.02.96 in Remagen. Promotion to Generalmajor 01.11.42. Attached to J.G. "Richthofen" 10.1935–05.1937, attached to J 88 as well as Staffelkapitan in "Legion Condor" 05.1937–06.1938, Adjutant to J.G. "Richthofen" 09.1938–10.1938, Staffelkapitan in I. Gruppe, J.G. "Richthofen" 11.1938–01.1939, Staffelkapitan in J.G. 52, 02.1939–06.1939. WWII: Staffelkapitan to 4.

Staffel, L.G. 2, 07.1939–09.1939, Adjutant to J.G. 27, 10.1939–03.1940, Commander of III. Gruppe, J.G. 26 "Schlageter" 06.1940–08.1940, Commander of J.G. 26 "Schlageter 08.1940–12.1941, Inspector and General of Jagdflieger 12.1941–01.1945, Commander of J.V. 44, 02.1945–04.1945, Honorary NSFK-Gruppenfuehrer, 104 Day Victories. Awards: Diamonds 28.01.42 (02), Swords 21.06.41 (1), Oak Leaves 24.09.40 (3), Knight's Cross 29.07.40, 1939 Iron Cross 1st and 2nd Class, Spanish Cross in Gold with Swords and Diamonds, Combined Pilot-Observer's Badge in Gold with Diamonds.

Generalleutnant Adolf Galland. (Roger James Bender)

Gallas, Paul: Generalmajor (01.09.44), (Heer); born 25.01.85 in Alt-Rahfelde, died 18.09.44 in action in Kasepaa. WWI: Leutnant in Ulan Regiment 10. WWII: Commander of Lehrer Gruppe Staff at Kriegsschule Munich 01.1935–08.1939, Commander of Transport Ersatz Bataillon 7, 09.1939–07.1941, Commandant of Feldkommandantur 247, 07.1941–06.1942, Commander of Special Purpose Regiment Staff of 281. Security Division 06.1942–09.1944. Awards: German Cross in Gold 23.04.44, Honor Roll Clasp 15.10.44, 1939 Clasps to the 1914 Iron Cross 1st and 2nd Class, Infantry Assault Badge in Silver, 1939 Wound Badge in Gold, 1914 Iron Cross 1st and 2nd Class, 1914 Wound Badge in Black, Cross of Honor.

Gallenkamp, Curt: General der Artillerie (01.04.42), (Heer); born 17.02.90 in Wesel, died 13.04.58 in Wiesbaden. WWI: Hauptmann attached to General Staff of Feld Armee. Promotions to Generalmajor 01.03.38, Generalleutnant 01.04.40. Attached to Heeres Service Office at Giessen 10.1934–10.1935, attached to Staff of Heeres Service Office 8, 10.1935–03.1936, attached to Staff of 34. Division 03.1936–05.1936, Commander of Heeres Service Office 8, 07.1936–10.1936, Commander of Heeres Service Office 11, 10.1936–04.1937, Commander of Artillerie 18, 05.1937–03.1938. WWII: Chief of Staff to III. Armee Korps 04.1938–09.1939, Commander of 78. Infanterie Division 09.1939–09.1941, Fuehrer Res. in O.K.H. 11.1941–03.1942, Commander of LXXX. Armee Korps 05.1942–08.1944, Fuehrer Res. in O.K.H. 08.1944–05.1945. Awards: Knight's Cross 19.11.41, 1939 Clasps to the 1914 Iron Cross 1st and 2nd Class, Infantry Assault Badge in Silver, 1914 Iron Cross 1st and 2nd Class, 1914 Wound Badge in Black, Cross of Honor.

Gallwitz, Karl: Ministerialdirektor (01.04.40), (Luftwaffe); born 29.01.82 in Pitschen, died 26.07.45 in Berlin. Civil Servant by profession. WWI: Hauptmann der Res. in 5. Infanterie Division. Department Leader in Construction Group of R.L.M. 05.1933–01.1939. WWII: Department Chief in Construction Group of

R.L.M. 02.1939–09.1939, Chief of Office Construction Group for Luftwaffe in R.L.M. 09.1939–05.1944, retired 08.1944. Awards: War Merit Cross 1st and 2nd Class with Swords, 1914 Iron Cross 1st and 2nd Class, 1914 Wound Badge in Black, Cross of Honor.

Gallwitz, Dr. Udo: Generalmajor (01.03.43), (Heer); born 22.05.92 in Reichenbach, died 31.03.43 in action in Ulyanovka. WWI: Leutnant in Feld Artillerie Regiment 21. WWII: Advisor and later Group Leader in Ballistic and Munitions Abteilung of Heeres Weapons Office Weapons Office of Reich War Ministry (later O.K.H.) 02.1935–10.1942, Commander of Artillerie Regiment 610, 10.1942–03.1943. Awards: 1939 Clasps to the 1914 Iron Cross 1st and 2nd Class, War Merit Cross 1st and 2nd Class with Swords, General Assault Badge, 1939 Wound Badge in Gold, Dr. Fritz Todt Prize in Gold 08.02.44, Silesian Eagle 1st and 2nd Class, 1914 Iron Cross 1st and 2nd Class, 1914 Wound Badge in Black, Cross of Honor.

Gallwitz, Werner von: Generalleutnant (01.05.44), (Heer); born 17.05.93 in Glogau, died 11.05.44 in action near Sevastopol. WWI: Oberleutnant in Feld Artillerie Regiment 76. Promotion to Generalmajor 01.10.43. WWII: Commander of II. Abteilung, Artillerie Regiment 19, 10.1934–08.1939, Commander of Artillerie Regiment 183, 08.1939–03.1942, Commander of Artillerie 133, 03.1942–02.1943, Senior Commander of Artillerie I 05.1943–01.1944, Commander of Gebirgs Artillerie 132, 04.1944–05.1944. Awards: 1939 Clasps to the 1914 Iron Cross 1st and 2nd Class, General Assault Badge, 1939 Wound Badge in Gold, RK-Hohenzollern, 1914 Iron Cross 1st and 2nd Class, Cross of Honor.

Gandert, Hans-Eberhard: Generalmajor (01.12.39), (Luftwaffe); born 02.09.92 in Sandberg, died 24.07.47 in Augsburg. WWI: in G.A.S. as Oberleutnant and Commander of Jagdgruppe 6. Attached to Staff of Reich Minister of R.L.M. 10.1934–01.1935, attached to Staff of Kampfflieger Schule Lechfeld 01.1935–03.1935, attached to Staff of Fliegerschule Cottbus 04.1935–05.1935, attached to Staff of Transport Kompanie III 05.1935–01.1936, Fliegerhorst Commandant of Quedlinburg 02.1936–07.1937, Commander of Fliegerschule (school unknown) 10.1937–06.1938. WWII: Department Chief in R.L.M. 07.1938–07.1941, Inspector of Clothing and Food Supply Affairs of Luftwaffe 07.1941–04.1942, Commander of Luftwaffe Practice Area in Zingst 05.1942–11.1944, Fuehrer Res. in O.K.L. 11.1944–02.1945. Awards: War Merit Cross 1st and 2nd Class with Swords, Pilot's Commemorative Badge, RK-Hohenzollern, 1914 Iron Cross 1st and 2nd Class, 1914 Wound Badge in Black, 1914 Pilot's Badge, Cross of Honor.

Gareis, Martin: General der Infanterie (01.04.45), (Heer); born 06.10.91 in Buch, died 26.02.76 in Kreuth. WWI: Oberleutnant and Adjutant to Infanterie Regiment 24. Promotions to Generalmajor 01.02.42, Generalleutnant 01.01.43. Commander of II. Bataillon, Infanterie Regiment at Allenstein 10.1934–10.1935, Commander of II. Bataillon, Infanterie Regiment 2, 10.1935–10.1937, Commander of Lehrer Gruppe B at Kriegsschule Munich 10.1937–03.1939. WWII: Commander of Infanterie Regiment 282, 09.1939–12.1941, Commander of 98. Infanterie Division 02.1942–02.1944, Commander of 264. Infanterie Division 05.1944–10.1944, Commander of XXXXVI. Panzer Korps 01.1945–05.1945. Awards: Knight's Cross 29.11.43, German Cross in Gold 18.10.41, 1939 Clasps to the 1914 Iron Cross 1st and 2nd Class, German Army High Command Commendation Certificate 22.09.41, Infantry Assault Badge in Silver, Eastern Front Medal, RK-Hohenzollern, 1914 Iron Cross 1st and 2nd Class, 1914 Wound Badge in Silver, Cross of Honor.

Garn, Dr. Alfred: General-Veterinar (01.07.42), (Heer); born 16.12.87 in Essen, died 23.03.52 in Giessen. Medical veterinarian by profession. WWI: Veterinar (unit unknown). WWII: Division Veterinar to 9. Division 08.1938–08.1939, Korps Veterinar to Wehrkreis IX 09.1939–1943, Fuehrer Res. in O.K.H. 1943–02.1944, retired 02.1944. Awards: War Merit Cross 1st and 2nd Class with Swords, 1914 Iron Cross 1st and 2nd Class, Cross of Honor.

Garski, Eugen: Generalmajor (01.09.42), (Heer); born 08.06.97 in Thorn, died 30.09.42 in action near Kostonossovo. WWI: Leutnant in Infanterie Regiment 18. Kompanie Chef in Infanterie Regiment 81, 03.1935–05.1935, Kompanie Chef in Infanterie Regiment 66, 06.1935–04.1937, Commander of II. Bataillon, Infanterie Regiment 33, 05.1937–04.1939. WWII: Commander of III. Bataillon, Infanterie Regiment "Grossdeutschland" 05.1939–08.1940, Commander of V. Bataillon, Infanterie Regiment "Grossdeutschland" 08.1940–09.1941, Course Commander at Doeberitz Infanterie Schule 09.1941–03.1942, Commander of Infanterie Regiment (mot.) "Grossdeutschland" 03.1942–09.1942. Awards: Knight's Cross 19.07.40, 1939 Clasps to the 1914 Iron Cross 1st and 2nd Class, Infantry Assault Badge in Silver, 1939 Wound Badge in Gold, 1914 Iron Cross 1st and 2nd Class, Cross of Honor.

Gaul, Hans: Generalmajor z.V. (01.02.42), (Heer); born 13.06.77 in Regensburg, died 01.09.57 in Reistenhausen. WWI: Hauptmann and Bataillon Commander in Bavarian Res. Infanterie Regiment 2. Attached to E-Officer Korps 03.1935–06.1937, retired 06.1937. WWII: recalled to military service 07.1940, Commander of P.O.W. District B 07.1940–08.1941, Commander of P.O.W. District N 08.1941–03.1942, Commandant of Feldkommandantur 679, 03.1942–08.1942, retired 09.1942. Awards: War Merit Cross 1st and 2nd Class with Swords, 1914 Iron Cross 1st and 2nd Class, Cross of Honor.

Gause, Alfred: Generalleutnant (01.04.43), (Heer); born 14.02.96 in Koenigsberg, died 30.09.67 in Bonn. WWI: Oberleutnant and Adjutant to 18. Pionier Bataillon.

Promotion to Generalmajor 01.06.41. Ia to Wehrkreis Kommando V (later V. Armee Korps) 10.1934–10.1937. WWII: attached to Wehrmacht Amt in Reich War Ministry (later O.K.W.) 10.1937–10.1939, Chief of Staff to X. Armee Korps 11.1939–05.1940, Chief of Staff to XXXVIII. Armee Korps 10.1940–01.1941, German Liaison to Italian Oberkommando in Africa 01.1941–09.1941, Chief of General Staff to Panzer Armee "Afrika" 09.1941–12.1942, Chief of General Staff to Heeresgruppe "Afrika" 03.1943.05.1943, Chief of General Staff to Heeresgruppe B 07.1943–04.1944, Chief of General Staff to Panzer Gruppe "West" and later 5. and 6. Panzer Armees 06.1944–11.1944, Fuehrer Res. in O.K.H. 11.1944–05.1945. Awards: Knight's Cross 13.12.41, 1939 Clasps to the 1914 Iron Cross 1st and 2nd Class, Tank Assault Badge in Bronze, Afrika Cuff Band, Kurland Cuff Band, 1914 Iron Cross 1st and 2nd Class, 1914 Wound Badge in Black, Cross of Honor.

Gautier, Theophil: Generalleutnant (01.04.41), (Luftwaffe); born 16.02.81 in Oels, died 08.09.53 in Frankfurt am Main. WWI: Korvettenkapitan and Commandant of torpedo boat *V 116*. Promotion to Generalmajor 01.06.38. Adjutant to Luftkreis Kommando VI in Kiel 07.1934–02.1936, Department Leader of Armaments Inspection in Dresden 04.1936–03.1938. WWII: Armaments Inspector for Vienna 04.1938–04.1944, retired 04.1944. Awards: War Merit Cross 1st and 2nd Class with Swords, 1939 Observer's Badge, Red Eagle Order IV. Class with Swords, RK-Hohenzollern, 1914 Iron Cross 1st and 2nd Class, 1914 Wound Badge in Black, Cross of Honor.

Gawantka, Georg: Generalmajor (01.08.38), (Heer); born 18.08.91 in Berlin, died 14.07.39 of natural causes in Prague. WWI: Rittmeister in Dragoon Regiment 22. Commander of Schuetzen Regiment 2, 10.1935–01.1938, Commander of 3. Schuetzen Brigade 02.1938–11.1938, Commander of 2. Schuetzen Brigade 11.1938–04.1939, Commander of 10. Panzer Division 05.1939–07.1939. Awards: 1914 Iron Cross 1st and 2nd Class, 1914 Wound Badge in Black, Cross of Honor.

Gebauer, Arthur: Generalmajor (01.06.42), (Heer); born 07.10.86 in Zattig, died 06.12.69 in Graz. WWI: Rittmeister and Kompanie Chef in Austrian Infanterie Regiment 59. Transferred to German Wehrmacht 03.1938, attached to Gruppen Kommando 5, 04.1938–07.1938. WWII: attached to Formation Staff of Infanterie Regiment 133, 08.1938–11.1939, Commander of Infanterie Regiment 158, 12.1939–03.1942, Wehrmacht Commander of Graz 04.1942–02.1945. Awards: 1939 Iron Cross 1st and 2nd Class, War Merit Cross 1st and 2nd Class with Swords, Infantry Assault Badge in Silver, Cross of Honor.

Gebb, Werner: Generalmajor (01.07.44), (Heer); born 08.06.96 in Heldenbergen, died 12.08.52 at Asbest P.O.W. Camp. WWI: Leutnant in Infanterie Regiment 118.

Kompanie Chef in Infanterie Regiment at Kassel 10.1934–10.1935, Adjutant to 9. Division 10.1935–04.1937. WWII: Advisor in Heeres Personnel Office of Reich War Ministry (later O.K.H.) 05.1937–06.1940, Department Chief in Heeres Personnel Department of O.K.H. 10.1940–01.1943, Commander of Grenadier Regiment 116, 02.1943–02.1944, Commander of 9. Infanterie Division 06.1944–08.1944, captured 08.1944. Awards: German Cross in Gold 14.05.44, 1939 Clasps to the 1914 Iron Cross 1st and 2nd Class, Infantry Assault Badge in Silver, 1914 Iron Cross 1st and 2nd Class, Cross of Honor.

Gebhardt, Prof. Dr. Karl: SS-Gruppenfuehrer und Generalleutnant der Waffen-SS (30.01.43); born 23.11.97 in Haag, died 02.06.48 (executed) at Landsberg Prison. Medical doctor by profession. P-1723317, SS-265894. WWI: NCO (unit unknown). Joined N.S.D.A.P. and S.S. in 1933. Promotion to SS-Brigadefuehrer 01.10.41. Orthopedic Surgeon and close personal friend of RFSS-Heinrich Himmler, z.b.V. RFSS 01.07.35, Leader on Staff of SS-Hauptamt 01.12.36–01.1238. WWII: attached to Personlicher Staff of RFSS 30.01.42, Chief of SS Lazarette Hohenlychen Orthopedic Clinic 15.05.43, Oberster Kliniker (Head of Clinics) in D. St. Reichsarzt-SS und Polizei 30.01.44–09.11.44. Awards: Knight's Cross of the War Merit Cross with Swords 31.05.44, German Cross in Silver 20.04.44, 1939 Clasps to the 1914 Iron Cross 1st and 2nd Class, War Merit Cross 1st and 2nd Class with Swords, 1939 Wound Badge in Black, Baltic Cross 1st and 2nd Class, 1914 Iron Cross 1st and 2nd Class, 1914 Wound Badge in Black, Cross of Honor, German Olympic Games Decoration 1st Class, Degen, Ring.

SS-Gruppenfuehrer Prof. Dr. Karl Gebhardt. (Josef Charita)

Gebler, Dr. Johannes: General-Stabsarzt (01.09.42), (Luftwaffe); born 30.06.91 in Magdeburg, died 25.01.59. Medical doctor by profession. WWI: Assistenz-Arzt in Res. Infanterie Regiment 37. Promotion to General-Arzt 20.08.40. Medical Advisor in Zentral Abteilung of R.L.M. 10.1933–07.1935, Chief Physician for Luftkreis Kommando III 08.1935–04.1938, Physician attached to Staff of Luftwaffen Kommando Osterreich 05.1938–01.1939, Physician attached to Luftwaffe Leadership Staff 88, 01.1939–06.1939. WWII: Chief Physician for Luftflotte 4, 07.1939–12.1942, Officer with Special Duties in R.L.M. 12.1942–01.1944, attached to Inspection of Luftwaffe Medical Matters in R.L.M. 02.1944–10.1944, retired 10.1944. Awards: War Merit Cross 1st and 2nd Class with Swords, 1914 Iron Cross 1st and 2nd Class, 1914 Wound Badge in Black, Cross of Honor.

Geerkens, Heinrich: Generalmajor (01.01.44), (Luftwaffe and Heer); born 15.09.93 in Buschenschachen, died 25.01.44 in action near Valassova. WWI: in G.A.S. as Oberleutnant (unit unknown). Attached to Air Office at Muenster 04.1934–04.1935, attached to Fliegerschule at Hildesheim 05.1935–12.1935, attached to Reich Air Ministry 01.1936–06.1936, attached to Legion Condor in Spain 07.1936–02.1937, attached to Staff of Flieger Training Regiment 47, 03.1937–03.1939. WWII: Commander of Flieger Training Regiment 33, 04.1939–10.1942, Commander of LW Jaeger Regiment in Holland 10.1942–08.1943, Commander of Luftwaffe Jager Regiment 17, 08.1943–01.1944, transferred to Heer 11.1943, Leader of 9. Luftwaffe Feld Division 01.1944–01.1944. Awards: 1939 Clasps to the 1914 Iron Cross 1st and 2nd Class, 1939 Wound Badge in Gold, Spanish Cross in Bronze with Swords, Pilot's Commemorative Badge, 1914 Iron Cross 1st and 2nd Class, 1914 Pilot's Badge, Cross of Honor.

Gehlen, Reinhard: Generalmajor (01.12.44), (Heer); born 03.04.02 in Erfurt, died 08.06.79 in Munich. Adjutant to Quartermaster I in Heeres General Staff 10.1935–07.1936, attached to Abteilung 1 of Heeres General Staff 07.1936–07.1937, attached to Abteilung 10 of Heeres General Staff 07.1937–11.1938. WWII: Chief of 8. Batterie, Artillerie Regiment 18, 11.1938–08.1939, Ia to 231. Infanterie Division 08.1939–10.1939, Group Leader of State Defenses in Heeres General Staff 10.1939–05.1940, First Adjutant to Chief of Heeres General Staff 06.1940–10.1940, Group Leader in Operations Department of Heeres General Staff 10.1940–05.1942, Department Chief of Foreign Armies East in O.K.W. 05.1942–04.1945. Awards: German Cross in Silver 28.03.45, War Merit Cross 1st and 2nd Class with Swords.

Geib, Theodor: General der Artillerie (01.12.41), (Heer); born 15.09.85 in Landau, died 26.11.44 of wounds in Freiburg Military Hospital. WWI: Hauptmann on Staff of Imperial War Ministry. Promotions to Generalmajor 01.04.37, Generalleutnant 01.01.39. Chief of Staff to Feldzeug Inspection of Reichswehr Ministry 04.1934–03.1935, Department Chief in Feldzeug Inspection of Reich War Ministry 04.1935–10.1937. WWII: Heeres Feld Equipment Master in General Office of Reich War Ministry (later O.K.H.) 10.1937–08.1943, Plenipotentiary General of Albania 09.1943–06.1944, Heeres Area Commander in France 06.1944–07.1944. Awards: German Cross in Silver 09.11.43, War Merit Cross 1st and 2nd Class with Swords, 1939 Wound Badge in Gold, 1914 Iron Cross 1st and 2nd Class, Cross of Honor.

Geier, Heinrich: General-Intendant (01.12.42), (Heer); born 16.09.95 in Berlin, died 04.03.75 in Puerto de la Cruz. Administrative Officer by profession. WWI: (rank and unit unknown). Attached to Wehrkreis Kommando IX 1935–1937, attached to Reich War Ministry 1937–01.1938, attached to Training Department in O.K.H. 02.1938–12.1944, Chief Intendant to X. Armee Korps 12.1944–05.1945. Awards: War Merit Cross 1st and 2nd Class with Swords, Cross of Honor.

Geiger, Franz: Generalleutnant (16.03.45), (Heer); born 19.12.94 in Landshut, died 05.1945 in action. WWI: Leutnant and Chief of 17. Pionier Kompanie. Promotion to Generalmajor 01.08.43. Commander of Pionier Bataillon 7, 10.1935–10.1936, Commander of Gebirgs Pionier Bataillon 54, 10.1936–06.1938. WWII: Commander of Pionier XVIII 08.1938–08.1939, Commander of Gebirgs Pionier Regiment Staff 620, 08.1939–05.1941, Department Chief (In 5) in O.K.H. 06.1941–08.1943, Commander of Special Staff Geiger 08.1943–01.1945, Fuehrer Res. in O.K.H. 01.1945–05.1945. Awards: German Cross in Silver 28.06.44, War Merit Cross 1st and 2nd Class with Swords, 1914 Iron Cross 1st and 2nd Class, Cross of Honor.

Geiger, Gustav: Generalmajor (01.09.44), (Heer); born 31.03.87 in Nuremberg, died 02.01.67. WWI: Hauptmann on Staff of Bavarian Infanterie Regiment 5. Training Leader at Weiden 02.1936–10.1936. WWII: Training Leader at Amberg 10.1936–10.1940, Commander of Infanterie Replacement Regiment 73, 10.1940–01.1942, Commander of Schuetzen Regiment 51, 03.1942–03.1943, Fuehrer Res. in O.K.H. 03.1943–02.1944, Commander of Truppenubungsplatz at Hohenfels 03.1944–05.1945. Awards: 1939 Clasps to the 1914 Iron Cross 1st and 2nd Class, Infantry Assault Badge in Silver, 1914 Iron Cross 1st and 2nd Class, Bavarian Military Service Order IV. Class with Swords, Cross of Honor.

Geiger, Rudolf: Generalmajor (01.12.44), (Heer); born 19.11.91 in Friedland, died 14.01.72 in Wels. WWI: Rittmeister and Bataillon Commander in Austrian Schuetzen Regiment 6. Transferred to German Wehrmacht 03.1938. WWII: Commander of III. Bataillon, Infanterie Regiment 133, 08.1938–06.1940, Commander of Infanterie Regiment 289, 06.1940–02.1943, Commander of Res. Infanterie Regiment 215, 05.1943–05.1944, Commander of Truppenubungsplatz at Brod 06.1944–02.1945. Awards: German Cross in Gold 22.11.41, 1939 Iron Cross 1st and 2nd Class, Infantry Assault Badge in Silver, Eastern Front Medal, Cross of Honor.

Geis, Hermann: Generalmajor z.V. (01.12.42), (Heer); born 20.01.78 in Munich, died 15.01.58 in Regensburg. WWI: Major and Commander of Senior Construction Staff Geis. WWII: recalled to military service 08.1939. Commander of Territorial Schuetzen Regiment 19 and later 131, 08.1939–02.1941, Commander of Patrol Services for Wehrkreis XIII 02.1941–01.1943, retired 01.1943. Awards: War Merit Cross 1st and 2nd Class with Swords, 1914 Iron Cross 1st and 2nd Class, Cross of Honor.

Geisler, Hans: General der Flieger (19.07.40), (Luftwaffe); born 19.04.91 in Hannover, died 25.06.66 in Koeln. WWI: in Naval G.A.S. as Oberleutnant zur See in I. Seeflieger Abteilung. Promotions to Generalmajor 01.04.37, Generalleutnant 01.04.39. Leader of Naval Aircraft 10.1935–03.1939, Officer attached to R.L.M. and O.B. der Luftwaffe 04.1939–05.1939. WWII: General z.b.V. attached to Luftflotte

2, 06.1939–09.1939, Commander of 10. Flieger Division 09.1939–10.1939, Commander of X. Flieger Korps 10.1939–08.1942, retired 10.1942. Awards: Knight's Cross 04.05.40, German Cross in Gold 09.11.42, 1939 Clasps to the 1914 Iron Cross 1st and 2nd Class, Combined Pilot/Observer's Badge, Naval Pilot's Commemorative Badge, 1914 Iron Cross 1st and 2nd Class, 1914 Naval Observer's Badge, Cross of Honor.

Geissler, Erich: Generalmajor (01.03.45), (Heer); born 11.12.95 in Buedingen, died 02.05.67 in Oldenburg. WWI: Leutnant and Adjutant to III. Bataillon, Infanterie Regiment 25. Adjutant to Infanterie Regiment at Kassel 10.1934–10.1935, Chief of 4. Kompanie, Infanterie Regiment 15, 10.1935–10.1937. WWII: Tactics Instructor at Kreigsschule Munich 10.1937–08.1939, Commander of III. Bataillon, Infanterie Regiment 87, 08.1939–01.1940, Commander of II. Bataillon, Infanterie Regiment 382, 01.1940–08.1941, Commander of Panzer Grenadier Regiment 200, 09.1941–12.1942, Department Chief (Org E/Tr) in O.K.H. 05.1943–05.1945. Awards: Knight's Cross 29.07.42, 1939 Clasps to the 1914 Iron Cross 1st and 2nd Class, Tank Assault Badge in Bronze, Afrika Cuff Band, 1914 Iron Cross 1st and 2nd Class, 1914 Wound Badge in Silver, Cross of Honor.

Geitner, Herbert: Generalleutnant (01.08.41), (Heer); born 25.01.88 in Berlin, died 22.01.42 of wounds in Freiburg Military Hospital. WWI: Hauptmann and Staff Officer in Prussian War Ministry. Promotion to Generalmajor 01.08.39. Commander of I. Bataillon, Infanterie Regiment 1, 08.1934–04.1936, Commander of Heeres Feuerwerkerschule 04.1936–03.1938. WWII: Commander of Infanterie Regiment 75, 04.1938–02.1940, Commander of 295. Infanterie Division until wounded 02.1940–12.1941. Awards: German Cross in Gold 10.12.41, 1939 Clasps to the 1914 Iron Cross 1st and 2nd Class, Infantry Assault Badge in Silver, 1939 Wound Badge in Gold, 1914 Iron Cross 1st and 2nd Class, Cross of Honor.

Geitner, Kurt Ritter von: Generalmajor der Res (01.04.44), (Heer); born 03.05.84 in Truppacher, died 06.09.68 in Munich. WWI: Hauptmann on Staff of Armee Gruppe South. WWII: attached to Infanterie Regiment 31, 10.1935–09.1939, Commander of Infanterie Replacement Regiment 209, 09.1939–02.1940, Ia to IV. followed by Wehrkreis VIII 02.1940–10.1940, Chief of Staff to Special Purpose A.O.K. XXXXV 10.1940–06.1941, Fuehrer Res. in O.K.H. 02.1942–07.1942, Chief of Staff to Wehrmacht Befehlshaber of Serbia 07.1942–08.1943, Chief of Staff to Wehrmacht Befehlshaber South-East 08.1943–09.1944, attached to O.K.W. 01.1944–05.1945. Awards: War Merit Cross 1st and 2nd Class with Swords, RK-Bavarian Military Max Joseph Order 19.06.16, RK-Hohenzollern, 1914 Iron Cross 1st and 2nd Class, Cross of Honor.

Gempp, Friedrich: Generalmajor z.V. (01.02.41), (Heer); born 06.07.73 in Freiburg, died 11.08.46 in Russian P.O.W. camp. WWI: Major and Abwehr Staff Officer.

WWII: recalled to military service 08.1939, attached to Ausland Abwehr of O.K.W. 08.1939–05.1943, retired 05.1943. Awards: War Merit Cross 1st and 2nd Class with Swords, 1914 Iron Cross 1st and 2nd Class, Cross of Honor.

Genee, Paul: Generalmajor z.V. (01.02.42), (Heer); born 23.03.78 in Paswalk, died 07.03.48 at Sohula P.O.W. Camp. WWI: in G.A.S. as Hauptmann and Commander of Feld Flieger Abteilung 3. Attached to Staff of Wehrkreis Kommando III 10.1933–09.1938, retired 09.1938. WWII: recalled to military service 09.1939, Commander of Military District Kommando II in Magdeburg 08.1940–07.1941, Commandant of Feld Section 580, 07.1941–09.1942, retired 09.1942. Awards: War Merit Cross 1st and 2nd Class with Swords, Pilot's Commemorative Badge, RK-Hohenzollern, 1914 Iron Cross 1st and 2nd Class, 1914 Pilot's Badge, Cross of Honor.

Genske, Wilhelm: Konteradmiral (01.02.42), (Kriegsmarine); born 31.10.85 in Weilburg, died 27.08.58 in Hamburg. WWI: Marine-oberingenieur and Engineer for 3. Submarine Halb Flotille. Welfare Leader attached to Marine Station North Sea 10.1933–06.1938. WWII: Commander of Wehrmacht Wehrkreis-Fursorge-und Versorgungs Abteilung for Wehrkreis X 06.1938–03.1944, retired 07.1944. Awards: War Merit Cross 1st and 2nd Class with Swords, 1914 Iron Cross 1st and 2nd Class, Cross of Honor.

Genthe, Friedrich: Generalleutnant z.V. (01.12.41), (Heer); born 25.07.73 in Gaimma, died 26.01.46 at Muehlberg P.O.W. Camp. WWI: Major and Commander of Uhlan Regiment 21. Promotion to Generalmajor z.V. 01.09.40. WWII: recalled to military service 12.1939, Commander of Division 445 z.b.V. 12.1939–01.1940, Commander of Division 412 z.b.V. 01.1940–10.1940, Commandant of P.O.W. Camp Oflag IV B 02.1941–04.1942, Fuehrer Res. in O.K.H. 04.1942–03.1943, retired 03.1943. Awards: War Merit Cross 1st and 2nd Class with Swords, RK-Hohenzollern, RK-Sachsen Military St. Heinrich's Order (date unknown), 1914 Iron Cross 1st and 2nd Class, Cross of Honor.

Genz, Dr. Paul: General-Arzt (01.03.42), (Heer); born 19.01.87 in Voelschow, died 13.05.47 in Eisenach. Medical doctor by profession. WWI: Physician (unit unknown). WWII: Division Physician to 2. Infanterie Division (mot.) 1938–03.1940, Corps Physician to XXXXII. Armee Korps 03.1940–04.1942, Army Physician to 18. Armee 09.1942–06.1944, retired 10.1944. Awards: 1939 Clasp to the 1914 Iron Cross 2nd Class, War Merit Cross 1st and 2nd Class with Swords, 1914 Iron Cross 2nd Class, Cross of Honor.

Genzken, Dr. Karl: SS-Gruppenfuehrer und Generalleutnant der Waffen-SS (30.01.43); born 08.06.85 in Holstein, died 10.10.57 in Hamburg. Medical doctor by profession. P-39913, SS-207954. WWI: Marine Oberassistezarzt attached to U-Boat Staff. Joined N.S.D.A.P. in 1926, joined S.A. in 1930, reached

SS-Gruppenfuehrer Dr. Karl Genzken. (Bundesarchiv)

rank of SA-Sanitats Standartenfuehrer, joined S.S. in 1933. Promotion to SS-Brigadefuehrer 01.08.41. Attached to SS-Sanitats Abteilung of SS-V.T. 01.12.36, Leader of SS-Sanitats Abteilung of SS-T.V.-K.L. 01.12.37–01.12.38. WWII: Division Physician to SS-Division "Totenkopf," Chief of Amt VIII (Sanitats Amt) of SS-Fuehrungshauptamt 30.01.42, Chief of Amtsgruppe D (Sanitatswesen der Waffen-SS) of SS-Fuehrungshauptamt 15.05.43–09.11.44. Awards: Golden Party Badge, War Merit Cross 1st and 2nd Class with Swords, 1914 Iron Cross 1st and 2nd Class, Cross of Honor, Degen, Ring.

Georgi, Richard: Generalmajor (01.12.44), (Heer); born 31.03.84 in Bremen, died 14.01.65 in Berlin. WWI: Hauptmann and Commander of II. Bataillon, Res. Infanterie Regiment 207. Attached to E-Officer Korps 03.1935–09.1935, Commander of Replacement Bataillon 58, 10.1935–10.1936, Commander of Supplementary Bataillon, Infanterie Regiment 65, 11.1936–03.1937. WWII: Training Leader at Luebeck 04.1937–08.1939, Commander of Infanterie Regiment 333, 09.1939–12.1940, Commander of Infanterie Replacement Regiment 20, 12.1940–12.1941, attached to Formation Staff of Infanterie Regiment 489, 12.1941–04.1942, Commander of Infanterie Replacement Regiment 20, 08.1942–08.1943, Commandant of P.O.W. Camp Oflag X B 08.1943–09.1944, Fuehrer Res. in O.K.H. 10.1944–01.1945. Awards: 1939 Clasps to the 1914 Iron Cross 1st and 2nd Class, Infantry Assault Badge in Silver, Eastern Front Medal, RK-Hohenzollern, 1914 Iron Cross 1st and 2nd Class, Austro-Hungarian Military Service Cross 3rd Class with War Decoration, 1914 Wound Badge in Black, Cross of Honor.

Gerber, Alexander Edler von Zabernberg: Generalmajor (01.09.42), (Heer); born 15.05.91 in Goerz, died 18.06.52 in Vienna. WWI: Hauptmann and Kompanie Chef in 2. Feld Jaeger Bataillon. Transferred to German Wehrmacht 03.1938. WWII: attached to Staff of Infanterie Regiment 25, 11.1938–08.1939, Commander of Infanterie Replacement Regiment 207, 10.1939–11.1939, Commander of Infanterie Regiment 314, 12.1939–12.1941, in hospital 12.1941–05.1942, Fuehrer Res. in O.K.H. 05.1942–01.1943, retired 01.1943. Awards: 1939 Iron Cross 1st and 2nd Class, Infantry Assault Badge in Silver, Cross of Honor.

Gercke, Hubert: General der Infanterie z.V. (0.1.12.42), (Heer); born 01.04.81 in Nikolaiken, died 07.12.42 of natural causes in Goerlitz. WWI: Hauptmann and Bataillon Commander in Infanterie Regiment 446. Promotions to Reichswehr Generalmajor 01.01.33, Generalleutnant 01.04.35. Commander of 2. Division

06.1935–03.1937. WWII: without assignment 04.1937–05.1940, Commander of 278. Infanterie Division 05.1940–07.1940, Commander of 401. Infanterie Division 01.1941–01.1942, retired 06.1942. Awards: 1939 Clasps to the 1914 Iron Cross 1st and 2nd Class, RK-Hohenzollern, 1914 Iron Cross 1st and 2nd Class, 1914 Wound Badge in Black, Cross of Honor.

Gercke, Rudolf: General der Infanterie (01.04.42), (Heer); born 17.08.84 in Nikolaiken, died 17.02.47 in Marburg. Brother of General der Infanterie Hubert Gercke. WWI: Hauptmann and Staff Officer in Armee Gruppe Kronprinz Rupprecht von Bayern. Promotions to Generalmajor 01.10.39, Generalleutnant 01.08.40. Group Leader in Reichswehr Ministry (later Reich War Ministry) 10.1933–10.1937. WWII: Department Chief in Heeres General Staff 10.1937–08.1939, Heeres Transport Chief in O.K.H. 08.1939–01.1940, Chief of Feld Transport Affairs in O.K.H. 01.1940–05.1945. Awards: Knight's Cross of the War Merit Cross with Swords 07.07.43, 1939 Clasps to the 1914 Iron Cross 1st and 2nd Class, War Merit Cross 1st and 2nd Class with Swords, Finnish Freedom Cross 1st Class with Breast Star and Swords, 1914 Iron Cross 1st and 2nd Class, Cross of Honor.

General der Infanterie Rudolf Gercke. (Josef Charita)

Gerhardt, Paul: Generalleutnant (01.02.41), (Heer); born 20.04.81 in Ruhrort, died 12.10.53 in Berlin. WWI: Hauptmann and Commander of III. Bataillon, Res. Infanterie Regiment 55. Promotion to Generalmajor 01.10.37. Commander of Military District Kommando at Eisenbach 10.1933–07.1936. WWII: Military Replacement Inspector for Allenstein 08.1936–11.1939, Commander of 311. Infanterie Division 11.1939–08.1940, Military Replacement Inspector for Allenstein 08.1940–01.1945, Fuehrer Res. in O.K.H. 01.1945–05.1945. Awards: War Merit Cross 1st and 2nd Class with Swords, RK-Hohenzollern, 1914 Iron Cross 1st and 2nd Class, Cross of Honor.

Gerke, Ernst: Generalleutnant (01.01.43), (Heer); born 07.06.90 in Altenburg, died 01.08.73 in Bartgeheide. WWI: Oberleutnant and Liaison on Staff of Chief of Signals Affairs in Sachsen High Command. Promotion to Generalmajor 01.02.41. Commander of Nachrichten Abteilung at Munich 10.1934–10.1935, Commander of Nachrichtentruppen V 10.1935–11.1938. WWII: Liaison between Wehrmacht Signals in O.K.W. and Reich Post Ministry 11.1938–04.1939, Signals Leader to 4. Armee 09.1939–10.1941, Signals Leader to Heeresgruppe Sud 10.1941–07.1942, Signals Leader to Heeresgruppe "Afrika" 03.1943–05.1943, Signals Leader to Heeresgruppe

B 06.1943–05.1945. Awards: Knight's Cross of the War Merit Cross with Swords 08.05.45, German Cross in Silver 15.02.43, 1939 Clasps to the 1914 Iron Cross 1st and 2nd Class, War Merit Cross 1st and 2nd Class with Swords, Eastern Front Medal, Afrika Cuff Band, 1914 Iron Cross 1st and 2nd Class, Cross of Honor.

Generalleutnant Ernst Gerke. (Josef Charita)

Gerlach, Adolf: Generalmajor (01.04.44), (Luftwaffe); born 5.01.94 in Singlis, died 14.05.53 in Bonn. WWI: Leutnant in Fuss Artillerie Bataillon 150. Batterie Chef in Flak Regiment 3, 10.1935–09.1936, Commander of II. Abteilung, Flak Regiment 4, 10.1936–11.1937, Commander of I. Abteilung, Flak Regiment 14, 12.1937–06.1938, Commander of Festung Flak Abteilung 33, 07.1938–10.1938. WWII: Commander of Flak Staff (later Flak Gruppe) Eifel 11.1938–08.1939, Commander of Flak Gruppe Euskirchen 11.1939–05.1940, Commander of Flak Regiment 40, 08.1939–11.1939, Commander of Flak Regiment 180, 10.1940–03.1941, Commander of Flak Regiment 42, 05.1941–09.1941, Commander of Flak Brigade Kanalinseln 11.1941–12.1943, Commander of 14. Flak Division 05.1944–05.1945. Awards: German Cross in Gold (date unknown), 1939 Iron Cross 1st Class, 1939 Clasp to the 1914 Iron Cross 2nd Class, Flak War Badge, German West Wall Medal, 1914 Iron Cross 2nd Class, Cross of Honor.

Gerlach, Arthur: Konteradmiral z.V. (01.02.43), (Kriegsmarine); born 07.03.90 in Erfurt, died 24.11.68 in Stuttgart. WWI: U-Boat Service as Marineingenieurober-aspirant and Chief Engineer on *U-39*. Advisor in Marineleitung 10.1931–10.1934, Engineer attached to Befehlshaber of Line Ships 10.1934–09.1936. WWII: Engineer Advisor in War Ship Construction 02.1937–11.1939, Leader of Commission for Boiler Protection and Feed Water Maintenance 01.1940–05.1942, Director of Naval Equipment and Repair Operations at Swinemuende 06.1942–05.1945. Awards: War Merit Cross 1st and 2nd Class with Swords, 1914 Iron Cross 1st and 2nd Class, 1914 Submarine Badge, 1914 Naval Wound Badge in Black, Cross of Honor.

Gerlach, Erwin: Generalmajor (01.07.43), (Heer); born 29.06.94 in Berlin, died 03.12.57 in Koenigstein. WWI: Leutnant and Adjutant to 32. Fuss Artillerie Bataillon. Commander of II. Abteilung, Artillerie Regiment at Halberstadt 10.1934–09.1935, Ia to Inspector of Artillerie 09.1935–08.1938. WWII: Ia to XI. Armee Korps 09.1938–10.1939, Ia to O.B. East (Poland) 10.1939–05.1940, Senior Quartermaster to 16. Armee 06.1940–12.1941, Senior Quartermaster to O.B. West 02.1942–12.1942, Commander of 389. Infanterie Division 04.1943–11.1943, Chief of Staff to Wehrkreis Kommando XII 12.1943–08.1944, Chief of Staff to Wehrkreis

Kommando IV 08.1944–05.1945. Awards: 1939 Clasps to the 1914 Iron Cross 1st and 2nd Class, War Merit Cross 1st and 2nd Class with Swords, 1939 Wound Badge in Black, 1914 Iron Cross 1st and 2nd Class, Austro-Hungarian Military Service Cross 3rd Class with War Decoration, Cross of Honor.

Gerlach, Joachim von: Konteradmiral (01.02.43), (Kriegsmarine); born 22.11.95 in Berlin, died 19.03.79 in Darmstadt. WWI: Leutnant zur See and Commandant of minesweeper. Attached to Staff of Marine Technische Schule in Berlin-Charlottenburg 10.1932–09.1934, Navigations Officer for battleship *Deutschland* 09.1934–10.1936, Advisor attached to Torpedo Inspection 11.1936–09.1937, Chief of Staff for Torpedo Inspectorate 10.1937–11.1938. WWII: Chief of Torpedo Abteilung in O.K.M. 11.1938–11.1939, Chief of Military Abteilung in Office Gruppe for Torpedo Weapons in O.K.M. 11.1939–04.1940, Commandant of Naval Section Wesermuende 07.1940–06.1942, Commander of Sea Defenses at Narvik 09.1942–04.1945. Awards: War Merit Cross 1st and 2nd Class with Swords, 1914 Iron Cross 1st and 2nd Class, Cross of Honor.

Gerlach, Karl: General-Stabsintendant (01.09.44), (Luftwaffe); born 07.08.83 in Boeken, died 17.10.51 in Altona. Administrative Officer by profession. WWI: Military Intendant Assessor. Promotion to General-Intendant 09.03.40. Intendant to Luftkreis Kommando II in Berlin 06.1934–03.1937. WWII: General-Intendant attached to R.L.M. 04.1937–11.1940, Intendant for Luftwaffe Befehlshaber Mitte (Central) 03.1941–03.1943, Chief Intendant to Oberbefehlshaber South-East 01.1943–09.1943, Chief Intendant to Luftgau Kommando XII 09.1943–03.1944, Chief Intendant to Luftflotte 10, 05.1944–09.1944, Officer with Special Duties attached to O.B. of Luftwaffe 09.1944–02.1945. Awards: War Merit Cross 1st and 2nd Class with Swords, 1914 Iron Cross 1st and 2nd Class, Cross of Honor.

Gerlach, Karl von: Generalmajor (01.06.41), (Luftwaffe); born 06.08.94 in Paulsdorf, died 24.06.41 in action in Linouo. WWI: in G.A.S. as Leutnant in Flieger Abteilung 241. Instructor at Luftwaffe Aufklarungs Schule at Braunschweig 07.1934–03.1935, Advisor in Ausbildungs Abteilung of Flieger Schulen 04.1935–02.1937, Fliegerhorst Commandant of Cottbus 03.1937–03.1938, Fliegerhorst Commandant of Braunschweig 04.1938–01.1939. WWII: Department Chief of Provisions Office in R.L.M. 02.1939–03.1941, Commander of Luftwaffe for Panzer Gruppe 2, 03.1941–06.1941. Awards: 1939 Clasps to the 1914 Iron Cross 1st and 2nd Class, 1939 Wound Badge in Gold, 1939 Observer's Badge, Pilot's Commemorative Badge, 1914 Iron Cross 1st and 2nd Class, 1914 Observer's Badge, Cross of Honor.

Gerloch, Bruno: Generalmajor (20.04.45), (Heer); born 11.11.90 in Teschen, died 03.09.54 in Vienna. WWI: Oberleutnant and Batterie Chef in Austrian Artillerie Regiment 50. Transferred to German Wehrmacht 03.1938, attached to

Artillerie Regiment 12, 07.1938–11.1938. WWII: Commander of II. Abteilung, Artillerie Regiment 116, 11.1938–11.1939, Commander of Artillerie Regiment 90, 11.1939–12.1942, Commander of Artillerie 2, 12.1942–03.1943, Commander of Artillerie 117, 08.1943–08.1944, attached to Staff of 708. Infanterie Division 08.1944–05.1945. Awards: Knight's Cross 04.09.40, German Cross in Gold 08.02.42, 1939 Clasps to the 1914 Iron Cross 1st and 2nd Class, General Assault Badge, Eastern Front Medal, 1914 Iron Cross 1st and 2nd Class, Cross of Honor.

Germar, Ulrich von: Generalmajor (01.03.41), (Heer); born 17.11.76 in Bromberg, died 27.02.48 in Blankenburg. WWI: Major and Commander of I. Bataillon, Res. Infanterie Regiment 233. WWII: Commander of Military District Kommando at Stolp 10.1933–08.1942, retired 08.1942. Awards: War Merit Cross 1st and 2nd Class with Swords, Pour le Mérite 22.04.18, RK-Hohenzollern, 1914 Iron Cross 1st and 2nd Class, 1914 Wound Badge in Silver, Cross of Honor.

Gerok, Kurt: Generalmajor (01.03.43), (Heer); born 24.02.82 in Ulm, died 24.04.46 in Karlsruhe. WWI: Hauptmann and Commander of II. Abteilung, Feld Artillerie Regiment 29. WWII: Commander of Military District Commando at Karlsruhe 04.1936–09.1939, Commander of Artillerie Replacement Regiment 5, 09.1939–05.1940, Commander of Military District Commando in Karlsruhe 06.1940–05.1941, Commander of Artillerie Replacement Regiment 25, 05.1941–02.1942, Commander of Artillerie Regiment 387, 02.1942–01.1943, Commander of 153. Feld Training Division 06.1943–06.1944, Commander of 207. Security Division 09.1944–01.1945. Awards: German Cross in Gold 29.03.44, 1939 Clasps to the 1914 Iron Cross 1st and 2nd Class, General Assault Badge, RK-Wuerttemberg Friedrich Order 1st Class with Swords, RK-Sachsen Albrecht Order 1st Class with Swords, 1914 Iron Cross 1st and 2nd Class, Bavarian Military Service Cross IV. Class with Swords, Austro-Hungarian Military Service Cross 3rd Class with War Decoration, Cross of Honor.

Gersdorff, Curt-Ulrich von: Generalmajor (20.04.45), (Heer); born 17.12.02 in Berleburg, died 02.07.68 in Hameln. Adjutant to Reiter Regiment at Gera 10.1934–10.1935, Adjutant to Schuetzen Regiment 1, 10.1935–05.1936, Chief of 1. Kompanie, Schuetzen Regiment 1, 05.1936–10.1937. WWII: Adjutant to 1. Schuetzen Brigade 10.1937–10.1939, Ic to XVI. Armee Korps 11.1939–10.1940, Ia to 20. Panzer Division 10.1940–08.1941, Ia to Heeresgruppe Nord 08.1941–10.1942, Ia to 32. Infanterie Division 10.1942–07.1943, Ia to Heeresgruppe Nord 07.1943–10.1944, Chief of General Staff to 16. Armee 10.1944–05.1945. Awards: Blood Order (unit unknown), German Cross in Gold 10.08.44, 1939 Iron Cross 1st and 2nd Class, Eastern Front Medal.

Gersdorff, Gero von: Generalmajor (01.01.43), (Heer); born 17.10.92 in Charlottenhof, died 15.11.67 in Munich. WWI: Leutnant in Fuss Garde Regiment 3, P.O.W. 09.1914–08.1919. Schwadron Chef in Reiter Regiment at Schwedt 10.1934–03.1935, attached to Staff of Military Commander of Hamburg 04.1935–10.1937. WWII: Commander of I. Bataillon, Infanterie Regiment 118, 10.1937–12.1939, Commander of Infanterie Regiment 166, 12.1939–09.1941, Commander of Infanterie Regiment 80, 09.1941–01.1942, Commander of Infanterie Replacement Regiment 246, 04.1942–12.1942, Commander of 401. Infanterie Division 12.1942–09.1944, attached to Staff of Inspector of Land Fortifications West 12.1944–05.1945. Awards: 1939 Clasps to the 1914 Iron Cross 1st and 2nd Class, Infantry Assault Badge in Silver, 1914 Iron Cross 1st and 2nd Class, Johann Ritter Order, 1914 Wound Badge in Black, Cross of Honor.

Gersdorff, Rudolf-Christoph Freiherr von: Generalmajor (08.03.45), (Heer); born 27.03.05 in Lueben, died 26.01.80 in Munich. Chief of 1. Schwadron, Reiter Regiment 7, 11.1934–05.1935, Chief of 3. Schwadron, Reiter Regiment 8, 10.1935–10.1936, Chief of 1. Schwadron, Kavallerie Regiment 8, 10.1936–08.1937, attached to Staff of Higher Kavallerie Officer 1, 10.1937–11.1938. WWII: Ic to Heeres Gruppen Kommando 5, 11.1938–08.1939, Ic to 14. Armee 08.1939–10.1939, Ic to XII. Armee Korps 11.1939–04.1940, Ia to 86. Infanterie Division 05.1940–04.1941, Ic to Heeresgruppe Mitte 06.1941–09.1943, Chief of Staff to LXXXII. Armee Korps 02.1944–07.1944, Chief of General Staff to 7. Armee 07.1944–08.1944. Awards: Knight's Cross 26.08.44, German Cross in Gold 25.10.43, 1939 Iron Cross 1st and 2nd Class, Infantry Assault Badge in Silver, Eastern Front Medal.

Gerstenberg, Alfred: Generalleutnant (01.09.43), (Luftwaffe); born 06.04.93 in Neudorf, died 04.01.59 in Garmisch. WWI: in G.A.S. as Leutnant in J.G. 2 "Richthofen." Promotion to Generalmajor 01.09.41. Chief of Staff of Luftwaffe Reserve 10.1934–07.1936, Tactics Instructor at Luftwaffe Kriegsschule Tutow 08.1936–05.1938. WWII: Luftwaffe Attaché in Bucharest 06.1938–08.1944, Befehlshaber of Luftwaffe in Romania 02.1942–08.1944, captured 08.1944. Awards: 1939 Clasps to the 1914 Iron Cross 1st and 2nd Class, War Merit Cross 1st and 2nd Class with Swords, Commander's Cross of the Order of the Star of Romania with Swords and Ring, Romanian Order of Michael the Brave 3rd Class, "J.G. Freiherr von Richthofen Nr. 1, 1917/18" Commemorative Cuff Band, Pilot's Commemorative Badge, RK-Hohenzollern, 1914 Iron Cross 1st and 2nd Class, 1914 Wound Badge in Black, 1914 Pilot's Badge, Cross of Honor.

Gerstmann, Josef: Generalmajor (01.04.44), (Heer); born 22.07.86 in Dzieditz, died 16.03.63 in Klagenfurt. WWI: Hauptmann and Adjutant to Landwehr Infanterie Regiment 4. Transferred to German Wehrmacht 03.1938. WWII: attached to Staff of Gebirgs Jaeger Regiment 137, 08.1938–08.1939, Commander of Gebirgs Replacement Regiment 2, 08.1939–02.1940, Commander of Infanterie Regiment 628, 02.1940–10.1940, Commander of Truppenubungsplatz at Suippes 11.1940–11.1943, Commander of Truppenubungsplatz at Sierady 12.1943–1944, Commander of Truppenubungsplatz at Chalons-sur-Marne 1944–08.1944, captured 08.1944. Awards: 1939 Iron Cross 1st and 2nd Class, War Merit Cross 1st and 2nd Class with Swords, Infantry Assault Badge in Silver, Cross of Honor.

Geschwandtner, Kurt: Generalmajor (01.10.42), (Heer); born 26.02.92 in Saarbruecken, died 03.12.53 in Goppingen. WWI: Oberleutnant in Fuss Artillerie Regiment 14. Commander of IV. Abteilung, Artillerie Regiment at Hannover 10.1934–10.1935, Commander of I. Abteilung, Artillerie Regiment 55, 10.1935–10.1936, Commander of I. Abteilung, Artillerie Regiment 67, 10.1936–01.1937. WWII: Commander of Artillerie Regiment 5, 02.1937–04.1940, Commander of Artillerie 130, 04.1940–10.1941, Commander of Artillerie 137, 04.1942–02.1943, attached to Wehrkreis VIII 10.1943–03.1944, attached to Feld Equipment Master in O.K.H. 03.1944–04.1945. Awards: 1939 Clasps to the 1914 Iron Cross 1st and 2nd Class, General Assault Badge, Silesian Eagle 2nd Class, RK-Baden Order of the Zaehringer Lion 2nd Class with Swords, 1914 Iron Cross 1st and 2nd Class, Austro-Hungarian Military Service Cross 3rd Class with War Decoration, Cross of Honor.

Geyer, Hermann: General der Infanterie (01.08.36), (Heer); born 07.07.82 in Stuttgart, died 10.04.46 (suicide) in Wildsee. WWI: Hauptmann attached to Chief of General Staff of Feld Armee. Promotions to Reichswehr Generalmajor 01.12.32, Reichswehr Generalleutnant 01.01.34. WWII: Commander of 5. Division and Wehrkreis Kommando V 08.1934–10.1939, Commander of IX. Armee Korps 10.1939–01.1942, Fuehrer Res. in O.K.H. 01.1942–12.1943, retired 12.1943. Awards: Knight's Cross 25.06.40, 1939 Clasps to the 1914 Iron Cross 1st and 2nd Class, Infantry Assault Badge in Silver, RK-Hohenzollern, 1914 Iron Cross 1st and 2nd Class, Cross of Honor.

General der Infanterie Hermann Geyer. (Bundesarchiv)

Geyer, Hugo: Ministerialdirigent (01.08.39), (Luftwaffe); born 06.04.84 in Hildburghausen, died 12.10.75 in Hildburghausen. Civil Servant by profession. WWI: in G.A.S. as Hauptmann and Commander of Kampfgeschwader 4. Member of N.S.D.A.P. Department Chief of GL/E5 in R.L.M. 05.1933–05.1945. Awards: War Merit Cross

1st and 2nd Class with Swords, Pilot's Commemorative Badge, RK-Hohenzollern, RK-Sachsen Ernestine House Order 1st Class with Swords, 1914 Iron Cross 1st and 2nd Class, Prussian Order of the Crown IV. Class with Swords, Bavarian Military Service Order IV. Class with Swords, 1914 Pilot's Badge, Cross of Honor.

Geyr von Schweppenburg, Leo Freiherr: General der Panzertruppe (01.04.40), (Heer); born 02.03.86 in Potsdam, died 27.01.74 in Irschenhausen. WWI: Hauptmann and Ia to 26. Landwehr Division. Promotions to Generalmajor 01.09.35, Generalleutnant 01.01.37. Military Attaché in the Hague and London 04.1933–10.1937. WWII: Commander of 3. Panzer Division 10.1937–02.1940, Commander of XXIV. Armee Korps 02.1940–01.1942, Commander of XXXX. Panzer Korps 07.1942–10.1942, Commander of LVIII. Panzer Korps 08.1943–01.1944, Commander of Panzer Gruppe West 04.1944–07.1944, Inspector of Panzertruppen in Replacement Armee 08.1944–05.1945. Awards: Knight's Cross 09.07.41, 1939 Clasps to the 1914 Iron Cross 1st and 2nd Class, Tank Assault Badge in Silver, Eastern Front Medal, 1914 Iron Cross 1st and 2nd Class, 1914 Wound Badge in Black, Cross of Honor.

Geyso, Eckkard von: Generalmajor (01.10.42), (Heer); born 25.05.91 in Charlottenburg, died 16.07.82 in Berlin. WWI: Oberleutnant der Res. in Infanterie Regiment 262. Adjutant to Heeres Service Office at Breslau 10.1934–04.1935, Commander of II. Bataillon, Infanterie Regiment at Crossen 05.1935–10.1935, Commander of II. Bataillon, Infanterie Regiment 29, 10.1935–11.1938. WWII: Commander of I. Bataillon, Grenz Infanterie Regiment 121, 11.1938–10.1939, Commander of Infanterie Regiment 121, 10.1939–02.1942, Commander of Infanterie Regiment 489, 04.1942–08.1942, Commander of Truppenubungsplatz at Doberitz 09.1942–07.1943, Commander of 709. Infanterie Division 07.1943–12.1943, Commander of 193. Infanterie Division 06.1944–05.1945. Awards: German Cross in Gold 18.01.41, 1939 Clasps to the 1914 Iron Cross 1st and 2nd Class, German Army High Command Commendation Certificate 04.10.41, Infantry Assault Badge in Silver, Eastern Front Medal, Crimea Shield, Romanian Commander's Cross of the Order of the Star with Swords and Ring, Bulgarian Bravery Order 1st Class with Swords, Prince Hohenzollern House Order Honor Cross 3rd Class with Swords, 1914 Iron Cross 1st and 2nd Class, 1914 Wound Badge in Black, Johann Ritter Order, Cross of Honor.

Giehrach, Bruno: Generalmajor (01.09.41), (Heer); born 27.01.82 in Berlin, died 12.04.63 in Forchheim. WWI: Hauptmann and Transport Chief of Railway Central Kiev. Leader of Welfare and Supply Department for Wehrkreis Kommando II 10.1935–05.1938. WWII: Leader of Welfare and Supply Department for Wehrkreis Kommando XVII 06.1938–02.1943, retired 02.1943. Awards: War Merit Cross 1st and 2nd Class with Swords, 1914 Iron Cross 1st and 2nd Class, Cross of Honor.

Gienanth, Curt-Ludwig Freiherr von: General der Kavallerie z.V. (01.09.40), (Heer); born 06.12.76 in Eisenberg, died 03.04.61 in Heidelberg. WWI: Major and Chief of General Staff to Military Plenipotentiary in Constantinople. Promotions to Reichswehr Generalmajor 01.02.29, Reichswehr Generalleutnant 01.02.31. Retired 09.1933. WWII: recalled to military service 09.1939, Commander of A.O.K. XXXVI 10.1939–05.1940, O.B. Ost (East) 05.1940–07.1940, Military Commander in General Government (occupied Poland) 07.1940–10.1942, Fuehrer Res. in O.K.H. 10.1942–06.1943, retired 06.1943. Awards: German Cross in Silver 30.06.43, 1939 Clasp to the 1914 Iron Cross 2nd Class, War Merit Cross 1st and 2nd Class with Swords, 1914 Iron Cross 1st and 2nd Class, 1914 Wound Badge in Black, Cross of Honor.

Giese, Herbert: Generalmajor (20.04.45), (Luftwaffe); born 02.09.99 in Ratibor, died 29.09.78 in Wiesbaden. WWI: Leutnant in Feld Artillerie Regiment 1. Schwadron Chef in Fahr Abteilung 3, 05.1934–03.1935, Batterie Chef and later Adjutant in Flak Regiment 6, 04.1935–09.1937, Ia on Staff of Senior Commander of Flak Artillerie VII 10.1937–11.1938, Tactics Instructor of Flak at Luftwaffe Kriegsschule Berlin 12.1938–07.1939. WWII: Ia to Commander of Luftwaffe Defense Zone West 10.1939–04.1940, Ia to Feld Luftgau Kommando Norway 04.1940–10.1941, Chief of Staff to Luftgau Kommando VIII 11.1941–10.1942, Chief of Staff to Luftgau Kommando XII 11.1942–03.1944, Chief of Staff to Luftflotte 10, 07.1944–12.1944, Commander of 31. Flak Division 01.1945–04.1945. Awards: 1939 Clasps to the 1914 Iron Cross 1st and 2nd Class, Flak War Badge, 1914 Iron Cross 1st and 2nd Class, Cross of Honor.

Giese, Karl-Hans: Generalmajor (01.04.45), (Heer); born 11.10.04 in Giesenfelde, died 19.09.80 in Oeynhausen. Adjutant to V. Abteilung, Artillerie Regiment at Ulm 10.1934–10.1935, Adjutant to II. Abteilung, Artillerie Regiment 51, 10.1935–10.1936, Adjutant to Artillerie Regiment 15, 10.1936–10.1937. WWII: Chief of 5. Batterie, Artillerie Regiment 29, 10.1937–08.1939, Commander of II. Abteilung, Artillerie Regiment 90, 08.1939–01.1940, attached to Staff of Heeresgruppe C 04.1940–08.1940, attached to Heeres General Staff in O.K.H. 01.1941–06.1942, attached to Organization Department in O.K.H. 08.1942–11.1943, Chief of Staff to XXIV. Panzer Korps 11.1943–08.1944, Commander of Grenadier Regiment 551, 09.1944–03.1945. Awards: German Cross in Gold (date unknown), Honor Roll Clasp 15.02.45, 1939 Iron Cross 1st and 2nd Class, War Merit Cross 1st and 2nd Class with Swords, Infantry Assault Badge in Silver.

Giessen, Erich: Generalmajor (15.02.45), (Heer); born 08.06.90 in Zweibruecken, died 04.04.50 in Grassau. WWI: Oberleutnant on Staff of XV. Armee Korps, attached to E-Officer Korps 03.1935–10.1936, attached to Artillerie Regiment 6,

11.1936–01.1937, Chief of 9. Batterie, Artillerie Regiment 6, 02.1937–02.1938. WWII: Commander of I. Abteilung, Artillerie Regiment 28, 03.1938–09.1939, Commander of Ersatz Artillerie Regiment 18, 09.1939–10.1939, Commander of Artillerie Regiment 8, 10.1939–1942, Commander of Kuesten Artillerie Regiment Staff 839, 03.1942–11.1942, Commander of Hoehere Kuesten Artillerie Nord 11.1942–09.1943, Commander of Heeres Kuesten Artillerie Schule 11.1943–11.1944, Fuehrer Res. in O.K.H. 11.1944–05.1945. Awards: 1939 Clasps to the 1914 Iron Cross 1st and 2nd Class, General Assault Badge, Eastern Front Medal, 1914 Iron Cross 1st and 2nd Class, 1914 Wound Badge in Black, Cross of Honor.

Gihr, Gustav: Generalmajor (01.10.43), (Heer); born 18.08.94 in Geisingen, died 31.10.59 in Freiburg. WWI: Oberleutnant and Chief of 11. Kompanie, Infanterie Regiment 98. Commander of I. Bataillon, Infanterie Regiment 109, 03.1936–10.1937. WWII: Commander of I. Bataillon, Infanterie Regiment 107, 10.1937–12.1939, Commander of Infanterie Regiment 367, 12.1939–09.1942, Commander of Fortress Grenadier Regiment 725, 09.1942–01.1943, Fuehrer Res. in O.K.H. 05.1943–10.1943, Commander of 707. Infanterie Division 05.1944–06.1944, captured 06.1944. Awards: German Cross in Gold (date unknown), 1939 Clasps to the 1914 Iron Cross 1st and 2nd Class, Infantry Assault Badge in Silver, Eastern Front Medal, 1914 Iron Cross 1st and 2nd Class, 1914 Wound Badge in Black, Cross of Honor.

Gilbert, Martin: Generalleutnant (01.01.42), (Heer); born 07.09.88 in Meissen, died 07.10.59 in Muehlheim. WWI: Hauptmann and Adjutant on Staff of General Government of Lomza. Promotion to Generalmajor 01.01.40. Chief of 6. Kompanie, Infanterie Regiment at Plauen 10.1934–10.1935, Commander of I. Bataillon, Infanterie Regiment 102, 10.1935–05.1936. WWII: Commander of Infanterie Regiment 79, 05.1936–12.1939, Commander of 167. Infanterie Division 12.1939–01.1940, Commander of 180. Infanterie Division 01.1940–01.1942, Commander of 110. Infanterie Division 01.1942–05.1943, Commander of 244. Infanterie Division 09.1943–04.1944, Fuehrer Res. in O.K.H. 04.1944–10.1944, Commander of 480. Infanterie Division 11.1944–05.1945. Awards: 1939 Clasps to the 1914 Iron Cross 1st and 2nd Class, Infantry Assault Badge in Silver, Eastern Front Medal, 1914 Iron Cross 1st and 2nd Class, 1914 Wound Badge in Silver, Cross of Honor.

Gille, Herbert-Otto: SS-Obergruppenfuehrer und General der Waffen-SS (09.11.44); born 08.03.97 in Gandersheim, died 26.12.66 in Stemmen. P-537337, SS-39854. WWI: Leutnant der Res. attached to Feld Artillerie Regiment 55. Joined N.S.D.A.P. in 1931, joined S.S. in 1932. Promotions to SS-Brigadefuehrer 01.12.42, SS-Gruppenfuehrer 09.11.43. Attached to III.

Sturmbann, SS-Standarte 1, 01.10.34–01.07.35, Leader on Staff of SS-Standarte 2 "Germania" 01.12.36, Leader of II. Sturmbann, SS-Standarte 2 "Germania" 01.12.37–01.12.38. WWII: Commander of I. Artillerie Sturmbann, SS-Artillerie Standarte V at Jueterbog, Commander of SS-Infanterie Regiment "Westland," SS-Division "Wiking" 30.01.42, Commander of SS-Artillerie Regiment, "Wiking" 15.05.43, Commander of the 5. SS-Panzer Grenadier (later Panzer Division) Division "Wiking," Commander of IV. SS-Panzer Korps 30.01.44–09.11.44. Awards: Diamonds 19.04.44 (12), Swords 20.02.44 (47), Oak Leaves 01.11.43 (315), Knight's Cross 08.10.42, German Cross in Gold 28.02.42, 1939 Clasps to the 1914 Iron Cross 1st and 2nd Class, General Assault Badge, Eastern Front Medal, Finnish Freedom Cross 1st Class with Swords, 1914 Iron Cross 1st and 2nd Class, Cross of Honor, Reich Sports Badge in Silver, SA-Sports Badge in Silver, Degen, Ring.

SS-Obergruppenfuehrer Herbert-Otto Gille. (Marc Rikmenspoel)

Gilsa, Werner Albrecht Freiherr von und zu: General der Infanterie (01.07.43), (Heer); born 04.03.89 in Berlin, died 08.05.45 (shot) in Lietmeritz. WWI: Hauptmann on Staff of 3. Landwehr Division. Promotions to Generalmajor 01.02.41, Generalleutnant 01.10.42. Commander of I. Bataillon, Infanterie Regiment at Luebeck 10.1934–10.1935, Commander of Wach Regiment Berlin 10.1935–10.1936. WWII: Commander of Infanterie Regiment 9, 10.1936–02.1941, Commander of 216. Infanterie Division 04.1941–05.1943, Commander of LXXXIX. Armee Korps 06.1943–11.1944, Commander of Defense District Dresden 11.1944–05.1945. Awards: Oak Leaves 24.01.42 (68), Knight's Cross 05.06.40, 1939 Clasps to the 1914 Iron Cross 1st and 2nd Class, Infantry Assault Badge in Silver, Eastern Front Medal, German Olympic Games Decoration 2nd Class, RK-Hohenzollern, 1914 Iron Cross 1st and 2nd Class, Cross of Honor.

Gimborn, Hermann von: Generalleutnant z.V. (01.02.41), (Heer); born 23.06.80 in Sigmaringen, died 15.02.53 in Bielfeld. WWI: Hauptmann and Commander of Pionier Staff 310. Promotion to Reichswehr Generalmajor 01.10.33. WWII: recalled to military service 08.1939, Chief of Investigation Staff Bremen 09.1939–07.1940, Commander of Fortifications for Lower Rhine 07.1940–06.1941, Commander of Division 177, 06.1941–09.1941, retired 12.1941. Awards: War Merit Cross 1st and 2nd Class with Swords, RK-Hohenzollern, 1914 Iron Cross 1st and 2nd Class, 1914 Wound Badge in Black, Cross of Honor.

Gimmler, Willy: Generalleutnant (01.04.43), (Heer); born 13.10.90 in Kontschwitz, died 19.08.63 in Hameln. WWI: Hauptmann attached to War Ministry. Promotion to Generalmajor 01.04.41. Commander of Nachrichten Abteilung at Koenigsberg 10.1934–10.1935, Commander of Nachrichten Abteilung 41, 10.1935–03.1936. WWII: Department Chief in Heeres Weapons Department of Reich War Ministry (later O.K.H.) 04.1936–04.1941, Signals Leader to 17. Armee 04.1941–08.1942, Signals Leader to Heeresgruppe D 08.1942–08.1944, Office Gruppe Chief of Wehrmacht Communications in O.K.W. 08.1944–05.1945. Awards: Knight's Cross of the War Merit Cross with Swords 08.05.45, German Cross in Silver 30.10.43, 1939 Clasps to the 1914 Iron Cross 1st and 2nd Class, War Merit Cross 1st and 2nd Class with Swords, 1914 Iron Cross 1st and 2nd Class, Cross of Honor.

Ginckel, Oskar von: Generalleutnant (01.02.41), (Heer); born 18.12.82 in Munich, died 14.11.49 at Vorkuta P.O.W. Camp. WWI: Hauptmann and Commander of I. Bataillon, Bavarian Feld Artillerie Regiment 7. Promotion to Generalmajor 01.04.36. Commander of Artillerie Regiment at Nuremberg 10.1934–10.1935, Commander of Artillerie 7, 10.1935–11.1936. WWII: Military Replacement Inspector for Munich 01.1937–03.1943, Commandant of Feldkommandantur 583, 06.1943–03.1945, Military Commander for Northern Kurland 03.1945–05.1945. Awards: War Merit Cross 1st and 2nd Class with Swords, Kurland Cuff Band, 1914 Iron Cross 1st and 2nd Class, 1914 Wound Badge in Black, Cross of Honor.

Gittner, Johannes: Generalmajor (01.08.44), (Heer); born 09.08.97 in Echartsberga, died 15.05.74 in Tutzing. WWI: Leutnant in 45. M.G. Bataillon. Attached to Staff of Wehrkreis Kommando II 10.1934–10.1935, attached to Staff of II. Armee Korps 10.1935–10.1936, Chief of 1. Batterie, Artillerie Regiment 5, 10.1936–10.1937. WWII: Ia to 5. Infanterie Division 10.1937–10.1939, Ia to XXXXIX. Armee Korps 02.1940–08.1940, Ia to XXVI. Armee Korps 08.1940–09.1941, Senior Quartermaster to 15. Armee 11.1941–05.1943, Commander of Artillerie Regiment 193, 06.1943–11.1943, Fuehrer Res. in O.K.H. 11.1943–06.1944, Commander of 292. Infanterie Division and later 302. Infanterie Division 06.1944–09.1944, Fuehrer Res. in O.K.H. 09.1944–05.1945. Awards: German Cross in Gold 17.09.44, 1939 Clasps to the 1914 Iron Cross 1st and 2nd Class, General Assault Badge, 1914 Iron Cross 1st and 2nd Class, 1914 Wound Badge in Black, Cross of Honor.

Gladisch, Walter: Admiral z.V. (01.02.41), (Kriegsmarine); born 02.01.82 in Berlin, died 23.03.54 in Bad Homburg. WWI: Korvettenkapitan and 2. Admiral Staff Officer with High Seas Fleet Kommando. Promotions to Reichsmarine Konteradmiral 01.10.28, Reichsmarine Vizeadmiral 01.10.31. Flottenkommando Chief 10.1931–09.1933. WWII: without assignment 09.1933–09.1939, Reich Commissioner of Jury Court in Berlin 09.1939–06.1943, retired 06.1943. Awards: War Merit Cross

1st and 2nd Class with Swords, Grand Cross of the Spanish Order for Service, 1914 Iron Cross 1st and 2nd Class, Oldenburg Friedrich-August Cross 1st and 2nd Class, Austro-Hungarian Military Service Cross 3rd Class with War Decoration, Turkish Half Moon, Cross of Honor.

Glaise von Horstenau, Edmund: General der Infanterie z.V. (01.09.43), (Heer); born 27.02.82 in Braunau, died 20.07.46 (suicide) in Langwasser. WWI: Major and General Staff Officer in Austrian Armee Supreme Command. Promotions to Generalmajor z.V. 01.03.41, Generalleutnant z.V. 01.08.42. Transferred to German Wehrmacht 03.1938. WWII: Minister z.b.V. for Ostmark 03.1938–11.1939, attached to O.K.W. 11.1939–04.1941, German Plenipotentiary General for Croatia 04.1941–09.1944, Military Historiographer for south-eastern part of war theater 09.1944–05.1945, SA-Gruppenfuehrer. Awards: Knight's Cross of the War Merit Cross with Swords 08.11.44, German Cross in Silver 08.03.43, War Merit Cross 1st and 2nd Class with Swords, Breast Star to the German Red Cross Decoration, 1914 Iron Cross 1st and 2nd Class, Cross of Honor.

General der Infanterie z.V. Edmund Glaise von Horstenau. (Josef Charita)

Glasl, Anton: Generalmajor (30.01.45), (Heer); born 13.02.97 in Freising, died 07.04.65 in Muehldorf am Inn. WWI: Leutnant in Bavarian Infanterie Regiment 13. Attached to Reichswehr Ministry (later Reich War Ministry) 05.1934–06.1935, attached to Abteilung 5 of Heeres General Staff 07.1935–10.1936, Chief of 11. Kompanie, Infanterie Regiment 20, 10.1936–10.1937. WWII: Ia to 10. Infanterie Division 10.1937–12.1939, Ia to XIII. Armee Korps 02.1940–07.1940, Department Chief in Office for Transport Affairs in O.K.H. 09.1940–09.1941, attached to War Sciences Office of O.K.H. 01.1942–03.1943, Commander of Gebirgs Jaeger Regiment 100, 03.1943–03.1944, Chief of Staff to Wehrkreis XVIII 07.1944–05.1945. Awards: Knight's Cross 11.10.43, 1939 Clasps to the 1914 Iron Cross 1st and 2nd Class, Infantry Assault Badge in Silver, Commander's Cross of the Romanian Order of the Crown with Swords, 1914 Iron Cross 1st and 2nd Class, Bavarian Military Service Order IV. With Swords, Cross of Honor.

Glasner, Johann: Generalmajor (01.01.38), (Heer); born 29.11.89 in Cilli, died 14.06.39 in Vienna. WWI: Hauptmann on Staff of Austrian Armee Gruppe "von Kaufmann." Transferred to German Wehrmacht 03.1938, Leader of Central Office in O.K.H. 04.1938–11.1938, attached to O.B. of Gruppen Kommando 5,

11.1938–04.1939, Defensive Replacement Inspector for Oppeln 05.1939–06.1939. Awards: Cross of Honor.

Gleim, Dr. Walter: General-Intendant (01.08.38), (Luftwaffe); born 18.08.90 in Treysa, died 17.11.44 in Drossen. Administrative Officer by profession. WWI: (rank and unit unknown). Intendant Official attached to R.L.M. 12.1933–06.1938, Chief Intendant for Luftgau Kommando IV in Muenster 08.1938–06.1939. WWII: Chief Intendant to Luftgau Kommando III in Berlin 07.1939–10.1940, Department Chief of (V5/6) in R.L.M. 10.1940–03.1944, Officer with Special Duties in R.L.M. 03.1944–11.1944. Awards: War Merit Cross 1st and 2nd Class with Swords.

Gleininger, Walter: Generalmajor (01.04.44), (Heer); born 12.03.92 in Rummelsburg, died 21.08.44 (suicide) near Gueret. WWI: Leutnant on Staff of Infanterie Regiment 82. Kompanie Chef in Kraftfahr Abteilung at Neuhammer 10.1934–10.1935. WWII: Commander of Panzer Jaeger Bataillon 18, 10.1935–10.1940, Commander of Infanterie Replacement Regiment 18, 01.1941–05.1941, Commander of Infanterie Replacement Regiment 128, 06.1941–03.1942, Fuehrer Res. in O.K.H. 03.1942–05.1942, Commander of 5. Panzer Grenadier Brigade 09.1942–11.1942, Fuehrer Res. in O.K.H. 11.1942–09.1943, Commandant of Feldkommandantur 586, 04.1944–08.1944. Awards: 1939 Clasps to the 1914 Iron Cross 1st and 2nd Class, 1914 Iron Cross 1st and 2nd Class, Cross of Honor.

Glodkowski, Erich: Generalmajor (01.04.41), (Heer); born 19.10.80 in Barten, died 04.01.58 in Essen. WWI: Hauptmann and Bataillon Commander in Queen Augusta Guard's Grenadier Regiment 4. WWII: Commander of Military District Kommando II in Essen 07.1936–10.1942, attached to Military District Kommando VI 11.1942–08.1943, retired 08.1943. Awards: War Merit Cross 1st and 2nd Class with Swords, RK-Hohenzollern, RK-Baden Order of the Zaehringer Lion 2nd Class with Swords, 1914 Iron Cross 1st and 2nd Class, 1914 Wound Badge in Silver, Cross of Honor.

Glokke, Gerhard: General der Infanterie (01.12.40), (Heer); born 26.11.84 in Posen, died 05.06.44 of natural causes in Muenster. WWI: Hauptmann and Ia to 107. Infanterie Division. Promotions to Reichswehr Generalmajor 01.10.34, Generalleutnant 01.10.36. Commander of 16. Division 10.1935–10.1937. WWII: attached to VI. Armee Korps 10.1937–08.1939, Commander of Wehrkreis Kommando VI 08.1939–06.1944. Awards: German Cross in Silver 01.08.43, War Merit Cross 1st and 2nd Class with Swords, RK-Hohenzollern, 1914 Iron Cross 1st and 2nd Class, Cross of Honor.

Gluecks, Richard: SS-Gruppenfuehrer und Generalleutnant der Waffen-SS (09.11.43), born 22.04.89 in Odenkirchen, died 10.05.45 (suicide) in Flensburg.

P-214805, SS-58706. WWI: Leutnant attached to Feld Artillerie Regiment 280. Joined N.S.D.A.P. in 1930, joined S.S. in 1932. Promotion to SS-Brigadefuehrer 20.04.41. Stabsfuehrer of SS-Oberabschnitte West 01.10.34, Leader of SS-Fuss Standarte 77, 01.07.35, attached to Staff of the SS-T.V. 01.12.36, attached to Staff of SS-T.V.-K.L. Inspectorate 01.12.37–01.12.38. WWII: Inspector of K.L. 30.01.42, Chief of Amtsgruppe D (Konzentrationslager) in W.V.H.A. 15.05.43–09.11.44. Awards: German Cross in Silver 25.01.45, War Merit Cross 1st and 2nd Class with Swords, 1914 Iron Cross 1st and 2nd Class, Cross of Honor, Degen, Ring.

Gnamm, Dr. Walter: Generalmajor (01.06.43), (Luftwaffe); born 28.05.95 in Alpirsbach, died 20.04.47 in Garmisch. WWI: in G.A.S. as Leutnant in Flieger Abteilung 23. Attached to Training Staff of Luftwaffe Kriegsschule Berlin 11.1935–09.1936, Staffelkapitan of Fernaufklarungs Staffel 123, 10.1937–09.1938, attached to Luftwaffe General Staff in Berlin 11.1938–01.1939. WWII: Commander of Fernaufklarungs Gruppe 21, 02.1939–08.1939, Ia to Luftwaffe Commander for 2. Armee 10.1939–03.1940, Luftwaffe Commander for Panzer Gruppe Kleist 03.1940–08.1940, Commander of Luftwaffe for 16. Armee 08.1940–06.1941, Luftwaffe Commander for Panzer Gruppe 1, 06.1941–10.1941, Commander of Luftwaffe for Heeresgruppe Sud 02.1942–06.1943, attached to Staff of Luftwaffe Commander South-East 06.1943–03.1944, attached to Luftgau Kommando XVII 04.1944–05.1945. Awards: 1939 Clasps to the 1914 Iron Cross 1st and 2nd Class, Eastern Front Medal, 1939 Observer's Badge, Pilot's Croatian Order of the Crown of King Zvonimir 1st Class with Swords, Commemorative Badge, RK-Wuerttemberg Friedrich Order 2nd Class with Swords, 1914 Iron Cross 1st and 2nd Class, 1914 Observer's Badge, Cross of Honor.

Godt, Eberhard: Konteradmiral (01.03.43), (Kriegsmarine); born 05.08.00 in Luebeck, died 13.09.95. WWI: Fahnrich on liner *Schlesien*, Commandant of torpedo boat G10, 09.1932–09.1934, Torpedo Officer on cruiser *Emden* 09.1934–09.1935, attached to U-Boat Training 09.1935–04.1936, Commandant of *U-25* and later *U-23*, 04.1936–01.1938. WWII: First Admiral Staff Officer attached to Befehlshaber of U-Boats 01.1938–09.1939, Chief of Operations Department with Submarine Kommando in O.K.M. 10.1939–02.1943, Chief of 2. Department in Submarine Kommando 03.1943–05.1945. Awards: German Cross in Gold 10.02.42, 1939 Iron Cross 1st Class, 1939 Clasp to the 1914 Iron Cross 2nd Class, 1914 Iron Cross 2nd Class, Cross of Honor.

Goebel, Karl: Generalmajor (01.03.45), (Heer); born 20.01.00 in Adelschlag, died 02.03.45 of wounds in Esslingen. WWI: Schuetze in Bavarian Infanterie Regiment 13. WWII: Kompanie Chef in Infanterie Regiment 119, 10.1936–08.1939, Kompanie Chef in Infanterie Regiment 420, 08.1939–12.1940, Commander of III. Bataillon, Infanterie Regiment 420, 12.1940–09.1942, Commander of Infanterie

Regiment 420, 12.1942–03.1944, Commander of Grenadier Regiment Boehmen 1 followed by Grenadier Regiment 305, 05.1944–09.1944, temporary Commander of 299. Infanterie Division until wounded 12.1944–02.1945 Awards: Oak Leaves 08.06.43 (252), Knight's Cross 10.09.42, German Cross in Gold 24.05.42, Honor Roll Clasp 17.11.44, 1939 Iron Cross 1st and 2nd Class, Close Combat Clasp in Bronze, Infantry Assault Badge in Silver, Eastern Front Medal, Kuban Shield, 1939 Wound Badge in Gold, Cross of Honor.

Goeckel, Guenther von: Generalmajor (01.02.41), (Heer); born 12.04.89 in Neustadt, died 20.12.79 in Bad Kissingen. WWI: Hauptmann on Staff of 44. Res. Division. Attached to Reichswehr Central Office in Hamburg 10.1934–04.1935, Military Replacement Inspector of Hamburg 05.1935–07.1936. WWII: Commander of Truppenubungsplatz at Ohrdruf 08.1936–02.1943, Fuehrer Res. in O.K.H. 02.1943–02.1944, Commander of P.O.W. Camp Oflag XIII B 05.1944–04.1945. Awards: War Merit Cross 1st and 2nd Class with Swords, 1914 Iron Cross 1st and 2nd Class, 1914 Wound Badge in Black, Cross of Honor.

Goedicke, Bruno: SS-Brigadefuehrer und Generalmajor der Waffen-SS (20.04.41); born 19.09.79 in Ploen, died 02.03.71 in Lohhof. P-2585288, SS-276066. WWI: Hauptmann and Commander of Feld Artillerie Regiment 250, retired as Major. Department Leader of Reich War Association, member of Stahlhelm, S.A. and N.S.K.O.V., Joined N.S.D.A.P. in 1933, joined S.S. in 1936. Leader on Staff of SS-Hauptamt 01.12.36–01.12.37, Leader on Staff of RFSS 01.12.38. WWII: Commander of SS-Artillerie Ersatz Regiment 30.01.42, SS-Standort Commandant of Vienna 15.05.43–09.11.44. Awards: War Merit Cross 1st and 2nd Class with Swords, 1914 Iron Cross 1st and 2nd Class, 1914 Wound Badge in Black, Cross of Honor, Degen, Ring.

Goehle, Herbert: Konteradmiral z.V. (01.07.42), (Kriegsmarine); born 04.03.78 in Krehlau, died 12.03.47 in Hof. WWI: Korvettenkapitan and Chief of X. Torpedobootsflotille. Chief of Economic Department in Marineleitung 10.1933–03.1936. WWII: no postings 03.1936–07.1941, attached to Senior Shipyard Staff for Eastern Territories 07.1941–11.1941, Senior Shipyard Director at La Pallice 12.1941–02.1944, retired 02.1944. Awards: War Merit Cross 1st and 2nd Class with Swords, Red Eagle Order IV. Class, RK-Hohenzollern, 1914 Iron Cross 1st and 2nd Class, Prussian Crown Order IV. Class with Swords, Cross of Honor.

Goeldel, Otto von: Generalmajor (01.02.41), (Heer); born 26.01.86 in Gut Schoenfeld, died 23.03.67 in Wiesbaden. WWI: Hauptmann and Commander of I. Bataillon, Infanterie Regiment 423. Attached to Heeres Service Office 5, 05.1936–10.1936, attached to Staff of Infanterie Regiment 10, 10.1936–10.1937. WWII: Commander of Infanterie Regiment 15, 10.1937–10.1939, Officer Judge attached to Reichs War Court 11.1939–06.1943, Commandant of Feldkommandantur 1038, 10.1943–01.1944, Fuehrer Res. in O.K.H. 02.1944–10.1944, retired 10.1944. Awards: War Merit Cross 1st and 2nd Class with Swords, 1914 Iron Cross 1st and 2nd Class, Cross of Honor.

Goeldner, Paul: Generalleutnant z.V. (01.02.41), (Heer); born 03.09.75 in Erfurt, died 13.12.45 at Teltow P.O.W. Camp. WWI: Major and Ia to I. Res. Korps. Promotion to Reichswehr Generalmajor 01.03.28. Recalled to military service 03.1939. WWII: attached to Heeres Library in Potsdam 03.1939–01.1940, Commander of 351. Infanterie Division 03.1940–05.1940, Chief of Military Administration in Paris 05.1940–03.1941, P.O.W. Commander for Wehrkreis III 03.1941–10.1942, Fuehrer Res. in O.K.H. 10.1942–04.1943, retired 04.1943. Awards: War Merit Cross 1st and 2nd Class with Swords, RK-Hohenzollern, 1914 Iron Cross 1st and 2nd Class, Cross of Honor.

Goerbig, Paul: Generalmajor (01.04.44), (Heer); born 23.05.95 in Saarbruecken, died 17.08.74 in Hamburg. WWI: Leutnant attached to Staff of Motor Affairs. Attached to Staff of Inspection of Transport Troops 08.1934–10.1935, attached to Staff Kommando of Panzertruppen 10.1935–03.1938, attached to Staff of XVI. Armee Korps (mot.) 04.1938–11.1938. WWII: Commander of Panzer Abteilung 67, 11.1938–10.1939, Chief of Truppenubungsplatz Abteilung in O.K.H. 11.1939–04.1943, Commandant of Feldkommandantur 509, 05.1943–06.1944, Commander of Truppenubungsplatz at Sennelager 07.1944–1945. Awards: War Merit Cross 1st and 2nd Class with Swords, 1914 Iron Cross 1st and 2nd Class, 1914 Wound Badge in Black, Cross of Honor.

Goering, Hermann: Reichsmarschall (19.07.40), (Luftwaffe); born 12.01.93 in Rosenheim, died 15.10.46 (suicide) in Nuremberg Prison. WWI: in G.A.S. as Oberleutnant and last Commander of "Richthofen" Geschwader. P-23. Promotions to General der Flieger 01.03.35, Generaloberst 20.04.45, Generalfeldmarschall 02.04.38. WWII: President of Reichstag 08.1932–04.1945, Reich Minister of R.L.M. 05.1933–04.1945, Oberbefehlshaber of Luftwaffe 06.1935–04.1945, Head of Four Year Plan 10.1936–04.1945. Awards: Golden Party Badge, Blood Order (Fuehrer of S.A.), 1939 Grand Cross 19.07.40, Knight's Cross 30.09.39, 1939 Clasps to the 1914 Iron Cross 1st and 2nd Class, Combined Pilot/Observer's Badge in Gold with Diamonds, 1939 Submarine War Badge with Diamonds, Grand Cross of the Italian Military Order of Savoy, Grand Cross of the Italian King's Order of Heiligen Mauritius and Lazzarus, Grand Cross of the Finnish Order of the White Rose with Breast Star and Swords, Grand Cross of the Finnish Cross of Freedom with Breast Star and Swords, Grand Cross of the King of Sweden with Swords and Kette, Danish Grand Cross of the Dannebrog Order with the Insignia in Diamonds, Romanian

Reichsmarschall Hermann Goering. (Roger James Bender)

Order of Michael the Brave (all three classes), Spanish Grand Cross and Breast Star of the Order of the Yolk and Arrows, Croatian Grand Cross and Breast Star of the Crown of King Zvonimir with Oak Leaves, Gau Berlin Commemorative Badge in Gold, Gau Essem Commemorative Badge in Gold, Gau Thuringen Commemorative Badge in Silver, Breast Star to the German Red Cross Decoration, German Olympic Games Decoration 1st Class, Danzig Cross 1st Class, Luftschutz Ehrenzeichen 1st Class in Gold, Badge of the Association of the National Motor and Aviation Organization in Silver, SA-Feldherrnhalle Dagger, "J.G. Freiherr von Richthofen Nr. 1, 1917/18" Commemorative Cuff Band, Pilot's Commemorative Badge, Pour le Mérite 02.06.28, Grand Cross of the Sachsen Ernestine House Order with Swords (Post-WWI), RK-Hohenzollern, RK-Baden Order of the Zaehring Lion 2nd Class with Swords, 1914 Iron Cross 1st and 2nd Class, Turkish Half Moon, 1914 Wound Badge in Black, 1914 Pilot's Badge, Cross of Honor.

Goeritz, Werner: Generalleutnant (01.01.43), (Heer); born 09.03.92 in Braunschweig, died 27.05.58 in Bad Toelz. WWI: Oberleutnant and 1. Ordnance Officer on Staff of 52. Infanterie Division. Promotion to Generalmajor 01.12.41. Attached to Staff of Infanterie Fuehrer VII 10.1934–10.1935, attached to Staff of 17. Division 10.1935–10.1936, Commander of III. Bataillon, Infanterie Regiment 35, 10.1936–11.1938. WWII: Commander of Infanterie Regiment 134, 11.1938–06.1940, Commander of Wehrmacht Railway Transport Department's Paris, East, North-East followed by Heeresgruppe Mitte 07.1940–05.1942, Commander of 291. Infanterie Division 06.1942–01.1944, Commander of 92. Infanterie Division 02.1944–06.1044, Fuehrer Res. in O.K.H. 07.1944–05.1945. Awards: Knight's Cross 06.11.43, German Cross in Gold 14.02.43, 1939 Clasps to the 1914 Iron Cross 1st and 2nd Class, Infantry Assault Badge in Silver, Eastern Front Medal, 1939 Wound Badge in Black, 1914 Iron Cross 1st and 2nd Class, 1914 Wound Badge in Black, Cross of Honor.

Goernnert, Dr. Friedrich: Ministerialdirigent (01.01.44), (Luftwaffe); born 18.03.07 in Karlsruhe, died 01.05.84 in Karlsruhe. Civil Servant by profession. Joined S.A., SA-Brigadefuehrer. WWII: Personal Adjutant to Reichsmarschall Hermann Goering 1937–1945. Awards: War Merit Cross 1st and 2nd Class with Swords, Combined Pilot/Observer's Badge in Gold with Diamonds.

Goesch, Martin: Generalmajor z.V. (01.04.43), (Heer); born 25.09.77 in Neuhof, died 10.12.45 in Plau. WWI: Hauptmann attached to Imperial Armee High Command. Recalled to military service 05.1938. WWII: without assignment 05.1938–05.1939, Commander of Landschuetzen Regiment 23, 09.1939–01.1943, retired 08.1943. Awards: War Merit Cross 1st and 2nd Class with Swords, Pour le Mérite 21.04.18, RK-Hohenzollern, 1914 Iron Cross 1st and 2nd Class, Cross of Honor.

Goeschen, Alex: Generalleutnant (01.08.43), (Heer); born 22.10.84 in Frankfurt am Main, died 07.04.70 in Bad Toelz. WWI: Rittmeister and Commander of I. Bataillon, Infanterie Regiment 79. Promotion to Generalmajor 01.08.41. Commander of Reiter (later Kavallerie) Regiment 2, 03.1934–03.1937. WWII: Commander of Military District Remonteschule XIII at Bamberg 04.1937–02.1942, attached to Rear of Heeresgruppe Sud 02.1942–08.1942, Commander of 213. Security Division 08.1942–05.1945. Awards: 1939 Clasps to the 1914 Iron Cross 1st and 2nd Class, War Merit Cross 1st and 2nd Class with Swords, 1914 Iron Cross 1st and 2nd Class, Cross of Honor.

Goette, Dr. Walther: Admiral-Arzt (01.04.43), (Kriegsmarine); born 11.03.94 in Wilhelmshaven, died 26.08.59 in Bremenhaven. Medical doctor by profession. WWI: Leutnant zur See and Watch Officer on torpedo boat. Physician for IV. Marine Artillerie Abteilung 12.1931–09.1934, Ship Physician for line ship *Schlesien* 09.1934–10.1935, Ship Physician for battleship *Deutschland* 10.1935–05.1936, Ship Physician for line ship *Schleswig-Holstein* 05.1936–09.1936. WWII: Physician on Staff of Second Admiral of Naval Station North Sea 09.1936–01.1940, Medical Inspector attached to Training Affairs of Navy in O.K.M. 01.1940–04.1941, Chief Physician of Naval Hospital at Wesermuende 05.1941–02.1944, attached to Wehrmacht Medical Office in O.K.H. 02.1944–01.1945. Awards: War Merit Cross 1st and 2nd Class with Swords, 1914 Iron Cross 1st and 2nd Class, Cross of Honor.

Goetting, Friedrich: Vizeadmiral (01.10.37), (Kriegsmarine); born 07.02.86 in Berlin, died 03.01.46 in Russian P.O.W. camp. WWI: U-boat service as Kapitanleutnant and Commandant of *U-93*. Promotion to Reichsmarine Konteradmiral 01.10.34. Commandant of Swinemuende 09.1933–09.1934, Inspector of Torpedo Boats and Mine Ships 10.1934–09.1936. WWII: Inspector of Torpedoes 10.1936–12.1939, Chief of Torpedo Weapons Amt in O.K.M. 12.1939–06.1940, placed at disposal of Kriegsmarine 06.1940–08.1942, Coastal Commander for Eastern Baltic Sea and Fortress Commander of Gotenhafen 09.1942–02.1943, retired 05.1943. Awards: War Merit Cross 1st and 2nd Class with Swords, 1914 Iron Cross 1st and 2nd Class, Oldenburg Friedrich-August Cross 1st and 2nd Class, 1914 Submarine Badge, Cross of Honor.

Goettke, Ernst: Generalleutnant (01.11.41), (Heer); born 12.10.85 in Magdeburg, died 22.10.66 in Duesseldorf. WWI: Hauptmann and Commander of II. Bataillon, Fuss Artillerie Regiment 20. Promotion to Generalmajor 01.04.40. Attached to Staff of Artillerie 3 in Reichswehr Ministry 10.1934–02.1935. WWII: Higher Artillery Officer attached to (In 4) in O.K.H. 02.1938–03.1941, Artillery Commander to XXXVI. Armee Korps 06.1941–09.1941, Higher Central Artillery attached to E-Officer Korps 03.1935–01.1938, Higher Artillery Officer attached to O.K.H. 02.1938–12.1941, Commander for Hoehere Kuesten Artillery Nord 01.1942–05.1943, General of Heeres Coastal and Fortress Artillery in O.K.H. 05.1943–05.1945. Awards: German Cross in Silver 23.02.43, 1939 Clasps to the 1914 Iron Cross 1st and 2nd Class, War Merit Cross 1st and 2nd Class with Swords, General Assault Badge, Finnish Freedom Cross 1st Class with Swords, RK-Hohenzollern, 1914 Iron Cross 1st and 2nd Class, 1914 Wound Badge in Black, Cross of Honor.

Goetz, Heinrich: Generalleutnant (01.04.45), (Heer); born 01.01.96 in Hannover, died 31.01.60 in Oberaudorf. WWI: Leutnant and Chief of 165. Motor Kompanie. Promotion to Generalmajor 01.08.44. Attached to 2. Kompanie, Infanterie Regiment at Potsdam 10.1934–10.1935, Chief of 2. Kompanie, Infanterie Regiment 9, 10.1935–04.1938. WWII: Adjutant on Staff of 3. Infanterie Division 05.1938–1940, Commander of Heer Flieger Interception Bataillon at Reichenberg 05.1940–06.1941, Commander of Infanterie Regiment 466, 08.1941–01.1944, Commander of 21. Infanterie Division 08.1944–09.1944 and again 01.1945–03.1945. Awards: Oak Leaves 05.03.45 (765), Knight's Cross 03.05.42, 1939 Clasps to the 1914 Iron Cross 1st and 2nd Class, Infantry Assault Badge in Silver, Eastern Front Medal, 1939 Wound Badge in Black, 1914 Iron Cross 1st and 2nd Class, 1914 Wound Badge in Black, Cross of Honor.

Goetze, Eberhard von: Konteradmiral (01.03.42), (Kriegsmarine); born 13.08.93 in Cosel, died 16.10.77 in Oberlauringen. WWI: Oberleutnant zur See on liner *Ostfriesland.* Advisor attached to Armor Department of Marineleitung (later O.K.M.) 07.1931–09.1936, Commandant of Artillerie Schule ship *Bremse* 09.1936–10.1938 and at same time attached to Marine Artillery Inspection 11.1937–06.1938. WWII: Leader of the Artillery Testing Command for Ships in the O.K.M. 10.1938–04.1940, Department Chief in Mechanical Artillery Section of O.K.M. 07.1940–08.1943, Office Group Chief for Artillery Development in O.K.M. 08.1943–02.1945. Awards: War Merit Cross 1st and 2nd Class with Swords, 1914 Iron Cross 2nd Class, Cross of Honor.

Gohrbandt, Dr. Erwin: General-Arzt (01.04.43), (Luftwaffe); born 20.09.90 in Schlawe, died 03.01.65 in Berlin. Medical doctor by profession. WWI: German medical service (rank and unit unknown). WWII: Advisory Specialist for Surgery for Medical Chief of Luftwaffe 08.1939–05.1945. Awards: Knight's Cross of the War Merit Cross with Swords 01.02.45, War Merit Cross 1st and 2nd Class with Swords, Cross of Honor.

Goldbeck-Loewe, Dr. Hans-Adolf: General-Arzt (01.12.44), (Luftwaffe); born 24.04.98 in Leipzig, died 09.01.77 in Itzehoe. Medical doctor by profession. WWI: Leutnant der Res. in Feld Artillerie Regiment 17. WWII: Mental Specialist in Psychology Department of Luftwaffe 10.1934–08.1939. Chief Physician of Luftwaffe Hospital in Wismar 09.1939–06.1940, Luftwaffe Liason Officer for Medical Matters with O.K.H. 07.1940–10.1944, Physician at Bad Nauheim 11.1944–05.1945. Awards: 1939 Clasp to the 1914 Iron Cross 2nd Class, War Merit Cross 1st and 2nd Class with Swords, 1914 Iron Cross 1st and 2nd Class, Cross of Honor.

Gollert, Werner: Ministerialdirigent (01.09.44), (Luftwaffe); born 20.01.00 in Neuruppin, died 10.03.61 in Oldenburg. Engineer by profession. WWI: Fahnenjunker in Pionier Bataillon 5. Oberregierungsbaurat in R.L.M. 01.1935–03.1937, Group Leader in Luftkreis Kommando IV in Muenster 04.1937–10.1937, Group Leader in Luftkreis Kommando VI in Kiel 10.1937–06.1938, Construction Group Leader for Luftgau Kommando IV in Dresden 07.1938–05.1939. WWII: Construction Group Leader for Luftgau Kommando III in Berlin 05.1939–04.1940, Group Leader in Office Group Construction and Deputy Chief of Luftwaffe Construction in R.L.M. 04.1940–10.1944. Awards: War Merit Cross 1st and 2nd Class with Swords, Cross of Honor.

Gollnick, Hans: General der Infanterie (01.10.43), (Heer); born 22.05.92 in Gut Gussen, died 15.02.70 in Hamburg. WWI: Oberleutnant and Adjutant to Res. Infanterie Regiment 21. Promotions to Generalmajor 01.06.41, Generalleutnant 01.01.43. Commander of I. Bataillon, Infanterie Regiment at Stargard 10.1934–10.1935, Commander of I. Bataillon, Infanterie Regiment 25, 10.1935–04.1939. WWII: Commander of Infanterie Regiment 76, 05.1939–06.1941, Komandeur of 36. Infanterie Division (mot.) 10.1941–08.1943, Commander of XXXXVI. Panzer Korps 08.1943–03.1944, Commander of XXVIII. Armee Korps 03.1944–05.1945. Awards: Oak Leaves 24.08.43 (282), Knight's Cross 27.11.42, 1939 Clasps to the 1914 Iron Cross 1st and 2nd Class, Infantry Assault Badge in Silver, Eastern Front Medal, 1914 Iron Cross 1st and 2nd Class, 1914 Wound Badge in Black, Cross of Honor.

Gollwitzer, Friedrich: General der Infanterie (01.12.43), (Heer); born 27.04.89 in Bullenheim, died 25.03.77 in Amberg. WWI: Hauptmann on Staff of Bavarian General of Pioniers. Promotions to Generalmajor 01.10.39, Generalleutnant 01.10.41. Commander of I. Bataillon, Infanterie Regiment at Amberg 10.1934–10.1935.

WWII: Commander of Infanterie Regiment 41, 10.1935–11.1939, Commander of Division 193, 11.1939–02.1940, Commander of 88. Infanterie Division 02.1940–03.1943, Commander of LIII. Armee Korps 06.1943–06.1944, captured 06.1944. Awards: Knight's Cross 08.02.43, German Cross in Gold 25.01.43, 1939 Clasps to the 1914 Iron Cross 1st and 2nd Class, Infantry Assault Badge in Silver, Eastern Front Medal, 1914 Iron Cross 1st and 2nd Class, Cross of Honor.

Goltz, Konrad: Generalleutnant (01.11.42), (Luftwaffe); born 08.10.81 in San Remo, died 10.01.47 in Prien. WWI: in Naval G.A.S. as Kapitanleutnant and Commander of Seeflieger in Turkey. Promotion to Generalmajor 01.04.41. Group Leader in LA II of R.L.M. 11.1933–03.1935, Group Leader and later Department Chief in Inspection of Marine Flieger in Luftwaffe Kommando VI in Kiel 04.1935–02.1939. WWII: Department Chief in (L In 8) of R.L.M. 03.1939–03.1941, Inspector of Sea Rescue Service (L In 6) in R.L.M. 04.1941–11.1942, retired 05.1943. Awards: War Merit Cross 1st and 2nd Class with Swords, 1939 Pilot's Badge, Naval Pilot's Commemorative Badge, RK-Sachsen Albrecht Order 2nd Class with Swords, 1914 Iron Cross 1st and 2nd Class, Prussian Crown Order IV. Class with Swords, 1914 Naval Wound Badge in Black, Turkish Half Moon, 1914 Naval Pilot's Badge, Cross of Honor.

Goltzsch, Rudolf: Generalmajor (01.12.44), (Heer); born 01.10.97 in Klein-Bautzen, died 18.03.74 in Bad Heilbronn. WWI: Leutnant in I. Bataillon, Infanterie Regiment 178. Attached to Staff of Ausbildungs Bataillon of Infanterie Regiment at Dresden 10.1934–10.1935, Regimental Signals Officer for Infanterie Regiment 101, 10.1935–10.1937. WWII: Tactics Instructor at Kriegsschule Potsdam 10.1937–08.1939, attached to Heeres Nachrichtenschule 10.1939–01.1940, Commander of I. Bataillon, Infanterie Regiment 174, 02.1940–01.1941, Course Commander of Instruction Department II for Infanterie Schule 01.1941–06.1942, Commander of Infanterie Schule V at Doberitz for Officer Aspirants 06.1942–10.1942, Commander of Grenadier Regiment 324, 11.1942–11.1943, Commander of Luftwaffe Jaeger Regiment 41, 11.1943–04.1944, Commander of Special Purpose Division Staff 606, 12.1944–03.1945. Awards: 1939 Clasps to the 1914 Iron Cross 1st and 2nd Class, Infantry Assault Badge in Silver, RK-Sachsen Albrecht Order 2nd Class with Swords, 1914 Iron Cross 1st and 2nd Class, Cross of Honor.

Gombart, Friedrich: Generalmajor z.V. (01.06.42), (Heer); born 08.01.77 in Lindau, died 06.05.49 in Lindau. WWI: Hauptmann and Flak Commander of 18. Armee. WWII: attached to E-Officer Korps 03.1935–08.1939, Commandant of Feldkommandantur for Lake Constance 08.1939–08.1941, Commandant of P.O.W. Camp Stalag 311, 11.1941–07.1942, Fuehrer Res. in O.K.H. 07.1942–04.1943, retired 04.1943. Awards: War Merit Cross 1st and 2nd Class with Swords, RK-Hohenzollern,

1914 Iron Cross 1st and 2nd Class, Bavarian Military Service Order IV. Class with Swords, Cross of Honor.

Gonell, Ernst: Generalmajor (30.01.45), (Heer); born 24.11.02 in Koenigsberg, died 23.02.45 (suicide) in Posen. Attached to Staff of Kriegsschule 10.1934–10.1936, Kompanie Chef in Infanterie Regiment 87, 10.1936–11.1938. WWII: Instructor at Kriegsschule Dresden 11.1938–08.1939, Commander of III. Bataillon, Infanterie Regiment 234, 08.1939–03.1940, Commander of III. Bataillon, Infanterie Regiment 433, 04.1940–08.1941, Commander of Replacement Grenadier Regiment 12, 01.1942–11.1942, Commander of Schule V in Posen for Officer Aspirants 06.1943–02.1945. Awards: Knight's Cross 22.02.45, German Cross in Gold 01.1945, 1939 Iron Cross 1st and 2nd Class, Infantry Assault Badge in Silver, 1939 Wound Badge in Gold.

Gorn, Walter: Generalmajor (01.10.44), (Heer); born 24.09.98 in Bieganin, died 10.07.68 in Rosenheim. WWI: Gefreiter in 1. Heavy M.G. Kompanie, Landwehr Infanterie Regiment 36. Chief of 5. Kompanie, Kradschuetzen Bataillon 3, 10.1935–06.1939. WWII: Commander of Staff Quarters for XIX. (Mot.) Armee Korps 07.1939–01.1940, Commander of Schuetzen Replacement Bataillon 10, 03.1940–10.1940, Commander of I. Bataillon, Schuetzen Regiment 10, 10.1940–01.1942, Commander of Kradschuetzen Bataillon 59, 01.1942–10.1942, Commander of Panzer Grenadier Regiment 10, 10.1942–03.1943, Commander of Panzertruppen Schule II at Krampnitz 01.1944–07.1944, Commander of 561. Volks Grenadier Division 07.1944–03.1945. Awards: Swords 08.06.43 (30), Oak Leaves 17.08.42 (113), Knight's Cross 20.04.41, German Cross in Gold 08.02.42, 1939 Iron Cross 1st Class, 1939 Clasp to the 1914 Iron Cross 2nd Class, Close Combat Clasp in Bronze, Tank Assault Badge in Bronze, Eastern Front Medal, 1939 Wound Badge in Silver, 1914 Iron Cross 2nd Class, Cross of Honor.

Gosewisch, Walter: Generalmajor (01.10.43), (Luftwaffe); born 13.06.96 in Hannover, died 06.03.73 in Hannover. WWI: Leutnant in Infanterie Regiment 136. Chief of 2. Training Kompanie at Luftwaffe Nachrichtenschule Halle-Saale 05.1935–03.1936, Group Leader and Chief of Signals Processing in R.L.M. 04.1936–02.1938. WWII: Department Chief with Chief of Communications in R.L.M. 03.1938–11.1941, Signals Leader to X. Flieger Korps 11.1941–06.1942, Senior Signals Leader of Luftflotte 5, 07.1942–12.1943, Chief of Air Signals of Inspector General of Luftwaffe in R.L.M. 04.1944–04.1945. Awards: German Cross in Silver (date unknown), 1939 Clasps to the 1914 Iron Cross 1st and 2nd Class, 1914 Iron Cross 1st and 2nd Class, Cross of Honor.

Gosslar, Konrad von: General der Kavallerie (01.02.38), (Heer); born 08.11.81 in Zichtau, died 09.09.39 in Berlin. WWI: Rittmeister and attached to Staff of

Feld Armee. Promotions to Reichswehr Generalmajor 01.04.34, Generalleutnant 01.01.36. Infantry Leader 02.1934–01.1935, Artillerie Fuehrer VI 02.1935–09.1935, Commander of 19. Division 10.1935–02.1938, Inspector of Kavallerie 03.1938–11.1938. WWII: attached to O.K.H. 11.1938–09.1939. Awards: 1914 Iron Cross 1st and 2nd Class, Cross of Honor.

Gossrau, Karl-Siegfried: General der Flieger (01.09.41), (Luftwaffe); born 14.01.87 in Stuttgart, died 27.11.72 in Stuttgart. WWI: Hauptmann on Staff of 52. Infanterie Division. Promotions to Generalmajor 01.03.38, Generalleutnant 01.03.40. Advisor in R.L.M. 10.1933–08.1934, Department Chief in Wehr Abteilung of R.L.M. 08.1934–03.1938. WWII: Military Replacement Inspector for Niederdonau in Vienna 06.1938–09.1939, Military Replacement Inspector for Posen 10.1939–05.1940, Chief of Luftwaffe Administration Office in R.L.M. 05.1940–08.1943, attached to Feld Luftgau Kommando Belgium and Northern France 03.1944–12.1944, retired 12.1944. Awards: War Merit Cross 1st and 2nd Class with Swords, 1939 Observer's Badge, RK-Hohenzollern, RK-Wuerttemberg Friedrich Order 1st Class with Swords, RK-Baden Order of the Zaehringer Lion 2nd Class with Swords, 1914 Iron Cross 1st and 2nd Class, 1914 Wound Badge in Gold, Cross of Honor.

Gothsche, Reinhold: Generalmajor (01.10.43), (Heer); born 23.11.93 in Erfurt, died 22.04.45 (shot by Army under martial law conditions) in Pressnitz. WWI: Leutnant and Ordinance Officer on Staff of 3. Infanterie Division. Half Regimental Commander of Reiter Regiment at Kamenz 05.1935–10.1935, Commander of I. Bataillon, Panzer Regiment 3, 10.1935–08.1937, attached to Reich War Ministry 08.1937–10.1937. WWII: Advisor in Inspectorate 6 (Motorized Transport) of Reich War Ministry (later O.K.H.) 10.1937–01.1940, Department Chief in Heeres General Department of O.K.H. 01.1940–05.1943, Fuehrer Res. in O.K.H. 11.1943–03.1944, Commandant of Feldkommandantur 520, 05.1944–02.1945, Commandant of Feldkommandantur 591, 02.1945–04.1945. Awards: War Merit Cross 1st and 2nd Class with Swords, 1914 Iron Cross 1st and 2nd Class, 1914 Wound Badge in Black, Cross of Honor.

Gottberg, Curt von: SS-Obergruppenfuehrer und General der Waffen-SS und Polizei (30.06.44); born 11.02.96 in East Prussia, died 31.05.45 (suicide) in Holstein P.O.W. Camp. P-948753, SS-45923. WWI: Leutnant attached to 1. Garde Regiment zu Fuss. Joined N.S.D.A.P. and S.S. in 1932. Promotions to SS-Brigadefuehrer 20.04.42, SS-Gruppenfuehrer 15.07.43. Leader of SS-Fuss Standarte 49, 01.07.35, Inspector of SS-Stammabt. Oberabschnitte Mitte 01.12.36, attached to Staff of R.u.S.H.A. 01.12.37–01.12.38. WWII: Chief of Amt III in SS-Hauptamt 30.01.42, S.S.P.F. of Minsk 15.05.43, attached to Generalkommissar District of Weissruthenien (White Ruthenia) of Reich Ministry for Occupied Eastern

Territories, H.S.S.P.F. of Russland-Mitte (Central Russia) and Weissruthenien 30.01.44, Commander of XII. SS-Armee Korps 09.11.44, Deputy Befehlshaber of Replacement Armee under control of Himmler. Awards: Knight's Cross 30.06.44, German Cross in Gold 07.08.43, 1939 Clasps to the 1914 Iron Cross 1st and 2nd Class, War Merit Cross 1st and 2nd Class with Swords, Anti-Partisan War Badge in Silver, 1914 Iron Cross 1st and 2nd Class, 1914 Wound Badge in Black, Cross of Honor, SA-Sports Badge in Silver, Degen, Ring.

SS-Obergruppenfuehrer Curt von Gottberg. (Michael Miller)

Gottschalk, Friedrich-Carl: Generalmajor (01.02.44), (Heer); born 30.09.92 in Brandenburg, died 14.02.60 in Berlin. WWI: in G.A.S. as Oberleutnant and Flieger Transport Officer at Luettich. Attached to Staff of Artillerie Regiment 6, 10.1935–10.1936. WWII: Tactics Instructor and later Instruction Group Leader at Heeres Feuerwerkerschule 10.1936–08.1939, Commander of I. Abteilung, Artillerie Regiment 297, 08.1939–09.1939, Commander of I. Abteilung, Artillerie Regiment 99, 09.1939–01.1940, Commander of Special Purpose Artillerie Regiment Staff 614, 10.1940–03.1942, Commander of Artillerie 126, 09.1942–11.942, Commander of Artillerie 103, 03.1943–09.1943, Commander of Artillerie 502, 09.1943–08.1944, attached to Military District in Prague 09.1944–05.1945. Awards: 1939 Clasps to the 1914 Iron Cross 1st and 2nd Class, General Assault Badge, Eastern Front Medal, Pilot's Commemorative Badge, 1914 Iron Cross 1st and 2nd Class, 1914 Observer's Badge, Cross of Honor.

Grabmann, Walter: Generalmajor (01.08.44), (Luftwaffe); born 20.09.05 in Bad Reichenhall, died 20.08.92 in Munich. Attached to Fliegerschule Lechfeld, Schleissheim and later Salzwedel 10.1934–03.1936, Adjutant to J.G. 134 "Horst Wessel" 03.1936–03.1937, Fliegerhorst Commandant of Koeln-Ostheim 03.1937–08.1938, Commander of Jagdgruppe 88 "Legion Condor" 09.1938–07.1939. WWII: Commander of V. Gruppe in 1. Training Jagdgeschwader 07.1939–04.1940, Commander of Z.G. 76 and Jagdfliegerfuehrer of Norway 04.1940–07.1941, Commander of Marine Zerstorer Schule 2 at Memmingen 08.1941–08.1942, Fighter Commander for Holland and Ruhr area 08.1942–11.1943, Commander of 3. Jagd Division 11.1943–04.1945. Awards: Knight's Cross 14.09.40, 1939 Iron Cross 1st and 2nd Class, Spanish Cross in Gold with Swords, Day Fighter Clasp in Gold, 1939 Wound Badge in Black, Combined Pilot-Observer's Badge, Spanish War Cross (Spain).

Grachegg, Gustav: Generalmajor z.V. (01.06.41), (Heer); born 17.11.82 in Spielfeld, died 05.1945 (missing in action). WWI: Major in Austrian Dragoon Regiment 8.

Transferred to German Wehrmacht 03.1938. WWII: P.O.W. Commander for Wehrkreis Kommando VIII 09.1940–04.1944, retired 05.1944. Awards: War Merit Cross 1st and 2nd Class with Swords, Cross of Honor.

Graeser, Fritz-Hubert: General der Panzertruppe (01.09.44), (Heer); born 03.11.88 in Frankfurt an der Oder, died 04.10.60 in Goettingen. WWI: Hauptmann and Ia to 1. Res. Division. Promotions to Generalmajor 01.10.41, Generalleutnant 01.03.43. Commander of I. Bataillon, Infanterie Regiment at Crossen 10.1934–10.1935. WWII: Commander of M.G. Bataillon 8, 10.1935–08.1939, Commander of Infanterie Regiment 29, 08.1939–07.1941, in hospital for severe wounds and placed in Fuehrer Res. in O.K.H. 07.1941–03.1943, Commander of 3. Panzer Grenadier Division 03.1943–03.1944, Commander of XXXXVIII. Panzer Korps 08.1944–09.1944, O.B. of 4. Panzer Armee 09.1944–05.1945. Awards: Swords 08.05.45 (154), Oak Leaves 26.06.44 (517), Knight's Cross 19.07.40, German Cross in Gold 08.02.42, 1939 Clasps to the 1914 Iron Cross 1st and 2nd Class, German Army High Command Commendation Certificate 30.07.41, Infantry Assault Badge in Silver, 1939 Wound Badge in Gold, 1914 Iron Cross 1st and 2nd Class, Cross of Honor.

Graessner, Walther: General der Infanterie (01.06.42), (Heer); born 31.01.91 in Magdeburg, died 16.07.43 at Troppau Military Hospital. WWI: Oberleutnant and Adjutant to 66. Infanterie Brigade. Promotions to Generalmajor 01.10.39, Generalleutnant 01.10.41. Attached to Kommando Staff of Military Commander of Leipzig 04.1934–10.1935, Ia to 14. Division 10.1935–10.1937, Commander of Infanterie Regiment 53, 10.1937–07.1939. WWII: Commander of Replacement Troops for Wehrkreis Kommando XVII 07.1939–11.1939, Commander of Division 187, 11.1939–02.1940, Commander of 298. Infanterie Division 02.1940–12.1941, Commander of XII. Armee Korps 02.1942–02.1943, Fuehrer Res. in O.K.H. 02.1943–07.1943. Awards: Knight's Cross 27.10.41, 1939 Clasps to the 1914 Iron Cross 1st and 2nd Class, Infantry Assault Badge in Silver, 1914 Iron Cross 1st and 2nd Class, Cross of Honor.

Graevenitz, Hans von: Generalleutnant (01.08.44), (Heer); born 14.07.94 in Frankfurt an der Oder, died 09.12.63 in Stuttgart. WWI: Oberleutnant in Grenadier Regiment 119. Promotion to Generalmajor 01.02.42. Attached to Reichswehr Ministry (later Reich War Ministry) 05.1932–10.1937, Commander of II. Bataillon, Infanterie Regiment 111, 10.1937–07.1938. WWII: Chief of Welfare and Supply Department in O.K.W. 08.1938–04.1943, Inspector for P.O.W. Affairs in O.K.W. 04.1943–04.1944, Commander of 237. Infanterie Division 07.1944–05.1945. Awards: German Cross in Silver (date unknown), 1939 Clasps to the 1914 Iron Cross 1st and 2nd Class, War Merit Cross 1st and 2nd Class with Swords, Infantry Assault Badge in Silver, 1914 Iron Cross 1st and 2nd Class, Cross of Honor.

Graewe, Ernst: Generalmajor (30.01.45), (Heer); born 14.07.94 in Koblenz, died 18.02.66 in Wiesbaden. WWI: Leutnant and Adjutant on the Artillerie Staff of A.O.K. 2. Commander of I. Bataillon, Artillerie Regiment at Rendsburg 10.1934–10.1935, Commander of I. Abteilung, Artillerie Regiment 20, 10.1935–11.1938. WWII: Commander of II. Abteilung, Artillerie Regiment 72, 11.1938–10.1939, Commander of 1. Rocket Artillerie Bataillon 11.1939–07.1940, Commander of Rocket Artillerie Regiment 51, 07.1940–08.1942, Commander of Rocket Artillerie Truppe 3, 08.1942–03.1944, Commander of 3. Rocket Artillerie Brigade 03.1944–09.1944, Commander of Rocket Artillery Troops for Replacement Armee 09.1944–05.1945. Awards: 1939 Clasps to the 1914 Iron Cross 1st and 2nd Class, General Assault Badge, Eastern Front Medal, 1914 Iron Cross 1st and 2nd Class, 1914 Wound Badge in Silver, Cross of Honor.

Graf, Karl: Generalleutnant z.V. (01.02.41), (Heer); born 08.11.83 in Passau, died 16.07.48 in Ingolstadt. WWI: Hauptmann on Staff of 4. Bavarian Infanterie Division. Promotion to Generalmajor z.V. 01.03.36. Commander of Infanterie Regiment at Munich 10.1934–07.1935, Military Replacement Inspector of Weimar 08.1935–05.1938, retired 06.1938. WWII: recalled to military service 09.1939, Commander of Replacement Troops for Wehrkreis Kommando VII 09.1939–11.1939, Commander of 157. Infanterie Division 11.1939–09.1942, Commander of Division 467, 10.1942–11.1943, attached to Wehrkreis Kommando VII 11.1943–09.1944, retired 09.1944. Awards: 1939 Clasps to the 1914 Iron Cross 1st and 2nd Class, Infantry Assault Badge in Silver, 1914 Iron Cross 1st and 2nd Class, 1914 Wound Badge in Black, Cross of Honor.

Graffen, Karl von: Generalleutnant (01.01.43), (Heer); born 06.06.93 in Ploen, died 01.11.64 in Groedersby. WWI: Oberleutnant in Res. Feld Artillerie Regiment 65. Promotion to Generalmajor 01.07.42. Commander of IV. Abteilung, Artillerie Regiment at Schwerin 10.1934–10.1935, Adjutant to Artillerie Schule Jueterbog 10.1935–10.1936. WWII: Staff Leader at Artillerie Schule Jueterbog 10.1936–09.1939, Administrator for Artillerie and Munitions Quarries in O.K.H. 10.1939–02.1941, Commander of Artillerie Regiment 129, 03.1941–11.1941, Commander of Artillerie 18, 11.1941–03.1942, Commander of 58. Infanterie Division 03.1942–09.1943, Senior Commander of Artillerie 316, 09.1943–04.1945. Awards: Knight's

Generalleutnant Karl von Graffen. (Bundesarchiv)

Cross 13.08.42, German Cross in Gold 24.12.41, 1939 Clasps to the 1914 Iron Cross 1st and 2nd Class, General Assault Badge, Eastern Front Medal, 1914 Iron Cross 1st and 2nd Class, Cross of Honor.

Grase, Martin: General der Infanterie (0.1.11.43), (Heer); born 03.05.91 in Schlochau, died 04.08.63 in Freiburg. WWI: Oberleutnant and Adjutant on Staff of 16. Landwehr Division. Promotions to Generalmajor 01.10.41, Generalleutnant 01.01.43. Attached to Kommando Staff of Military Commander of Berlin 10.1934–10.1935, Commander of III. Jaeger Bataillon, Infanterie Regiment 30, 10.1935–10.1936. WWII: 1. Adjutant to the I. Armee Korps 10.1936–08.1939, Adjutant to A.O.K. 16, 10.1939–02.1940, Commander of Infanterie Regiment 1, 03.1940–01.1942, Commander of 1. Infanterie Division 01.1942–07.1943, Commander of I. Armee Korps 11.1943–01.1944, Commander of XXVI. Armee Korps 01.1944–02.1944, Fuehrer Res. in O.K.H. 02.1944–07.1944, Wehrmacht Commander of Belgium and Northern France 07.1944–09.1944, Commander of III. Feldjager Korps 09.1944–03.1945. Awards: Oak Leaves 23.05.43 (248), Knight's Cross 18.10.41, 1939 Clasps to the 1914 Iron Cross 1st and 2nd Class, Infantry Assault Badge in Silver, Eastern Front Medal, 1914 Iron Cross 1st and 2nd Class, 1914 Wound Badge in Black, Cross of Honor.

Grasser, Anton: General der Infanterie (01.05.44), (Heer); born 03.11.91 in Bossendorf, died 03.11.76 in Stuttgart. WWI: Leutnant der Res. in Replacement Bataillon, Infanterie Regiment 132. Promotions to Generalmajor 01.04.42, Generalleutnant 01.01.43. Attached to Infanterie Regiment 110, 03.1936–05.1936, attached to Staff of III. Bataillon, Infanterie Regiment 13, 05.1936–10.1936, Chief of 9. Kompanie, Infanterie Regiment 119, 10.1936–10.1937, attached to Staff of Infanterie Regiment 119, 10.1937–11.1938. WWII: Commander of I. Bataillon, Infanterie Regiment 119, 11.1938–02.1940, Commander of Infanterie Regiment 119, 02.1940–01.1942, Commander of 25. Panzer Grenadier Division 01.1942–11.1943, Commander of XXVI. Armee Korps 02.1944–07.1944, Commander of LXXII. Armee Korps 01.1945–05.1945. Awards: Oak Leaves 05.12.43 (344), Knight's Cross 16.06.40, German Cross in Gold 11.03.43, 1939 Clasps to the 1914 Iron Cross 1st and 2nd Class, Infantry Assault Badge in Silver, Eastern Front Medal, 1914 Iron Cross 1st and 2nd Class, 1914 Wound Badge in Silver, Cross of Honor.

Grassmann, Gerhard: Generalmajor (01.03.43), (Heer); born 20.10.93 in Neisse, died 23.09.75 in Aschaffenburg. WWI: Leutnant and Adjutant to I. Bataillon, Feld Artillerie Regiment 16. Commander of I. Abteilung, Artillerie Regiment at Koenigsberg 10.1934–10.1935, Commander of I. Abteilung, Artillerie Regiment 1, 10.1935–11.1938. WWII: Leader of Lehrer Gruppe A at Artillerie Schule Jueterbog 11.1938–09.1939, Artillery Officer on Staff of Heeresgruppe C 09.1939–10.1940,

Commander of Artillerie Regiment 26, 11.1940–03.1942, Commander of Artillerie 122, 03.1942–11.1942, Commander of 333. Infanterie Division 12.1942–03.1943, attached to General of Artillerie in O.K.H. 04.1943–06.1943, attached to Commander of Artillerie Schule I 07.1943–08.1943, Higher Commander of Artillerie 311, 09.1943–11.1943, Higher Commander of Artillerie 309, 01.1944–11.1944, Higher Commander of Artillerie 321, 11.1944–05.1945. Awards: German Cross in Gold 17.11.41, 1939 Clasps to the 1914 Iron Cross 1st and 2nd Class, General Assault Badge, Eastern Front Medal, 1914 Iron Cross 1st and 2nd Class, Cross of Honor.

Grassmann, Werner: Vizeadmiral (01.01.40), (Kriegsmarine); born 09.03.88 in Berlin, died 20.10.43 in Berlin. WWI: Kapitanleutnant and Watch Officer on *M-141*. Promotion to Konteradmiral 01.10.37. Chief of Shipyard Department in Marineleitung 07.1933–09.1934, Chief of General Artillery Matters in Marineleitung 10.1934–09.1935, Commander of Schiff Artillerie Schule 09.1935–09.1937, Inspector attached to Marine Artillerie in O.K.M. 09.1937–01.1939, Chief of Warship Construction Amt in O.K.M. 04.1939–06.1939. WWII: Chief of Naval Commando Office in O.K.M. 08.1939–06.1941, Coastal Commander for Western Baltic Sea 06.1941–02.1943, retired 05.1943. Awards: War Merit Cross 1st and 2nd Class with Swords, 1914 Iron Cross 1st and 2nd Class, Cross of Honor.

Grau, Ernst: Generalmajor (01.10.43), (Heer); born 21.01.92 in Magdeburg, died 17.10.43 of wounds in Nowo-Alekejewka. WWI: Leutnant der Res. in Infanterie Regiment 131. Kompanie Chef in Infanterie Regiment 58, 10.1935–11.1938. WWII: attached to Staff of Military Commander of Koeln 11.1938–09.1939, Bataillon Commander in Infanterie Regiment 412, 10.1939–08.1941, wounded and in hospital 08.1941–01.1942, Commander of Grenadier Regiment 2, 07.1942–10.1943. Awards: 1939 Clasps to the 1914 Iron Cross 1st and 2nd Class, Infantry Assault Badge in Silver, 1939 Wound Badge in Gold, Cross of Honor.

Grauert, Ulrich: Generaloberst (19.07.40), (Luftwaffe); born 06.03.89 in Berlin, died 15.05.41 in action in St. Omer. WWI: in G.A.S. as Hauptmann and Commander of Flieger Abteilung 17. Promotions to Generalmajor 01.10.36, Generalleutnant 20.04.38, General der Flieger 01.10.39. Department Leader P I in R.L.M. 11.1933–03.1937, Senior Flieger Commander II 07.1937–06.1938. WWII: Commander of 1. Flieger Division 07.1938–10.1939, Commander of I. Flieger Korps 10.1939–05.1941. Awards: Knight's Cross 29.05.40, 1939 Clasps to the 1914 Iron Cross 1st and 2nd Class, 1939 Wound Badge in Gold, Combined Pilot/Observer's Badge in Gold with Diamonds, Pilot's Commemorative Badge, RK-Hohenzollern, 1914 Iron Cross 1st and 2nd Class, Austro-Hungarian Military Service Cross 3rd Class with War Decoration, 1914 Observer's Badge, Cross of Honor.

Gravenstein, Hans: Generalmajor (01.01.45), (Heer); born 16.07.90 in Berlin, died 03.05.47 (executed) in Belgrade. WWI: Hauptmann and Adjutant to Commander of Artillerie 117. Attached to Staff of I. Abteilung, Artillerie Regiment 59, 07.1936–10.10.1936, Batterie Chef in Artillerie Regiment 59, 10.1936–10.1937. WWII: Commander of I. Abteilung, Artillerie Regiment 70, 10.1937–02.1940, Commander of Artillerie Regiment 225, 02.1940–09.1942, Commander of Artillerie Regiment 252, 10.1942–05.1943, Commander of Artillerie 415, 09.1943–10.1944, Commander of 373. Croatian Infanterie Division 10.1944–05.1945. Awards: 1939 Clasps to the 1914 Iron Cross 1st and 2nd Class, General Assault Badge Eastern Front Medal, Croatian Order of the Crown of King Zvonimir 1st Class with Oak Leaves and Crown, RK-Hohenzollern, 1914 Iron Cross 1st and 2nd Class, Cross of Honor.

Grawitz, Prof. Dr. Ernst-Robert: SS-Obergruppenfuehrer und General der Waffen-SS (20.04.44); born 08.06.99 in Berlin, died 24.04.45 (suicide) with family in Berlin. Medical doctor by profession. P-1102844, SS-27483. WWI: Fahnrich attached to Hannover Jaeger Bataillon 10. Joined N.S.D.A.P. in 1931, joined S.S. in 1932. Promotions to SS-Brigadefuehrer 20.04.37, SS-Gruppenfuehrer 01.10.41. Attached to Staff of SS-Oberabschnitte Ost 01.10.34, Reichsarzt-SS (Head Doctor of S.S.) 01.07.35–01.12.37. WWII: Reichsarzt-SS und Polizei (Head Doctor of S.S. and Police) 01.12.38–09.11.44, DRK-Generalhauptfuehrer. Awards: 1939 Clasp to the 1914 Iron Cross 2nd Class, War Merit Cross 1st and 2nd Class with Swords, Breast Star to the German Red Cross Decoration, Luftschutz Ehrenzeichen 1st Class, German West Wall Medal, Commander's Cross of the Order of the White Rose of Finland with Swords, Grand Officer's Cross of the Italian Order of the Crown, 1914 Iron Cross 2nd Class, Cross of Honor, Reich Sports Badge in Silver, SA-Sports Badge in Bronze, Degen, Ring.

Greiff, Kurt von: General der Infanterie (01.09.40), (Heer); born 24.02.76 in Stuttgart, died 06.03.45 of natural causes in Isny. WWI: Major and Chief of Staff to XXV. Res. Korps. Promotions to Reichswehr Generalmajor 01.11.27, Reichswehr Generalleutnant 01.06.29 WWII: recalled to military service 08.1939, Commandant of Feldkommandantur 592, 12.1939–03.1940, Commander of XXXXV. Higher Kommando 03.1940–04.1942, retired 08.1942. Awards: War Merit Cross 1st and 2nd Class with Swords, Pour le Mérite 09.06.18, RK-Hohenzollern, Prussian Red Eagle Order IV Class, 1914 Iron Cross 1st and 2nd Class, Cross of Honor.

Greiffenberg, Hans von: General der Infanterie (01.04.44), (Heer); born 12.10.93 in Tschebiatkow, died 30.06.51 in Koenigstein. WWI: Oberleutnant and Adjutant to Infanterie Regiment 14. Promotions to Generalmajor 01.08.40, Generalleutnant 01.04.42. Ia to Wehrkreis Kommando IV 11.1934–10.1935, Ia to IV. Armee Korps

10.1935–10.1936, Commander of I. Bataillon, Infanterie Regiment 103, 10.1936–10.1937, Instruction Group Leader at Wehrmacht Schule 10.1937–01.1938, Department Chief T-4 in Heeres General Staff 02.1938–09.1938. WWII: Chief of Abteilung 1 in Operations Abteilung of Heeres General Staff 10.1938–08.1939, Chief of Operations Abteilung in O.K.W. 08.1939–10.1940, Chief of General Staff to 12. Armee 01.1941–05.1941, Chief of General Staff to Heeresgruppe Mitte 06.1941–04.1942, Chief of General Staff to Heeresgruppe A 05.1942–07.1943, Military Attaché to Budapest 10.1943–04.1944, Wehrmacht Plenipotentiary for Hungary 04.1944–05.1945. Awards: Knight's Cross 18.05.41, 1939 Clasps to the 1914 Iron Cross 1st and 2nd Class, Eastern Front Medal, 1914 Iron Cross 1st and 2nd Class, 1914 Wound Badge in Silver, Cross of Honor.

General der Infanterie Hans von Greiffenberg. (Bundesarchiv)

Greim, Robert Ritter von: Generalfeldmarschall (25.04.45), (Luftwaffe); born 22.06.92 in Bayreuth, died 24.05.45 (suicide) in Salzburg while in custody. WWI: in G.A.S. as Oberleutnant and Leader of Jasta 34. Promotions to Generalmajor 01.02.38, Generalleutnant 01.06.40, General der Flieger 19.07.40, Generaloberst 16.02.43. Fliegerhorst Commandant of Doeberitz 04.1934–03.1935, Inspector of Jagd and Sturzkampfflieger 04.1935–02.1936, Inspector of Air Traffic Control 02.1936–05.1937, Chief of Luftwaffe Personnel Office in R.L.M. 06.1937–01.1939. WWII: Commander of 5. Flieger Division 02.1939–10.1939, Commander of V. Flieger Korps 10.1939–03.1942, Commander of Luftwaffe Kommando Ost (East) 04.1942–05.1943, Oberbefehlshaber of Luftflotte 6, 05.1943–04.1945, Oberbefehlshaber of Luftwaffe 04.1945–05.1945. Awards: Golden Party Badge (honorary), Swords 28.08.44 (92), Oak Leaves 02.04.43 (216), Knight's Cross 24.06.40, 1939 Clasps to the 1914 Iron Cross 1st and 2nd Class, Combined Pilot-Observer's Badge in Gold with Diamonds, Pilot's Commemorative Badge, Pour le Mérite 14.10.18, RK-Bavarian Military Max Joseph Order: 23.10.18, RK-Hohenzollern, 1914 Iron Cross 1st and 2nd Class, 1914 Pilot's Badge, Cross of Honor.

Generalfeldmarschall Robert Ritter von Greim. (Roger James Bender)

Greiner, Heinrich: Generalleutnant (01.01.43), (Heer); born 12.08.95 in Amberg, died 19.11.77 in Rottach-Egern. WWI: Leutnant on Staff of Bavarian Infanterie Regiment 13. Promotion to Generalmajor 01.03.42. WWII: Instructor at Infanterie Schule in Munich 10.1934–01.1940, Commander of Infanterie Regiment 63, 02.1940–09.1940, Leader of Missing in Action Office in O.K.H. 09.1940–04.1941, Commander of Infanterie Regiment 499, 04.1941–01.1942, Commander of 268. Infanterie Division 01.1942–09.1943, Commander of 362. Infanterie Division 11.1943–01.1945. Awards: Oak Leaves 05.09.44 (572), Knight's Cross 22.09.41, 1939 Clasps to the 1914 Iron Cross 1st and 2nd Class, Infantry Assault Badge in Silver, Eastern Front Medal, 1914 Iron Cross 1st and 2nd Class, 1914 Wound Badge in Black, Cross of Honor.

Greul, Dr. Emil: Admiral-Stabsarzt (01.10.43), (Kriegsmarine); born 29.12.95 in Neubissingen, died 30.10.93 in Bremen. Medical doctor by profession. WWI: Leutnant der Res. in a Bavarian field artillery regiment. Promotion to Admiral-Arzt 01.09.42. Attached to Sanitats Amt for Naval Station North Sea and at same time Family Physician at Wilhelmshaven 03.1930–10.1934, Chief Physician at Naval Hospital in Cuxhaven 10.1934–03.1939. WWII: Chief Physician of Naval Hospital at Wesermuende 04.1939–04.1941, Commander of Naval Medical Academy 04.1941–09.1943, Chief of Naval Medical Office of Kriegsmarine and Medical Chief 10.1943–05.1945. Awards: Knight's Cross of the War Merit Cross with Swords 20.04.45, War Merit Cross 1st and 2nd Class with Swords, 1914 Iron Cross 2nd Class, 1914 Wound Badge in Black, Cross of Honor.

Admiral-Stabsarzt Dr. Emil Greul. (Josef Charita)

Griesbach, Franz: Generalmajor (01.08.44), (Heer); born 21.12.92 in Brueck, died 24.09.84 in Lage. WWI: Leutnant der Res. in Infanterie Regiment 27. Attached to Infanterie Regiment 12, 04.1936–05.1939. WWII: Kompanie Chef in Infanterie Regiment 12, 06.1939–08.1939, Chief of 10. Kompanie, Infanterie Regiment 467, 08.1939–05.1940, Staff Officer Course at Koenigsbrueck 05.1940–06.1941, Commander of Replacement Bataillon, Infanterie Regiment 467, 06.1941–09.1941, Commander of I. Bataillon, Infanterie Regiment 391, 09.1941–10.1941, attached to Formation Staff of Infanterie Regiment 391, 10.1941–04.1942, attached to Formation Staff of Grenadier Regiment 399, 04.1942–07.1942, Commander of Grenadier Regiment 399, 08.1942–02.1944, in hospital and Fuehrer Res. remainder of war due to injuries 02.1944–05.1945. Awards: Swords 06.03.44 (53), Oak Leaves 17.0.5.43 (242), Knight's Cross 14.03.42, 1939 Clasps to the 1914 Iron Cross 1st and 2nd Class, Infantry Assault Badge in Silver, Eastern Front Medal, Crimea Shield, 1939 Wound Badge in Gold, 1914 Iron Cross 1st and 2nd Class, Cross of Honor.

Generalmajor Franz Griesbach. (Bundesarchiv)

Grieshammer, Fritz: Generalmajor (01.04.44), (Luftwaffe); born 30.03.99 in Rehau, died 26.12.56 in Munich. WWI: Leutnant der Res. in Bavarian Feld Artillerie Regiment 8. Batterie Chef of 1. Batterie, Flak Regiment 8, 10.1935–03.1936, Batterie Chef of 1. Batterie, Flak Regiment 18, 04.1936–09.1936, Commander of II. Abteilung, Flak Regiment 25, 10.1936–06.1938. WWII: Commander of Festung Flak Abteilung 32, 07.1938–09.1939, Commander of Flak Gruppe at Kassel 10.1939–1940, Commander of Flak Brigade's IX 01.1941–05.1941, Commander of Flak Brigade VI 05.1941–07.1942, Commander of Flak Brigade in Vienna 10.1942–12.1942, Commander of Flak Brigade XVI 12.1942–12.1943, Commander of 24. Flak Division 01.1944–01.1945. Awards: Knight's Cross 12.04.45, 1939 Iron Cross 1st Class, 1939 Clasps to the 1914 Iron Cross 2nd Class, Flak War Badge, 1914 Iron Cross 2nd Class, Bavarian Military Service Order IV. Class with Swords, 1914 Wound Badge in Black, Cross of Honor.

Grimme, Hugo: General der Flak Artillerie (01.01.41), (Luftwaffe); born 06.11.72 in Goslar, died 02.11.43 in Schwerin. WWI: in G.A.S. as Major and Chief of Air Intelligence Department. Promotions to Reichswehr Generalmajor 01.03.28, Heer Generalleutnant 01.05.35. President of R.L.B. 04.1933–04.1936. WWII: Assistant in Kriegswissenschaftliche Abteilung of Luftwaffe 05.1936–12.1940, placed at disposal of Luftwaffe 01.1941–05.1943, retired 05.1943. Awards: War Merit Cross 1st and 2nd Class with Swords, German Social Welfare Decoration 1st Class, RK-Hohenzollern, RK-Sachsen Albrecht Order 1st Class with Swords, 1914 Iron Cross 1st and 2nd Class, Bavarian Military Service Cross IV. Class with Swords, Oldenburg Friedrich-August Cross 1st and 2nd Class, 1914 Wound Badge in Black, Turkish Silver Liakat Medal with Sabre, Turkish Half Moon, Cross of Honor.

Grimmeiss, Maxmilian: General der Artillerie (01.01.45), (Heer); born 27.02.93 in Erlangen, died 31.03.72 in Erlangen. WWI: Oberleutnant and Adjutant to Bavarian Feld Artillerie Regiment 10. Promotions to Generalmajor 01.02.42, Generalleutnant 01.04.43. Attached to Abwehr Abteilung of Reichswehr Ministry (later Reich War

Ministry) 07.1934–10.1936, Ia to XI. Armee Korps 10.1936–11.1938. WWII: Commander of Artillerie Regiment 78, 11.1938–08.1939, Chief of Staff to XII. Armee Korps 08.1939–09.1939, Chief of Staff to IX. Armee Korps 10.1939–01.1941, Chief of General Staff to 15. Armee 01.1941–11.1941, attached to Staff of Reichsmarschall Goering 12.1941–07.1944, Fuehrer Res. in O.K.H. 07.1944–01.1945. Awards: 1939 Clasps to the 1914 Iron Cross 1st and 2nd Class, 1914 Iron Cross 1st and 2nd Class, 1914 Wound Badge in Black, Cross of Honor.

Grobholz, Dr. Franz-Josef: Generalmajor (01.10.42), (Heer); born 11.04.93 in Zweibruecken, died 06.11.52 in Berlin. WWI: Oberleutnant on Staff of Trains in Heeresgruppe "Linsingen." Attached to Abwehr Abteilung in Reichswehr Ministry (later Reich War Ministry) 06.1934–11.1938. WWII: Commander of Kraftfahr Abteilung 8, 11.1938–08.1939, Heeres Nachschub Fuehrer 581, 08.1939–07.1940, Officer Judge at Reichs War Court 07.1940–11.1944, attached to Chief of Wehrmacht Patrol Services in O.K.W. 12.1944–05.1945. Awards: 1939 Clasp to the 1914 Iron Cross 2nd Class, War Merit Cross 1st and 2nd Class with Swords, 1914 Iron Cross 1st and 2nd Class, Cross of Honor.

Groddeck, Karl-Albrecht von: Generalleutnant (01.01.44), (Heer); born 18.02.94 in Berlin, died 10.01.44 of wounds at Breslau Hospital. WWI: Oberleutnant and temporary Commander of I. Bataillon, Grenadier Regiment 5. Promotion to Generalmajor 01.08.42. Commander of III. Bataillon, Infanterie Regiment 12, 10.1934–09.1937. WWII: Commander of Psych Evaluation Office for Wehrkreis Kommando VIII 10.1937–10.1939, Commander of Infanterie Regiment 120 (mot.) 10.1939–05.1942, wounded and placed in Fuehrer Res. 05.1942–07.1943, Commander of 161. Infanterie Division 08.1943–08.1943 until wounded again. Awards: Knight's Cross 08.09.41, 1939 Clasps to the 1914 Iron Cross 1st and 2nd Class, Infantry Assault Badge in Silver, Eastern Front Medal, 1939 Wound Badge in Gold, Romanian Order of Michael the Brave 3rd Class, RK-Hohenzollern, RK-Wuerttemberg Friedrich Order 2nd Class with Swords, 1914 Iron Cross 1st and 2nd Class, 1914 Wound Badge in Black, Cross of Honor.

Groeben, Peter von der: Generalmajor (01.03.45), (Heer); born 09.12.03 in Langheim, died 29.05.02 in Kiel. Attached to Kriegsschule 10.1935–10.1937, attached to Heeres Gruppen Kommando 1, 10.1937–03.1939. WWII: attached to Staff of Heeres Gruppen Kommando 1, 04.1939–08.1939, Chief Supply Officer (Ib) to Heeresgruppe Nord 08.1939–10.1939, Chief Supply Officer (Ib) to Heeresgruppe B 10.1939–04.1941, Ia to 86. Infanterie Division 04.1941–11.1942, Ia to A.O.K. 2, 11.1942–07.1943, Ia to Heeresgruppe Mitte 07.1943–11.1944, Commander of 3. Kavallerie Brigade and later Division 12.1944–05.1945. Awards: German Cross in Gold 08.01.43, 1939 Iron Cross 1st and 2nd Class, Eastern Front Medal.

Groeneveldt, Egon: Generalmajor z.V. (01.02.42), (Heer); born 25.06.76 in Platenrode, died 17.11.45 in Bad Hersfeld. WWI: Major in 55. Infanterie Brigade, P.O.W. 08.1914–09.1918. Commander of Military District Kommando at Konstanz 10.1933–09.1937, retired 09.1937. WWII: recalled to military service and placed at disposal of Heeres 08.1939–07.1941, Commandant of Feldkommandantur 684, 07.1941–03.1942, retired 05.1942, SS-Brigadefuehrer on Staff of SS-Abschnitte XXXXV. Awards: War Merit Cross 2nd Class with Swords, 1914 Iron Cross 1st and 2nd Class, 1914 Wound Badge in Black, Cross of Honor.

Grolig, Oswin: Generalmajor (01.11.43), (Heer); born 06.01.94 in Altona, died 18.08.44 from accident in Lotz. WWI: Leutnant in Hussar Regiment 11. Adjutant to Reiter Regiment at Erfurt 10.1934–10.1935, Adjutant to Kradschuetzen Bataillon 3, 10.1935–04.1936, attached to Reich War Ministry (later O.K.H.) 05.1936–11.1938. WWII: Commander of Aufklarungs Abteilung 8, 11.1938–12.1939, Commander of Schuetzen Ersatz Regiment 83, 12.1939–07.1940, Commander of Schuetzen Regiment 33, 07.1940–02.1942, Commander of 1. Panzer Grenadier Brigade 07.1942–12.1942, Commander of Panzertruppen Schule II at Krampnitz 05.1943–01.1944, Commander of 25. Panzer Division 06.1944–08.1944. Awards: German Cross in Gold 02.01.42, 1939 Clasps to the 1914 Iron Cross 1st and 2nd Class, Tank Assault Badge in Bronze, Eastern Front Medal, 1939 Wound Badge in Gold, 1914 Iron Cross 1st and 2nd Class, 1914 Wound Badge in Black, Cross of Honor.

Grolman, Helmuth von: Generalleutnant (01.11.44), (Heer); born 06.11.98 in Reinsheim, died 18.01.77 in Hannover. WWI: in G.A.S. as Leutnant in Flieger Abteilung 29. Promotion to Generalmajor 01.12.43. Advisor in Zentral Abteilung of Heeres General Staff 07.1935–10.1937, Chief of 4. Schwadron, Kavallerie Regiment 9, 10.1937–05.1938. WWII: Ia to 28. Infanterie Division 07.1938–10.1940, Ia in Operations Department of O.K.H. 10.1940–11.1942, Commander of 1. Panzer Regiment 01.1943–08.1943, Chief of General Staff to 2. Panzer Armee 08.1943–07.1944, Chief of General Staff to Heeresgruppe Sud Ukraine followed by Heeresgruppe Sud 07.1944–03.1945, Commander of 4. Kavallerie Division 03.1945–05.1945. Awards: German Cross in Gold 12.08.44, 1939 Clasps to the 1914 Iron Cross 1st and 2nd Class, War Merit Cross 1st and 2nd Class with Swords, Tank Assault Badge in Silver, Pilot's Commemorative Badge, 1914 Iron Cross 1st and 2nd Class, 1914 Wound Badge in Black, 1914 Pilot's Badge, Cross of Honor.

Gronau, Wolfgang von: Generalmajor (01.07.43), (Luftwaffe); born 25.02.93 in Berlin, died 17.03.77 in Fransdorf. WWI: Naval G.A.S. as Oberleutnant zur See and Adjutant to Commander of Hochseeflotte. Managing Director of Aero Clubs of Germany 04.1934–12.1938, attached to Staff of L.G. Greifswald 01.1939–04.1939.

WWII: Luftwaffe Attaché to Japan 04.1939–01.1945. Awards: War Merit Cross 1st and 2nd Class with Swords, Combined Pilot/Observer's Badge in Gold with Diamonds, German Olympic Games Decoration 1st Class, Naval Pilot's Commemorative Badge, RK-Hohenzollern, 1914 Iron Cross 1st and 2nd Class, 1914 Naval Pilot's Badge, Cross of Honor.

Groos, Dr. Otto: Admiral z.V. (01.09.41), (Kriegsmarine); born 17.07.82 in Juelich, died 29.05.70 in Bremen. WWI: Korvettenkapitan and Admiral Staff Officer attached to IV. Aufklarungs Gruppe. Promotions to Reichsmarine Konteradmiral 01.12.30, Reichsmarine Vizeadmiral 01.04.34. Chief of Marine Kommando Amt in Marineleitung 09.1931–09.1934, Inspector of Wehrmacht Academy 1935–date unknown. WWII: Chief of Special Staff War Economics and Economic Combat Measures in O.K.W. and at same time Leader of Military Commission of Tripartite 06.1940–06.1944, Chief of Staff of War Economic and Economic Combat Measures in O.K.W. 10.1944–05.1945. Awards: War Merit Cross 1st and 2nd Class with Swords, RK-Hohenzollern, 1914 Iron Cross 1st and 2nd Class, Turkish Half Moon, Cross of Honor.

Groppe, Theodor: Generalleutnant (01.11.39), (Heer); born 16.08.82 in Trier, died 28.04.73 in Trier. WWI: Hauptmann and Commander of II. Bataillon, Grenadier Regiment 1. Promotion to Generalmajor 01.10.37. WWII: Landwehr Commander of Hanau 10.1936–08.1939, Commander of 214. Infanterie Division 08.1939–02.1940, Fuehrer Res. in O.K.H. 02.1940–12.1941, never held another command due to being politically unreliable, lost rank and was later arrested by Gestapo. Awards: 1939 Clasps to the 1914 Iron Cross 1st and 2nd Class, Pour le Mérite 06.11.18, RK-Hohenzollern, 1914 Iron Cross 1st and 2nd Class, 1914 Wound Badge in Black, Cross of Honor.

Grosch, Walther: Generalleutnant (01.06.43), (Luftwaffe); born 14.04.91 in Coburg, died 22.11.72 in Berg. WWI: in G.A.S. as Hauptmann in Jagdflieger Schule 1. Promotion to Generalmajor 01.06.41. Department Leader in R.L.M. 02.1934–07.1935, Instruction Group Leader at Fliegerschule Fassberg 08.1935–11.1937, attached to Sonderstab W in O.K.W. 02.1939–07.1939. WWII: Quartermaster of Luftgau Kommando XI 07.1939–03.1941, Senior Quartermaster for Luftflotte 5, 05.1941–05.1943, Inspector of Construction Troops and P.O.W.s (L In 17) in R.L.M. 05.1943–06.1944, General of Foreign Personnel of Luftwaffe in R.L.M. 06.1944–02.1945. Awards: German Cross in Silver 02.04.43, War Merit Cross 1st and 2nd Class with Swords, 1939 Observer's Badge, "J.G. Freiherr von Richthofen Nr. 1, 1917/18" Commemorative Cuff Band, Pilot's Commemorative Badge, 1914 Iron Cross 1st and 2nd Class, 1914 Wound Badge in Black, 1914 Observer's Badge, Cross of Honor.

Groschupf, Ernst: Generalleutnant (01.07.42), (Heer); born 18.08.78 in Fuerstenberg, died 14.07.64 in Verden. WWI: Hauptmann and Commander of II. Abteilung, Feld Artillerie Regiment 8. Promotion to Generalmajor 01.04.40. Attached to Staff of Military Replacement Inspection of Berlin 11.1934–08.1935. WWII: Commander of Military District Kommando I in Potsdam 09.1935–04.1940, Commander of Truppenubungsplatz at Senne 04.1940–11.1941, Commander of Truppenubungsplatz at Doberitz 11.1941–08.1942, retired 04.1943. Awards: War Merit Cross 1st and 2nd Class with Swords, 1914 Iron Cross 1st and 2nd Class, Cross of Honor.

Grosse, Erich: Generalmajor (01.12.42), (Heer); born 23.06.85 in Bremen, died 01.12.42 in action at Stalingrad. WWI: Hauptmann and Ic on Staff of Coastal Fortifications. Attached to Training Regiment at Ludwigsburg 11.1934–12.1936, attached to Legion Condor in Spain as Training Leader at Heeres Offizier Schule 01.1937–05.1939. WWII: attached to Kriegsschule Wiener-Neustadt 07.1939–03.1940, Commander of Infanterie Regiment West 03.1940–07.1941, Commander of Infanterie Regiment 276, 06.1941–12.1942. Awards: German Cross in Gold 25.01.43, 1939 Clasps to the 1914 Iron Cross 1st and 2nd Class, Infantry Assault Badge in Silver, Eastern Front Medal, 1939 Wound Badge in Gold, Spanish Cross in Bronze with Swords, 1914 Iron Cross 1st and 2nd Class, 1914 Wound Badge in Black, Cross of Honor.

Grosse, Dr. Hermann: General-Stabsarzt (01.10.41), (Heer); born 27.10.86 in Hannover, died 18.11.66 in Bad Reichenhall. Medical doctor by profession. WWI: Assistenz-Arzt (unit unknown). Promotion to General-Arzt 01.04.39. Division Physician to 7. Division 1935–03.1938. WWII: Corps Physician to XVIII. Armee Korps 04.1938–08.1939, Corps Physician to XVII. Armee Korps 08.1939–10.1940, Army Physician to 1. Armee 01.1941–06.1941, Army Physician to 11. Armee 06.1941–11.1942, Corps Physician to Wehrkreis VII 12.1942–01.1945. Awards: 1939 Clasp to the 1914 Iron Cross 2nd Class, War Merit Cross 1st and 2nd Class with Swords, 1914 Iron Cross 2nd Class, Cross of Honor.

Grosse, Dr. Walther: Generalmajor (01.04.43), (Heer); born 01.01.84 in Marienburg, died 20.09.69 in Muehlheim. WWI: Hauptmann and Commander of II. Bataillon, Infanterie Regiment 151. Pionier Advisor to Wehrgau in Koenigsberg 07.1934–03.1935, Pionier Advisor to Fortress Commander of Koenigsberg 05.1935–07.1939. WWII: attached to German Russian Military Commission 10.1939–04.1940, Commander of Bau Truppen 38, 04.1940–07.1940, attached to Staff of General of Pioniers in O.K.H. 12.1940–05.1942, Commander of Senior Construction Staff 18, 05.1942–08.1943, Higher Pionier Leader 18, 08.1943–05.1945. Awards: 1939 Clasps to the 1914 Iron Cross 1st and 2nd Class, General Assault Badge, 1914 Iron Cross 1st and 2nd Class, Cross of Honor.

Grosskreutz, Hans: Ministerialdirigent (01.04.41), (Luftwaffe); born 09.05.81 in Hanshagen, died 19.07.48. Civil Servant by profession. WWI: Hauptmann (unit unknown). WWII: Department Chief of (L/13) in R.L.M. 11.1936–03.1944, retired 03.1944. Awards: War Merit Cross 1st and 2nd Class with Swords, 1914 Iron Cross 1st and 2nd Class, Cross of Honor.

Grossmann, Horst: General der Infanterie (09.11.44), (Heer); born 19.11.91 in Sybba, died 04.05.72 in Ruesselheim. WWI: Oberleutnant and Adjutant to Infanterie Regiment 175. Promotions to Generalmajor 01.01.42, Generalleutnant 01.01.43. Commander of II. Bataillon, Infanterie Regiment at Gumbinnen 10.1934–10.1935, Commander of II. Bataillon, Infanterie Regiment 22, 10.1935–02.1938. WWII: Commander of Lehrer Gruppe B at Kriegsschule Potsdam 03.1938–10.1939, Commander of Infanterie Regiment 84, 10.1939–12.1941, Commander of 6. Infanterie Division 01.1942–12.1943, Leader of LV. Armee Korps 01.1944–05.1944, Commander of VI. Armee Korps 08.1944–05.1945. Awards: Oak Leaves 04.09.43 (292), Knight's Cross 23.08.41, German Cross in Gold 11.02.43, 1939 Clasps to the 1914 Iron Cross 1st and 2nd Class, Infantry Assault Badge in Silver, Eastern Front Medal, RK-Hohenzollern, 1914 Iron Cross 1st and 2nd Class, 1914 Wound Badge in Black, Cross of Honor.

Grote, Waldemar Freiherr: Generalleutnant (01.11.39), (Heer); born 02.07.77 in Trendelburg, died 16.04.57 in Braunschweig. WWI: Major and Commander of II. Bataillon, Infanterie Regiment 98. Promotion to Generalmajor 01.10.37. Office Leader IV at Giessen 12.1934–05.1935, Leader of Replacement Troops at Darmstadt 06.1935–03.1936. WWII: Landwehr Commander for Berlin 10.1936–08.1939, Commander of 218. Infanterie Division 08.1939–12.1941, Fuehrer Res. in O.K.H. 12.1941–08.1942, retired 08.1942. Awards: 1939 Clasps to the 1914 Iron Cross 1st and 2nd Class, Infantry Assault Badge in Silver, RK-Hohenzollern, 1914 Iron Cross 1st and 2nd Class, 1914 Wound Badge in Black, Cross of Honor.

Groth, Dr. Walter: General-Arzt (01.09.41), (Luftwaffe); born 12.09.83 in Berlin, died 12.04.47 in Mattenwald. Medical doctor by profession. WWI: Stabs-Arzt and Chief of Feldlazarett 52. WWII: Advisor and later Department Chief attached to Luftwaffe Medical Services in R.L.M. 10.1935–05.1940, Chief Physician to Luftgau Kommando VII 06.1940–03.1942, Chief Physician to Luftgau Kommando XII and XIII 06.1942–03.1943, Fuehrer Res. in O.K.L. 03.1943–01.1944, retired 01.1944. Awards: War Merit Cross 1st and 2nd Class with Swords, Silesian Eagle 1st and 2nd Class, 1914 Iron Cross 1st and 2nd Class, Cross of Honor.

Grothe, Hermann-Ernst: Generalmajor (01.03.45), (Heer); born 10.12.94 in Koenigsberg, died 05.04.59 in Berlin. WWI: Leutnant der Res. and Adjutant to III. Bataillon, Infanterie Regiment 24. Attached to Kriegsschule Hannover 10.1935–05.1936, Batterie Chef in Nebelwerfer Abteilung 2, 06.1936–02.1938, attached to Staff of Werfer Abteilung 2, 03.1938–11.1938. WWII: Commander of Nebelwerfer Bataillon 5, 11.1938–08.1940, Commander of Nebelwerfer Regiment Staff z.b.V. 1, 09.1940–01.1941, Commander of Nebelwerfer Artillerie Regiment 52, 01.1941–09.1942, Commander of Rocket Troops 1 and later 1. Rocket Artillerie Brigade 09.1942–05.1945. Awards: German Cross in Silver (date unknown), 1939 Clasps to the 1914 Iron Cross 1st and 2nd Class, War Merit Cross 1st and 2nd Class with Swords, General Assault Badge, Eastern Front Medal, RK-Hohenzollern, 1914 Iron Cross 1st and 2nd Class, 1914 Wound Badge in Black, Cross of Honor.

Grube, Helmut: Konteradmiral (01.02.42), (Kriegsmarine); born 07.05.93 in Hohensprenz, died 05.12.78 in Schleswig. WWI: Marineingenieuroberaspirant and Engineer on heavy cruiser *Furst Bismarck*. Lead Engineer for cruiser *Karlsruhe* 12.1930–03.1933, attached to Chief for Marine Station Eastern Sea 03.1933–09.1933, Advisor attached to Marineleitung 09.1933–09.1935, Advisor attached to Ship Machine Inspection 10.1935–09.1938. WWII: Advisor for Testing in War Ship Construction 10.1938–11.1939, Chief of Staff of Test Command for new warship construction in O.K.M. 11.1939–01.1941, Department Chief in Office Group for Ship Machine Operations in O.K.M. 01.1941–01.1943, Director of Supply Department in O.K.M. 01.1943–12.1944. Awards: German Cross in Silver 28.08.44, War Merit Cross 1st and 2nd Class with Swords, 1914 Iron Cross 2nd Class, Cross of Honor.

Gruber, Dr. Karl: General-Richter (01.09.38), (Heer); born 21.09.78 in Prague, died 15.03.58 in Vienna. Civil Servant by profession. WWI: Hauptmann (Auditor). Transferred to German Wehrmacht 03.1938. WWII: attached to Reichs War Court 09.1938–10.1939, retired 10.1939. Awards: unknown.

Gruen, Dr. Alfred: General-Richter (1944), (Heer); born 07.02.96 in Augsburg, died 01.07.59 in Verdun. Jurist by profession. WWI: Leutnant der Res. (unit unknown). WWII: Chief Judge to 12. Armee 01.1941–06.1942, Chief Judge to Heeresgruppe A 07.1942–01.1944, Judge with Reichs War Court 01.1944–05.1945. Awards: War Merit Cross 1st and 2nd Class with Swords, 1914 Iron Cross 1st and 2nd Class, Cross of Honor.

Gruen, Otto: General der Artillerie (01.08.36), (Heer); born 29.05.82 in Deggendorf, died 26.03.46 in Tegernsee. WWI: Hauptmann attached to A.O.K. 6. Promotions to Reichswehr Generalmajor 01.02.33, Reichswehr Generalleutnant 01.02.34. Inspector of Artillerie in Reichswehr Ministry (later Reich War Ministry) 10.1934–09.1937, retired 09.1937, recalled to military service 11.1938. WWII: Inspector of Artillerie on Staff of O.B. of Replacement Armee 08.1939–05.1944,

Fuehrer Res. in O.K.H. 05.1944–08.1944, retired 08.1944. Awards: German Cross in Silver 29.05.44, War Merit Cross 1st and 2nd Class with Swords, 1914 Iron Cross 1st and 2nd Class, Cross of Honor.

Gruenewald, Dr. Otto: General-Richter (01.08.44), (Heer); born 29.03.97 in Bad Wimpfen, died 29.07.80 in Murnau. Jurist by profession. WWI: service unknown. Attached to Heeres Justice Service Division 09.1937–1938. WWII: Advisor in Legal Department of O.K.H. 1938–06.1940, Judge to 1. Armee 12.1940–06.1942, attached to Heeres Field Justice Department of O.K.H. 11.1942–05.1945. Awards: War Merit Cross 1st and 2nd Class, with Swords, 1914 Wound Badge in Black, Cross of Honor.

Grun, Edgar: Generalmajor z.V. (01.02.42), (Heer); born 06.09.76 in Dostorff, died 06.11.62 in Garmisch-Partenkirchen. WWI: Major and Adjutant on Staff of XXXXIV. Res. Korps. WWII: Commander of Military District Kommando at Naumburg/Saale 10.1933–08.1939, Commander of Military District Kommando for Halle-Saale 09.1939–07.1942, retired 08.1942. Awards: War Merit Cross 1st and 2nd Class with Swords, 1914 Iron Cross 1st and 2nd Class, Cross of Honor.

Grund, Hans: Generalmajor (01.01.44), (Luftwaffe); born 01.2.96 in Eisleben, died 08.07.76 in Hamburg. WWI: in G.A.S. as Leutnant in Flieger Abteilung A 262. Staffelkapitan in K.G. 3, 07.1936–03.1938, Gruppen Commander in K.G. 3, 04.1938–06.1939. WWII: Flughafenbereichs Commandant of several facilities 06.1939–06.1941, assigned to Staff of Feldluftgau Kommando Moscow, Minsk and later Southern Russia 10.1941–09.1943, Flughafenbereichs Commandant of 3-VIII 09.1943–09.1944, Commander of Troops in Luftgau Kommando XI 11.1944–05.1945. Awards: 1939 Clasp to the 1914 Iron Cross 2nd Class, War Merit Cross 1st and 2nd Class with Swords, Eastern Front Medal, 1939 Observer's Badge, Reich Senate Culture Honor Badge, Reich Sports Badge in Gold, Pilot's Commemorative Badge, 1914 Iron Cross 1st and 2nd Class, 1914 Observer's Badge, Cross of Honor.

Gruner, Erich: Generalmajor (01.09.43), (Heer); born 10.09.94 in Berlin, died 12.05.44 in action in Crimea. WWI: Oberleutnant and Adjutant to District Kommando in Thorn. Kompanie Chef in Infanterie Regiment 39, 10.1935–05.1936, Commander of I. Bataillon, Infanterie Regiment 78, 05.1936–10.1937. WWII: Commander of III. Bataillon, Infanterie Regiment 78, 10.1937–02.1940, Commander of Infanterie Regiment 517, 02.1940–12.1940, Commander of Infanterie Regiment 589, 12.1940–07.1941, Commander of Infanterie Regiment 429, 07.1941–10.1942, Fuehrer Res. in O.K.H. 10.1942–12.1942, Leader of 62. Infanterie Division 12.1942–01.1943, attached to Heeresgruppe A 05.1943–11.1943, Commander of 111. Infanterie Division 11.1943–05.1944.

Awards: German Cross in Gold 09.10.42, Honor Roll Clasp 05.10.42, 1939 Clasps to the 1914 Iron Cross 1st and 2nd Class, German Army High Command Commendation Certificate 25.05.42, Infantry Assault Badge in Silver, Eastern Front Medal, 1939 Wound Badge in Gold, 1914 Iron Cross 1st and 2nd Class, 1914 Wound Badge in Black, Cross of Honor.

Guderian, Heinz: Generaloberst (19.07.40), (Heer); born 17.06.88 in Culm, died 14.05.54 in Schwangau. WWI: Hauptmann and Ia to General Staff in Italy. Promotions to Generalmajor 01.08.36, Generalleutnant 10.02.38, General der Panzertruppe 23.11.38. Chief of Staff to Commander of Transport Troops 07.1934–01.1938, Commander of XVI. Armee Korps (mot.) 04.1938–11.1938. WWII: Chief of Schnelltruppen 11.1938–08.1939, Commander of XIX. Armee Korps (mot.), 08.1939–11.1940, Commander of Panzer Gruppe 2 (later Panzer Armee) 11.1940–12.1941, placed in Fuehrer Res. in O.K.H. and attached to Wehrkreis Kommando III 01.1942–02.1943, Inspector General of Panzertruppen in O.K.H. 02.1943–04.1945, Chief of Heeres General Staff 07.1944–03.1945. Awards: Oak Leaves 17.07.41 (24), Knight's Cross 27.10.39, 1939 Clasps to the 1914 Iron Cross 1st and 2nd Class, Tank Assault Badge in Silver, 1914 Iron Cross 1st and 2nd Class, Cross of Honor.

Generaloberst Heinz Guderian. (Bundesarchiv)

Gudowius, Erich: Generalleutnant z.V. (01.06.42), (Heer); born 06.03.73 in Schoenheide, died 01.105.44 of natural causes in Berlin. WWI: Major and Chief of Staff to XIV. Armee Korps. Promotion to Reichswehr Generalmajor 01.11.27. WWII: recalled to military service 08.1939, Deputy Chief of War History Department in O.K.H. 09.1939–03.1942, retired 06.1942. Awards: War Merit Cross 1st and 2nd Class with Swords, Pour le Mérite 04.08.18, RK-Hohenzollern, 1914 Iron Cross 1st and 2nd Class, Cross of Honor.

Guembel, Karl: Generalleutnant (01.01.43), (Heer); born 24.06.88 in Finstingen, died 28.10.70 in Heidelberg. WWI: Oberleutnant and Adjutant to Res. Infanterie Regiment 64. Promotion to Generalmajor 01.02.42. Attached to Staff of Infanterie Regiment 27, 10.1935–05.1936, Commander of III. Bataillon, Infanterie Regiment 110, 05.1936–06.1938. WWII: Commander of Infanterie Regiment 118, 07.1938–02.1940, Commander of Infanterie Regiment 516, 02.1940–12.1941, Commander of 295. Infanterie Division 12.1941–04.1942, Commander of 257. Infanterie Division 05.1942–05.1942, Commander of 182.

Infanterie Division 07.1942–09.1942, Commander of 348. Infanterie Division 09.1942–02.1944, Commander of Division 152, 03.1944–05.1945. Awards: Knight's Cross 30.10.41, 1939 Clasps to the 1914 Iron Cross 1st and 2nd Class, Infantry Assault Badge in Silver, Eastern Front Medal, 1914 Iron Cross 1st and 2nd Class, Cross of Honor.

Guendell, Walther von: Generalleutnant (01.12.43), (Heer); born 05.03.92 in Hannover, died 10.02.73 in Hannover. WWI: Oberleutnant and 2. Ordnance Officer on Staff of 95. Infanterie Division. Promotion to Generalmajor 01.12.41. Commander of II. Bataillon, Infanterie Regiment at Luebeck 10.1934–10.1935, Commander of II. Bataillon, Infanterie Regiment 6, 10.1935–05.1937, Military Commander of Hannover 06.1937–10.1937, attached to Staff of Infanterie Regiment 73, 10.1937–11.1938. WWII: Commander of Infanterie Regiment 73, 11.1938–08.1939, Commander of Infanterie Replacement Regiment 13, 08.1939–09.1941, Headquarters Commandant of O.K.H. 09.1941–05.1945. Awards: War Merit Cross 1st and 2nd Class with Swords, 1914 Iron Cross 1st and 2nd Class, Cross of Honor.

Guenther, Erich: Generalmajor (01.05.44), (Heer); born 16.01.98 in Wilhelmshaven, died 03.05.44 in action near Slobozzia. WWI: Gefreiter in Fusilier Regiment 86. Kompanie Chef in Infanterie Regiment 67, 10.1935–07.1938. WWII: Commander of II. Bataillon, Infanterie Regiment 67, 08.1938–10.1941, Commander of Infanterie Regiment 680, 10.1941–05.1944. Awards: German Cross in Gold 02.07.44, 1939 Iron Cross 1st Class, 1939 Clasp to the 1914 Iron Cross 2nd Class, German Army High Command Commendation Certificate 17.02.44, Infantry Assault Badge in Silver, Eastern Front Medal, 1939 Wound Badge in Gold, 1914 Iron Cross 2nd Class, Cross of Honor.

Guenther, Dr. Ernst: General-Stabsarzt (01.04.42), (Heer); born 24.11.88 in Quedlinburg, died 15.11.49 in Oberfrohe. Medical doctor by profession. WWI: Assistenz-Arzt (unit unknown). Promotion to General-Arzt 01.04.40. WWII: Division Physician to 24. Infanterie Division 1938–10.1939, Corps Physician to IV. Armee Korps 10.1939–01.1941, Army Physician to 15. Armee 01.1941–11.1944, Fuehrer Res. in O.K.H. 11.1944–03.1945. Awards: 1939 Clasp to the 1914 Iron Cross 2nd Class, War Merit Cross 1st and 2nd Class with Swords, Eastern Front Medal, 1914 Iron Cross 2nd Class, Cross of Honor.

Guenther, Dr. Kurt: General-Arzt (01.04.41), (Heer); born 24.12.89 in Quedlinburg, died 24.03.41 of natural causes in Ludwigsburg. Medical doctor by profession. WWI: service unknown. WWII: Division Physician to 25. Division 1938–08.1939, Corps Physician to V. Armee Korps 08.1939–03.1941. Awards: 1939 Clasp to the 1914 Iron Cross 2nd Class, 1914 Iron Cross 2nd Class, Cross of Honor.

Guentzel, Ernst: Generalleutnant (01.10.41), (Heer); born 09.03.88 in Wittslock, died 17.12.42 of natural causes in Hamm. WWI: Hauptmann and Bataillon Commander in Feld Artillerie Regiment 63. Promotion to Generalmajor 01.10.39. Commander of Beobachter Abteilung 1, 10.1934–09.1936, Commander of Artillerie Regiment 52, 10.1936–10.1937. WWII: Commander of Artillerie Regiment 16, 11.1937–08.1939, Commander of Artillerie 103, 08.1938–12.1940, Commander of 113. Infanterie Division 12.1940–06.1941, Fuehrer Res. in O.K.H. 06.1941–12.1942, Commander of Division 462, 12.1942. Awards: 1939 Clasps to the 1914 Iron Cross 1st and 2nd Class, General Assault Badge, 1914 Iron Cross 1st and 2nd Class, Cross of Honor.

Guhl, Konrad: Generalleutnant z.V. (01.02.41), (Heer); born 17.07.70 in Neisse, died 24.10.44 of natural causes in Gut. WWI: Oberstleutnant and Commander of Artillerie 33. Promotion to Reichswehr Generalmajor 01.12.23. WWII: recalled to military service 09.1939, placed at disposal of Heeres 09.1939, Commander of 174. Infanterie Division 06.1940–04.1942, retired 05.1942. Awards: 1939 Clasps to the 1914 Iron Cross 1st and 2nd Class, Infantry Assault Badge in Silver, RK-Hohenzollern, 1914 Iron Cross 1st and 2nd Class, Cross of Honor.

Gullmann, Otto: Generalleutnant (01.01.43), (Heer); born 07.11.87 in Ingolstadt, died 02.01.63 in Saalfeld. WWI: Hauptmann on Staff of Staging Inspection VI. Promotion to Generalmajor 01.02.41. Attached to Staff of Infanterie Regiment 36, 10.1935–10.1936, attached to IX. Armee Korps 10.1936–01.1937. WWII: Military Commander of Muenster 02.1937–08.1939, Commander of Infanterie Replacement Regiment 16, 08.1939–02.1940, Commandant of Feldkommandantur 520, 02.1940–11.1943, Fuehrer Res. in O.K.H. 11.1943–03.1944, Area Commandant then German Plenipotentiary General for Albania 03.1944–10.1944, attached to Wehrkreis Kommando VII 01.1945–05.1945. Awards: War Merit Cross 1st and 2nd Class with Swords, 1914 Iron Cross 1st and 2nd Class, 1914 Wound Badge in Black, Cross of Honor.

Gundelach, Herbert: Generalmajor (30.01.45), (Heer); born 15.06.99 in Metz, died 04.11.71 in Hochdahl. WWI: Leutnant in Guards Pionier Replacement Bataillon. Attached to Staff of Artillerie Fuehrer II 04.1935–10.1935, attached to Staff of 2. Division 10.1935–04.1936, 2. Staff Officer of 2. Division 04.1936–10.1937, Chief of 3. Kompanie, Pionier Bataillon 31, 10.1937–06.1938, Ia to Kommando Staff Upper Rhein 06.1938–11.1938, Ia to Senior Commander of Grenztruppen Oberrhein 11.1938–05.1939. WWII: Ia to 16. Infanterie Division (later Motorized) 06.1939–01.1942, Senior Quartermaster to 1. Armee 03.1942–09.1943, Commander of Grenadier Regiment 24, 12.1943–01.1944, Chief of Staff to XXVIII. Armee Korps 02.1944–11.1944, Chief of Staff to General of Pioniers in O.K.H.

11.1944–05.1945. Awards: German Cross in Gold 26.01.42, 1939 Clasps to the 1914 Iron Cross 1st and 2nd Class, Eastern Front Medal, 1914 Iron Cross 1st and 2nd Class, 1914 Wound Badge in Black, Cross of Honor.

Gunderloch, Dr. Rudolf: General-Stabsarzt (01.01.41), (Heer); born 14.10.85 in Freiburg, died 25.06.62 in Wiesbaden. Medical doctor by profession. WWI: Assistenz-Arzt (unit unknown). Promotion to General-Arzt 01.03.37. WWII: Commandant of Heeres Medical Academy 05.1934–08.1939, Army Physician to 5. Armee 08.1939–10.1939, Armee Arzt to 18. Armee 11.1939–09.1942, Army Physician to Heeresgruppe Nord 09.1942–02.1943, Corps Physician to Wehrkreis XII 04.1943–09.1944, retired 11.1944. Awards: 1939 Clasp to the 1914 Iron Cross 2nd Class, War Merit Cross 1st and 2nd Class with Swords, 1914 Iron Cross 1st and 2nd Class, 1914 Wound Badge in Black, Cross of Honor.

Gunzelmann, Emil-Heinrich: Generalleutnant (01.10.41), (Heer); born 17.07.87 in Munich, died 14.12.75 in Oberammergau. WWI: Hauptmann and Bataillon Commander in Bavarian Replacement Regiment 11. Promotion to Generalmajor 01.10.38. Attached to Staff of Heeres Service Office 7, 10.1935–05.1936, attached to Staff of Infanterie Regiment 40, 05.1936–03.1938, Commander of Infanterie Regiment 34, 05.1938–04.1939. WWII: Military Replacement Inspector for Mannheim 05.1939–05.1941, Military Replacement Inspector for Graz 05.1941–01.1943, Fuehrer Res. in O.K.H. 01.1943–02.1944, P.O.W. Commander for General-Government (occupied Poland) 05.1944–09.1944, P.O.W. Commander for Wehrkreis Kommando VI 09.1944–05.1945. Awards: War Merit Cross 1st and 2nd Class with Swords, 1914 Iron Cross 1st and 2nd Class, Bavarian Military Service Cross IV. Class with Swords, Cross of Honor.

Gurran, Paul: Generalleutnant (01.02.44), (Heer); born 11.01.93 in Zauche, died 22.04.44 of wounds near Majevo. WWI: Vizefeldwebel in Grenadier Regiment 12. Promotion to Generalmajor 01.10.43. Attached to Staff of Commander of Truppenubungsplatz at Stablack 10.1934–09.1937. WWII: Commander of III. Bataillon, Infanterie Regiment 45, 10.1937–02.1940, Commander of Infanterie Regiment 506, 02.1940–11.1942, Commander of Schule for Heeresgruppe Nord 11.1942–03.1943, attached to Heeresgruppe Nord 11.1942–09.1943, Commander of 24. Infanterie Division until wounded 09.1943–02.1944. Awards: Knight's Cross 12.09.41, 1939 Clasps to the 1914 Iron Cross 1st and 2nd Class, Infantry Assault Badge in Silver, Eastern Front Medal, 1939 Wound Badge in Gold, 1914 Iron Cross 1st and 2nd Class, Cross of Honor.

Guse, Guenther: Admiral (01.01.40), (Kriegsmarine); born 30.08.86 in Stettin, died 06.05.53 at Vladmir P.O.W. Camp. WWI: Kapitanleutnant and torpedo boat Commandant in 18. Torpedoboots Halbflotille. Promotions to

Konteradmiral 01.04.35, Vizeadmiral 01.11.37. Chief of Flotten Abteilung in Marineleitung 09.1932–09.1934, Chief of Marine Kommando Amt in Marineleitung (later O.K.M.) 09.1934–10.1938 and at same time Chief of Staff for Seekriegsleitung 04.1937–10.1938. WWII: Deputy Commander of Naval Station Baltic Sea 05.1939–03.1943, retired 05.1943. Awards: German Cross in Silver 19.02.43, 1939 Clasps to the 1914 Iron Cross 1st and 2nd Class, 1914 Iron Cross 1st and 2nd Class, Oldenburg Friedrich-August Cross 1st and 2nd Class, Cross of Honor.

Admiral Guenther Guse. (Bundesarchiv)

Gusovius, Richard von: Generalmajor z.V. (01.06.42), (Heer); born 13.07.73 in Koenigsberg, died 06.07.42 of natural causes in Koenigsberg. WWI: Major and Chairman of 2. Remonte Committee. WWII: attached to Remote Matters in O.K.H. 08.1939–05.1942, attached to Staff of Wehrmacht Befehlshaber of Netherlands 07.1941–12.1941. Awards: War Merit Cross 1st and 2nd Class with Swords, 1914 Iron Cross 1st and 2nd Class, Cross of Honor.

Gutenberger, Karl: SS-Obergruppenfuehrer und General der Waffen-SS und Polizei (01.08.44); born 18.04.05 in Essen, died 08.07.61 in Essen. P-25249, SS-372303. Joined N.S.D.A.P. and S.A. in 1925, reached rank of SA-Brigadefuehrer and Leader of SA-Brigade 73, joined S.S. in 1940. Promotions to SS-Brigadefuehrer 01.06.40, SS-Gruppenfuehrer 09.11.42. WWII: Fuehrer of SS-Oberabschnitte West and H.S.S.P.F. 30.01.42–09.11.44, Polizei President, Member of Reichstag (WK 23 Duesseldorf-West). Awards: Golden Party Badge, 1939 Iron Cross 2nd Class, War Merit Cross 1st and 2nd Class with Swords, 1939 Wound Badge in Black, Gau Essen Commemorative Badge, German Horseman's Badge in Bronze, Degen, Ring.

SS-Obergruppenfuehrer Karl Gutenberger. (Bundesarchiv)

Guth, Kurt: Generalmajor (10.08.43), (Heer); born 24.07.98 in Kirchheim, died 11.03.43 of wounds in hospital in Riga. WWI: Leutnant in Feld Artillerie Regiment 80. Batterie Chef in Artillerie Regiment at Jueterbog 10.1934–09.1935, Batterie Chef in Artillerie Lehr Regiment at Jueterbog 10.1935–11.1938. WWII: Commander of I. Abteilung, Artillerie Regiment 24, 11.1938–11.1940, Commander of Artillerie Regiment 24 until wounded 11.1940–02.1943. Awards: German Cross in Gold 04.09.42, 1939 Clasps to the 1914 Iron Cross 1st and 2nd Class, General Assault Badge, Eastern Front Medal, 1939 Wound Badge in Gold, 1914 Iron Cross 1st and 2nd Class, Cross of Honor.

Gutjahr, Karl-Otto: Konteradmiral (01.04.43), (Kriegsmarine); born 29.06.95 in Voerde, died 21.06.75 in Bielefeld. WWI: U-boat service as Leutnant zur See and Watch Officer on *U-139*. Leader at Torpedoschule 03.1932–09.1934, Chief of 1. Torpedoboots Halbflotille 09.1934–09.1935, Chief of 1. Torpedobootsflotille 10.1935–08.1936, First Admiral Staff Officer attached to Leader of Torpedo Boats 08.1936–10.1937, attached to Staff of Marine Station Eastern Sea 10.1937–09.1938. WWII: Advisor in Marinepersonal Office of O.K.M. 10.1938–11.1939, Chief of Military Department in Torpedo Weapons Office of O.K.M. 11.1939–03.1943, Chief of Torpedo Weapons Office in O.K.M. 03.1943–05.1945. Awards: German Cross in Silver 16.04.45, War Merit Cross 1st and 2nd Class with Swords, Baltic Cross 1st and 2nd Class, 1914 Iron Cross 1st and 2nd Class, 1914 Submarine Badge, 1914 Naval Wound Badge in Black, Cross of Honor.

Gutknecht, Alfred: Generalmajor (01.07.42), (Heer); born 20.06.88 in Badingen, died 12.11.46 (suicide) while in custody in Berlin. WWI: Hauptmann with protection troops in German East Afrika. Attached to Staff of 1. Panzer Division 05.1935–10.1936. WWII: attached to Staff of I. Armee Korps 10.1936–03.1940, attached to Staff of XXII. Armee Korps 03.1940–05.1940, Higher Officer for Transport Services attached to A.O.K. 12, 05.1940–02.1941, Armee Transport Officer for A.O.K. 15, 04.1941–09.1942, Transport Officer on Staff of Wehrmacht O.B. West 09.1942–09.1944, Transport Officer attached to Heeresgruppe D 09.1944–04.1945. Awards: 1939 Clasp to the 1914 Iron Cross 2nd Class, War Merit Cross 1st and 2nd Class with Swords, 1914 Iron Cross 1st and 2nd Class, Cross of Honor.

Gutzeit, Hans: Generalmajor (01.08.43), (Heer); born 18.11.94 in Plantieres, died 05.06.75 in Quickborn. WWI: Leutnant in Infanterie Regiment 98. Instruction Group Leader at Kavallerie Schule in Hannover 10.1935–09.1936. WWII: Commander of Kraftfahr Abteilung 9, 10.1936–08.1939, Army Supply Leader to 1. Armee 08.1939–03.1940, Army Supply Leader to Panzergruppe von Kleist (XXII. Armee Korps mot.) 03.1940–07.1940, attached to O.K.H. 09.1940–07.1941, Commander of Supply District Central 07.1941–04.1942, Commander of Supply District for Heeresgruppe B 04.1942–10.1942, in hospital due to illness 12.1942–03.1943, Commander of Nachschubtruppen Schule at Otwock 03.1943–04.1944, held supply positions in Heeresgruppe Sud 04.1944–05.1945. Awards: German Cross in Silver 29.04.45, War Merit Cross 1st and 2nd Class with Swords, 1914 Iron Cross 1st and 2nd Class, Cross of Honor.

Gutzeit, Prof. Dr. Kurt: General-Arzt der Res. (01.08.44), (Heer); born 02.06.93 in Berlin, died 29.10.57 in Marburg. Medical doctor by profession. WWI: German medical service (rank and unit unknown). WWII: Consultant Internist with Heeres Medical Inspectorate in O.K.H. 08.1939–05.1945. Awards: Knight's Cross of the War Merit Cross with Swords 16.05.44, 1939 Iron Cross 2nd Class, War Merit Cross 1st and 2nd Class with Swords, Cross of Honor.

Gyldenfeldt, Georg von: Generalmajor (01.01.45), (Luftwaffe); born 01.05.97 in Putz, died 23.05.77 in Muenster. WWI: Leutnant in Garde Fuss Artillerie Regiment 1. Batterie Chef in Flak Abteilung Lankwitz 06.1935–09.1935, Batterie Chef in Flak Regiment 7, 10.1935–09.1937, Chief of Flak Stammbatterie Regensburg 10.1937–03.1938, Chief of Flak Stammbatterie Steyr 03.1938–05.1938. WWII: Commander of I. Abteilung, Flak Regiment 38, 05.1938–03.1940, Commander of Flak Regiment 6, 08.1940–09.1941, Commander of Flak Regiment 104, 09.1941–04.1942, Commander of Eisenbahn Flak Regiment 122, 04.1942–01.1943, Inspector of Special Weapons of Flak Artillerie (V1 and V2) on Staff of Flak Artillerie in R.L.M. 11.1943–05.1945. Awards: German Cross in Gold 27.04.42, 1939 Iron Cross 1st Class, 1939 Clasp to the 1914 Iron Cross 2nd Class, Flak War Badge, 1914 Iron Cross 2nd Class, Cross of Honor.

Gyldenfeldt, Heinz von: Generalleutnant (09.11.44), (Heer); born 15.08.99 in Bromberg, died 23.08.71 in Hamburg. WWI: Leutnant in Guards Feld Artillerie Regiment 1. Promotion to Generalmajor 01.07.43. Attached to Abteilung T1 of Reichswehr Ministry 05.1934–04.1935, attached to General Staff of Heeres 07.1935–10.1937, Chief of 2. Batterie, Artillerie Regiment 52, 10.1937–07.1938, Ia to 16. Division 07.1938–05.1939. WWII: attached to Abteilung 11 of Heeres General Staff 06.1939–08.1939, Ia to 212. Infanterie Division 08.1939–04.1940, Ia to 9. Armee 05.1940–3.1941, 1. General Staff Officer to O.B. of Heeres 06.1941–12.1941, Ia to Heeresgruppe A 05.1942–07.1942, Fuehrer Res. in O.K.H. 07.1942–07.1943, German Chief of General Staff to Italian 11. Armee 07.1943–10.1943, Chief of General Staff to 4. Armee 10.1943–05.1944, Chief of General Staff to Heeresgruppe G 05.1944–09.1944, Chief of General Staff to Heeresgruppe F 10.1944–03.1945, Chief of General Staff to Heeresgruppe Sud 03.1945–05.1945. Awards: German Cross in Gold 28.07.43, 1939 Clasps to the 1914 Iron Cross 1st and 2nd Class, 1914 Iron Cross 1st and 2nd Class, Cross of Honor.

APPENDIX I

German General Officers who held the rank of Generalmajor to Generalfeldmarschall or Konteradmiral to Grossadmiral during World War I

Note: Included is the highest rank achieved during WWI, their name, and the date they were promoted to that rank. PLM indicates Pour le Mérite Order, and EL indicates Oak Leaves to the Pour le Mérite Order.

Imperial Generals and Admirals

Generalleutnant Viktor Albrecht (18.04.16) / PLM: 09.04.18
Generalmajor Gustaf Reinhold von Arnim (27.01.17)
General der Infanterie Ernst von Bachmeister (24.12.14) / PLM: 08.10.17
Generalleutnant William Balck (22.03.17) / PLM: 09.03.18
Generalmajor Franz, Prinz von Bayern (10.09.14) / PLM: 16.05.18
Generalfeldmarschall Leopold, Prinz von Bayern (01.08.16) / 1914 Grand Cross: 04.03.18, EL: 25.07.17, PLM: 05.08.15
Generalfeldmarschall Ludwig III, Koenig von Bayern (26.06.15) / PLM: 08.12.16
Generalfeldmarschall Rupprecht, Kronprinz von Bayern (01.08.16) / EL: 20.12.16, PLM: 22.08.15
Vizeadmiral Paul Behncke (25.11.16) / PLM: 04.12.17
General der Infanterie Eduard von Below (22.03.17) / PLM: 18.08.17
Generalmajor Ernst von Below (27.01.17) / EL: 13.10.18, PLM: 24.11.17
General der Infanterie Fritz von Below (13.09.12) / EL: 11.08.16, PLM: 03.1915
Generalleutnant Hans von Below (18.04.18) / PLM: 24.11.17
General der Infanterie Otto von Below (30.08.14) / EL: 27.04.17, PLM: 16.02.15
Generalmajor Richard von Berendt (27.01.17) / EL: 24.11.17, PLM: 14.01.17
Generalmajor Karl Berger (24.07.15) / PLM: 17.04.18
Generalleutnant Walter von Bergmann (15.07.18) / PLM: 08.05.18
General der Kavallerie Friedrich von Bernhardi (27.01.08) / EL: 15.05.18, PLM: 20.08.16

Generalleutnant Albert von Berrer (18.02.13) / PLM: 27.08.17
Generaloberst Hans Hartwig von Beseler (27.01.18) / EL: 20.08.15, PLM: 10.10.14
Generalleutnant Alfred von Boeckmann (06.06.16) / EL: 01.06.17, PLM: 08.10.16
Generaloberst Max von Boehn (22.03.18) / EL: 20.05.17, PLM: 24.08.16
General der Infanterie Curt von dem Borne (18.04.18) / EL: 03.11.18, PLM: 09.04.18
Generalleutnant Karl von Borries (03.03.15) / PLM: 13.06.18
Generalmajor Rudolf von Borries (18.08.16) / PLM: 04.08.17
Generaloberst Felix Graf von Bothmer (09.04.18) / EL: 25.07.17, PLM: 07.07.15
Generalmajor Otto Freiherr von Brandenstein (18.10.18) / PLM: 15.05.18
Generalmajor Johann Ritter und Edler von Braun (20.09.18)
Generalleutnant Anatol Graf von Bredow (23.07.15) / PLM: 23.07.15
Generalmajor Ludwig Bressler (22.03.17) / PLM: 09.10.18
Generalleutnant Carl Briese (22.03.18) / PLM: 30.08.18
Generalmajor Bernhard Bronsart von Schellendorf (20.09.18) / PLM: 16.09.16
Geenralfeldmarschall Karl Wilhelm Paul von Bulow (27.01.15) / PLM: 04.04.15
Generalleutnant Hermann Ritter von Burkhardt (19.10.16) / PLM: 12.05.17
Generalmajor Johannes von Busse (22.03.15) / PLM: 16.04.18
Admiral Eduard von Capelle (12.04.13) / PLM: 09.01.18
General der Infanterie Adolf von Carlowitz (05.04.17) / EL: 25.05.18, PLM: 29.07.17
Generalleutnant Chales de Beaulieu (25.06.13) / PLM: 05.09.17
Generalleutnant Siegfried von la Chevallerie (18.08.18) / EL: 05.10.18, PLM: 20.01.18
General der Infanterie Eberhard von Clear (22.03.14) / PLM: 29.06.15
Generalleutnant Eugen Ritter von Claus (14.12.17)
General der Infanterie Richard von Conta (18.08.18) / EL: 26.03.18, PLM: 15.10.16
Generalmajor Rudolf Daenner (22.01.15) / PLM: 26.10.18
Generalleutnant Viktor Dallmer (03.08.16) / EL: 08.06.18, PLM: 26.04.17
Generalmajor Johannes von Dassel (18.06.17) / PLM: 25.10.18
General der Infanterie Berthold von Deimling (22.03.14) / PLM: 28.08.16
Generalleutnant Hermann von Desler und Scharfenstein (18.05.18) / PLM: 08.11.17
Generalleutnant Carl Dieffenbach (18.04.15) / PLM: 26.04.17
Generalmajor Otto Freiherr von Diepenbroick-Grueter (18.08.16) / PLM: 13.06.18
Generalmajor Wilhelm von Dommes (22.03.18) / PLM: 08.06.18
General der Infanterie Johannes von Eben (30.08.14) / EL: 22.09.17, PLM: 07.10.16
General der Infanterie Magnus von Eberhardt (18.08.14) / EL: 25.04.18, PLM: 20.05.17
General der Infanterie Oskar von Ehrenthal (28.08.16) / PLM: 15.06.17
Generalmajor Johannes Ehrhardt (18.12.17)

Generalfeldmarschall Hermann von Eichhorn (18.12.17) / EL: 28.09.15, PLM: 18.08.15
Generaloberst Karl von Einem gen. von Rothmaler (27.01.15) / EL: 17.10.16, PLM: 16.03.15
Generalmajor Ernst von Eisenhart-Rothe (18.08.16)
General der Infanterie Karl d' Elsa (23.09.08) / PLM: 01.09.16
Generalleutnant Hugo Elstermann von Elster (18.06.15) / PLM: 22.09.17
General der Infanterie Otto von Emmich (25.09.09) / EL: 14.05.15, PLM: 07.08.14
Generalleutnant Siegfried Freiherr von Ende (05.11.16) / PLM: 31.10.17
Generalleutnant Nikolaus Ritter von Endres (19.05.15) / EL: 04.08.18, PLM: 17.04.18
Generalleutnant George von Engelbrechten (22.03.17) / PLM: 08.07.18
Generalmajor Hans von der Esch (24.07.15) / PLM: 13.10.18
Generalleutnant Ludwig von Estorff (06.06.16) / PLM: 06.09.17
Generalleutnant Guenther von Etzel (27.01.18) / EL: 25.10.18, PLM: 04.08.18
Generalmajor Karl von Fabeck (20.09.18)
General der Infanterie Max von Fabeck (13.01.10) / PLM: 23.08.15
Generaloberst Ludwig Freiherr von Falkenhausen (24.12.14) / EL: 15.04.16, PLM: 23.08.15
General der Infanterie Erich von Falkenhayn (20.01.15) / EL: 03.06.15, PLM: 16.02.15
General der Kavallerie Eugen von Falkenhayn (24.09.14) / EL: 13.11.15, PLM: 28.08.15
General der Infanterie Karl Ritter von Fassbender (11.10.14) / PLM: 13.09.16
Generalmajor Bernhard Graf Fink von Finckenstein (18.08.16) / PLM: 09.04.18
Generalleutnant Paul Fleck (19.08.14) / PLM: 16.03.15
Generalleutnant Sigismund von Foerster (01.03.13) / PLM: 28.05.17
General der Infanterie Hermann von Francois (19.08.14) / EL: 27.07.17, PLM: 14.05.15
Generalleutnant Adolf Franke (20.04.09) / PLM: 18.10.18
Generalleutnant Erich Freyer (22.03.17) / PLM: 17.04.18
Generalleutnant Friedrich von Friedeburg (25.02.18) / PLM: 20.09.18
Generalleutnant Albert von Fritsch (17.12.16) / PLM: 03.09.18
Generalmajor Georg Frotscher (22.07.18) / PLM: 05.05.18
Generalleutnant Georg Fuchs (03.02.14) / PLM: 18.08.17
Generalmajor Arthur von Gabain (03.05.14) / EL: 17.04.18, PLM: 08.11.17
General der Infanterie Dr. Hans Emil Alexander Gaede (24.12.14) / PLM: 25.08.70
General der Artillerie Max von Gallwitz (04.04.11) / EL: 28.09.15, PLM: 24.07.15
General der Kavallerie Otto von Garnier (03.12.17) / PLM: 12.10.16
Generalleutnant Georg Freiherr von Gayl (24.04.04) / PLM: 08.05.18

General der Kavallerie Ludwig Freiherr von Gebsattel (19.03.14) / PLM: 04.10.16
General der Infanterie Friedrich von Gerok (12.09.14) / PLM: 07.07.15
Generalmajor Rudiger Graf von der Goltz (18.08.16) / PLM: 15.05.18
Generalleutnant Friedrich von Gontard (18.04.16) / EL: 04.08.18, PLM: 09.04.18
General der Infanterie Konrad von Gossler (11.09.07) / PLM: 10.08.16
Generalmajor Wilhelm von Groddeck (18.04.15) / PLM: 09.04.18
General der Artillerie Hans von Gronau (02.09.14) / EL: 06.08.18, PLM: 04.10.16
Generalleutnant Wilhelm Groener (11.11.16) / PLM: 11.09.15
General der Infanterie Erich von Gruendell (02.09.14) / PLM: 28.08.16
Generalleutnant Paul von Gruenert (27.01.18) / PLM: 03.05.18
Generalleutnant Hans von Guretzky-Cornitz (21.04.11) / PLM: 09.03.16
Generalmajor Otto Haas (16.09.17)
Generalleutnant Rudolf Hammer (17.06.18) / PLM: 24.11.17
Generalmajor Hans Freiherr von Hammerstein-Gesmold (18.10.17) / PLM: 06.11.18
Generalmajor Walter von Haxthausen (18.07.17) / PLM: 13.06.18
Generaloberst Josias von Heeringen (27.01.14) / EL: 25.08.16, PLM: 25.08.15
Generalmajor Georg von Heimburg (22.03.18)
Generalmajor Siegfried von Held (18.04.17) / PLM: 07.11.18
Generalmajor Emil Hell (20.05.17) / EL: 11.01.17, PLM: 21.09.16
Generalleutnant Friedrich-Wilhelm von Hertzberg (22.04.12) / PLM: 04.11.18
Generalmajor Emil Hesse (19.08.14)
Generalmajor Hans Hesse (18.10.18) / PLM: 11.12.16
Generalfeldmarschall Paul von Hindenburg (27.11.14) / Breast Star to the Grand Cross of the 1914 Iron Cross: 24.03.18, 1914 Grand Cross: 19.12.16, EL: 23.02.15, PLM: 08.09.14
Admiral Franz Ritter von Hipper (11.08.18) / PLM: 05.06.16
Generalmajor Karl Hoefer (25.02.18) / EL: 14.04.18, PLM: 23.07.16
Generalleutnant Ernst von Hoeppner (18.04.15) / PLM: 08.04.17
Generalleutnant Eberhard von Hofacker (01.11.16) / EL: 24.11.17, PLM: 26.04.17
Generalmajor Max Hoffmann (29.10.17) / EL: 25.07.17, PLM: 07.10.16
Generalleutnant Heinrich von Hofmann (25.02.18) / EL: 18.09.18, PLM: 12.11.17
General der Infanterie Max Hofmann (27.01.18) / EL: 05.07.18, PLM: 28.08.15
Grossadmiral Henning von Holtzendorff (31.05.18) / EL: 01.02.18, PLM: 22.03.17
Generalmajor Rudolf von Horn (18.08.17) / PLM: 21.09.18
General der Infanterie Otto Freiherr von Huegel (30.09.14) / PLM: 28.08.16
Generalleutnant Walter von Huelsen (22.03.18) / PLM: 09.04.18
General der Infanterie Oskar von Hutier (27.01.17) / EL: 23.03.18, PLM: 06.09.17
Generalleutnant Emil Ilse (18.04.16) / PLM: 28.08.16
General der Infanterie Alban von Jacobi (13.09.12) / PLM: 12.04.17
Generalmajor Wilhelm Jahn (18.10.18)

Generalmajor Georg Johow (27.01.18) / PLM: 21.09.16
Generalmajor Fritz-Hans Juerst (22.03.17)
Generalmajor Ernst Kabisch (18.06.17) / PLM: 09.10.18
General der Infanterie Hugo von Kathen (22.03.14) / EL: 27.08.17, PLM: 28.08.16
Generalmajor Wilhelm Kaupert (27.01.17) / PLM: 29.10.18
Obergeneral-Arzt (Generalleutnant) Prof. Dr. Berthold von Kern (1915)
Generalleutnant Christoph Ritter von Kiefhaber (19.11.16) / PLM: 24.11.17
Generalmajor Georg Kipping (18.08.17)
Generaloberst Guenther Graf von Kirchbach (27.01.18) / PLM: 27.08.17
Generaloberst Hans von Kirchbach (23.01.18) / PLM: 11.08.16
Generalleutnant Alfred von Kleist (06.11.17) / PLM: 08.10.18
Generaloberst Alexander von Kluck (27.01.14) / PLM: 28.03.15
Generalleutnant Paul Ritter von Kneussl (19.05.15) / EL: 11.0.17, PLM: 03.06.15
Generalmajor Johannes Koch (15.07.18)
General der Kavallerie Goetz Freiherr von Koenig (14.11.15) / PLM: 23.07.15
General der Infanterie Robert Kosch (18.08.16) / EL: 27.11.5, PLM: 20.02.15
General der Artillerie Konrad Krafft von Dellmensingen (08.08.18) / EL: 11.12.16, PLM: 07.09.16
Generalmajor Maximilian Friedrich Krahmer (19.08.14)
General der Infanterie Alfred Krauss (01.08.17) / PLM: 12.11.17
Generalmajor Eduard Kreuter (15.07.18) / PLM: 14.10.18
General der Kavallerie Hans Krug von Nidda (10.09.14) / PLM: 07.10.18
Generalleutnant Viktor Kuehne (27.01.15) / PLM: 11.12.16
Generalleutnant Dr. Hermann von Kuhl (18.04.15) / EL: 20.12.16, PLM: 28.08.16
Generalmajor Friedrich Kundt (07.11.17) / PLM: 12.10.18
General der Kavallerie Maximilian von Laffert (22.05.13) / PLM: 01.09.16
Generalleutnant Felix Langer (27.01.18) / EL: 07.11.18, PLM: 08.10.17
Vizeadmiral Wilhelm von Lans (27.01.13) / PLM: 25.06.00
General der Infanterie Alfred von Larisch (25.06.18) / PLM: 25.08.18
Generalmajor Hans Lepper (24.07.15)
Generalleutnant Arnold Lequis (15.07.18) / EL: 05.12.17, PLM: 11.10.17
Generalmajor Paul von Lettow-Vorbeck (29.10.17) / EL: 10.10.17, PLM: 04.11.16
Generalleutnant Karl von Lewinski (10.06.18) / PLM: 02.05.17
General der Infanterie Eduard von Liebert (25.02.17) / PLM: 06.06.17
General der Kavallerie Otto Liman von Sanders (06.03.15) / EL: 10.01.16, PLM: 23.08.15
Generalleutnant Arthur von Lindequist (06.11.17) / EL: 07.11.18, PLM: 23.12.17
Generaloberst Alexander von Linsingen (07.04.18) / EL: 03.07.15, PLM: 14.05.15
Generalmajor Georg von der Lippe (18.10.18)
General der Infanterie Karl Litzmann (24.12.14) / EL: 18.08.15, PLM: 29.11.14
General der Infanterie Ewald von Lochow (16.06.13) / EL: 13.11.15, PLM: 14.01.15

Generalleutnant Robert Loeb (20.03.15) / PLM: 17.06.18
Generalmajor Friedrich Karl von Lossberg (03.08.17) / EL: 24.04.17, PLM: 21.09.16
Generalmajor Otto von Lossow (14.12.17)
General der Infanterie Erich Ludendorff (28.08.16) / 1914 Grand Cross: 24.03.18, EL: 23.02.15, PLM: 08.08.14
Generalleutnant Arthur Freiherr von Luettwitz (27.01.18) / PLM: 08.11.17
General der Infanterie Walther Freiherr von Luettwitz (18.08.18) / EL: 26.03.18, PLM: 24.08.16
Generaloberst Moritz Freiherr von Lyncker (10.04.18) / PLM: 02.11.17
Generalfeldmarschall August von Mackensen (22.06.15) / 1914 Grand Cross: 09.01.17, EL: 14.06.15, PLM: 27.11.14
Generalmajor Georg Maercker (18.08.17) / EL: 03.05.18, PLM: 01.10.17
Generalmajor Gottfried Marquard (18.08.17) / PLM: 27.09.16
General der Kavallerie Wolfgang von Marschall Freiherr von Altengotten (18.04.15) / EL: 16.05.18, PLM: 21.09.16
General der Kavallerie Georg von der Marwitz (19.08.14) / EL: 14.05.15, PLM: 07.03.15
Generalmajor Willi Matthias (18.12.17) / PLM: 22.11.17
Generalmajor Dr. Heinrich von Maur (27.01.16) / PLM: 20.05.17
Generalleutnant Wilhelm Meckel (20.09.18) / PLM: 26.08.17
Generalleutnant Johann Meister (17.06.18) / PLM: 02.11.05
Generalmajor Arnold Ritter von Moehl (08.04.15) / PLM: 09.10.18
Generaloberst Helmuth von Moltke (27.01.14) / PLM: 07.08.15
Generalleutnant Kurt von Morgen (19.08.14) / EL: 11.12.16, PLM: 01.12.14
Generalleutnant Otto von Moser (18.08.15) / PLM: 26.04.17
General der Infanterie Bruno von Mudra (13.09.11) / EL: 17.10.16, PLM: 13.01.15
Generalmajor Georg Muehry (22.03.15) / PLM: 25.10.18
Admiral Georg-Alexander von Mueller (29.08.10) / PLM: 24.03.18
Generalleutnant Albert von Mutius (15.07.18) / PLM: 04.09.18
Generalmajor Carl Nehbel (18.05.18) / PLM: 30.09.18
Generalleutnant Horst Ritter und Edler von Oetinger (27.01.15) / PLM: 26.03.18
Generalmajor Martin Freiherr von Oldershausen (30.11.17) / PLM: 20.05.17
General der Infanterie Adolf von Oven (13.09.12) / PLM: 22.09.18
Generalleutnant Ernst von Oven (27.01.15) / PLM: 25.10.18
General der Infanterie Guenther von Pannwitz (27.01.15) / PLM: 13.09.16
Generalleutnant Axel von Petersdorff (18.05.18) / PLM: 22.04.18
General der Infanterie Horst Edler von der Planitz (05.04.17) / PLM: 20.05.17
Generaloberst Hans von Plessen (18.09.08) / PLM: 24.03.18
General der Infanterie Karl Frieherr von Plettenberg (12.04.10) / PLM: 14.05.15
General der Infanterie Otto von Plueskow (30.08.14) / PLM: 11.05.17

Generalmajor Georg Pohlmann (22.03.18) / PLM: 04.10.18
Generalmajor Eitel Friedrich, Prinz von Preussen (18.05.18) / EL: 14.05.15, PLM: 22.03.15
Generaloberst Heinrich, Prinz von Preussen (04.09.09) / EL: 24.01.18, PLM: 01.08.16
Generalmajor Kurt Freiherr Prinz von Buchau (18.08.17) / PLM: 11.05.18
General der Infanterie Kurt von Pritzelwitz (13.09.11) / PLM: 15.01.16
Generalleutnant Wilhelm von Puttkamer (19.08.16) / PLM: 26.10.18
General der Infanterie Ferdinand von Quast (19.08.14) / EL: 10.04.18, PLM: 11.08.16
Generalleutnant Otto Ritter von Rauchenberger (17.01.17) / EL: 19.10.18, PLM: 06.09.17
Generalmajor Theodor Renner (22.03.18) / PLM: 01.09.18
Generalmajor Wilhelm Ribbentrop (18.10.17) / PLM: 18.09.18
General der Kavallerie Manfred Freiherr von Richthofen (16.09.17) / PLM: 18.01.18
General der Infanterie Julius Riemann (27.01.15) / PLM: 16.05.15
Generalmajor Dietrich von Roeder (18.06.17) / PLM: 17.04.18
Generalleutnant Rudolf Rusche (27.01.18) / PLM: 03.11.18
Generalfeldmarschall Friedrich August III, Koenig von Sachsen (11.09.12) / PLM: 29.12.16
General der Infanterie Ernst II, Herzog von Sachsen-Altenburg Herzog zu Sachsen (19.08.14) / PLM: 30.05.15
Generalleutnant Traugott von Sauberzweig (15.07.18) / EL: 23.03.18, PLM: 06.09.17
Admiral Reinhard Scheer (05.06.16) / EL: 01.02.18, PLM: 05.06.16
General der Infanterie Reinhold Freiherr von Scheffer-Boyadel (05.03.08) / PLM: 02.12.14
General der Infanterie Dedo von Schenck (13.09.12) / PLM: 04.10.16
Generalleutnant Heinrich Scheuch (09.10.18) / PLM: 08.04.18
Generalleutnant Eberhard Graf von Schmettow (18.08.16) / EL: 04.08.18, PLM: 11.12.16
Generalleutnant Egon Graf von Schmettow (20.05.14) / PLM: 04.11.17
Admiral Erhard Schmidt (27.01.18) / PLM: 31.10.17
General der Infanterie Konstantin Schmidt von Knobelsdorf (18.10.18) / EL: 21.08.16, PLM: 17.10.15
Generalleutnant Roderich von Schoeler (06.06.16) / PLM: 30.06.18
General der Artillerie Friedrich von Scholtz (13.09.12) / EL: 01.06.17, PLM: 03.09.15
Admiral Ludwig von Schroeder (27.01.11) / EL: 23.12.17, PLM: 20.10.15
Generaloberst Richard von Schubert (27.01.17) / PLM: 28.08.16

Generalleutnant Georg von Schuessler (18.08.17) / PLM: 22.04.18
Generalmajor Hans von Seeckt (26.06.15) / EL: 27.11.15, PLM: 14.05.15
Generalleutnant Ludwig Sieger (03.02.14) / EL: 03.11.18, PLM: 27.04.18
General der Infanterie Friedrich Sixt von Arnim (07.04.13) / EL: 03.08.17, PLM: 10.08.16
General der Infanterie Franz Freiherr von Soden (17.12.16) / PLM: 27.07.17
Admiral Wilhelm Souchen (11.08.18) / PLM: 29.10.16
General der Infanterie Hermann von Staabs (03.12.17) / EL: 15.05.18, PLM: 11.12.16
General der Infanterie Hermann von Stein (01.11.16) / EL: 08.04.18, PLM: 01.09.16
General der Artillerie Hermann Freiherr von Stein zu Nord- und Ostheim (28.05.18) / EL: 24.11.17, PLM: 20.08.17
General der Kavallerie Otto von Stetten (17.01.17) / PLM: 22.09.16
General der Infanterie Cuno von Steuben (19.08.14) / PLM: 13.10.15
Generalleutnant Paul von Stolzmann (15.07.18) / PLM: 07.07.15
General der Infanterie Hermann von Strantz (07.04.11) / PLM: 22.08.15
Generalleutnant Karl von Stumpff (06.11.17) / PLM: 22.04.18
Generalmajor Gerhard Tappen (26.06.15) / EL: 27.01.16, PLM: 11.09.15
Generalmajor Theodor Teetzmann (18.04.15) / PLM: 11.10.17
Generalmajor Paul Tiede (18.04.16) / EL: 25.10.18, PLM: 17.04.18
Grossadmiral Alfred von Tirpitz (27.01.11) / PLM: 10.08.15
Konteradmiral Adolf von Trotha (17.12.16) / PLM: 10.06.16
Generalmajor Ludwig Ritter von Tutschek (08.04.15) / PLM: 08.12.17
Generalmajor Ernst von Uechtritz und Steinkirch (18.06.17) / PLM: 21.10.18
Admiral Guido von Usedom (27.01.16) / EL: 23.08.15, PLM: 05.04.02
Generalleutnant Detlev Vett (10.06.18) / PLM: 04.10.18
Generalleutnant Emil Waldorf (24.12.14) / PLM: 01.11.18
Generalleutnant Oskar Freiherr von Watter (06.11.17) / EL: 03.11.18, PLM: 23.12.17
General der Infanterie Theodor Freiherr von Watter (18.08.16) / PLM: 01.09.16
Generalleutnant Hasso von Wedel (30.06.18) / EL: 24.11.17, PLM: 27.08.17
Generalleutnant Richard Wellmann (27.01.17) / EL: 26.10.18, PLM: 23.12.17
Generalleutnant Karl Ritter von Wenninger (10.09.14) / PLM: 01.05.17
General der Infanterie Georg Wichura (22.03.17) / EL: 08.06.18, PLM: 26.04.17
Generalleutnant Adolf Wild von Hohenborn (20.01.15) / EL: 11.10.18, PLM: 02.08.15
Generalfeldmarschall Wilhelm II, Deutscher Kaiser und Koenig von Preussen (03.05.00) / 1914 Grand Cross: 11.12.16, EL: 12.05.15, PLM: 15.02.15
General der Infanterie Wilhelm, Kronprinz von Preussen (27.01.17) / EL: 08.09.16, PLM: 22.08.15

Generalfeldmarschall Wilhelm II, Koenig von Wurttemberg (23.07.16) / PLM: 24.01.17

General der Infanterie Arnold von Winckler (22.03.17) / EL: 15.06.17, PLM: 27.11.15

Generalfeldmarschall Remus von Woyrsch (01.08.16) / EL: 23.07.15, PLM: 25.10.14

Generalmajor Ernst von Wrisberg (06.11.17) / PLM: 08.04.18

Generalfeldmarschall Albrecht Herzog von Wurttemberg (01.08.16) / EL: 25.02.18, PLM: 22.08.15

General der Infanterie Oskar Ritter und Edler von Xylander (27.03.13) / PLM: 20.08.16

Generalleutnant Alfred Ziethen (06.11.17) / PLM: 14.06.15

General der Infanterie Johann von Zwehl (02.09.14) / EL: 17.10.16, PLM: 08.09.14

APPENDIX II

Glossary of Terms

1-IV: Luftwaffe abbreviation for Commander or Flughafenbereichs Commandant of Section 1, attached to Luftgau Kommando 1.

Abschnitte: SS Sub District within an SS-Oberabschnitte which incorporated a few SS-Fuess Standarten and Support Units. It was usually led by an SS-Oberfuehrer or SS-Brigadefuehrer.

Abteilung: Department, or battalion in military formation or office branch in administrative formation.

Abwehr: Intelligence branch of the German Wehrmacht.

Afrika Korps: The German Africa Corps.

Amt: Office.

Armee: Army formation comprising several army corps.

Armee Gruppe: Army group comprising several army-sized formations.

Armee Oberkommando (A.O.K.): Army High Command.

Artillerie: Artillery.

Artillerie Commander 130: Artillery commander at corps or army level. The number represents the independent artillery formation unit number or the formation attached to the corps and/or army itself.

Arzt: Medical doctor.

Aufklarungs Abteilung: Reconnaissance battalion.

Ausbildungs: Training.

Bandenkampfverbaende: Anti-partisan units.

Bataillon: Battalion-sized formation.

Befehlshaber: Senior military commander.

Befehlshaber der Waffen-SS (BdW-SS): Senior Waffen-SS commander of an occupied territory.

Beobachter: Observer.

Bild: Photo.

Blindflugschule: Luftwaffe Instrument Flight School for Pilots and Wireless Operators.

Bombengeschwader: Bomber wing formation.

Brigade: Brigade-sized formation consisting of at least two regiments.
Chef: Chief, utilized in military and office type commands.
Chef des General Stab: Term given to the senior staff officer of a corps- or army-sized formation as well as the senior general officer of the Wehrmacht High Command (O.K.W.) of the Heer, Luftwaffe, Kriegsmarine, and Waffen-SS.
Deutschen Luftsportverbande (DLV): German Air Sports Association, the precursor to the Luftwaffe and was used to disguise its real purpose following the Treaty of Versailles.
Division: Division-sized formation consisting of several regimental-sized formations and support units.
Division 190: Infantry divisions in this format (as opposed to those which state their unit number first) were usually newly formed units that were still being compiled and were divisions in name only.
East Truppen: Foreign volunteer troops from occupied or allied countries in Eastern Europe.
Eisenbahn Pionier: Railroad Engineer Unit.
E-Officer Korps: Officers who were attached to the Replacement Officer Corps, not of reserve status.
Ersatz: Replacement.
Fahnrich: Officer candidate (Imperial Army).
Fallschirmjaeger (F.S.J.): Parachute troops.
Fallschirmtruppe: Parachute troops.
Feldherrnhalle: Unit title of the German Army Panzer Brigade and later Division.
Feldkommandantur: A sub area of a field command unit used for security in occupied territories.
Feldpost: Field postal service.
Feld Section: Rear area of an armee-sized formation.
Feldzeug Kommando: Ordnance troop command.
Feldzeugtruppen: Ordnance troops.
Festung: Fortress.
Flak: Anti-aircraft artillery.
Flak Abteilung: Anti-aircraft battalion-sized formation.
Flak Brigade: Anti-aircraft brigade-sized formation.
Flak Korps: Anti-aircraft corps-sized formation.
Flak Regiment: Anti-aircraft regiment-sized formation.
Fliegerfuehrer: Flying leader.
Fliegerhorst Kommandant: Air base commander.
Flieger Korps: Luftwaffe corps-sized formation.
Flottille: Small fleet of ships or U-boats.
Flughafenbereichs Kommandant: Flight airport range commander.
Flugzeugfuehrer: Flight section leader.
Feldzeugmeisterei: Heeres Ordnance Command.

Feldzeugmeister: Heeres Ordnance Chief, usually with the rank of a Generalleutnant.
Fernaufklarungsgruppe: Luftwaffe Air Reconnaissance Group.
Feuerwerker Schule: Heeres Ordnance School for NCOs.
Fliegertruppen: Flying Troops of the German Air Service, a general term used for all flight personnel.
Freiwilligen: Volunteer.
Fuehrer: Leader. Also a term used for a temporary Commander.
Fuehrer Reserve O.K.H., O.K.L. or O.K.M.: Senior Heer, Luftwaffe or Marine officers who had no command and were placed on reserve status until a command became available (or while they recovered from wounds or illness).
Fusilier: Light infantry.
Fuss Artillerie: Foot artillery.
GAS: German Air Service, the Imperial Air Force during WWI.
Gebirgstruppe: Mountain troops.
General Government: Occupied Poland.
General Kommissar: General Commissioner.
Generalluftzeugmeister: Title given to Luftwaffe General Erhard Mich, as the general responsible for the development, testing and procurement of all materials needed for the Luftwaffe. His staff was part of the R.L.M.
Geschwader: Flight formation.
Grenadier: Traditional military name for elite infantry.
Grenztruppen Kommando: Border Troops Command.
Gruppe: Group.
Gruppe Leiter: Group Leader.
Harko: Senior artillery commander.
Heer: German Army.
Heeres-Feldzeugmeisterei: Office of the Army Field Equipment Master.
Heeres Gruppe: Army group consisting of several army-sized formations.
Heeres Gruppen Kommando: Army group command.
Hoehere Kommando: Higher Command.
Hoehere SS -und Polizeifuehrer (H.S.S.P.F.): Senior SS and police commander.
Ia: First staff officer or chief of operations.
Ib: Supply officer.
Ic: Intelligence officer.
IIa: Adjutant.
Infanterie: Infantry.
Ingenieur: Engineer.
Inspekteur or Inspektor: Inspector for the inspection of troops or fortifications.
Intendant: Administrative officer.
Jaeger: Light infantry.
Jagd Division: Luftwaffe fighter division.

Jagdfuehrer: (Fighter leader) was the title given to a Luftwaffe commander of fighter aircraft who was responsible for the defense of a large region or occupied country.
Jagdgeschwader (J.G.): Fighter wing formation.
Jagdverbaende (J.V.): Jet Fighter wing formation.
Junker: Officer candidate.
Junkerschule: Officer Candidate School.
Kampfflieger Schule: Bomber Air Crew School.
Kampfgeschwader (K.G.): Bomber wing formation.
Kampfgruppe (K.G.): Battle group formation.
Kavallerie: Cavalry.
Kommandant (Kdt.): Commander of a U-boat or sea vessel.
Kommandeur: Commander.
Kommando: Commando or command.
Kompanie: Company-sized formation.
Korps: Corps-sized formation consisting of two or more divisions.
Kradschuetzen Abteilung: Motorcycle battalion.
Kraftfahr: Motor Transport.
Kraftfahrparktruppen: Motor park troops.
Kraftfahr Schule: Motor Transport School.
Kriegsmarine: German Navy.
Kriegsschule: War School.
Landwehr: Militias.
Lazarette: Military hospital.
Lehr: Training unit.
Leichte: Light.
Leitender: Leading.
Leiter: Leader.
Luftflotte: Air Fleet.
Luftgau: Luftwaffe regional districts.
Luftkreis: Early term for Luftwaffe districts.
Luftwaffe: German Air Force.
Luftwaffe Gruppen Kommando: Luftwaffe group command.
Luftzeuggruppe: Air equipment group.
Marine Artillerie Abteilung: Naval artillery battalion.
Marine Artillerie Schule: Naval Artillery School.
Marine Division: Naval land division.
Marine Flak Abteilung: Naval anti-aircraft battalion.
Marine Gruppen Kommando: Naval group command.
Marine-oberbaudirektor: Naval senior construction director.
Marine Stamm Regiment: Naval Cadre Regiment.
Ministerialdirektor: Ministry director.

Ministerialdirigent: Ministry regent.
Ministerialrat: Ministry official.
Nachrichtenfuehrer: Signals leader.
Nachrichtenschule: Signals school.
Nachrichtentruppe: Signals troops.
Nachschub: Supplies.
Nachtaufklarungsgeschwader (N.A.G.): Night reconnaissance wing.
Nachtjagdgeschwader (N.J.G.): Night fighter wing.
Nationalsozialistische Deutsche Arbeiter Partei (N.S.D.A.P.): National Socialist German Workers' Party.
Nebelwerfer: Smoke mortar that came in the form of a six-barrel rapid fire rocket launcher.
Nord: North and divisional title of the 6th SS-Gebirgs Division.
Oberbefehlshaber (O.B.): Supreme Military Commander of an army, army group or air fleet.
Oberkommando der Luftwaffe (O.K.L.): High Command of the German Air Force.
Oberkommando der Marine (O.K.M.): High Command of the German Navy, the successor to the Marineleitung.
Oberkommando der Wehrmacht (O.K.W.): Supreme High Command of the Armed Forces.
Oberkommando des Heeres (O.K.H.): High Command of the German Army.
Observer Abteilung: Artillery observation battalion.
Office Group: Comprising of several smaller offices within an administration.
Oflag: Prisoner-of-war camp for officers.
Ordnungstruppen: Security troops.
Ost: East.
Ostland: Occupied Eastern territories.
P: National Socialist German Workers' Party membership number.
Panzer: Tank.
Panzer Abteilung: Tank-battalion-sized formation.
Panzer Abwehr Abteilung: Anti-Tank Battalion .
Panzer Aufklarungs Abteilung: Tank Reconnaissance Battalion.
Panzer Division: Tank-division-sized formation with at least one full-strength panzer regiment.
Panzer Grenadier: Tank support troops.
Panzer Korps: Tank-corps-sized formation.
Panzer Regiment: Tank-regiment-sized formation.
Panzertruppen: Tank troops.
Pionier: Engineer.
Pionieretruppen: Engineer troops.
Quartermaster: Senior supply leader.

Rasse-und Siedlungshauptamt (R.u.S.H.A): The SS Race and Resettlement Main Office was responsible for the racial purity of the SS. It played a major role in expansion into Eastern Europe with Germans from Germany itself as well as racial Germans from other parts of Europe.
Rear Area: The rear of an armee formation.
Reconnaissance Abteilung: Reconnaissance battalion.
Regiment: Regimental-sized formation.
Reichsluftfahrtministerium (R.L.M.): Reich Ministry of Aviation.
Reichsmarineamt: Naval Main Office of the Reichswehr.
Reichswehr: Germany's peacetime army, 1919–1935.
Reich War Ministry (R.K.M.): Later renamed O.K.H.
Repl.: Replacement.
Replacement Regiment or Battalion: Units that maintain reserves and/or new recruits to help fill the gaps of their parent units.
Richter: Judge.
Rittmeister: Cavalry captain.
Sanitats: Medical unit or service.
Sanitatstruppen: Medical troops.
Schiff: Ship.
Schiff Stamm Regiment: Naval Ship Cadre Regiment.
Schlachtgeschwader (S.G.): Ground assault wing "Stuka" formation.
Schlacht "Stuka" geschwader (S.G.): Assault fighter wing.
Schnelle Truppen: Fast or rapid troops.
Schuetzen: Rifle formation.
Schule/Schulen: School/schools.
Schutzstaffel (S.S.): Guard echelon, the bodyguard protecting Adolf Hitler which developed and grew into its own entity under Reichsfuehrer-SS Heinrich Himmler.
Seeflieger Abteilung: Flying battalion.
Schwadron: Company-size formation in a cavalry regiment regiment.
Schwere: Heavy.
Sonderstab: Special staff.
Sperrversuchkommando: Naval experimental mine command.
S.S.: Membership number in the SS.
SS-Dienstalterliste (SS-DAL): SS Officer List issued annually 1934–1944 except for 1940–1941.
SS-Fuehrungshauptamt: Operational command of the Waffen-SS.
SS-Fuess Standarte: SS-Foot Regiments of the Allgemeine-SS.
SS-Hauptamt: SS Main Office.
SS-und Polizeifuehrer (S.S.P.F.): SS and police commander.
Stab: Staff.
Stabsfuehrer: Staff leader.

Staffel: Section of a fighter, Stuka, or bomber wing formation.
Staffelkpt.: Squadron leader or squadron captain.
Standort Kommandant: Garrison commander.
Sturmgeschutz: Assault gun.
Technische Amt: Technical Office.
Transportflieger: Transport Flyers.
Transport Geschwader: Transport Wing of the Luftwaffe.
Truppenubungplatz: Troop exercise grounds.
U-Boat: Unterseeboote or submarine.
Unteroffizierschule: Training school for future non-commissioned officers.
Verwaltungstruppen: Administrative troops.
Veterinartruppen: Veterinary troops.
Volks Grenadier Division: German Army divisions (not to be confused with the *Volkssturm*) that were formed in the fall of 1944 comprising the last levy of German manpower, such as non-essential military personnel and other non-infantry formations. Despite being named a division they fell short of the full complement of troops needed for such a formation.
Volkssturm: Home Defense Guard set up by Goebbels towards the end of the war and placed under the control of the military or local N.S.D.A.P. leaders. It mainly comprised civilians made up of war wounded no longer in the military, WWI veterans and those who did not qualify for military service.
Waffen Meister: Weapons Master.
Waffen-SS: Armed SS.
Wasserversorgungstruppen: Water supply troops.
Wehrersatz: Defensive replacement.
Wehrkreis: German Army regional districts.
Zerstorer: Destroyer.
Zerstorergeschwader (Z.G.): Heavy/destroyer fighter wing formation.
Zugfuehrer: Section leader.

APPENDIX III

Glossary of Awards

1914 Iron Cross 1st Class: Awarded for bravery during WWI and ranked above the Iron Cross 2nd Class; worn on the center of the left breast pocket.

1914 Iron Cross 2nd Class: Awarded for bravery during WWI and ranked below the Iron Cross 1st Class; worn on a ribbon through the 2nd buttonhole of the tunic or above the left breast pocket.

1914 Naval Observer's Badge: Same criteria as the 1914 Observer's Badge, but of a different design; worn on the lower left breast pocket.

1914 Naval Pilot's Badge: Same criteria as the 1914 Pilot's Badge, but of a different design; worn on the lower left breast pocket.

1914 Naval Wound Badge: Same criteria as the 1914 Wound Badge, but of a different design; worn on the lower left breast pocket.

1914 Observer's Badge: WWI German Air Service Observer qualification badge given to Army Observers upon completion of training; worn on the lower left breast pocket.

1914 Pilot's Badge: WWI German Air Service Pilot qualification badge given to Army Pilots upon completion of training; worn on the lower left breast pocket.

1914 Submarine Badge: WWI Submarine Badge awarded for several patrols to eligible crews; worn on the lower left breast pocket.

1914 Wound Badge: WWI Wound Badge awarded in Black, Silver or Gold depending on the number and/or severity of wounds received—if combatant was killed in action or died of wounds, presentation of the Wound Badge in Gold was automatic; worn on the lower left breast pocket.

1921 Panzer Badge: Commemorative badge awarded to former members of tank crews from WWI; worn on the lower left breast pocket.

1929 Nuremberg Badge of Honor: Presented to those who had participated in the 1929 Nuremberg party rally; worn on the left breast pocket.

1939 Grand Cross: Highest Third Reich military award bestowed only once to Reichsmarschall Hermann Goering; worn on a ribbon at the neck.

1939 Iron Cross 1st Class: Awarded for bravery during WWII, ranked above the Iron Cross 2nd Class but below the German Cross in Gold or Knight's Cross; worn on the center of the left breast pocket.

1939 Clasp to the 1914 Iron Cross 1st Class: Awarded to those who had earned the 1939 Iron Cross 1st Class but had already received the 1914 version during WWI; worn above the 1914 Iron Cross 1st Class.

1939 Iron Cross 2nd Class: Awarded for bravery during WWII and ranked below the Iron Cross 1st Class; worn on a ribbon through the second buttonhole of the tunic or above the left breast pocket.

1939 Clasp to the 1914 Iron Cross 2nd Class: Awarded to those who had earned the 1939 Iron Cross 2nd Class but had already received the 1914 version during WWI; worn on the ribbon of the 1914 Iron Cross 2nd Class.

1939 Wound Badge: Awarded in Black, Silver or Gold depending on the number and/or severity of wounds received. If the combatant was killed in action or died of wounds, presentation of the Wound Badge in Gold was automatic. Wounds received during WWI counted towards higher grades if wounded again during WWII; worn on the lower left breast pocket.

1939 Pilot's Badge: Luftwaffe qualification badge presented upon completion of pilot training; worn on the lower left breast pocket.

1939 Observer's Badge: Luftwaffe qualification badge presented upon completion of observer training; worn on the lower left breast pocket.

1939 Combined Pilot-Observer's Badge: Luftwaffe qualification badge presented to those who had qualified as both a pilot and observer; worn on the lower left breast pocket.

1939 Submarine War Badge: Awarded to submarine crews who successfully took part in two patrols and/or had been wounded during a patrol; worn on the lower left breast pocket.

20.07.44 Wound Badge: Awarded to those who were wounded in the 20 July 1944 assassination attempt on Hitler's life—as with other wound badges, the grade awarded depended upon the number and/or severity of wounds received; worn on the lower left breast pocket.

Afrika Cuff Band: Awarded to those who had served at least six months in the African campaign—the time requirement was waived if the individual was wounded in action or had received an award; worn above the left cuff of the tunic.

Airship Commemorative Badge: Commemorative badge awarded by the Weimar Government to crews of airships from WWI; worn on the lower left breast pocket.

Anti-Aircraft War Badge (Heer): Awarded on a point system where a total of 16 points were needed for the award in shooting down, assisted in downing and/or spotting an aircraft with searchlights; worn on the lower left breast pocket.

Anti-Partisan War Badge: Awarded in Bronze (20 days), Silver (50 days) or Gold (100 days) for engagements against partisan formations; worn on the lower left breast pocket.

Austro-Hungarian military awards presented to medium- and lower-ranking officers during WWI:
Austro-Hungarian Military Service Cross 3rd Class with War Decoration.
Austrian Pilot's Badge.

Auxiliary Cruiser's War Badge: Awarded to crew members of a successful long voyage—the time requirement was waived if a crew member had been wounded in action; worn on the lower left breast.

Baltic Cross: Awarded for 3–6 months of service in the Baltic region while a member of a Freikorps unit. Officially, there was only a 1st Class version worn on the center of the left breast pocket. Unofficially, there was a 2nd Class version worn on a ribbon above the left breast pocket.

Blood Order: Awarded to participants of the 9 November 1923 Munich Beer Hall Putsch. It was also later awarded to those who had sacrificed for the movement; worn on a ribbon through the buttonhole of the right breast pocket.

Bulgarian military awards presented to German general officers during WWII:
Grand Officer Cross of the Bulgarian Order of Heligen Alexander with Swords.
Grand Officer Cross of the Bulgarian Military Service Order.
Bulgarian Military Service Order 1st Class with War Decoration.
Bulgarian Order for Bravery I. Class.
Bulgarian Order for Bravery II. Class.
Bulgarian Order for Bravery III. Class.
Bulgarian Order for Bravery IV. Class.

Cholm Shield: Awarded to those who had participated and/or been wounded during the battle of Cholm; worn on the upper left sleeve of the tunic.

Close Combat Clasp: Awarded in Bronze (15 days), Silver (30 days) and Gold (50 days) for close combat with the enemy such as hand to hand combat and without the support of armor. The award criteria were lessened if the soldier had been badly wounded. Due to its late institution date (November 1942), the award criteria were retroactive to the start of the Russian campaign (22 June 1941). The gold class was considered by Hitler to be the highest infantry award and when possible, was bestowed by him personally; worn above the left breast pocket.

Coastal Artillery War Badge: Awarded for leadership, a single act of merit for which no other award was given, or to those who had earned eight points in action against enemy aircraft and/or naval targets or had been killed in action; worn on the lower left breast pocket.

Combined Pilot-Observer's Badge in Gold with Diamonds: A special decoration created by and awarded at the discretion of Reichsmarschall Hermann Goering. It was presented to senior Luftwaffe generals, select Luftwaffe aces, senior generals of the Heer, Kriegsmarine, SS and to foreign dignitaries and/or heads of state; worn above all other medals (except for the Golden Party Badge) on the left breast pocket.

Commemorative Pilot's Badge: Awarded by the Weimar Government to pilots who had served in the German Air Service during WWI. This included fighter, bomber, and reconnaissance pilots, and was worn on the lower left breast pocket.

Crimea Shield: Awarded to those who had served at least three months, taken part in one major operation, received a decoration or had been wounded during the Crimea campaign; worn on the upper left sleeve of the tunic.

Croatian Military Awards presented to German General Officers during WWII:

Order of the Iron Trefoil 1st Class.

Order of the Iron Trefoil 2nd Class.

Order of the Iron Trefoil 3rd Class.

Grand Cross of the Order of the Crown of King Zvonimir with Breast Star and Swords.

Order of the Crown of King Zvonimir 1st Class (Commander) with Breast Star, Oak Leaves and Swords.

Order of the Crown of King Zvonimir 1st Class (Commander) with Breast Star and Swords.

Order of the Crown of King Zvonimir 1st Class (Commander) with Breast Star and Oak Leaves.

Order of the Crown of King Zvonimir 1st Class (Commander) with Breast Star.

Order of the Crown of King Zvonimir 1st Class (Commander).

Cross of Honor: Awarded to those who had taken part in WWI. The version with swords was for combative personnel while the one without swords was for non-combative personnel; worn on a ribbon above the left breast pocket.

Degen: Honor Sword of the SS given to SS-Junkerschule Graduates and ranking SS Leaders.

Demjansk Shield: Awarded for sixty days of service in the Demjansk pocket, having been wounded or received a decoration. Luftwaffe personnel had to have flown 50 combat missions or landed 50 supply missions into the pocket to qualify for the award; worn on the upper left sleeve of the tunic.

Destroyer's War Badge: Awarded for 12 operational missions, 3 separate engagements with the enemy, having served on a ship sunk by the enemy, heroic action or for being wounded in action; worn on the lower left breast pocket.

Diamonds: Knight's Cross with Oak Leaves, Swords and Diamonds was awarded for outstanding acts of persona bravery and/or leading of a military formation. It ranked above the Swords but below the Golden Oak Leaves, Swords, and Diamonds; worn at the neck above the Knight's Cross.

Eastern Front Medal: Awarded for participation in the Russian campaign between 15 November 1941 and 26 April 1942. Criteria was 14 days of combat, 60 days in a combat zone but not in direct combat, 30 sorties if a pilot or crew member in the Luftwaffe, having been wounded, received severe frostbite, or was killed in action; worn on a ribbon through the second buttonhole of the tunic.

Finnish military awards presented to German general officers during WWII:

Finnish Order of the Grand Cross of the White Rose with Breast Star and Swords.

Finnish Order of the Grand Cross of Liberty (Freedom) with Breast Star and Swords.

Finnish Order of the Cross of Liberty (Freedom) Gold Medal of Merit.

Finnish Order of the Cross of Liberty (Freedom) 1st Class with Breast Star, Oak Leaf and Swords.

Finnish Order of the Cross of Liberty (Freedom) 1st Class with Breast Star and Swords.

Finnish Order of the Cross of Liberty (Freedom) 1st Class with Oak Leaf and Swords.

Finnish Order of the Cross of Liberty (Freedom) 1st Class with Swords.

Finnish Order of the Cross of Liberty (Freedom) 1st Class without Swords

Finnish Order of the Cross of Liberty (Freedom) 2nd Class with Swords.

Finnish Order of the Cross of Liberty (Freedom) 2nd Class without Swords

Finnish Order of the Lion 1st Class with Breast Star and Swords.

Finnish Order of the Lion 1st Class with Swords.

Finnish Order of the Lion 1st Class without Swords.

Flak War Badge: Luftwaffe award presented on a point system for the location, participation and/or downing of an aircraft or for outstanding leadership; worn on the lower left breast pocket.

General Assault Badge: Awarded to non-infantry personnel such as tank assault gun crews, artillery and engineers. Criteria was three combat engagements with the enemy, or for the single-handed destruction of a tank prior to the institution of the Tank Destruction Badge. As the war progressed, the grades of the award were expanded to 25, 50, 75 and 100 respectively; worn on the lower left breast pocket.

German Army High Command Commendation Certificate: Awarded to officers, NCOs and EMs who had distinguished themselves in combat for a particular action and/or actions and as a result, were personally recognized by the O.B. of the Heer and/or the Fuehrer. As a pre-requisite, they had to have already received the 1939 Iron Cross 1st and 2nd Class or Clasps to the 1914 Iron Cross 1st and 2nd Class. When instituted, they were also allowed to wear the Honor Roll Clasp.

German Cross in Gold: Awarded for outstanding acts of personal bravery and/or leading of a military formation. It ranked above the 1939 Iron Cross 1st Class but below the Knight's Cross of the Iron Cross; worn on the center of the right breast pocket.

German Cross in Silver: Awarded to those in non-combative roles such as staff officers, medical staff, support personnel and to those who contributed towards the war effort. It ranked above the War Merit Cross 1st Class but below the Knight's Cross of the War Merit Cross and was worn on the center of the right breast pocket. If the recipient had received both the German Cross in Gold and Silver, then the gold class would be worn above the silver one.

German Horseman's Badge: Awarded to all riding formations for the care of horses and was presented in bronze, silver, and gold classes; worn on the lower left breast pocket.

German Motor Sports Badge: Awarded to all motor formations for the care and maintenance of their vehicles in bronze, silver and gold classes; worn on the lower left breast pocket.

German Olympic Games Decoration: Awarded to those who had participated in the formation and support of the 1936 Olympic Games (not to the athletes). It came in three classes; the 1st class was worn on a ribbon at the neck, while the 2nd and 3rd classes were worn on a ribbon above the left breast pocket.

German Order: The highest political award of the N.S.D.A.P. which was awarded at the discretion of Adolf Hitler. The 1st and 2nd class awards were worn on a ribbon at the neck, while the 3rd class was a pinback cross worn on the center of the left breast pocket.

German Red Cross Decorations: Social awards that came in several classes where the level of the award depended on the rank and/or position of the recipient.

German Social Welfare Decorations: Social awards that replaced the traditional German Red Cross Decorations and as such, came in several classes. Level of awards depended on the rank and/or position of the recipient.

Golden HJ Honor Badge with Oak Leaves: Highest award of the Hitler Youth given to select Party/military leaders by the Reichsjugenfuehrer (Reich Youth Leader); worn above all other awards (except for the Golden Party Badge) on the left breast pocket.

Golden HJ Honor Badge: Awarded to H.J. and B.D.M. members who had joined prior to 2 October 1932 and had five years of unbroken service in the Hitler Youth and/or another party formation following Hitler Youth service; worn on the left breast pocket.

Golden Party Badge: Awarded by the N.S.D.A.P. to the first 100,000 party members with unbroken membership. It was also later presented as an honorary award to those who contributed towards the movement; worn above all awards, military or political, on the left breast pocket.

Golden Prussian Military Service Cross: Imperial German award presented by the Kingdom of Prussia as the highest military award to NCOs for personal bravery. Since they did not hold officer rank, they were not eligible to receive the Pour le Mérite; worn on a ribbon through the second buttonhole of the tunic or above the left breast pocket.

Ground Combat Badge (Luftwaffe): Awarded for 3 separate engagements on separate days; being wounded during an engagement; receiving a decoration because of an engagement; or being killed in action. Worn on the lower left breast pocket.

Heer Bergfuehrer Badge: Awarded to Heer Gebirgstruppen (Army Mountain Troops) who had qualified as a mountain guide for at least one year. It could be worn on either the left or right breast pocket of the tunic.

High Seas Fleet War Badge: Awarded for 12 weeks of service on a ship with good conduct, successful voyages, or having been wounded in action; worn on the lower left breast pocket.

Honor Roll Clasp: Awarded to those mentioned in the Honor Roll of the German Wehrmacht for acts of heroism and/or leadership prior to and after the institution of the clasp in 1944. The recipient had to have already received the 1939 Iron Cross 1st and 2nd Class or the 1939 Clasps to the 1914 Iron Cross 1st and 2nd Class; worn on the ribbon of the 1939 Iron Cross 2nd Class through the second buttonhole of the tunic.

Hungarian military awards presented to German general officers during WWII:
Commander's Cross of the Hungarian Service Order with Breast Star.
Grand Officer's Cross of the Hungarian Service Order.
Knight's Cross of the Hungarian Service Order.

Imperial German military awards presented by German kingdoms and states to medium- and lower-ranking officers during WWI:

Anhalt: RK-Anhalt Albrecht Order of the Bear 2nd Class with Swords.

Baden: RK-Baden Order of the Zaehringer Lion 2nd Class with Swords.

Bavaria: RK-Bavarian Military Max Joseph Order, Bavarian Military Service Order IV. Class with Swords, Bavarian Military Service Order 3rd Class with Swords.

Braunschweig: War Service Cross 1st and 2nd Class.

Mecklenburg-Schwerin: Military Service Cross 1st and 2nd Class.

Oldenburg: Friedrich-August Cross 1st and 2nd Class.

Prussia: Pour le Mérite with Oak Leaves, Pour le Mérite, Red Eagle Order IV. Class with Swords, Golden Prussian Military Service Cross, RK-House Order of Hohenzollern with Swords, RK-Princely House Order of Hohenzollern, Prussian Crown Order IV, with Swords.

Saxony: Grand Cross of the Sachsen Ernestine House Order with Swords and Ring, RK-Sachsen Ernestine House Order 1st Class with Swords, RK-Sachsen Ernestine House Order 2nd Class with Swords, RK-Sachsen Military St. Heinrich's Order, RK-Sachsen Albrecht Order 1st Class with Swords, RK-Sachsen Albrecht Order 2nd Class with Swords, RK-Sachsen Order of the White Falcon 2nd Class with Swords, RK-Sachsen Military Service Order 2nd Class with Swords.

Wuerttemberg: RK-Wuerttemberg Friedrich Order 1st Class with Swords, RK-Wuerttemberg Friedrich Order 2nd Class with Swords, RK-Wuerttemberg Military Service Order.

Infantry Assault Badge: Awarded to the infantry in Silver or motorized infantry in Bronze for three combat engagements with the enemy on separate days; worn on the lower left breast pocket.

Italian military awards presented to German general officers during WWII:
Commander's Cross of the Order of the Crown of Italy.
Commander's Cross of the Italian Colonial Order with Breast Star.

Jagdstaffel Boelcke Nr. 2, 1916/18 Cuff Band: Worn by Luftwaffe personnel who served in this fighter unit during WWI.

J.G. Freiherr von Richthofen Nr. 1, 1917/18 Cuff Band: Worn by Luftwaffe personnel who served in this fighter unit during WWI.

Knight's Cross: Knight's Cross of the 1939 Iron Cross awarded for outstanding acts of personal bravery and/or leading of a military formation. It was below the Oak Leaves to the Knight's Cross but ranked above the German Cross in Gold or 1939 Iron Cross 1st Class; worn on a ribbon at the neck.

Knight's Cross of the War Merit Cross: Awarded to civil, political/government personnel for outstanding contribution towards the war effort as well as to members of the military in supportive/staff positions. Military personnel received the version with swords while all others received the award without swords. The Knight's Cross of the War Merit Cross ranked above the German Cross in Silver or the War Merit Cross 1st Class but below the version in gold, which was only awarded twice on 20 April 1945; worn on a ribbon at the neck.

Kreta Cuff Band: Awarded to those who had taken part in the air, sea, and land operations during the battle for Crete; worn above the left cuff of the tunic.

Kuban Shield: Awarded to those who had served 60 days at the Kuban bridgehead, taken part in at least one major operation, or had been wounded in action; worn on the upper left sleeve of the tunic.

Kurland Cuff Band: Manufactured and awarded in the Kurland pocket to those who had participated and/or been wounded in its defense; worn above the left cuff of the tunic.

Metz Cuff Band: Awarded for seven days of action or to those who had been wounded during the battle for Metz; worn above the left cuff of the tunic.

Minesweepers-Sub Chasers-Escort Vessel War Badge: Awarded for 3 engagements, excellent performance over a 6-month period, hazardous duty, or 23 days of escort duty; worn on the lower left breast pocket.

Narvik Shield: Awarded to those who had participated or had been wounded during the battle for Narvik; worn on the upper left sleeve of the tunic.

Naval Combat Clasp: Awarded for a total of five meritorious actions; worn above the left breast pocket.

Naval Pilot's Commemorative Badge: Same criteria as the Pilot's Commemorative Badge, but of a different design; worn on the lower left breast pocket.

Oak Leaves: Knight's Cross with Oak Leaves awarded for outstanding acts of personal bravery and/or leading of a military formation. It ranked above the Knight's Cross but below the Swords to the Knight's Cross; worn above the Knight's Cross at the neck.

Parachute Badge: Awarded upon completion of parachute training; worn on the lower left breast pocket.

Pilot's Commemorative Badge: Awarded by the Weimar Government to former pilots of WWI German Air Service; worn on the lower left breast pocket.

Pour le Mérite: Imperial German award presented by the Kingdom of Prussia to officers for outstanding acts of bravery and/or leading of a military formation. The Pour le Mérite ranked above the Knight's Cross of the House Order of Hohenzollern but below the Oak Leaves to the Pour le Mérite; worn on a ribbon at the neck.

Princely House Order of Hohenzollern: The equivalent of the military version of the Knight's Cross of the House Order of Hohenzollern with Swords. The only difference being that this award was presented by the actual princely house of Hohenzollern, and not its namesake taken by Kaiser Wilhelm of Prussia.

Red Eagle Order: Imperial German award bestowed by the Kingdom of Prussia that came in several classes depending on the rank and/or position of the recipient. It was awarded for bravery, the leading of a military formation, or for diplomatic reasons, until the end of WWI.

Reich Senate Culture Honor Badge: Presented to members of the Reich Cultural Senate whose head was Dr. Joseph Goebbels; worn on the left breast pocket.

Reich Sports Badge: Awarded to all formations for athletic achievement, in bronze, silver, or gold classes; worn on the lower left breast pocket.

Ring: Death's Head Ring of the SS awarded to the first 10,000 members of the SS and later expanded to those who held officer rank for at least three years; worn on the left ring finger.

RK-Bavarian Military Max Joseph Order: Imperial German award presented by the Kingdom of Bavaria to officers for outstanding acts of personal bravery that would warrant along the same lines as the Pour le Mérite Order. It came with the title of nobility and was worn on a ribbon through the second buttonhole of the tunic or above the left breast.

RK-Hohenzollern: Imperial German award presented by the Kingdom of Prussia to officers for outstanding acts of bravery. It ranked above the 1914 Iron Cross 1st Class but below the Pour le Mérite Order; worn on a ribbon through the second buttonhole of the tunic or above the left breast.

RK-Military Maria Theresia Order: Imperial award presented by the Kingdom of Austria-Hungary to officers for outstanding acts of bravery; worn on a ribbon through the second buttonhole of the tunic or above the left breast.

Romanian military awards presented to German general officers during WWII:
Commander's Cross of the Romanian Order with Breast Star and Swords.
Commander's Cross of the Romanian Order with Crown and Swords.
Commander's Cross of the Order of the Star with Swords and Ring.
Order of Michael the Brave III. Class.

SA-Rally at Braunschweig Badge of Honor: Presented to those who had taken part in the SA Rally at Braunschweig in 1931; worn on the left breast pocket.

SA-Sports Badge: Awarded by the SA to SA and SS formations for athletic achievement in bronze, silver, or gold classes; worn on the lower left breast pocket.

Silesian Eagle: Awarded for service in a Freikorps unit in Silesia and came in 2nd class for 3 months of service and 1st class for 6 months of service. The 1st class was worn on the lower left breast pocket, while the 2nd class was worn on a ribbon above the left breast pocket.

Spanish Cross: Awarded to German personnel for bravery and/or length of service in Spain during the Spanish Civil War. It came in several classes (gold with swords and diamonds, gold with swords, silver with and without swords and bronze with and without swords) and was worn on the center of the right breast pocket, either by itself or below the German Cross in gold/silver if both had been awarded.

Swords: Knight's Cross with Oak Leaves and Swords awarded for outstanding acts of personal bravery and/or leading of a military formation. It ranked above the Oak Leaves but below the Diamonds to the Knight's Cross; worn at the neck between the Oak Leaves and Knight's Cross.

Tank Assault Badge: Awarded to panzer crews in silver and to armored car personnel/ panzer grenadier troops in bronze for engagements with the enemy. As the war progressed, this award was expanded to include 25, 50, 75 and 100 grades and was awarded accordingly depending on the number of engagements; worn on the lower left breast pocket.

Tank Destruction Badge: Awarded for single-handed destruction of a tank with a grenade satchel, magnetic mine or panzerfaust. For a single kill, a silver/grey threaded badge was worn on the upper right sleeve. If the recipient had five kills to his credit, he could choose to wear a yellow/gold threaded badge in place of five single ones on his sleeve.

Turkish imperial awards presented to Germans during WWI:
Turkish Golden Liakat Medal with Sabre.
Turkish Silver Liakat Medal with Sabre.
Turkish Half Moon (Iron Half Moon).
Turkish Pilot's Badge.

U-Boat Combat Clasp: Awarded in silver or bronze depending on the number of sorties and/or acts of bravery by the individual; worn above the left breast pocket.

War Merit Cross 1st Class: Awarded to civilians and government personnel for contributions towards the war effort, as well as to military personnel in a supportive and/or staff position. It was awarded with swords to the military and without swords to civilian/government personnel. It ranked above the War Merit Cross 2nd Class but below the German Cross in Silver and was worn on the center of the left breast pocket.

War Merit Cross 2nd Class: As noted above but ranked below the War Merit Cross 1st Class; worn on a ribbon through the second buttonhole of the tunic or above the left breast pocket.

West Wall Medal: Awarded to those who took part in planning and construction of fortifications along Germany's western borders; worn on a ribbon through the second buttonhole of the tunic or above the left breast pocket.

APPENDIX IV

Tables of Ranks

Heer

Generalfeldmarschall	General Field Marshal
Generaloberst	Colonel-General
General der	Full General
Panzertruppe/Artillerie/Gebirgstruppe/Infanterie/ Kavallerie/Nachrichtentruppe/Pioniere	
General-Oberstabsarzt (Medical)	
General-Oberstabsrichter (Judicial)	
General-Oberstabsintendant (Administrative)	
General-Oberstabsveterinar (Veterinary)	
Generalleutnant	Lieutenant-General
General-Stabsarzt (Medical)	
General-Stabsrichter (Judicial)	
General-Stabsintendant (Administrative)	
Genereral-Stabsveterinar (Veterinary)	
Generalmajor	Major-General
General-Arzt (Medical)	
General-Richter (Judicial)	
General-Intendant (Administrative)	
General-Veterinar (Veterinary)	
Oberst	Colonel
Oberstarzt (Medical)	
Oberstrichter (Judicial)	
Oberstleutnant	Lieutenant-Colonel
Oberfeldarzt (Medical)	
Oberfeldrichter (Judicial)	
Major	Major
Oberstabsarzt (Medical)	
Oberstabsrichter (Judicial)	

Hauptmann	Captain
Stabsarzt (Medical)	
Stabsrichter (Judicial)	
Oberleutnant	First Lieutenant
Ober-Arzt (Medical)	
Leutnant	Second Lieutenant
Assistenzarzt (Medical)	
Stabsfeldwebel	Sergeant Major
Obefeldwebel	Master Sergeant
Feldwebel	Staff Sergeant
Unterfeldwebel	Technical Sergeant
Unteroffizier	Sergeant
Obergefreiter	Corporal
Gefreiter	Private First Class
Obersoldat	Private
Soldat	Soldier, Grenadier

Luftwaffe

Generalfeldmarschall	General Field Marshal
Generaloberst	Colonel-General
General der	Full General
Flieger/Flak/Fallschirmtruppe/Nachrichtentruppe	
General-Oberstabsarzt (Medical)	
General-Oberstabsrichter (Judicial)	
General-Oberstabsintendant (Administrative)	
Generaloberstabs-Veterinar (Veterinary)	
Generalleutnant	Lieutenant-General
General-Stabsarzt (Medical)	
General-Stabsrichter (Judicial)	
General-Stabsintendant (Administrative)	
General-Stabsveterinar (Veterinary)	
Generalmajor	Major-General
General-Arzt (Medical)	
General-Richter (Judicial)	
General-Intendant (Administrative)	
General-Veterinar (Veterinary)	
Oberst	Colonel
Oberstarzt (Medical)	
Oberstrichter (Judicial)	

Oberstleutnant	Lieutenant-Colonel
Oberfeldarzt (Medical)	
Oberfeldrichter (Judicial)	
Major	Major
Oberstabsarzt (Medical)	
Oberstabsrichter (Judicial)	
Hauptmann	Captain
Stabsarzt (Medical)	
Stabsrichter (Judicial)	
Oberleutnant	First Lieutenant
Ober-Arzt (Medical)	
Leutnant	Second Lieutenant
Assistenzarzt (Medical)	
Stabsfeldwebel	Sergeant Major
Oberfeldwebel	Master Sergeant
Feldwebel	Staff Sergeant
Unterfeldwebel	Technical Sergeant
Unteroffizier	Sergeant
Obergefreiter	Corporal
Gefreiter	Private First Class
Oberflieger	Private
Flieger	Flyer

Kriegsmarine

Grossadmiral	Grand Admiral
Generaladmiral	Colonel-General
Admiral	Full General
General der Marine	
Admiral-Oberstabsarzt (Medical)	
Admiral-Oberstabsrichter (Judicial)	
Admiral-Oberstabsintendant (Administrative)	
Vizeadmiral	Lieutenant-General
Generalleutnant der Marine	
Admiral-Stabsarzt (Medical)	
Admiral-Stabsrichter (Judicial)	
Admiral-Stabsintendant (Administrative)	
Konteradmiral	Major-General
Generalmajor der Marine	
Admiral-Arzt (Medical)	

Admiral-Richter (Judicial)	
Admiral-Intendant (Administrative)	
Marine-Oberbaudirektor	
Kapitan zur See	Colonel
Fregattenkapitan	Lieutenant-Colonel
Korvettenkapitan	Major
Kapitanleutnant	Captain
Oberleutnant zur See	First Lieutenant
Leutnant zur See	Second Lieutenant
Obersteuermannsmaat	Petty Officer Second Class—Quartermaster
Steuermannsmaat	Petty Officer Third Class—Quartermaster
Oberbootsmannsmaat	Petty Officer Second Class—Coxswain
Bootsmannsmaat	Petty Officer Third Class—Coxswain
Matrosenhauptgefreiter	Seaman First Class with 4½ years' service
Matrosenobergefreiter	Seaman First Class
Matrosengefreiter	Seaman Second Class
Matrose	Seaman

Waffen-SS

SS-Oberst-Gruppenfuehrer und Generaloberst der Waffen-SS	Colonel-General
SS-Obergruppenfuehrer und General der Waffen-SS	General
SS-Gruppenfeuhrer und Generalleutnant der Waffen-SS	Lieutenant-General
SS-Brigadefuehrer und Generalmajor der Waffen-SS	Major-General
SS-Oberfuehrer	Senior Colonel
SS-Standartenfuehrer	Colonel
SS-Obersturmbannfuehrer	Lieutenant-Colonel
SS-Sturmbannfuehrer	Major
SS-Hauptsturmfuehrer	Captain
SS-Obersturmfuehrer	First Lieutenant
SS-Untersturmfuehrer	Second Lieutenant
SS-Sturmscharfuehrer	Sergeant Major
SS-Hauptscharfuehrer	Master Sergeant
SS-Oberscharfuehrer	Staff Sergeant
SS-Scharfuehrer	Technical Sergeant
SS-Unterscharfuehrer	Sergeant
SS-Rottenfuehrer	Corporal
SS-Sturmmann	Private First Class
SS-Oberschuetze	Private
SS-Schuetze	Soldier, Grenadier

APPENDIX V

Fate of Heer Generals

Died of natural causes during World War II

H-Generalmajor Moritz Basler
H-Generalleutnant Arnold Freiherr von Biegeleben
H-Generlmajor Friedrich Ritter von Bogendoerfer
H-General-Arzt Dr. Richard Brekle
H-General der Infanterie Walter Graf von Brockdorff-Ahlefeldt
H-Generalmajor Ernst Buchterkirch
H-Generalmajor Robert Buehrmann
H-General-Arzt Dr. Wilhelm Dietrich
H-Generaloberst Friedrich Dollmann
H-Generalstabs-Veterinar Dr. Julius Eckert
H-Generaloberst Kurt Freiherr von Hammerstein-Equard
H-General der Artillerie Max Foehrenbach
H-Generalmajor z.V. Dr. Alfons Fonck
H-General-Stabsveterinar Dr. Philipp Fritsch
H-Generalleutnant z.V. Victor Gaissert
H-Generalmajor Georg Gawantka
H-General der Infanterie z.V. Hubert Gercke
H-General der Infanterie Gerhard Glokke
H-General der Infanterie Kurt von Greiff
H-Generalleutnant z.V. Erich Gudowius
H-General-Arzt Dr. Kurt Guenther
H-Generalleutnant Ernst Guentzel
H-Generalleutnant z.V. Konrad Guhl
H-Generalmajor z.V. Richard von Gusovius
H-Generalmajor Werner Haack
H-Generaloberst Curt Haase
H-Generalmajor Hans-Joachim Haupt
H-Generalamjor z.V. Karl Hausser
H-Generaloberst Walter Heitz
H-Generalleutnant Georg Hewelke
H-Generalmajor Karl Joerling
H-General-Intendant z.V. Theodor Hontschik
H-Generalmajor z.V. Otto von Huepeden
H-General-Stabsarzt Dr. Johannes Kaefer
H-Generalmajor Hugo Karl
H-General der Infanterie Friedrich Karmann
H-Generalmajor z.V. Hugo Kiehl

H-Generalmajor z.V. Hans von Knauer
H-General der Kavallerie Wilhelm Knochenhauer
H-Generalleutnant z.V. Rudolf Krantz
H-General-Veterinar Dr. Alferd Kunke
H-Generalmajor z.V. Otto Kuntze
H-Generalleutnant Franz Landgraf
H-Generalmajor Georg Lang
H-Generalmajor z.V. Wilhelm Lindemann
H-Generalmajor z.V. Karl-August Moeslinger
H-Generalleutnant Josef Ritter von Molo
H-Generalmajor Friedrich Moro
H-Generalmajor z.V. Kurt Mueller
H-Generalleutnant z.V. Kurt Mueller
H-Generalmajor Georg Naegelsbach
H-Generalmajor Willi Plewig
H-General der Kavallerie Guenther von Pogrell
H-Generalleutnant Ludwig Ritter von Radlmeier
H-Generalfeldmarschall Walther von Reichenau
H-Generalleutnant Karl Rudolph
H-Generalmajor Richard Schack
H-Generalmajor Arthur Schade
H-Generalleutnant Heinrich von Schenckendorff
H-General der Infanterie z.V. Max von Schenckendorff
H-Generalleutnant Guenther Schwantes
H-Generalleutnant z.V. Manfred von Schwerin
H-Generalmajor z.V. Theodor Stahl
H-Generalmajor Otto Stamm
H-Generalmajor z.V. Georg Graf von Stillfried und Rattonitz
H-Generalleutnant Heinrich Strack
H-Generalmajor Wilhelm Stubenrauch
H-Generalmajor Eberhard Freiherr von der Tann-Rathsamhausen
H-Generalmajor Friedrich von Tempelhoff
H-Generalmajor Maximilian Thaeter
H-Generalmajor z.V. Anton Unger
H-General-Arzt z.V. Dr. Gerhard Voth
H-Generalmajor Wolfgang Freiherr von Waldenfels
H-Generalleutnant Friedrich Zickwolff
H-Generalleutnant Karl Zwengauer

Killed in action

H-Generalmajor Edgar Arndt
H-Generalmajor Harry von Arnim
H-Generalmajor Karl Arnold
H-Generalmajor Karl Baer
H-Generalmajor Erich Balla
H-Generalmajor Viktor Bartcky
H-General-Veterinar Dr. Erich Bartsch
H-Generalmajor Adolf Berger
H-Generalleutnant Friedrich Bergmann
H-Generalleutnant Erich Bernecker
H-Generalleutnant Gerhard Berthold
H-Generalmajor Paul Betz
H-Generalleutnant Clemens Betzel
H-Generalmajor Otto Beutler
H-Generalmajor Otto Biermann
H-Generalleutnant Georg von Bismarck
H-General der Infanterie Johannes Block

H-Generalfeldmarschall Fedor von Bock
H-Generalleutnant Georg Braun
H-General der Infanterie Kurt von Briesen
H-Generalleutnant Fritz von Brodowski
H-Generalmajor Heinrich-Walter Bronsart von Schellendorf
H-Generalmajor Wolfgang Bucher
H-Generalmajor Albert Buck
H-Generalmajor Andreas Buechting
H-Generalmajor Cord von Buelow
H-Generalmajor Werner von Buelow
H-Generalmajor Otto Buesing
H-Generalmajor Horst Christiani
H-Generalmajor Bruno Chrobeck
H-Generalleutnant Wilhelm Crisolli
H-Generalmajor Willi Daube
H-Generalmajor Hans Daubert
H-Generalmajor Joachim von der Damerau-Dombrowski
H-Generalmajor Sigismund-Hellmut Rittter und Edler von Dawans
H-Generalmajor Guenther von Dewitz gen von Krebs
H-Generalmajor Constantin Freiherr von Digeon von Monteton
H-Generalmajor Berndt von Doering
H-Generalmajor Kurt Domansky
H-Generalmajor Robert Ritter von Doser
H-Generalleutnant Viktor von Drabich-Waechter
H-Generalleutnant Otto Drescher
H-Generalleutnant Rene Eberle
H-General der Infanterie Karl Eibl
H-Generalmajor Max Eichstaedt
H-Generalmajor Werner Eichstaedt
H-Generalmajor Wolfgang Elster
H-Generalleutnant Harald Freiherr von Elverfeldt
H-Generalleutnant Wilhelm Falley
H-Generalmajor Arthur Finger
H-Generalmajor Karl Fischer
H-General der Panzertruppe Wolfgang Fischer
H-Generalmajor Hans-Joachim Fouquet
H-Generalmajor Botho von Frantzius
H-Generalmajor Lothar Freutel
H-Generalleutnant Rudolf Friedrich
H-Generaloberst Werner Freiherr von Fritsch
H-Generalmajor Egon Fuchs
H-Generalmajor Otto Gabcke
H-Generalleutnant Franz Gall
H-Generalmajor Paul Gallas
H-Generalmajor Dr. Udo Gallwitz
H-Generalleutnant Werner von Gallwitz
H-Generalmajor Eugen Garski
H-Generalmajor Heinrich Geerkens
H-Generalmajor Erich Gross
H-Generalmajor Erich Gruner
H-Generalmajor Erich Guenther
H-Generalleutnant Ernst Haccius
H-Generalmajor Oskar von dem Hagen
H-Generalmajor Hans Hahne
H-General-Arzt Dr. Walter Hanspach
H-General der Infanterie Alexander von Hartmann
H-Generalmajor Georg Haus
H-Generalmajor Willi Heinrich
H-Generalleutnant Conrad-Oskar Heinrichs
H-Generalmajor Alfred Heisig
H-Generalleutnant Heinz Hellmich
H-Generalmajor Richard Hellmich
H-Generalmajor Walter Herold

H-Generalmajor Fritz Hertzsch
H-Generalmajor Hans-Christoph von Heydebrand und der Lasa
H-Generalmajor Edgar Hieber
H-Generalmajor Bruno Hippler
H-Generalleutnant Harald von Hirschfeld
H-Generalmajor Georg Hoecherl
H-Generalmajor Johannes Hoelz
H-Generalmajor Heinrich Hohmeyer
H-Generalmajor Helmuth von Hufenbach
H-Generalleutnant Walter Jost
H-Generalleutnant Hans Kaellner
H-Generalleutnant Kurt Kalmukoff
H-Generalmajor Hans Kamecke
H-Generalleutnant Harry von Kirchbach
H-Generalmajor Ludwig Kirschner
H-Generalmajor Ernst-Richard Knecht
H-Generalleutnant Viktor Koch
H-Generalmajor Otto Koehler
H-Generalmajor Paul Kohwalt
H-Generalmajor Botho Kollberg
H-General der Infanterie Joachim von Kortzfleisch
H-Generalmajor Dr. Karl Koske
H-Generalmajor Georg Kossmala
H-Generalleutnant Dietrich Kraiss
H-Generalmajor Wilhelm Kraut
H-Generalleutnant Franz Krech
H-Generalleutnant Hermann Kress
H-Generalmajor Theodor Kretzschmer
H-Generalmajor Otto von Kries
H-General der Infanterie Ernst-Anton von Krosigk
H-Generalmajor zV Kurt Kuehme
H-General der Panzertruppe Friedrich Kuehn
H-Generalmajor August-Wilhelm Kuester
H-Generalmajor Friedrich Kussin
H-Generalleutnant Otto Lancelle
H-Generalmajor Joachim-Friedrich Lang
H-General der Panzertruppe Willibald Freiherr von Langermann und Erlenkamp
H-Generalleutnant Adolf Lechner
H-Generalmajor Wilhelm von Lengerke
H-Generalmajor Karl Freiherr von Lersner
H-Generalmajor Rudolf Lippert
H-Generalmajor Max-Hermann von Loefen
H-Generalmajor Carl Lohmeyer
H-Generalmajor Ernst Michael
H-Generalleutnant Johann Mickl
H-General der Infanterie Friedrich Mieth
H-Generalmajor Alexander Moeckel
H-Generalleutnant Kurt Moehring
H-Generalleutnant Max Muehlmann
H-Generalleutnant Richard Mueller
H-Generalmajor Wilhelm Muench
H-Generalmajor Walter Mylo
H-Generalleutnant Egon von Neindorff
H-Generalmajor Andreas Nelsuer
H-Generalmajor Dr. Herbert Olbrich
H-Generalleutnant Hans Oschmann
H-Generalmajor Friedrich-Wilhelm Otte
H-Generalmajor Christian Pagels
H-Generalleutnant Rudolf Peschel
H-General der Artillerie Dr. Georg Pfeiffer
H-Generalleutnant Hellmuth Pfeiffer
H-General der Infanterie Hellmuth Priess
H-Generalleutnant Heinrich von Prittwitz und Gaffron

H-Generalmajor Job-Detlef von Raczeck
H-Generalleutnant Heinz von Randow
H-General der Infanterie Hermann Recknagel
H-Generalleutnant Siegfried Rein
H-Generalleutnant Kurt Renner
H-Generalmajor Richard-Heinrich von Reuss
H-Generalmajor Gustav-Adolf Riebel
H-Generalmajor Gottfried Ries
H-Generalleutnant Stephan Rittau
H-Generalleutnant Hans-Guenther von Rost
H-Generalmajor Karl Rothenberg
H-Generalleutnant Karl Ruebel
H-Generalmajor Siegfried Runge
H-Generalleutnant Ernst Rupp
H-Generalleutnant Hans de Salengre-Drabbe
H-Generalmajor Walter Schade
H-Generalmajor Dr. Gotthold Schaefer
H-Generalmajor Franz Scheidies
H-Generalmajor Otto Schell
H-Generalleutnant Walther Scheller
H-Generalleutnant Gerd Scherbening
H-Generalleutnant Walter Schilling
H-Generalmajor Gerd Schmidhuber
H-Generalmajor Axel Schmidt
H-Generalleutnant Friedrich Schmidt
H-Generalleutnant Gustav Schmidt
H-Generalmajor Josef Schmidt
H-Generalleutnant Kurt Schmidt
H-Generalmajor Carl-August von Schoenfeld
H-Generalleutnant Otto Schuenemann
H-Generalmajor Ulrich Schuetze
H-Generalmajor Adalbert Schulz
H-Generalmajor Dr. Johannes Schulz
H-Generalleutnant Borgislav Graf von Schwerin
H-Generalmajor Erich Freiherr von Seckendorff
H-Generalmajor Erich Seidel
H-General der Artillerie Hermann Ritter von Speck
H-Generalleutnant Rudolf Stegmann
H-General der Artillerie Wilhelm Stemmermann
H-Generalmajor Hermann Stempel
H-Generalleutnant Richard Stempel
H-Generalleutnant Walter Stettner Ritter von Grabenhofen
H-Generalmajor Helmuth Strempel
H-General der Panzertruppe Georg Stumme
H-Generalmajor Erich Sudau
H-Generalmajor Max Suemmermann
H-Generalleutnant Arnold Szelinski
H-Generalmajor Ernst-Heinrich Voss
H-General der Artillerie Martin Wandel
H-Generalmajor August-Heinrich Wassmuth
H-Generalmajor Gerhard Weber
H-General der Infanterie Wilhelm Wegener
H-Generalmajor Guenther Weichhardt
H-Generalmajor der Res. Maximilian Wengler
H-Generalleutnant Marion von Wessely
H-Generalmajor Horst von Wolff
H-Generalmajor Helmut Wortmann
H-Generalleutnnat Albrecht Wuestenhagen
H-Generalmajor Eduard Zorn
H-General der Infanterie Hans Zorn

Died of wounds

H-Generalleutnant Ernst-Guenther Baade
H-Generalleutnant Johannes Baessler
H-Generalmajor Hans Berger
H-Generalmajor Friedrich Bluemke
H-Generalmajor Heinz Brandt
H-Generalleutnant Werner Duerking
H-General der Artillerie Theodor Geib
H-Generalleutnant Herbert Geitner
H-Generalmajor Karl Goebel
H-Generalmajor Ernst Grau
H-Generalleutnant Karl-Albrecht von Groddek
H-Generalleutnant Paul Gurran
H-Generalmajor Kurt Guth
H-General der Infanterie Wilhelm Hasse
H-Generalleutnant Kurt Himer
H-Generalleutnant Walther von Huenersdorff
H-Generalmajor Werner Jacob
H-Generalmajor Ernst Juengling
H-Generalmajor Erich Kahsnitz
H-Generalmajor Richard Kanzler
H-Generalmajor Erich von Kirchbach
H-Generalmajor Fritz Kistner
H-Generalmajor Ernst Knebel
H-Generalmajor Guenter Leopold
H-Generalmajor Wilhelm Lorenz
H-Generalmajor Georg von Neufville
H-Generalleutnant Walter Neumann-Silkow
H-Generalmajor Gustav-Adolf von Nostitz-Wallwitz
H-Generalmajor Hugo Ribstein
H-Generalleutnant Werner Richter
H-Generalleutnant Heinrich Roth
H-Generalmajor Hans-Georg Schmidt von Altenstadt
H-General der Infanterie Rudolf Schmundt
H-General der Infanterie Wilhelm Schneckenburger
H-Generalmajor Ernst Schreder
H-Generalmajor Lothar von Seydlitz-Kurzbach
H-Generalleutnant Friedrich Sieburg
H-Generalmajor Siegfried Voigt
H-Generalmajor Karl Ritter von Weber
H-Generalmajor Hermann von Wedel
H-Generalmajor z.V. Gustav-Adolf von Wulffen

Killed in accidents

H-Generalmajor Julius von Bernuth
H-Generalleutnant Franz-Karl Cranz
H-Generalleutnant Friedrich-Wilhelm Deutsch
H-Generaloberst Eduard Dietl
H-General der Gebirgstruppe Karl Eglseer
H-Generalmajor Oswin Grolig
H-General der Infanterie Arthur Hauffe
H-Generalmajor Werner Heyden
H-Generaloberst Hans Hube
H-General der Infanterie Hans Jordan
H-Generalmajor Ernst Klueg
H-Generalmajor Gerhard Koerner
H-Generalmajor Oskar Kubitza
H-General der Infanterie Paul Laux

H-Generalleutnant Ludwig Loeweneck
H-Generalleutnant Karl Loewrick
H-Generalmajor Helmut Michalik
H-General-Stabsarzt Dr. Wilhelm Osterland
H-Generalmajor Wilhelm Otzen
H-Generalmajor Peter-Paul Petersen
H-Generalleutnant Georg Rosenbusch
H-Generalleutnant Franz Rossi
H-Generalleutnant Joachim Freiherr von Schleinitz
H-Generalmajor Walther Schloesser
H-Generaloberst Eugen Ritter von Schobert
H-Generalmajor Georg Schott
H-General der Infanterie Walther Schroth
H-Generalmajor Dr. Albert Seekirchner
H-Generalleutnant Bogislav von Studnitz
H-Generalleutnant Kurt Thomas
H-Generalmajor Hermann Ulbrich
H-Generalmajor Helmuth Voelter
H-General der Infanterie Hellmuth Volkmann
H-Generalleutnant Walter Wessel
H-General der Infanterie Thomas-Emil von Wickede
H-Generalleutnant Wolf-Dietrich Ritter und Edler von Xylander
H-Generalmajor z.V. Max Zunehmer

Committed suicide during World War II

H-Generalleutnant Guenther Angern
H-Generalmajor Erich Baerenfanger
H-Genralmajor Konrad Barde
H-Generaloberst Ludwig Beck
H-General der Artillerie Prof. Dr. Karl Becker
H-Generalmajor Siegfried von Blanckensee
H-Generalleutnant Erpo Freiherr von Bodenhausen
H-Generalmajor Richard von Bothmer
H-General der Kavallerie Georg Brandt
H-Generalleutnant Karl von Buelowius
H-General der Infanterie Wilhelm Burgdorf
H-Generalleutnant Conrad von Cochenhausen
H-General der Panzertruppe Karl Decker
H-General-Arzt Dr. Josef Ebbert
H-Generalmajor Walter Gleininger
H-Generalmajor Ernst Gonell
H-Generalmajor Erich Hassenstein
H-Generalamjor Carl Henke
H-Generalmajor Paul Hoffmann
H-General-Stabsarzt Dr. Karl Holm
H-Generalleutnant Arno Jahr
H-Generalmajor Friedrich Kammel
H-Generalfeldmarschall Guenther von Kluge
H-Generalleutnant Arthur Kobus
H-General der Infanterie Hans Krebs
H-Generalleutnant zV Georg Kuehn
H-General-Arzt Dr. Guenther Lenz
H-General-Arzt Dr. Johannes Lieschke
H-General-Stabsrichter Werner Lueben
H-Generalfeldmarschall Walter Model

H-General der Infanterie z.V. Hans Petri
H-Generalleutnant Ernst Philipp
H-Generalfeldmarschall Erwin Rommel
H-Generalmajor Dr. Gotthold Schaefer
H-Generalleutnant z.V. Wolfgang Schmidt-Logan
H-Generalmajor Georg Scholze
H-Generalleutnant z.V. Winfried von der Schulenburg
H-Generalmajor Rudolf Sieckenius
H-Generalleutnant Ralf Sodan
H-Generalmajor Henning von Tresckow
H-General der Artillerie Eduard Wagner
H-Generalleutnant Erich Weingart
H-Generalleutnant Karl Zutavern

Executed during World War II

H-Generalmajor Karl von Dewitz gen von Krebs
H-Generalmajor Heinrich Burggraf und Graf zu Dohna-Schlobitten
H-General der Nachrichtentruppe Erich Fellgiebel
H-Generaloberst Friedrich Fromm
H-Generalmajor Reinhold Gothsche
H-Generalleutnant Paul von Hase
H-Generalleutnant Gustav Heistermann von Ziehlberg
H-Generalmajor Otto Herfurth
H-Generaloberst Erich Hoepner
H-Generalleutnant z.V. Hans Knuth
H-General der Infanterie Friedrich Olbricht
H-Generalmajor Hans Oster
H-General der Artillerie Friedrich von Rabenau
H-Generalmajor Fritz Reinhardt
H-General-Stabsrichter Dr. Karl Sack
H-Generalleutnant Hans Graf von Sponeck
H-Generalmajor Hellmuth Stieff
H-Generalmajor Martin Strahammer
H-General der Infanterie Carl-Heinrich von Stuelpnagel
H-Generalleutnant Fritz Thiele
H-Generalleutnant Karl Freiherr von Thuengen
H-Generalfeldmarschall Erwin von Witzleben

Committed suicide after World War II

H-Generaloberst Johannes Blaskowitz
H-Generalleutnant Erpo Freiherr von Bodenhausen
H-General der Gebirgstruppe Franz Boehme
H-Generalmajor Kurt Eberhard
H-Generalmajor z.V. Paul Genee
H-General der Infanterie Hermann Geyer
H-General der Infanterie Edmund Glaise von Horstenau
H-Generalmajor Alfred Gutknecht
H-General der Infanterie Eberhard Kinzel

H-Generalmajor Kuno Klemm
H-Generalleutnant Rudolf Schrader
H-General der Infanterie Otto von Stuelpnagel
H-Generalmajor Otto Willigmann

Executed after World War II

H-Generalleutnant Friedrich-Gustav Bernhard
H-Generalleutnant Karl Burckhardt
H-Generalmajor Stanislaus von Dewitz gen von Krebs
H-Generalleutnant Albrecht Freiherr Digeon von Monteton
H-Generalleutnant Wolfgang von Ditfurth
H-General der Infanterie Anton Dostler
H-Generalmajor Gottfried von Erdmannsdorff
H-General der Infanterie Werner von Erdmannsdorff
H-General der Panzertruppe Gustav Fehn
H-Generalmajor Adolf Fischer
H-Generalleutnant Johann Fortner
H-Generalmajor Hans Gravenstein
H-Generalleutnant Adolf Hamann
H-Generalleutnant zV Hans von Hoesslin
H-Generaloberst Alfred Jodl
H-Generalmajor Emil Just
H-Generalfeldmarschall Wilhelm Keitel
H-Generalleutnant Josef Kuebler
H-General der Infanterie Ludwig Kuebler
H-Generalmajor Hans Kuepper
H-Generalmajor Adalbert Lontschar
H-Generalleutnant Hartwing von Ludwiger
H-General der Infanterie Friedrich-Wilhelm Mueller
H-Generalleutnant Fritz Niedholdt
H-Generalmajor Bronislaw Pawel
H-Generalleutnant Fritz-Georg von Rappard
H-Generalmajor Heinrich Remlinger
H-Generalleutnant Johann-Georg Richert
H-Generalleutnant Siegfried Ruff
H-Generalleutnant z.V. Hugo Schaefer
H-Generalleutnant Friedrich Stephan
H-Generalmajor Hubert Strohmaier
H-Generalmajor Eckart von Tschammer und Osten
H-Generalmajor Friedrich Werther
H-Generalleutnant Hermann Winkler
H-Generalleutnant Eugen Wurster

Died in prisoner-of-war camps after World War II

H-Generalleutnant z.V. Wilhelm Adam
H-Generalmajor Hans-Henning von Alten
H-Generalleutnant Dr. Friedrich Altrichter
H-Generalmajor Hans-Adolf von Arenstorff

H-Generalmajor Erwin Barends
H-Generalmajor Hans-Joachim Baumeister
H-Generalleutnant Friedrich Bayer
H-Generalmajor Gerd Paul von Below
H-Generalleutnant Hans Boeckh-Behrens
H-Generalleutnant Walter von Boltenstern
H-Generalleutnant Willibald Borowietz
H-Generalleutnant Josef Brauner von Haydringen
H-Generalfeldmarschall Ernst Busch
H-Generalmajor Julius Dauber
H-Generalmajor Otto Deindl
H-Generalmajor Ludwig Drees
H-General-Intendant Dr. Max Dutzmann
H-Generalmajor Walther Dybilasz
H-Generalmajor Anton Eberth
H-Generalmajor Gerhard von Enckevort
H-Generalmajor Joachim Engel
H-General-Veterinar Dr. Walter Fischer
H-Generalmajor Werner Gebb
H-Generalmajor z.V. Friedrich Gempp
H-Generalmajor z.V. Paul Genee
H-Generalleutnant z.V. Friedrich Genthe
H-Generalleutnant Oskar von Ginckel
H-Generalleutnant z.V. Paul Goeldner
H-General der Infanterie Siegfried Haenicke
H-General der Infanterie Wilhelm Hasse
H-Generaloberst Walter Heitz
H-General der Artillerie Kurt Herzog
H-Generaloberst Karl Hilpert
H-General der Infanterie Friedrich Hochbaum
H-Generalleutnant Edmund Hoffmeister
H-General-Arzt Prof. Dr. Friedrich Jungblut
H-General-Arzt Dr. Hermann Kayser
H-General-Arzt Dr. Paul Kern
H-Generalmajor Werner Kirsten
H-Generalfeldmarschall Ewald von Kleist
H-General-Arzt z.V. Dr. Werner Kluge
H-Generalleutnant Gerhard Kuehne
H-General der Infanterie Arthur Kullmer
H-Generalmajor Ernst von Kurnatowski
H-Generalmajor z.V. Karl Ritter von Kurz
H-Generalleutnant Kurt Lahode
H-Generalmajor Richard Lepper
H-General der Gebirgstruppe Karl von Le Suire
H-General der Infanterie Erich Luedke
H-General der Infanterie Rudolf Lueters
H-Generalmajor Robert Macher
H-Generalleutnant Gerhard Medem
H-Generalleutnant Robert Meissner
H-Generalmajor Karl Meltzer
H-General der Artillerie Willi Moser
H-Generalmajor Claus Mueller-Buelow
H-Generalmajor Werner Mummert
H-Generalmajor Franz Neumayr
H-Generalmajor Georg Neymann
H-Generalmajor z.V. Georg von Niebecker

H-Generalleutnant Guenther von Niebelschuetz
H-Generalmajor Prof. Dr. Oskar Ritter von Niedermayer
H-Generalleutnant Heinrich Niehoff
H-Generalmajor Otto Niemann
H-Generalmajor Rudolf Noack
H-General-Stabsarzt Dr. Curt Oehlmann
H-Generalleutnant Curt von Oesterreich
H-Generalleutnant Kurt Oppenlaender
H-General der Infanterie z.V. Hans Petri
H-General der Artillerie Max Pfeffer
H-Generalleutnant z.V. Plotho, Wolfgang Edler Herr und Freiherr von Plotho
H-Generalleutnant Gerhard Poel
H-Generalleutnant Georg Postel
H-General der Infanterie Erich Raschick
H-Generalleutnant Anton Rathke
H-General-Stabsintendant Walter Reich
H-Generalmajor Kurt Ruehle von Lilienstern
H-Generalmajor Wilhelm Runge
H-Generalmajor Josef Rupprecht
H-General der Pioniere Karl Sachs
H-Generalleutnant Werner Sanne
H-Generalleutnant z.V. Oskar Schellbach
H-Generalleutnant Paul Scheuerpflug
H-General-Arzt Dr. Walter Schleusener
H-Generalmajor Friedrich Schneider
H-Generalmajor Friedrich Schoenfelder
H-Generalleutnant z.V. Otto Schroeder
H-Generalmajor Hans-Georg Schuberth
H-Generalleutnant Hans-Heinrich Sixt von Armin
H-General-Arzt Dr. Heinrich Smend
H-General der Infanterie Karl-Wilhelm Specht
H-Generalleutnant Hans Stieler von Heydekampf
H-Generalleutnant Herbert Stimmel
H-Generalleutnant Paul Stoewer
H-Generalleutnant Mauritz Freiherr von Strachwitz
H-Generalleutnant Heinrich Thoma
H-Generalmajor z.V. Walter Traenckner
H-Generalmajor Louis Tronnier
H-Generalleutnant Christian Usinger
H-General der Infanterie Paul Voelckers
H-General der Artillerie Helmuth Weidling
H-Generalmajor Ernst Wening
H-General der Artillerie Peter Weyer
H-Generalleutnant Heinrich Wintzer
H-Generalmajor Heinrich Wittkopf
H-Generalmajor Hans von Ziegesar
H-Generalmajor Arthur Zierold
H-Generalleutnant Alexander von Zuelow

Bibliography

Primary Sources

Dienstalterliste der Schutzstaffel der N.S.D.A.P. stand vom 9 November 1944, Berlin, 1944.
Dienstalterliste der Schutzstaffel der N.S.D.A.P. stand vom 1 Oktober 1944, Berlin, 1944.
Dienstalterliste der Waffen-SS stand vom 01.07.44, Berlin, 1944.
Dienstalterliste der Schutzstaffel der N.S.D.A.P. stand vom 30 Januar 1944, Berlin, 1944.
Dienstalterliste der Schutzstafffel der N.S.D.A.P. stand vom 1 Oktober 1943, Berlin, 1943.
Dienstalterliste der Schutzstaffel der N.S.D.A.P. stand vom 15 Mai 1943, Berlin, 1943.
Dienstalterliste der Schutzstaffel der N.S.D.A.P. stand vom 1 Oktober 1942, Berlin, 1942.
Dienstalterliste der Schutzstaffel der N.S.D.A.P. stand vom 30 Januar 1942, Berlin, 1942.
Dienstalterliste der Schutzstaffel der N.S.D.A.P. stand vom 1 Dezember 1938, Berlin, 1938.
Dienstalterliste der Schutzstaffel der N.S.D.A.P. stand vom 1 Dezember 1937, Berlin, 1937.
Dienstalterliste der Schutzstaffel der N.S.D.A.P. stand vom 1 Dezember 1936, Berlin, 1936.
Dienstalterliste der Schutzstaffel der N.S.D.A.P. stand vom 1 Juli 1935, Berlin, 1935.
Dienstalterliste der Schutzstaffel der N.S.D.A.P. stand vom 1 Oktober 1934, Berlin, 1934.
Gerbet, Klaus & Johnst, David: *Generalfeldmarschall Fedor von Bock: The War Diary 1939–1945*, Schiffer Publishing Ltd., 1996.
Guderian, Heinz: *Panzer Leader*, London, 1952.
Halder, Franz (edited by Burdieck, Charles & Jacobsen, Hans-Adolf): *The Halder War Diary 1939–1942*, Greenhill Books, 1988.
Keitel, Wilhelm: *Memoirs of Field Marshall Wilhelm Keitel*, New York, 1966.
Kesselring, Albert (edited by Macksey, Kenneth): *The Memoirs of Field Marshal Albert Kesselring*, Greenhill Books, 2007.
Manstein, Erich von: *Lost Victories*, London, 1959.
Speer, Albert: *Inside the Third Reich: Memoirs by Albert Speer*, Scribner Publishing, 1981.
The Nuremberg Trials—The Complete Proceedings Volume 1: The Indictment and Opening Statements, Coda Books Ltd., 2011.
The Nuremberg Trials—The Complete Proceedings Volume 2: The Indictment—The Four Charges, Coda Books Ltd., 2011.
The Nuremberg Trials—The Complete Proceedings Volume 3: The Policy to Exterminate the Jews, Coda Books Ltd., 2011.
The Nuremberg Trials—*The Complete Proceedings Volume 4: Individual Responsibility of the Defendants*, Coda Books Ltd., 2011.
Wood, James A. editor: *Army of the West: The Weekly Reports of German Army Group B, from Normandy to the West Wall 1944*, Stackpole Books, 2007.

Secondary Sources

Barnett, Correlli: *Hitler's Generals*, Grove Weidenfeld Publishing, 1989.

Beevor, Antony: *Stalingrad: The Final Siege 1942–1943*, Penguin Group Publishing, New York, 1998.

Beevor, Antony: *The Battle for Spain: The Spanish Civil War 1936–1939*, Orion Publishing, 2009.

Beevor, Antony: *Ardennes 1944: Hitler's Last Gamble*, Viking Publishing, 2015.

Beevor, Antony: *D-Day: The Battle for Normandy*, Penguin Books, 2010.

Bennett, Roy & Bennett, G. H.: *Hitler's Admirals*, Naval Institute Press, 2004.

Bidwell, Shelford: *Hitler's Generals and their Battles*, Salamander Books, 1978.

Bradley, Dermot, Hildebrand, Karl-Friedrich and Roevekamp, Markus: *Die Generale des Heeres 1921–1945, Volumes I–VII*, Biblio Verlag, Osnabrueck, 1993–2004.

Carruthers, Bob: *Wolf Pack: The U-Boats at War*, Pen & Sword Publishing, 2013.

Cooper, Mathew: *German Army 1933–1945*, Scarborough House Publishing, 1990.

Davis, Clyde R.: *The Wehrmacht and the Golden Party Badge, Military Advisor, Volume 22, Number 2*, Roger James Bender Publishing, San Jose, CA, 2011.

Deighton, Len: *Fighter: The True Story of the Battle of Britain*, Random House, 2008.

Deutsch, Harold C.: *Hitler and his Generals: The Hidden Crises January–June 1938*, University of Minnesota Press, 1974.

Dimbleby, Jonathan: *Operation Barbarossa: The History of a Cataclysm*, Oxford University Press, 2021.

Doerr, Manfred and Thomas, Franz: *Die Traeger der Nahkampfspange in Gold 1943–1945: Heer, Luftwaffe, Waffen-SS*, Biblio-Verlag, Osnabrueck, 1986.

Dorr, Manfred: *Die Inhaber der Annerkenungsurkunde des Oberbefehlshaber des Heeres 1941–1945*, Biblio-Verlag, Osnabrueck, 1993.

Dupuy, T. N.: *A Genius for War: The German Army and the General Staff 1807–1945*, Prentice Hall Publishing, 1977.

Engel, Gerhard: *At the Heart of the Reich: The Secret Diary of Hitler's Army Adjutant*, Greenhill Books, 2006.

Fellgiebel, Walther-Peer: *Die Traeger der Ritterkreuz des Eisernen Kreuzes 1939–1945*, Podzun-Pallas Verlag, Friedberg, 1988.

Forczyk, Robert: *Case White: The Invasion of Poland, 1939*, Osprey Publishing, Oxford, 2019.

Galante, Pierre: *Operation Valkyrie: The German Generals' Plot against Hitler*, Cooper Square Press, 2002.

Gericke, Bernd: *Die Inhaber des Deutschen Kreuzes in Gold, des Deutschen Kreuzes in Silber der Kriegsmarine und die Inhaber der Ehrentafelspange der Kriegsmarine*, Biblio-Verlag, Osnabrueck, 1993.

Glantz, David: *Hitler and his Generals: Military Conferences 1942–1945*, Enigma Books, 2002.

Goerlitz, Walter: *History of the German General Staff, 1657–1945*, Westview Press, 1985.

Hildebrand, Hans H. and Henriot, Ernest: *Deutschland Admirale 1849–1945, Bands I–III*, Biblio Verlag, Osnabrueck, 1988–1996.

Hildebrand, Karl-Friedrich: *Die Generale der Deutschen Luftwaffe 1935–1945, Bands I–III*, Biblio Verlag, Osnabrueck, 1990.

Hildebrand, Karl-Friedrich and Zweng, Christian: *Die Ritter des Ordens Pour le Mérite des I. Weltkriegs, Volumes I–III*, Biblio Verlag, Osnabrueck, 1999–2011.

Irving, David: *The Rise and Fall of the Luftwaffe: The Life of Field Marshal Erhard Milch*, Brown and Company Publishing, 1974.

Iziowski, Richard: *The Enigma of General Blaskowitz*, Hippocrene Books, 1997.

Kaufmann, H. W. & Kaufmann, J. E.: *Hitler's Blitzkrieg Campaigns: The Invasion and Defense of Western Europe*, Da Capo Press, 1993.

Keilig, Wolf: *Die Generale des Heeres und die Sanitatsoffizier im Generalsrang*, Podzun-Pallas Verlag, Friedberg, 1983.

Kursietis, Andris J.: *The Wehrmacht at War 1939–1945: The Units and Commanders of the German Ground Forces during World War II*, Aspekt Publishing, The Netherlands, 1999.

Lohmann, W. and Hildebrand, H.: *Die Deutsche Kriegsmarine*, Verlag Hans-Henning Podzun, Bad Nauheim, 1956.

MacDonald, Charles B.: *A Time for Trumpets: The Untold Story of the Battle of the Bulge*, Bantam Books, 1985.

Mitcham, Jr., Samuel W.: *Hitler's Legions: The German Army Order of Battle, World War II*, Stein & Day Publishing, 1985.

Mitcham Jr., Samuel W.: *Men of the Luftwaffe*, Presidio Press, Novato, CA, 1988.

Mitcham, Jr., Samuel W.: *Triumphant Fox: Erwin Rommel and the Rise of the Afrika Corps*, Penguin Publishing Group, 1990.

Mosley, Leonard: *The Reich Marshal: A Biography of Hermann Goering*, Doubleday Publishing, 1974.

Mueller, Michael: *Nazi Spymaster: The Life and Death of Admiral Wilhelm Canaris*, Skyhorse Publishing, 2017.

O'Hara, Vincent P.: *The German Fleet at War 1939–1945*, Naval Institute Press, Annapolis, MD, 2004.

Patzwall, Klaus D. and Scherzer, Veit: *Das Deutschen Kreuz 1941–1945: Geschichte und Inhaber*, Patzwall-Verlag, Norderstedt, 2007.

Petrow, Richard: *The Bitter Years: The Invasion and Occupation of Denmark and Norway, April 1940–May 1945*, William Morrow and Co., London, 1974.

Ryan, Cornelius: *Last Battle: The Battle for Berlin*, Simon, and Schuster, 1995.

Scheibert, Horst: *Die Traeger der Ehrenblattspange des Heeres und Waffen-SS: Die Traeger der Ehrentaffelspange der Kriegsmarine: Die Inhaber des Ehrenpokals fur Besondere im Luftkreig*, Biblio-Verlag, Osnabrueck, 1986.

Scherzer, Veit: *Die Ritterkreuztraeger: Die Inhaber des Ritterkreuzes des Eisernen Kreuzes 1939–1945*, Scherzers Militaire-Verlag, Ranis/Jena, 2005.

Schulz, Andreas. Wegman, Guenter and Zinke, Dieter: *Die Generale der Waffen-SS und Polizei, Volumes I–IV*, Biblio-Verlag, Bissendorf, 2003–2009.

Schulz, Andreas. Wegman, Guenter and Zinke, Dieter: *Die Generale der Waffen-SS und Polizei, Volumes V–VI*, Biblio-Verlag, Bissendorf, 2003–2009.

Spaeter, Helmut: *Panzerkorps Grossdeutschland*, Schiffer Publishing Ltd., 1990.

Stahel, David: *Operation Barbarossa and Germany's Defeat in the East*, Cambridge University Press, 2011.

Stahel, David: *Operation Typhoon: Hitler's March on Moscow*, October 1941, Cambridge University Press, 2015.

Stein, George H.: *The Waffen-SS: Hitler's Elite Guard at War*, Cornell University Press Ltd., London, 1966.

Tarrant, V. E.: *The Last Year of the Kriegsmarine May 1944–May 1945*, Naval Institute Press, 1994.

Tucker-Jones, Anthony: *Stalin's Revenge: Operation Bagration and the Annihilation of Army Group Centre*, Pen & Sword Publishing, 2009.

Turner, Barry: *Karl Doenitz and the Last Days of the Third Reich*, Icon Publishing, London, 2015.

Williamson, Gordon and Charita, Josef: *The War Merit Cross*, Roger James Bender Publishing, San Jose, CA, 2008.

Institutions

Bundesarchiv
Denver Public Library Interlibrary Loan

Websites

Axis Biographical Research
Axis History Forum
Generale des Heeres 1939–1945
Lexikon der Wehrmacht